W9-DAL-793

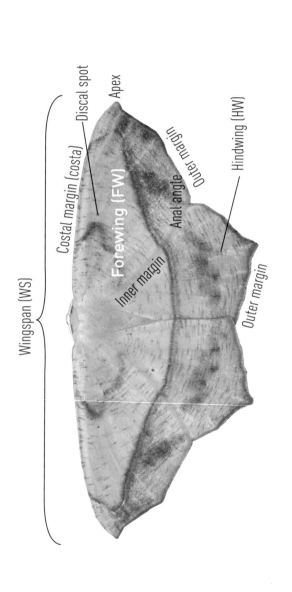

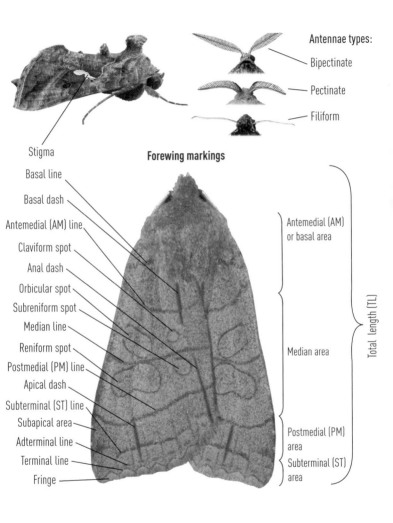

Antennae types:
- Bipectinate
- Pectinate
- Filiform

Stigma

Forewing markings

Basal line
Basal dash
Antemedial (AM) line
Claviform spot
Anal dash
Orbicular spot
Subreniform spot
Median line
Reniform spot
Postmedial (PM) line
Apical dash
Subterminal (ST) line
Subapical area
Adterminal line
Terminal line
Fringe

Antemedial (AM) or basal area

Median area

Postmedial (PM) area

Subterminal (ST) area

Total length (TL)

PETERSON FIELD GUIDE
TO
MOTHS
of Northeastern North America

PETERSON FIELD GUIDE
TO
MOTHS
of Northeastern North America

FIRST EDITION

DAVID BEADLE
SEABROOKE LECKIE

HOUGHTON MIFFLIN HARCOURT
BOSTON   NEW YORK   2012

Sponsored by
ROGER TORY PETERSON INSTITUTE
NATIONAL WILDLIFE FEDERATION

AURORA PUBLIC LIBRARY

Copyright © 2012 by David Beadle and Seabrooke Leckie

All rights reserved

For information about permission to reproduce selections from this book,
write to Permissions, Houghton Mifflin Harcourt Publishing Company,
215 Park Avenue South, New York, New York 10003.

www.hmhbooks.com

Library of Congress Cataloging-in-Publication Data
Beadle, David, date.
Peterson field guide to moths of northeastern
North America / by David Beadle and Seabrooke Leckie.
p. cm.
Includes bibliographical references and index.
ISBN 978-0-547-23848-7
1. Moths—Northeastern States—Identifiaction. 2. Moths—Canada,
Eastern—Identification. I. Leckie, Seabrooke. II. Title.
QL548.B43 2012
595.780974—dc
2011016059

Printed in China

SCP 10 9 8 7 6 5 4 3 2 1

Preceding images:
Rosewing, *Sideridis rosea*
Squash Vine Borer, *Melittia cucurbitae*

*To Francis Solly and Phil Milton, the great "Moth Men of Thanet";
and to the memory of Paul McGaw.*
—David Beadle

*For Mom and Dad, who planted the seed of curiosity and gave it
water and sunlight and plenty of room to grow.*
—Seabrooke Leckie

Burdock Seedhead Moth

THE LEGACY OF AMERICA'S GREATEST NATURALIST AND CREATOR of the field guide series, Roger Tory Peterson, is kept alive through the dedicated work of the Roger Tory Peterson Institute of Natural History (RTPI). Established in 1985, RTPI is located in Peterson's hometown of Jamestown, New York, near Chautauqua Institution in the southwestern part of the state.

Today RTPI is a national center for nature education that maintains, shares, and interprets Peterson's extraordinary archive of writings, art, and photography. The Institute, housed in a landmark building by world-class architect Robert A. M. Stern, continues to transmit Peterson's zest for teaching about the natural world through leadership programs in teacher development as well as outstanding exhibits of contemporary nature art, natural history, and the Peterson Collection.

Your participation as a steward of the Peterson Collection and supporter of the Peterson legacy is needed. Please consider joining RTPI at an introductory rate of 50 percent of the regular membership fee for the first year. Simply call RTPI's membership department at (800) 758-6841 ext. 226, or e-mail membership@rtpi.org to take advantage of this special membership offered to purchasers of this book. For more information, please visit the Peterson Institute in person or virtually at www.rtpi.org.

Eastern Panthea

Rose Plume Moth

CONTENTS

PETERSON FIELD GUIDE
TO
MOTHS
of Northeastern North America

Yellow-collared Scape Moth

Faint-spotted Palthis

INTRODUCTION

For most people, moths are a mysterious group. They fly under cover of darkness, hidden in a world in which our own eyes can't see. Our only interaction with them is usually in watching them flutter in confusion at our porch lights, or gathering on the outside of the house windows at night. Most are small, and while they're fluttering around in wild circles it's difficult to see anything but drab paleness. If one slips inside our home, we probably toss it back outside without giving it a second look.

So it was for Seabrooke until she found herself away from home one summer a few years ago, waiting for some permits to be resolved for a job she had been contracted to do. With time on her hands, she discovered a black light in her host's garage, and on a whim strung up a sheet in the yard to see what might turn up that warm August evening. That single decision completely changed her opinion of moths. A new world was opened up, one that included incredible color and pattern, amazing diversity.

David, meanwhile, had been "mothing" for some 25 years. He'd first become interested in moths while working at Sandwich Bay Bird Observatory in Kent, U.K. Many bird observatories in Great Britain also run live traps for moths every night as part of their regular monitoring activities, and sorting through the night's catch was part of each day's routine. A few years later, after David immigrated to Ontario, his mother-in-law gave him an unusual birthday present—the *Peterson Field Guide to Eastern Moths* by Charles V. Covell, Jr. The spark was rekindled, and the fire still burns brightly. The catching and photographing of moths became an all-consuming passion, often pushing aside birds during the summer months. Amazing what one seminal book can do!

Prior to our book, there existed a few printed field guides, including Covell's older Peterson Field Guide, but all of these previous books treated the moths as an insect collector would, with the specimens displayed spread-winged, and not as the moth would be seen while alive and at rest. A few websites have been started in recent years that display moths at rest, but they can be time-consuming to browse through and of course require that you be at a computer. With all his years of experience, David proved a font of knowledge and a very patient friend. He would occasionally send Seabrooke photos of his own to help support an identification—images he had taken of live moths he had caught himself over the years. It didn't take Seabrooke long to ask, "Have you thought about producing a field guide with these?" And from there, a guide was born.

More than 11,000 species of moths are currently recognized in North America. This is an overwhelming number, far greater than even the most ambitious field guide might be able to cover in one volume. In order to offer the most useful field guide to moths that we could, we limited our scope to just northeastern North America. Even this much smaller region still contains a few thousand species. Many of these are small, however, or very rare, or very localized in occurrence. We selected nearly 1,500 of the most common or most eye-catching of the moths in this area to include in this guide. The majority of the species you are likely to encounter on any given night will be present in these pages; for those that aren't, we provide additional resources at the end of the book.

The purpose of this guide is not to provide an exhaustive life history for each species, but rather to be an introduction to them. We have selected photographs that depict representative individuals for each species, and we have included basic information that will help in reaching an identification. If you wish to know more about any of these species, additional information can be found in the resources at the end of the guide.

For both of us, moths are our hobby, not our profession. While we have made every effort to ensure that the content of this guide is as accurate as possible, there may still be errors present. Moths have not had the benefit of decades of hobbyists collecting data in the same way some other taxonomic groups, such as birds or butterflies, have had. There are still many gaps in our knowledge. We hope that by providing a comprehensive, user-friendly guide we may be able to fill in some of these gaps through introducing new enthusiasts to this amazing group of insects. We would be interested in receiving feedback on errors and omissions so that future editions of this guide might be corrected and improved.

Maple Zale

HOW TO USE
THIS BOOK

Canadian Sphinx

How to See Moths

Moths are everywhere. You don't need to stray far from home to see them; even the tiniest urban lot has moths present, providing there are plants around for the caterpillars to feed on. Observing moths can be as easy as turning on the porch light on a warm summer evening and stepping out once in a while to see what might have come in.

In the same way that one's birdwatching experience is improved with a pair of binoculars, so too can a little bit of equipment greatly increase the enjoyment you take in looking for moths. You don't need to spend very much, either—a simple outlay of $15 can dramatically increase the number of moths you might see. Of course, as with any hobby, if you discover a passion for it, it's definitely possible to spend quite a bit more.

The Basics
Lightbulbs. While a simple incandescent light might draw in a few moths, the most effective bulbs are ones that project some light in the UV spectrum. There is some debate over why moths are attracted to light, and why UV light should make a difference. One theory suggests that moths navigate by the light of the moon and that artificial light disorients them; another holds that the wavelengths of UV light stimulate pheromone receptors on the moths' antennae, luring them in. Whatever the reason, artificial lights will draw in the greatest number of species.

A black light is an inexpensive option for attracting moths. Black lights are often sold at home renovation centers or other stores that provide a wide array of bulbs as party accessories. Similar in nature are grow bulbs, designed for plants or aquariums, and bug zappers (make sure you disable the zapper if you purchase one of these!). A more expensive, but much more effective, option is a mercury or sodium vapor bulb. These powerful, high-wattage bulbs broadcast a very bright light, attracting more individuals and drawing moths in from farther away. They are the sort of bulbs found in typical outdoor security lights and usually need to be ballasted in an appropriate fixture (although some are sold as self-ballasted). Be careful using these—they get very hot and can present a fire risk if knocked over or if your sheet falls across them.

White cotton sheet. A light bulb may be set up in front of a wall or other smooth surface that reflects the light and also provides a place for moths to settle. Pale surfaces work best, as it's easier to detect the moths. A cotton sheet has the additional advantage of reflecting UV rays (synthetic fibers such as polyester do not), creating a broader surface area for attracting moths. This is especially true when using a black light, which is much more effective when used in combination with a white sheet. Figure 1 shows a typical sheet and light setup.

Light trap. This is an essential piece of equipment for serious moth enthusiasts. A light trap holds the moths drawn to the light until the moth-er can return to check them. This has the great benefit of allowing you to get some sleep overnight! Light traps can be purchased online or can be easily made from household components. Figure 2 shows three different types of light traps.

At its most basic, a trap consists of a container in which to hold the moths, egg cartons for the moths to hide in while inside, a lid to keep them from escaping, a funnel in the lid to let moths in, and a light bulb to sit in the funnel. The exact pieces you use to accomplish these goals are determined by what's available to you and how much you want to spend. An image search on the Internet for "moth trap" will provide many different examples of this same general setup. If you choose to run a trap, be sure to check it first thing in the morning and remove the moths that have settled on the top and surrounding area, or the birds will thank you for the breakfast buffet!

Fig 1. One of the authors checking a typical sheet setup. Used here is a plain white sheet and inexpensive black light CFL bulb. The bulb is clamped to a simple tripod. A headlamp is often helpful when checking a sheet, as the black light tends to obscure colors and patterns.

Sugar bait. Some species of moths are not very attracted to artificial light but are nectar-feeders and will come to sugar bait, as shown in Figure 3. The combination of ingredients you use is flexible and can be determined by what you have on hand in the kitchen. A particularly effective mixture is to blend one soft banana, a scoop of brown sugar, a dollop of molasses, and a glug or two of beer (flat or cheap

Fig 2. Three styles of light trap. From top to bottom: commercially available Robinson trap with clear lid and circular funnel; David's homemade Skinner trap with clear lid and linear funnel-like gap; and Seabrooke's homemade Robinson-type trap with solid lid and circular funnel. The clear lids are thought to help moths settle more quickly within the trap, possibly avoiding damage to delicate wing scales, but many moth enthusiasts use solid-topped traps with few or no adverse effects. Note the egg cartons inside, which provide a resting substrate.

Fig 3. A selection of moths visiting sugar bait near Long Point, Ontario, in September.

is fine). Paint this sticky concoction onto tree trunks with a brush. It may stain wood, so avoid using it on your deck or other structures. Another option is to soak a thick rope (at least 0.5 in./1.25 cm in diameter, so the moths can land on it) in the mixture and then string it between two supports. You need to check the trees regularly, just as you would do with your cotton sheet, in order to see what the bait has attracted.

Jars or containers. The moth photographs in this guide were all taken during daylight, which allows for better photos since you don't need to use a flash. Moths can be cooled in the refrigerator (not the freezer) for one night if necessary; the low temperature puts them into a state of torpor, which keeps them calm and lowers their metabolism. Pill bottles such as those provided by a pharmacist make ideal containers as they are small and don't take up much room in the fridge, and clear so that you can see what you have inside. You can order them from websites or ask at your local pharmacy.

In "the Wild"

Not all moths are nocturnal. Some nectar-feeders can be seen supping at flowers during the daytime as well. A few species are almost exclusively diurnal and are rarely encountered at night. You can encourage day-fliers to visit your gardens by planting nectar-rich flowers, which are often sold at garden centers as being appealing to butterflies or hummingbirds.

Don't forget to keep your eyes peeled while out hiking. The moths that visit your garden plants can also be found on wildflowers. Watch for small pale shapes that rise up out of the grass or off the forest floor ahead of you. All of those moths that come to your sheet at night have to spend the day somewhere; examine tree trunks and bark crevices, rock ledges, and other protected places. Don't overlook your house and garage—moths can turn up in the strangest places.

Caterpillars and Cocoons

This guide helps only with the identification of adults, but moths actually spend a larger percentage of their lifetime in the larval stage. Some caterpillars are very cryptic, blending in with the plants on which they feed. Others have behaviors or patterns that make them instantly recognizable, such as the springtime tents made by the Eastern Tent Caterpillar or the fuzzy black-and-brown Woolly Bear Caterpillars of the Isabella Tiger Moth. We do not provide any information on caterpillars or cocoons, but if you are interested in learning to identify moth caterpillars, check out the resources at the end of the book.

How to Photograph Moths

Another great tool in a moth enthusiast's arsenal is a digital camera. While you might initially have considered taking pictures of the moths that come to your light as a way to record what you see, photography is also useful for identification purposes, as the camera often captures detail that is imperceptible to the human eye. The identification of micromoths (see p. 22) in particular benefits greatly from this. In most cases, photography can do away with the need for collecting specimens, just as binoculars meant that bird enthusiasts could pack away their shotguns.

Even a compact point-and-shoot can produce good results. Simply snap photos of the species at your white sheet or trap and study your photos at leisure later, with available references at hand. If using flash, note that it can sometimes alter the color tones of your subjects or reflect off the scales, creating washed-out images that may be difficult to use for identification purposes.

While this is the easiest approach to moth photography, the best results are achieved with a small investment of time and patience. Most of the moths in this guide were photographed using the following method. It may seem like a lot of effort, but the results can be very rewarding.

Indirect natural daylight is the best lighting for photographing moths. Since few moths are active during the day, this requires holding the moths that come to your light overnight. Using a small container, carefully capture the moth and place it in the fridge until the morning (for more on holding moths, see the section on jars or containers, p. 9). The next day, carefully tip the moth from its container onto a suitable substrate. Natural items such as bark or leaves make aesthetically pleasing backgrounds, and graph paper can provide a useful size reference. Most large moths will remain still, often appearing dead, potentially for many minutes. (Don't worry, they're not dead, simply torpid—place them in the sun and they'll soon fly off.) Micromoths and some geometers, because of their large ratio of surface area to body volume, warm up quickly and may give you only a few seconds to snap a photo before they fly away.

To obtain crisp images, it is best to mount your camera on a tripod, especially if using a digital SLR with a macro lens. If photographing outdoors, a solid substrate such as a branch or rock that won't move in the breeze is also useful. Lower light levels sometimes require longer shutter speeds; you can eliminate the vibration caused by pressing the shutter button by using a shutter release or by simply setting the camera to a two-second delay. In situations of directional light (such as beside a window), small white or metallic reflecting boards, or even a square of aluminum foil, can reflect light onto the moth to reduce shadows. Mid- to low-range f-stops on SLR cameras will produce evenly blurred backgrounds for moths on twigs or leaves.

How to Identify Moths

With such a vast array of possibilities, it's easy to feel a bit overwhelmed when first learning to identify moths. Many of them seem to look the same, and even learning to tell one family or subfamily from another can seem a daunting challenge. It is only through constant practice and regular exposure that you will start to be able to discern differences, and practice takes time. Don't give up! It takes most moth enthusiasts a few years before they start feeling comfortable with their local species.

When you're beginning, it is easiest to select a subset of the moths at your lights and set about learning them first. Which subset you decide to start with is entirely up to you, but we recommend concentrating on the common species first, the ones you see many of on a given night. Once you feel comfortable with the common species, it will be easier to spot the less common species. Another approach is to begin with the flashy or brightly colored species, as these are easily remembered and tend to stand out from the rest. In subsequent seasons you can build on the skills you developed the year before, and each summer you'll be able to identify a few more species without having to refer to your guidebooks. We strongly recommend ignoring the smaller moths to begin with, and just focusing on the larger ones, which are usually easier to identify. When you feel comfortable with the larger moths, you can turn to the smaller ones without feeling overwhelmed.

Another good way to familiarize yourself with the different species is simply to spend some time flipping through your field guide. If you've often looked at an illustration in your book, when the species finally turns up at your light you'll already know what it is, or at least have a fair idea of where to find it in the guide.

Appearance

When trying to identify a particular individual, first make sure that the lepidopteran you're looking at is in fact a moth. Some diurnal moths resemble butterflies in color and habit, and some drab butterflies might bring to mind a moth. The easiest way to tell them apart is by the antennae: if they are clubbed at the tip, it's a butterfly; if they are threadlike or feathery, it's a moth.

There are many questions you should ask yourself, even before you begin looking at the patterns of lines and spots on the moth's wings. How large is it? How does it pose while at rest? What shape is it? What color is it? Knowing the answers to these questions can help you narrow down which group a moth is in. A medium-sized moth that rests with its wings spread out to its sides is most likely in the family Geometridae, whereas one that sits with its wings folded tentlike over its back is probably in the family Noctuidae. A noctuid that is long and thin is most likely in a different subfamily than one that is more triangular. As with anything, there are exceptions, but it is a helpful place to start. The endpapers of this guide show many different moth silhouettes.

Size is a very important key in identifying moths. Not only can it help you determine which group of moths an individual belongs to, but it also can often help in separating two very similar species. All of the species on a plate are sized relative to each other, so larger species will be shown larger. We have placed a life-sized gray silhouette of one of the moths on each plate to give you a sense of actual size. The scale might be different from one plate to the next, even within the same family, so make sure to refer to the silhouette on each page.

Once you have narrowed down the possibilities to a few families, you can look more closely at the patterns. In this guide we refer to the different spots and lines (often called bands when they are wider) that can be seen on the wing. Each has its own unique name, and knowing the terminology for the structure and patterns of the wing will be very helpful when reading the species accounts. Figure

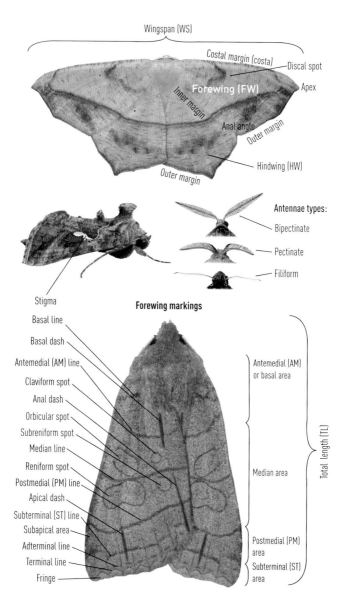

Wingspan (WS)

Costal margin (costa) — Discal spot

Forewing (FW) — Apex

Inner margin

Anal angle

Outer margin

Hindwing (HW)

Outer margin

Stigma

Antennae types:

Bipectinate

Pectinate

Filiform

Forewing markings

Basal line

Basal dash

Antemedial (AM) line

Claviform spot

Anal dash

Orbicular spot

Subreniform spot

Median line

Reniform spot

Postmedial (PM) line

Apical dash

Subterminal (ST) line

Subapical area

Adterminal line

Terminal line

Fringe

Antemedial (AM) or basal area

Median area

Postmedial (PM) area

Subterminal (ST) area

Total length (TL)

Fig 4. Wing structures, antennae types, and forewing markings referred to in the species accounts.

4 shows the different markings and parts of the wing that we refer to when describing species, as well as the different types of moth antennae. This figure is repeated on the inside front cover for convenience.

To conserve space, we frequently use abbreviations when referring to commonly referenced parts or structures. Forewing and hindwing are shortened to FW and HW, respectively. Likewise, the antemedial line, postmedial line, and subterminal line are the AM, PM, and ST lines. These abbreviations are also used when referring to the areas of the wing with the same name. Measurements are given as either wingspan (WS) or total length (TL), with the former from wingtip to wingtip and the latter from head to tail.

Some additional moth-specific terminology is used throughout the accounts. These words and phrases have been defined in the glossary at the back of this book.

Some species of moths, such as Harris's Three-Spot, are unique and impossible to mistake for any other species, while others, such as the two habrosynes, can be separated only by a relatively subtle field mark. The markings that help distinguish a given species from similar ones are indicated on the plates using arrows, the unique and innovative system of identification pioneered by Roger Tory Peterson in his first field guide to birds. Clarification is also provided in the text. It is helpful to refer to both when trying to find an identification.

Just as in humans, even within the same species of moth there is often quite a bit of individual variation. Some individuals might be lighter in color than others, or darker, or a different color altogether; some might be well marked while others are very faint. A few individuals may be melanic: completely dark due to an excess of pigment. In some species there are multiple color patterns; in others, females look very different from males. Furthermore, some species of moths may live for a few weeks, and over time some scales may be rubbed off from the wings, affecting their appearance. Some very worn individuals may not be identifiable at all.

Flight Periods

The species composition of the moths that come to your light will change over the course of a season. The majority of the moths you see in May will be different from those you see in September. Knowing when the adults of a certain species are on the wing can help narrow down an identification. If you are considering between a species that flies in spring and one that flies in summer, and it's August, it's clear which of the two your moth is.

The length of time a species might be present varies among species. Some can be encountered nearly all year, whereas others fly during only a three- or four-week window. Several species raise two broods, meaning adults are encountered in two different non-overlapping periods; others emerge from their cocoons in the fall and then overwinter as adults, waking from hibernation to fly again in the spring.

Flight periods are shown as a visual representation to the left of the species account where the information can be seen at a quick glance. The three colored boxes represent spring, summer, and fall, and roughly correspond to three months each from March through November. The black line below the boxes indicates when the species is present. The range given represents the average flight period for the region covered by this guide; users in the south of our area might expect moths to fly a little bit earlier, or for longer, than indicated here, while users to the north will likely see the opposite. Flight periods are assumed to refer to a single brood unless otherwise indicated.

Range

Knowing where a moth occurs is every bit as important as knowing when it occurs. Previous field guides to moths have provided only a written description of the range for each species. Such descriptions are vague at best, as much is left to the interpretation of the user. In this guide we have endeavored to provide range maps for as many species as possible. The maps are easy to interpret and can quickly tell you whether to expect a species in your area. For those species where there is not enough available information to create a range map, we include a written description of range in the species account.

The paucity of data on moth species compared with other, more familiar groups, such as birds or trees, presented a challenge when preparing these maps. While the range of many common species is well known, there were insufficient data to create maps for some of the less abundant moths. Even where there was a good data set, it was impossible to draw a map with precision.

To get around these difficulties, we relied heavily on the use of ecoregions in mapping ranges. Unlike vertebrates, moths are strongly tied to the food plants their caterpillars eat—if these host plants aren't present, the moth won't be either. The host plants, in turn, are often restricted to certain environments, whether by temperature, soil type, drainage, etc. Similar environments and plant communities can be broadly grouped into large areas called ecoregions.

The ecoregion map we used to create the range maps in this guide is shown in Figure 5. This map was adapted from the North American Atlas, a project completed by the Commission for Environmental Cooperation in joint partnership with the three North American governments.

Although some plant species may be found in one part of an ecoregion but not another, in general this system allowed us to extrapolate a range from known data points. For instance, if a moth has been recorded in southern Michigan, there is a good chance it also occurs in southern Wisconsin and southern Ontario, and we have depicted it as such, even if we had no data from these latter two regions.

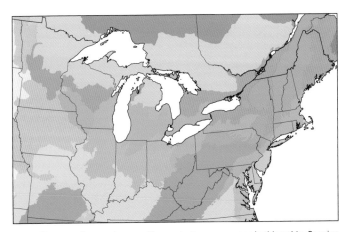

Fig 5. The map of ecoregions used to create the range maps in this guide. Species ranges were inferred by matching known data points to ecoregions and extrapolating to those ecoregions' boundaries. Map adapted from the North American Atlas by the Commission for Environmental Cooperation and the three North American governments. For a detailed explanation of the ecoregions, including region labels, visit http://www.cec.org/.

This approach is of course not without its own problems, and undoubtedly there will be instances in which the maps either over- or underrepresent the actual distribution. Also, the transition between habitat types is rarely a sharp line, and depending on the requirements of a given species it may be found slightly beyond the boundaries of its main ecoregion. Please bear this in mind when interpreting the maps. Additionally, moths are winged creatures, and many are capable of flying long distances. A range map is never a hard and fast rule, as birdwatchers can attest—species may show up out of range from time to time.

Maps are depicted in one of two colors. The darker shade indicates typical range, while the lighter shade represents migratory or vagrant range. In some instances, where the lighter shade borders a darker one, it is an indication of an expanding range; this is usually noted in the text.

Habitat and Host Plants

A moth species is rarely distributed evenly across its range. With few exceptions, most species can be found only in or near habitats that contain their larval food plants. Even though a species may be shown to occur throughout an entire state, there will be some locations in that state where the moth is abundant, and others where it cannot be found at all.

Habitat is another important tool in moth identification. Knowing that one species is found only in bogs and marshes while another frequents upland forests can make your decision easier. Likewise, if a species feeds on tamarack but there are no tamarack trees anywhere near you, you are unlikely to have the species turn up (but see the caveat above regarding winged organisms!).

Some moth species are very specific in their requirements. Their larvae may feed exclusively on only one or two plant species, and the distribution of such moths is often nearly identical to that of their host plants. Other species are generalists, whose caterpillars are not fussy about what they eat. These moths may be encountered across a broad range of habitats and ecoregions. Many (though not all) of the moths found throughout our coverage area are generalists, whereas those restricted to small ranges are often picky eaters.

Abundance

As you develop an interest in moths, one of the first things you are likely to notice is that some species are more abundant than others. This is true across all taxons—some species are just more common. We have tried to indicate relative abundance for each species to give you a sense of the likelihood of occurrence. However, the relative abundance of the different species attracted to a light may change from one location to another; what is plentiful in one locale may not be plentiful in another. This is partly determined by the host plants the larvae favor, with generalists being on average more abundant than specialists, and with specialists more abundant when their host plant is more abundant. Abundance is also affected by flight periods: a species will be more abundant in the middle of its flight period than at either end. Dozens may be seen in a night at the peak of the flight period, and a few weeks later you might find only one in an entire evening.

A large part of species identification in any taxon is knowing what to expect. By combining information on appearance, range, flight period, habitat, and abundance, it is usually possible to reach a probable or definitive identification.

Moth Taxonomy

There are two basic approaches to organizing a field guide: by grouping species of similar appearance together, or by organizing species taxonomically. Although a beginner often finds it easier to use a book in which similar species are presented side by side, this approach is frustrating once you have enough experience to be able to recognize taxonomic groups. If you know the moth you are looking at is a pinion because of its size and shape, but you don't know which one, you want to be able to flip to the section on pinions and compare them all. Books organized by similar appearance will have you flipping back and forth and back again to compare the different pinions in order to determine which yours is. Becoming familiar with the different taxonomic groups may take some time, but in the long run it will greatly aid your ability to identify different species.

The organization of this guide follows the most recent taxonomic updates as of this writing. Taxonomy is always changing as new research and studies reveal more about the relationships between species; species are moved from one group to another or are lumped or split to form new species. Major changes don't happen often, however, so the taxonomic organization used here should provide a firm base for learning.

Hodges and MPG Numbers

Every species of moth in North America is represented by a unique identification number in addition to its scientific and common names. The first series of numbers used originated from a publication by lepidopterist Ronald Hodges in which he assigned a number to every known moth species north of Mexico, and as such are called the Hodges numbers. This paper was published in 1983, and many taxonomic changes have taken place since then. Some numbers no longer exist because the species that bore them were lumped with others; new species have been described, requiring new numbers which in turn resulted in decimals being used; and some species have been moved to new groups, resulting in the numbers being out of order taxonomically. Despite this, the Hodges numbers are often useful to know, as once assigned, a number will remain with a species permanently, even through taxonomic revisions, renamings, and reorderings. Most websites and many publications organize their lists by Hodges number.

More recently, a new numbering system was created by Robert Patterson of the Moth Photographers Group website (we have used the label "MPG numbers" for this new scheme). This system assigns a two-digit prefix to each superfamily, and to each species a four-digit suffix, unique within the superfamily. This allows superfamilies to be numbered independently and quickly helps identify to which group a species belongs. As of 2010 only one superfamily, the Noctuoidea, had been formally assigned MPG numbers. Other superfamilies will be assigned MPG numbers as new taxonomic revisions are published.

The MPG numbers for the Noctuoidea reflect the current taxonomic order and are therefore less confusing than the original Hodges numbers. The order of species in this superfamily, as presented in this guide, follows that of the MPG numbers. For moths outside of the Noctuoidea, we have endeavored to present the families in current taxonomic order, but within each family the species remain ordered by Hodges number to avoid confusion.

Only the Noctuoidea superfamily has received an official prefix (93); however, in the checklist at the back of this guide we provide unofficial numbers in parentheses for all of the other groups. These two-digit numbers may be used as a prefix, in combination with the four-digit Hodges number as suffix, to create a similar six-digit number for personal uses such as labeling files or organizing checklists, in order to help sort them by current taxonomy. Although the prefix for the Noctuoidea is assigned at the superfamily level, our unofficial numbers are given at the family level, which is necessary to ensure proper taxonomic organization.

In the species accounts, the numbers are shown following the common and scientific names. For all groups up to the superfamily Noctuoidea, only the Hodges number is given. Beginning with the Noctuoidea, both the MPG and Hodges numbers are provided, with the latter in parentheses.

Common Names

A few taxonomic groups, such as birds and butterflies, have publications providing standardized common names, as decided by a committee of scientists with expertise in the field. No such publication yet exists for moths. While some species, such as the Luna Moth, are so familiar that they are known everywhere by a single name, many species have no commonly accepted name and can be found in different places with different names. To complicate matters, the common name of many moth species includes the genus the moth belongs to; however, taxonomic changes that move the species into another genus require that the common name be changed to reflect this.

The common names we use in this guide come largely from existing publications, primarily *A Field Guide to the Moths of Eastern North America* by Charles V. Covell, Jr. When multiple common names exist for a species, we have selected the one we feel is most representative or easiest to remember. In a few instances, we could find no evidence of a previously given common name and have coined our own.

Micros versus Macros

If you happen to attend a moth night with experienced moth enthusiasts, you might hear them refer to "macromoths" and "micromoths," or simply "macros" and "micros." For the most part, micromoths are relatively small moths and macromoths relatively large, but each group has a few exceptions that are closer in size to those of the other group.

The distinction between the two groups has more to do with taxonomy than it does with size, but the terms are handy labels. Taxonomy usually orders species according to their evolutionary age, with the oldest groups presented first, and the youngest—those that have diverged most recently—presented last. Strictly speaking, micromoths are those moths that appear on the first half of taxonomic lists, from the Goldcap Moss-Eater through the Mournful Thyris. The moths from Hodges #6235, Lettered Habrosyne, through to the end of the list are labeled macromoths. Conveniently for lepidopterists, the two groups also split by size, providing easy labels.

Moths and Conservation

Although we don't often see them, moths are an important part of the environment. Adult moths provide a valuable source of food for bats, many species of which feed almost exclusively while in flight, and caterpillars are a vital part of the diet that adult songbirds feed their nestlings. Some species of moths have periodic "outbreak" years, and certain types of birds are so tied to these outbreaks for their breeding success that their populations are seminomadic. As moth outbreaks have been suppressed for the benefit of the forestry industry, so too have we seen their dependent bird populations decline. There is some anecdotal evidence that insect populations have been declining for several decades, and especially those of flying insects, including moths. Most species of birds that feed exclusively on the wing, such as swallows and nighthawks, are in sharp decline. Although we typically think of bees as the pollinators of our fruits and vegetables, many species of moths are also pollinators, and their decline could have repercussions for us, too.

A large part of the problem is that we simply don't know very much about our moths, or insects in general. Unlike for birds, which have millions of enthusiasts across the continent and for which there are several national and international monitoring schemes, there are few programs to track insect populations. Most of those that exist in North America are either local or limited to a few species. Great Britain has developed the National Moth Recording Scheme (NMRS), a citizen science project that invites anyone anywhere in the country to submit their observations to a national database used to help track moth populations and learn more about their distribution. There are several excellent guides to the moths of Great Britain, and mothing is a popular activity as a result. Since the NMRS's inception in 2007, more than 8 million records have been collected for it.

Currently in North America we lack even a solid grasp of the distribution of many moth species. While state and county lists exist for birds and butterflies and even dragonflies, there are few such inventories for moths, and many are incomplete. Because so little is known about our moths and their distribution, every time you put your lights out at night you have the potential to contribute something valuable—that dart could be new for the county, or your July date for that sallow could be the earliest on record.

The more we know, the better our understanding, and the better able we are to design and implement conservation efforts. Our hope is that this guide will not only open up the world of moths to budding naturalists and enthusiasts, but will also help ensure the future of these beautiful insects for generations to come.

Columbine Borer

SPECIES
ACCOUNTS

MOSS-EATERS   Family Micropterigidae

Among North America's tiniest moths; only one species occurs in our area. Larvae feed on liverworts. Adults rarely come to light and are best sought at liverwort beds in early summer.

 GOLDCAP MOSS-EATER

Epimartyria auricrinella   0001   Uncommon

TL 4–6 mm. Dark gray FW is peppered with golden scales and has a coppery or purplish sheen when fresh. Top of head is golden yellow. **HOSTS:** Liverwort. **RANGE:** Se. Canada and ne. U.S.

GHOST MOTHS   Family Hepialidae

Medium to large moths. Wings are covered with tiny spinelike scales that give some species a slightly hairy aspect. Adults lack mouthparts and do not feed. Many species are crepuscular and can sometimes be found in mating swarms at dusk. They are rarely attracted to lights, but the introduced Lupulina Ghost Moth is an exception.

 SILVER-SPOTTED GHOST MOTH

Sthenopis argenteomaculatus   0018   Uncommon

TL 40–55 mm. Grayish FW is crossed by oblique bronzy brown bands. Two chunky white spots mark AM area. **HOSTS:** Primarily roots of partly submerged alder. **RANGE:** Se. Canada and ne. U.S.

 FOUR-SPOTTED GHOST MOTH

Sthenopis purpurascens   0019   Uncommon

TL 40–55 mm. FW is either purplish gray or brown with a complex pattern of dark and light oblique bands. Basal area is marked with two white dots. **HOSTS:** Primarily roots of poplar, also alder and willow. **RANGE:** S. Canada and ne. U.S. **NOTE:** The two color types were once considered to be separate species.

 WILLOW GHOST MOTH *Sthenopis thule*   0021   Uncommon

TL 40 mm. Yellow FW has brown shading along costa. Elongated, brown-edged white spots mark basal, median, and PM areas. **HOSTS:** Willow. **RANGE:** Se. Canada and ne. U.S.

MOSS-EATERS

actual size

GOLDCAP MOSS-EATER

GHOST MOTHS

actual size

**SILVER-SPOTTED
GHOST MOTH**

**FOUR-SPOTTED
GHOST MOTH**

WILLOW GHOST MOTH

GOLD-SPOTTED GHOST MOTH

Sthenopis auratus 0022 **Uncommon**
TL 34–38 mm. Brown FW has a brassy luster. Chunky gold spots mark AM, median, and ST areas. Costa and PM line are overlaid with pink lines. **HOSTS:** Ferns. **RANGE:** Se. Canada and extreme ne. U.S.

GRACEFUL GHOST MOTH

Korscheltellus gracilis 0031 **Uncommon**
TL 18–22 mm. Mottled brown FW has silvery gray patches in inner basal area and an oblique silvery gray band extending from inner margin to apex. **HOSTS:** Primarily roots of balsam fir and red spruce, also white spruce, birch, aspen, and ferns. **RANGE:** S. Canada and ne. U.S.

LUPULINA GHOST MOTH

Korscheltellus lupulina 0031.1 **Uncommon**
TL 14–18 mm. Brown or orange FW has an irregular, silvery white basal dash and oblique fragmented band extending from inner margin to apex. Male is smaller than female. **HOSTS:** Herbaceous plants, including chicory, lettuce, potato, and strawberry. **RANGE:** Mostly s. ON, but range expanding. **NOTE:** Introduced from Europe.

WHITE EYE-CAP AND YUCCA MOTHS
Families Opostegidae and Prodoxidae

Gooseberry Barkminer has broadly fringed, lanceolate wings and a shaggy head. Its larvae mine in stems and leaves of currants. Yucca Moth is stout-bodied with rounded white FW; often found in gardens with ornamental yucca plants. Adults of both species are mostly nocturnal and will come to lights in small numbers.

GOOSEBERRY BARKMINER

Opostega quadristrigella 0122 **Uncommon**
TL 10 mm. White FW has a brown blotch at midpoint of inner margin and a tiny black dot at apex. **HOSTS:** Currant and gooseberry. **RANGE:** Se. Canada and e. U.S.

YUCCA MOTH *Tegeticula yuccasella* 0198 **Uncommon**
TL 12–13 mm. White FW is dark brown on underside. Grayish brown HW is fringed white. **HOSTS:** Yucca. **RANGE:** S. Canada and e. U.S.

GHOST MOTHS

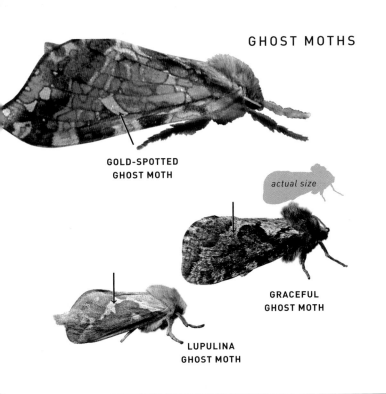

GOLD-SPOTTED
GHOST MOTH

actual size

GRACEFUL
GHOST MOTH

LUPULINA
GHOST MOTH

WHITE EYE-CAP AND
YUCCA MOTHS

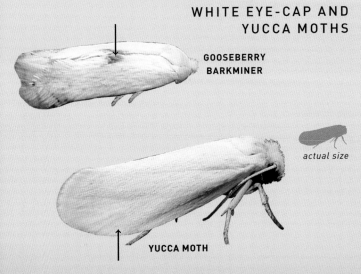

GOOSEBERRY
BARKMINER

actual size

YUCCA MOTH

29

Fairy Moths   Family Adelidae

Delicate moths with broad, boldly patterned FW. Many species have remarkably long antennae. Sometimes found taking nectar from flowers during daytime. Also nocturnal and will come to lights in small numbers.

RIDINGS' FAIRY MOTH *Adela ridingsella*   0228   Uncommon
TL 7–8 mm. Golden brown FW has a silver median band. Inner ST area is boldly marked with silver-edged black spots. Long antennae. **HOSTS:** Unknown. **RANGE:** Se. Canada and ne. U.S.

PURPLE FAIRY MOTH *Adela purpurea*   0229   Uncommon
TL 7–8 mm. Dark purplish FW has a black-edged white median band and incomplete white ST line. Very long antennae. **HOSTS:** Unknown. **RANGE:** Se. Canada and ne. U.S.

Fungus and Tube Moths
Families Tineidae and Acrolophidae

Small, streamlined moths with variably patterned FW markings. Many species have FW fringe slightly flared with hairlike scales. Larvae of many species are detritus feeders. Adults are mostly nocturnal and will come to lights in small numbers.

YELLOW WAVE MOTH *Hybroma servulella*   0300   Uncommon
TL 4–6 mm. Yellow FW has peppery brown patches along inner margin, costa, and in ST area. Head is yellow. **HOSTS:** Unknown. **RANGE:** Se. Canada and e. U.S.

SPECKLED XYLESTHIA
Xylesthia pruniramiella   0317   Common
TL 6–7 mm. Mottled brown FW is marked with pale bands. Tufts of raised scales create a lumpy appearance. **HOSTS:** Plum. **RANGE:** Se. Canada and ne. U.S.

BURROWING WEBWORM *Amydria effrentella*   0334   Common
TL 10–11 mm. Shiny tan FW is blotched with dark brown spots along costa. Thorax is dark brown. Hornlike labial palps are densely hairy at base. **HOSTS:** Unknown. **RANGE:** Se. Canada and e. U.S.

DARK GRASS-TUBEWORM *Acrolophus morus*   0367   Common
TL 15 mm. Brown FW has faint black patches in median area and paler patches along inner margin. **HOSTS:** Birch. **RANGE:** Se. Canada and e. U.S.

FAIRY MOTHS

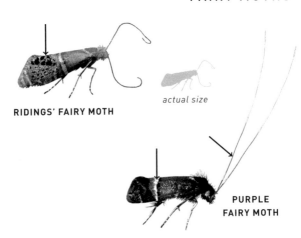

RIDINGS' FAIRY MOTH

actual size

**PURPLE
FAIRY MOTH**

FUNGUS AND TUBE MOTHS

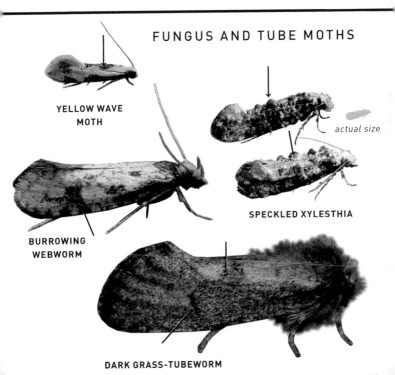

**YELLOW WAVE
MOTH**

actual size

**BURROWING
WEBWORM**

SPECKLED XYLESTHIA

DARK GRASS-TUBEWORM

DARK-COLLARED TINEA *Tinea apicimaculella* 0392 **Common**
TL 7–8 mm. Shiny tan FW has a narrow black streak extending through central area and a black dot in inner median area. Thorax is black. **HOSTS:** Unknown. **RANGE:** Widespread.

SAFFRON-HEADED MONOPIS
Monopis crocicapitella 0415 **Common**
TL 5–7 mm. Blackish FW has a jagged cream-colored stripe along inner margin and a white triangular patch at midpoint of costa. Shaggy-looking head is pale. **HOSTS:** Dead vegetable and animal matter. **RANGE:** Widespread.

PAVLOVSKI'S MONOPIS *Monopis pavlovski* 0418.1 **Common**
TL 7–10 mm. Grayish FW has a large white U-shaped patch covering outer median and ST area. Head and thorax are white. Raised tufts create a lumpy appearance. **HOSTS:** Dead vegetable and animal matter. **RANGE:** Se. Canada and ne. U.S. **NOTE:** Introduced from E. Asia.

ORANGE-HEADED MONOPIS *Monopis spilotella* 0421 **Common**
TL 8–10 mm. Bluish FW has white patches at midpoint of costa and inner ST area. Head is dull orange. **HOSTS:** Unknown. **RANGE:** Se. Canada and ne. U.S.

Ribbed Cocoon-making Moths
Family Bucculatricidae

Tiny, streamlined moths that have flared, feathery tips to FW. Head is topped with a tuft of hairlike scales. Larvae are either leaf miners or leaf skeletonizers on a variety of woody plants and deciduous trees. Some species will come to lights in very small numbers, but most adults are best observed by collecting and raising them from larval stages.

MOUNTAIN BUCCULATRIX
Bucculatrix montana 0486 **Common**
TL 5–6 mm. White FW is marked with a long tawny basal dash and fragmented angled lines. Fringe is peppered with black scales. **HOSTS:** Sweet Gale. **RANGE:** Se. Canada and ne. U.S.

NARROW BUCCULATRIX
Bucculatrix angustata 0522 **Uncommon**
TL 4–5 mm. Tawny brown FW is marked with a long white basal dash and fragmented, angled lines. Often has black dashes in inner median area and near apex. **HOSTS:** Aster and goldenrod. **RANGE:** Widespread.

FUNGUS AND TUBE MOTHS

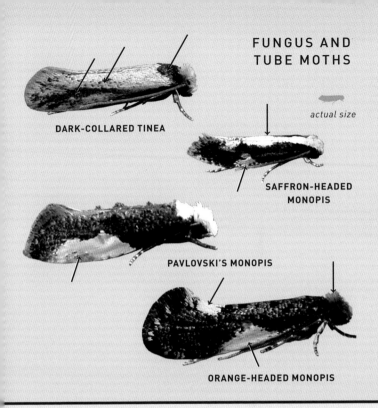

DARK-COLLARED TINEA

actual size

SAFFRON-HEADED MONOPIS

PAVLOVSKI'S MONOPIS

ORANGE-HEADED MONOPIS

RIBBED COCOON-MAKING MOTHS

MOUNTAIN BUCCULATRIX

actual size

NARROW BUCCULATRIX

CROWNED BUCCULATRIX

Bucculatrix coronatella 0559 **Uncommon**
TL 4–5 mm. Tawny FW has three slanting brown patches along costa. Midpoint of inner margin is accented with a raised tuft of black scales. **HOSTS:** Unknown. **RANGE:** Se. Canada and ne. U.S.

OAK SKELETONIZER *Bucculatrix ainsliella* 0572 **Common**
TL 4–5 mm. Brown FW is marked with three wide, fragmented white bands. Midpoint of inner margin is accented with a raised tuft of black scales. **HOSTS:** Oak. **RANGE:** Se. Canada and ne. U.S.

LEAF BLOTCH MINER MOTHS
Family Gracillariidae

Very small, streamlined moths that usually rest propped up on their fore-legs. In early instars the larvae are leafminers on a variety of deciduous trees. Later instars are leafrollers. Adults are nocturnal and freely visit lights in small numbers.

DOGWOOD CALOPTILIA

Caloptilia belfragella 0594 **Common**
TL 7 mm. Brown FW has elongated pale costal streak that widens in AM area. **HOSTS:** Dogwood. **RANGE:** Se. Canada and ne. U.S.

MAPLE CALOPTILIA

Caloptilia bimaculatella 0595 **Common**
TL 7 mm. Shiny purple FW has two golden yellow triangles jutting in from costa. **HOSTS:** Maple. **RANGE:** Se. Canada and ne. U.S.

WALNUT CALOPTILIA

Caloptilia blandella 0596 **Common**
TL 7 mm. Dark brown FW has a wide pale yellow costal streak interrupted by slanting brown AM line. **HOSTS:** Black walnut. **RANGE:** Se. Canada and ne. U.S.

ASH LEAF CONE ROLLER

Caloptilia fraxinella 0606 **Common**
TL 7–8 mm. Peppery brown FW is speckled with a few white scales along inner margin. **HOSTS:** Ash. **RANGE:** Se. Canada and ne. U.S.

RIBBED COCOON-MAKING MOTHS

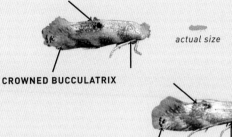

actual size

CROWNED BUCCULATRIX

OAK SKELETONIZER

LEAF BLOTCH MINER MOTHS

actual size

DOGWOOD CALOPTILIA

MAPLE CALOPTILIA

WALNUT CALOPTILIA

ASH LEAF CONE ROLLER

BOX-ELDER LEAFROLLER

Caloptilia negundella   0615   **Common**
TL 7 mm. Brown FW has mottled pale yellow costal streak.
HOSTS: Box elder. **RANGE:** Se. Canada and ne. U.S.

PACKARD'S CALOPTILIA

Caloptilia packardella   0620   **Common**
TL 7 mm. Bronzy FW has a large golden yellow triangle at midpoint of costa. **HOSTS:** Sugar maple. **RANGE:** Se. Canada and ne. U.S.

CHERRY LEAF CONE ROLLER

Caloptilia serotinella   0637   **Common**
TL 8–9 mm. Large. Dark brown FW is boldly mottled white.
HOSTS: Black cherry. **RANGE:** Se. Canada and ne. U.S.

POPLAR CALOPTILIA   *Caloptilia stigmatella*   0639   **Common**
TL 7 mm. Dark brown FW has a pale, hooked triangle at midpoint of costa. **HOSTS:** Poplar and willow. **RANGE:** Se. Canada and ne. U.S.

WITCH-HAZEL CALOPTILIA

Caloptilia superbifrontella   0641   **Common**
TL 7 mm. Tawny FW has a large golden yellow costal patch. Head, thorax, and basal section of inner margin are yellow.
HOSTS: Witch hazel. **RANGE:** Se. Canada and ne. U.S.

TICK-TREFOIL CALOPTILIA

Caloptilia violacella   0644   **Common**
TL 7 mm. Bronzy brown FW has a broad pale yellow costal streak and black dot in central median area. **HOSTS:** Tick trefoil.
RANGE: Se. Canada and ne. U.S.

LILAC LEAFMINER   *Caloptilia syringella*   0645   **Common**
TL 7 mm. Brown FW has a marbled pattern of black, gray, and white. Usually has small pale spots along costa. **HOSTS:** Unknown. **RANGE:** Se. Canada and ne. U.S.

WILLOW LEAF BLOTCH MINER

Micrurapteryx salicifoliella   0647   **Common**
TL 6 mm. Dark brown FW is broadly edged white along inner margin. Costa is marked with white streaks. Head and thorax are white. **HOSTS:** Willow. **RANGE:** Se. Canada and ne. U.S.

LEAF BLOTCH MINER MOTHS

BOX-ELDER LEAFROLLER

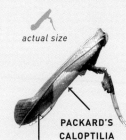

actual size

PACKARD'S CALOPTILIA

CHERRY LEAF CONE ROLLER

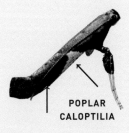

POPLAR CALOPTILIA

WITCH-HAZEL CALOPTILIA

TICK-TREFOIL CALOPTILIA

LILAC LEAFMINER

WILLOW LEAF BLOTCH MINER

LOCUST DIGITATE LEAFMINER

Parectopa robiniella   0657   **Common**
TL 5–6 mm. Golden brown FW has a pattern of incomplete, slanting white bands. Fringe has tufts of white scales. **HOSTS:** Fleabane and plantain. **RANGE:** Se. Canada and ne. U.S.

FINITE-CHANNELED LEAFMINER

Neurobathra strigifinitella   0663   **Common**
TL 5 mm. Gray FW has a fine pattern of angled, black-edged white lines. Apex is marked with a black dot. **HOSTS:** Oak. **RANGE:** Se. Canada and ne. U.S.

PARORNIX SPECIES COMPLEX

Parornix spp.   0686.97   **Common**
TL 4–5 mm. A complex of several species that cannot be identified without the aid of a microscope. Gray FW is marked with thin white dashes along costa and inner margin, with a black dot near apex. **HOSTS:** Deciduous trees and woody plants, depending on species. **RANGE:** Widespread.

SNAKEROOT LEAFMINER

Leucospilapteryx venustella   0698   **Uncommon**
TL 4 mm. Peppery brown FW has narrow, black-edged white bands. Top of head and thorax is white. **HOSTS:** White snakeroot. **RANGE:** Se. Canada and e. U.S.

GOLDENROD LEAFMINER

Cremastobombycia solidaginis   0723   **Uncommon**
TL 5–6 mm. Pale orange FW is weakly marked with angled white median and PM lines. Edging to lines is sprinkled with black scales. **HOSTS:** Goldenrod. **RANGE:** Se. Canada and e. U.S.

LESSER MAPLE LEAF BLOTCH MINER

Phyllonorycter lucidicostella   0765   **Uncommon**
TL 5–6 mm. White FW is weakly marked with angled tan lines. Terminal line has a black dot at apex. **HOSTS:** Maple. **RANGE:** Se. Canada and ne. U.S.

CHERRY BLOTCH MINER

Phyllonorycter propinquinella   0784   **Uncommon**
TL 5–6 mm. Golden FW is boldly patterned with black-edged white lines and wedges. White basal dash and black apical dash are noticeable. **HOSTS:** Black cherry. **RANGE:** Se. Canada and ne. U.S.

LEAF BLOTCH MINER MOTHS

actual size

LOCUST DIGITATE LEAFMINER

PARORNIX SPECIES COMPLEX

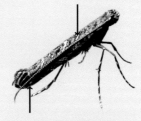

FINITE-CHANNELED LEAFMINER

GOLDENROD LEAFMINER

SNAKEROOT LEAFMINER

LESSER MAPLE LEAF BLOTCH MINER

CHERRY BLOTCH MINER

BLACK LOCUST LEAFMINER
Phyllonorycter robiniella 0790 **Uncommon**
TL 5–6 mm. Golden FW is boldly patterned with angled silvery lines. Short black bar in inner median area and black apical spot are noticeable. **HOSTS:** Black locust. **RANGE:** Se. Canada and ne. U.S.

HORNBEAM LEAFMINER
Cameraria ostryarella 0832 **Uncommon**
TL 5–6 mm. Golden brown FW is boldly patterned with almost straight, black-edged white bands. Angled ST line is fragmented. **HOSTS:** Eastern hornbeam and ironwood. **RANGE:** Se. Canada and ne. U.S.

ERMINE AND NEEDLEMINER MOTHS
Families Lyonetiidae and Yponomeutidae

Small to tiny moths with long, narrow wings. Ailanthus Webworm resembles Ornate Moth (tiger moth family). The ermines are distinctive, white with many small black spots that are variable in number and placement. The *Argyresthia* are tiny species whose white and gold coloration is the most distinguishing feature when viewed with the naked eye. The adults of all species are nocturnal and frequently visit lights in small to moderate numbers.

CLEMENS' PHILONOME
Philonome clemensella 0462 **Uncommon**
TL 5 mm. Peppery brown FW has a white basal dash connected to fragmented white AM line. Thorax is white. **HOSTS:** Hickory. **RANGE:** Sw. ON and ne. U.S.

AILANTHUS WEBWORM *Atteva aurea* 2401 **Common**
TL 11–15 mm. Reddish orange FW is boldly patterned with wide black-edged bands of pale yellow spots. **HOSTS:** Ailanthus, also other deciduous trees and shrubs. **RANGE:** Sw. ON and e. U.S.

GRAY-BLUE SWAMMERDAMIA
Swammerdamia caesiella 2413 **Common**
TL 7 mm. Mottled gray FW has a darker fringe and indigo terminal line. Head and dorsal surface of thorax are white. **HOSTS:** Birch, cherry, and hawthorn. **RANGE:** Se. Canada and ne. U.S.

LEAF BLOTCH MINER MOTHS

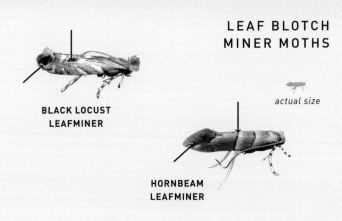

BLACK LOCUST LEAFMINER

actual size

HORNBEAM LEAFMINER

ERMINE AND NEEDLEMINER MOTHS

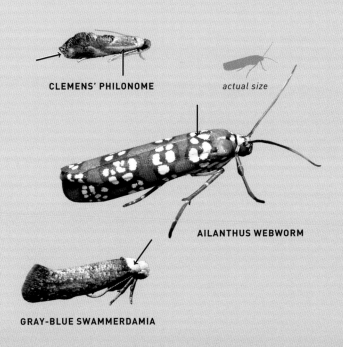

CLEMENS' PHILONOME

actual size

AILANTHUS WEBWORM

GRAY-BLUE SWAMMERDAMIA

AMERICAN ERMINE
Yponomeuta multipunctella   2420   **Common**
TL 11–13 mm. White FW is evenly covered with three or four rows of tiny black dots. HW is white. **HOSTS:** Running strawberry bush. **RANGE:** Se. Canada and e. U.S.

ORCHARD ERMINE   *Yponomeuta padella*   2421   **Common**
TL 10–11 mm. Resembles American Ermine but has fewer dots and central area of FW is unmarked. HW is gray. **HOSTS:** Cherry, hawthorn, mountain ash, and serviceberry. **RANGE:** Se. Canada. **NOTE:** Introduced from Europe.

SPINDLE ERMINE   *Yponomeuta cagnagella*   2423.1   **Common**
TL 10–13 mm. Resembles Orchard Ermine but has more black dots around edges of FW. HW is dark gray. **HOSTS:** Spindle. **RANGE:** Se. Canada and extreme ne. U.S. **NOTE:** Introduced from Europe.

PINE NEEDLE SHEATHMINER
Zelleria haimbachi   2427   **Common**
TL 7–8 mm. Fawn-colored FW has a white stripe extending through central part of wing. Head and dorsal surface of thorax are white. **HOSTS:** Pine. **RANGE:** Se. Canada and e. U.S.

HONEY-COMB MICRO
Argyresthia alternatella   2435   **Common**
TL 5–6 mm. Fawn-colored FW is marked with a netlike pattern of brown lines. Dorsal surface of head is white. **HOSTS:** Unknown. **RANGE:** Se. Canada and ne. U.S.

BRONZE ALDER MOTH
Argyresthia goedartella   2457   **Common**
TL 6–7 mm. Satin white FW is boldly marked with three metallic bronze bands. Median band is Y-shaped. Adopts a headstand resting position. **HOSTS:** Alder and birch. **RANGE:** Widespread.

CHERRY SHOOT BORER
Argyresthia oreasella   2467   **Common**
TL 6 mm. Resembles Bronze Alder Moth but lacks bronzy basal band and often incomplete median band is not Y-shaped. Adopts a headstand resting position. **HOSTS:** Chokecherry, pin cherry, and Saskatoon berry. **RANGE:** Widespread.

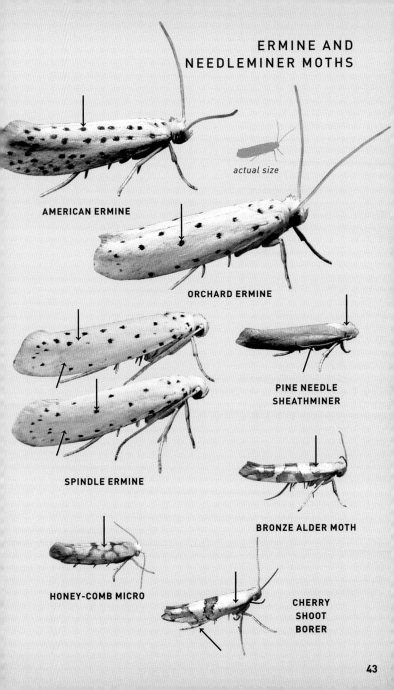

ERMINE AND NEEDLEMINER MOTHS

AMERICAN ERMINE

actual size

ORCHARD ERMINE

SPINDLE ERMINE

PINE NEEDLE
SHEATHMINER

BRONZE ALDER MOTH

HONEY-COMB MICRO

CHERRY
SHOOT
BORER

43

FALCATE-WINGED MOTHS   Family Ypsolophidae

Small, narrow-winged moths that typically rest with their antennae held forward from the body. The wings curl up at the tips. Adults are nocturnal and come to lights in small numbers.

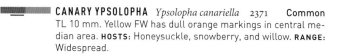

CANARY YPSOLOPHA   *Ypsolopha canariella*   2371   **Common**
TL 10 mm. Yellow FW has dull orange markings in central median area. **HOSTS:** Honeysuckle, snowberry, and willow. **RANGE:** Widespread.

EUROPEAN HONEYSUCKLE MOTH
Ypsolopha dentella   2375   **Common**
TL 10–11 mm. Chocolate brown FW has a pale stripe along inner margin that curves into inner PM area. **HOSTS:** Honeysuckle. **RANGE:** Se. Canada and ne. U.S. **NOTE:** Introduced from Europe.

SCYTHED YPSOLOPHA
Ypsolopha falciferella   2380   **Uncommon**
TL 10 mm. Gray FW is marked with oblique brownish bands in median and ST areas. Typically has a speckled appearance. Outer margin of FW has a deep notch. **HOSTS:** Chokecherry. **RANGE:** Widespread.

SEDGE, DIAMONDBACK, AND FALSE DIAMONDBACK MOTHS
Families Glyphipterigidae, Plutellidae, and Acrolepiidae

Small, narrow-winged moths. The *Plutella* species rest with their antennae held forward from the body. The flared wings may appear to curl up at the tips. Adults are nocturnal and come to lights in small numbers.

YELLOW NUTSEDGE MOTH
Diploschizia impigritella   2346   **Uncommon**
TL 4–5 mm. Bronzy FW has a backward-pointing white crescent at midpoint of inner margin. Five short silver bars mark subapical area. **HOSTS:** Yellow nutsedge. **RANGE:** Se. Canada and e. U.S.

DAME'S ROCKET MOTH   *Plutella porrectella*   2363   **Uncommon**
TL 7–8 mm. Pale FW is streaked with brown. Terminal line is blackish. Antennae have three dusky bands near tip. **HOSTS:** Dame's rocket. **RANGE:** Se. Canada and ne. U.S.

FALCATE-WINGED MOTHS

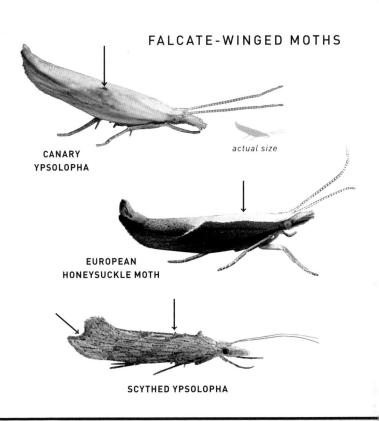

**CANARY
YPSOLOPHA**

actual size

**EUROPEAN
HONEYSUCKLE MOTH**

SCYTHED YPSOLOPHA

SEDGE, DIAMONDBACK, AND
FALSE DIAMONDBACK MOTHS

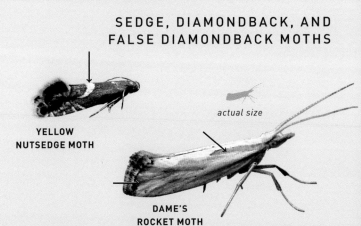

**YELLOW
NUTSEDGE MOTH**

actual size

**DAME'S
ROCKET MOTH**

45

DIAMONDBACK MOTH *Plutella xylostella* 2366 **Common**
TL 7–8 mm. Sexually dimorphic. FW of male is brown with a jagged ochre stripe along inner margin. Paler female shows less contrast. **HOSTS:** Various plants in the Brassicaceae. **RANGE:** Widespread. **NOTE:** Introduced from Europe before the 1850s.

CARRIONFLOWER MOTH
Acrolepiopsis incertella 2490 **Uncommon**
TL 6 mm. Purplish brown FW is marked with a bold white tooth at midpoint of inner margin. Midpoint of fringe has a white spot. **HOSTS:** Bristly greenbrier and lily. **RANGE:** Sw. ON and e. U.S.

Grass Miner Moths Family Elachistidae

A distinctive group of small, flattish moths with long upward-curving labial palps. Several species overwinter as adults and can be encountered in early spring. All species are nocturnal and visit lights in small numbers.

RED AGONOPTERIX *Agonopterix lythrella* 0857 **Common**
TL 7–9 mm. Reddish FW is peppered gray along costa and AM and PM lines. Two tiny black dots (sometimes fused) mark AM area. **HOSTS:** Loosestrife and Saint John's wort. **RANGE:** Se. Canada and ne. U.S.

CURVE-LINED AGONOPTERIX
Agonopterix curvilineella 0859 **Common**
TL 8–10 mm. Gray FW is speckled whitish along costa. Median area is marked with a short curved black bar and white discal dot. **HOSTS:** Unknown. **RANGE:** Se. Canada and ne. U.S.

CLEMENS' AGONOPTERIX
Agonopterix clemensella 0862 **Common**
TL 8–10 mm. Brown FW is mottled whitish along costa. Two white dots accent blackish central median patch. **HOSTS:** Parsnip. **RANGE:** Se. Canada and ne. U.S.

BROWN-COLLARED AGONOPTERIX
Agonopterix atrodorsella 0864 **Common**
TL 10–13 mm. Pale FW has small blackish basal patch and blackish mottling along costa. Darker median area has a white discal dot. Head and thorax are black. **HOSTS:** Boneset, coreopsis, beggar ticks, and sweet fern. **RANGE:** Se. Canada and e. U.S.

SEDGE, DIAMONDBACK, AND FALSE DIAMONDBACK MOTHS

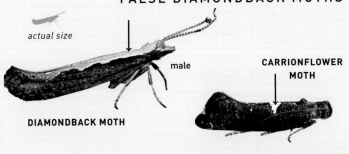

actual size

male

DIAMONDBACK MOTH

CARRIONFLOWER MOTH

GRASS MINER MOTHS

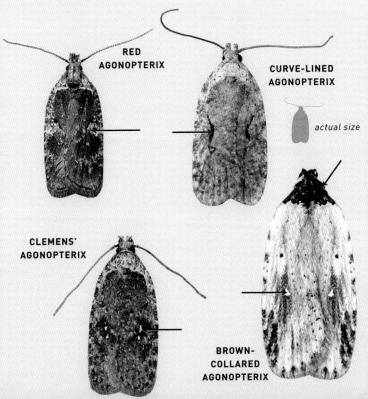

RED AGONOPTERIX

CURVE-LINED AGONOPTERIX

actual size

CLEMENS' AGONOPTERIX

BROWN-COLLARED AGONOPTERIX

FEATHERDUSTER AGONOPTERIX
Agonopterix pulvipennella 0867 **Common**
TL 10–12 mm. Mottled brown FW is streaked blackish in median and ST areas. A white discal dot marks median area. **HOSTS:** Goldenrod and nettle. **RANGE:** Se. Canada and ne. U.S.

POISON HEMLOCK AGONOPTERIX
Agonopterix alstromeriana 0874.1 **Common**
TL 10–12 mm. Milky brown FW is scattered with dusky scales. Costa is white basally. Large blackish median patch is bordered red on inner side. **HOSTS:** Poison hemlock. **RANGE:** Se. Canada and ne. U.S. **NOTE:** Introduced from Europe in the 1800s.

CANADIAN AGONOPTERIX
Agonopterix canadensis 0878 **Common**
TL 10–12 mm. Pale FW is mottled and streaked brown in median and ST areas. Costa is whitish basally. Black blotch in median area is flanked with smaller dots. **HOSTS:** Ragwort. **RANGE:** Se. Canada and ne. U.S.

FOUR-DOTTED AGONOPTERIX
Agonopterix robiniella 0882 **Common**
TL 8–12 mm. Pale orange FW is peppered with rusty scales. Darker zigzag bar extends through inner median area. A black dot marks AM area. **HOSTS:** Black locust. **RANGE:** Se. Canada and ne. U.S.

BOG BIBARRAMBLA *Bibarrambla alenella* 0911 **Common**
TL 10–12 mm. Pale gray FW is speckled with darker scales. Short lines of black-edged raised scales mark faint AM and PM lines. **HOSTS:** Alder and birch. **RANGE:** Se. Canada and ne. U.S.

PACKARD'S SEMIOSCOPIS
Semioscopis packardella 0912 **Common**
TL 12–15 mm. Silvery FW has a sinuous black line extending from base to central median area. An ochre streak extends through center of wing. **HOSTS:** Possibly rosaceous plants. **RANGE:** Se. Canada and ne. U.S.

PLAIN SEMIOSCOPIS *Semioscopis inornata* 0914 **Common**
TL 12–16 mm. Whitish FW is finely peppered with blackish scales. Short lines of black-edged raised scales along faint AM and PM lines. **HOSTS:** Poplar and willow. **RANGE:** Se. Canada and ne. U.S.

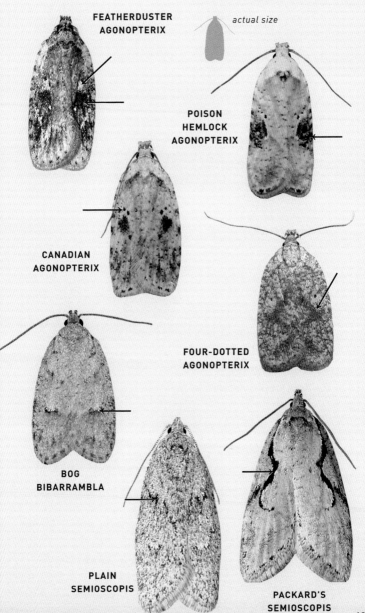

GRASS MINER MOTHS

FEATHERDUSTER
AGONOPTERIX

actual size

POISON
HEMLOCK
AGONOPTERIX

CANADIAN
AGONOPTERIX

FOUR-DOTTED
AGONOPTERIX

BOG
BIBARRAMBLA

PLAIN
SEMIOSCOPIS

PACKARD'S
SEMIOSCOPIS

49

AURORA SEMIOSCOPIS *Semioscopis aurorella* 0916 **Common**
TL 12–15 mm. Grayish brown FW has paler costal streak. A fragmented black line extends from base to central median area. **HOSTS:** Unknown, possibly birch. **RANGE:** Se. Canada and ne. U.S.

PARSNIP WEBWORM *Depressaria pastinacella* 0922 **Common**
TL 10–14 mm. Yellowish brown FW has blackish streaks extending along veins. Thorax and head are straw colored. **HOSTS:** Umbellifers, including parsnip and angelica. **RANGE:** Widespread.

YARROW WEBWORM *Depressaria alienella* 0926 **Common**
TL 9–11 mm. Reddish brown FW is speckled with pale gray scales. Thorax and head are whitish. **HOSTS:** Yarrow. **RANGE:** S. Canada and ne. U.S.

GOLD-STRIPED LEAFTIER
Machimia tentoriferella 0951 **Common**
TL 12–14 mm. Yellowish tan FW is marked with three black dots in AM area and fragmented median band. Apex is pointed. **HOSTS:** Deciduous trees, including ash, birch, elm, oak, maple, and poplar. **RANGE:** Se. Canada and e. U.S.

DOTTED LEAFTIER *Psilocorsis reflexella* 0957 **Common**
TL 7–12 mm. Light brown FW is brindled with thin brown lines. A black discal spot marks median area. **HOSTS:** Deciduous trees, including beech, birch, hickory, oak, maple, and poplar. **RANGE:** Se. Canada and e. U.S.

VIPER'S BUGLOSS MOTH *Ethmia bipunctella* 0986 **Common**
TL 10–14 mm. White FW is mostly black toward costa with an irregular inner edge. Terminal line is a row of black dots. **HOSTS:** Viper's bugloss. **RANGE:** Se. Canada and e. U.S.

ZELLER'S ETHMIA *Ethmia zelleriella* 0992 **Common**
TL 11–14 mm. White FW is boldly marked with black spots and streaks. Abdomen and legs are pale yellow. Gray HW has a pale fringe. **HOSTS:** *Phacelia* species. **RANGE:** Se. Canada and e. U.S.

STREAKED ETHMIA *Ethmia longimaculella* 0999 **Common**
TL 10–14 mm. Resembles Zeller's Ethmia, but FW is more evenly streaked. Terminal line is a row of black dots. HW is pearly gray. **HOSTS:** Puccoon. **RANGE:** S. Canada and e. U.S.

GRASS MINER MOTHS

AURORA
SEMIOSCOPIS

YARROW WEBWORM

PARSNIP
WEBWORM

GOLD-STRIPED
LEAFTIER

actual size

DOTTED
LEAFTIER

VIPER'S
BUGLOSS MOTH

ZELLER'S ETHMIA

STREAKED ETHMIA

SCHLAEGER'S FRUITWORM MOTH
Antaeotricha schlaegeri 1011 **Common**
TL 11–15 mm. White FW has pale gray bands in basal, median, and ST areas. Thorax has an erect tuft of blue-black scales. **HOSTS:** Oaks, primarily white oak. **RANGE:** Se. Canada and e. U.S.

LINDEN BARK-BORER
Chrysoclista linneella 1463 **Uncommon**
TL 6 mm. Pointed FW is orange with a blackish border. Three raised silver spots mark median area. Thorax and head are silver. **HOSTS:** European linden, possibly basswood. **RANGE:** Se. Canada and extreme ne. U.S. **NOTE:** A European species, first discovered in NY in 1928.

CONCEALER AND SCAVENGER MOTHS
Families Xyloryctidae, Oecophoridae, and Autostichidae

Small moths with long, narrow wings; those of a few species are flared. Many species are brightly or distinctively marked. Larvae of most species feed on dead leaves and fungi. Adults are nocturnal and will come to lights in small numbers.

RETICULATED DECANTHA
Decantha boreasella 1042 **Common**
TL 5–6 mm. Pale orange FW has a netlike pattern of white lines and patches of peppery brown shading. **HOSTS:** Unknown, possibly fungus on deadwood. **RANGE:** Se. Canada and e. U.S.

ORANGE-HEADED EPICALLIMA
Epicallima argenticinctella 1046 **Common**
TL 6–7 mm. Yellow FW has brown basal area and shading in ST area. Silver lines are slightly bent. **HOSTS:** Elm. **RANGE:** Se. Canada and ne. U.S.

BEAUTIFUL DAFA *Dafa formosella* 1048 **Uncommon**
TL 6–7 mm. Pale orange FW has irregular brown median band and shading along outer margin. **HOSTS:** Birch. **RANGE:** Se. Canada and ne. U.S. **NOTE:** Introduced from Europe.

THE SKUNK *Polix coloradella* 1058 **Uncommon**
TL 11 mm. Sooty black FW has pale yellow streak along inner margin that extends along inner PM line. **HOSTS:** Dead and decaying wood and bark. **RANGE:** S. Canada and n. U.S.

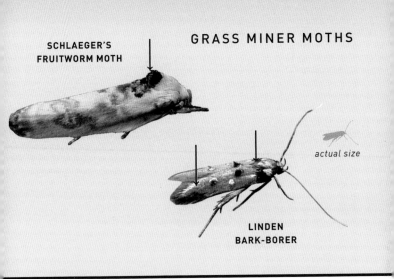

GRASS MINER MOTHS

SCHLAEGER'S FRUITWORM MOTH

actual size

LINDEN BARK-BORER

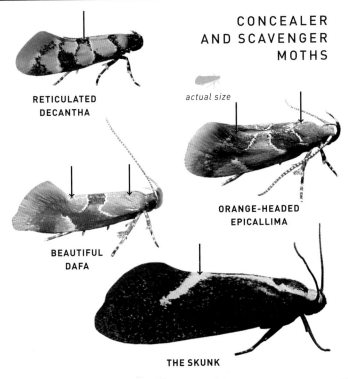

CONCEALER AND SCAVENGER MOTHS

RETICULATED DECANTHA

actual size

BEAUTIFUL DAFA

ORANGE-HEADED EPICALLIMA

THE SKUNK

THREE-SPOTTED CONCEALER MOTH

Eido trimaculella 1068 **Common**

TL 6–7 mm. Grayish brown FW is lightly peppered whitish. Two white costal patches and checkered fringe are noticeable when fresh. Rests in a shallow headstand position. **HOSTS:** Reported on bracket fungus and elm. **RANGE:** S. Canada and n. U.S.

FOUR-SPOTTED YELLOWNECK

Oegoconia novimundi 1134 **Common**

TL 7–9 mm. Peppery blackish FW is boldly marked with fragmented pale yellow bands. **HOSTS:** Detritus in leaf litter. **RANGE:** S. Canada and n. U.S.

GERDANA MOTH *Gerdana caritella* 1144 **Common**

TL 7–8 mm. Peppery yellow FW has blackish basal patch and fragmented PM and ST lines. AM line is reduced to two dots. **HOSTS:** Unknown. **RANGE:** Se. Canada and e. U.S.

ACORN MOTH *Blastobasis glandulella* 1162 **Common**

TL 8–13 mm. Gray FW has a kinked whitish AM band bordering a blackish median patch. Two black dots in reniform area are usually noticeable. **HOSTS:** Larvae feed inside acorns and chestnuts. **RANGE:** Se. Canada and e. U.S.

CASEBEARER MOTHS Family Coleophoridae

Small, streamlined moths, usually with long forward-pointing antennae. Larvae mine in leaves and seeds, living in cases made from plant material and frass. Most species are difficult to identify as adults and are best identified by the larval cases. Adults are mostly nocturnal and will come to lights in small numbers.

AMERICAN PISTOL CASEBEARER

Coleophora atromarginata 1257 **Common**

TL 10 mm. White FW is speckled brown toward apex. Antennae are banded with gray. **HOSTS:** Red oak and swamp oak, also birch, cherry, hazelnut, hickory, and ironwood. **RANGE:** Se. Canada and e. U.S.

CHERRY CASEBEARER *Coleophora pruniella* 1271 **Common**

TL 6–8 mm. FW is whitish to slate gray with a granular look. Antennae are banded black and white. **HOSTS:** Deciduous trees and woody plants, including alder, apple, birch, cherry, myrtle, poplar, and sweet fern. **RANGE:** Se. Canada and e. U.S.

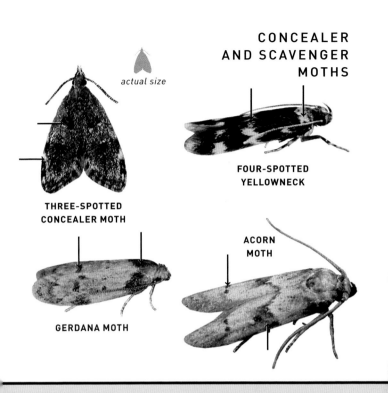

CONCEALER AND SCAVENGER MOTHS

actual size

THREE-SPOTTED CONCEALER MOTH

FOUR-SPOTTED YELLOWNECK

GERDANA MOTH

ACORN MOTH

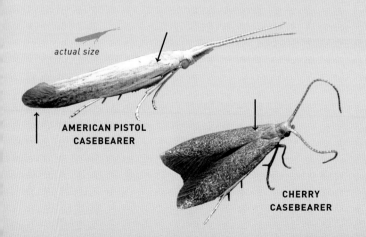

CASEBEARER MOTHS

actual size

AMERICAN PISTOL CASEBEARER

CHERRY CASEBEARER

METALLIC CASEBEARER

Coleophora mayrella 1387 **Common**

TL 8 mm. Metallic bronzy green FW has a reddish sheen near apex. White-tipped antennae are thickened at base. **HOSTS:** Clover seeds. **RANGE:** Se. Canada and e. U.S.

LARGE CLOVER CASEBEARER

Coleophora trifolii 1388 **Common**

TL 8 mm. Resembles Metallic Casebearer, but antennae lack thickened basal section. **HOSTS:** Sweet clover. **RANGE:** Se. Canada and e. U.S. **NOTE:** Introduced from Europe.

RED-STREAKED MOMPHA *Mompha eloisella* 1443 **Common**

TL 6–8 mm. White FW has reddish V-shaped lines and tufts of gray hairlike scales toward pointed apex. Black spots mark median area, inner margin, and thorax. **HOSTS:** Stems of evening primrose. **RANGE:** Se. Canada and e. U.S.

CHENOPODIUM SCYTHRIS *Scythris limbella* 1673 **Common**

TL 8–9 mm. Shiny pale tan FW is marked with brown blotches. Flared fringe is blackish. **HOSTS:** Goosefoot and orach. **RANGE:** Se. Canada and ne. U.S. **NOTE:** Introduced from Europe.

COSMET MOTHS   Family Cosmopterigidae

Small moths with moderately narrow wings. Larvae are predominantly miners of leaves or stems, or feed on flower buds or seed heads. Caterpillars of Shy Cosmet are usually responsible for fluffy cattail heads observed in midwinter. Adults are nocturnal and will come to lights, though a few species may also be observed during the day.

KERMES SCALE MOTH

Euclemensia bassettella 1467 **Common**

TL 5–7 mm. Black FW has a broad orange stripe along costa and basal area. Raised tufts of silvery scales mark AM and PM areas. **HOSTS:** Larvae parasitize oak-inhabiting scale insects in the genus *Kermes*. **RANGE:** Extreme se. Canada and e. U.S.

CHAMBERS' COSMOPTERIX

Cosmopterix pulchrimella 1472 **Common**

TL 4–5 mm. Dark brown FW has an even, dull orange median band edged with silver. Four silvery streaks pass through AM area. **HOSTS:** Clearweed and Pennsylvania pellitory. **RANGE:** Se. Canada and e. U.S.

CASEBEARER MOTHS

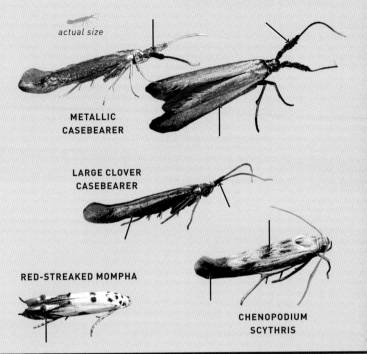

actual size

METALLIC CASEBEARER

LARGE CLOVER CASEBEARER

RED-STREAKED MOMPHA

CHENOPODIUM SCYTHRIS

COSMET MOTHS

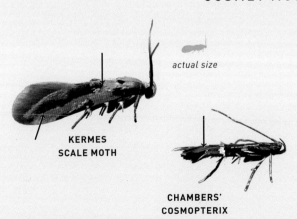

actual size

KERMES SCALE MOTH

CHAMBERS' COSMOPTERIX

MOUNTAIN COSMOPTERIX

Cosmopterix montisella   1476   **Uncommon**

TL 6–7 mm. Resembles Chambers' Cosmopterix but has a pale orange L-shaped median band edged distally with two separate silvery spots. **HOSTS:** Unknown. **RANGE:** Se. Canada, w. and n.e. U.S.

SHY COSMET   *Limnaecia phragmitella*   1515   **Common**

TL 7–11 mm. Shiny, pale tan FW is streaked with brown near apex. Two white-ringed brown spots mark AM and PM areas. **HOSTS:** Flowers and developing seeds of cattail. **RANGE:** Se. Canada and ne. U.S.

HOG-PEANUT LEAF-SEWER

Stilbosis tesquella   1609   **Uncommon**

TL 4–6 mm. Silvery gray FW is tinged purplish bronze at base and apex. Three tufts of raised gold and brown scales accent median area. **HOSTS:** Hog peanut. **RANGE:** Extreme se. Canada and ne. U.S.

SWEETCLOVER ROOT BORER

Walshia miscecolorella   1615   **Uncommon**

TL 6–10 mm. Mottled FW has a wide pale tan median band. Two tufts of raised blackish scales mark basal area, with another tuft in PM area. **HOSTS:** Lupine, sweet clover, thistle, and other leguminous plants. **RANGE:** Widespread.

PERIMEDE SPECIES COMPLEX

Perimede ricina/falcata   1631/1632   **Uncommon**

TL 5–7 mm. Two species are nearly identical. Gray FW is marked with three black spots in AM and PM areas. Whitish ST line is broken in middle. Fringe has a patch of yellowish scales just below apex. Rests in a headstand position. **HOSTS:** Unknown. **RANGE:** Se. Canada and e. U.S.

COSMET MOTHS

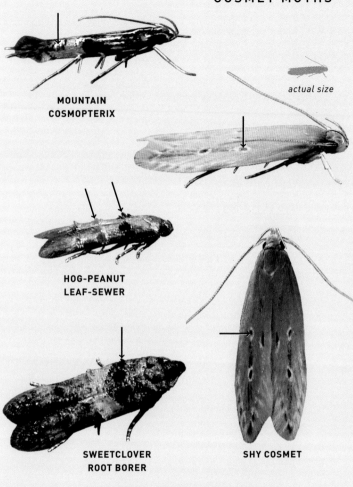

actual size

MOUNTAIN COSMOPTERIX

HOG-PEANUT LEAF-SEWER

SWEETCLOVER ROOT BORER

SHY COSMET

PERIMEDE SPECIES COMPLEX

59

TWIRLER MOTHS   Family Gelechiidae

A huge assemblage of small and very small moths, with upward-pointing labial palps that curve over the head like tiny horns. A varied group; some are remarkably colorful or metallic, whereas others are relatively plain and difficult to identify. Larvae of the Goldenrod Gall Moth are among three insect species responsible for the galls observed on goldenrod stems. Adults of most species come to light in small to moderate numbers. Some, such as Pink-washed Aristotelia, are also commonly observed during the day.

BURDOCK SEEDHEAD MOTH
Metzneria lappella   1685   **Common**
TL 8–10 mm. Tan FW is streaked rusty brown with a tiny black discal spot. **HOSTS:** Burdock seeds. **RANGE:** Se. Canada and e. U.S. **NOTE:** Introduced from Eurasia.

SILVER-BANDED MOTH
Chrysoesthia lingulacella   1718   **Common**
TL 4–5 mm. Golden yellow FW is marked with silver streaks and bands. Blackish fringe is hairy. Head and thorax are silver. **HOSTS:** Orach and goosefoot. **RANGE:** Widespread, but local and erratic.

ORANGE-CRESCENT MOTH
Enchrysa dissectella   1721   **Uncommon**
TL 6 mm. Bronzy FW has an orange streak along inner margin beyond silvery median band. **HOSTS:** Unknown. **RANGE:** Se. Canada and ne. U.S.

PINK-WASHED ARISTOTELIA
Aristotelia roseosuffusella   1761   **Common**
TL 7 mm. Brown FW has a bold pattern of oblique black and white bars. Light brown inner margin is marked with pink spots. **HOSTS:** Clover. **RANGE:** Widespread.

LESSER BUD MOTH   *Recurvaria nanella*   1783   **Common**
TL 6–7 mm. Peppery gray FW has a curving black AM line and fragmented black crescent arching through ST area. **HOSTS:** Unknown. **RANGE:** Se. Canada and e. U.S.

SOUTHERN NEEDLEMINER
Coleotechnites australis   1793   **Common**
TL 5 mm. Pale tan FW is dotted with tufts of raised black and white scales. Slanting black lines are obvious only along costa. White ST line is V-shaped. **HOSTS:** Unknown. **RANGE:** Se. Canada and e. U.S.

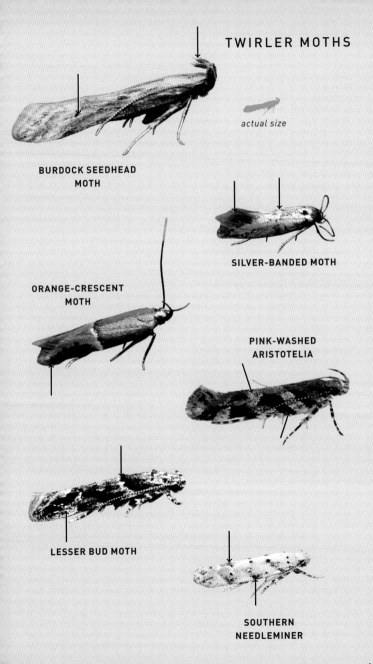

TWIRLER MOTHS

actual size

BURDOCK SEEDHEAD MOTH

SILVER-BANDED MOTH

ORANGE-CRESCENT MOTH

PINK-WASHED ARISTOTELIA

LESSER BUD MOTH

SOUTHERN NEEDLEMINER

WHITE STRIPE-BACKED MOTH
Arogalea cristifasciella 1851 **Common**
TL 5 mm. Whitish FW has a broad black AM band that slants inward toward inner margin. **HOSTS:** Unknown. **RANGE:** Se. Canada and e. U.S.

TEN-SPOTTED HONEYSUCKLE MOTH
Athrips mouffetella 1852 **Common**
TL 8–9 mm. Peppery gray FW is marked with five black dots in central median area. **HOSTS:** Honeysuckle. **RANGE:** Se. Canada and ne. U.S.

WHITE-BANDED TELPHUSA
Telphusa latifasciella 1857 **Common**
TL 5–7 mm. Grayish FW typically has a black basal area and wide white median band. Sometimes FW is mostly grayish. **HOSTS:** Unknown. **RANGE:** Se. Canada and e. U.S.

Y-BACKED TELPHUSA *Telphusa longifasciella* 1858 **Common**
TL 8–9 mm. Black FW has sharply contrasting white streak along inner margin continuing as an oblique AM line. **HOSTS:** Unknown. **RANGE:** Se. Canada and e. U.S.

WALSINGHAM'S MOTH
Pseudochelaria walsinghami 1864 **Uncommon**
TL 7–8 mm. Gray FW is boldly patterned with black patches in basal half of inner margin and outer ST area. A black streak passes through central ST area. **HOSTS:** Unknown. **RANGE:** Se. Canada and e. U.S.

ELM LEAF-SEWER *Carpatolechia fugitivella* 1874.2 **Common**
TL 7 mm. Peppery grayish brown FW has a mottled blackish patch in central median area. **HOSTS:** Elm. **RANGE:** Se. Canada and e. U.S.

CREPUSCULAR ROCK-ROSE MOTH
Neotelphusa sequax 1881 **Common**
TL 8 mm. Peppery gray FW is marked with lines of black raised scales. Median and ST bands are whitish. **HOSTS:** Unknown. **RANGE:** Se. Canada and e. U.S.

GOLDENROD GALL MOTH
Gnorimoschema gallaesolidaginis 1986 **Common**
TL 12–14 mm. Frosty gray FW has chocolate brown patches in basal, median, and ST areas. **HOSTS:** Goldenrod. **RANGE:** Widespread.

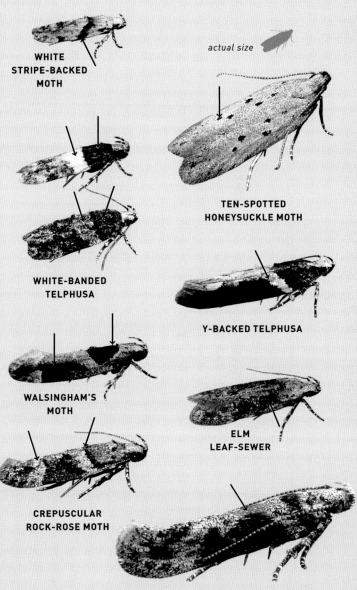

TWIRLER MOTHS

WHITE
STRIPE-BACKED
MOTH

actual size

TEN-SPOTTED
HONEYSUCKLE MOTH

WHITE-BANDED
TELPHUSA

Y-BACKED TELPHUSA

WALSINGHAM'S
MOTH

ELM
LEAF-SEWER

CREPUSCULAR
ROCK-ROSE MOTH

GOLDENROD GALL MOTH

SPRING OAK LEAFROLLER

Chionodes formosella 2077 **Common**

TL 7–9 mm. Gray FW has fragmented black median band and ST area. White ST band is broken at midpoint. **HOSTS:** Oak. **RANGE:** Se. Canada and ne. U.S.

BLACK-SMUDGED CHIONODES

Chionodes mediofuscella 2093 **Common**

TL 5–8 mm. Light brown FW has darker brown shading in outer half. Pale AM line is edged black. **HOSTS:** Giant ragweed. **RANGE:** Widespread.

RED-NECKED PEANUTWORM MOTH

Stegasta bosqueella 2209 **Common**

TL 7–8 mm. Black FW is boldly marked with irregular orange patch along inner margin and a white subapical spot. **HOSTS:** Unknown. **RANGE:** Sw. ON and e. U.S.

MUSIC-LOVING MOTH *Battaristis concinusella* 2225 **Common**

TL 4–5 mm. Gray FW has a V-shaped white ST line. Apex is highlighted with a black dot. **HOSTS:** Unknown. **RANGE:** Se. Canada and e. U.S.

ORANGE STRIPE-BACKED MOTH

Battaristis vittella 2229 **Common**

TL 5–6 mm. Orange FW is marked with three silvery gray bands. Eyes are blood red. **HOSTS:** Unknown. **RANGE:** Se. Canada and e. U.S.

DARK-HEADED ASPEN LEAFROLLER

Anacampsis innocuella 2237 **Common**

TL 12 mm. Gray FW is marked with three rows of double black spots. ST line is broadly edged black. **HOSTS:** Poplar. **RANGE:** Se. Canada and ne. U.S.

UNSTRIPED ANACAMPSIS

Anacampsis nonstrigella 2244 **Common**

TL 12 mm. Pale gray FW is blackish beyond midpoint. Terminal line is edged white. Eyes are blood red. **HOSTS:** Unknown. **RANGE:** Se. Canada and ne. U.S.

PEACH TWIG BORER *Anarsia lineatella* 2257 **Common**

TL 6–7 mm. Small. Peppery gray FW is marked with blackish streaks between veins. **HOSTS:** Unknown, possibly peach trees. **RANGE:** Se. Canada and ne. U.S.

TWIRLER MOTHS

**SPRING OAK
LEAFROLLER**

actual size

**BLACK-SMUDGED
CHIONODES**

**RED-NECKED
PEANUTWORM MOTH**

**MUSIC-LOVING
MOTH**

**ORANGE
STRIPE-BACKED
MOTH**

**DARK-HEADED ASPEN
LEAFROLLER**

**UNSTRIPED
ANACAMPSIS**

PEACH TWIG BORER

FERNALD'S HELCYSTOGRAMMA
Helcystogramma fernaldella   2267   **Common**
TL 8–10 mm. Pale FW is peppered with brown scales between veins. Three tiny brown dots mark central median area. **HOSTS:** Grasses. **RANGE:** S. Canada and n. U.S.

LANCEOLATE MOTH
Helcystogramma hystricella   2268   **Common**
TL 6–9 mm. Pale FW has bold brown streaks between veins. A tiny black dot highlights median area. Apex is sharply pointed. **HOSTS:** Grasses. **RANGE:** Se. Canada and ne. U.S.

PALMERWORM MOTH   *Dichomeris ligulella*   2281   **Common**
TL 8–11 mm. Sexually dimorphic. FW is either brown (female) or blackish with a cream-colored costal streak (male). Narrow, pointed wing shape. **HOSTS:** Oak, apple, plum, and cherry. **RANGE:** Widespread. **NOTE:** Adults overwinter.

JUNIPER WEBWORM   *Dichomeris marginella*   2282   **Common**
TL 8–9 mm. Chocolate brown FW has broad whitish stripes along inner margin and costa. Top of head and thorax is whitish. **HOSTS:** Juniper. **RANGE:** Se. Canada and ne. U.S. **NOTE:** Introduced from Europe.

SPOTTED DICHOMERIS
Dichomeris punctidiscella   2283   **Common**
TL 7–9 mm. Pale FW is darker beyond curved PM line. Central median area is marked with brown spots. **HOSTS:** Unknown. **RANGE:** Se. Canada and e. U.S.

SHINING DICHOMERIS
Dichomeris ochripalpella   2289   **Common**
TL 7–8 mm. Black FW has irregular metallic silvery blue patches. Labial palps are orange. **HOSTS:** Aster and goldenrod. **RANGE:** Se. Canada and ne. U.S.

BILOBED DICHOMERIS   *Dichomeris bilobella*   2291   **Common**
TL 7–9 mm. Gray or tan FW has a black bar along basal half of inner margin that juts into median area. Black discal spot and ST line are edged yellow. **HOSTS:** Goldenrod and aster. **RANGE:** Se. Canada and ne. U.S.

COPA DICHOMERIS   *Dichomeris copa*   2291.2   **Common**
TL 8–9 mm. Slate gray FW has orange streak along basal half of costa. Central median area is marked with yellow-edged black dots. **HOSTS:** Goldenrod. **RANGE:** Se. Canada and ne. U.S.

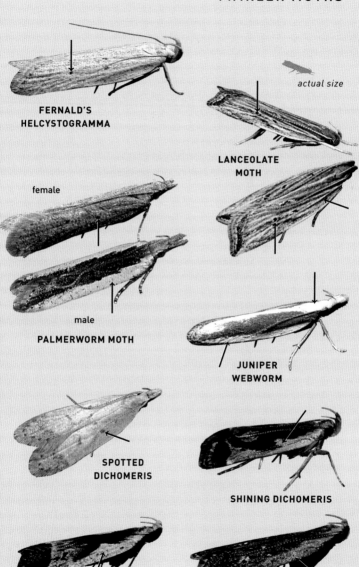

TWIRLER MOTHS

FERNALD'S HELCYSTOGRAMMA

actual size

LANCEOLATE MOTH

female

male

PALMERWORM MOTH

JUNIPER WEBWORM

SPOTTED DICHOMERIS

SHINING DICHOMERIS

BILOBED DICHOMERIS

COPA DICHOMERIS

CREAM-EDGED DICHOMERIS

Dichomeris flavocostella 2295   **Common**
TL 8–9 mm. Black FW has a broad creamy costal stripe that has a spur extending into PM area. **HOSTS:** Goldenrod and aster. **RANGE:** Se. Canada and e. U.S.

INDENTED DICHOMERIS *Dichomeris inserrata* 2297   **Common**

TL 7–9 mm. Resembles Cream-edged Dichomeris, but creamy costal streak lacks PM spur. **HOSTS:** Goldenrod. **RANGE:** Se. Canada and e. U.S.

TOOTHED DICHOMERIS

Dichomeris serrativittella 2301   **Common**
TL 7–9 mm. Slate gray FW has a sawtooth edge to whitish costal streak. A black streak extends through central median area. **HOSTS:** Possibly *Brassica* species. **RANGE:** Se. Canada and e. U.S.

TWO-SPOTTED DICHOMERIS

Dichomeris leuconotella 2299   **Common**
TL 6–9 mm. Dusky FW is marked with a thick black ST line. Central median area is accented with yellow dots. **HOSTS:** Goldenrod and aster. **RANGE:** S. Canada and n. U.S.

LITTLE DEVIL *Dichomeris nonstrigella* 2307   **Common**

TL 7–9 mm. Shiny bluish black FW is without obvious markings. Labial palps are bright orange. **HOSTS:** Aster. **RANGE:** Se. Canada and ne. U.S.

BLACK-EDGED DICHOMERIS

Dichomeris picrocarpa 2309   **Common**
TL 9–10 mm. Golden brown FW has blackish outer margin bordered with a white terminal line and orange fringe. **HOSTS:** Cherry and peach. **RANGE:** Se. Canada and ne. U.S. **NOTE:** Introduced from Asia.

INVERSED DICHOMERIS

Dichomeris inversella 2310.1   **Common**
TL 6–8 mm. Peppery silvery gray FW has faint darker bands and a curved whitish ST line. Labial palps are brushy. **HOSTS:** Possibly hickory. **RANGE:** Se. Canada and e. U.S.

TWIRLER MOTHS

actual size

CREAM-EDGED DICHOMERIS

INDENTED DICHOMERIS

TOOTHED DICHOMERIS

TWO-SPOTTED DICHOMERIS

LITTLE DEVIL

BLACK-EDGED DICHOMERIS

INVERSED DICHOMERIS

LEAF SKELETONIZERS   Family Zygaenidae

These two species might be mistaken for members of the tiger moth family: Grapeleaf Skeletonizer for Yellow-collared Scape Moth, and Orange-patched Smoky Moth for Black-and-yellow Lichen Moth. Members of this family produce hydrogen cyanide, and their bright coloration is a warning to predators. Most are active at flowers during the day, though both of these species will also come to lights at night.

GRAPELEAF SKELETONIZER
Harrisina americana   4624   **Common**
TL 10–15 mm. Abdomen and semitranslucent FW are smoky black. Thorax has bright vermillion collar. **HOSTS:** *Ampelopsis*, grape, redbud, and Virginia creeper. **RANGE:** Se. Canada and e. U.S.

ORANGE-PATCHED SMOKY MOTH
Pyromorpha dimidiata   4639   **Common**
TL 8–12 mm. Smoky black FW has a contrasting pale orange patch in outer basal area. **HOSTS:** Oak leaves. **RANGE:** E. U.S.

SLUG MOTHS   Family Limacodidae

Small, chunky moths that hold their rounded wings in a tentlike position when at rest. Some species curl their abdomen upward above the level of the wings. Larvae of many species are bizarre in form and color and often have stinging hairs. Adults are strictly nocturnal and visit lights in small numbers.

EARLY BUTTON SLUG MOTH
Tortricidia testacea   4652   **Common**
TL 8–12 mm. Orange FW has darker veins in ST area. Slanting rusty median band ends at apex. **HOSTS:** Beech, birch, black cherry, chestnut, oak, and witch hazel. **RANGE:** E. Canada and e. U.S.

ABBREVIATED BUTTON SLUG MOTH
Tortricidia flexuosa   4654   **Common**
TL 8–12 mm. Yellowish FW has indistinct PM and ST lines fused at costa, forming a U-shape. **HOSTS:** Deciduous trees, including apple, black cherry, chestnut, oak, and plum. **RANGE:** E. Canada and e. U.S.

LEAF SKELETONIZERS

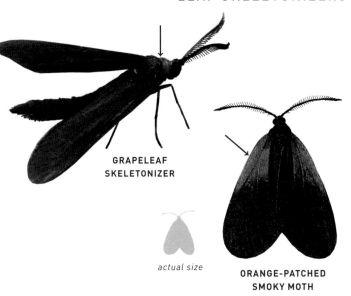

GRAPELEAF SKELETONIZER

actual size

ORANGE-PATCHED SMOKY MOTH

SLUG MOTHS

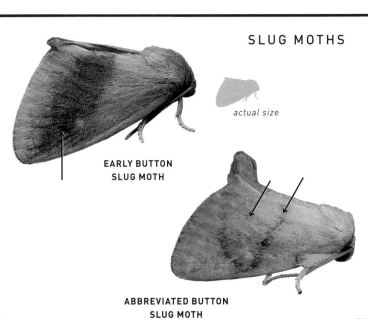

actual size

EARLY BUTTON SLUG MOTH

ABBREVIATED BUTTON SLUG MOTH

JEWELED TAILED SLUG MOTH

Packardia geminata   4659   **Common**
TL 8–12 mm. Peppery pale tan FW has darker brown median area. Inner ST line is marked with a string of three white dots. **HOSTS:** Trees and shrubs, including birch, hickory, oak, and spruce. **RANGE:** E. Canada and e. U.S.

ELEGANT TAILED SLUG MOTH

Packardia elegans   4661   **Common**
TL 10–12 mm. Peppery gray FW has indistinct white lines. Inner ST line is marked with two black dots. **HOSTS:** Unknown. **RANGE:** S. Canada and e. U.S.

YELLOW-SHOULDERED SLUG MOTH

Lithacodes fasciola   4665   **Common**
TL 10–13 mm. Peppery yellow FW has kinked white median line edged gray and black. ST line angles across apex. **HOSTS:** Deciduous trees and shrubs, including apple, beech, elm, oak, and willow. **RANGE:** Widespread.

YELLOW-COLLARED SLUG MOTH

Apoda y-inversum   4667   **Common**
TL 11–15 mm. Pale orange FW has brown median and ST lines that converge toward costa. Two indistinct lines form an X-shape near anal angle. Darker individuals have brown shading within lines, forming a Y-shape. **HOSTS:** Beech, hickory, ironwood, and oak. **RANGE:** Se. Canada and e. U.S.

SHAGREENED SLUG MOTH   *Apoda biguttata*   4669   **Common**

TL 10–15 mm. Grayish brown FW is marked with white-edged chestnut patches at apex and anal angle. **HOSTS:** Ironwood, hickory, and oak. **RANGE:** E. Canada and e. U.S.

SKIFF MOTH   *Prolimacodes badia*   4671   **Common**

TL 12–17 mm. Milky coffee-colored FW has a rounded, white-edged brown median patch that continues along costa to base of wing. **HOSTS:** Trees and woody plants, including birch, blueberry, oak, poplar, and willow. **RANGE:** Sw. ON and e. U.S.

SPUN GLASS SLUG MOTH

Isochaetes beutenmuelleri   4675   **Common**
TL 10–12 mm. Pale orange-brown FW is marked with indistinct wavy brown lines and scattered patches of gray scales. Legs are adorned with tufts of pale scales. **HOSTS:** Swamp oak. **RANGE:** E. U.S.

SLUG MOTHS

**JEWELED TAILED
SLUG MOTH**

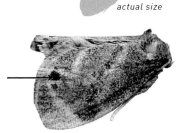

actual size

**ELEGANT TAILED
SLUG MOTH**

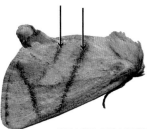

**YELLOW-COLLARED
SLUG MOTH**

**SHAGREENED
SLUG MOTH**

**YELLOW-SHOULDERED
SLUG MOTH**

SKIFF MOTH

**SPUN GLASS
SLUG MOTH**

HAG MOTH *Phobetron pithecium* 4677 **Common**
TL 10–15 mm. Sexually dimorphic. Translucent FW of male (not shown) has black veins and discal spot, whereas female is purplish gray with irregular black and yellow lines. Legs of both sexes adorned with tufts of pale scales. **HOSTS:** Trees and woody plants, including apple, ash, dogwood, oak, and willow. **RANGE:** Se. Canada and e. U.S.

CROWNED SLUG MOTH *Isa textula* 4681 **Common**
TL 9–16 mm. Peppery light brown FW has diffuse pale gray median band and apical patch. **HOSTS:** Trees and shrubs, including elm, hickory, maple, and oak. **RANGE:** Sw. ON and e. U.S.

PURPLE-CRESTED SLUG MOTH
Adoneta spinuloides 4685 **Common**
TL 8–12 mm. Rusty brown FW has a wide blackish streak through median area and black dots along ST line. White basal dash almost joins incomplete white median line near inner margin. **HOSTS:** Trees and shrubs, including basswood, beech, birch, chestnut, and willow. **RANGE:** Se. Canada and e. U.S.

SPINY OAK-SLUG MOTH *Euclea delphinii* 4697 **Common**
TL 10–15 mm. Chocolate brown FW is marked with chestnut and black patches. Isolated mint green patches in inner median and subapical areas can be fused or even absent on some individuals. **HOSTS:** Trees and woody plants, including apple, beech, chestnut, maple, and oak. **RANGE:** Se. Canada and e. U.S.

SMALLER PARASA *Parasa chloris* 4698 **Common**
TL 10–14 mm. Brown FW has a wide apple green median band. Brown ST area is relatively wide. Thorax and head are apple green. **HOSTS:** Deciduous trees, including apple, dogwood, elm, and oak. **RANGE:** E. U.S.

STINGING ROSE CATERPILLAR MOTH
Parasa indetermina 4699 **Common**
TL 12–15 mm. Resembles Smaller Parasa, but larger green median patch has an evenly rounded outer margin. Midpoint of narrow brown terminal line is often marked with a blackish patch. **HOSTS:** Trees and shrubs, including apple, dogwood, hickory, maple, and rose. **RANGE:** E. U.S.

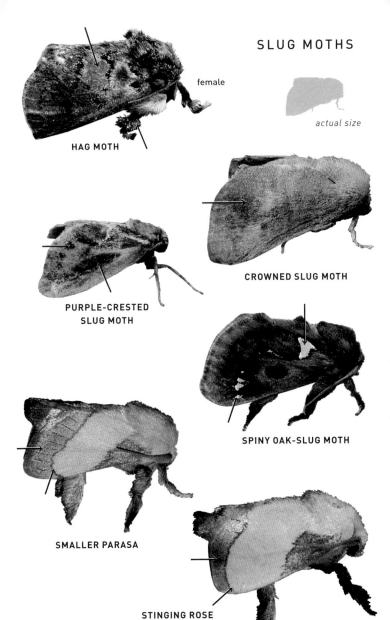

SLUG MOTHS

female

actual size

HAG MOTH

CROWNED SLUG MOTH

PURPLE-CRESTED
SLUG MOTH

SPINY OAK-SLUG MOTH

SMALLER PARASA

STINGING ROSE
CATERPILLAR MOTH

75

SADDLEBACK CATERPILLAR MOTH

Acharia stimulea   4700   **Common**
TL 14–22 mm. Chocolate brown FW is marked with peppery ash
gray streaks. A short black basal dash ends at a small white
dot. **HOSTS:** Various, including apple, blueberry, elm, maple,
and oak. **RANGE:** E. U.S.

CLEARWING BORERS   Family Sesiidae

A remarkable group of colorful, diurnal moths that closely resemble bees
and wasps, but differ in antennal structure and lack of a constricted waist.
Larvae bore into roots, branches, and trunks of a wide variety of trees and
into stems of many herbaceous plants. Several species bore into commercial fruit trees such as apple and peach and can be serious pests. Inconspicuous and hard to find; only one species, Maple Callus Borer, is regularly
encountered at lights. The best way to see most others is to purchase commercially available pheromone lures.

RASPBERRY CROWN BORER

Pennisetia marginatum   2513   **Common**
TL 13–16 mm. Transparent FW has a brown border and black
veins. Abdomen is banded black and pale yellow with raised
band of black scales on third segment. Male has bipectinate
antennae. **HOSTS:** Blackberry, raspberry, and boysenberry.
RANGE: S. Canada and e. U.S.

VIRGINIA CREEPER CLEARWING

Albuna fraxini   2532   **Common**
TL 15–18 mm. Partly black FW is marked with red or orange
discal bar. Black abdomen has a flared brushy tuft at tip. Antennae have wide white band near tip. **HOSTS:** Virginia creeper.
RANGE: Se. Canada and e. U.S.

SQUASH VINE BORER   *Melittia cucurbitae*   2536   **Common**
TL 17 mm. Large. Black FW. Thorax is gray. Abdomen is red
with a row of black dots dorsally. Hind legs are adorned with
large tufts of reddish scales. **HOSTS:** Squash, gourds, and
pumpkin. **RANGE:** Se. Canada and e. U.S.

EUROPEAN HORNET MOTH   *Sesia apiformis*   2542   **Common**
TL 18–22 mm. Large. Transparent FW has reddish brown border and veins. Thorax has large yellow tegulae. Abdomen is
banded black and yellow, with fourth segment mostly black.
HOSTS: Poplar. **RANGE:** New England and s. ON, but incompletely known. **NOTE:** Introduced from Europe.

SLUG MOTHS

**SADDLEBACK
CATERPILLAR MOTH**

actual size

CLEARWING
BORERS

female

**RASPBERRY
CROWN BORER**

male

female

**EUROPEAN HORNET
MOTH**

**VIRGINIA CREEPER
CLEARWING**

actual size

SQUASH VINE BORER

AMERICAN HORNET MOTH *Sesia tibiale* 2543 **Common**
TL 16 mm. Large. Transparent FW is tinted amber with reddish brown border and veins. Abdomen is banded black and yellow, often with third and forth segments largely black. Thorax has thin yellow dorsal stripes and collar. **HOSTS:** Poplar and willow. **RANGE:** Widespread.

RED MAPLE BORER *Synanthedon acerrubri* 2546 **Common**
TL 12 mm. Transparent FW has black border and discal bar. Blue-black abdomen has an orange-tipped, fanned tuft at tip. **HOSTS:** Red maple and sugar maple. **RANGE:** Se. Canada and e. U.S.

DOGWOOD BORER *Synanthedon scitula* 2549 **Common**
TL 8–12 mm. Transparent FW has black border and discal bar with yellow patch near tip and thin yellow streaks inside costa. Thorax has wide yellow tegulae. Banded, black-and-yellow abdomen has a fanned tuft at tip. **HOSTS:** Deciduous trees, including apple, birch, dogwood, oak, and willow. **RANGE:** Se. Canada and e. U.S.

LESSER PEACHTREE BORER
Synanthedon pictipes 2550 **Common**
TL 16 mm. Transparent FW has thin black border and veins. Sides of neck white. Head has small white dots in front of eyes. Blue-black abdomen has a tapered tuft at tip. **HOSTS:** Fruit-bearing trees, including wild cherry and plum. **RANGE:** Se. Canada and e. U.S.

RILEY'S CLEARWING *Synanthedon rileyana* 2552 **Common**
TL 10–15 mm. Transparent FW has narrow reddish brown border and red discal bar. Thorax has yellow patches at base of wings and narrow yellow collar. Black abdomen has yellow bands on each segment. **HOSTS:** Horse nettle. **RANGE:** Se. Canada and e. U.S.

CURRANT CLEARWING
Synanthedon tipuliformis 2553 **Common**
TL 8–12 mm. Transparent FW has black border and discal bar and streaks of yellow extending between veins at tip. Black abdomen has narrow yellow bands on some segments and a fan-like tuft at tip. **HOSTS:** Cultivated currant, gooseberry, and raspberry. **RANGE:** S. Canada and n. U.S.

CLEARWING BORERS

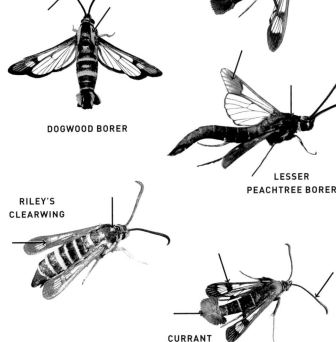

actual size

AMERICAN HORNET MOTH

RED MAPLE BORER

DOGWOOD BORER

LESSER PEACHTREE BORER

RILEY'S CLEARWING

CURRANT CLEARWING

MAPLE CALLUS BORER *Synanthedon acerni* 2554 **Common**
TL 12–13 mm. Transparent FW has black border and discal bar and pale yellow streaks at tip. Head is red. Slender abdomen has a fanned orange tuft at tip. **HOSTS:** Maple. **RANGE:** Se. Canada and e. U.S. **NOTE:** The only clearwing likely to be encountered at lights.

PEACHTREE BORER *Synanthedon exitiosa* 2583 **Common**
TL 15–20 mm. Sexually dimorphic. Male resembles Lesser Peachtree Borer but is larger with thicker black borders and veins on wings. Female has black FW and a wide orange band on two segments of abdomen. **HOSTS:** Fruit-bearing trees, including cultivated cherry, peach, and plum. **RANGE:** Widespread.

LILAC BORER *Podosesia syringae* 2589 **Common**
TL 17 mm. Purplish blue FW has some red scales at base. Thorax has a red collar. Slightly constricted abdomen is black. Long legs are tipped yellow. Antennae are reddish. **HOSTS:** Ash, fringe tree, lilac, and other related species. **RANGE:** Widespread.

EUPATORIUM BORER *Carmenta bassiformis* 2596 **Common**
TL 8–14 mm. Transparent FW has brown border and reddish discal bar with yellow streaks extending between veins at tip. Brown abdomen has narrow yellowish bands on alternate segments and a brushy yellow tip. Antennae have wide white band near tip. **HOSTS:** Ironweed. **RANGE:** E. U.S.

METALMARK MOTHS Family Choreutidae

Very small moths with broad wings that often bear metallic scales (though not present in the one species here). Wings are usually held above the body while at rest. Adults are active during the day and can be found visiting flowers or resting among vegetation.

APPLE LEAF SKELETONIZER
Choreutis pariana 2650 **Uncommon**
TL 9 mm. Orange-brown FW has pale lilac median band and dark jagged lines. **HOSTS:** Crab apple. **RANGE:** Se. Canada and ne. U.S. **NOTE:** Introduced from Europe about 1917.

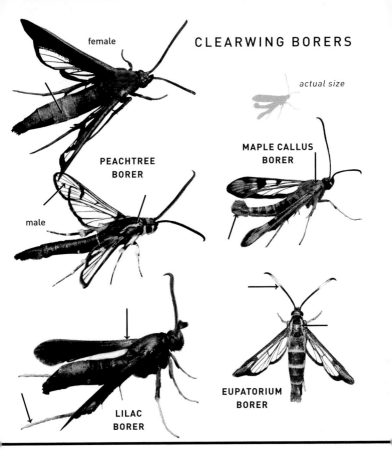

CLEARWING BORERS

female

actual size

**MAPLE CALLUS
BORER**

**PEACHTREE
BORER**

male

**LILAC
BORER**

**EUPATORIUM
BORER**

METALMARK MOTHS

**APPLE LEAF
SKELETONIZER**

actual size

CARPENTERWORM AND LEOPARD MOTHS   Family Cossidae

Exceptionally large micromoths that superficially resemble small sphinx moths in size and shape. Most are strongly sexually dimorphic, with females being considerably larger and bulkier than males. Most have thin wings that are semi-translucent and fray easily. Males (and in some species females) have bipectinate antennae. Larvae are borers in trunks and branches of various trees, taking several years to complete their development. The larval galleries of some species may weaken the host tree, making it vulnerable to drought. Adults occasionally visit lights in small numbers.

POPLAR CARPENTERWORM

Acossus centerensis   2675   Uncommon
TL 22–27 mm. Semi-translucent sooty FW has brindled pattern of black lines. Thinly scaled HW is pale gray. Thorax has a white collar. **HOSTS:** Poplar. **RANGE:** S. Canada and e. U.S.

ROBIN'S CARPENTERWORM

Prionoxystus robiniae   2693   Uncommon
TL 27–45 mm. Semi-translucent whitish FW has a dense network of black veins and lines. Blackish blotches of variable size mark basal and median areas. HW of smaller male is yellow with black outer margin. **HOSTS:** Ash, chestnut, locust, oak, poplar, and willow. **RANGE:** Widespread.

LITTLE CARPENTERWORM

Prionoxystus macmurtei   2694   Uncommon
TL 23–40 mm. Resembles Poplar Carpenterworm but is less densely marked with black lines. Translucent HW is pale gray in both sexes. Thorax has a whitish collar. **HOSTS:** Ash, maple, and oak. **RANGE:** Se. Canada and e. U.S.

LEOPARD MOTH   *Zeuzera pyrina*   2700   Uncommon
TL 24–40 mm. Semi-translucent white FW is evenly marked with black spots between white veins. Fluffy white thorax is marked with black spots. Long abdomen protrudes beyond folded wings. **HOSTS:** Trees and woody plants, including apple, hawthorn, and pear. **RANGE:** Extreme se. Canada and ne. U.S. **NOTE:** Introduced from Europe in the mid-1800s.

CARPENTERWORM AND LEOPARD MOTHS

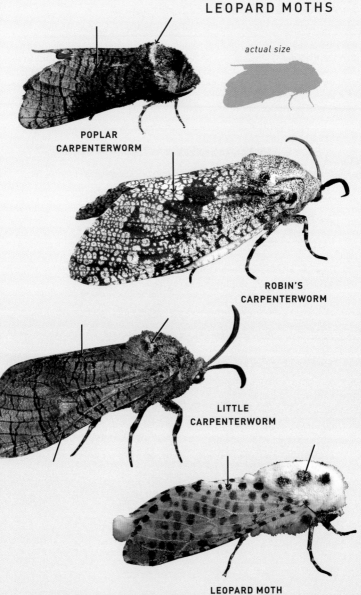

actual size

POPLAR CARPENTERWORM

ROBIN'S CARPENTERWORM

LITTLE CARPENTERWORM

LEOPARD MOTH

Tortrix Leafrollers
Family Tortricidae, Subfamily Tortricinae,
Tribes Tortricini, Euliini, and Cnephasiini

Small, flat moths with straight or slightly rounded wings that form a shallow point at the apex. Many species show a dark triangle on the outer edge of the FW. A few, such as Hasty Acleris, are incredibly variable, with different individuals of the same species bearing wildly different FW patterns. Larvae are typically leafrollers. Some species hibernate as adults and fly early the following spring. Adults are nocturnal and will come to light in small numbers.

HAIRNET ACLERIS *Acleris forskaleana* 3501 **Common**
TL 9 mm. Cream-colored FW is boldly marked with an orange netlike pattern. Sometimes has a dusky blotch at midpoint of inner margin. **HOSTS:** Maple and sycamore. **RANGE:** Se. Canada and ne. U.S.

OAK LEAFSHREDDER *Acleris semipurpurana* 3503 **Common**
TL 8 mm. FW is variably white with yellowish bands or mottled gray-brown with a whitish central costal streak. **HOSTS:** Oak. **RANGE:** Se. Canada and ne. U.S.

MACDUNNOUGH'S ACLERIS
Acleris macdunnoughi 3506 **Common**
TL 9–10 mm. Silvery gray FW has large chestnut brown patch at midpoint of costa. Sometimes appears rather speckled. **HOSTS:** Unknown. **RANGE:** Se. Canada and e. U.S.

SNOWY-SHOULDERED ACLERIS
Acleris nivisellana 3510 **Common**
TL 7 mm. Mottled pale gray FW has white basal half of costa. Reddish tufts mark AM and ST areas. Indented costa is accented with a gray triangle at midpoint. **HOSTS:** Apple. **RANGE:** Se. Canada and ne. U.S.

COMMON ACLERIS *Acleris subnivana* 3517 **Common**
TL 7 mm. White FW has a grayish brown triangle at midpoint of strongly indented costa. Some individuals are tan-colored with a fragmented dark triangle at midpoint of straight costa. **HOSTS:** Red oak. **RANGE:** Se. Canada and ne. U.S.

SMALL ASPEN LEAFTIER *Acleris fuscana* 3520 **Common**
TL 8 mm. Mottled gray FW has darker shading in basal area and midpoint of costa. **HOSTS:** Aspen. **RANGE:** Se. Canada and ne. U.S.

TORTRIX LEAFROLLERS

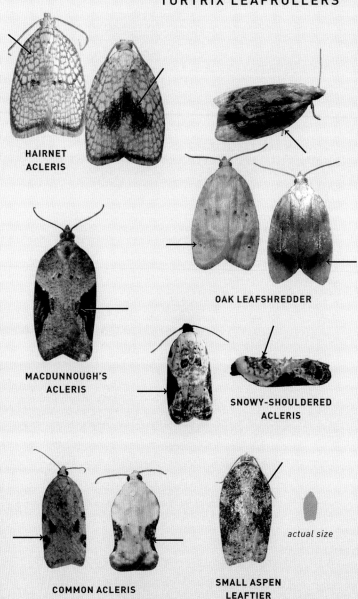

HAIRNET ACLERIS

OAK LEAFSHREDDER

MACDUNNOUGH'S ACLERIS

SNOWY-SHOULDERED ACLERIS

COMMON ACLERIS

SMALL ASPEN LEAFTIER

actual size

HALF-RINGED ACLERIS *Acleris semiannula* 3521 **Common**
TL 7–8 mm. Pale tan FW has a hollow, brown-edged triangular patch at midpoint of costa. Wings are sometimes boldly speckled black. **HOSTS:** Unknown. **RANGE:** Se. Canada and ne. U.S.

SPECKLED ACLERIS *Acleris negundana* 3526 **Common**
TL 8–9 mm. Straw-colored FW is boldly speckled with black scales. Sometimes has a faint, fragmented brown patch at midpoint of slightly indented costa. **HOSTS:** Box elder. **RANGE:** Se. Canada and e. U.S.

HASTY ACLERIS *Acleris hastiana* 3531 **Common**
TL 10–11 mm. Polymorphic. Gray or brown FW can show lengthwise streaks of pale orange or chestnut. Sometimes has whitish basal area or AM band. **HOSTS:** Poplar and willow. **RANGE:** S. Canada and ne. U.S.

STRAWBERRY ACLERIS *Acleris fragariana* 3532 **Common**
TL 8–9 mm. Mottled brown FW has contrasting pale yellow or whitish basal half. **HOSTS:** Members of Myricaceae; perhaps sweet fern and sweet gale. **RANGE:** Se. Canada and ne. U.S.

CELIANA'S ACLERIS *Acleris celiana* 3533 **Common**
TL 10 mm. Dark chestnut brown FW typically has mottled whitish AM band and darker basal patch. Some individuals are darker with bold white and chestnut streaks extending along costa. **HOSTS:** Unknown. **RANGE:** Se. Canada and ne. U.S.

LESSER MAPLE LEAFROLLER
Acleris chalybeana 3539 **Common**
TL 9 mm. Silvery gray FW is variably marked with indistinct black and brown lines. Sometimes has a blackish basal bar. **HOSTS:** Apple, beech, birch, maple, and oak. **RANGE:** Se. Canada and ne. U.S.

BLACK-HEADED BIRCH LEAFROLLER
Acleris logiana 3540 **Common**
TL 10 mm. Whitish or pale gray FW is dotted with tufts of raised dusky scales. Darker costal triangle is often reduced to a bar in central median area. **HOSTS:** Alder, birch, and viburnum. **RANGE:** Se. Canada and ne. U.S.

TORTRIX LEAFROLLERS

HALF-RINGED ACLERIS

SPECKLED ACLERIS

actual size

HASTY ACLERIS

CELIANA'S ACLERIS

STRAWBERRY ACLERIS

BLACK-HEADED BIRCH LEAFROLLER

LESSER MAPLE LEAFROLLER

87

MULTIFORM LEAFROLLER

Acleris flavivittana   3542   **Common**
TL 10–11 mm. Polymorphic. Gray or brown FW can have fine or bold white streaks along costa. Sometimes has a black basal dash. Some individuals are mostly black with mottled white AM band and basal area. **HOSTS:** Alder, birch, and viburnum. **RANGE:** Se. Canada and ne. U.S.

EASTERN BLACK-HEADED BUDWORM

Acleris variana   3548   **Common**
TL 8–9 mm. Polymorphic. Typically has orange FW marked with white and chestnut lengthwise streaks. Sometimes has mottled gray FW with a bold orange streak. Others are gray with mottled dusky bands. **HOSTS:** Unknown. **RANGE:** Se. Canada and ne. U.S.

YOUNG'S ACLERIS   *Acleris youngana*   3550   **Common**
TL 10 mm. Gray FW has a bold orange or chestnut basal dash. Sometimes has an additional streak in subapical area. **HOSTS:** Unknown. **RANGE:** Se. Canada and ne. U.S.

DARK-SPOTTED ACLERIS   *Acleris inana*   3551   **Common**
TL 10 mm. Gray FW is largely brown beyond slanting AM line. Inner basal area is marked with a large chestnut spot. **HOSTS:** Unknown. **RANGE:** Se. Canada and ne. U.S.

BLACK-LINED ACLERIS   *Acleris nigrolinea*   3556   **Common**
TL 11–14 mm. Large. Pale gray FW is mottled with darker scales. Thin black streak extending through median area is crossed with lines of raised scales. **HOSTS:** Willow, also birch and cherry. **RANGE:** Se. Canada and ne. U.S.

GREAT ACLERIS   *Acleris maximana*   3557   **Uncommon**
TL 12–15 mm. Large. Gray FW is variably striated with dusky lines. Some individuals are marbled with brown and pale gray. **HOSTS:** Poplar and willow. **RANGE:** S. Canada and ne. U.S.

FERRUGINOUS EULIA   *Eulia ministrana*   3565   **Uncommon**
TL 9.5–11.5 mm. Rusty orange FW has a pale yellow costal streak that sweeps through ST area. Midpoint of inner margin is marked with a lilac-colored patch. **HOSTS:** Deciduous trees and shrubs, including birch, rose, and willow. **RANGE:** Se. Canada and ne. U.S.

TORTRIX LEAFROLLERS

EASTERN BLACK-HEADED BUDWORM

**MULTIFORM
LEAFROLLER**

**YOUNG'S
ACLERIS**

**DARK-SPOTTED
ACLERIS**

**BLACK-LINED
ACLERIS**

actual size

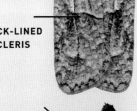

**GREAT
ACLERIS**

**FERRUGINOUS
EULIA**

89

GRAY-MARKED TORTRICID

Decodes basiplagana   3573   **Common**
TL 9 mm. Gray FW is lightly barred with black scales. Dark gray
bands mark basal, median, and ST areas. **HOSTS:** Oak. **RANGE:**
Se. Canada and ne. U.S.

COCHYLID MOTHS
Family Tortricidae, Subfamily Tortricinae, Tribe Cochylini

Small moths with flared wings that are kept folded at rest. The head, with
its fuzzy labial palps, is usually tucked downward, creating a snouty, hunch-
backed appearance. Larvae are seed, flower, and stem borers. Adults are
nocturnal and will come to light in small numbers.

SILVER-BORDERED AETHES

Aethes argentilimitana   3754.2   **Common**
TL 6–7 mm. Cream-colored FW is boldly banded with olive
brown bands. Bands are edged with silvery scales. **HOSTS:** Unknown. **RANGE:** Se. Canada and ne. U.S.

TWO-SPOTTED AETHES   *Aethes atomosana*   3754.3   **Common**
TL 9–10 mm. Creamy yellow FW is lightly peppered with brown
scales. Median and terminal areas are variably speckled black.
HOSTS: Unknown. **RANGE:** Se. Canada and ne. U.S.

REDDISH AETHES   *Aethes biscana*   3755.1   **Common**
TL 8–10 mm. Pale orange FW is lightly brindled brown. Dark
brown streak through inner AM area and slanting PM line are
well defined. **HOSTS:** Unknown. **RANGE:** Se. Canada and ne. U.S.

DARK-SPOTTED AETHES   *Aethes mymara*   3758.2   **Common**
TL 8–9 mm. Pale FW has sharply defined black-edged brown
line slanting from inner basal area. Inner PM line forms a distinct black triangle. **HOSTS:** Unknown. **RANGE:** Se. Canada and
ne. U.S.

PATRICIA'S AETHES   *Aethes patricia*   3759   **Common**
TL 7–8 mm. Whitish FW is boldly patterned with fragmented
warm brown lines. Angled PM line is broken at midpoint.
HOSTS: Unknown. **RANGE:** Se. Canada and ne. U.S.

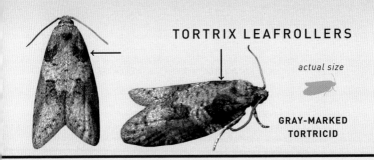

TORTRIX LEAFROLLERS

actual size

**GRAY-MARKED
TORTRICID**

COCHYLID MOTHS

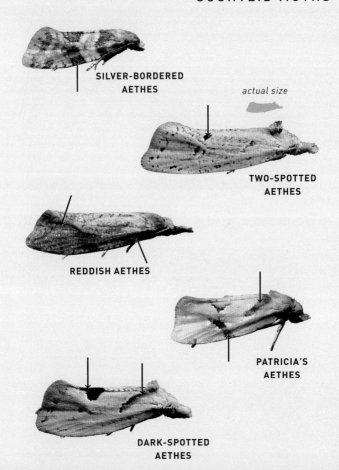

**SILVER-BORDERED
AETHES**

actual size

**TWO-SPOTTED
AETHES**

REDDISH AETHES

**PATRICIA'S
AETHES**

**DARK-SPOTTED
AETHES**

SIX-TOOTHED AETHES *Aethes sexdentata* 3760.2 **Common**
TL 7–8 mm. Peppery grayish brown FW is boldly marked with angled dark brown AM and PM bands. Costal area between bands is whitish. **HOSTS:** Unknown. **RANGE:** Se. Canada and ne. U.S.

PINK-MOTTLED COCHYLID
Cochylis aurorana 3767 **Common**
TL 6–7 mm. Warm brown FW is marked with poorly defined pinkish bands. Median band has a blackish spot at midpoint. **HOSTS:** Unknown. **RANGE:** Se. Canada and ne. U.S.

HORNED COCHYLID *Cochylis bucera* 3769 **Common**
TL 4–5 mm. Orange FW has silver-studded brown median band that widens toward inner margin. ST line is weakly defined or absent. **HOSTS:** Unknown. **RANGE:** Se. Canada and ne. U.S.

BANDED SUNFLOWER MOTH *Cochylis hospes* 3777 **Common**
TL 6–7 mm. Pale yellow FW has silver-studded brown median band that widens toward inner margin. Incomplete ST line is dark brown. **HOSTS:** Unknown. **RANGE:** Se. Canada and ne. U.S.

BROAD-PATCH COCHYLID *Cochylis nana* 3778 **Common**
TL 6–7 mm. Pinkish FW is boldly marked with wide gray bands in basal and median areas. ST area is marked with yellowish and brown lines. **HOSTS:** Unknown. **RANGE:** Se. Canada and ne. U.S.

RINGS' COCHYLID *Cochylis ringsi* 3780 **Common**
TL 6–8 mm. Whitish FW is boldly patterned with earth brown basal and median bands edged silver. Terminal line is edged brown. **HOSTS:** Unknown. **RANGE:** Se. Canada and ne. U.S.

BROWN-PATCHED PHALONIDIA
Phalonidia lepidana 3807 **Common**
TL 6–7 mm. Whitish FW blends to pale orange in ST area. An oblique russet brown median band fades before reaching costa. **HOSTS:** Unknown. **RANGE:** Se. Canada and ne. U.S.

BIRD'S COCHYLID *Phtheochroa birdana* 3813 **Common**
TL 12–13 mm. Large. Gray FW is boldly patterned with an oblique brown AM band and blackish ST band. Basal area is whitish. **HOSTS:** Unknown. **RANGE:** Se. Canada and ne. U.S.

COCHYLID MOTHS

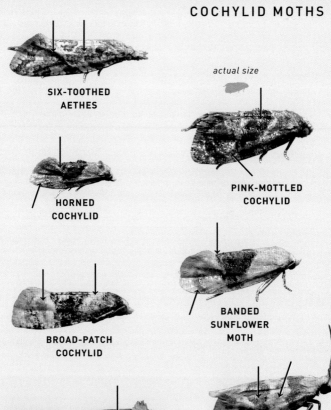

**SIX-TOOTHED
AETHES**

actual size

**PINK-MOTTLED
COCHYLID**

**HORNED
COCHYLID**

**BROAD-PATCH
COCHYLID**

**BANDED
SUNFLOWER
MOTH**

BIRD'S COCHYLID

RINGS' COCHYLID

BROWN-PATCHED PHALONIDIA

MARBLED COCHYLID *Phtheochroa riscana* 3822 **Common**
TL 8–9 mm. Mottled FW has contrasting pale basal area. AM line slants inward toward inner margin. **HOSTS:** Unknown. **RANGE:** Se. Canada and ne. U.S.

SILVER-LINED COCHYLID
Phtheochroa vitellinana 3825 **Common**
TL 5–7 mm. Yellow FW is banded with wavy silver-edged rusty lines. Median and PM lines converge at midpoint. **HOSTS:** Unknown. **RANGE:** Se. Canada and ne. U.S.

KEARFOTT'S ROLANDYLIS *Rolandylis maiana* 3837 **Common**
TL 5–7 mm. Cream-colored FW has olive brown median and ST bands. Terminal line is checkered brown. Head is often mottled with black scales. **HOSTS:** Unknown. **RANGE:** Se. Canada and ne. U.S.

DARK-BANDED COCHYLID *Thyraylia bana* 3843 **Common**
TL 5–7 mm. Pale FW is variably banded light brown and yellowish. Median band is darker with a blackish bar at midpoint. **HOSTS:** Unknown. **RANGE:** Se. Canada and ne. U.S.

HOLLAND'S COCHYLID
Thyraylia hollandana 3847 **Common**
TL 5–7 mm. Whitish FW is strongly suffused with pink in ST and terminal areas. Wide brown median band is edged blackish at inner margin. **HOSTS:** Unknown. **RANGE:** Se. Canada and ne. U.S.

PRIMROSE COCHYLID *Atroposia oenotherana* 3848 **Common**
TL 5–6 mm. Rose pink FW has large ochre patch covering AM and basal area. Fringe is cream-colored. **HOSTS:** Unknown. **RANGE:** Se. Canada and ne. U.S.

COCHYLID MOTHS

actual size

MARBLED COCHYLID

SILVER-LINED COCHYLID

KEARFOTT'S ROLANDYLIS

DARK-BANDED COCHYLID

HOLLAND'S COCHYLID

PRIMROSE COCHYLID

Archips Leafrollers
Family Tortricidae, Subfamily Tortricinae, Tribe Archipini

Small, flat moths with rounded or curvy wings, especially in the case of Omnivorous Leafroller. Many species show darker bands or fine lines running across the wing, though some are mottled with no defined pattern. Larvae are typically leafrollers, though a few, such as Ugly-nest Caterpillar Moth, build large communal webs resembling those of tent caterpillars. Many species are serious crop pests, particularly in orchards. Adults are nocturnal and will come to light in small numbers.

THREE-LINED LEAFROLLER
Pandemis limitata   3594   **Common**
TL 10–12 mm. FW is variably pale tan to brown with darker base, median band, and subapical patch. Darker areas are edged yellowish. **HOSTS:** Deciduous trees and shrubs, including alder, apple, birch, maple, and oak. **RANGE:** Se. Canada and ne. U.S.

RED-BANDED LEAFROLLER
Argyrotaenia velutinana   3597   **Common**
TL 9 mm. Whitish FW is mottled gray and brown in basal and ST areas. Chestnut median band is often broken with a black bar. **HOSTS:** Trees and shrubs, including apple, cherry, grape, and spruce. **RANGE:** Se. Canada and ne. U.S.

FOUR-LINED LEAFROLLER
Argyrotaenia quadrifasciana   3621   **Common**
TL 9 mm. Creamy FW is blotched orange, creating a netlike pattern. Slanting AM, PM, and ST lines are purplish. **HOSTS:** Apple, cherry, hawthorn, and serviceberry. **RANGE:** Se. Canada and ne. U.S.

LINED OAK LEAFROLLER
Argyrotaenia quercifoliana   3623   **Common**
TL 13 mm. Creamy FW is heavily blotched light brown, creating a netlike pattern. Narrow brown AM and PM lines are indistinct. **HOSTS:** Oak and witch hazel. **RANGE:** Se. Canada and ne. U.S.

WHITE-SPOTTED LEAFROLLER
Argyrotaenia alisellana   3624   **Common**
TL 12 mm. Chocolate brown FW is marked with large whitish patches along costa and in basal and ST areas. **HOSTS:** Oak. **RANGE:** Se. Canada and ne. U.S.

ARCHIPS LEAFROLLERS

**THREE-LINED
LEAFROLLER**

**RED-BANDED
LEAFROLLER**

actual size

**FOUR-LINED
LEAFROLLER**

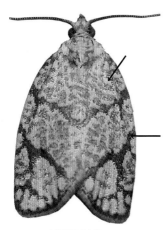

**LINED OAK
LEAFROLLER**

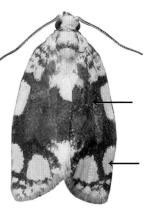

**WHITE-SPOTTED
LEAFROLLER**

97

GRAY-BANDED LEAFROLLER

Argyrotaenia mariana   3625   **Common**
TL 11 mm. Whitish FW has warm brown shading in basal and median areas. Hollow black costal triangle is sharply defined. **HOSTS:** Deciduous trees and woody plants, including apple, beech, blueberry, oak, and willow. **RANGE:** Se. Canada and ne. U.S.

BROKEN-BANDED LEAFROLLER

Choristoneura fractivittana   3632   **Common**
TL 11–12 mm. Yellowish tan FW is overlaid with a faint network of brown scales. Brown median band is broken at midpoint. Some individuals are darker with a complete median band. **HOSTS:** Apple, birch, elm, oak, and raspberry. **RANGE:** Se. Canada and ne. U.S.

OBLIQUE-BANDED LEAFROLLER

Choristoneura rosaceana   3635   **Common**
TL 12 mm. Yellowish tan FW is marked with an oblique brown median band and subapical patch. **HOSTS:** Trees and woody plants, including apple, blueberry, oak, and pine. **RANGE:** Se. Canada and ne. U.S.

LARGE ASPEN TORTRIX

Choristoneura conflictana   3637   **Common**
TL 18 mm. Large. Gray FW has darker basal area and thick slanting median band. **HOSTS:** Primarily trembling aspen. **RANGE:** Se. Canada and ne. U.S.

SPRUCE BUDWORM   *Choristoneura fumiferana*   3638   **Common**
TL 11–15 mm. FW is variably pale gray or orange overlaid with a darker, marbled pattern. Usually has a short black bar in central median area. **HOSTS:** Balsam fir and white spruce, also other coniferous trees. **RANGE:** Se. Canada and ne. U.S.

JACK PINE BUDWORM   *Choristoneura pinus*   3643   **Common**
TL 11–15 mm. Orange FW is overlaid with a faint network of rusty scales. Silvery gray bands in median and ST areas are fragmented. **HOSTS:** Jack pine and Scotch pine. **RANGE:** Se. Canada and ne. U.S.

FRUIT TREE LEAFROLLER   *Archips argyrospila*   3648   **Common**
TL 8–12 mm. Reddish brown FW is mottled with irregular bluish gray bands. Two cream-colored spots mark costa. **HOSTS:** Fruit-bearing trees and plants, including apple, blueberry, peach, and pear. **RANGE:** Se. Canada and ne. U.S.

ARCHIPS LEAFROLLERS

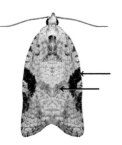

GRAY-BANDED LEAFROLLER

actual size

BROKEN-BANDED LEAFROLLER

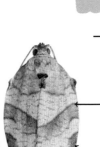

OBLIQUE-BANDED LEAFROLLER

SPRUCE BUDWORM

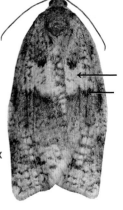

LARGE ASPEN TORTRIX

FRUIT TREE LEAFROLLER

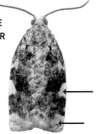

JACK PINE BUDWORM

WHITE-SPOTTED OAK LEAFROLLER

Archips semiferana 3653 **Common**
TL 9–11 mm. Pinkish FW is marked with irregular whitish bands and marbling in basal area. **HOSTS:** Oak, also apple and witch hazel. **RANGE:** Se. Canada and ne. U.S.

OAK WEBWORM *Archips fervidana* 3655 **Common**

TL 8–12 mm. Pale orange and brown FW has grayish ST area. Two black spots mark costa, with another in central median area. **HOSTS:** Hickory and oak. **RANGE:** Se. Canada and ne. U.S.

OMNIVOROUS LEAFROLLER

Archips purpurana 3658 **Common**
TL 14 mm. Brownish tan FW is overlaid with a faint network of brown scales. Darker individuals have dusky shading in basal, median, and ST areas. Has fishtail-shaped outline. **HOSTS:** Deciduous trees and low plants, including apple, blueberry, goldenrod, violets, and willow. **RANGE:** Se. Canada and ne. U.S.

UGLY-NEST CATERPILLAR MOTH

Archips cerasivorana 3661 **Common**
TL 12 mm. Orange FW has irregular lilac-colored bands. Two hollow brown spots mark costa, with another in central median area. **HOSTS:** Chokecherry, also apple, black cherry, hawthorn, and roses. **RANGE:** Se. Canada and ne. U.S.

STRIATED TORTRIX *Archips strianus* 3664 **Uncommon**

TL 12 mm. Brown FW is boldly patterned with black and cream streaks along veins. **HOSTS:** Black spruce and white spruce. **RANGE:** Se. Canada and ne. U.S.

BOLDLY-MARKED ARCHIPS *Archips dissitana* 3666 **Common**

TL 12 mm. White FW is boldly patterned with fragmented black bands. **HOSTS:** Unknown, possibly coniferous trees. **RANGE:** Se. Canada and ne. U.S.

SPRING SPRUCE NEEDLE *Archips pachardiana* 3667 **Common**

TL 10 mm. Whitish FW is finely brindled gray with fragmented blackish bands creating a marbled appearance. **HOSTS:** Primarily spruce, also balsam fir. **RANGE:** Se. Canada and ne. U.S.

BLACK-AND-GRAY BANDED LEAFROLLER

Syndemis afflictana 3672 **Common**
TL 10 mm. Silvery gray FW has contrasting black-edged pale gray median band. **HOSTS:** Trees, including balsam fir, birch, maple, and spruce. **RANGE:** Se. Canada and ne. U.S.

ARCHIPS LEAFROLLERS

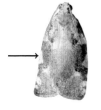

WHITE-SPOTTED OAK LEAFROLLER

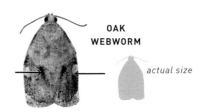

OAK WEBWORM

actual size

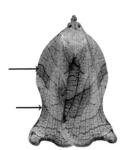

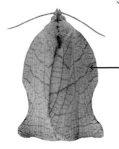

OMNIVOROUS LEAFROLLER

UGLY-NEST CATERPILLAR MOTH

STRIATED TORTRIX

BOLDLY-MARKED ARCHIPS

SPRING SPRUCE NEEDLE

BLACK-AND-GRAY BANDED LEAFROLLER

WHITE-TRIANGLE CLEPSIS *Clepsis persicana* 3682 **Common**
TL 10–11 mm. Orange FW has lilac band along ST line and contrasting white triangle at midpoint of costa. **HOSTS:** Various trees, including alder, apple, birch, maple, and spruce. **RANGE:** Se. Canada and ne. U.S.

CLEMENS' CLEPSIS *Clepsis clemensiana* 3684 **Common**
TL 10–11 mm. Pale yellow FW has hint of darker scaling along veins. **HOSTS:** Primarily grasses, also aster and goldenrod. **RANGE:** Se. Canada and ne. U.S.

BLACK-PATCHED CLEPSIS
Clepsis melaleucanus 3686 **Common**
TL 11–12 mm. Creamy white FW has extensive patch of grayish brown shading along inner margin and a dark subapical patch. **HOSTS:** Apple, blue cohosh, mandrake, Solomon's seal, and trillium. **RANGE:** Se. Canada and ne. U.S.

GARDEN TORTRIX *Clepsis peritana* 3688 **Common**
TL 8 mm. Pinkish brown FW has an oblique brown median band and a rounded dusky subapical patch. **HOSTS:** Strawberry and other low plants, with a preference for dying leaves. **RANGE:** Se. Canada and ne. U.S.

SHIMMERING ADOXOPHYES
Adoxophyes negundana 3691 **Common**
TL 10 mm. Creamy white FW is overlaid with a faint network of brown scales. Wide brown median band and ST line are boldest markings. **HOSTS:** Unknown. **RANGE:** Se. Canada and ne. U.S.

SPARGANOTHID LEAFROLLERS Family
Tortricidae, Subfamily Tortricinae, Tribe Sparganothidini

Small moths, similar in appearance to other members of the subfamily, but with longer labial palps that give them a snouty appearance. Many species are brightly colored. Larvae are typically leafrollers. Adults are nocturnal and will readily come to light.

SPARGANOTHIS FRUITWORM
Sparganothis sulphureana 3695 **Common**
TL 10 mm. Yellow FW is overlaid with a faint network of orange scales. Reddish AM and PM lines merge at inner margin, forming a V-shape. **HOSTS:** Various trees and plants, including apple, clover, corn, cranberry, pine, and willow. **RANGE:** Se. Canada and ne. U.S.

ARCHIPS LEAFROLLERS

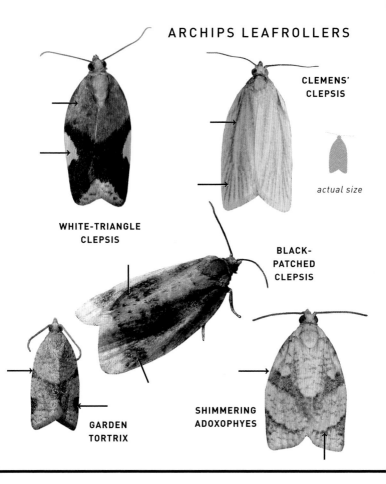

**CLEMENS'
CLEPSIS**

actual size

**WHITE-TRIANGLE
CLEPSIS**

**BLACK-
PATCHED
CLEPSIS**

**GARDEN
TORTRIX**

**SHIMMERING
ADOXOPHYES**

SPARGANOTHID
LEAFROLLERS

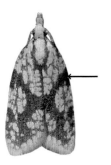

actual size

**SPARGANOTHIS
FRUITWORM**

103

THREE-STREAKED SPARGANOTHIS

Sparganothis tristriata   3699   **Uncommon**
TL 10 mm. Bright yellow FW has striking reddish streaks that are studded with metallic silvery gray scales. **HOSTS:** Unknown. **RANGE:** Se. Canada and ne. U.S.

ONE-LINED SPARGANOTHIS

Sparganothis unifasciana   3711   **Common**
TL 10–12 mm. Golden yellow FW has oblique reddish median band and fragmented ST patches. **HOSTS:** Various trees and herbaceous plants, including ash and pine. **RANGE:** Se. Canada and ne. U.S.

OAK CENOPIS   *Cenopis diluticostana*   3716   **Common**
TL 7–8 mm. Shiny FW is variably light brown to chestnut. Darker AM and PM bands cut through yellow costal margin. **HOSTS:** Ash, possibly oak. **RANGE:** Se. Canada and e. U.S.

RETICULATED FRUITWORM

Cenopis reticulatana   3720   **Common**
TL 10–12 mm. Creamy yellow FW is overlaid with a network of orange scales. Oblique median band is fused to thinner Y-shaped ST line. **HOSTS:** Various trees and shrubs, including alder, apple, blueberry, maple, and oak. **RANGE:** Se. Canada and ne. U.S.

MAPLE-BASSWOOD LEAFROLLER

Cenopis pettitana   3725   **Common**
TL 10–13 mm. FW is variably whitish to pale yellow, often with fragmented brown lines. **HOSTS:** Apple, basswood, and maple. **RANGE:** Se. Canada and ne. U.S.

APRONED CENOPIS   *Cenopis niveana* 3727   **Common**
TL 10 mm. Chocolate brown FW has yellow patches along costa and band along outer margin. **HOSTS:** Unknown. **RANGE:** Se. Canada and ne. U.S.

TUFTED APPLE BUD MOTH

Platynota idaeusalis   3740   **Common**
TL 10–13 mm. Gray FW has chocolate brown shading along inner margin. Three lines of raised scales cross median area. **HOSTS:** Various trees and low plants, including apple, black walnut, box elder, clover, and pine. **RANGE:** Se. Canada and ne. U.S.

SPARGANOTHID LEAFROLLERS

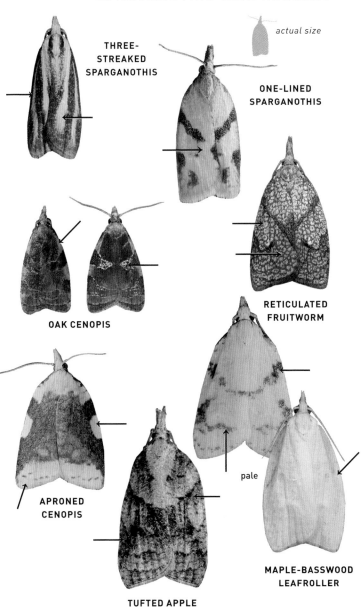

actual size

THREE-STREAKED SPARGANOTHIS

ONE-LINED SPARGANOTHIS

RETICULATED FRUITWORM

OAK CENOPIS

APRONED CENOPIS

pale

MAPLE-BASSWOOD LEAFROLLER

TUFTED APPLE BUD MOTH

SINGED PLATYNOTA *Platynota semiustana* 3741 **Common**
TL 8–10 mm. Sooty black FW has contrastingly paler terminal line. Raised tufts of scales in median area are sometimes tipped whitish. **HOSTS:** Unknown. **RANGE:** Se. Canada and ne. U.S.

EXASPERATING PLATYNOTA
Platynota exasperatana 3743 **Common**
TL 10–13 mm. Pale gray FW has darker median area overlaid with black lines. Three thicker lines of raised scales cross median area. **HOSTS:** Unknown. **RANGE:** Se. Canada and ne. U.S.

WHITE-LINE LEAFROLLER
Amorbia humerosana 3748 **Common**
TL 11–15 mm. Gray FW is speckled with blackish scales. A streak of chocolate brown shading extends along inner margin. Has very broad FW with sharply pointed apex. **HOSTS:** Various trees and shrubs, including apple, huckleberry, poison ivy, and sumac. **RANGE:** Se. Canada and ne. U.S.

OLETHREUTINE MOTHS
Family Tortricidae, Subfamily Olethreutinae

As in other tortricid moths, the FW margin is usually slightly curved, but it is narrower at the base, giving the moth a more tapered appearance. Wings are often held slightly curled or tight to the body. Many species have fuzzy labial palps. Where head shape and wing posture are similar to those of species in the tribe Cochylini, the olethreutine moths can be told by their higher head profile and resulting straighter "back." Most species are leafrollers; a few, such as Codling Moth, are crop pests of commercial importance. Adults will come to light, sometimes in moderate numbers.

JAVELIN MOTH *Bactra verutana* 2707 **Common**
TL 8 mm. Mottled, pale tan FW has median area marked with two brown blotches. **HOSTS:** *Cyperus* (flatsedge). **RANGE:** Widespread.

GRAPE BERRY MOTH *Paralobesia viteana* 2712 **Common**
TL 6 mm. Lead gray FW has a large straw-colored patch along inner margin and bronze brown median and PM patches. **HOSTS:** Grape. **RANGE:** Se. Canada and e. U.S.

SPARGANOTHID LEAFROLLERS

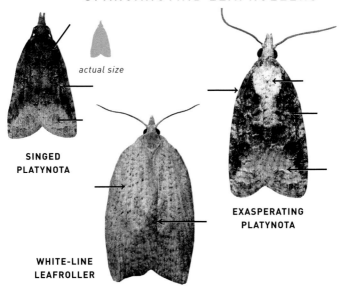

actual size

**SINGED
PLATYNOTA**

**WHITE-LINE
LEAFROLLER**

**EXASPERATING
PLATYNOTA**

OLETHREUTINE MOTHS

actual size

JAVELIN MOTH

GRAPE BERRY MOTH

DULL-BARRED ENDOTHENIA

Endothenia hebesana 2738 **Common**

TL 8 mm. Marbled FW has two-pronged dusky median band. Three black-edged spots form PM band. **HOSTS:** Low plants, including iris, speedwell, and vervain. **RANGE:** Se. Canada and e. U.S.

IMPUDENT HULDA *Hulda impudens* 2747 **Common**

TL 7 mm. Pale gray FW has contrasting sooty gray basal patch that continues along costa. Inner margin is marked with a two-lobed brown patch. **HOSTS:** Unknown. **RANGE:** Se. Canada and ne. U.S.

SCULPTURED MOTH *Eumarozia malachitana* 2749 **Common**

TL 7 mm. Gray FW is tinged with reddish pink distally. A large white-edged, mossy green median patch is conspicuous. Worn individuals may appear brownish. **HOSTS:** Persimmon. **RANGE:** Se. Canada and e. U.S.

DECEPTIVE APOTOMIS *Apotomis deceptana* 2765 **Common**

TL 10–12 mm. Gray FW is finely vermiculated with a network of black lines. **HOSTS:** Poplar and willow. **RANGE:** Se. Canada and ne. U.S.

POPLAR LEAFROLLER

Pseudosciaphila duplex 2769 **Common**

TL 9–12.5 mm. Mottled blue-gray FW has a broad white median band. A sharp backward-pointing white spike cuts into dark PM line. **HOSTS:** Poplar, also alder, birch, maple, and willow. **RANGE:** Se. Canada and ne. U.S.

DUSKY LEAFROLLER *Orthotaenia undulana* 2770 **Common**

TL 9 mm. Grayish brown FW has a whitish median band and edging to copper-tinged PM band. **HOSTS:** Poplar, also birch and willow. **RANGE:** Widespread.

SHINING OLETHREUTES *Olethreutes nitidana* 2775 **Common**

TL 7–8.5 mm. Pale orange FW is overlaid with darker orange-brown markings. Median band has long backward-pointing prongs. **HOSTS:** Maple. **RANGE:** Se. Canada and ne. U.S.

PUNCTUATED OLETHREUTES

Olethreutes punctanum 2786 **Common**

TL 9 mm. Pale, violet gray FW has short blackish basal bar and tiny black discal spot. **HOSTS:** Dogwood. **RANGE:** Se. Canada and ne. U.S.

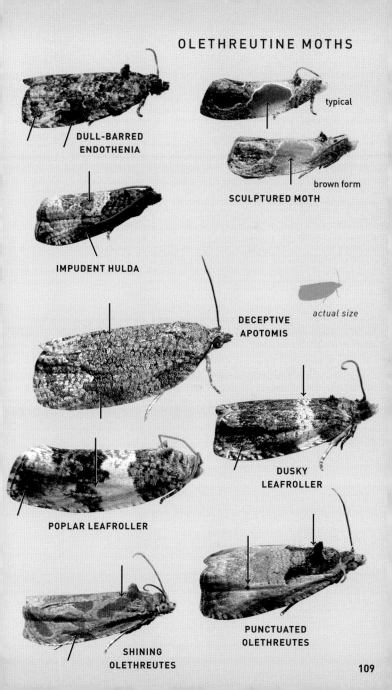

OLETHREUTINE MOTHS

DULL-BARRED ENDOTHENIA

typical

brown form

SCULPTURED MOTH

IMPUDENT HULDA

DECEPTIVE APOTOMIS

actual size

POPLAR LEAFROLLER

DUSKY LEAFROLLER

SHINING OLETHREUTES

PUNCTUATED OLETHREUTES

INORNATE OLETHREUTES

Olethreutes inornatana 2788 **Common**

TL 10.5 mm. Uniform tan FW has paler basal dash and reddish shading along costa and outer margin. **HOSTS:** Black cherry and chokecherry. **RANGE:** Se. Canada and e. U.S.

WRETCHED OLETHREUTES

Olethreutes exoletum 2791 **Common**

TL 8 mm. Pale gray FW has slanting blackish basal bar and dusky shading along costa and outer margin. **HOSTS:** Currant. **RANGE:** Se. Canada and ne. U.S.

QUARTERED OLETHREUTES

Olethreutes quadrifidum 2794 **Common**

TL 8–9 mm. Pale gray FW has white veins and reddish shading in basal area and along costa and outer margin. **HOSTS:** Dogwood. **RANGE:** Se. Canada and ne. U.S.

DARK OLETHREUTES *Olethreutes nigranum* 2800 **Common**

TL 12 mm. FW is variable but typically is straw-colored with contrasting blackish bar along inner margin and rusty shading along costa. **HOSTS:** Sugar maple. **RANGE:** Se. Canada and ne. U.S.

MALANA LEAFROLLER *Olethreutes malana* 2820 **Common**

TL 8 mm. White FW has some mottled blackish shading in inner basal, costal, and ST areas. Incomplete black median bar falls short of black discal spot. **HOSTS:** Apple. **RANGE:** Se. Canada and ne. U.S.

BANDED OLETHREUTES *Olethreutes fasciatana* 2823 **Common**

TL 8 mm. Dark brown FW has olive highlights along silvery lines. AM line is broadly edged white. **HOSTS:** Poplar and willow. **RANGE:** Se. Canada and e. U.S.

HYDRANGEA LEAFTIER *Olethreutes ferriferana* 2827 **Common**

TL 8.5 mm. Pale violet gray FW has contrasting chestnut brown basal area and trapezoidal subapical patch. **HOSTS:** Wild hydrangea. **RANGE:** Se. Canada and ne. U.S.

IRON-LINED OLETHREUTES

Olethreutes ferrolineana 2838.1 **Common**

TL 10 mm. Yellowish tan FW is finely vermiculated black and studded with lines of metallic silver dots. **HOSTS:** Unknown. **RANGE:** Se. Canada and ne. U.S.

OLETHREUTINE MOTHS

INORNATE OLETHREUTES

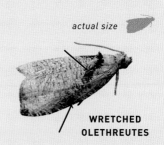

actual size

WRETCHED OLETHREUTES

QUARTERED OLETHREUTES

DARK OLETHREUTES

MALANA LEAFROLLER

BANDED OLETHREUTES

HYDRANGEA LEAFTIER

IRON-LINED OLETHREUTES

FROSTY OLETHREUTES *Olethreutes glaciana* 2847 **Common**
TL 8 mm. FW is banded black and white, often with an isolated white spot in black median band. **HOSTS:** Deciduous trees, including birch, chokecherry, maple, and willow. **RANGE:** Widespread.

DIVIDED OLETHREUTES
Olethreutes bipartitana 2848 **Common**
TL 9.5 mm. White FW has mottled bluish basal patch and median band. **HOSTS:** *Spermolepis* (scaleseed). **RANGE:** Se. Canada and ne. U.S.

PINK-WASHED LEAFROLLER
Metendothenia separatana 2860 **Common**
TL 8 mm. Pinkish FW has blue-gray edging to irregular black AM and median bands. Isolated black discal spot is noticeable. **HOSTS:** Black cherry, blackberry, and rose. **RANGE:** Se. Canada and e. U.S.

GREEN BUDWORM *Hedya nubiferana* 2862 **Common**
TL 11 mm. Mottled gray-brown FW is whitish beyond median area. **HOSTS:** Apple and hawthorn. **RANGE:** Widespread. **NOTE:** Introduced from Europe.

EUROPEAN PINE SHOOT MOTH
Rhyacionia buoliana 2867 **Common**
TL 11 mm. Orange FW is boldly marked with pale silvery gray lines. **HOSTS:** Pine. **RANGE:** Widespread. **NOTE:** Introduced from Europe.

NORTHERN PITCH TWIG MOTH
Retinia albicapitana 2892 **Common**
TL 10 mm. Rusty brown FW is marked with narrow silvery gray lines and spots. **HOSTS:** Jack pine. **RANGE:** Se. Canada and ne. U.S.

GRAY RETINIA *Retinia gemistrigulana* 2898 **Uncommon**
TL 11 mm. Ash gray FW is finely banded with crisp black dashes. **HOSTS:** Unknown. **RANGE:** Se. Canada and e. U.S.

SHADED PHANETA *Phaneta umbrastriana* 2913 **Common**
TL 8–9 mm. Streaky straw-colored FW blends to chestnut in ST area. Silvery gray lines mark inner ST area. **HOSTS:** Unknown. **RANGE:** Se. Canada and ne. U.S.

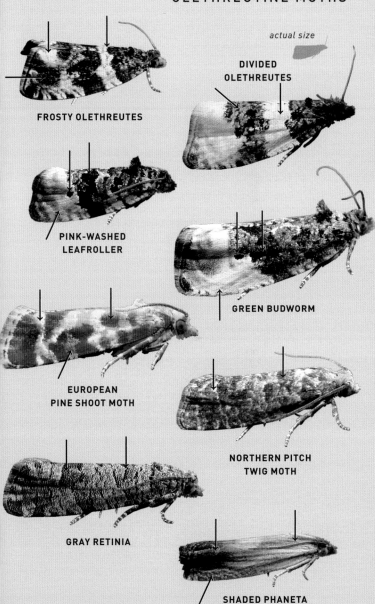

OLETHREUTINE MOTHS

actual size

FROSTY OLETHREUTES

DIVIDED OLETHREUTES

PINK-WASHED LEAFROLLER

GREEN BUDWORM

EUROPEAN PINE SHOOT MOTH

NORTHERN PITCH TWIG MOTH

GRAY RETINIA

SHADED PHANETA

PALE-HEADED PHANETA

Phaneta ochrocephala   2927   **Common**

TL 7 mm. Creamy FW is heavily mottled warm brown. A sinuous blackish band extends through median area. **HOSTS:** Rough cocklebur. **RANGE:** Se. Canada and e. U.S.

REDDISH PHANETA   *Phaneta raracana*   2928   **Common**

TL 6 mm. Brick red FW has contrasting whitish patch in inner ST area. Head and thorax are mostly white. **HOSTS:** Goldenrod. **RANGE:** Se. Canada and e. U.S.

BUFF-TIPPED PHANETA

Phaneta ochroterminana   2929   **Common**

TL 6 mm. Dark blue-gray FW has contrasting pale orange outer margin. Head and thorax are mostly dull orange. **HOSTS:** Canada goldenrod. **RANGE:** Se. Canada and e. U.S.

ASTER-HEAD PHANETA   *Phaneta tomonana*   2936   **Common**

TL 6 mm. Gray FW has two sharply defined black wedges along inner margin. **HOSTS:** New England aster. **RANGE:** Se. Canada and e. U.S.

ROBINSON'S EUCOSMA

Eucosma robinsonana   3009   **Common**

TL 8 mm. Brown FW is boldly patterned with black-edged white bands. Head is white. **HOSTS:** Unknown. **RANGE:** Se. Canada and e. U.S.

WHITE PINE CONE BORER

Eucosma tocullionana   3074   **Common**

TL 8 mm. Marbled FW is mottled with pale gray and brown. Pale orange bands in median area are edged silver. **HOSTS:** White pine, also balsam fir, spruce, and tamarack. **RANGE:** Se. Canada and ne. U.S.

TRIANGLE-BACKED EUCOSMA

Eucosma dorsisignatana   3116   **Common**

TL 10 mm. Gray FW is finely vermiculated chestnut. Two separate blackish brown patches extend through median area. **HOSTS:** Goldenrod. **RANGE:** Widespread.

SIMILAR EUCOSMA   *Eucosma similiana*   3116.1   **Common**

TL 10 mm. Pale pinkish gray FW is finely vermiculated brown. A U-shaped chestnut patch extends through median area. **HOSTS:** Goldenrod. **RANGE:** Se. Canada and e. U.S.

OLETHREUTINE MOTHS

PALE-HEADED PHANETA

REDDISH PHANETA

BUFF-TIPPED PHANETA

ASTER-HEAD PHANETA

ROBINSON'S EUCOSMA

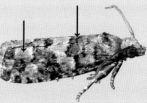

WHITE PINE CONE BORER

TRIANGLE-BACKED EUCOSMA

SIMILAR EUCOSMA

actual size

DERELICT EUCOSMA *Eucosma derelicta* 3120 **Common**
TL 8 mm. Pale pinkish brown FW is finely vermiculated chestnut. Slanting median line is broadly edged brown. **HOSTS:** Goldenrod. **RANGE:** Widespread.

THREE-PARTED EPIBLEMA
Epiblema tripartitana 3184 **Common**
TL 8–10 mm. Mottled gray-brown FW has contrasting white median band. **HOSTS:** Great coneflower. **RANGE:** Se. Canada and e. U.S.

SCUDDER'S EPIBLEMA
Epiblema scudderiana 3186 **Common**
TL 8–9 mm. White FW has contrasting blue-gray basal patch. A black spot marks grayish inner ST area. **HOSTS:** Goldenrod. **RANGE:** Se. Canada and e. U.S.

BIDENS BORER *Epiblema otiosana* 3202 **Common**
TL 6–8 mm. Dark grayish brown FW has a large U-shaped white patch at midpoint of inner margin. Inner ST area is paler gray. **HOSTS:** Beggar ticks and annual ragweed. **RANGE:** Se. Canada and e. U.S.

BRIGHTON'S EPIBLEMA
Epiblema brightonana 3203 **Common**
TL 7 mm. Blue-gray FW is marked with white-edged black patch at midpoint of inner margin. Slanting black PM line is constricted near inner margin. **HOSTS:** Unknown. **RANGE:** Se. Canada and ne. U.S.

DIRTY NOTOCELIA *Notocelia illotana* 3210 **Common**
TL 11 mm. Whitish FW has contrasting dark brown basal patch. Front of head is orange. **HOSTS:** Unknown. **RANGE:** Widespread.

ASHY SULEIMA *Suleima cinerodorsana* 3217 **Common**
TL 7–8 mm. Grayish brown FW has wide irregular white stripe along inner margin. Head is white. **HOSTS:** Sunflower. **RANGE:** Se. Canada and ne. U.S.

CANADIAN SONIA *Sonia canadana* 3219 **Common**
TL 8 mm. Light brown FW has darker brown shading along angled median line and inner ST area. Whitish lines are obvious only near inner margin. **HOSTS:** Goldenrod. **RANGE:** Se. Canada and ne. U.S.

OLETHREUTINE MOTHS

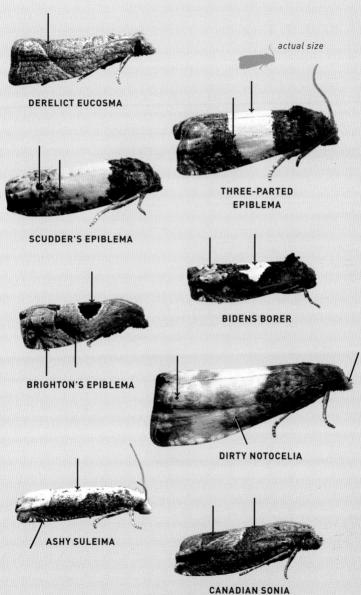

DERELICT EUCOSMA

actual size

THREE-PARTED
EPIBLEMA

SCUDDER'S EPIBLEMA

BIDENS BORER

BRIGHTON'S EPIBLEMA

DIRTY NOTOCELIA

ASHY SULEIMA

CANADIAN SONIA

COTTONWOOD TWIG BORER

Gypsonoma haimbachiana   3226   **Common**
TL 7 mm. Whitish FW has sharply angled border to darker basal area. Apex is marked with a black spot. **HOSTS:** Cottonwood. **RANGE:** Se. Canada and e. U.S.

MAPLE TWIG BORER   *Proteoteras aesculana*   3230   **Common**
TL 8 mm. Gray FW is mottled pale green when fresh. Blackish crescent that arcs toward apex is fragmented. Raised tufts of scales give FW a lumpy appearance. **HOSTS:** Maples. **RANGE:** Widespread.

BLACK-CRESCENT PROTEOTERAS

Proteoteras crescentana   3233   **Common**
TL 8 mm. Pale gray FW is tinted warm brown when fresh. A thick black crescent arcs toward apex. Raised tufts give the FW a lumpy appearance. **HOSTS:** Box elder. **RANGE:** Widespread.

MAPLE SHOOT BORER   *Proteoteras moffatiana*   3235   **Common**
TL 8 mm. Resembles Maple Twig Borer but is greener when fresh and has less distinct blackish lines. **HOSTS:** Maple. **RANGE:** Se. Canada and ne. U.S.

SHAGBARK HICKORY LEAFROLLER

Pseudexentera cressoniana   3246   **Common**
TL 10 mm. Peppery gray FW is typically marked with faint darker lines. Basal area is often slightly darker than rest of wing. **HOSTS:** Shagbark hickory. **RANGE:** Se. Canada and e. U.S.

PALE APPLE LEAFROLLER

Pseudexentera mali   3247   **Common**
TL 10 mm. Gray FW has orange shading in basal and median areas. Lines are indistinct apart from inner part of angled AM line. **HOSTS:** Apple. **RANGE:** Se. Canada and ne. U.S.

BANDED PSEUDEXENTERA

Pseudexentera maracana   3254   **Common**
TL 10 mm. Pale gray FW is boldly marked with blackish basal area and thick dark median band. **HOSTS:** Hawthorn. **RANGE:** Se. Canada and e. U.S.

VIRGINIA PSEUDEXENTERA

Pseudexentera virginiana   3258   **Common**
TL 10 mm. Silvery FW has large rounded brown patch in central median area that extends toward apex. **HOSTS:** Unknown. **RANGE:** Se. Canada and e. U.S.

OLETHREUTINE MOTHS

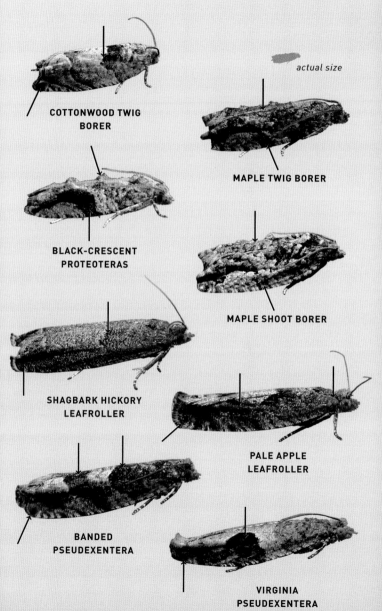

actual size

COTTONWOOD TWIG BORER

MAPLE TWIG BORER

BLACK-CRESCENT PROTEOTERAS

MAPLE SHOOT BORER

SHAGBARK HICKORY LEAFROLLER

PALE APPLE LEAFROLLER

BANDED PSEUDEXENTERA

VIRGINIA PSEUDEXENTERA

LIKEABLE GRETCHENA *Gretchena amatana* 3264 **Common**
TL 10 mm. Mottled grayish brown FW has an irregular pale gray streak along inner margin. A black streak extends through central median and ST areas. **HOSTS:** Unknown. **RANGE:** Se. Canada and ne. U.S.

YELLOW-HEADED ASPEN LEAFTIER
Epinotia nisella 3306 **Common**
TL 8 mm. FW is variable but typically is gray with contrasting dark basal patch inside sharply angled AM line. Sometimes has chestnut along inner margin or median area. **HOSTS:** Poplar, also alder, birch, maple, and willow. **RANGE:** Widespread.

WALKER'S EPINOTIA *Epinotia transmissana* 3310 **Common**
TL 9 mm. Grayish brown FW has contrasting whitish patch at midpoint of inner margin. Fragmented reddish lines slant inward near apex. **HOSTS:** Willow. **RANGE:** Se. Canada and ne. U.S.

MAPLE TRUMPET SKELETONIZER
Catastega aceriella 3334 **Common**
TL 10–12 mm. Peppery whitish FW often has darker basal area within angled AM line. Fragmented blackish lines are often edged brown. **HOSTS:** Sugar maple and red maple. **RANGE:** Se. Canada and ne. U.S.

DIAMONDBACK EPINOTIA *Epinotia lindana* 3351 **Common**
TL 11 mm. Blackish brown FW has a saw-toothed pale stripe extending along inner margin. **HOSTS:** Dogwood. **RANGE:** Widespread.

LITTLE CLOUD ANCYLIS *Ancylis nubeculana* 3354 **Common**
TL 9 mm. FW is whitish with contrasting darker gray shading at midpoint of inner margin and along outer margin. Note the two isolated brown spots near apex. **HOSTS:** Deciduous trees, including apple, hawthorn, pear, and serviceberry. **RANGE:** Se. Canada and ne. U.S.

HALF-OVAL ANCYLIS *Ancylis semiovana* 3361 **Uncommon**
TL 9 mm. White FW has dark brown patch along inner margin. An oblique white bar slants inward through brown ST area. **HOSTS:** Probably New Jersey tea. **RANGE:** Se. Canada and ne. U.S.

SYCAMORE LEAFFOLDER *Ancylis platanana* 3370 **Uncommon**
TL 9 mm. Fawn-colored FW has a pale costal stripe that is interrupted by a slanting bar at its midpoint. **HOSTS:** Sycamore. **RANGE:** Se. Canada and ne. U.S.

OLETHREUTINE MOTHS

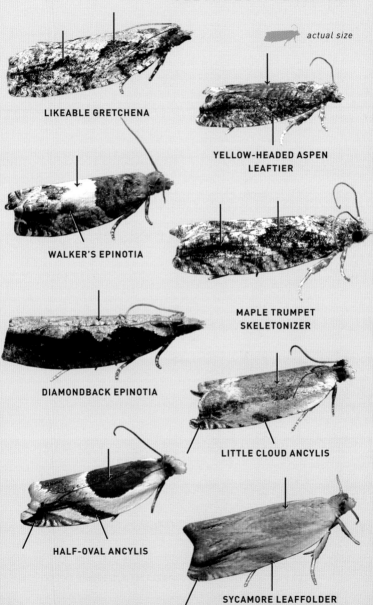

actual size

LIKEABLE GRETCHENA

YELLOW-HEADED ASPEN LEAFTIER

WALKER'S EPINOTIA

MAPLE TRUMPET SKELETONIZER

DIAMONDBACK EPINOTIA

LITTLE CLOUD ANCYLIS

HALF-OVAL ANCYLIS

SYCAMORE LEAFFOLDER

SHATTERED ANCYLIS

Ancylis diminutana 3379 **Uncommon**

TL 9 mm. Ash gray FW has a sharply defined jagged brown stripe extending from base to apex. **HOSTS:** Willow. **RANGE:** Widespread.

VARIABLE DICHRORAMPHA SPECIES COMPLEX

Dichrorampha simulana/bittana 3404/3406 **Uncommon**

TL 9 mm. Two virtually identical species. Dull orange FW has a contrasting brown basal patch as far as angled median line. Sometimes has a pale orange patch at midpoint of inner margin. **HOSTS:** Unknown. **RANGE:** Se. Canada and ne. U.S.

HAPPY PAMMENE *Pammene felicitana* 3419 **Uncommon**

TL 7 mm. Grayish FW has contrasting white basal patch and inner margin. Median and ST areas are crossed with silvery blue lines. **HOSTS:** Unknown. **RANGE:** Se. Canada and ne. U.S.

ORIENTAL FRUIT MOTH

Grapholita molesta 3426 **Uncommon**

TL 5–7 mm. Peppery gray FW has indistinct silvery lines that are obvious only along costa. Typically has a whitish dot in central median area. **HOSTS:** Fruit-bearing trees, including apple, cherry, pear, and peach; sometimes a serious pest. **RANGE:** Widespread. **NOTE:** Accidentally introduced from Japan prior to 1915.

CHERRY FRUITWORM

Grapholita packardi 3428 **Uncommon**

TL 5 mm. Small. Gray FW has wavy black lines accented with silvery blue bands. **HOSTS:** Fruit-bearing trees, including apple, cherry, pear, and peach. **RANGE:** Se. Canada and ne. U.S.

CLOVER HEAD CATERPILLAR MOTH

Grapholita interstinctana 3439 **Uncommon**

TL 6 mm. Grayish brown FW is marked with oblique metallic stripes along costa. Two slanting silver stripes mark midpoint of inner margin. **HOSTS:** Clover and sunflower. **RANGE:** Se. Canada and ne. U.S.

WHITE-MARKED CYDIA

Cydia albimaculana 3461 **Uncommon**

TL 7 mm. Gray FW is finely speckled white. Large white patch at midpoint of inner margin is conspicuous. Pairs of silvery blue bands cross median area. **HOSTS:** Poplar. **RANGE:** Se. Canada and ne. U.S.

OLETHREUTINE MOTHS

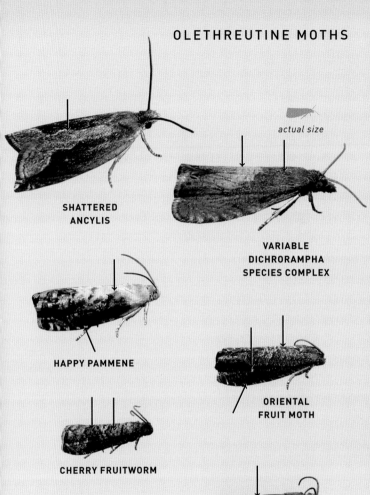

actual size

SHATTERED ANCYLIS

VARIABLE DICHRORAMPHA SPECIES COMPLEX

HAPPY PAMMENE

ORIENTAL FRUIT MOTH

CHERRY FRUITWORM

CLOVER HEAD CATERPILLAR MOTH

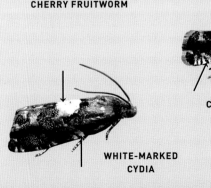

WHITE-MARKED CYDIA

EASTERN PINE SEEDWORM
Cydia toreuta   3486   **Uncommon**
TL 8 mm. Purplish gray FW is finely vermiculated gold. Thick, black-edged, silvery gray bands cross median area. **HOSTS:** Pine. **RANGE:** Se. Canada and ne. U.S.

CODLING MOTH   *Cydia pomonella*   3492   **Common**
TL 12 mm. Ash gray FW is finely brindled with dark gray bands. Large black patch in inner ST area contains fragmented bronze bars. **HOSTS:** Apple, pear, and plum. **RANGE:** Widespread. **NOTE:** Introduced from Europe. An important pest of fruit trees.

FILBERTWORM MOTH   *Cydia latiferreana*   3494   **Common**
TL 11 mm. FW is variably orange or reddish brown, finely speckled pale yellow. Two broad silvery bands cross median area. **HOSTS:** Beech, filbert, hazelnut, and oak. **RANGE:** Widespread.

DOTTED GYMNANDROSOMA
Gymnandrosoma punctidiscanum   3495   **Common**
TL 11 mm. Grayish brown FW has marbled appearance. Curved blackish median band contains a white discal dot. **HOSTS:** Locust. **RANGE:** E. N. America.

LOCUST TWIG BORER
Ecdytolopha insiticiana   3497   **Common**
TL 12 mm. Mottled, grayish brown FW has large whitish patch in ST area. Inner ST line is fragmented into black dashes. **HOSTS:** Black locust. **RANGE:** Widespread.

FALSE BURNET AND MANY-PLUMED MOTHS   Families Urodidae and Alucitidae

Shaggy-spotted Wockia resembles phycitine moths, with long curved wings and tufted scales along the median line. Six-plume Moth is distinctive, with wings made up of multiple feathery plumes, which it usually holds spread while at rest. Both will come to light in small numbers.

SIX-PLUME MOTH   *Alucita montana*   2313   **Common**
WS 12–14 mm. Wings are divided into six plumelike branches. Darker brown bands on wings create a zigzag pattern. Plume shafts on HW are banded black and white. **HOSTS:** Snowberry. **RANGE:** Widespread.

OLETHREUTINE MOTHS

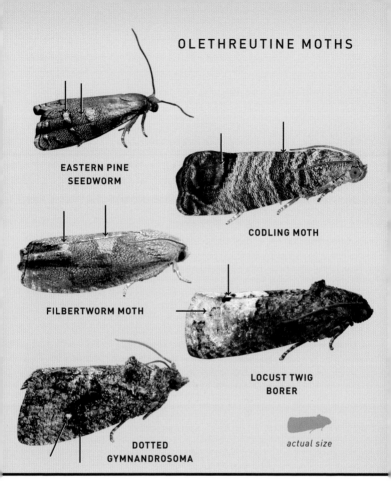

EASTERN PINE SEEDWORM

CODLING MOTH

FILBERTWORM MOTH

LOCUST TWIG BORER

DOTTED GYMNANDROSOMA

actual size

MANY-PLUMED MOTHS

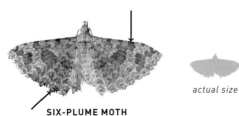

SIX-PLUME MOTH

actual size

SHAGGY-SPOTTED WOCKIA

Wockia asperipunctella   2415.1   **Rare**
TL 10 mm. Silvery gray FW has distinct median band of raised black scales. Median and ST areas are mottled brown. **HOSTS:** Unknown. **RANGE:** E. Great Lakes region.

PLUME MOTHS   Family Pterophoridae

Spindly-legged moths that have a characteristic "airplane" posture at rest. A notch at the tip of the FW divides the wing into two lobes. FW patterns are often very similar, and species can sometimes be difficult to tell apart. Most are nocturnal and will often visit lights in small numbers. Sometimes they can be found resting outdoors on walls or among plants during the daytime.

GRAPE PLUME MOTH

Geina periscelidactylus   6091   **Common**
WS 16–20 mm. Small. Peppery orange FW has a white crescent in the mouth of the notch and two thin white lines slanting in from costa near apex. Brown abdomen has white lateral lines on most segments. **HOSTS:** Grape and Virginia creeper. **RANGE:** Se. Canada and e. U.S.

BUCK'S PLUME MOTH   *Geina bucksi*   6093   **Common**
WS 17 mm. Rusty FW has two white lines (inner line thicker) slanting in from costa near apex. Abdomen is brown with white lateral lines on some segments and a broad white band at base. **HOSTS:** Unknown. **RANGE:** Se. Canada and e. U.S.

LOBED PLUME MOTH   *Dejongia lobidactylus*   6102   **Common**
WS 18 mm. Bronzy brown FW has a white costal streak at apex. Lower lobe has three white spots in outer fringe. Brown abdomen has white teardrop-shaped spots on middle segments. Thorax has a thin white band. **HOSTS:** Unknown. **RANGE:** Se. Canada and ne. U.S.

ROSE PLUME MOTH

Cnaemidophorus rhododactyla   6105   **Common**
WS 24–26 mm. Large. Orange FW has a white line slanting across the mouth of the notch. A broken white band slants through median area. Abdomen has two tiny white dots and a broad white band at base. **HOSTS:** Rose. **RANGE:** Holarctic; in N. America found mostly in Great Lakes region.

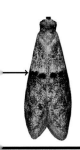

FALSE BURNET MOTHS

SHAGGY-SPOTTED WOCKIA

actual size

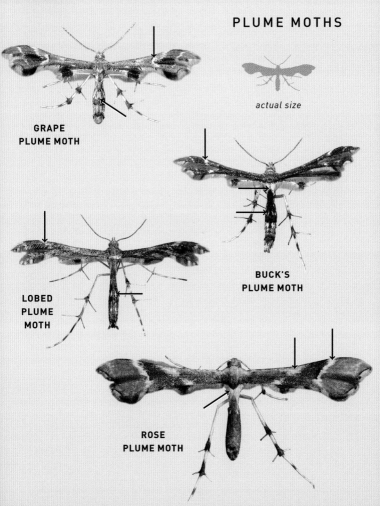

PLUME MOTHS

actual size

GRAPE PLUME MOTH

BUCK'S PLUME MOTH

LOBED PLUME MOTH

ROSE PLUME MOTH

YARROW PLUME MOTH
Gillmeria pallidactyla   6107   **Common**
WS 24–27 mm. Pale tan FW has brown shading in basal and median areas. A pale streak slants through central median area. Abdomen is pale, sometimes with a darker dorsal stripe. **HOSTS:** Yarrow, possibly tansy. **RANGE:** Holarctic; widespread.

ARTICHOKE PLUME MOTH
Platyptilia carduidactylus   6109   **Common**
WS 18–27 mm. Grayish brown FW has a triangular brown patch along costa in PM area. Terminal line on both lobes is brown with a whitish fringe. Abdomen is whitish at base with two inverted V-shaped bands on inner segments. **HOSTS:** Artichoke and thistle. **RANGE:** Widespread.

GERANIUM PLUME MOTH   *Amblyptilia pica*   6118   **Common**
WS 18 mm. Small. FW is variably whitish to light brown, boldly marked with fine lines and spots. Dark triangle along costa in PM area and slanting ST line are well defined. **HOSTS:** Low plants and greenhouse ornamentals, including geranium and snapdragon. **RANGE:** W. N. America. Occurs in ON and ne. U.S. as a greenhouse pest. **NOTE:** Overwinters as an adult.

MOUNTAIN PLUME MOTH   *Adaina montanus*   6157   **Common**
WS 15–16 mm. Small. Straw-colored FW has peppery brown bands in basal and median areas. Abdomen is uniformly pale. **HOSTS:** Canada cocklebur and New York aster. **RANGE:** Se. Canada and ne. U.S.

EUPATORIUM PLUME MOTH
Oidaematophorus eupatorii   6168   **Common**
WS 21 mm. Light grayish brown FW has three thin blackish streaks along costa near apex. A white V in the mouth of the notch is narrowly bordered black. Pale abdomen has an oddly swollen and kinked midsection. **HOSTS:** Probably boneset. **RANGE:** Se. Canada and e. U.S.

BLACK-MARKED PLUME MOTH
Hellinsia inquinatus   6186   **Common**
WS 18 mm. Whitish FW is heavily peppered with dark scales. Small blackish streaks extend along costa near apex, with another in the mouth of the notch. Median area is marked with a blackish dot. Grayish abdomen has a dorsal row of paired blackish streaks. **HOSTS:** Unknown. **RANGE:** Se. Canada and e. U.S.

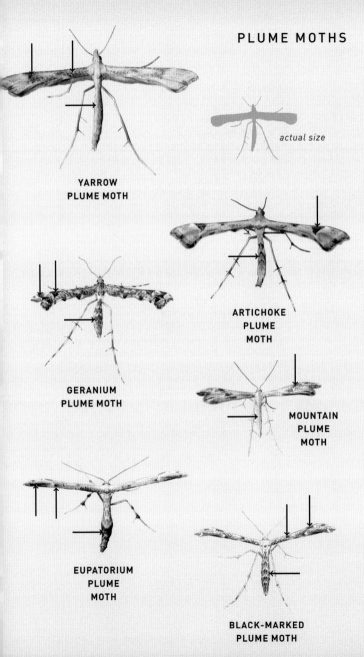

PLUME MOTHS

actual size

YARROW PLUME MOTH

ARTICHOKE PLUME MOTH

GERANIUM PLUME MOTH

MOUNTAIN PLUME MOTH

EUPATORIUM PLUME MOTH

BLACK-MARKED PLUME MOTH

PLAIN PLUME MOTH
Hellinsia homodactylus   6203   **Common**
WS 23 mm. FW is pure white. Abdomen is uniformly pure white,
sometimes with a tinge of pale yellow. **HOSTS:** Unknown.
RANGE: Se. Canada and e. U.S.

MORNING-GLORY PLUME MOTH
Emmelina monodactyla   6234   **Common**
WS 25 mm. Peppery FW is pale gray to pinkish brown with a
darker spot in the mouth of the notch. Pale abdomen has a dorsal row of tiny black dots. Wings are normally rolled tight at
rest. **HOSTS:** Morning glory, lamb's quarters, orach, smartweed, and joe-pye weed. **RANGE:** Holarctic; widespread.

FRUITWORM MOTHS   Family Carposinidae

Very small deltoid moths with strongly pointed wings. Both species have
raised tufts of metallic scales on the FW. Larvae feed within fruits and galls.
Adults are rarely attracted to lights.

CURRANT FRUITWORM MOTH
Carposina fernaldana   2315   **Uncommon**
TL 8–9 mm. Silvery gray FW is whitish basally with several tufts
of raised scales. Blackish bar is present in median area. **HOSTS:**
Fruits of trees and plants, including currant and hawthorn.
RANGE: Se. Canada and ne. U.S.

CRESCENT-MARKED BONDIA
Bondia crescentella   2319   **Uncommon**
TL 8 mm. Silvery gray FW is lightly peppered and streaked
black. Tufts of darker raised scales are accented with silver.
HOSTS: Presumably fruits of various trees and plants. **RANGE:**
Se. Canada and ne. U.S.

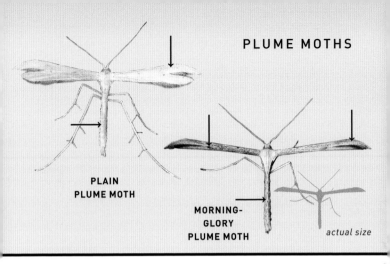

PLUME MOTHS

PLAIN PLUME MOTH

MORNING-GLORY PLUME MOTH

actual size

FRUITWORM MOTHS

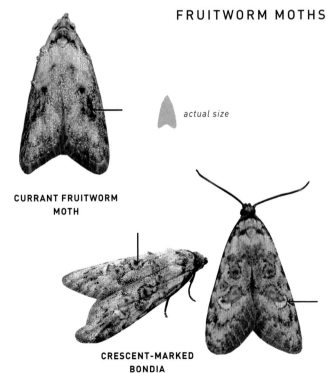

actual size

CURRANT FRUITWORM MOTH

CRESCENT-MARKED BONDIA

ASSORTED PYRALIDS Family Pyralidae, Subfamilies Pyralinae, Epipaschiinae, and Galleriinae

Small broad-winged, deltoid pyralid moths. The larvae of some species live mostly indoors and feed on stored grains, dried vegetable matter, or even dead animals. A few species rest with their wings spread open and abdomen slightly raised. Many are nocturnal and come freely to lights. Some can be found indoors as adults and may be encountered year-round.

MEAL MOTH *Pyralis farinalis* 5510 **Common**
TL 14–16 mm. Chestnut brown FW has a wide fawn-colored median area bordered with white lines. **HOSTS:** Stored grain products. **RANGE:** Se. Canada and e. U.S.

CALICO PYRALID *Aglossa costiferalis* 5511 **Common**
TL 10–11 mm. Shiny pinkish tan FW is marked with peppery black lines and discal spot. **HOSTS:** Unknown. **RANGE:** Se. Canada and e. U.S.

PINK-MASKED PYRALID *Aglossa disciferalis* 5512 **Common**
TL 11 mm. Resembles Calico Pyralid but dark AM and PM lines are well defined and more jagged, and discal spot is smaller. **HOSTS:** Unknown. **RANGE:** Se. Canada and e. U.S.

LARGE TABBY *Aglossa pinguinalis* 5516 **Uncommon**
TL 15–20 mm. Grayish FW is peppered with coarse hairlike scales. Darker lines are most obvious at costa. **HOSTS:** Animal dung and hay refuse in barns. **RANGE:** Se. Canada and e. U.S. **NOTE:** Introduced from Europe.

STORED GRAIN MOTH *Aglossa caprealis* 5517 **Common**
TL 12–14 mm. Shiny brown FW is mottled with coarse, straw-colored hairlike scales. **HOSTS:** Stored foods, grain chaff, fungi, and dead animals. **RANGE:** Se. Canada and e. U.S.

GREASE MOTH *Aglossa cuprina* 5518 **Common**
TL 17 mm. Shiny pinkish brown FW is marked with pale-edged jagged black lines. Note large bulge in AM line and black-edged discal spot. **HOSTS:** Stored foods, grain chaff, fungi, and dead animals. **RANGE:** Se. Canada and e. U.S.

CLOVER HAYWORM *Hypsopygia costalis* 5524 **Common**
TL 10 mm. Peppery vinaceous wings have wide yellow fringes. Outer margin yellow. FW costa is marked with two large yellow spots. **HOSTS:** Mostly dried plant material and stored hay. **RANGE:** Se. Canada and e. U.S.

ASSORTED PYRALIDS

MEAL MOTH

CALICO PYRALID

actual size

PINK-MASKED PYRALID

LARGE TABBY

STORED GRAIN MOTH

GREASE MOTH

CLOVER HAYWORM

133

RED-SHAWLED MOTH

Pseudasopia intermedialis   5526   **Common**

TL 12 mm. Reddish FW has hairlike scales, creating a slightly mottled effect. Slightly jagged lines are incompletely edged pale yellow. **HOSTS:** Unknown. **RANGE:** Se. Canada and e. U.S.

YELLOW-FRINGED DOLICHOMIA

Dolichomia olinalis   5533   **Common**

TL 10 mm. Purplish wings have narrow yellow fringes. Outer margin purple. Narrow lines widen at costa, forming yellow triangles. **HOSTS:** Oak. **RANGE:** Se. Canada and e. U.S.

BOXWOOD LEAFTIER   *Galasa nigrinodis*   5552   **Common**

TL 11 mm. Brick red FW has scarlet basal area and fragmented pale lines that converge at costa, forming a pale patch. Costal margin is concave at midpoint. **HOSTS:** Box wood. **RANGE:** Se. Canada and e. U.S.

DIMORPHIC TOSALE   *Tosale oviplagalis*   5556   **Common**

TL 8–9 mm. Sexually dimorphic. Male has pinkish brown FW with wide chestnut brown bands and whitish lines. Female has similar pattern but is paler and grayer. **HOSTS:** Unknown. **RANGE:** Se. Canada and e. U.S.

DRAB CONDYLOLOMIA

Condylolomia participalis   5571   **Common**

TL 7–8 mm. Pinkish FW has paler yellow basal area and costal streak. Note patch of raised scales near midpoint of costal margin. **HOSTS:** Presumably sweet gale. **RANGE:** Se. Canada and e. U.S.

DIMORPHIC EPIPASCHIA

Epipaschia superatalis   5577   **Common**

TL 10–12 mm. Straw-colored FW (sometimes tinted green) has contrasting chocolate brown shading beyond angled PM line. **HOSTS:** Unknown. **RANGE:** Se. Canada and e. U.S.

ZELLER'S MACALLA   *Macalla zelleri*   5579   **Common**

TL 12–14 mm. Light brown FW has contrasting dark brown basal patch. Median area is speckled white, especially along AM line. **HOSTS:** Unknown. **RANGE:** Se. Canada and e. U.S.

ORANGE-TUFTED ONEIDA   *Oneida lunulalis*   5588   **Common**

TL 12 mm. Silvery FW has AM line of raised orange scales edged with green. Curved outer PM line borders blackish apical patch. **HOSTS:** Oak. **RANGE:** Se. Canada and e. U.S.

ASSORTED PYRALIDS

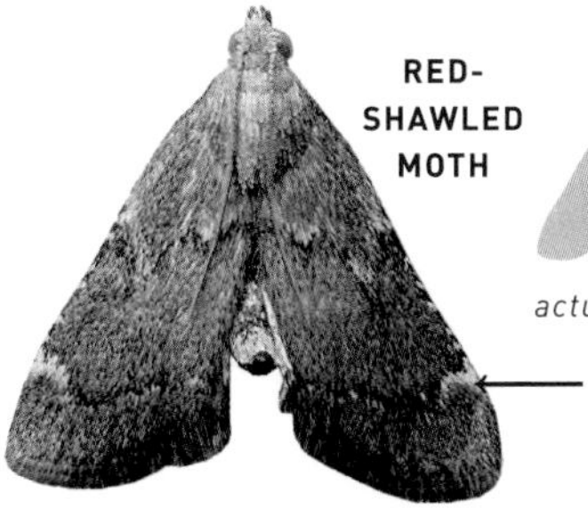

RED-
SHAWLED
MOTH

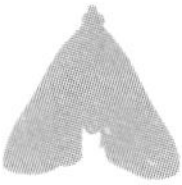

actual size

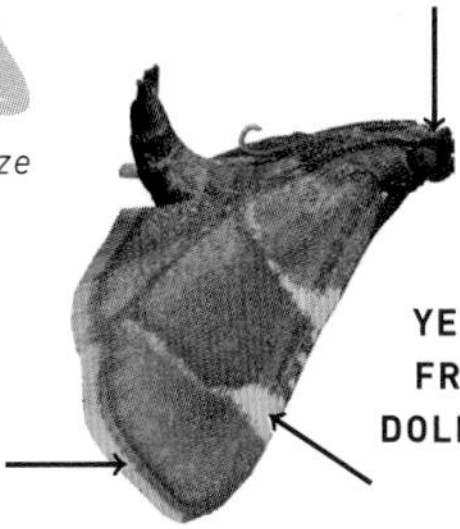

YELLOW-
FRINGED
DOLICHOMIA

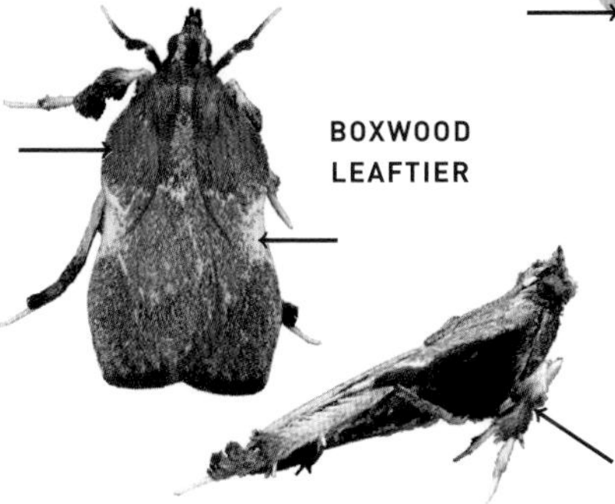

BOXWOOD
LEAFTIER

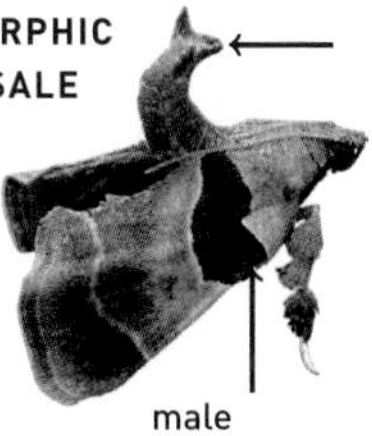

DIMORPHIC
TOSALE

male

DRAB
CONDYLOLOMIA

DIMORPHIC EPIPASCHIA

ZELLER'S MACALLA

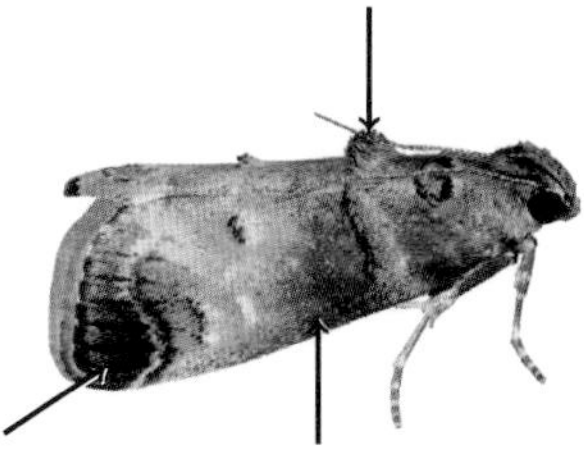

ORANGE-TUFTED ONEIDA

SYCAMORE WEBWORM *Pococera militella* 5604 **Common**
TL 12–14 mm. Pinkish FW has a white median band and double black AM line broken by a translucent panel. Black tuft of raised scales in basal area. **HOSTS:** Sycamore. **RANGE:** Se. Canada and e. U.S.

MAPLE WEBWORM *Pococera asperatella* 5606 **Common**
TL 12–14 mm. Peppery gray FW has a wide whitish median band. Black AM and PM lines are double. **HOSTS:** Maple. **RANGE:** Se. Canada and e. U.S.

STRIPED OAK WEBWORM
Pococera expandens 5608 **Common**
TL 14–15 mm. Gray FW has contrasting ochre basal patch. Black lines edged with peppery white scales near inner margin. **HOSTS:** Unknown. **RANGE:** Se. Canada and e. U.S.

GREATER WAX MOTH *Galleria mellonella* 5622 **Common**
TL 13–18 mm. Grayish brown FW has a streaky pattern of black and white dashes, especially along PM line. Outer margin of wing is concave. Female is larger than male. **HOSTS:** Beeswax. **RANGE:** Cosmopolitan.

BEE MOTH *Aphomia sociella* 5629 **Common**
TL 15–18 mm. Sexually dimorphic. FW pattern is highly variable, often with shades of green and brown. Males are brighter than females. Note two black spots in median area. **HOSTS:** Beeswax. **RANGE:** Se. Canada and e. U.S. **NOTE:** Introduced from Europe.

Phycitine Moths
Family Pyralidae, Subfamily Phycitinae

A large, homogenous group of narrow-winged pyralid moths that appear streamlined and small-headed at rest. Most species have short, upturned labial palps. Some species, most notably in the genera *Acrobasis* and *Dioryctria,* have rows of raised scales on the FW, usually adjacent to the AM line. Most are nocturnal and will come freely to lights. A few are prone to long-range northbound immigration during periods of drought or favorable winds, sometimes appearing far out of their normal ranges.

LEAF CRUMPLER MOTH *Acrobasis indigenella* 5651 **Common**
TL 9–12 mm. Whitish FW has dark brown lines and incomplete buff median band. **HOSTS:** Apple, cherry, hawthorn, and plum. **RANGE:** Widespread.

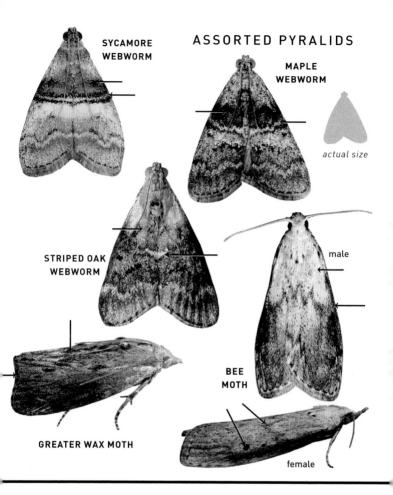

ASSORTED PYRALIDS

SYCAMORE WEBWORM

MAPLE WEBWORM

actual size

STRIPED OAK WEBWORM

male

BEE MOTH

GREATER WAX MOTH

female

PHYCITINE MOTHS

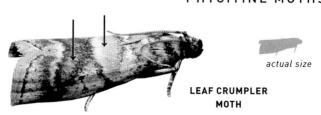

actual size

LEAF CRUMPLER MOTH

CRANBERRY FRUITWORM *Acrobasis vaccinii* 5653 **Common**
TL 9–12 mm. Gray FW has white costal streak interrupted by an incomplete blackish median bar. **HOSTS:** Blueberry, cranberry, and huckleberry. **RANGE:** E. Canada and e. U.S.

TRICOLORED ACROBASIS
Acrobasis tricolorella 5655 **Common**
TL 9–12 mm. Gray FW has bold black patches at midpoint of costa and in subapical area. AM line is edged with white and red bands. **HOSTS:** Fruit-bearing trees, including apple, cherry, and plum. **RANGE:** Se. Canada and e. U.S.

MANTLED ACROBASIS *Acrobasis palliolella* 5659 **Common**
TL 8–10 mm. Gray FW has whitish basal area. Inner margin is reddish inside slanting median line. Head and thorax are white. **HOSTS:** Hickory. **RANGE:** Widespread.

PECANLEAF CASEBEARER
Acrobasis juglandis 5661 **Common**
TL 9–10 mm. Peppery gray FW has a slanting median line ending as a triangular blackish patch at midpoint of costa. Modest scale ridge is blackish. **HOSTS:** Black walnut, butternut, and pecan. **RANGE:** Se. Canada and e. U.S.

HICKORY SHOOT BORER *Acrobasis caryae* 5664 **Common**
TL 10–12 mm. Gray FW has narrow reddish bands on either side of raised black scale ridge. **HOSTS:** Hickory. **RANGE:** Se. Canada and e. U.S.

PIGEON ACROBASIS *Acrobasis aurorella* 5670 **Common**
TL 10–12 mm. Uniformly pinkish white FW has contrasting dark brown basal area. Head is whitish. **HOSTS:** Unknown. **RANGE:** S. ON and ne. U.S.

HICKORY LEAFSTEM BORER
Acrobasis angusella 5673 **Common**
TL 10–13 mm. Purplish gray FW has reddish bands in basal and ST areas. Raised black scale ridge is edged brown and white. **HOSTS:** Hickory. **RANGE:** Se. Canada and ne. U.S.

WALNUT SHOOT MOTH *Acrobasis demotella* 5674 **Common**
TL 10–13 mm. Pinkish FW has wide gray median area. Raised reddish scale ridge is edged with narrow orange and white bands. Head and thorax are white. **HOSTS:** Black walnut. **RANGE:** Se. Canada and e. U.S.

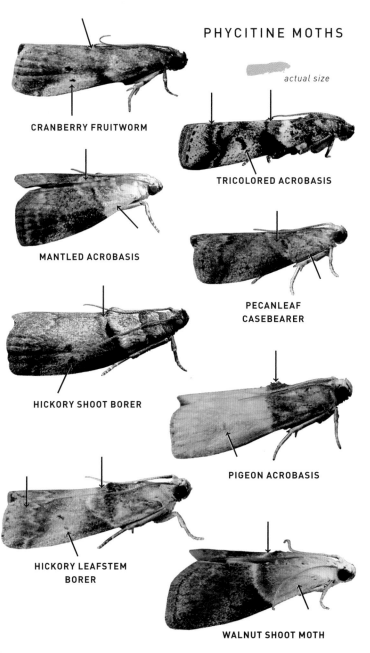

PHYCITINE MOTHS

actual size

CRANBERRY FRUITWORM

TRICOLORED ACROBASIS

MANTLED ACROBASIS

PECANLEAF CASEBEARER

HICKORY SHOOT BORER

PIGEON ACROBASIS

HICKORY LEAFSTEM BORER

WALNUT SHOOT MOTH

TWO-STRIPED APOMYELOIS

Apomyelois bistriatella   5721   **Common**

TL 9–12 mm. Peppery gray FW is blackish along inner margin. Jagged white AM line is most obvious near inner margin. **HOSTS:** Fungi on deadwood. **RANGE:** Widespread.

GOLD-BANDED ETIELLA   *Etiella zinckenella*   5744   Uncommon

TL 9–13 mm. Lilac gray FW has a white costal streak. Narrow chestnut scale ridge is edged with a wide ochre median band. Upturned labial palps are long and brushy. **HOSTS:** Immature seeds of legumes. **RANGE:** Sw. U.S.; a rare immigrant to ne. N. America.

BLACK-BANDED IMMYRLA

Immyrla nigrovittella   5766   **Common**

TL 11–12 mm. Gray FW has paler median area. Raised black scale ridge is edged with black and white lines. **HOSTS:** Hickory and eastern hornbeam. **RANGE:** Se. Canada and e. U.S.

ENGEL'S SALEBRIARIA   *Salebriaria engeli*   5773   **Common**

TL 8–10 mm. Uniform dark grayish brown FW has contrasting white patch at midpoint of inner margin. **HOSTS:** Oak. **RANGE:** Widespread.

STRIPED BIRCH PYRALID

Ortholepis pasadamia   5783   **Common**

TL 10–13 mm. Peppery dark gray FW is boldly marked with white zigzag lines. Basal area is brownish. **HOSTS:** Unknown. **RANGE:** Widespread.

BELTED LEAFROLLER   *Sciota vetustella*   5794   **Common**

TL 12–13 mm. Purplish gray FW has contrasting reddish basal area. Thick black median band is edged pale gray. **HOSTS:** Basswood. **RANGE:** Se. Canada and e. U.S.

LOCUST LEAFROLLER   *Sciota subcaesiella*   5796   **Common**

TL 10–15 mm. Mottled gray FW is tinted purplish brown in basal and median areas. Thick black median band is edged with white zigzag line. **HOSTS:** Black locust. **RANGE:** Se. Canada and e. U.S.

BLACK-SPOTTED LEAFROLLER

Sciota virgatella   5797   **Common**

TL 10–15 mm. Gray FW is tinted brown in basal and inner median areas. Fragmented jagged lines create a spotted appearance. **HOSTS:** Black locust. **RANGE:** Se. Canada and e. U.S.

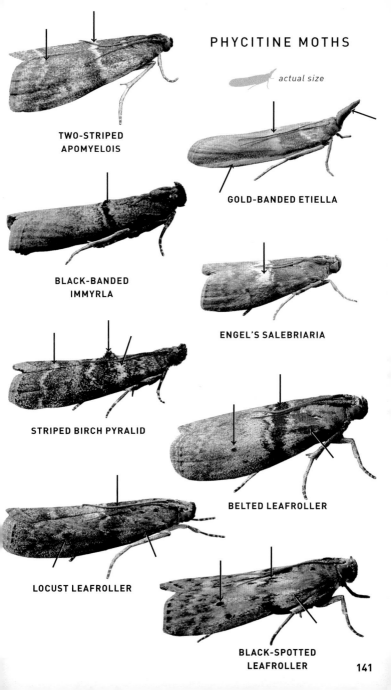

PHYCITINE MOTHS

actual size

TWO-STRIPED APOMYELOIS

GOLD-BANDED ETIELLA

BLACK-BANDED IMMYRLA

ENGEL'S SALEBRIARIA

STRIPED BIRCH PYRALID

BELTED LEAFROLLER

LOCUST LEAFROLLER

BLACK-SPOTTED LEAFROLLER

141

YELLOW-SHOULDERED LEAFROLLER
Sciota basilaris 5799 **Common**
TL 11–14 mm. Blue-gray FW has red and ochre basal area. Kinked white AM line is narrowly edged black. **HOSTS:** Poplar and willow. **RANGE:** Se. Canada and ne. U.S.

TLASCALA MOTH *Tlascala reductella* 5808 **Common**
TL 9–11 mm. Pale gray FW is marked with three parallel AM lines. Basal and ST areas are tinged reddish. **HOSTS:** Honey locust. **RANGE:** Se. Canada and e. U.S.

OVAL TELETHUSIA *Telethusia ovalis* 5812 **Common**
TL 12–14 mm. Peppery pale gray FW is marked with white-edged light brown bands. **HOSTS:** Pussytoes and woolly yellow daisy. **RANGE:** Widespread.

SPECKLED BLACK PYLA *Pyla fusca* 5829 **Common**
TL 12–14 mm. Peppery sooty gray FW has indistinct wavy black lines. Median line is whitish at inner margin. **HOSTS:** Low plants, including blueberry. **RANGE:** Widespread.

EVERGREEN CONEWORM
Dioryctria abietivorella 5841 **Common**
TL 12–15 mm. Peppery gray FW has pattern of raised black scale ridges and broad brown bands. **HOSTS:** Fir, pine, and spruce. **RANGE:** Se. Canada and ne. U.S.

SPRUCE CONEWORM
Dioryctria reniculelloides 5843 **Common**
TL 12–15 mm. Peppery fawn-colored FW has complex pattern of white-edged zigzag lines. **HOSTS:** Primarily spruce, also other coniferous trees. **RANGE:** Se. Canada and ne. U.S.

WEBBING CONEWORM *Dioryctria disclusa* 5847 **Common**
TL 11–15 mm. Orange FW is marked with three jagged white lines. Median and ST areas are tinged reddish. **HOSTS:** Pine. **RANGE:** Se. Canada and e. U.S.

ZIMMERMAN PINE MOTH
Dioryctria zimmermani 5852 **Common**
TL 14–18 mm. Reddish-tinged FW has three rows of raised black and chestnut scale ridges. **HOSTS:** Primarily white pine. **RANGE:** Se. Canada and e. U.S.

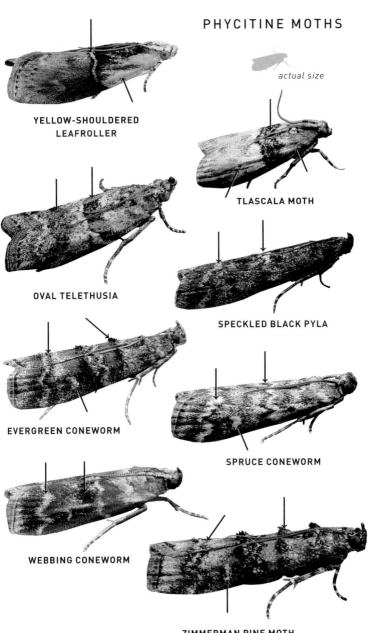

PHYCITINE MOTHS

actual size

YELLOW-SHOULDERED
LEAFROLLER

TLASCALA MOTH

OVAL TELETHUSIA

SPECKLED BLACK PYLA

EVERGREEN CONEWORM

SPRUCE CONEWORM

WEBBING CONEWORM

ZIMMERMAN PINE MOTH

143

LESSER CORNSTALK BORER
Elasmopalpus lignosellus 5896 **Common**
TL 8–12 mm. Shiny straw-colored FW has peppery brown shading along costa and inner margin. Reniform area is spotted black. Upturned labial palps are black. **HOSTS:** Various low plants. **RANGE:** Extreme s. ON and e. U.S.

AMERICAN PLUM BORER
Euzophera semifuneralis 5995 **Common**
TL 13 mm. Crimson FW has incomplete blackish median band and pale gray zigzag lines. Terminal line is dotted. **HOSTS:** Deciduous trees, including apple, cherry, peach, pear, sweet gum, and walnut. **RANGE:** Widespread.

ROOT COLLAR BORER
Euzophera ostricolorella 5997 **Common**
TL 19 mm. Resembles American Plum Borer but is brighter red and considerably larger. Zigzag lines are white. **HOSTS:** Tulip tree. **RANGE:** Sw. ON and e. U.S.

BROAD-BANDED EULOGIA
Eulogia ochrifrontella 5999 **Common**
TL 7–8 mm. Reddish brown FW is marked with a broad, yellow-edged, blackish median band. All lines are slightly wavy. **HOSTS:** Apple, oak, and pecan. **RANGE:** Widespread.

DARKER MOODNA *Moodna ostrinella* 6005 **Common**
TL 8 mm. Small. Brick red FW has blackish median band broadly edged white. Reniform spot is speckled white. **HOSTS:** Trees and low plants, including apple, birch, cotton, iris, oak, pine, and sumac. **RANGE:** Widespread.

DRIED-FRUIT MOTH *Vitula edmandsii* 6007 **Common**
TL 13 mm. Peppery pale gray FW has fragmented, jagged black lines and reniform dot. Inner margin is tinted reddish. **HOSTS:** Pollen, honey, and immature hymenoptera in bee colonies. **RANGE:** Se. Canada and e. U.S.

BROWER'S VITULA *Vitula broweri* 6011 **Common**
TL 7–9 mm. Light brown FW has darker median and ST areas edged with white zigzag lines. **HOSTS:** Unknown. **RANGE:** Se. Canada and ne. U.S.

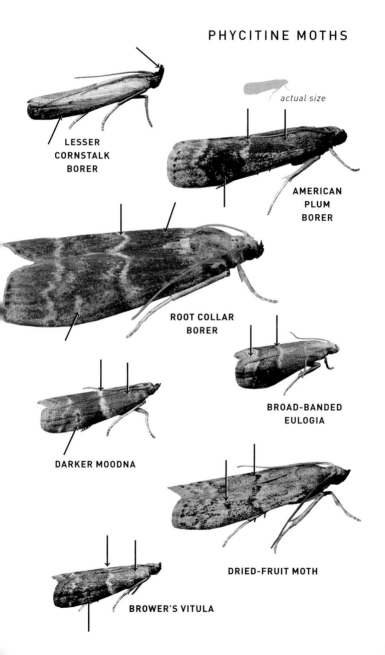

PHYCITINE MOTHS

actual size

LESSER CORNSTALK BORER

AMERICAN PLUM BORER

ROOT COLLAR BORER

BROAD-BANDED EULOGIA

DARKER MOODNA

DRIED-FRUIT MOTH

BROWER'S VITULA

CARMINE SNOUT MOTH

Peoria approximella   6053   **Common**

TL 8 mm. Bright carmine FW has cream-colored streaks along costa and inner margin. Upturned labial palps are brushy-looking. **HOSTS:** Unknown. **RANGE:** Se. Canada and e. U.S.

MOSS-EATING CRAMBIDS
Family Crambidae, Subfamily Scopariinae

Small, narrowly deltoid moths with monochromatic, pointed wings. Indistinct dark tufts of scales are present on the FW; they are absent in other crambids. Adults frequently visit lights.

DOUBLE-STRIPED SCOPARIA

Scoparia biplagialis   4716   **Common**

TL 7–9 mm. Peppery gray FW has two white-edged dusky bands crossing median area. **HOSTS:** Possibly roots and mosses. **RANGE:** Widespread.

MANY-SPOTTED SCOPARIA *Scoparia basalis*   4719   **Common**

TL 7–9 mm. Whitish FW has gray basal area. Black dashes accent grayish ST area. **HOSTS:** Possibly roots and mosses. **RANGE:** S. Canada and ne. U.S.

STRIPED EUDONIA *Eudonia strigalis*   4738   **Common**

TL 6–8 mm. Peppery whitish FW has thin black longitudinal streaks extending through median and ST areas. **HOSTS:** Possibly mosses. **RANGE:** Se. Canada and e. U.S.

GRASS-VENEERS
Family Crambidae, Subfamily Crambinae

Small, narrow moths that are commonly found in grassy woodlands and old fields. They rest with their wings tight to the body, forming a tubular shape. Long fuzzy palps give them a snouty look. Predominantly golden brown, often with satin white streaks. Adults are regular visitors to lights and can frequently be flushed from vegetation during the daytime.

BIDEN'S GRASS-VENEER *Crambus bidens*   5342   **Common**

TL 14 mm. Shiny brown FW has pointed white streak (sometimes shaded brown) that has sharp spur protruding from inner edge. **HOSTS:** Unknown. **RANGE:** Se. Canada and ne. U.S.

PHYCITINE MOTHS

CARMINE SNOUT MOTH

actual size

MOSS-EATING CRAMBIDS

actual size

DOUBLE-STRIPED SCOPARIA

STRIPED EUDONIA

MANY-SPOTTED SCOPARIA

GRASS-VENEERS

actual size

BIDEN'S GRASS-VENEER

IMMACULATE GRASS-VENEER

Crambus perlella   5343   **Common**
TL 10–12 mm. White FW is without markings. **HOSTS:** Grasses, including sheep fescue and wavy hairgrass. **RANGE:** S. Canada and n. U.S.

WIDE-STRIPE GRASS-VENEER

Crambus unistriatellus   5344   **Common**
TL 12–17 mm. Shiny tan FW has wide white streak that flares at outer margin. **HOSTS:** Various grasses and grass roots. **RANGE:** S. Canada and n. U.S.

COMMON GRASS-VENEER

Crambus praefectellus   5355   **Common**
TL 15–16 mm. Shiny brown FW has pointed white streak that sometimes has a tiny spur projecting from inner edge. **HOSTS:** Grasses and cereal grains. **RANGE:** Widespread.

LEACH'S GRASS-VENEER *Crambus leachellus*   5357   **Common**
TL 15–16 mm. Shiny brown FW has a pointed white streak that touches basal section of costa. **HOSTS:** Grasses. **RANGE:** Widespread.

SMALL WHITE GRASS-VENEER

Crambus albellus   5361   **Common**
TL 8–9 mm. White FW has sharply angled median and ST lines and a row of black dots along terminal line. **HOSTS:** Grasses. **RANGE:** Se. Canada and ne. U.S.

DOUBLE-BANDED GRASS-VENEER

Crambus agitatellus   5362   **Common**
TL 13–14 mm. Golden brown FW has large white patch covering outer basal half of wing. White streak is interrupted by angled silver ST line. **HOSTS:** Grasses and low plants. **RANGE:** Se. Canada and e. U.S.

PASTURE GRASS-VENEER *Crambus saltuellus* 5363   **Common**
TL 14 mm. Shiny brown FW has wide white streak divided by brown stripe. Thin black-edged silver streaks extend along inner margin. **HOSTS:** Grasses. **RANGE:** S. ON and ne. U.S.

GIRARD'S GRASS-VENEER

Crambus girardellus   5365   **Uncommon**
TL 15 mm. White FW has golden brown streak parallel to inner margin that is sometimes connected to costa. **HOSTS:** Possibly grass roots. **RANGE:** Se. Canada and ne. U.S.

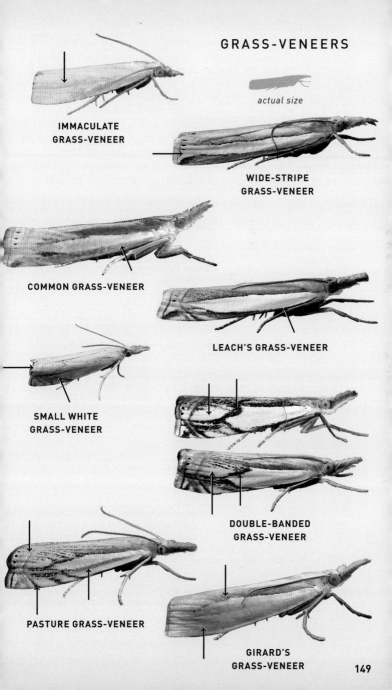

GRASS-VENEERS

IMMACULATE GRASS-VENEER

actual size

WIDE-STRIPE GRASS-VENEER

COMMON GRASS-VENEER

LEACH'S GRASS-VENEER

SMALL WHITE GRASS-VENEER

DOUBLE-BANDED GRASS-VENEER

PASTURE GRASS-VENEER

GIRARD'S GRASS-VENEER

149

EASTERN GRASS-VENEER

Crambus laqueatellus   5378   **Common**
TL 15 mm. Shiny tan FW has wide white streak divided by brown stripe. Thin black lines pass through ST area. **HOSTS:** Grasses. **RANGE:** Se. Canada and e. U.S.

MOTTLED GRASS-VENEER

Neodactria luteolellus   5379   **Common**
TL 10–15 mm. Mottled FW is variably yellowish or brown. Angled lines are often dotted. **HOSTS:** Probably grasses. **RANGE:** Widespread.

TOPIARY GRASS-VENEER

Chrysoteuchia topiarius   5391   **Common**
TL 12 mm. Shiny tan FW is orange beyond angled silver ST line. Darker streaks extend along veins. **HOSTS:** Grasses and herbaceous plants, including blueberry and cranberry. **RANGE:** Widespread.

LESSER VAGABOND SOD WEBWORM

Agriphila ruricolellus   5399   **Common**
TL 12 mm. Pale tan FW has faint dusky streaks along veins. Angled median and ST lines are usually conspicuous. **HOSTS:** Grasses and common sheep sorrel. **RANGE:** Widespread.

VAGABOND CRAMBUS   *Agriphila vulgivagellus*   5403   Common
TL 18 mm. Pale tan FW has bold streaky pattern. Terminal line is accented with black and gold dots. **HOSTS:** Grasses and grains, including wheat and rye. **RANGE:** Widespread.

THREE-SPOTTED CRAMBUS

Catoptria latiradiellus   5408   **Uncommon**
TL 10–12 mm. Brown FW has bold white streak obliquely crossed by two blackish bars. **HOSTS:** Possibly mosses. **RANGE:** S. Canada and n. U.S.

SOD WEBWORM   *Pediasia trisecta*   5413   **Common**
TL 14–18 mm. Tawny FW has ash gray streak along inner margin. Two black dashes mark fragmented median and ST lines. **HOSTS:** Grasses. **RANGE:** Widespread.

GOLD-STRIPE GRASS-VENEER

Microcrambus biguttellus   5419   **Common**
TL 8 mm. White FW has angled lines obvious near costa. Median line is accented with black dots at midpoint and inner margin. **HOSTS:** Grasses. **RANGE:** Se. Canada and e. U.S.

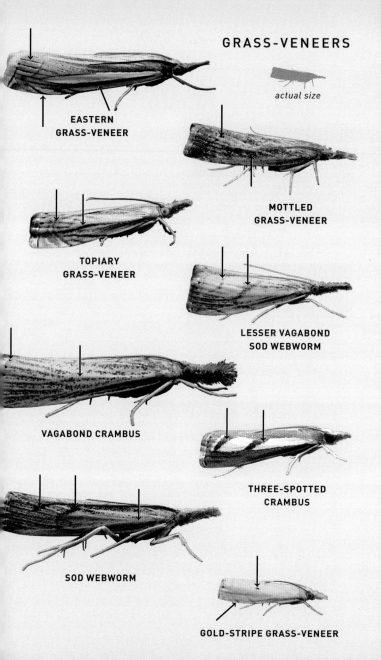

GRASS-VENEERS

actual size

EASTERN GRASS-VENEER

MOTTLED GRASS-VENEER

TOPIARY GRASS-VENEER

LESSER VAGABOND SOD WEBWORM

VAGABOND CRAMBUS

THREE-SPOTTED CRAMBUS

SOD WEBWORM

GOLD-STRIPE GRASS-VENEER

ELEGANT GRASS-VENEER

Microcrambus elegans 5420 **Common**

TL 8–10 mm. White FW is variably peppered brown. White-edged ST line is straight. Backward-pointing wedge along inner margin is conspicuous. **HOSTS:** Grasses. **RANGE:** Se. Canada and e. U.S.

CHANGEABLE GRASS-VENEER

Fissicrambus mutabilis 5435 **Common**

TL 12 mm. Gray FW has tawny streak along inner margin. Median and ST lines are jagged. Rests in a headstand position. **HOSTS:** Grasses. **RANGE:** Se. Canada and e. U.S.

WOOLLY GRASS-VENEER

Thaumatopsis pexellus 5439 **Common**

TL 18 mm. Grayish FW has tawny streaks along costa and inner margin. Dark streak in median area extends to apex. Male (shown) has large bipectinate antennae. **HOSTS:** Unknown. **RANGE:** S. Canada and e. U.S.

BLUEGRASS WEBWORM

Parapediasia teterrella 5451 **Common**

TL 12 mm. Tawny FW has pattern of gray streaks between veins as far as angled orange ST line. Often shows blackish blotches inside median line. **HOSTS:** Grasses, including bluegrass and tall fescue. **RANGE:** Se. Canada and e. U.S.

BELTED GRASS-VENEER

Euchromius ocelleus 5454 **Common**

TL 12–14 mm. Pearly gray FW is crossed by two golden bands in median area. Angled ST line is accented with black dots. **HOSTS:** Grain products. **RANGE:** S. U.S.; an occasional immigrant to ne. N. America.

SNOWY UROLA *Urola nivalis* 5464 **Common**

TL 12 mm. Satin white FW has tiny black spot midway along inner margin and black-dashed terminal line. **HOSTS:** Grasses. **RANGE:** Se. Canada and e. U.S.

CURVE-LINED ARGYRIA *Vaxi auratella* 5465 **Common**

TL 8–10 mm. Satin white FW has golden median and terminal lines that connect along inner margin. **HOSTS:** Unknown. **RANGE:** Se. Canada and e. U.S.

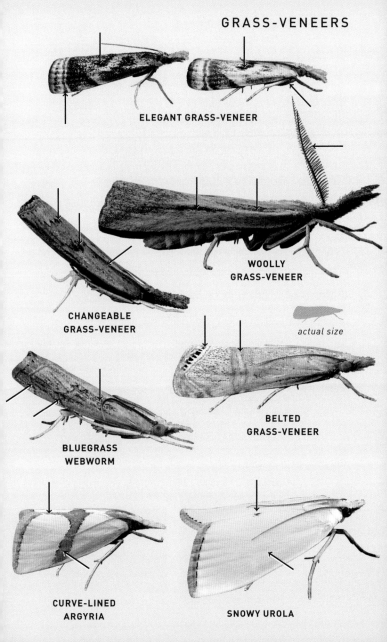

GRASS-VENEERS

ELEGANT GRASS-VENEER

WOOLLY GRASS-VENEER

CHANGEABLE GRASS-VENEER

actual size

BELTED GRASS-VENEER

BLUEGRASS WEBWORM

CURVE-LINED ARGYRIA

SNOWY UROLA

STRAIGHT-LINED ARGYRIA

Vaxi critica 5466 **Common**

TL 8–12 mm. Resembles Curve-lined Argyria, but median and terminal lines do not meet along inner margin. **HOSTS:** Unknown. **RANGE:** Se. Canada and e. U.S.

SILVERED HAIMBACHIA

Haimbachia albescens 5488 **Common**

TL 15 mm. Whitish FW is finely peppered with dusky scales. Brown median line has black dot at midpoint. Double ST line is strongly curved. **HOSTS:** Unknown. **RANGE:** S. ON and e. U.S.

DONACAULAS

Family Crambidae, Subfamily Schoenobiinae

Very similar to grass-veneers, the donacaulas typically have pointier wings and are generally a more uniformly brownish orange. Adults regularly visit lights.

DELIGHTFUL DONACAULA

Donacaula melinellus 5316 **Uncommon**

TL 21 mm. Pale orange FW has a brown streak extending through median area. Slanting apical dash and reniform dot are often noticeable. Sometimes has a pale costal streak. **HOSTS:** Unknown. **RANGE:** Se. Canada and e. U.S.

LONG-BEAKED DONACAULA

Donacaula longirostrallus 5319 **Uncommon**

TL 20 mm. Orange FW has a brown costal streak and slanting apical dash. Median area is mottled with brown spots. **HOSTS:** Unknown. **RANGE:** Se. Canada and ne. U.S.

BROWN DONACAULA

Donacaula roscidellus 5321 **Uncommon**

TL 18 mm. Uniform grayish brown FW has slightly darker shading along veins in ST area. Blackish reniform dot is the only noticeable marking. **HOSTS:** Unknown. **RANGE:** Se. Canada and e. U.S.

GRASS-VENEERS

actual size

STRAIGHT-LINED ARGYRIA

SILVERED HAIMBACHIA

DONACAULAS

DELIGHTFUL DONACAULA

actual size

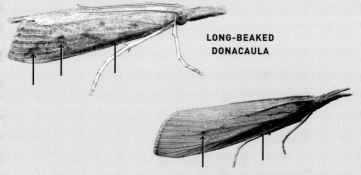

LONG-BEAKED DONACAULA

BROWN DONACAULA

155

Aquatic Crambids
Family Crambidae, Subfamily Acentropinae

Small deltoid moths that often have beautifully complex wing markings. Resting posture may either be with wings spread, or folded, sometimes quite tightly, to form a deltoid shape. Larvae are aquatic, feeding on water lilies and other aquatic vegetation. They will come to light in small numbers and can sometimes be seen fluttering above lily pads or other vegetation in ponds.

NYMPHULA MOTH *Nymphula ekthlipsis* 4747   Common
TL 13–17 mm. White wings have an ornate pattern of swirling, black-edged buff bands. **HOSTS:** Yellow water lily and bur reed. **RANGE:** Se. Canada and ne. U.S.

PONDSIDE CRAMBID *Elophila icciusalis* 4748   Common
TL 8–15 mm. Creamy yellow FW has intricate pattern of black-edged white bands and spots. **HOSTS:** Aquatic plants, including buckbean, duckweed, eelgrass, and sedges. **RANGE:** Widespread.

WATERLILY BORER *Elophila gyralis* 4751   Common
TL 10–16 mm. Grayish brown (sometimes all dark) FW has complex pattern of white-edged lines and spots. Black patch at midpoint of inner margin contains a white dot. **HOSTS:** Water lilies. **RANGE:** Se. Canada and e. U.S.

BLACK DUCKWEED MOTH
Synclita tinealis 4754   Uncommon
TL 4–6 mm. Very small. Blackish FW often has diffuse whitish spot in median area. Antennae are short. **HOSTS:** Duckweed. **RANGE:** Se. Canada and e. U.S.

WATERLILY LEAFCUTTER *Synclita obliteralis* 4755   Common
TL 7–11 mm. Sexually dimorphic. Mottled pale brown FW has jagged white median band widening toward costa. Female is larger and paler. **HOSTS:** Aquatic plants, including duckweed, pondweed, and water lilies. **RANGE:** Se. Canada and e. U.S.

POLYMORPHIC PONDWEED MOTH
Parapoynx maculalis 4759   Common
TL 8–15 mm. Grayish brown FW is boldly marked with large white spots. Darker individuals are uniformly gray or brown. **HOSTS:** Various aquatic plants. **RANGE:** Se. Canada and e. U.S.

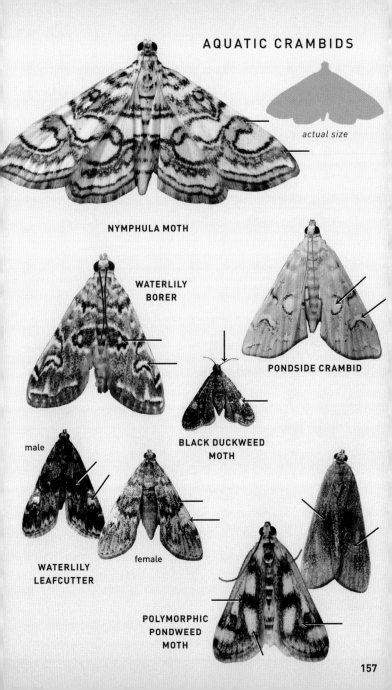

AQUATIC CRAMBIDS

actual size

NYMPHULA MOTH

WATERLILY BORER

PONDSIDE CRAMBID

BLACK DUCKWEED MOTH

male

female

WATERLILY LEAFCUTTER

POLYMORPHIC PONDWEED MOTH

157

OBSCURE PONDWEED MOTH

Parapoynx obscuralis 4760 **Common**

TL 6–12 mm. Peppery FW has black blotches in median area. Banded HW has gold terminal line. **HOSTS:** Aquatic plants, including eelgrass, pondweed, and yellow water lily. **RANGE:** Se. Canada and e. U.S.

CHESTNUT-MARKED PONDWEED MOTH

Parapoynx badiusalis 4761 **Common**

TL 8–12 mm. White wings are marked with bold black bands. Terminal line on all wings is golden yellow. Wings spread outward at rest. **HOSTS:** Aquatic plants, including pondweed. **RANGE:** Se. Canada and e. U.S.

WATERMILFOIL LEAFCUTTER

Parapoynx allionealis 4764 **Common**

TL 8–14 mm. Whitish wings are variably streaked brown and marked with wavy black lines. Terminal line is brown on all wings. **HOSTS:** Aquatic plants, including broadleaf water milfoil and spikerush. **RANGE:** Widespread.

TWO-BANDED PETROPHILA

Petrophila bifascialis 4774 **Common**

TL 7–12 mm. Peppery white FW has double brown median band and three angled dashes at apex. HW has a row of black and silver spots along outer margin. **HOSTS:** Diatoms and algae scraped from rocks. **RANGE:** Widespread.

PLEVIE'S AQUATIC MOTH

Eoparargyractis plevie 4787 **Common**

TL 7–9 mm. Banded brown and white FW has a black-edged, backward-pointing subapical dash. HW has a row of black and silver spots along outer margin. **HOSTS:** Unknown. **RANGE:** Se. Canada and ne. U.S.

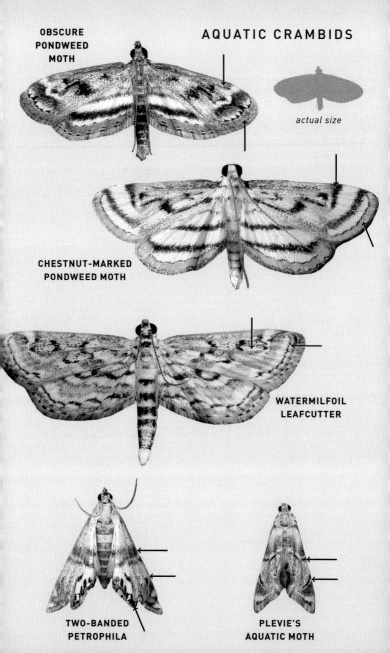

OBSCURE PONDWEED MOTH

AQUATIC CRAMBIDS

actual size

CHESTNUT-MARKED PONDWEED MOTH

WATERMILFOIL LEAFCUTTER

TWO-BANDED PETROPHILA

PLEVIE'S AQUATIC MOTH

Assorted Crambids
Family Crambidae, Subfamilies Odontiinae, Glaphyriinae, and Evergestinae

Small moths that superficially resemble members of the Pyraustinae. Broad, triangular wings are usually held flat but in a few species may be curved over the body. Larvae of a few species, such as Cabbage Webworm, feed on Brassicaceae and may be crop pests. Adults will come to light in small numbers.

OYSTERSHELL METREA *Metrea ostreonalis* 4789 Uncommon
TL 10–12 mm. White FW has broad grayish median band broken at midpoint. Pale gray ST line is incomplete. **HOSTS:** Black buckthorn and possibly leatherwood. **RANGE:** Se. Canada and ne. U.S.

SPOTTED PEPPERGRASS MOTH
Eustixia pupula 4794 Common
TL 8–9 mm. White FW is marked with evenly spaced black dots. Face and labial palps are black. **HOSTS:** Peppergrass, field pennycress, and cabbage. **RANGE:** Se. Canada and e. U.S.

YELLOW-VEINED MOTH
Microtheoris ophionalis 4796 Uncommon
TL 6–7 mm. Dull, brick red FW has curved yellow ST line. Yellow veins extend from basal area to dusky PM line. **HOSTS:** Unknown. **RANGE:** Se. Canada and ne. U.S.

RUFOUS-BANDED CRAMBID
Mimoschinia rufofascialis 4826 Rare
TL 6–11 mm. Yellowish FW has broad reddish brown AM and PM bands. Brown spots mark midpoint of costa and apex. **HOSTS:** Mallow and hollyhock. **RANGE:** W. Canada and s. U.S; uncommon in sw. ON.

CABBAGE WEBWORM *Hellula rogatalis* 4846 Uncommon
TL 9–12 mm. Peppery tan FW has darker median area between whitish AM and PM lines. Reniform spot is blackish. **HOSTS:** Brassicaceae, including cabbage, kale, rape, and horseradish. **RANGE:** S. U.S; an irregular fall immigrant to ne. N. America.

WHITE-ROPED GLAPHYRIA
Glaphyria sequistrialis 4870 Common
TL 8–10 mm. Peppery tan FW is marked with wavy white bands with a brown fringe. **HOSTS:** Unknown. **RANGE:** Se. Canada and e. U.S.

ASSORTED CRAMBIDS

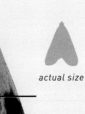

actual size

OYSTERSHELL METREA

YELLOW-VEINED MOTH

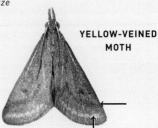

SPOTTED PEPPERGRASS MOTH

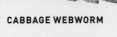

RUFOUS-BANDED CRAMBID

CABBAGE WEBWORM

WHITE-ROPED GLAPHYRIA

BLACK-PATCHED GLAPHYRIA
Glaphyria fulminalis 4873 **Common**
TL 6–7 mm. Cream-colored FW has faint zigzag lines that cut through large dark brown median patch. **HOSTS:** Unknown. **RANGE:** Se. Canada and e. U.S.

XANTHOPHYSA MOTH
Xanthophysa psychialis 4879 **Common**
TL 7–9 mm. Orange FW has zigzag silvery gray lines and fringe. **HOSTS:** Unknown. **RANGE:** Se. Canada and e. U.S.

SOOTY LIPOCOSMODES
Lipocosmodes fuliginosalis 4888 **Common**
TL 6–7 mm. White FW has extensive dusky patch in median area. Wavy blackish lines are inconspicuous. **HOSTS:** Unknown. **RANGE:** Se. Canada and e. U.S.

JULIA'S DICYMOLOMIA
Dicymolomia julianalis 4889 **Common**
TL 8–11 mm. Pale FW has reddish bands and peppery gray median area. Reniform spot is white. **HOSTS:** Cattail heads, dead cotton bolls, prickly pear, and eggs of bagworm moths. **RANGE:** Se. Canada and e. U.S.

SOOTY-WINGED CHALCOELA
Chalcoela iphitalis 4895 **Common**
TL 8–10 mm. Pale orange FW has large silvery gray patch covering most of median and ST area. HW has a row of black and silver dots along terminal line. **HOSTS:** Larvae of paper wasps. **RANGE:** A western species whose range extends into s. ON and MI.

PEGASUS CHALCOELA
Chalcoela pegasalis 4896 **Uncommon**
TL 8–10 mm. Chocolate brown FW has a silvery gray median patch between curved AM and PM line. HW has a row of black and silver dots along terminal line. **HOSTS:** Larvae of paper wasps. **RANGE:** Se. Canada and e. U.S.

PURPLE-BACKED CABBAGEWORM
Evergestis pallidata 4897 **Common**
TL 13–15 mm. Straw-colored FW is marked with angled brown lines. ST area is blotched with brown scales. A heart-shaped loop cuts through median line. **HOSTS:** Brassicaceae, including bittercress, cabbage, and horseradish. **RANGE:** S. Canada and ne. U.S.

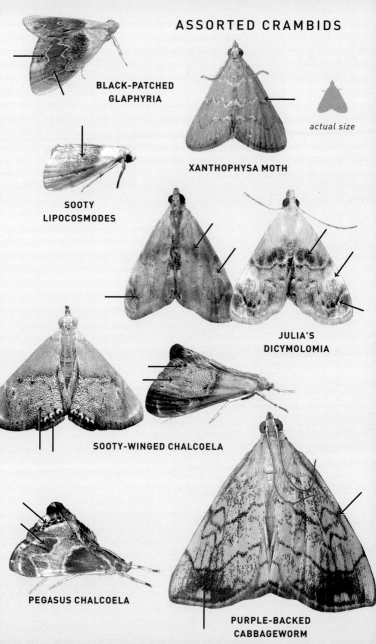

ASSORTED CRAMBIDS

BLACK-PATCHED
GLAPHYRIA

XANTHOPHYSA MOTH

actual size

SOOTY
LIPOCOSMODES

JULIA'S
DICYMOLOMIA

SOOTY-WINGED CHALCOELA

PEGASUS CHALCOELA

PURPLE-BACKED
CABBAGEWORM

LARGE-SPOTTED EVERGESTIS

Evergestis unimacula 4901   **Common**
TL 10–13 mm. Shiny grayish brown FW has fragmented band of cream-colored spots ending as a larger patch at costa. **HOSTS:** Unknown. **RANGE:** Se. Canada and ne. U.S.

Pyraustine Moths
Family Crambidae, Subfamily Pyraustinae

A large group of small to medium-sized deltoid moths. Many are plainly attired in shades of gray or brown, whereas others are strikingly colorful. The broad wings are typically folded flat when at rest, but others keep their wings spread. Common in a variety of habitats, nearly all will come to lights at night in small to moderate numbers. White-spotted Sable is diurnal and usually found at flowers or among vegetation during the day. Celery Leaftier and Lucerne Moth are also commonly disturbed from low vegetation during daytime.

DOGBANE SAUCROBOTYS

Saucrobotys futilalis 4936   **Common**
TL 13–14 mm. Peppery brown or orange FW is faintly marked with scalloped brown AM and PM lines. **HOSTS:** Dogbane and milkweed. **RANGE:** Se. Canada and e. U.S.

STREAKED ORANGE MOTH

Nascia acutella 4937   **Uncommon**
TL 12 mm. Smooth fawn FW has slightly paler veins and conspicuous white fringe. **HOSTS:** Presumably grasses and sedges. **RANGE:** Se. Canada and e. U.S.

PALE-WINGED CROCIDOPHORA

Crocidophora tuberculalis 4945   **Common**
TL 8–10 mm. Shiny, pale tan FW has an unusual creased appearance to central median area. Brown lines are indistinct. **HOSTS:** Unknown. **RANGE:** Se. Canada and e. U.S.

EUROPEAN CORN BORER *Ostrinia nubilalis* 4949   **Common**
TL 14–16 mm. Sexually dimorphic. FW of male is mostly brown with a yellowish band beyond jagged PM line. Yellowish female is marked with jagged brown lines. **HOSTS:** Low plants and crops, including aster, bean, corn, millet, and potato. **RANGE:** E. Canada and e. U.S. **NOTE:** This abundant crop pest was introduced from Europe.

ASSORTED CRAMBIDS

LARGE-SPOTTED EVERGESTIS

actual size

PYRAUSTINE MOTHS

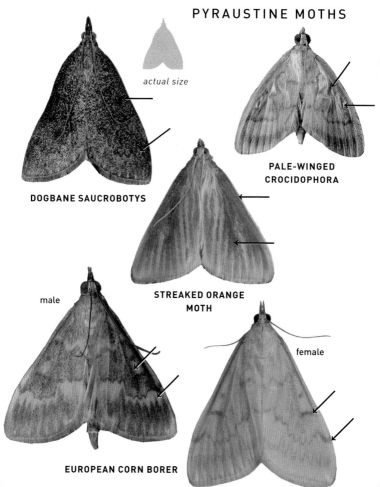

actual size

PALE-WINGED CROCIDOPHORA

DOGBANE SAUCROBOTYS

STREAKED ORANGE MOTH

male

EUROPEAN CORN BORER

female

MINT ROOT BORER *Fumibotys fumalis* 4950 Common
TL 11–13 mm. Rusty orange FW has slightly scalloped brown lines and a brown blotch surrounding paler reniform spot. **HOSTS:** Mint. **RANGE:** Widespread.

TITIAN PEALE'S CRAMBID
Perispasta caeculalis 4951 Uncommon
TL 7–10 mm. Violet gray FW has indistinct blackish lines. Male has a rectangular semi-translucent panel in outer median area. Outer margin is concave near apex. **HOSTS:** Unknown. **RANGE:** S. Canada and e. U.S.

SMALL MAGPIE *Eurrhypara hortulata* 4952 Common
WS 25 mm. White wings have brown borders and spotted lines. Thorax and head are mostly pale orange. **HOSTS:** Nettle, also bindweed and mint. **RANGE:** Se. Canada and ne. U.S. **NOTE:** Introduced from Eurasia.

CROWNED PHLYCTAENIA
Phlyctaenia coronata 4953 Common
TL 13 mm. Grayish brown FW is marked with pale yellow spots and accents along jagged lines. **HOSTS:** Deciduous trees and plants, including alder, elderberry, hickory, and viburnum. **RANGE:** Widespread.

WHITE-SPOTTED SABLE *Anania funebris* 4958 Common
TL 11 mm. Black wings are marked with large white spots. Thorax has yellow tegulae. **HOSTS:** Goldenrod. **RANGE:** S. Canada and n. U.S.

GARDEN WEBWORM *Achyra rantalis* 4975 Common
TL 10–11 mm. FW is variably pale tan to dark brown with a pale patch between dusky orbicular and reniform spots. Sometimes has paler band beyond PM line. **HOSTS:** Low plants and crops, including alfalfa, bean, corn, and strawberry. **RANGE:** Widespread.

CARROT SEED MOTH *Sitochroa palealis* 4986.1 Uncommon
TL 11–13 mm. Pale yellow FW has slightly darker veins. Sometimes has a dusky smudge in median area. **HOSTS:** Seed heads of wild carrot. **RANGE:** Se. Canada and e. U.S. **NOTE:** Introduced from Europe.

PYRAUSTINE MOTHS

actual size

MINT ROOT BORER

TITIAN PEALE'S CRAMBID

SMALL MAGPIE

CROWNED PHLYCTAENIA

WHITE-SPOTTED SABLE

GARDEN WEBWORM

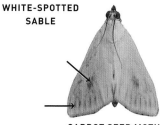

CARROT SEED MOTH

167

BEET WEBWORM *Loxostege sticticalis* 5004 **Common**
TL 13 mm. Brown FW has a patchwork of pale gray spots and lines. Brown-edged orbicular and reniform spots are separated by pale patch. **HOSTS:** Low plants, including beet, flax, spinach, and wormwood. **RANGE:** Widespread.

ALFALFA WEBWORM *Loxostege cerealis* 5017 **Common**
TL 10–13 mm. Tan FW has streaky pattern of brown and black lines. **HOSTS:** Low plants and crops, including alfalfa. **RANGE:** Widespread.

RASPBERRY PYRAUSTA *Pyrausta signatalis* 5034 **Common**
TL 8–11 mm. Bright pinkish red FW has fragmented cream-colored lines and reniform spot. **HOSTS:** Horsemint. **RANGE:** Widespread.

BICOLORED PYRAUSTA *Pyrausta bicoloralis* 5040 **Common**
TL 10 mm. Golden yellow wings are shaded purple beyond wavy PM line. **HOSTS:** Unknown. **RANGE:** Se. Canada and e. U.S.

ORANGE-SPOTTED PYRAUSTA
Pyrausta orphisalis 5058 **Common**
TL 7–10 mm. Dark crimson FW has golden yellow patches in basal and ST areas. HW is black with broad yellow median band. **HOSTS:** Mint. **RANGE:** Widespread. **NOTE:** Often frequents roadside puddles during daytime.

MINT-LOVING PYRAUSTA
Pyrausta acrionalis 5071 **Common**
TL 7–10 mm. Reddish FW has variable golden yellow mottling in median area. HW is reddish with narrow yellow median band. **HOSTS:** Mint. **RANGE:** Se. Canada and e. U.S.

CELERY LEAFTIER *Udea rubigalis* 5079 **Common**
TL 10 mm. FW is variably pale tan to reddish brown with crisp dusky lines. Reniform spot is figure eight–shaped. **HOSTS:** Low plants and crops, including bean, beet, celery, and spinach. **RANGE:** Widespread.

MERRICK'S CRAMBID
Loxostegopsis merrickalis 5117 **Common**
TL 9–12 mm. Peppery dark gray FW has pale yellow subapical patch. Head and labial palps are pale yellow. **HOSTS:** Unknown. **RANGE:** Se. Canada and e. U.S.

PYRAUSTINE MOTHS

BEET WEBWORM

actual size

ALFALFA WEBWORM

dark

BICOLORED PYRAUSTA

RASPBERRY PYRAUSTA

ORANGE-SPOTTED PYRAUSTA

MINT-LOVING PYRAUSTA

MERRICK'S CRAMBID

CELERY LEAFTIER

PALER DIACME *Diacme elealis* 5142 **Common**
WS 20 mm. Yellow FW is marked with irregular purplish brown bands. All wings have a broad dark border. **HOSTS:** Unknown. **RANGE:** Extreme se. Canada and e. U.S.

DARK DIACME *Diacme adipaloides* 5143 **Common**
WS 18 mm. Resembles Paler Diacme, but darker FW is grayish brown with irregular pale orange bands. HW is paler yellow with a wide brown border. **HOSTS:** Unknown. **RANGE:** Se. Canada and ne. U.S.

LUCERNE MOTH *Nomophila nearctica* 5156 **Common**
TL 15 mm. Long, narrow FW is brown with contrasting blackish spots and streaks. **HOSTS:** Low plants, including alfalfa, celery, clover, and smartweed. **RANGE:** Widespread.

GRAPE LEAFFOLDER *Desmia funeralis* 5159 **Common**
TL 16 mm. Black FW is marked with two large white spots in median area. HW has a broad white median band. Top of head is either all black or has a few white scales. **HOSTS:** Evening primrose, grape, and redbud. **RANGE:** Widespread.

WHITE-HEADED GRAPE LEAFFOLDER
Desmia maculalis 5160 **Common**
TL 10–14 mm. Resembles Grape Leaffolder but is smaller. HW often has a stepped white median band. Top of head is dusted with white scales. **HOSTS:** Grape. **RANGE:** Se. Canada and e. U.S.

SPOTTED BEET WEBWORM
Hymenia perspectalis 5169 **Common**
TL 10–12 mm. Brown FW has pattern of broken white lines and spots. HW has a jagged white median band. **HOSTS:** Low plants, including beet, chard, and potato. **RANGE:** Se. Canada and e. U.S.; a regular fall immigrant to the north part of range.

HAWAIIAN BEET WEBWORM
Spoladea recurvalis 5170 **Common**
TL 9–11 mm. Brown FW has white median band ending with a point before reaching costa. Subapical patch is white. HW is marked with a broad white median band. **HOSTS:** Low plants, including beet, chard, and spinach. **RANGE:** Se. Canada and e. U.S.; an irregular fall immigrant to the north part of range.

PYRAUSTINE MOTHS

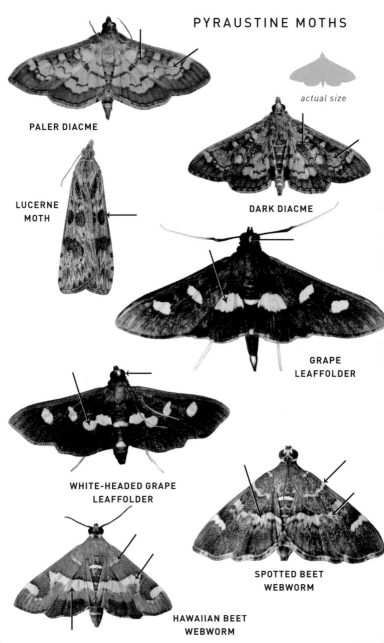

actual size

PALER DIACME

LUCERNE MOTH

DARK DIACME

GRAPE LEAFFOLDER

WHITE-HEADED GRAPE LEAFFOLDER

SPOTTED BEET WEBWORM

HAWAIIAN BEET WEBWORM

171

HARLEQUIN WEBWORM

Diathrausta harlequinalis   5175   **Uncommon**
TL 6.5–9 mm. Blackish FW has pattern of orange lines and square white spots in median area. HW has white median band that widens toward outer margin. Wings are spread open at rest. **HOSTS:** Unknown. **RANGE:** Se. Canada and U.S.

YELLOW-SPOTTED WEBWORM

Anageshna primordialis   5176   **Common**
TL 6 mm. Very small. Dusty brown FW is marked with black-edged yellow lines and spots. HW has pale yellow bands. **HOSTS:** Unknown. **RANGE:** Se. Canada and e. U.S.

HOLLOW-SPOTTED BLEPHAROMASTIX

Blepharomastix ranalis   5182   **Common**
TL 10 mm. Shiny yellowish tan FW has bold pattern of brown lines and outlines to spots. PM line is sharply kinked. **HOSTS:** Goosefoot. **RANGE:** Se. Canada and e. U.S.

MELONWORM MOTH *Diaphania hyalinata*   5204   **Uncommon**
TL 10–15 mm. Semi-translucent FW is bordered with brown along costa and outer margin. Has an eye-catching brushy tuft at tip of abdomen. **HOSTS:** Cucumber, melon, and squash. **RANGE:** Mostly tropical, but common in extreme se. U.S.; a rare late fall immigrant to ne. North America.

KIMBALL'S PALPITA *Palpita kimballi*   5219   **Uncommon**
TL 14–15 mm. Semi-translucent satin white FW has narrow orange streak along costa. **HOSTS:** Unknown. **RANGE:** E. U.S.

SPLENDID PALPITA *Palpita magniferalis*   5226   **Common**
TL 15 mm. Whitish FW is variably speckled and blotched with dusky brown. Median band is usually obvious. **HOSTS:** Ash. **RANGE:** Se. Canada and e. U.S.

IRONWEED ROOT MOTH

Polygrammodes flavidalis   5228   **Common**
TL 12–17 mm. Pale yellow FW has wavy orange-brown lines and orbicular spot. Pattern rapidly fades with wear. **HOSTS:** Ironweed. **RANGE:** Se. Canada and e. U.S.

BASSWOOD LEAFROLLER *Pantographa limata* 5241 **Common**
WS 38 mm. Pale FW is marked with crisp pattern of brown lines and outlines to spots. Inner margin and central ST area are shaded purplish brown. **HOSTS:** Basswood, oak, and rock elm. **RANGE:** Se. Canada and e. U.S.

PYRAUSTINE MOTHS

HARLEQUIN WEBWORM

actual size

YELLOW-SPOTTED WEBWORM

HOLLOW-SPOTTED BLEPHAROMASTIX

MELONWORM MOTH

KIMBALL'S PALPITA

SPLENDID PALPITA

IRONWEED ROOT MOTH

BASSWOOD LEAFROLLER

BOG LYGROPIA *Lygropia rivulalis* 5250 **Common**
WS 17 mm. Pale wings are marked with intricate pattern of brown lines and outlines to spots. **HOSTS:** Unknown. **RANGE:** Se. Canada and ne. U.S.

WHITE-SPOTTED BROWN MOTH
Diastictis ventralis 5255 **Uncommon**
TL 15 mm. Brown FW has isolated clusters of small white spots in median and ST areas. **HOSTS:** Unknown, but usually occurs in fens and wetlands. **RANGE:** Se. Canada and e. U.S. **NOTE:** Can be flushed from sedge meadows in daytime.

BOLD-FEATHERED GRASS MOTH
Herpetogramma pertextalis 5275 **Common**
WS 28 mm. Semi-translucent wings have violet sheen and pattern of scalloped brown lines. **HOSTS:** Low plants, including violets. **RANGE:** Se. Canada and e. U.S.

ZIGZAG HERPETOGRAMMA
Herpetogramma thestealis 5277 **Common**
WS 35 mm. Resembles Bold-feathered Grass Moth but has darker FW with bolder jagged lines and white bands and spots. **HOSTS:** Hazelnut, basswood, and strawberry bush. **RANGE:** Se. Canada and e. U.S.

SCRAPED PILOCROCIS
Pilocrocis ramentalis 5281 **Uncommon**
TL 12–15 mm. Brown FW has brassy sheen when fresh. Yellow-edged PM line is strongly curved. **HOSTS:** False nettle. **RANGE:** Se. Canada and e. U.S.

WINDOW-WINGED MOTHS Family Thyrididae

Chunky day-flying moths that habitually spread their wings when alighting on flower heads. The wings have translucent panels or spots forming windows. Larvae are leafrollers or borers. Adults take nectar from flowers.

SPOTTED THYRIS *Thyris maculata* 6076 **Common**
TL 7–10 mm. Blackish wings and body speckled orange. FW and HW have small translucent white spots in central median area. **HOSTS:** *Clematis* and *Houstonia* species. **RANGE:** Se. Canada and e. U.S.

PYRAUSTINE MOTHS

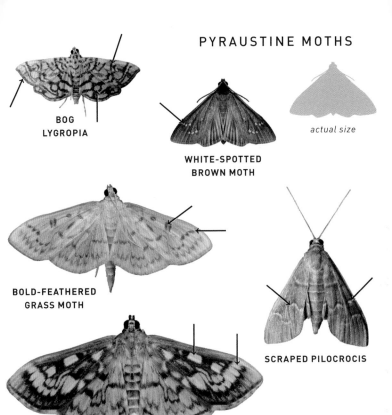

BOG LYGROPIA

WHITE-SPOTTED BROWN MOTH

actual size

BOLD-FEATHERED GRASS MOTH

SCRAPED PILOCROCIS

ZIGZAG HERPETOGRAMMA

WINDOW-WINGED MOTHS

actual size

SPOTTED THYRIS

MOURNFUL THYRIS *Thyris sepulchralis* 6077 **Common**
TL 8–13 mm. Black wings and body with creamy white spots. FW and HW spots are larger than in Spotted Thyris. **HOSTS:** Clematis and grape. **RANGE:** Sw. ON and e. U.S.

HABROSYNES, THYATIRIDS, AND HOOKTIPS Family Depranidae

The habrosynes and thyatirids are beautifully patterned noctuid-like moths. All have raised thoracic crests, rest in a "tented" position, and could possibly be mistaken for prominents. The hooktips are small-headed, geometrid-like moths. All but Two-lined Hooktip rest with wings spread, and only Northern Eudeilinia lacks hooked tips to the FW. They are nocturnal and will visit lights in small numbers.

LETTERED HABROSYNE *Habrosyne scripta* 6235 **Common**
TL 20–21 mm. Metallic gray FW has complex pattern of brown-edged whitish lines. Midpoint of PM line is slightly kinked. **HOSTS:** Birch, black raspberry, and purple-flowering raspberry. **NOTE:** Two broods.

GLORIOUS HABROSYNE *Habrosyne gloriosa* 6236 **Uncommon**
TL 20–21 mm. Resembles Lettered Habrosyne but midpoint of PM line is bent at 90 degrees. **HOSTS:** Unknown, presumably *Rubus* species. **NOTE:** Two broods.

TUFTED THYATIRID
Pseudothyatira cymatophoroides 6237 **Common**
TL 23–25 mm. Pale FW has a contrasting black triple AM line and black patch beyond inner ST line. Form "expultrix" has ash gray FW with pinkish shading in basal and median areas. **HOSTS:** Deciduous trees and shrubs, including alder, birch, maple, poplar, and willow. **NOTE:** Two broods.

DOGWOOD THYATIRID *Euthyatira pudens* 6240 **Common**
TL 23–25 mm. Gray FW is marked with large pinkish patches in basal, costal, and apical areas. Individuals of form "pennsylvanicus" are mostly gray with weakly defined ghostlike markings. **HOSTS:** Flowering dogwood.

ARCHED HOOKTIP *Deprana arcuata* 6251 **Common**
WS 27–40 mm. Rusty-edged ST line on hooked orange FW curves toward apex. Reniform spot is two black dots. **HOSTS:** Alder and birch. **NOTE:** Two broods.

WINDOW-WINGED MOTHS

MOURNFUL THYRIS

actual size

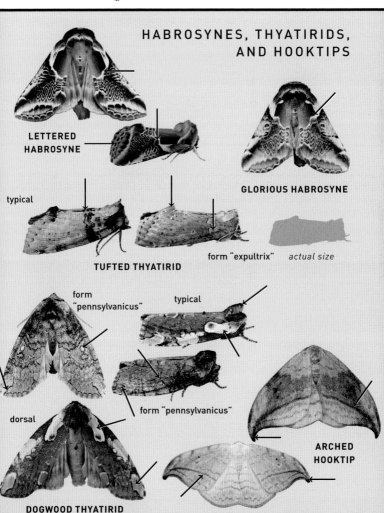

HABROSYNES, THYATIRIDS, AND HOOKTIPS

LETTERED HABROSYNE

GLORIOUS HABROSYNE

typical

form "expultrix"   *actual size*

TUFTED THYATIRID

form "pennsylvanicus"

typical

form "pennsylvanicus"

ARCHED HOOKTIP

dorsal

DOGWOOD THYATIRID

177

TWO-LINED HOOKTIP *Deprana bilineata* 6252   Common
TL 16–21 mm. Pale orange FW is marked with slanting, parallel AM and PM lines. Spring brood brindled with brown; summer brood more uniform. Single reniform dot. **HOSTS:** Alder, birch, elm, and poplar. **NOTE:** Two broods.

NORTHERN EUDEILINIA
Eudeilinia herminiata 6253   Common
WS 27 mm. White wings have dotted brown AM and PM lines of varying intensity. **HOSTS:** Dogwood.

ROSE HOOKTIP *Oreta rosea* 6255   Common
WS 25–35 mm. FW is variable in color. Typically is rusty brown with a broad yellow band between PM and ST lines. Some individuals are uniformly pinkish or rusty brown on all wings. Two tiny white dots mark median area. **HOSTS:** Birch and viburnum. **NOTE:** Two broods.

SCOOPWINGS   Family Uraniidae

Two flat-winged moths that resemble members of the Geometridae. Both species habitually crease their scalloped HW, creating a gap that lends them a tailed shape. They are nocturnal and will occasionally come to lights.

GRAY SCOOPWING *Callizzia amorata* 7650   Uncommon
WS 15–22 mm. Gray FW has rusty-edged AM and PM lines that are connected with short bar near inner margin. Brown triangular patch at midpoint of outer margin is edged black. **HOSTS:** Honeysuckle.

BROWN SCOOPWING
Calledapteryx dryopterata 7653   Uncommon
WS 18–22 mm. Orange-brown FW has dark edging to scooped-out section along outer margin. AM and PM lines are incomplete. Rectangular patch at midpoint of inner margin is edged blackish. **HOSTS:** Nannyberry and wild-raisin.

HABROSYNES, THYATIRIDS, AND HOOKTIPS

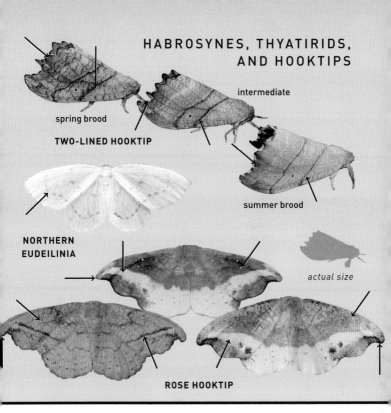

spring brood

TWO-LINED HOOKTIP

intermediate

summer brood

NORTHERN EUDEILINIA

actual size

ROSE HOOKTIP

SCOOPWINGS

GRAY SCOOPWING

BROWN SCOOPWING

CARPETS AND PUGS
Family Geometridae, Subfamily Larentiinae

A large group of flimsy, broad-winged moths. Most species adopt a flat position when resting, plastering themselves on tree trunks and branches, where they can be extremely cryptic and hard to find. A few, notably in the genus *Eulithis,* rest with their slender abdomen raised above the level of the wings. Most are woodland species, though some can be found in gardens, even in urban areas. The group is largely nocturnal and will come freely to lights, though a small number are diurnal and are to be sought along woodland trails or around bogs and fens.

DARK MARBLED CARPET *Dysstroma citrata* 7182 **Common**
WS 26–32 mm. Variable. Peppery gray FW is typically marked with brown bands along jagged black lines. Median area is sometimes largely white or warm brown. Outer PM line is edged white. **HOSTS:** Deciduous trees and low plants, including alder, willow, and Rubus spp. **NOTE:** Two broods.

ORANGE-BARRED CARPET

Dysstroma hersiliata 7189 **Common**
WS 25–29 mm. Variable. Dark gray FW has a wide orange band in AM area. Usually has orange shading in outer ST area. Outer PM line has an inward-pointing tooth jutting into median area. Rarely, entire median area is orange. **HOSTS:** Currant.

LESSER GRAPEVINE LOOPER

Eulithis diversilineata 7196 **Common**
WS 28–33 mm. Pale orange FW is crossed by fine brown lines. Inner median area is often tinted lilac. Midpoint of PM line forms a long outward-pointing spike. **HOSTS:** Grape and Virginia creeper. **NOTE:** Two broods.

GREATER GRAPEVINE LOOPER

Eulithis gracilineata 7197 **Common**
WS 28–30 mm. Resembles Lesser Grapevine Looper (many individuals are indistinguishable), but FW has double AM and PM lines that are often filled with brown shading. Median area is uniformly pale. **HOSTS:** Grape and Virginia creeper.

THE CHEVRON *Eulithis testata* 7201 **Common**
WS 22–25 mm. FW is variably pale orange to brown with gray shading in median and ST areas. Short white apical dash borders an orange triangle along outer margin. **HOSTS:** Poplar and willow.

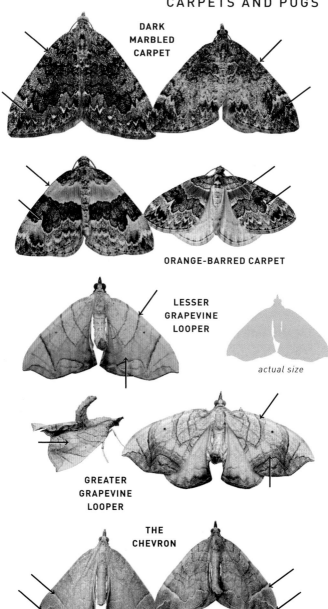

DARK MARBLED CARPET

ORANGE-BARRED CARPET

LESSER GRAPEVINE LOOPER

actual size

GREATER GRAPEVINE LOOPER

THE CHEVRON

DIMORPHIC EULITHIS

Eulithis molliculata   7203   **Uncommon**

WS 28 mm. Sexually dimorphic. FW of male (shown) is purplish brown, whereas that of female is pale orange. Lines are frosted with white shading. Notched white apical dash borders a conspicuous reddish patch. **HOSTS:** Ninebark.

WHITE EULITHIS   *Eulithis explanata*   7206   **Common**

WS 22–28 mm. Gray FW has darker shading in basal and median areas. Median area is sometimes fragmented. Scalloped lines are broadly edged white. **HOSTS:** Blueberry.

SERRATED EULITHIS   *Eulithis serrataria*   7208   **Common**

WS 22–30 mm. Grayish FW is shaded purple in basal and median areas. AM and basal lines are jagged. PM line has a rounded bulge at midpoint and gently curving outer section. **HOSTS:** Unknown. **RANGE:** Se. Canada and ne. U.S.

BLACK-BANDED CARPET

Eustroma semiatrata   7210   **Uncommon**

WS 28–32 mm. Pale gray FW has blackish shading in basal and median areas. Slightly scalloped lines are edged white. Outer section of PM line is wavy. Some individuals are entirely blackish with whitish lines. **HOSTS:** Willow herb.

SMALL PHOENIX   *Ecliptopera silaceata*   7213   **Uncommon**

WS 24–28 mm. Blackish FW is marked with paler gray bands in AM and ST areas. White basal and AM lines are slightly jagged. PM line has two inward-pointing spikes. Outer section of PM line is relatively straight. **HOSTS:** Impatiens and willow herb. **NOTE:** Two broods.

GEORGE'S CARPET   *Plemyria georgii*   7216   **Uncommon**

WS 27–30 mm. Peppery pale gray FW has brown chainlike median band that divides before reaching costa. Discal spot is accented with white scales. **HOSTS:** Deciduous trees, including birch, poplar, and willow. **RANGE:** S. Canada and n. U.S.

JUNIPER CARPET   *Thera juniperata*   7217   **Uncommon**

WS 24–30 mm. Pale brown FW has darker brown basal and median areas. Angular AM line is often connected to scalloped PM line by a bar in central median area. Fragmented black apical dash almost touches bulge in PM line. **HOSTS:** Juniper. **RANGE:** S. Canada and n. U.S.

CARPETS AND PUGS

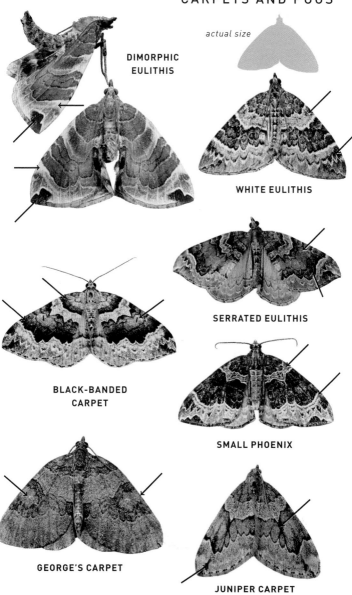

actual size

DIMORPHIC EULITHIS

WHITE EULITHIS

SERRATED EULITHIS

BLACK-BANDED CARPET

SMALL PHOENIX

GEORGE'S CARPET

JUNIPER CARPET

CONTRACTED SPANWORM

Thera contractata   7218   **Uncommon**

WS 23–25 mm. Pale gray FW has crisp black AM and PM lines that converge at inner margin. Jagged white ST line is edged with black dashes and warm brown shading. **HOSTS:** Juniper and white birch. **RANGE:** E. Canada and ne. U.S.

SHATTERED HYDRIOMENA

Hydriomena perfracta   7229   **Common**

WS 30 mm. Peppery gray FW has wide pink median area edged with chestnut bands. **HOSTS:** Tamarack and trembling aspen. **RANGE:** Se. Canada and ne. U.S.

BLACK-DASHED HYDRIOMENA

Hydriomena divisaria   7235   **Common**

WS 24–30 mm. Grayish brown FW has variable pattern of scalloped blackish lines. Basal line is usually thick and strongly kinked. Grayish band in AM area usually reaches costa. Terminal line is usually blurred paired dots. **HOSTS:** Balsam fir, pine, and white spruce.

RENOUNCED HYDRIOMENA

Hydriomena renunciata   7236   **Uncommon**

WS 27–30 mm. Resembles Black-dashed Hydriomena; many individuals show intermediate characteristics and may be indistinguishable. Basal line is usually narrower and rarely kinked. Grayish band in AM area usually fades before reaching costa. Terminal line is usually distinct paired dots. **HOSTS:** Alder.

TRANSFIGURED HYDRIOMENA

Hydriomena transfigurata   7237   **Uncommon**

WS 26–33 mm. Resembles Black-dashed and Renounced Hydriomenas, but wings are usually narrower and grayish band in AM area is more distinct. Terminal line may be variable. **HOSTS:** Pine.

TISSUE MOTH *Triphosa haesitata*   7285   **Uncommon**

WS 35–40 mm. Grayish FW is marked with parallel, scalloped lines and chestnut bands. Outer section of PM line has outward-pointing blunt point. Often has an orange patch in central median area. **HOSTS:** Buckthorn, barberry, hawthorn, oak, and wild plum. **NOTE:** Two broods. Some adults hibernate over the winter and fly again in Apr.

BARBERRY GEOMETER *Coryphista meadii*   7290   **Common**

WS 30–36 mm. FW is variably pale gray to brown. Outer section of PM line has outward-pointing tooth. Sometimes marked with orange bands. **HOSTS:** Barberry. **NOTE:** Three broods.

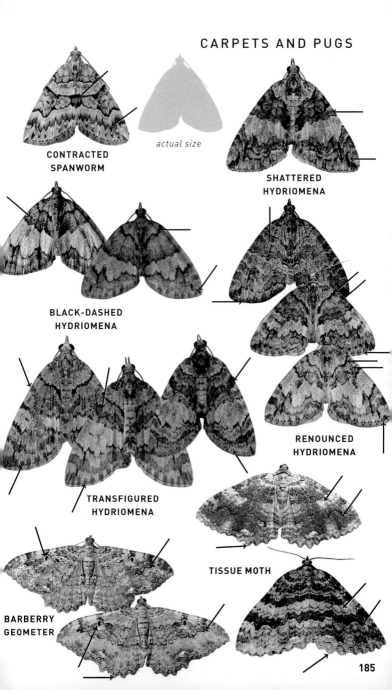

CARPETS AND PUGS

CONTRACTED SPANWORM

actual size

SHATTERED HYDRIOMENA

BLACK-DASHED HYDRIOMENA

RENOUNCED HYDRIOMENA

TRANSFIGURED HYDRIOMENA

TISSUE MOTH

BARBERRY GEOMETER

185

CHERRY SCALLOP SHELL

Rheumaptera prunivorata 7292 **Common**
WS 35–41 mm. Straw-colored wings are overlaid with dense pattern of undulating lines. Jagged white ST line is edged orange. **HOSTS:** Azalea, meadowsweet, and willow. **NOTE:** Two broods.

SPEAR-MARKED BLACK *Rheumaptera hastata* 7293 **Common**

WS 25–36 mm. Black wings are variably marked with fragmented white lines. Always has a broad white PM band on FW that has outward-pointing spearhead-like marking at its midpoint. **HOSTS:** Deciduous trees and shrubs, including alder, birch, blueberry, poplar, and willow. **NOTE:** Two broods.

WHITE-BANDED BLACK

Rheumaptera subhastata 7294 **Uncommon**
WS 30–34 mm. Resembles Spear-marked Black but tends to have more extensive white lines and bands on wings, some individuals showing more white than black. **HOSTS:** Alder, northern bayberry, and sweet gale.

WHITE-RIBBONED CARPET

Mesoleuca ruficillata 7307 **Common**
WS 23–28 mm. White FW has mottled blue-black basal and subapical patches. PM line is finely scalloped. ST area is marked with faded blue scalloped lines. **HOSTS:** Birch and blackberry. **NOTE:** Two broods.

DOUBLE-BANDED CARPET

Spargania magnoliata 7312 **Common**
WS 19–27 mm. Pale gray FW is marked with jagged white-edged lines. Darker median band and subapical patch are edged black. **HOSTS:** Willow herb and evening primrose. **NOTE:** Two broods.

SMALL RIVULET *Perizoma alchemillata* 7320 **Common**

WS 14–24 mm. Brown FW is mottled with gray and white scales along veins. Jagged PM line is broadly edged white on both sides, forming a wide band. **HOSTS:** Hemp nettle. **RANGE:** Se. Canada and possibly ne. U.S.

VARIABLE CARPET *Anticlea vasiliata* 7329 **Common**

WS 30 mm. Pale purplish gray FW has brown bands along basal, AM, and outer PM lines. Midpoint of PM line is marked with a rounded W-shape. Black apical dash almost touches outer part of PM line. **HOSTS:** Raspberry and Carolina rose.

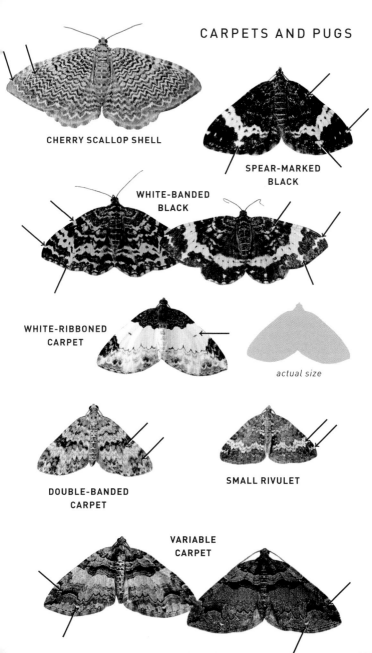

CARPETS AND PUGS

CHERRY SCALLOP SHELL

SPEAR-MARKED
BLACK

WHITE-BANDED
BLACK

WHITE-RIBBONED
CARPET

actual size

DOUBLE-BANDED
CARPET

SMALL RIVULET

VARIABLE
CARPET

MANY-LINED CARPET *Anticlea multiferata* 7330   **Common**
WS 19–25 mm. Purplish brown FW is crossed by many parallel yellowish lines. AM, ST, and terminal lines are white. **HOSTS:** Willow herb.

SHINY GRAY CARPET *Stamnodes gibbicostata* 7333 **Uncommon**
WS 25–31 mm. Shiny grayish brown FW is uniform apart from two white patches along costa. Underside of HW is mottled with fragmented black bands in basal and median areas. All wings have checkered fringe when fresh. Usually rests with its wings held tight above its abdomen. **HOSTS:** Maple, oak, and poplar.

LABRADOR CARPET *Xanthorhoe labradorensis* 7368 **Common**
WS 20–24 mm. Pale gray FW has broad orange median band. Almost straight AM line is boldly marked in black. **HOSTS:** A variety of plants, including cabbage, hemlock, peppergrass, and radish. **NOTE:** Two broods.

RED TWIN-SPOT *Xanthorhoe ferrugata* 7388   **Common**
WS 18–25 mm. Grayish brown FW has reddish brown basal area and subapical patch. Wide median area is variably blackish or dark crimson. Outer ST line is accented with two black spots. **HOSTS:** Low plants, including chickweed and ground ivy. **NOTE:** Two broods.

TOOTHED BROWN CARPET
Xanthorhoe lacustrata 7390   **Common**
WS 20–26 mm. Pale gray FW has warm brown inner basal patch and shading beyond scalloped white ST line. Wide median band is brown with blackish edges and discal spot. Brown subapical patch and ST spots are diffuse. **HOSTS:** Birch, blackberry, hawthorn, impatiens, and willow. **NOTE:** Two broods.

WHITE-BANDED TOOTHED CARPET
Epirrhoe alternata 7394   **Common**
WS 19–26 mm. Resembles Toothed Brown Carpet, but FW has AM and PM lines thickly edged white, forming wide bands. ST and terminal area are brownish. **HOSTS:** Bedstraw.

SHARP-ANGLED CARPET
Euphyia intermediata 7399   **Common**
WS 20–27 mm. Resembles Toothed Brown Carpet, but wide dark median band has distinctly sharp tooth projecting backward from otherwise straight PM line. Blackish subapical patch is well defined. **HOSTS:** Chickweed, elm, impatiens, and mustard. **NOTE:** Two broods.

CARPETS AND PUGS

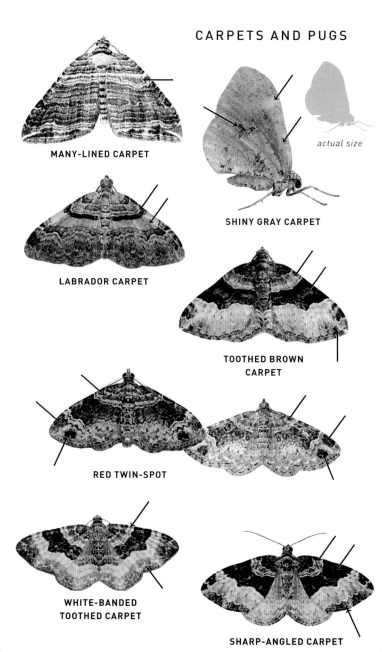

MANY-LINED CARPET

SHINY GRAY CARPET

actual size

LABRADOR CARPET

TOOTHED BROWN
CARPET

RED TWIN-SPOT

WHITE-BANDED
TOOTHED CARPET

SHARP-ANGLED CARPET

189

THE GEM *Orthonama obstipata* 7414 **Common**
WS 15–23 mm. Sexually dimorphic. FW of male is pale tan with a broken dusky median band and blackish apical dash. FW of female is maroon with dotted white lines and a white-edged discal spot. **HOSTS:** Low plants, including dock and ragwort. **NOTE:** Two or more broods. Cannot survive cold winters; northern individuals are immigrants from farther south.

BENT-LINE CARPET
Costaconvexa centrostrigaria 7416 **Common**
WS 17–23 mm. Sexually dimorphic. FW of male is pale gray with a blackish AM line and outer section of PM line. Female is similar but has darker gray median band. Both sexes show a black discal dot. **HOSTS:** Low plants, including knotweed and smartweed. **NOTE:** Two or more broods.

SOMBER CARPET *Disclisioprocta stellata* 7417 **Uncommon**
WS 25–33 mm. FW is variably pale straw colored to dark brown with incomplete white edges to scalloped lines. Median area is often slightly darker. Midpoint of PM line has two rounded teeth within the bulge. **HOSTS:** Amaranth and devil's claws. **NOTE:** A tropical species that regularly immigrates northward, occasionally reaching ne. N. America in the fall.

UNADORNED CARPET *Hydrelia inornata* 7422 **Common**
WS 17–22 mm. Peppery white FW has grayish brown shading in basal area and along ST line. AM and PM lines are edged chestnut. Black discal dots mark all wings. **HOSTS:** White birch and yellow birch.

FRAGILE WHITE CARPET *Hydrelia albifera* 7423 **Common**
WS 16–17 mm. White FW is crossed by wavy yellowish tan lines. ST line is often fragmented. All wings are marked with tiny black discal dots. **HOSTS:** Alternate-leaf dogwood, red osier dogwood, and white birch. **NOTE:** Two broods.

THE WELSH WAVE *Venusia cambrica* 7425 **Uncommon**
WS 23–25 mm. Peppery pale gray FW has double AM and PM lines blackish toward costa. Brown-tinged ST area is marked with black and white dashes along veins. **HOSTS:** Deciduous trees, including alder, apple, birch, serviceberry, and willow. **NOTE:** Two broods.

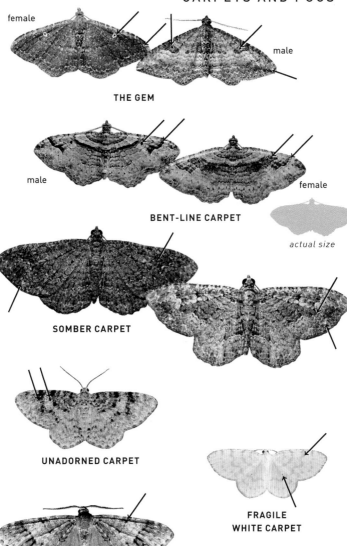

female

male

THE GEM

male

female

BENT-LINE CARPET

actual size

SOMBER CARPET

UNADORNED CARPET

**FRAGILE
WHITE CARPET**

THE WELSH WAVE

BROWN-SHADED CARPET

Venusia comptaria 7428 **Common**
WS 17–22 mm. Pale gray FW has faint pattern of brown-edged wavy lines. Black outer half of median line connects with a short black dash at midpoint of PM line. Terminal line is checkered black and white. **HOSTS:** Alder, beech, and birch.

WHITE-STRIPED BLACK

Trichodezia albovittata 7430 **Common**
WS 20–25 mm. Black FW is marked with broad white median band that has an extension reaching inner fringe. HW is black with a partly white fringe. **HOSTS:** Impatiens. **NOTE:** Two broods. Often seen during daytime along wooded trails.

AUTUMNAL MOTH *Epirrita autumnata* 7433 **Common**
WS 25–36 mm. Pale gray FW has double AM and PM lines often filled with brown shading. Thick black veins in central median area form inverted V. Terminal line is paired black dots. **HOSTS:** Deciduous and coniferous trees, including ash, birch, maple, oak, and pine.

BRUCE SPANWORM *Operophtera bruceata* 7437 **Common**
WS 25–30 mm. Resembles Autumnal Moth, but FW is variably pale gray to sooty brown. Small black discal spot present. Terminal line is single black dots. Female has undeveloped wings and is flightless. **HOSTS:** Deciduous trees, including aspen, beech, maple, and willow.

THE BEGGAR *Eubaphe mendica* 7440 **Common**
WS 21–30 mm. Semi-translucent yellowish FW has wide purplish gray AM and PM bands fragmented into spots by pale veins. Basal section of costa is tinged orange. **HOSTS:** Maple and violet. **NOTE:** Two or more broods.

THE LITTLE BEGGAR *Eubaphe meridiana* 7441 **Common**
WS 18–25 mm. Resembles The Beggar but is smaller and has deeper orange FW with smaller spots forming purplish gray AM and PM bands. **HOSTS:** Unknown. **RANGE:** E. U.S.

BROWN BARK CARPET *Horisme intestinata* 7445 **Common**
WS 21–33 mm. Pale tan FW is marked with fine parallel lines. PM and ST lines are deeply scalloped. Wide costal streak is almost unmarked. **HOSTS:** Possibly clematis. **NOTE:** Two broods.

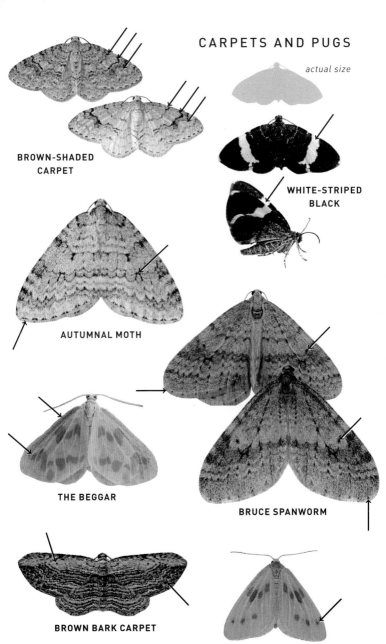

CARPETS AND PUGS

actual size

BROWN-SHADED CARPET

WHITE-STRIPED BLACK

AUTUMNAL MOTH

THE BEGGAR

BRUCE SPANWORM

BROWN BARK CARPET

THE LITTLE BEGGAR

COLUMBIA PUG *Eupithecia columbiata* 7459 **Common**
WS 12–20 mm. Yellowish brown FW is marked with blackish parallel lines and speckling on veins. Scalloped ST line is accented with white, usually with a spot near inner margin. Second abdominal segment is black. **HOSTS:** Deciduous trees and plants, including alder, buckthorn, dogwood, poplar, maple, and willow. **RANGE:** S. Canada and n. U.S.

COMMON PUG *Eupithecia miserulata* 7474 **Common**
WS 12–20 mm. Pale gray FW is tinted green when fresh. Black discal spot is conspicuous. Inner ST line is marked with a white spot. Last few segments of abdomen are often whitish. **HOSTS:** Trees and low plants, including aster, clover, juniper, oak, and willow. **RANGE:** Widespread.

WHITE-SPOTTED PUG
Eupithecia tripunctaria 7488 **Common**
WS 21–23 mm. Grayish brown FW has faint lines and black and white dashes along veins. Discal spot touches bulge in median line. Inner ST line and inner corner of HW are marked with bold white dots. Thorax is marked with a small white triangle. **HOSTS:** Umbellifers, including wild-raisin, wild carrot, and parsnip. **RANGE:** Widespread.

JUNIPER PUG
Eupithecia interruptofasciata 7551 **Uncommon**
WS 15–20 mm. Pale gray FW is patterned with strongly angled lines. Black discal spot touches median line. Three black wedges mark outer ST area. Second abdominal segment is black. **HOSTS:** Juniper. **RANGE:** S. Canada and n. U.S.

CLOAKED PUG *Eupithecia mutata* 7575 **Common**
WS 17–22 mm. Whitish FW has faint black AM and PM lines that widen toward costa. Broad reddish bands mark basal and ST areas. Large black discal spot touches median line. **HOSTS:** Seeds of spruce cones. **RANGE:** S. Canada and n. U.S.

WORMWOOD PUG *Eupithecia absinthiata* 7586.1 **Common**
WS 22–26 mm. Large. Pale gray FW is tinged violet. Faint dotted lines are obvious only at costa. Elongated black discal spot is conspicuous. Second abdominal segment is blackish. **HOSTS:** A wide variety of plants, including aster, goldenrod, and wormwood. **RANGE:** Holarctic; se. Canada and ne. U.S.

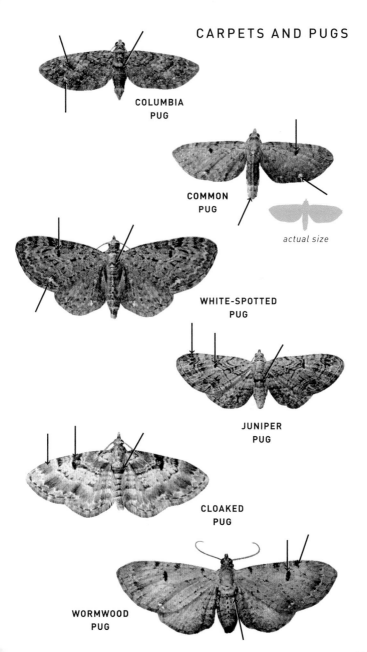

CARPETS AND PUGS

COLUMBIA
PUG

COMMON
PUG

actual size

WHITE-SPOTTED
PUG

JUNIPER
PUG

CLOAKED
PUG

WORMWOOD
PUG

TAWNY PUG *Eupithecia ravocostaliata* 7605 **Common**
WS 20–25 mm. Pearly gray FW has purplish costal streak interrupted by white-edged lines. Large black discal crescent almost touches costal shading. Black veins mark central median area. Abdomen is tipped white. **HOSTS:** Deciduous trees, including birch, poplar, and willow. **RANGE:** S. Canada and n. U.S.

GREEN PUG *Pasiphila rectangulata* 7625 **Common**
WS 19–23 mm. Green FW is marked with wavy black AM and PM lines. ST area has two black patches near apex. The green color fades quickly with wear. **HOSTS:** In Europe, host plants include apple, blackthorn, cherry, and pear. **RANGE:** Holarctic; se. Canada and ne. U.S.

OLIVE-AND-BLACK CARPET
Acasis viridata 7635 **Common**
WS 18–20 mm. Grayish FW has mottled dusky bands broken by black and white dashes along veins. Fresh individuals are streaked mossy green along veins. **HOSTS:** Northern wild-raisin.

MOTTLED GRAY CARPET *Cladara limitaria* 7637 **Common**
WS 21–28 mm. Pale gray FW has wavy lines often edged with fragmented bands of brown, yellow, or green shading. Bulging PM line is broadly edged dark brown. HW is pearly gray. **HOSTS:** Sheep laurel and coniferous trees.

THE SCRIBBLER *Cladara atroliturata* 7639 **Common**
WS 23–30 mm. Whitish FW is overlaid with dense pattern of crisp wavy black lines typically intermixed with bands of mint green; a rare form exists with gray bands. **HOSTS:** Alder, birch, maple, and willow.

POWDERED BIGWING
Lobophora nivigerata 7640 **Common**
WS 21–25 mm. Powdery whitish FW is marked with indistinct lines ending as blurry patches along costa. Elongated black discal spot is noticeable. **HOSTS:** Trembling aspen, also balsam poplar, alder, birch, and willow.

THREE-PATCHED BIGWING
Heterophleps refusaria 7645 **Uncommon**
WS 23–30 mm. Pale grayish brown FW is finely peppered with white scales. Faint AM, PM, and ST lines end as brown patches along costa. **HOSTS:** Unknown.

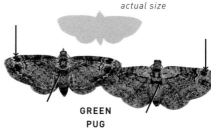

TAWNY PUG

actual size

GREEN PUG

OLIVE-AND-BLACK CARPET

MOTTLED GRAY CARPET

gray form

THE SCRIBBLER

typical

POWDERED BIGWING

THREE-PATCHED BIGWING

THREE-SPOTTED FILLIP

Heterophleps triguttaria   7647   **Common**
WS 18–24 mm. Pale yellowish tan FW is marked with two large chocolate brown patches along costa. **HOSTS:** Maple.

THE BAD-WING   *Dyspteris abortivaria*   7648   **Common**

WS 20–29 mm. Bluish green FW has faint whitish AM and PM lines that fade before reaching costa. Small white discal spots mark all wings. Rounded HW is much smaller, resulting in a long-winged appearance. **HOSTS:** Grape. **NOTE:** Two broods.

WAVES   Family Geometridae, Subfamily Sterrhinae

Small to medium-sized geometers that are usually pale and rest with wings flat and spread wide. The males of some species have bipectinate antennae. Most are nocturnal and will come freely to lights. A few, such as Chickweed Geometer and Cross-lined Wave, are also active in daylight.

DRAB BROWN WAVE   *Lobocleta ossularia*   7094   **Common**

WS 13–19 mm. Wings are variably pale tan or brown with peppery blackish lines. Median line on FW is kinked near inner margin. Terminal line is usually dotted. All wings are marked with small black discal dots. **HOSTS:** Chickweed and possibly bedstraw, clover, and strawberry.

RED-BORDERED WAVE   *Idaea demissaria*   7114   **Common**

WS 14–19 mm. Straw-colored wings have reddish shading in basal area and beyond PM line. Slightly scalloped lines are reddish brown. All wings are marked with tiny black discal dots. **HOSTS:** Unknown.

SINGLE-DOTTED WAVE   *Idaea dimidiata*   7126   **Common**

WS 18–21 mm. Cream-colored wings have indistinct purplish lines. Inner ST line of FW is accented with a row of four blackish spots. Terminal line is dotted. **HOSTS:** In Europe, host plants include cow parsley, burnet-saxifrage, hedge bedstraw, and dandelion. **RANGE:** Holarctic; se. Canada and ne. U.S. **NOTE:** One or two broods; introduced from Europe.

COMMON TAN WAVE   *Pleuroprucha insulsaria*   7132   **Common**

WS 14–20 mm. Grainy pale tan wings are faintly marked with scalloped yellow-edged lines. Diffuse median line is often most noticeable marking. Pale ST line is laced with tiny black dots. **HOSTS:** Trees and low plants, including bedstraw, chestnut, corn, goldenrod, and oak. **NOTE:** Three broods.

CARPETS AND PUGS

THREE-SPOTTED FILLIP

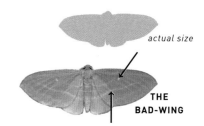

actual size

THE BAD-WING

WAVES

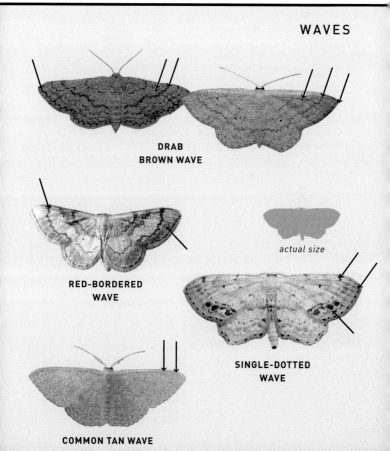

DRAB BROWN WAVE

RED-BORDERED WAVE

actual size

SINGLE-DOTTED WAVE

COMMON TAN WAVE

199

PACKARD'S WAVE *Cyclophora packardi* 7136 **Common**
WS 17–23 mm. Pale orange wings are densely peppered red-dish. AM and PM lines are dotted. Sometimes has smudgy dark median band. All wings are marked with small hollow discal spots. **HOSTS:** Unknown; possibly oak or sweet fern.

SWEETFERN GEOMETER
Cyclophora pendulinaria 7139 **Common**
WS 17–24 mm. Whitish wings are variably peppered gray. AM and PM lines are dotted. Sometimes has darker gray median band. All wings are marked with large hollow discal spots. **HOSTS:** Deciduous trees and low plants, including alder, beech, blueberry, and sweet fern. **NOTE:** Three broods.

CHICKWEED GEOMETER
Haematopis grataria 7146 **Common**
WS 18–26 mm. Deep yellow wings have wide pink median and weaker ST lines. FW has pink discal dot. Fringe on all wings is pink. Male has bipectinate antennae. **HOSTS:** Low plants, in-cluding chickweed, clover, knotweed, and smartweed. **NOTE:** Two broods.

CROSS-LINED WAVE *Timandra amaturaria* 7147 **Common**
WS 20–28 mm. Yellowish wings are finely speckled gray. Oblique red PM line of FW connects with grayish ST line at apex and continues onto HW, forming continuous line across wings. HW has sharply pointed outer margin. **HOSTS:** Buckwheat, crested bindweed, and dock. **NOTE:** Sometimes active during daytime.

FROSTED TAN WAVE *Scopula cacuminaria* 7157 **Common**
WS 18–23 mm. Whitish wings have inner ST line heavily ac-cented with black spots. All wings show small black discal dots and dotted terminal lines. HW has sharply pointed outer mar-gin. **HOSTS:** Dandelion and lettuce. **NOTE:** Two broods.

LARGE LACE-BORDER *Scopula limboundata* 7159 **Common**
WS 20–31 mm. Whitish wings are marked with faint wavy brown lines. Some individuals show variable blackish shading beyond PM line, sometimes forming a continuous band. All wings have small black discal dots. **HOSTS:** Trees and low plants, including apple, bedstraw, blueberry, dandelion, and meadow beauty. **NOTE:** Two broods.

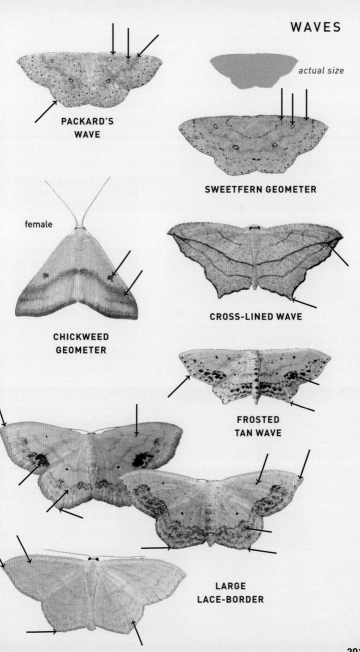

WAVES

PACKARD'S WAVE

actual size

SWEETFERN GEOMETER

female

CHICKWEED GEOMETER

CROSS-LINED WAVE

FROSTED TAN WAVE

LARGE LACE-BORDER

SIMPLE WAVE *Scopula junctaria* 7164 **Common**
WS 20–26 mm. Resembles Large Lace-Border, but creamy white wings are marked with wavy brown lines that are roughly parallel. Usually lacks obvious discal dots. **HOSTS:** Deciduous trees and plants, including chickweed, clover, and elm.

FOUR-LINED WAVE *Scopula quadrilineata* 7165 **Uncommon**
WS 20–26 mm. Satin white wings are finely peppered with brown scales. Faint yellowish brown lines are straight and roughly parallel. **HOSTS:** Clover and chokeberry.

FRIGID WAVE *Scopula fridgidaria* 7166 **Common**
WS 18–26 mm. Whitish wings are densely peppered brown. Faint yellowish brown lines are roughly parallel and slightly wavy. Usually lacks obvious discal dots. **HOSTS:** Possibly blueberry.

SOFT-LINED WAVE *Scopula inductata* 7169 **Common**
WS 17–24 mm. Resembles Frigid Wave, but creamy white wings are lightly peppered brown. Soft brownish lines are roughly parallel. All wings have tiny black discal dots. Some individuals are brownish. **HOSTS:** Low plants, including aster, clover, dandelion, ragweed, and sweet clover. **NOTE:** Two broods.

LIGHT-RIBBONED WAVE
Leptostales ferruminaria 7180 **Common**
WS 14–20 mm. Dull orange wings are marked with wavy black lines. Broad reddish brown median band is often blackish at costa of FW. Wavy ST line is dotted. **HOSTS:** Unknown.

EMERALDS
Family Geometridae, Subfamily Geometrinae

Predominantly green geometers that rest on flat, widely spread wings. The males of some species have bipectinate antennae. A few species also have brown forms; in the case of Red-fringed Emerald, this is seen only in the spring. All are nocturnal and will come to lights in small numbers.

RED-BORDERED EMERALD *Nemoria lixaria* 7033 **Common**
WS 20–30 mm. Pale green wings are marked with slightly jagged, faint whitish AM and PM lines. Tiny black discal spots mark all wings. Terminal line is red. Fringe is boldly checkered with red. **HOSTS:** Deciduous trees and woody plants, including oak, red maple, and sweet fern. **NOTE:** Two or more broods.

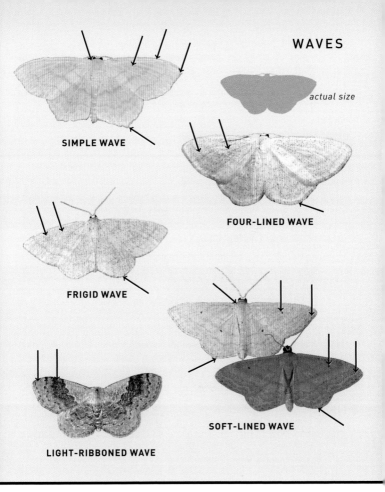

WAVES

actual size

SIMPLE WAVE

FOUR-LINED WAVE

FRIGID WAVE

SOFT-LINED WAVE

LIGHT-RIBBONED WAVE

EMERALDS

actual size

RED-BORDERED EMERALD

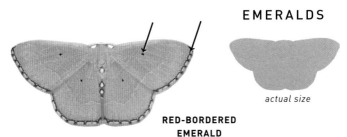

RED-FRINGED EMERALD *Nemoria bistriaria* 7046 **Common**
WS 22–25 mm. Resembles Red-bordered Emerald but usually lacks obvious black discal spots on wings. Terminal line and outlines to abdominal spots are more pinkish. A brown spring form occurs in the far north. **HOSTS:** Birch, oak, sweet fern, and walnut. **NOTE:** Two broods.

RED-FRONTED EMERALD
Nemoria rubrifrontaria 7047 **Common**
WS 21–25 mm. Bluish green FW has pink scales at base of costa and almost straight white AM and PM lines. Fringes are whitish, sometimes tinged pink. Head has pinkish front surface. **HOSTS:** Northern bayberry, sheep laurel, winged sumac, sweet fern, and sweet gale. **NOTE:** Two broods.

WHITE-FRINGED EMERALD
Nemoria mimosaria 7048 **Common**
WS 20–25 mm. Bluish green wings have almost straight white AM and PM lines. Fringe on all wings is white. Abdomen has single white spot on basal segment and a white line on dorsal surface of most other segments. **HOSTS:** Various trees, including birch, maple, white pine, and willow.

SHOWY EMERALD *Dichorda iridaria* 7053 **Common**
WS 20–30 mm. Pale bluish green wings have broad white AM and PM lines that blend into ground color. White costal streak is mottled gray near base. Tiny black discal spots mark all wings. **HOSTS:** Poison ivy, staghorn sumac, and winged sumac. **NOTE:** Two broods.

WAVY-LINED EMERALD *Synchlora aerata* 7058 **Common**
WS 13–24 mm. Pale green wings have slightly wavy white AM and PM lines. Dotted whitish ST line is sometimes noticeable. Fringe on all wings is tinged pale green. Abdomen has narrow white dorsal stripe running entire length. **HOSTS:** Low plants, including aster, coneflower, goldenrod, and ragweed. **NOTE:** Two or more broods.

SOUTHERN EMERALD *Synchlora frondaria* 7059 **Common**
WS 15 mm. Resembles Wavy-lined Emerald, but AM and PM lines are more jagged. Faint white veins are sometimes obvious in median and ST areas. Fringe on all wings is tinged green. **HOSTS:** Low plants, including blackberry, chrysanthemum, and Spanish needles.

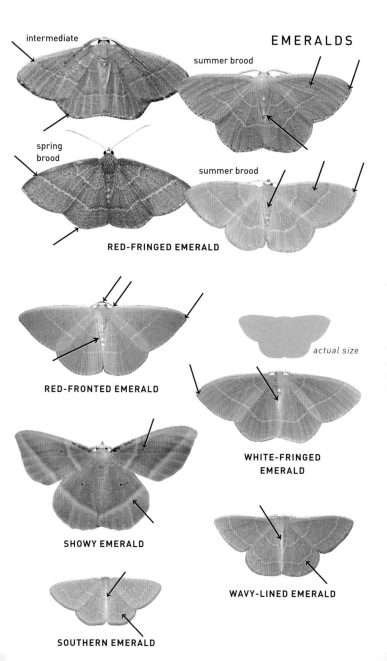

intermediate

EMERALDS

summer brood

spring brood

summer brood

RED-FRINGED EMERALD

RED-FRONTED EMERALD

actual size

WHITE-FRINGED EMERALD

SHOWY EMERALD

WAVY-LINED EMERALD

SOUTHERN EMERALD

BLACKBERRY LOOPER

Chlorochlamys chloroleucaria   7071   **Common**
WS 14–23 mm. Grainy bluish green FW has wide cream-colored
AM and PM lines and costal streak. HW has a single cream-colored median PM line. Cream-colored dorsal stripe extends
from thorax to tip of abdomen. Male has broadly bipectinate antennae. **HOSTS:** Blackberry and strawberry fruits, also petals of
composite flowers. **NOTE:** Two broods.

PISTACHIO EMERALD

Hethemia pistasciaria   7084   **Common**
WS 16–31 mm. Wings are variably deep grayish green when
fresh to dull orange-brown when worn, with fragmented white
AM and PM lines. Costa and fringe on all wings are tinged copper. HW has bluntly pointed outline. **HOSTS:** Blueberry and oak.

INFANTS   Family Geometridae, Subfamily Archiearinae

Diurnal geometrids that fly on warm sunny afternoons in early spring, often
before the snow has completely melted. Both are more likely to be confused
with early spring butterflies than with other moths. Usually found in birch-
dominated woodlands along dirt roads, open paths, or clearings.

THE INFANT   *Archiearis infans*   6256   **Common**
WS 30–33 mm. Warm brown FW has an almost complete whit-
ish median band and small white subapical patch. HW has a
large orange patch and small discal spot. **HOSTS:** Birch, also
willow and poplar.

SCARCE INFANT   *Leucobrephos brephoides*   6257   **Rare**
WS 29–30 mm. Dusky gray (sometimes paler gray) FW has a
complete white ST band and a less obvious broken basal band.
HW is mostly white with a broad black border. Appears rather
hairy. **HOSTS:** Aspen, birch, and alder.

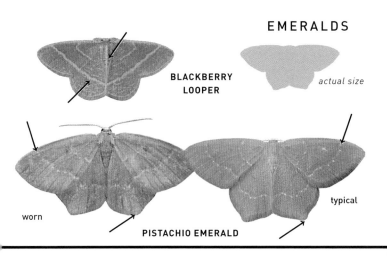

EMERALDS

BLACKBERRY LOOPER

actual size

worn

PISTACHIO EMERALD

typical

INFANTS

THE INFANT

SCARCE INFANT

207

TYPICAL GEOMETERS
Family Geometridae, Subfamily Ennominae

Flimsy, broad-winged moths that typically rest with their wings flat, although several species habitually close their wings (or almost do) over the abdomen. Females of some species are wingless, or nearly so. Wing patterns vary tremendously; several groups are difficult to identify. All will come to lights, some in large numbers. A few species, such as Fall Cankerworm, may also be observed during the day.

FALL CANKERWORM MOTH
Alsophila pometaria   6258   **Common**
TL 26–32 mm. Gray FW of male (shown) has faint white-edged AM and PM lines. PM line bends at a right angle near costa, forming a white subapical patch. Female is wingless. **HOSTS:** A wide variety of trees and members of the rose family.

COMMON SPRING MOTH   *Heliomata cycladata* 6261   **Common**
WS 17–22 mm. Mottled brown FW is marked with large white patches in inner margin and subapical areas. White HW has dark border. **HOSTS:** Black locust and honey locust.

ORANGE WING   *Mellilla xanthometata*   6271.1   **Common**
WS 16–21 mm. Grayish brown FW is marked with faint yellowish lines. Males have darker brown shading beyond almost straight PM line and a blackish spot at midpoint of ST line. HW is bright orange in males, paler in females. **HOSTS:** Locust.
NOTE: Active both day and night.

BROWN-BORDERED GEOMETER
Eumacaria madopata   6272   **Uncommon**
WS 20–25 mm. Pale lilac wings are marked with crisp brown lines. Mottled brown ST area is crossed with white veins. Apex of FW is sharply pointed. **HOSTS:** Apple, cherry, and plum.

LESSER MAPLE SPANWORM
Speranza pustularia   6273   **Common**
WS 18–28 mm. White FW is crossed with variably fragmented orange-brown lines that widen toward the costa. **HOSTS:** Maple, also birch, cherry, poplar, and coniferous trees.

CURRANT SPANWORM   *Speranza ribearia* 6274   **Uncommon**
WS 29–31 mm. Pale yellow wings are variably marked with fragmented brown lines. Midpoint of PM line is marked with a smudgy brown patch. **HOSTS:** Currant and gooseberry.

TYPICAL GEOMETERS

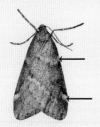

FALL CANKERWORM MOTH

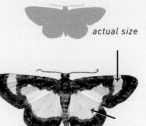

actual size

COMMON SPRING MOTH

BROWN-BORDERED GEOMETER

male

ORANGE WING

LESSER MAPLE SPANWORM

CURRANT SPANWORM

SULPHUR GRANITE *Speranza sulphurea* 6283 **Uncommon**
WS 20–25 mm. Creamy yellow to bright yellow wings have rusty brown fringe and blotches along costa and inner margin. Discal spot is often well defined. **HOSTS:** Blueberry and sweet gale.

RANNOCH LOOPER *Speranza brunneata* 6286 **Uncommon**
WS 25 mm. Yellowish brown wings are faintly marked with four darker lines. Fringes are checkered gray and brown. Often rests with wings almost closed above abdomen. **HOSTS:** Primarily blueberry but also recorded feeding on aspen, birch, and buffalo berry.

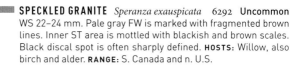

SPECKLED GRANITE *Speranza exauspicata* 6292 **Uncommon**
WS 22–24 mm. Pale gray FW is marked with fragmented brown lines. Inner ST area is mottled with blackish and brown scales. Black discal spot is often sharply defined. **HOSTS:** Willow, also birch and alder. **RANGE:** S. Canada and n. U.S.

FOUR-SPOTTED GRANITE
Speranza coortaria 6299 **Uncommon**
WS 22–26 mm. Purplish gray FW with four brown patches evenly spaced along costa. **HOSTS:** Apple, cherry, hawthorn, pear, and willow.

BARRED GRANITE *Speranza subcessaria* 6303 **Common**
WS 20–28 mm. Gray FW is variably peppered with blackish scales. Pattern of four dark patches along costa resembles Four-spotted Granite, but median bar is twice as long as other bars. **HOSTS:** Currant and gooseberry.

BLACK-BANDED ORANGE *Epelis truncataria* 6321 **Uncommon**
WS 12–20 mm. Brindled pale orange wings are marked with three white-edged black bands. **HOSTS:** Bearberry and leatherleaf. **NOTE:** This attractive diurnal moth can often be found flitting among low plants in bogs.

SPLIT-LINED GRANITE *Speranza bitactata* 6304 **Common**
WS 20–28mm. Resembles Barred Granite but midpoint of extended median bar is kinked at right angle. **HOSTS:** Alder and gooseberry.

COMMON ANGLE *Macaria aemulataria* 6326 **Common**
WS 20–22 mm. Straw-colored FW has faint brown lines accented darker on veins and at costa. Midpoint of ST area is marked with a large blackish paw-print mark. Outer margin has shallow indentation near apex. **HOSTS:** Maple.

TYPICAL GEOMETERS

female

actual size

male

SULPHUR GRANITE

RANNOCH LOOPER

SPECKLED GRANITE

BARRED GRANITE

SPLIT-LINED GRANITE

FOUR-SPOTTED GRANITE

BLACK-BANDED ORANGE

COMMON ANGLE

211

BIRCH ANGLE *Macaria notata* 6330 Uncommon
WS 25–30 mm. Resembles Common Angle but is larger with whiter wings. Large chestnut subapical patch is noticeable. **HOSTS:** Birch and alder.

BLURRY CHOCOLATE ANGLE
Macaria transitaria 6339 Uncommon
WS 23–28 mm. Purplish gray FW has faint blackish lines obvious only at costa. Warm brown ST band blends into ground color. HW is whitish with ST band of brown shading. **HOSTS:** Pine.

MINOR ANGLE *Macaria minorata* 6340 Common
WS 17–21 mm. Peppery violet gray FW has jagged lines most obvious at costa. Warm brown ST band is most obvious in subapical area. **HOSTS:** Red pine and white pine. **NOTE:** Two broods.

BICOLORED ANGLE *Macaria bicolorata* 6341 Uncommon
WS 27–32 mm. Resembles Blurry Chocolate Angle but is usually larger. Purplish gray wings are shaded brown beyond PM line, appearing two-toned. **HOSTS:** Pine.

RED-HEADED INCHWORM *Macaria bisignata* 6342 Common
WS 25–30 mm. Whitish wings are lightly peppered with gray scales. Faint brown ST line is marked with a brown spot at midpoint, ending at large blackish subapical patch. **HOSTS:** Pine.

SIX-SPOTTED ANGLE *Macaria sexmaculata* 6343 Uncommon
WS 16–24 mm. Peppery pale gray FW is marked with three even lines. Midpoint of PM and ST lines is accented with black spots. **HOSTS:** Tamarack. **NOTE:** Two broods.

PALE-MARKED ANGLE *Macaria signaria* 6344 Common
WS 20–30 mm. Pale gray FW has wavy brown lines, often most obvious at costa. Midpoint of ST area is marked with a fractured black blotch. **HOSTS:** Coniferous trees.

WHITE PINE ANGLE *Macaria pinistrobata* 6347 Common
WS 24–28 mm. Peppery whitish FW is marked with fragmented wavy black lines. ST area is marked with fractured black spot at midpoint and large black subapical patch. **HOSTS:** White pine.

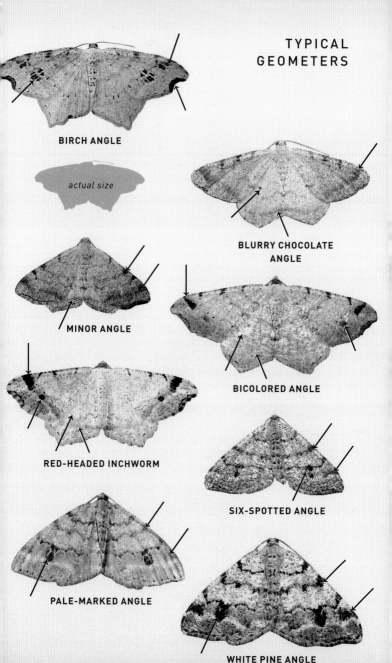

TYPICAL
GEOMETERS

BIRCH ANGLE

actual size

**BLURRY CHOCOLATE
ANGLE**

MINOR ANGLE

BICOLORED ANGLE

RED-HEADED INCHWORM

SIX-SPOTTED ANGLE

PALE-MARKED ANGLE

WHITE PINE ANGLE

HEMLOCK ANGLE *Macaria fissinotata* 6348 **Common**

WS 22–25 mm. Resembles White Pine Angle, but FW often lacks median band, except at costa. Blackish spots at midpoint of ST area and brown subapical patch are usually well developed. **HOSTS:** Hemlock and balsam fir.

OWEN'S ANGLE *Macaria oweni* 6351 **Uncommon**

WS 22–25 mm. White FW is boldly marked with fragmented black lines that widen at costa. Large black spot at midpoint of PM and ST area usually contains two thin white dashes. **HOSTS:** Tamarack.

CURVE-LINED ANGLE *Digrammia continuata* 6362 **Common**

WS 20–24 mm. Brindled whitish or gray FW is boldly marked with gently curving double AM and PM lines. Diffuse median band is sometimes present. **HOSTS:** White cedar and red cedar. **NOTE:** Two broods.

FAINT-SPOTTED ANGLE *Digrammia ocellinata* 6386 **Common**

WS 24–27 mm. Ash gray wings are marked with wide brown bands, especially in ST area. All lines are accented with black dashes along yellowish veins. **HOSTS:** Locust. **NOTE:** Two broods.

YELLOW-LINED ANGLE

Digrammia mellistrigata 6397 **Common**

WS 21–28 mm. Bluish gray FW has bold yellow-edged lines and a band of darker shading beyond kinked PM line. Median area is marked with small blackish discal spot. **HOSTS:** Willow. **RANGE:** S. Canada and n. U.S. **NOTE:** Two broods.

HOLLOW-SPOTTED ANGLE

Digrammia gnophosaria 6405 **Common**

WS 18–23 mm. Brindled grayish brown FW is faintly marked with wavy lines that widen at costa. Elliptical blackish reniform spot has a pale center. **HOSTS:** Tamarack and willow. **NOTE:** Two broods.

YELLOW-VEINED GEOMETER

Orthofidonia flavivenata 6430 **Common**

WS 26 mm. Peppery gray FW is mottled with mossy green scales when fresh. All lines are indistinct. Conspicuous yellow or orange veins extend through central median area. **HOSTS:** Blueberry. **RANGE:** Se. Canada and ne. U.S.

TYPICAL GEOMETERS

actual size

HEMLOCK ANGLE

OWEN'S ANGLE

CURVE-LINED ANGLE

YELLOW-LINED ANGLE

FAINT-SPOTTED ANGLE

HOLLOW-SPOTTED ANGLE

YELLOW-VEINED GEOMETER

SULPHUR WAVE *Hesperumia sulphuraria* 6431 **Common**
WS 29–35 mm. Pale yellow to orange FW is typically marked with fragmented brown lines, though sometimes median area is shaded brown. Large hollow discal spot is usually conspicuous. **HOSTS:** Various trees and shrubs, including cherry and snowberry. **NOTE:** Active by day and night.

CRANBERRY SPANWORM *Ematurga amitaria* 6436 **Common**
WS 25–30 mm. Bronzy brown FW is marked with dark brown lines. Female has whitish speckling along FW lines. HW is tawny with darker lines and peppering. **HOSTS:** Cranberry and rosaceous plants. **NOTE:** Mostly diurnal.

DOTTED GRAY *Glena cribrataria* 6449 **Common**
WS 23–31 mm. Whitish wings are marked with evenly spaced dotted lines. Abdomen has pairs of black spots on each segment. **HOSTS:** Poplar, spruce, and willow. **NOTE:** Two broods.

FOUR-BARRED GRAY *Aethalura intertexta* 6570 **Common**
WS 21–25 mm. Gray wings have four evenly spaced, often slightly fragmented, blackish lines that widen toward costa. Jagged ST line is edged white. **HOSTS:** Alder and birch. **NOTE:** Two broods.

LARGE PURPLISH GRAY *Iridopsis vellivolata* 6582 **Common**
WS 30–36 mm. Purplish gray FW has warm brown bands in basal and ST areas. Black AM and PM lines converge and often merge near inner margin. HW has elliptical hollow discal spot. **HOSTS:** Fir, pine, spruce, and tamarack.

PALE-WINGED GRAY *Iridopsis ephyraria* 6583 **Common**
WS 23–34 mm. Pale gray FW often has fragmented brown bands in basal and ST areas. Wavy black lines widen toward costa. PM line has a large bulge near costa before merging with wider median band. Elliptical hollow discal spots mark all wings. **HOSTS:** Trees and woody plants, including ash, balsam fir, elm, gooseberry, maple, and willow.

SMALL PURPLISH GRAY *Iridopsis humaria* 6584 **Common**
WS 24–28 mm. Resembles Large Purplish Gray but is smaller with more rounded FW. Indistinct median line merges with PM line near inner margin. **HOSTS:** Trees and low plants, including alfalfa, white birch, clover, hickory, and soybean.

TYPICAL GEOMETERS

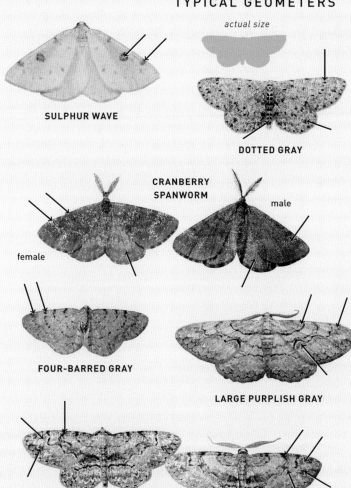

actual size

SULPHUR WAVE

DOTTED GRAY

CRANBERRY SPANWORM

female

male

FOUR-BARRED GRAY

LARGE PURPLISH GRAY

PALE-WINGED GRAY

SMALL PURPLISH GRAY

BENT-LINE GRAY *Iridopsis larvaria*   6588   **Common**
WS 26–36 mm. Resembles Pale-winged Gray, but wings tend to have sharper black lines and outlines to elliptical spots. HW has a sharp kink in PM line. **HOSTS:** Deciduous trees, including alder, birch, black cherry, maple, and willow. **NOTE:** Two broods.

COMMON GRAY *Anavitrinella pampinaria*   6590   **Common**
WS 23–34 mm. Peppery pale gray FW is marked with crisp black lines that often widen toward inner margin. Abdomen has white band at base. **HOSTS:** Deciduous trees and plants, including apple, ash, clover, cotton, and poplar. **NOTE:** Two broods.

DOUBLE-LINED GRAY *Cleora sublunaria*   6594   **Common**
WS 25–30 mm. Resembles Common Gray, but whitish or gray FW has double AM line. Midpoint of ST area is often marked with a whitish patch, especially on darker individuals. Elliptical hollow discal spots mark all wings. **HOSTS:** Sweet fern.

SMALL ENGRAILED *Ectropis crepuscularia*   6597   **Common**
WS 26–37 mm. Variable. Peppery wings are marked with toothed black lines, often heaviest on veins. Midpoint of ST area has two sharp wedges. Pale extremes are whitish with wide PM band. Melanics are sooty brown with white ST line. **HOSTS:** Various trees, including apple, birch, elm, hemlock, oak, poplar, spruce, tamarack, and willow. **NOTE:** Two broods.

PORCELAIN GRAY *Protoboarmia porcelaria*   6598   **Common**
WS 26–35 mm. Peppery gray wings are marked with bold blackish lines. PM and whitish zigzag ST lines are accented with black wedges on veins. **HOSTS:** Deciduous and coniferous trees, including cedar, balsam fir, hemlock, pine, birch, elm, and oak.

TULIP-TREE BEAUTY *Epimecis hortaria*   6599   **Common**
WS 43–57 mm. Large. Peppery gray FW has white-edged scalloped lines, sometimes accented with brown scales. Blackish median band merges with PM line. Melanics are slaty with white-edged lines. **HOSTS:** Deciduous trees, including pawpaw, poplar, sassafras, and tulip tree.

CANADIAN MELANOLOPHIA
Melanolophia canadaria   6620   **Common**
WS 36–39 mm. Pale gray FW is marked with fragmented lines. Wavy PM line is double at midpoint and inner margin, forming two darker patches. **HOSTS:** Various trees and shrubs, including alder, ash, birch, blueberry, elm, locust, maple, pine, tamarack, and willow.

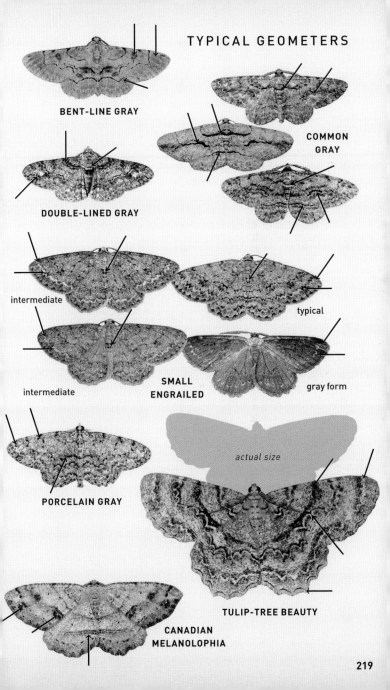

TYPICAL GEOMETERS

BENT-LINE GRAY

COMMON GRAY

DOUBLE-LINED GRAY

intermediate

typical

intermediate

SMALL ENGRAILED

gray form

PORCELAIN GRAY

actual size

TULIP-TREE BEAUTY

CANADIAN MELANOLOPHIA

SIGNATE MELANOLOPHIA

Melanolophia signataria   6621   **Common**

WS 30–35 mm. Resembles Canadian Melanolophia, but light brown FW is more uniform, with straighter PM line that is double only at inner margin. **HOSTS:** Various trees, including alder, birch, elm, fir, maple, oak, spruce, and tamarack.

POWDER MOTH   *Eufidonia notataria*   6638   **Common**

WS 20–26 mm. Mottled white FW has diffuse brown bands along jagged lines. Female is less heavily marked than male. HW is pale with fragmented lines. Large black discal spots mark all wings. **HOSTS:** Coniferous trees, including fir, hemlock, pine, spruce, and tamarack.

SHARP-LINED POWDER MOTH

Eufidonia discospilata   6639   **Common**

WS 20–26 mm. Resembles Powder Moth (many individuals cannot be safely identified) but typically has wide sooty bands along lines and in terminal area. HW is more peppery than in Powder Moth and often shows three bold lines. Female is less heavily marked than male. **HOSTS:** Deciduous trees and shrubs, including alder, birch, blueberry, Labrador tea, laurel, and willow.

PEPPER-AND-SALT GEOMETER

Biston betularia   6640   **Common**

WS 40–45 mm. Long wings of typical form are peppered pale gray with wavy black AM and PM lines. Melanics are sooty black. **HOSTS:** Various trees and shrubs, including alder, birch, cherry, dogwood, elm, tamarack, and willow. **NOTE:** One or two broods.

STOUT SPANWORM   *Lycia ursaria*   6651   **Common**

WS 30–35 mm. Peppery pale gray FW is marked with closely spaced, almost parallel, black AM, median, and PM lines. Female (not shown) has wings but is flightless. Abdomen and thorax are extremely hairy. **HOSTS:** Deciduous trees and woody plants, including alder, ash, birch, cherry, cranberry, maple, and poplar.

TYPICAL GEOMETERS

SIGNATE MELANOLOPHIA

actual size

POWDER MOTH

male

female

male

SHARP-LINED POWDER MOTH

female

PEPPER-AND-SALT GEOMETER

typical

melanic

STOUT SPANWORM

ONE-SPOTTED VARIANT

Hypagyrtis unipunctata 6654 **Common**

WS 20–47 mm. Sexually and seasonally variable. In typical form, peppery FW is pale gray or yellowish brown marked with fragmented black lines. Spring broods typically more contrastingly colored than summer broods. Melanics are sooty with brown ST band. Both forms nearly always have midpoint of ST line accented with one or more pale spots. Outer margin of wings is scalloped, especially in larger female. **HOSTS:** Various trees, including alder, birch, fir, hickory, oak, pine, and willow. **NOTE:** Two or more broods.

PINE MEASURINGWORM MOTH

Hypagyrtis piniata 6656 **Common**

WS 28–32 mm. Resembles One-spotted Variant but is typically smaller and grayer with indistinct blackish lines. Whitish ST line is accented with a larger white spot at midpoint. Large black discal spots mark all wings. **HOSTS:** Coniferous trees, including fir, hemlock, pine, and tamarack.

THE HALF-WING *Phigalia titea* 6658 **Common**

WS 30–40 mm. Typically, peppery pale gray FW has wavy AM and PM lines that are sometimes doubled. Straight median band does not touch PM line. Melanics are sooty with black veins. Female (not shown) is wingless. **HOSTS:** Deciduous trees and woody plants, including basswood, blueberry, elm, hickory, maple, and oak.

TOOTHED PHIGALIA *Phigalia denticulata* 6659 **Common**

WS 30–37 mm. Resembles The Half-Wing but is usually smaller; PM line on FW is jagged, especially near costa. Slightly wavy median line almost touches PM line at inner margin. Flightless female (not shown) has vestigial wings. **HOSTS:** Unknown.

SMALL PHIGALIA *Phigalia strigataria* 6660 **Common**

WS 30–38 mm. Resembles Toothed Phigalia, but often fragmented PM line is straighter near inner margin. Flightless female (not shown) has tiny wings. **HOSTS:** Elm, and probably other deciduous trees.

SPRING CANKERWORM *Paleacrita vernata* 6662 **Common**

TL 16–19 mm. Silvery FW of male is marked with pattern of incomplete black lines and veins. Apical dash is connected to outer PM line. Female (not shown) is wingless. **HOSTS:** Deciduous trees, including apple, birch, cherry, elm, maple, and oak.

TYPICAL GEOMETERS

typical

ONE-SPOTTED VARIANT

melanic

PINE MEASURINGWORM MOTH

actual size

melanic

typical

THE HALF-WING

TOOTHED PHIGALIA

SMALL PHIGALIA

SPRING CANKERWORM

LINDEN LOOPER *Erannis tiliaria* 6665   **Common**

WS 32–42 mm. Wings of male are light brown, often with darker bands along wavy AM and PM lines. Wingless female (not shown) has pale abdomen blotched black. **HOSTS:** Deciduous trees, including ash, birch, beech, elm, maple, oak, and poplar.

BLUISH SPRING MOTH

Lomographa semiclarata 6666   **Common**

WS 23–28 mm. Wings are usually closed tightly above abdomen at rest. Underside of wings is white with dotted ST and terminal lines and bold black discal spots. Upper surface of FW is bluish gray with diffuse brownish lines. **HOSTS:** Trees and low plants, including alder, Juneberry, chokeberry, hawthorn, and poplar. **NOTE:** Mostly diurnal.

WHITE SPRING MOTH

Lomographa vestaliata 6667   **Common**

WS 15–26 mm. Semi-translucent white wings are without obvious marking. Underside of FW is tinged yellowish brown along costa. **HOSTS:** Deciduous trees and shrubs, including apple, beech, cherry, hawthorn, maple, and snowberry.

GRAY SPRING MOTH

Lomographa glomeraria 6668   **Common**

WS 22–25 mm. Peppery pale gray wings are marked with faint scalloped lines and blackish discal spots. **HOSTS:** *Prunus* species.

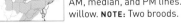

YELLOW-DUSTED CREAM

Cabera erythemaria 6677   **Common**

WS 27–30 mm. Whitish wings are patterned with wide yellowish AM, median, and PM lines. **HOSTS:** Birch, blueberry, poplar, and willow. **NOTE:** Two broods.

THE VESTAL *Cabera variolaria* 6678   **Common**

WS 22–25 mm. All wings are uniformly satin white. Front of head and forelegs are tinted yellow or orange. **HOSTS:** Poplar and willow. **NOTE:** Up to three broods. Also known as Pink-striped Willow Spanworm.

BLACK-DOTTED RUDDY *Ilecta intractata* 6711   **Common**

WS 21–31 mm. Wings are variably dark brown, reddish brown, or ochre, and have three, often indistinct, dark lines. Small black discal spots on all wings. **HOSTS:** American holly.

TYPICAL GEOMETERS

LINDEN LOOPER

BLUISH SPRING MOTH

actual size

WHITE SPRING MOTH

GRAY SPRING MOTH

YELLOW-DUSTED CREAM

THE VESTAL

BLACK-DOTTED RUDDY

COMMON LYTROSIS *Lytrosis unitaria* 6720 **Common**
WS 45–57 mm. Wings are variably pale gray or yellowish with reddish brown shading beyond PM line. Fine black lines create a barklike pattern. Larger females are generally grayer than males. **HOSTS:** Hawthorn, pin oak, and sugar maple.

THE SAW-WING *Euchlaena serrata* 6724 **Common**
WS 40–53 mm. Pale yellow wings are shaded chocolate brown beyond straight PM line. Incomplete AM line and small discal spots are present on all wings. **HOSTS:** Apple, blueberry, and maple.

MUZARIA EUCHLAENA *Euchlaena muzaria* 6725 **Common**
WS 27–48 mm. Peppery purplish brown wings are often slightly darker beyond curved PM line. Tiny black discal spots mark all wings. **HOSTS:** Black cherry and chokecherry. **NOTE:** One or two broods.

JOHNSON'S EUCHLAENA
Euchlaena johnsonaria 6729 **Common**
WS 26–37 mm. Resembles Muzaria Euchlaena, but tawny brown wings are marked with sharper black lines and veins. ST line is often marked with blackish blotches. **HOSTS:** Deciduous trees and shrubs, including ash, birch, elm, hawthorn, and willow. **NOTE:** Two broods.

DEEP YELLOW EUCHLAENA
Euchlaena amoenaria 6733 **Common**
WS 30–49 mm. Peppery yellowish wings are shaded rusty brown along AM line and beyond median line. Apex of FW and outer margin of HW are speckled whitish. Small discal dots mark all wings. **HOSTS:** Unknown. **NOTE:** Two broods.

MOTTLED EUCHLAENA *Euchlaena tigrinaria* 6737 **Common**
WS 33–41 mm. Variably earth brown to orange, speckled and blotched blackish. AM and PM lines are crisply edged yellow. Black apical dash on FW is edged with a pale patch. **HOSTS:** White birch, also oak, poplar, and willow.

LEAST-MARKED EUCHLAENA
Euchlaena irraria 6739 **Common**
WS 37–48 mm. Yellowish brown FW has diffuse brown shading beyond inner section of curved PM line. Tiny black discal dots mark all wings. **HOSTS:** Oak.

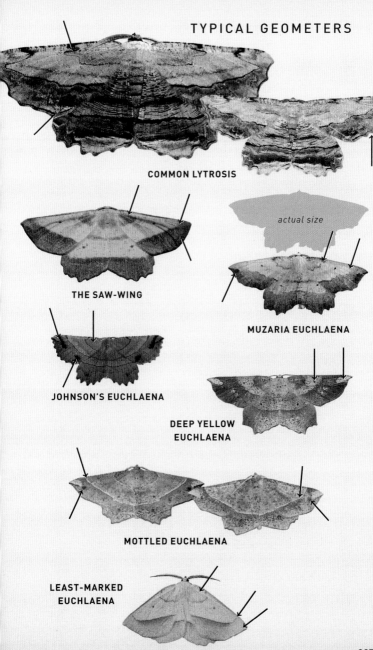

TYPICAL GEOMETERS

COMMON LYTROSIS

actual size

THE SAW-WING

MUZARIA EUCHLAENA

JOHNSON'S EUCHLAENA

DEEP YELLOW EUCHLAENA

MOTTLED EUCHLAENA

LEAST-MARKED EUCHLAENA

227

FALSE CROCUS GEOMETER

Xanthotype urticaria　6740　　　　　　　　**Common**
WS 30–40 mm. Yellow wings are variably speckled and blotched purplish brown. PM line is sometimes a complete band. Males are typically more heavily patterned than larger females. **HOSTS:** Various trees and low plants, including catnip, goldenrod, ground ivy, and dogwood. **NOTE:** One or two broods.

CROCUS GEOMETER　*Xanthotype sospeta*　6743　　**Common**

WS 35–48 mm. Resembles False Crocus Geometer (many individuals cannot be reliably identified to species) but is typically paler yellow with sparse brown blotching. **HOSTS:** Deciduous trees and shrubs, including basswood, blueberry, cherry, currant, elm, maple, rose, and viburnum. **NOTE:** One or two broods.

HONEST PERO　*Pero honestaria*　6753　　　　**Common**

WS 34–36 mm. Broad FW is variably gray (male) or violet brown (female) with paler ST area beyond wavy black PM line. Inner PM line is relatively straight. Has a pronounced costal fold in outer third of FW at rest. **HOSTS:** Black cherry, black locust, and tamarack. **NOTE:** Two broods.

MORRISON'S PERO　*Pero morrisonaria*　6755　　**Common**

WS 34–40 mm. Resembles Honest Pero, but FW is light brown in both sexes, often heavily speckled darker. Costa is typically paler. PM line has a small indentation before reaching costa. **HOSTS:** Coniferous trees, including fir, pine, spruce, and tamarack. **NOTE:** Two broods.

OAK BEAUTY　*Phaeoura quernaria*　6763　　　**Common**

WS 37–56 mm. Charcoal gray wings of male (shown) are variably mottled brown and white along jagged lines. Larger females tend to show wider white bands. Dark individuals are sooty with white edges on lines restricted to costa. **HOSTS:** Deciduous trees, including basswood, birch, elm, oak, and poplar. **NOTE:** Two broods.

PALE BEAUTY　*Campaea perlata*　6796　　　　**Common**

WS 28–51 mm. Whitish wings are suffused pale green to varying degrees. White-edged green AM and PM lines curve inward at costa. **HOSTS:** Deciduous trees, including alder, birch, elm, oak, and willow. **NOTE:** One or two broods.

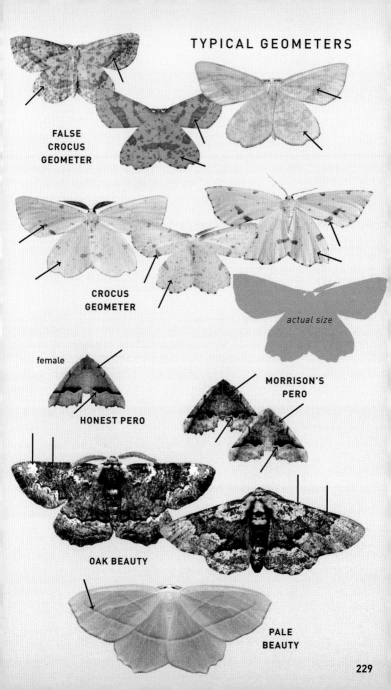

TYPICAL GEOMETERS

FALSE CROCUS GEOMETER

CROCUS GEOMETER

actual size

female

HONEST PERO

MORRISON'S PERO

OAK BEAUTY

PALE BEAUTY

229

MAPLE SPANWORM *Ennomos magnaria* 6797 **Common**
WS 43–60 mm. Unevenly scalloped wings are pale orange, variably speckled and blotched brown. Rests with its wings raised about 45 degrees above the horizontal. **HOSTS:** Deciduous trees, including alder, basswood, maple, oak, and poplar.

ELM SPANWORM *Ennomos subsignaria* 6798 **Common**
WS 35–40 mm. White wings are often tinged greenish along costa. Undersides of wings are marked with small black discal spots. Bipectinate antennae are lime green. Rests with its wings held tightly compressed above abdomen. **HOSTS:** Deciduous trees and shrubs, including apple, birch, elm, maple, and oak.

NORTHERN PETROPHORA
Petrophora subaequaria 6804 **Common**
WS 19 mm. Speckled tan FW has yellowish veins and brown shading inside uneven ST line. White-edged AM and PM lines are parallel. Pale HW is marked with faintly dotted lines. All wings show tiny black discal dots. **HOSTS:** Ferns.

NORTHERN PALE ALDER
Tacparia atropunctata 6806 **Common**
WS 24 mm. Violet gray FW is marked with speckled blackish AM and PM lines. Diffuse brown PM band continues onto HW. Tiny black discal dots are faint. ST area is tinged brown. **HOSTS:** Sweet gale and sweet fern.

PALE ALDER *Tacparia detersata* 6807 **Common**
WS 19 mm. Whitish FW is faintly brindled with brown lines. Diffuse brown PM band is accented with black dots. Pale HW has faint brown median band. ST area is tinged brown. **HOSTS:** Alder.

PALE HOMOCHLODES
Homochlodes fritillaria 6812 **Common**
WS 28–30 mm. FW is variably pale tan to grayish brown with faint dotted lines. A diffuse brown band in PM area is accented with white dots, usually forming a patch at midpoint. **HOSTS:** Ferns.

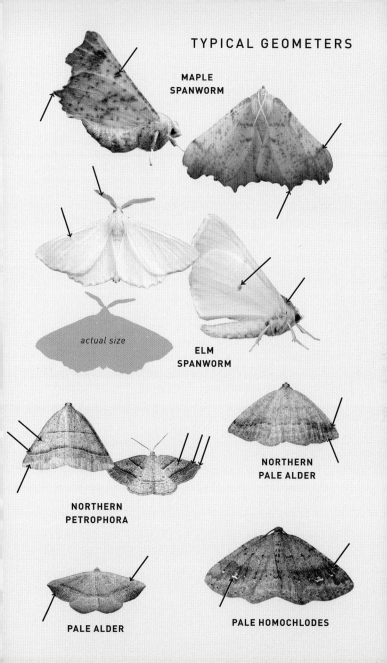

TYPICAL GEOMETERS

**MAPLE
SPANWORM**

**ELM
SPANWORM**

actual size

**NORTHERN
PETROPHORA**

**NORTHERN
PALE ALDER**

PALE ALDER

PALE HOMOCHLODES

NORTHERN THORN *Selenia alciphearia* 6817 Uncommon

WS 35 mm. Wings are closed tightly above abdomen at rest. Underside of HW has a straight black median line and white PM line with a white crescent between them. Underside of FW is similar but with costa speckled white. Upper surfaces of wings are orange with brown lines. **HOSTS:** Deciduous trees and woody plants, including alder, birch, cherry, currant, hickory, and maple. **NOTE:** Two broods.

KENT'S GEOMETER *Selenia kentaria* 6818 Uncommon

WS 33–52 mm. Resembles Northern Thorn, but underside of HW has broader black median line and wider white band beyond PM line. Upper surface of FW typically has more white along costa and wider white band beyond PM line. **HOSTS:** Deciduous trees, including basswood, beech, birch, elm, maple, and oak. **NOTE:** One or two broods.

PALE METANEMA *Metanema inatomaria* 6819 Common

WS 26–36 mm. Dove gray wings are marked with paler veins and rust-edged yellowish lines. PM line ends before apex. Discal spot on FW is orange. **HOSTS:** Poplar and willow. **NOTE:** Two broods.

DARK METANEMA *Metanema determinata* 6820 Common

WS 23–30 mm. Resembles Pale Metanema but is darker and more peppery. Whitish veins are often prominent. Bold PM line ends at apex. Discal dot on FW is black. **HOSTS:** Ash, aspen, and willow. **NOTE:** One or two broods.

WARNER'S METARRANTHIS

Metarranthis warneri 6821 Uncommon

WS 32–35 mm. Grayish brown FW has pale-edged AM and PM lines that converge toward inner margin. Median area is shaded brown along lines. Tiny blackish discal dots mark all wings. **HOSTS:** Cherry, dogwood, and willow. **RANGE:** S. Canada and n. U.S.

RUDDY METARRANTHIS

Metarranthis duaria 6822 Common

WS 35–40 mm. Resembles Warner's Metarranthis, but wings are tinted purplish or reddish. Blackish lines are often fragmented across veins. Short black apical dash is often present. **HOSTS:** Deciduous trees and shrubs, including alder, birch, blueberry, hawthorn, rose, and willow.

TYPICAL GEOMETERS

NORTHERN THORN

KENT'S GEOMETER

PALE METANEMA

ACTUAL SIZE

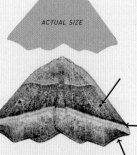

DARK METANEMA

**WARNER'S
METARRANTHIS**

RUDDY METARRANTHIS

SCALLOPED METARRANTHIS COMPLEX

Metarranthis sp.   6823/25   **Common**

WS 32–43 mm. *Metarranthis hypocharia, angularia,* and *inde-clinata* overlap greatly in appearance; many can only be identi-fied by genitalia. Median area is generally darker than PM area and marked by four small, dark discal spots. Angled (*M. angu-laria*) is often more rusty on average, while Pale (*M. indeclinata*) tends toward straw-colored, but many intermediates exist and Scalloped (*M. hypocharia*) may resemble either. **HOSTS:** Includes apple, blueberry, cherry, persimmon, and sassafras.

YELLOW-WASHED METARRANTHIS

Metarranthis obfirmaria   6832   **Common**

WS 26–36 mm. Peppery brown wings often have contrasting paler median area. Rusty-edged AM and PM lines converge to-ward inner margin on FW. **HOSTS:** Blueberry, chokecherry, and oak.

DARK SCALLOP MOTH   *Cepphis decoloraria*   6834   **Common**

WS 26–33 mm. Dark bluish gray wings are marked with con-trasting blackish median bands. Other lines are lightly brindled with pale scales. All wings have black-edged scalloped inden-tations along outer margin. **HOSTS:** Blackberry. **NOTE:** One or two broods.

SCALLOP MOTH   *Cepphis armataria*   6835   **Common**

WS 26–33 mm. Brindled tawny FW has paler costal streak and slightly wavy parallel brown lines. PM line is double. HW is suf-fused purple beyond median line. **HOSTS:** Trees and shrubs, in-cluding apple, birch, gooseberry, and maple. **NOTE:** One or two broods.

AMERICAN BARRED UMBER

Plagodis pulveraria   6836   **Common**

WS 26–32 mm. Purplish brown or straw-colored FW has darker maroon median area between straight AM and bulging PM lines. **HOSTS:** Deciduous trees, including birch, hazelnut, haw-thorn, and willow.

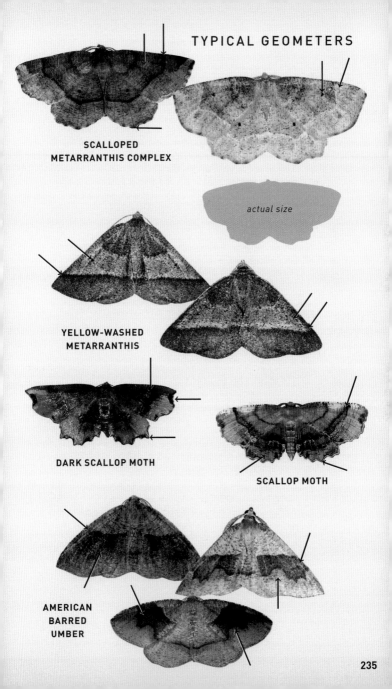

TYPICAL GEOMETERS

SCALLOPED
METARRANTHIS COMPLEX

actual size

YELLOW-WASHED
METARRANTHIS

DARK SCALLOP MOTH

SCALLOP MOTH

AMERICAN
BARRED
UMBER

ALIEN PROBOLE *Probole alienaria* 6837 **Common**
WS 23–34 mm. Variable. Wings are typically whitish, brindled with brown streaks and with darker veins. Midpoint of PM line on FW is sharply pointed. Many Probole individuals are not reliably identified to species and are best left as *Probole* sp. **HOSTS:** Various deciduous trees, shrubs, and woody plants. **NOTE:** Two broods.

FRIENDLY PROBOLE *Probole amicaria* 6838 **Common**
WS 23–34 mm. Strongly resembles Alien Probole and is likewise highly variable in appearance but wings may be more consistently shaded purple beyond PM line, with stronger black markings. Tooth of PM line is typically blunted, not sharp. **HOSTS:** Red osier dogwood. **NOTE:** Two broods, Apr.–Aug.

LEMON PLAGODIS *Plagodis serinaria* 6840 **Common**
WS 30–38 mm. Pale lemon yellow FW is faintly marked with brown lines and pinkish shading along costa and inner ST area. PM line is boldest near inner margin. **HOSTS:** Deciduous trees, including aspen, basswood, black cherry, and oak.

PURPLE PLAGODIS *Plagodis kuetzingi* 6841 **Uncommon**
WS 22–26 mm. Light brown FW is suffused deep purple beyond curved PM line. Costal streak and inner ST area are speckled with whitish scales. **HOSTS:** Ash.

STRAIGHT-LINED PLAGODIS

Plagodis phlogosaria 6842 **Common**
WS 21–33 mm. Seasonally variable. FW of spring brood is pale tan, suffused with purple shading along lines; summer brood is more uniformly orange with blackish scaling in inner ST area. Solid black discal spots mark all wings. **HOSTS:** Deciduous trees, including alder, basswood, birch, black cherry, and chokecherry. **NOTE:** Two broods.

FERVID PLAGODIS *Plagodis fervidaria* 6843 **Common**
WS 23–31 mm. Seasonally variable. FW of spring brood is yellowish, strongly brindled with thin brown lines with purple shading along inner PM line. Summer brood is more uniformly light brown with fragmented PM line. Black discal spots mark all wings in summer brood. **HOSTS:** Various trees, including ash, birch, maple, oak, and spruce. **NOTE:** Two broods.

TYPICAL GEOMETERS

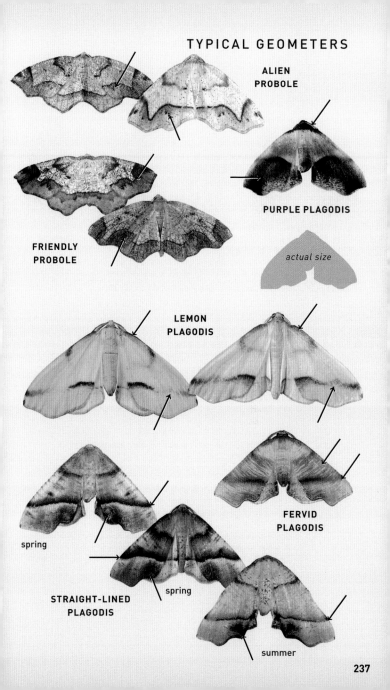

ALIEN PROBOLE

PURPLE PLAGODIS

FRIENDLY PROBOLE

actual size

LEMON PLAGODIS

FERVID PLAGODIS

spring

STRAIGHT-LINED PLAGODIS

spring

summer

HOLLOW-SPOTTED PLAGODIS

Plagodis alcoolaria   6844   **Common**

WS 26–35 mm. Resembles Straight-lined Plagodis but is not so seasonally variable. Well-defined PM line often curves outward slightly toward apex. Discal spots are often hollow. Median area is often strongly brindled with brown streaks. **HOSTS:** Deciduous trees, including basswood, beech, chestnut, maple, and oak. **NOTE:** Two broods.

GRAY SPRUCE LOOPER   *Caripeta divisata*   6863   **Common**

WS 27–38 mm. Grayish brown FW is lightly brindled darker. Darker median area (sometimes fragmented) bordered with jagged, white-edged AM and PM lines. Large white discal spot is conspicuous. **HOSTS:** Coniferous trees, including hemlock, spruce, and white pine.

NORTHERN PINE LOOPER   *Caripeta piniata*   6864   **Common**

WS 27–38 mm. Pale orange FW has darker shading along sinuous white PM line. ST area is streaked white along veins. Basal and median areas are marked with white dashes. **HOSTS:** Pine.

BROWN PINE LOOPER   *Caripeta angustiorata*   6867   **Common**

WS 28–31 mm. Rusty brown FW with thick white lines and pale costal streak. Sharply pointed AM line protrudes into median area. Discal spot is white. Basal and ST areas are speckled pale gray. **HOSTS:** Pine, also fir, spruce, and tamarack.

STRAW BESMA   *Besma endropiaria*   6884   **Common**

WS 30–36 mm. Semi-translucent pale tan wings are often faintly peppered brown. Brown lines are often incomplete, apart from well-defined PM line on FW. Lacks discal spots on wings. **HOSTS:** Maple, also alder, birch, and oak.

OAK BESMA   *Besma quercivoraria*   6885   **Common**

WS 27–41 mm. Sexually dimorphic. Females are paler and less boldly patterned than males and can resemble Straw Besma. Pale FW is often finely peppered brown. AM and PM lines are often noticeable, whereas ST line is faint. Some individuals show prominent orange or brown veins or have brown shading in inner ST area. Tiny black discal spots usually mark all wings. **HOSTS:** Oak, birch, elm, poplar, willow, and white spruce. **NOTE:** Two broods.

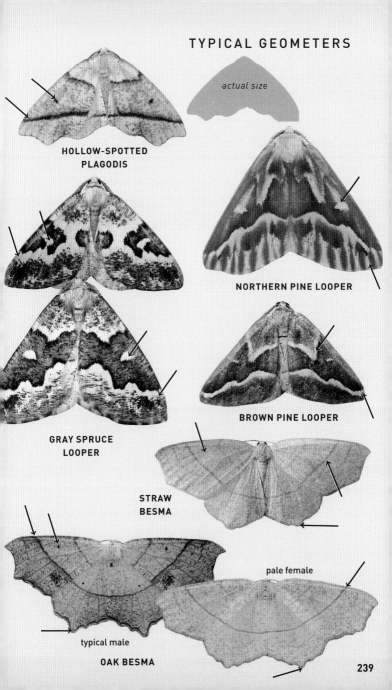

TYPICAL GEOMETERS

actual size

HOLLOW-SPOTTED PLAGODIS

NORTHERN PINE LOOPER

GRAY SPRUCE LOOPER

BROWN PINE LOOPER

STRAW BESMA

pale female

typical male

OAK BESMA

HEMLOCK LOOPER *Lambdina fiscellaria* 6888 **Common**
WS 29–45 mm. Semi-translucent grayish brown FW is heavily peppered darker. Yellow-edged purplish PM line is strongly kinked. **HOSTS:** Various trees, including hemlock, balsam fir, white spruce, and oak.

CURVE-LINED LOOPER *Lambdina fervidaria* 6894 **Common**
WS 25–37 mm. Resembles Hemlock Looper, but wide, purplish brown AM and PM lines are slightly curved. Head is pale yellow. **HOSTS:** Deciduous trees, including ironwood, birch, and oak. **NOTE:** Two broods.

CHAIN-DOTTED GEOMETER *Cingilia catenaria* 6898 **Common**
WS 30–40 mm. White or pearly gray wings have finely etched jagged black lines. Terminal line is dotted. Head and "shoulders" are pale orange. **HOSTS:** Trees and low plants, including alder, blueberry, goldenrod, maple, oak, pine, and willow.

FALSE HEMLOCK LOOPER *Nepytia canosaria* 6906 **Common**
WS 23–30 mm. Peppery FW is variably white to dark gray, boldly marked with toothed black lines and veins. Black discal spot is conspicuous. **HOSTS:** Coniferous trees, including fir, hemlock, and spruce.

SHARP-LINED YELLOW *Sicya macularia* 6912 **Common**
WS 24–35 mm. Speckled yellow FW has large cinnamon brown patch in inner ST area. Basal and median areas are marked with tiny black dots. Rests with wings tented. **HOSTS:** Trees and shrubs, including alder, blueberry, poplar, and willow. **NOTE:** Two broods.

CONFUSED EUSARCA *Eusarca confusaria* 6941 **Common**
WS 30–40 mm. Peppery FW is variably pale gray or straw-colored, sometimes shaded darker in median area. Faint AM line is rounded. Straight yellow-edged PM line fades before reaching apex. All wings are marked with tiny black discal spots. **HOSTS:** Composites, including aster, dandelion, and goldenrod.

YELLOW SLANT-LINE *Tetracis crocallata* 6963 **Common**
WS 25–45 mm. Creamy yellow FW has a thick brown PM line that slants from midpoint of inner margin to apex. In second brood, slightly paler HW has a brown median line. Tiny black discal dots mark all wings. **HOSTS:** Alder, chestnut, sumac, and willow. **NOTE:** Two broods.

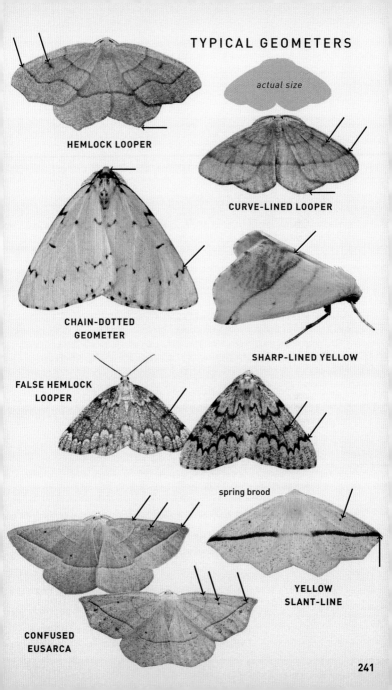

TYPICAL GEOMETERS

actual size

HEMLOCK LOOPER

CURVE-LINED LOOPER

CHAIN-DOTTED GEOMETER

SHARP-LINED YELLOW

FALSE HEMLOCK LOOPER

spring brood

CONFUSED EUSARCA

YELLOW SLANT-LINE

241

WHITE SLANT-LINE *Tetracis cachexiata* 6964 **Common**
WS 34–50 mm. White FW has bold pale orange PM line that slants from midpoint of inner margin to apex. HW is uniformly white. **HOSTS:** Deciduous trees and shrubs, including alder, birch, poplar, and willow.

SNOWY GEOMETER *Eugonobapta nivosaria* 6965 **Common**
WS 21–33 mm. Snowy white wings are without markings. Outer margin of HW has distinctive point. Sometimes shows tiny black discal spots on undersides of all wings. **HOSTS:** Unknown. **NOTE:** Two broods.

CURVE-TOOTHED GEOMETER
Eutrapela clemataria 6966 **Common**
WS 38–56 mm. FW is variably light brown to dark purplish brown, shaded darker in median area. Yellow PM line curves sharply inward near costa. Slightly scalloped HW has yellow median line. **HOSTS:** Deciduous trees, including ash, basswood, birch, elm, and poplar. **NOTE:** Two broods, spring generation more numerous.

JUNIPER-TWIG GEOMETER
Patalene olyzonaria 6974 **Common**
WS 32–39 mm. FW is variably grayish tan to orange with faint AM line and bold blackish PM line that kinks inward before reaching costa. Often shows blackish blotches in ST area. Apex is hooked, especially in female. **HOSTS:** Juniper, also white cedar and possibly pine. **NOTE:** Two or more broods.

LARGE MAPLE SPANWORM
Prochoerodes lineola 6982 **Common**
WS 43–46 mm. Variable. Pale yellow to purplish brown FW is marked with pale-edged AM and PM lines. Often has zigzag or dotted ST line. HW has straight median line. Tiny black discal dots mark all wings. **HOSTS:** Deciduous trees and low plants, including apple, birch, blueberry, cherry, grasses, oak, and poplar.

VARIABLE ANTEPIONE *Antepione thisoaria* 6987 **Common**
WS 27–40 mm. Seasonally and sexually dimorphic. Both sexes of spring brood have brown FW marked with black triangular subapical patch and a dusky smudge along inner PM line. Wings are yellow in summer brood, with male having reddish brown shading beyond PM line. **HOSTS:** Deciduous trees and shrubs, including apple, maple, and sumac. **NOTE:** Two broods.

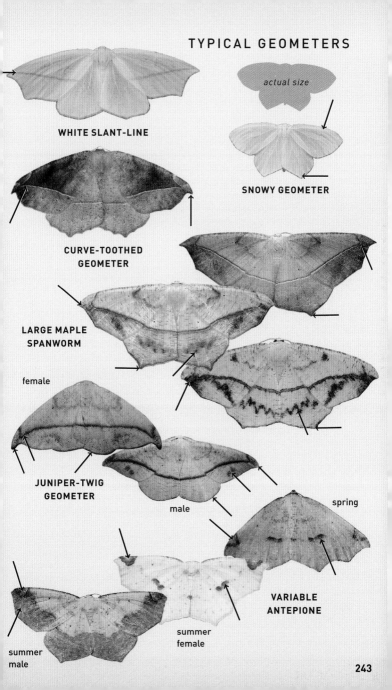

TYPICAL GEOMETERS

actual size

WHITE SLANT-LINE

SNOWY GEOMETER

CURVE-TOOTHED GEOMETER

LARGE MAPLE SPANWORM

female

JUNIPER-TWIG GEOMETER

male

spring

VARIABLE ANTEPIONE

summer female

summer male

HORNED SPANWORM *Nematocampa resistaria* 7010 **Common**
WS 19–25 mm. Yellowish wings have a network pattern of brown veins and lines. Median and PM lines converge twice before veering apart at costa. ST area is extensively shaded purplish brown on all wings. **HOSTS:** Deciduous trees and plants, including apple, birch, maple, oak, and strawberry. **NOTE:** One or two broods.

SACK-BEARERS Family Mimallonidae

Two hairy, stout-bodied moths that rest with their wings flat or slightly drooped. Both have an indentation in outer margin of the FW, creating a hook-tipped appearance. Larvae build open-ended "sacks" of silk and leaves in which they overwinter and pupate in the spring. Both species are generally uncommon in their oak woodland habitat. Strictly nocturnal, adults will come to lights in small numbers.

SCALLOPED SACK-BEARER
Lacosoma chiridota 7659 Uncommon
WS 20–32 mm. Pale orange FW has darker shading (brown in male, orange in female) in median area. Brown PM line is sinuous. Elongated reniform spot is boldly marked in black. **HOSTS:** Oak.

MELSHEIMER'S SACK-BEARER
Cicinnus melsheimeri 7662 Uncommon
TL 21–26 mm. Ghostly pearl gray FW is sprinkled with dusky scales and flushed pinkish orange in median area and along veins. Black PM line curves inward near costa. Bar-shaped reniform spot is black. **HOSTS:** Oak, mainly scrub oak northward.

APATELODID MOTHS Family Apatelodidae

Two medium-sized woodland moths that rest in spectacular, acrobatic headstand positions with the abdomen raised high above the thorax. The Angel holds its wings flatly together, whereas Spotted Apatelodes fans its wings apart. Both are nocturnal and will visit lights in small numbers.

SPOTTED APATELODES *Apatelodes torrefacta* 7663 **Common**
TL 18–22 mm. Gray FW is marked with faint blackish lines that widen near inner margin and a black basal patch. Translucent dot near apex is more obvious from underside. Thorax has thick black band. **HOSTS:** Deciduous trees, including ash, maple, and oak. **NOTE:** Two broods.

TYPICAL GEOMETERS

HORNED SPANWORM

actual size

SACK-BEARERS

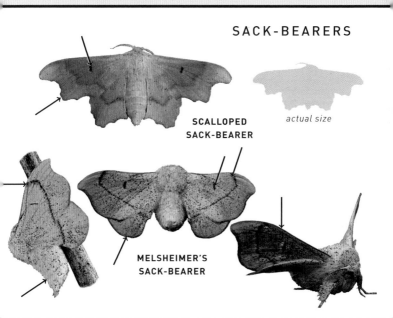

SCALLOPED SACK-BEARER

actual size

MELSHEIMER'S SACK-BEARER

APATELODID MOTHS

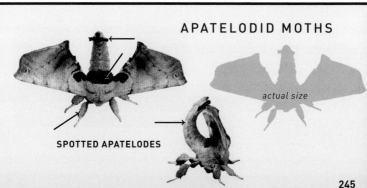

SPOTTED APATELODES

actual size

245

THE ANGEL *Olceclostera angelica* 7665 **Common**
TL 18–22 mm. Gray FW has brown bands along dotted lines. Midpoint of ST line is marked with two large translucent spots. Outer margin is slightly scalloped. Thorax has sharp brown dorsal ridge. **HOSTS:** Ash and lilac.

TENT CATERPILLAR AND LAPPET MOTHS Family Lasiocampidae

Small to medium-sized, extremely hairy moths. Females are often considerably larger than males. They adopt a tentlike position while resting, with some species sprawling their hairy forelegs in front of them. The tolypes have a distinctive "mohawk" of blue and black scales. Eastern Tent Caterpillar Moth in particular is well known for its showy communal webs that house the developing larvae. All will visit lights, sometimes in large numbers.

LARGE TOLYPE *Tolype velleda* 7670 **Common**
TL 17–28 mm. Gray FW has contrasting white veins. AM and double PM lines are whitish. ST line is evenly curved along its length. Females are paler and less well marked than males. **HOSTS:** Deciduous trees, including apple, ash, birch, elm, oak, and plum.

LARCH TOLYPE *Tolype laricis* 7673 **Common**
TL 17–21 mm. Resembles Large Tolype, but FW of much smaller male is blackish with smoky gray veins. Larger and paler female has ST line that is noticeably pinched-in at its midpoint. **HOSTS:** Coniferous trees, including fir, pine, and tamarack.

SMALL TOLYPE *Tolype notialis* 7674 **Common**
TL 16–20 mm. Resembles Large Tolype but is darker and smaller and has ST line with two bulges along its length. Sexes are generally alike, but some females can be larger and paler than males. **HOSTS:** Coniferous trees.

DOT-LINED WHITE MOTH
Artace cribrarius 7683 **Common**
TL 14–31 mm. Pearly gray FW is marked with rows of black dots or dashes on contrasting white veins. Woolly thorax and abdomen are gleaming white. Male has pectinate antennae. **HOSTS:** Oak, also cherry and rose.

APATELODID MOTHS

THE ANGEL

actual size

TENT CATERPILLAR AND LAPPET MOTHS

actual size

female

male

LARGE TOLYPE

LARCH TOLYPE

SMALL TOLYPE

DOT-LINED WHITE MOTH

RILEY'S LAPPET MOTH *Heteropacha rileyana* 7685 **Common**
TL 15–19 mm. Peppery grayish brown FW is slightly translucent. Median area and dotted ST line are darker. Jagged white AM line borders paler basal area. Thorax has darker dorsal stripe. **HOSTS:** Honey locust. **NOTE:** Two broods.

LAPPET MOTH *Phyllodesma americana* 7687 **Common**
TL 15–25 mm. Peppery FW is variably yellowish brown, reddish, or bluish gray. At rest, scallop-edged HW is held below level of FW, imparting a unique appearance. **HOSTS:** Alder, birch, oak, poplar, and rose. **NOTE:** Two broods.

FOREST TENT CATERPILLAR MOTH
Malacosoma disstria 7698 **Common**
TL 17–21 mm. Yellowish to rusty brown FW has hairlike quality to it. Median area between parallel rusty AM and PM lines is sometimes darker brown. **HOSTS:** Deciduous trees, including alder, aspen, basswood, birch, cherry, maple, and oak. **NOTE:** Two broods.

EASTERN TENT CATERPILLAR MOTH
Malacosoma americana 7701 **Common**
TL 15–24 mm. Hairy-looking brown FW has broad cream-colored AM and PM lines. Some individuals have a paler median area. Females sometimes have paler yellowish wings. **HOSTS:** Deciduous trees, especially apple, cherry, and crab apple.

Royal Silkworm Moths
Family Saturniidae, Subfamily Ceratocampinae

Medium to large, strikingly beautiful moths. These silkworms are more narrow-winged than the other groups, and most rest with their wings folded back in an inverse V or deltoid shape. Larvae of all species but Pine Devil and northern form of Imperial Moth feed on deciduous trees and shrubs, limiting the extent of the group's northern distribution. Adults are nocturnal and will come to light in small numbers.

IMPERIAL MOTH *Eacles imperialis* 7704 **Uncommon**
WS 80–174 mm. Mustard yellow wings are variably blotched and speckled purplish brown in basal and ST areas. Males marked more heavily than females, especially in south part of range. **HOSTS:** Deciduous trees, including basswood, birch, alder, cedar, elm, hickory, maple, oak, and walnut. **NOTE:** Northern subspecies *E. i. pini,* also shown, is smaller and less heavily marked. Its larvae feed on pines.

TENT CATERPILLAR AND LAPPET MOTHS

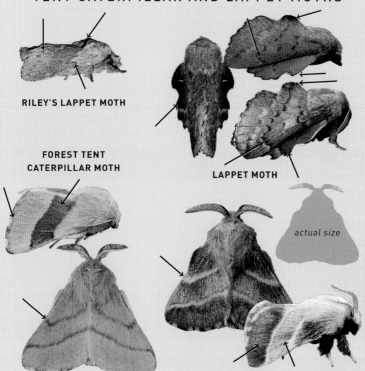

RILEY'S LAPPET MOTH

FOREST TENT CATERPILLAR MOTH

LAPPET MOTH

actual size

EASTERN TENT CATERPILLAR MOTH

ROYAL SILKWORM MOTHS

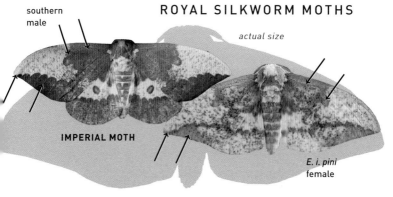

southern male

actual size

IMPERIAL MOTH

E. i. pini female

REGAL MOTH *Citheronia regalis* 7706   **Uncommon**
WS 95–155 mm. Lead gray FW is marked with bright orange veins and bold creamy spots. Orange thorax has pale yellow lateral stripes. **HOSTS:** Deciduous trees, including ash, butternut, hickory, sycamore, and walnut.

PINE DEVIL *Citheronia sepulcralis* 7708   **Uncommon**
WS 70–135 mm. Dark violet gray FW is faintly marked with pale crimson veins and dusky reniform spot and ST line. HW has rose-colored basal area and veins. **HOSTS:** Pine, including pitch pine and eastern white pine.

HONEY LOCUST MOTH *Syssphinx bicolor* 7709   **Common**
TL 26–35 mm. Dimorphic. FW is either gray or orange, lightly speckled darker. Slightly scalloped PM line reaches costa in subapical area. Two white dots in reniform area may be reduced or absent. HW is pink with a crimson flush. **HOSTS:** Honey locust and Kentucky coffee tree. **NOTE:** Up to three broods.

BISECTED HONEY LOCUST MOTH
Syssphinx bisecta 7712   **Uncommon**
TL 28–40 mm. Resembles Honey Locust Moth, but oblique, straight PM line extends from inner margin to apex. Well-defined AM line curves inward near costa. No white reniform dots. HW is orange with a crimson flush along inner margin. **HOSTS:** Honey locust and Kentucky coffee tree. **NOTE:** Two broods.

ROSY MAPLE MOTH *Dryocampa rubicunda* 7715   **Common**
TL 26 mm. FW has bright pink basal area and broad pale yellow median band that reaches apex. ST area may be yellow or pink. Plush yellow thorax is densely hairy. **HOSTS:** Maple and oak.

SPINY OAKWORM MOTH *Anisota stigma* 7716   **Common**
TL 22–38 mm. FW is golden yellow to russet brown, variably speckled with dusky scales. Straight PM line extends from inner margin to apex. AM line curves inward before reaching costa. FW has a round white reniform spot. Female (not shown) is larger but otherwise nearly identical. **HOSTS:** Primarily oak, also basswood and hazelnut.

ORANGE-TIPPED OAKWORM MOTH
Anisota senatoria 7719   **Common**
TL 17–28 mm. Sexually dimorphic. Pale orange FW of female is lightly speckled. Smaller male (not shown) resembles Spiny Oakworm Moth, but deep red FW is straighter and mostly translucent; may or may not show speckling. Both sexes have a round white reniform spot. **HOSTS:** Primarily oak.

ROYAL SILKWORM MOTHS

actual size

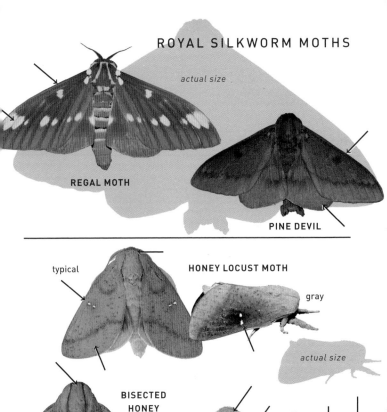

REGAL MOTH

PINE DEVIL

typical

HONEY LOCUST MOTH

gray

actual size

**BISECTED
HONEY
LOCUST
MOTH**

**ROSY MAPLE
MOTH**

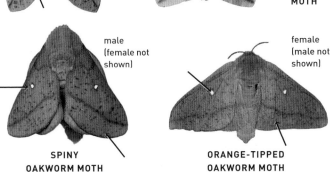

male
(female not
shown)

female
(male not
shown)

**SPINY
OAKWORM MOTH**

**ORANGE-TIPPED
OAKWORM MOTH**

PINK-STRIPED OAKWORM MOTH

Anisota virginiensis   7723 **Common**

TL 20–35 mm. Sexually dimorphic. Russet FW of female has a pink outer margin beyond PM line. FW of smaller male (not shown) is straighter with a translucent median patch but is otherwise similar to that of female. Both sexes have a round white reniform spot. **HOSTS:** Red oak.

BUCK MOTHS
Family Saturniidae, Subfamily Hemileucinae

Medium-large, brightly colored moths. Eastern Buck Moth is a diurnal species that can sometimes be flushed or encountered flying in oak forests on warm autumn days. At rest, it folds its wings tented over its back. The Io Moth holds its wings folded closed and flat while at rest. The large eyespot on the HW is likely flashed to frighten predators.

EASTERN BUCK MOTH *Hemileuca maia*   7730   Uncommon

WS 50–75 mm. Wings are black with a white median band. Black reniform spot on FW is fused to black basal area. Densely hairy thorax is black with a white collar. Hairy abdomen is tipped orange in male, black in female (not shown). **HOSTS:** Primarily scrub oak, also other oaks.

IO MOTH *Automeris io*   7746   **Common**

WS 50–80 mm. Sexually dimorphic. FW is largely yellow in male and bronzy gray to purplish pink in female. Yellow HW has a red streak along inner margin and a large blue eyespot boldly outlined black. **HOSTS:** Deciduous trees, shrubs, and plants, including clover, corn, maple, oak, and willow.

ROYAL SILKWORM MOTHS

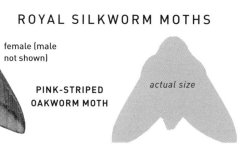

female (male not shown)

PINK-STRIPED OAKWORM MOTH

actual size

BUCK MOTHS

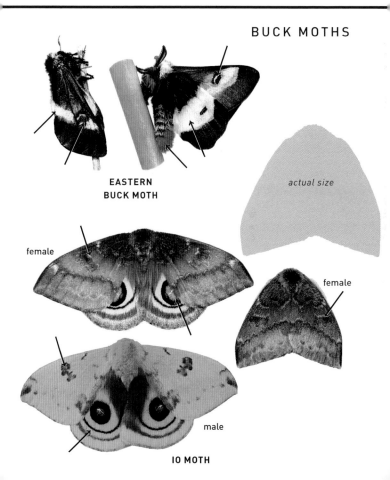

EASTERN BUCK MOTH

actual size

female

female

male

IO MOTH

Giant Silkworm Moths
Family Saturniidae, Subfamily Saturniinae

Spectacular large to very large flat-winged moths found in woodlands. They are characterized by their strikingly beautiful and colorful wing patterns, often with eyespots. Males have feathery, bipectinate antennae which are used to detect female pheromones; female antennae shape varies with species. Some species will rest with their wings closed tight over the abdomen and will drop to the ground like a fallen leaf if disturbed; others, like the Luna Moth, rest with flat wings. They are mostly nocturnal, often appearing a few hours after dusk, and are attracted to lights in small numbers.

POLYPHEMUS MOTH *Antheraea polyphemus* 7757 **Common**
WS 100–150 mm. Pinkish cinnamon wings are marked with transparent eyespots surrounded by concentric yellow and blue rings. **HOSTS:** Trees and shrubs, including ash, birch, grape, hickory, maple, oak, and pine.

LUNA MOTH *Actias luna* 7758 **Common**
WS 75–105 mm. Apple green wings are marked with sleepy-looking elliptical eyespots outlined yellow, white, and black. HW has dramatically long, slightly twisted tails. **HOSTS:** Deciduous trees, including alder, beech, cherry, hazelnut, hickory, and willow.

PROMETHEA MOTH *Callosamia promethea* 7764 **Common**
WS 75–95 mm. Sexually dimorphic. Male has blackish wings with cream-colored band beyond ST line. Female has wings largely reddish brown with a wavy white PM line. Irregularly shaped pale reniform spots mark all wings. Pale border of HW is accented with a row of blackish (male) or reddish (female) bars. **HOSTS:** Deciduous trees and shrubs, including apple, ash, basswood, birch, cherry, maple, spicebush, sweet gum, and tulip tree.

TULIP-TREE SILKMOTH
Callosamia angulifera 7765 **Common**
WS 80–110 mm. Both sexes resemble female Promethea Moth, but male is darker overall and female is paler orange. Large T-shaped reniform spots mark all wings of both sexes. Pale border of HW is accented with a row of blackish (male) or orange (female) spots. **HOSTS:** Tulip tree, also black cherry and sassafras.

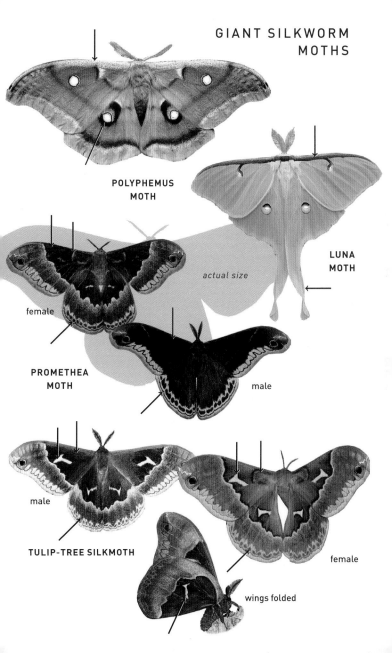

GIANT SILKWORM MOTHS

POLYPHEMUS MOTH

LUNA MOTH

actual size

female

PROMETHEA MOTH

male

male

TULIP-TREE SILKMOTH

female

wings folded

CECROPIA MOTH *Hyalophora cecropia* 7767 **Common**

WS 110–150 mm. Grayish brown wings have tear-shaped reniform spots and broad white and red ST bands. Red thorax has a white collar. **HOSTS:** Deciduous trees and shrubs, including apple, ash, beech, birch, elm, maple, oak, and willow.

COLUMBIA SILKMOTH

Hyalophora columbia 7768 **Uncommon**

WS 80–100 mm. Resembles Cecropia Moth but is smaller and has more extensive maroon shading in basal half of gray FW. PM line lacks reddish shading. HW lacks red edging to white ST band. **HOSTS:** Tamarack.

LARGE SPHINX MOTHS
Family Sphingidae, Subfamily Sphinginae

Robust, medium-sized to large moths. Most species have long pointed wings and a long tapering abdomen. They are powerful fliers. Adults feed on nectar taken from tubular flowers, employing their well-developed and often very long proboscis. Most species are nocturnal and are attracted to lights.

PINK-SPOTTED HAWKMOTH

Agrius cingulata 7771 **Common**

TL 55–65 mm. FW has variegated pattern of gray and brown with blackish lines and dashes. Darker median patch surrounds small white reniform spot. HW has a pink basal patch. Abdomen has pairs of pink and black lateral spots. **HOSTS:** Low plants and shrubs, including sweet potato and jimsonweed. **NOTE:** An irregular late autumn stray to the north part of region.

CAROLINA SPHINX *Manduca sexta* 7775 **Common**

TL 55–65 mm. Gray FW has obscure blackish lines and brown shading. Inner half of ST line is jagged. Gray HW has black and white bands. Abdomen has six pairs of yellow spots along sides. **HOSTS:** Crops, including potato, tobacco, and tomato.

FIVE-SPOTTED HAWKMOTH

Manduca quinquemaculatus 7776 **Common**

TL 50–70 mm. Resembles Carolina Sphinx, but inner half of ST line is slightly wavy. HW has widely separated, jagged black bands. Abdomen typically has five, sometimes six, pairs of yellow spots along sides. **HOSTS:** Crops, including potato, tobacco, and tomato.

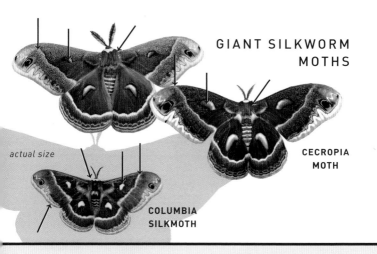

GIANT SILKWORM MOTHS

actual size

CECROPIA MOTH

COLUMBIA SILKMOTH

LARGE SPHINX MOTHS

PINK-SPOTTED HAWKMOTH

CAROLINA SPHINX

actual size

FIVE-SPOTTED HAWKMOTH

RUSTIC SPHINX *Manduca rustica* 7778 **Common**
TL 50–80 mm. Brownish FW has jagged white-edged lines. Darker median patch surrounds small white reniform spot. White-spotted abdomen has three pairs of yellow spots near base. **HOSTS:** Fringe tree, jasmine, and bignonia. **NOTE:** Two broods; a rare fall stray to the north part of region.

 ASH SPHINX *Manduca jasminearum* 7783 **Common**
TL 48–58 mm. Gray FW is marked with thick black line that extends through median area from costa to midpoint of outer margin. Warm brown patch covers area behind small white reniform spot. **HOSTS:** Ash. **NOTE:** Two broods.

 PAWPAW SPHINX *Dolba hyloeus* 7784 **Common**
TL 30–35 mm. Gray FW is peppered with white, brown, and olive scales. Wide dusky bands border jagged AM and PM lines. **HOSTS:** Pawpaw, holly, sweet fern, possum haw, and inkberry.

 ELM SPHINX *Ceratomia amyntor* 7786 **Common**
TL 50–60 mm. Brown FW is streaked olive in median area. Black dashes extend from base to apex. White reniform spot is bar-shaped. **HOSTS:** Elm, birch, basswood, and cherry.

 WAVED SPHINX *Ceratomia undulosa* 7787 **Common**
TL 45–60 mm. Gray FW has double, jagged black lines. Oblique apical dash touches jagged ST line. Conspicuous white reniform spot. **HOSTS:** Ash, privet, oak, hawthorn, and fringe tree.

 CATALPA SPHINX *Ceratomia catalpae* 7789 **Common**
TL 42–47 mm. Yellowish brown FW has double scalloped ST line. Short black apical dash is conspicuous. Pale brown reniform spot is outlined black. **HOSTS:** Catalpa. **NOTE:** Two broods.

 PLEBIAN SPHINX *Paratrea plebeja* 7793 **Common**
TL 33–38 mm. Streaky gray FW has a series of short black dashes extending from base to apex. White reniform spot is outlined black. All wings have checkered fringe. **HOSTS:** Trumpet creeper, yellow trumpetbush, passionflower, and lilac. **NOTE:** Two broods.

 HERMIT SPHINX *Lintneria eremitus* 7796 **Common**
TL 35–40 mm. Grayish brown FW has inconspicuous wavy blackish lines. Black dashes extend from median area to apex. Black-edged reniform spot (sometimes double) is white. **HOSTS:** Bee balm, mint, bugleweed, and sage.

LARGE SPHINX
MOTHS

RUSTIC
SPHINX

ASH
SPHINX

PAWPAW
SPHINX

ELM
SPHINX

WAVED
SPHINX

CATALPA
SPHINX

PLEBIAN
SPHINX

HERMIT
SPHINX

259

GREAT ASH SPHINX *Sphinx chersis* 7802 **Common**
TL 50–70 mm. Gray FW has crisp black dashes extending between veins from inner median area to apex. Thorax shows two thin black dorsal lines. **HOSTS:** Ash, lilac, privet, quaking aspen, and *Prunus* spp.

CANADIAN SPHINX *Sphinx canadensis* 7807 **Common**
TL 45–50 mm. Resembles much larger Great Ash Sphinx. ST line is fragmented into a row of white dashes. **HOSTS:** White ash and blueberry.

LAUREL SPHINX *Sphinx kalmiae* 7809 **Common**
TL 40–55 mm. Fawn-colored FW has dark brown shading along inner margin and veins. Tiny reniform spot is black. ST line is a row of white-edged black wedges. **HOSTS:** Laurel, lilac, ash, poplar, and others. **NOTE:** Two broods.

NORTHERN APPLE SPHINX
Sphinx poecila 7810.1 **Common**
TL 40–50 mm. Gray FW has black dashes extending between veins in median area. Conspicuous white reniform spot is outlined black. Gray HW has a thick terminal band. Thorax is black. **HOSTS:** Apple, sweet fern, blueberry, white spruce, and alder.

CLEMENS' SPHINX *Sphinx luscitiosa* 7811 **Uncommon**
TL 30–40 mm. Yellowish gray (male) or pale gray (female, not shown) FW has black shading beyond PM line. Median area is marked with crisp black veins. White discal spot is usually evident. HW is deep yellow in male (paler yellow in female) with a broad black terminal line. **HOSTS:** Apple, ash, birch, poplar, and willow.

WILD CHERRY SPHINX *Sphinx drupiferarum* 7812 **Common**
TL 45–60 mm. Dark gray FW has contrasting pale streak along costal margin. Terminal line is edged white. Thin black streaks extend between veins from inner median area to apex. Thorax is blackish. **HOSTS:** Wild cherry, plum, lilac, hackberry, and apple.

SOUTHERN PINE SPHINX
Lapara coniferarum 7816 **Common**
TL 30–35 mm. Grayish FW has warm brown shading along inner margin. Two black dashes cut through inner median area; longest touches jagged ST line. Grayish brown thorax has pale "mushroom-shaped" central stripe. **HOSTS:** Pine, including loblolly pine and longleaf pine.

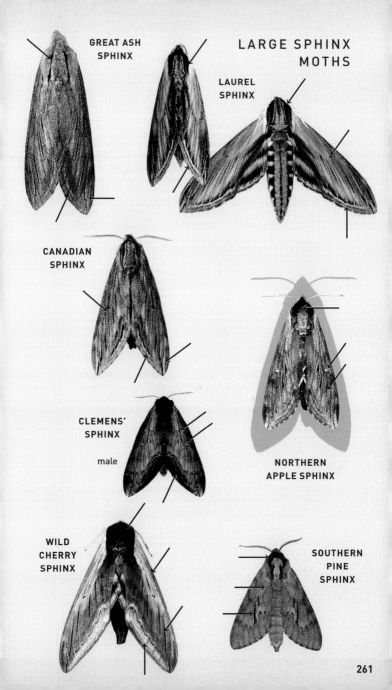

GREAT ASH
SPHINX

LARGE SPHINX
MOTHS

LAUREL
SPHINX

CANADIAN
SPHINX

CLEMENS'
SPHINX

male

NORTHERN
APPLE SPHINX

WILD
CHERRY
SPHINX

SOUTHERN
PINE SPHINX

NORTHERN PINE SPHINX

Lapara bombycoides 7817 **Common**

TL 27–35 mm. Slate gray FW is peppered with white scales. Three black dashes extend through median area; longest touches jagged ST line. Reniform spot is black. **HOSTS:** Pine and tamarack.

EYED SPHINX MOTHS
Family Sphingidae, Subfamily Smerinthinae

Medium-sized to large sphinx moths with scalloped wings that are held elevated and slightly away from the body. In most species, HW has a blue-filled eyespot. All are nocturnal and will regularly visit lights in small numbers.

TWIN-SPOTTED SPHINX

Smerinthus jamaicensis 7821 **Common**

TL 38–45 mm. Lilac gray FW has blackish median bar fused to angled AM line, creating a Y-shape. Whitish apex is accented with black semicircle. Rosy pink HW has black-edged blue eyespot divided by black line. Thorax has blackish dorsal patch. **HOSTS:** Deciduous trees, including apple, ash, elm, poplar, and birch.

ONE-EYED SPHINX *Smerinthus cerisyi* 7822 **Common**

TL 45–55 mm. Violet gray FW has blackish shading in inner median area and along outer margin. Pale pinkish veins extend through median area. Rosy pink HW has black-edged blue eyespot with a black spot in center. Thorax has black dorsal patch. **HOSTS:** Poplar and willow.

BLINDED SPHINX *Paonias excaecata* 7824 **Common**

TL 35–50 mm. Light brown FW has darker brown and violet shading in median area and along scalloped outer margin. Thick black bar in inner median area connects to black AM line. Rosy pink HW has black-edged blue eyespot. **HOSTS:** Deciduous trees, including basswood, willow, birch, and poplar.

SMALL-EYED SPHINX *Paonias myops* 7825 **Common**

TL 32–35 mm. Slate-colored FW has bold blackish lines and orange spots. HW has yellow patch surrounding black-edged blue eyespot. Thorax has a flaming orange dorsal stripe. **HOSTS:** Deciduous trees, including black cherry, serviceberry, and basswood.

LARGE SPHINX MOTHS

NORTHERN PINE SPHINX

EYED SPHINX MOTHS

actual size

TWIN-SPOTTED SPHINX

ONE-EYED SPHINX

BLINDED SPHINX

SMALL-EYED SPHINX

WALNUT SPHINX *Amorpha juglandis* 7827 **Common**
TL 30–40 mm. FW is variably pale pinkish gray to brown with darker shading in median area and beyond PM line. Wavy AM and PM lines converge toward inner margin. Holds HW forward, beyond costa of FW at rest. **HOSTS:** Deciduous trees, including walnut, butternut, hickory, alder, and beech.

MODEST SPHINX *Pachysphinx modesta* 7828 **Common**
TL 45–65 mm. Bluish gray FW has dark gray median band surrounding small white reniform spot. Outer margin is scalloped. HW has a slash of crimson in median area. **HOSTS:** Poplar, aspen, cottonwood, and willow. **NOTE:** Also known as Big Poplar Sphinx.

SMALL SPHINX MOTHS
Family Sphingidae, Subfamily Macroglossinae

Similar in shape and habit to the large sphinx moths, this group is, as a whole, more colorful and varied. Some are crepuscular and can be found feeding on flowers at dusk. A small number are strictly diurnal, being found flitting among patches of flowers in meadows and gardens on sunny afternoons. All but the clearwings and Nessus Sphinx may come to light.

HUMMINGBIRD CLEARWING *Hemaris thysbe* 7853 **Common**
TL 25–30 mm. Mostly transparent wings have jagged chestnut borders and veins. Thorax is uniformly light brown. Dark chestnut abdomen has yellowish segments at base. **HOSTS:** Honeysuckle, snowberry, hawthorn, cherry, and plum. **NOTE:** Two broods. Diurnal, often found taking nectar from flowers.

SNOWBERRY CLEARWING *Hemaris diffinis* 7855 **Common**
TL 22–30 mm. Transparent FW has thin black border with smooth inner edge. Apical spot and stripe along inner margin are orange. Cream-colored thorax has a brown dorsal stripe. Blackish abdomen has a broken yellow band near tip. **HOSTS:** Snowberry, dogbane, and honeysuckle. **NOTE:** Two broods. Diurnal.

PANDORUS SPHINX *Eumorpha pandorus* 7859 **Common**
TL 45–60 mm. Pale green FW has complex pattern of darker green patches and pink veins extending through inner ST area. Thorax is pale green with dark tegulae. **HOSTS:** Grape, *Ampelopsis*, and Virginia creeper.

EYED SPHINX MOTHS

WALNUT SPHINX

MODEST SPHINX

SMALL SPHINX MOTHS

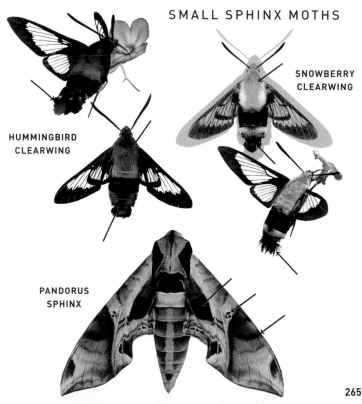

HUMMINGBIRD CLEARWING

SNOWBERRY CLEARWING

PANDORUS SPHINX

ACHEMON SPHINX *Eumorpha achemon* 7861 Uncommon
TL 45–55 mm. Pinkish brown FW has darker brown patches along inner margin and near apex. HW has large rosy pink basal patch and dotted brown ST band. Thorax has dark brown tegulae. **HOSTS:** Grape and *Ampelopsis*.

ABBOTT'S SPHINX *Sphecodina abbottii* 7870 Common
TL 30–40 mm. Violet gray FW has barklike pattern of swirling black lines. Outer margin is deeply scalloped. HW has a broad yellow basal patch. Wide abdomen has a brushy, three-pronged tip. **HOSTS:** Grape and *Ampelopsis*.

LETTERED SPHINX *Deidamia inscriptum* 7871 Common
TL 25–38 mm. Ash gray FW is marked with thick dusky bands. Scalloped outer margin is accented with black crescents. Abdomen is typically curled upward when moth is at rest. **HOSTS:** Grape, *Ampelopsis,* and Virginia creeper.

NESSUS SPHINX *Amphion floridensis* 7873 Common
TL 22–28 mm. Chocolate brown FW has darker bands in median area and beyond PM line. Rusty HW has a yellow spot at costa. Two thin yellow bands on abdomen are eye-catching. **HOSTS:** Grape, *Ampelopsis,* and cayenne pepper. **NOTE:** One or two broods. Diurnal, often found taking nectar from flowers.

HYDRANGEA SPHINX *Darapsa versicolor* 7884 Uncommon
TL 35–45 mm. Bronzy green FW has swirling pattern of curved pinkish mauve lines. Orange HW has pale greenish border and stripe along inner margin. **HOSTS:** Smooth hydrangea, buttonbush, and water-willow. **NOTE:** One or two broods.

VIRGINIA CREEPER SPHINX
Darapsa myron 7885 Common
TL 28–38 mm. FW is variably light brown to pale green with a thin orange border and wide bands of darker shading, boldest beyond outer PM line. Dull orange HW has a brown or greenish patch at anal angle. **HOSTS:** Virginia creeper, grape, *Ampelopsis,* and viburnum. **NOTE:** Two broods.

AZALEA SPHINX *Darapsa choerilus* 7886 Common
TL 30–40 mm. Pinkish mauve FW has reddish brown shading beyond straight median line. Dull orange HW has purplish border. **HOSTS:** Azalea, blueberry, sour gum, and viburnum. **NOTE:** Two broods.

SMALL SPHINX MOTHS

ACHEMON SPHINX

ABBOTT'S SPHINX

NESSUS SPHINX

LETTERED SPHINX

HYDRANGEA SPHINX

AZALEA SPHINX

VIRGINIA CREEPER SPHINX

TERSA SPHINX *Xylophanes tersa* 7890 Uncommon

TL 35–45 mm. Tawny brown FW is marked with thin longitudinal lines. Brown HW has a black median band studded with yellowish wedges. Long, sharply tapering abdomen is brown with yellow lateral stripes. **HOSTS:** Madder, starcluster, and Virginia buttonweed. **NOTE:** A rare stray to the north part of the region.

SPURGE HAWKMOTH *Hyles euphorbiae* 7892 Uncommon

TL 38–50 mm. Olive brown FW has an irregular pinkish stripe extending from base to apex. Pale areas are usually peppered darker. Pink HW has black base and ST line. **HOSTS:** Leafy spurge. **NOTE:** Introduced from Europe to combat the invasive leafy spurge.

GALLIUM SPHINX *Hyles gallii* 7893 Uncommon

TL 38–50 mm. Resembles Spurge Hawkmoth, but jagged cream-colored stripe on FW is clean-cut, without any dark peppering. Black HW has a broad pink median band. **HOSTS:** Bedstraw, willow weed, woodruff, and godetia.

WHITE-LINED SPHINX *Hyles lineata* 7894 Common

TL 35–50 mm. Resembles Gallium Sphinx, but FW is marked with whitish veins cutting through central ochre stripe. **HOSTS:** Various trees and low plants, including apple, elm, evening primrose, grape, tomato, and purslane. **NOTE:** Two broods. An irregular immigrant to northern part of range, where strays can show up as late as mid-Oct.

SUPERFAMILY NOCTUOIDEA

The Noctuoidea are a massive assemblage of stout-bodied, often hairy moths, considered taxonomically as the most evolutionarily recent moth lineage. Members of this superfamily are generally medium-small to large, but a few are very tiny and could be confused for micromoths. Many fold their wings over their abdomen when at rest, while others rest with their wings spread like members of the Geometridae. A large number are nondescript or even somber in appearance, clad in shades of gray or brown, often with intricate and contrasting patterns on the FW. Some, notably the underwing moths in the genus *Catocala,* have vividly colorful wing patterns. Most are nocturnal and likely to be found only at lights or sugar bait, though a small number are habitual day fliers. The Noctuoidea are well represented in ne. North America, and usually make up a large portion of the moths encountered on any given night.

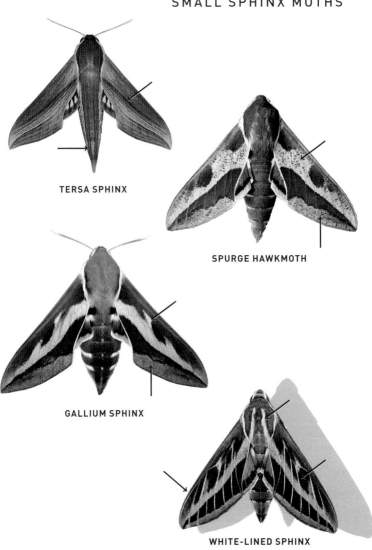

TERSA SPHINX

SPURGE HAWKMOTH

GALLIUM SPHINX

WHITE-LINED SPHINX

PROMINENTS Family Notodontidae

A varied assortment of stout, often beautifully patterned noctuid moths. Some have a short thoracic crest or tufts of hairlike scales along the inner margin of the FW. Moths in the genus *Schizura* mimic twigs by rolling their wings into a tube. Most prominents are found in mature woodlands, though some also occur in well-established gardens. All are strictly nocturnal and will visit lights in small numbers.

SIGMOID PROMINENT

Clostera albosigma   93-0003 (7895)   **Common**

TL 16–20 mm. Grayish brown FW has pale parallel lines. Chestnut subapical patch extends beyond white S-shaped outer PM line. Outer half of ST area is shaded with violet gray. **HOSTS:** Aspen, poplar, and willow. **NOTE:** Two broods.

ANGLE-LINED PROMINENT

Clostera inclusa   93-0004 (7896)   **Common**

TL 17–19 mm. Gray FW has large patch of dusky shading that extends through outer half of slightly kinked PM line. Oblique median line is straight. Pale orange subapical patch is relatively small. **HOSTS:** Aspen, poplar, and willow. **NOTE:** Two broods.

STRIPED CHOCOLATE-TIP

Clostera strigosa   93-0006 (7898)   **Common**

TL 15–16 mm. Peppery gray-brown FW is marked with curvy lines. Blackish streak cuts through midpoint of PM line. Kinked outer PM line borders a cream-colored subapical patch. **HOSTS:** Poplar and willow.

APICAL PROMINENT

Clostera apicalis   93-0009 (7901)   **Common**

TL 17–19 mm. Gray FW has an oblique median line that is slightly kinked. Wavy outer PM line borders an extensive rusty subapical patch. **HOSTS:** Willow and poplar. **NOTE:** Two broods.

GEORGIAN PROMINENT

Hyperaeschra georgica   93-0010 (7917)   **Common**

TL 19–24 mm. Grayish brown FW has irregular white-edged lines and black dashes in ST area. Basal area has a straw-colored oval patch. A tuft of black hairlike scales projects midway along inner margin. **HOSTS:** Oak. **NOTE:** Two broods.

PROMINENTS

SIGMOID PROMINENT

actual size

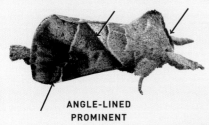

**ANGLE-LINED
PROMINENT**

STRIPED CHOCOLATE-TIP

APICAL PROMINENT

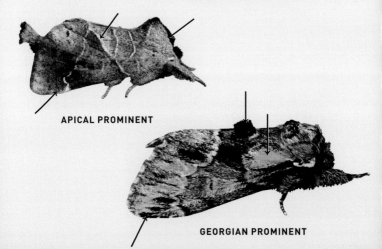

GEORGIAN PROMINENT

BLACK-RIMMED PROMINENT

Pheosia rimosa   93-0012 (7922)   **Common**
TL 25–32 mm. Creamy gray FW has a thick white streak arcing
from base to apex. Black dashes extend along white veins near
inner margin. Black apical dash is noticeable. **HOSTS:** Poplar
and willow. **NOTE:** Two or more broods.

ELEGANT PROMINENT

Odontosia elegans   93-0013 (7924)   **Common**
TL 27–32 mm. Sepia brown FW blends to ash gray near outer
margin. Black veins are peppered with white scales. Bold white
basal dash borders a fawn-colored streak along inner margin.
A tuft of gray scales projects midway along inner margin.
HOSTS: Poplar. **NOTE:** Two broods.

FINNED-WILLOW PROMINENT

Notodonta scitipennis   93-0015 (7926)   **Uncommon**
TL 18–25 mm. Lead gray FW has cream-colored inner margin
and basal areas streaked with rust and black. Scalloped AM
and ST lines are edged with pale yellow and rust. **HOSTS:** Poplar
and willow. **NOTE:** Two broods.

NORTHERN FINNED PROMINENT

Notodonta torva   93-0017 (7928)   **Uncommon**
TL 22–27 mm. Uniform dark gray FW is strongly peppered with
white scales. Bar-shaped reniform spot is outlined with whitish
scales. **HOSTS:** Poplar and willow. **NOTE:** One or two broods.

DOUBLE-TOOTHED PROMINENT

Nerice bidentata   93-0018 (7929)   **Common**
TL 20–21 mm. Ash gray FW has a black double-toothed longitudinal bar that blends into brown toward costa. Black subapical
dash is edged white. **HOSTS:** Elm. **NOTE:** Two broods.

COMMON GLUPHISIA

Gluphisia septentrionis   93-0019 (7931)   **Common**
TL 14–17 mm. Peppery gray FW has warm brown patches in inner median and basal areas. Basal line is strongly toothed.
Wavy AM and PM lines are roughly parallel. Some individuals
have blackish median band. **HOSTS:** Poplar. **NOTE:** Two or more
broods.

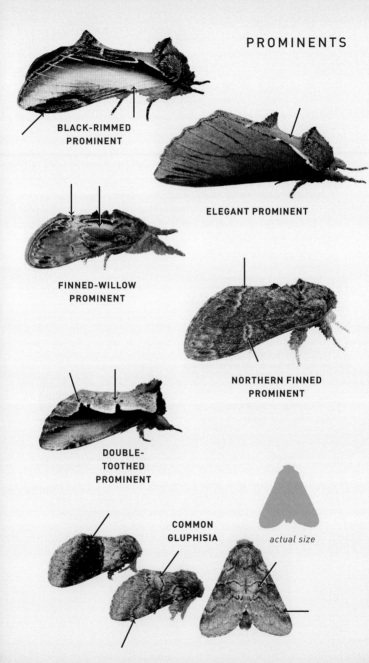

PROMINENTS

BLACK-RIMMED PROMINENT

ELEGANT PROMINENT

FINNED-WILLOW PROMINENT

NORTHERN FINNED PROMINENT

DOUBLE-TOOTHED PROMINENT

COMMON GLUPHISIA

actual size

FOUR-SPOTTED GLUPHISIA

Gluphisia avimacula   93-0021 (7933)   **Common**
TL 18–22 mm. Peppery gray FW has sharply defined cream-colored spots in median and basal areas. Inner median area is variably shaded warm brown. Slightly wavy black AM line is conspicuous. Sometimes has basal and median areas shaded black. **HOSTS:** Poplar.

LINTNER'S GLUPHISIA

Gluphisia lintneri   93-0022 (7934)   **Common**
TL 20 mm. Peppery gray FW has extensive ochre shading in median area that bleeds into almost straight AM line. Basal area is clouded with ochre shading. Some individuals have wide blackish median band. **HOSTS:** Poplar.

WHITE FURCULA   *Furcula borealis*   93-0024 (7936)   **Common**

TL 18–23 mm. White FW is marked with black spots along lines. Peppery dark gray median band and subapical patch are accented with orange and metallic blue spots. Thorax has topknot of orange and metallic blue scales. **HOSTS:** Cherry. **NOTE:** Two broods.

GRAY FURCULA   *Furcula cinerea*   93-0025 (7937)   **Common**

TL 17–22 mm. Pearly gray FW is sparingly marked with blackish spots along lines. Peppery median band and shading along ST line are only slightly darker, weakly accented with orange and metallic blue spots. **HOSTS:** Aspen, poplar, and willow. **NOTE:** Two broods.

WESTERN FURCULA

Furcula occidentalis   93-0027 (7939)   **Common**
TL 17–22 mm. White FW has narrow, peppery gray median and ST bands. Toothed PM line is double. Wavy edges of median patch and ST line are accented with orange and dull blue spots. **HOSTS:** Willow. **NOTE:** Two broods.

MODEST FURCULA

Furcula modesta   93-0029 (7941)   **Common**
TL 18–23 mm. Creamy white FW is sparsely marked with black dots along lines. Blackish median band is hourglass-shaped or broken in the middle. Large black subapical patch borders outer ST line. **HOSTS:** Poplar and willow. **NOTE:** Two broods.

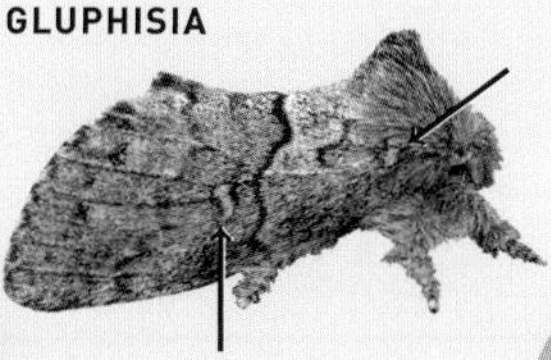

PROMINENTS

FOUR-SPOTTED
GLUPHISIA

actual size

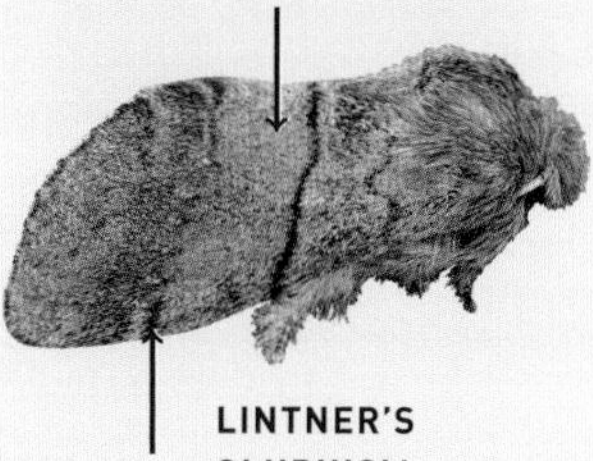

LINTNER'S
GLUPHISIA

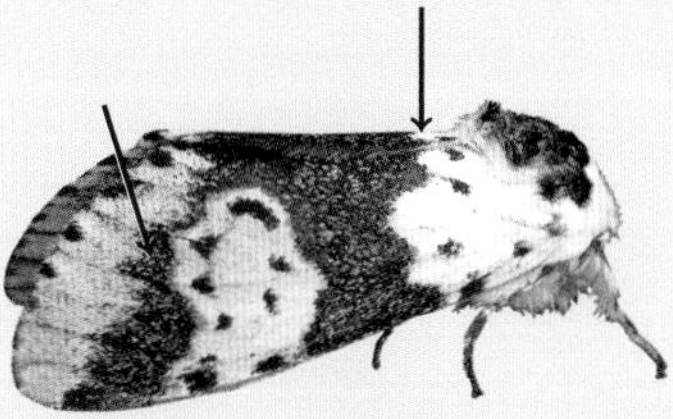

WHITE FURCULA

defensive
posture

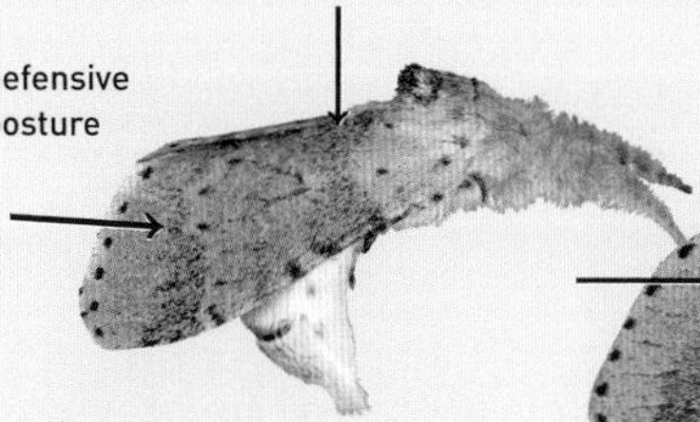

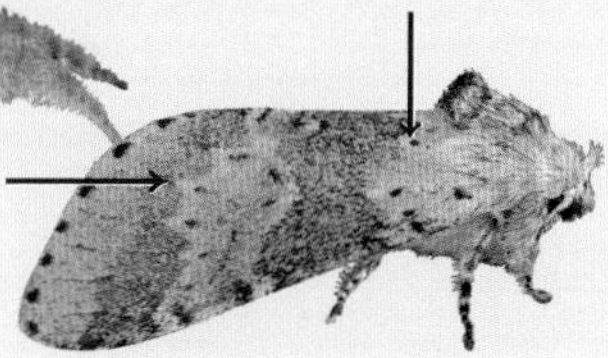

GRAY FURCULA

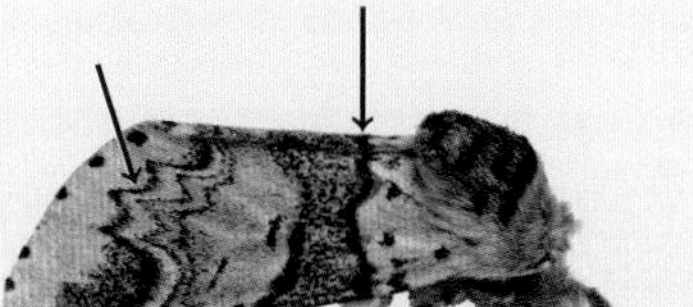

WESTERN FURCULA

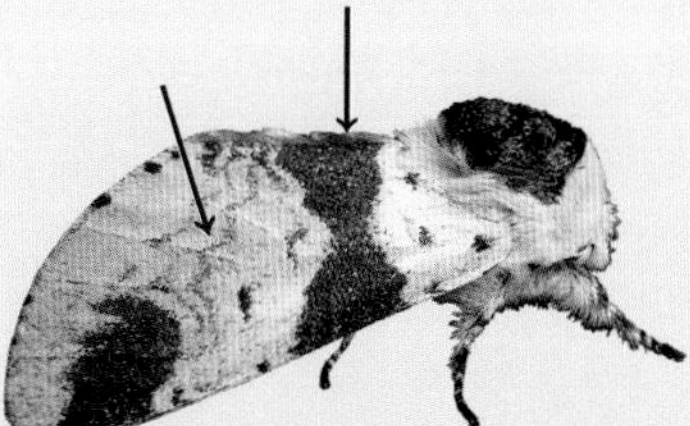

MODEST FURCULA

275

BLACK-ETCHED PROMINENT

Cerura scitiscripta   93-0030 (7942)   **Uncommon**

TL 15–22 mm. White FW has finely etched black lines and veins. AM and ST lines are double, sometimes filled with gray shading. Crescent-shaped reniform spot is outlined in black. **HOSTS:** Cherry, poplar, and willow. **NOTE:** Two broods

YELLOW-NECKED CATERPILLAR MOTH

Datana ministra   93-0033 (7902)   **Common**

TL 22–26 mm. Tawny brown FW has blackish lines that are almost parallel. Outer margin is deeply scalloped when fresh. Orbicular spot is faint or absent. **HOSTS:** Trees and woody shrubs, including apple, oak, birch, and willow. **NOTE:** One or two broods.

ANGUS' DATANA

Datana angusii   93-0034 (7903)   **Uncommon**

TL 20–25 mm. Darker than other Datana species. Coppery brown FW has parallel blackish lines. Orbicular spot is sometimes present. Outer margin is slightly scalloped. **HOSTS:** Deciduous trees, including butternut, hickory, and walnut.

DREXEL'S DATANA

Datana drexelii   93-0035 (7904)   **Uncommon**

TL 22–27 mm. Tawny brown FW often has reddish shading along costa. Brown lines are almost parallel. Blackish orbicular spot and apical dash are often noticeable. Outer margin is slightly scalloped. **HOSTS:** Birch, blueberry, basswood, sassafras, and witch hazel.

CONTRACTED DATANA

Datana contracta   93-0037 (7906)   **Common**

TL 21–27 mm. Tawny brown FW has dark brown, almost parallel, yellow-edged lines. Outer margin is not scalloped. **HOSTS:** Primarily chestnut and oak, also blueberry, hickory, and witch hazel.

WALNUT CATERPILLAR MOTH

Datana integerrima 93-0038 (7907)   **Common**

TL 21–28 mm. Tawny brown FW has dark brown, almost parallel lines, narrowly edged with pale yellow. Outer margin is not scalloped. **HOSTS:** Butternut, hickory, pecan, and walnut.

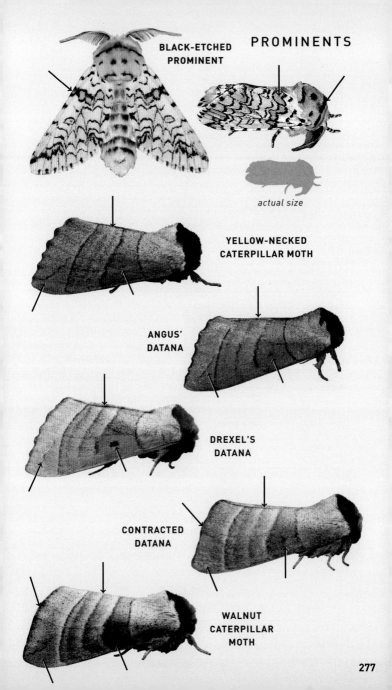

PROMINENTS

BLACK-ETCHED
PROMINENT

YELLOW-NECKED
CATERPILLAR MOTH

actual size

ANGUS'
DATANA

DREXEL'S
DATANA

CONTRACTED
DATANA

WALNUT
CATERPILLAR
MOTH

277

SPOTTED DATANA
Datana perspicua 93-0039 (7908) **Common**
TL 25–30 mm. Bright golden yellow FW has almost parallel lines. Small orbicular and larger brown reniform spot are conspicuous. Apical dash is often present. Outer margin is slightly scalloped. **HOSTS:** Sumac. **NOTE:** One or two broods.

WHITE-DOTTED PROMINENT
Nadata gibbosa 93-0046 (7915) **Common**
TL 20–30 mm. Orange FW is peppered with brown scales, except along inner margin and median area. Apex is often paler. AM and PM lines converge toward inner margin. Reniform spot consists of two round white spots. **HOSTS:** Primarily oak, also birch, cherry, and maple. **NOTE:** Two or more broods.

OVAL-BASED PROMINENT
Peridea basitriens 93-0048 (7919) **Common**
TL 19–26 mm. Gray FW has billowing AM line that follows outlines of brown-tinged, ovate basal markings. PM line is scalloped. ST line is a row of brown dashes between black veins. **HOSTS:** Unknown.

ANGULOSE PROMINENT
Peridea angulosa 93-0049 (7920) **Common**
TL 19–26 mm. Gray FW often has incomplete whitish median band. Wavy brown AM line is edged pale orange. PM line is a fragmented row of black and white dashes. **HOSTS:** Oak. **NOTE:** Two or more broods.

CHOCOLATE PROMINENT
Peridea ferruginea 93-0050 (7921) **Common**
TL 20–27 mm. Grayish brown FW has chocolate brown shading in basal, median, and ST areas. Wavy AM and PM lines are edged white. Reniform spot is white. **HOSTS:** Birch.

LINDEN PROMINENT
Ellida caniplaga 93-0051 (7930) **Common**
TL 19–24 mm. Silvery gray FW has three parallel black lines forming outer section of AM line. White reniform spot is incompletely edged black. ST line is a row of black dots. **HOSTS:** Basswood. **NOTE:** Two broods.

DRAB PROMINENT
Misogada unicolor 93-0066 (7974) **Common**
TL 24–26 mm. Gray FW has a greenish tint when fresh. Inconspicuous, scalloped PM line is accented with tiny white dots. **HOSTS:** Cottonwood and sycamore.

PROMINENTS

SPOTTED DATANA

actual size

OVAL-BASED PROMINENT

WHITE-DOTTED PROMINENT

ANGULOSE PROMINENT

CHOCOLATE PROMINENT

LINDEN PROMINENT

DRAB PROMINENT

279

MOTTLED PROMINENT

Macrurocampa marthesia   93-0067 (7975)   **Common**

TL 24–28 mm. Gray FW has black veins sprinkled with white scales. Patches of green shading are present in basal and median areas. Scalloped PM and ST lines are double and edged white. Basal area is darker than rest of wing. **HOSTS:** Primarily oak, also poplar and maple.

OBLIQUE HETEROCAMPA

Heterocampa obliqua   93-0075 (7983)   **Common**

TL 20–28 mm. Grayish brown FW has green and rust shading in basal area and along ST line. Thin black basal dash and curved black line extends from barlike reniform spot to inner ST line. Oblique subapical patch is either white (male) or orange (female). **HOSTS:** Oak.

SMALL HETEROCAMPA

Heterocampa subrotata   93-0077 (7985)   **Uncommon**

TL 16–20 mm. FW is variably gray or brown, often with a strong greenish tint. Scalloped AM and PM lines are double, filled with orange scales. Oblique subapical patch is white with thin black streaks along veins. **HOSTS:** Hickory, maple, birch, and other deciduous trees.

WHITE-BLOTCHED HETEROCAMPA

Heterocampa umbrata   93-0082 (7990)   **Common**

TL 23–33 mm. Gray FW is often strongly clouded with moss green shading. Lines are obscure apart from curved black bar extending from top of reniform crescent to inner ST line. Large white subapical patch is often tinged pale green. **HOSTS:** Oak.

SADDLED PROMINENT

Heterocampa guttivitta   93-0086 (7994)   **Common**

TL 23–25 mm. FW is variably gray to yellowish green, often paler near apex. Inconspicuous, scalloped AM and PM lines are marked with tiny white dashes. Wavy ST line is dotted. **HOSTS:** Trees and woody plants, including maple, oak, apple, beech, and sumac. **NOTE:** Two broods.

WAVY-LINED HETEROCAMPA

Heterocampa biundata   93-0087 (7995)   **Common**

TL 25–30 mm. FW is variably grayish brown to mossy green. Scalloped AM and PM lines are double, often filled with orange scales. Wavy ST line is a row of black wedges. **HOSTS:** Deciduous trees and woody plants, including apple, willow, and hickory. **NOTE:** Two or more broods.

MOTTLED PROMINENT

actual size

OBLIQUE
HETEROCAMPA

SMALL
HETEROCAMPA

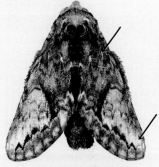

WHITE-BLOTCHED
HETEROCAMPA

SADDLED PROMINENT

WAVY-LINED
HETEROCAMPA

VARIABLE OAKLEAF CATERPILLAR MOTH

Lochmaeus manteo   93-0090 (7998)   **Common**

TL 20–27 mm. Gray FW has outer median area variably shaded dark gray. Scalloped AM line is double, often filled with pale gray scales. PM line is often indistinct. Reniform spot is usually white with a thin black crescent in center. **HOSTS:** Primarily beech, chestnut, and oak, also birch, elm, and walnut.

DOUBLE-LINED PROMINENT

Lochmaeus bilineata   93-0091 (7999)   **Common**

TL 18–23 mm. Gray FW has slightly darker outer median area. Double AM and PM lines are filled with pale gray scales. Inconspicuous reniform spot is a thin black crescent. **HOSTS:** A variety of deciduous trees, including elm, basswood, oak, birch, beech, and walnut.

MORNING-GLORY PROMINENT

Schizura ipomoeae   93-0098 (8005)   **Common**

TL 20–25 mm. Grayish brown FW is variably marked with dark streaking between veins. Reniform spot is a thin black crescent outlined in white. Jagged AM and PM lines are double but sometimes indistinct. Darker individuals have blackish FW, often with a pale costal streak and reniform spot. **HOSTS:** Trees and woody plants, including basswood, beech, birch, maple, and oak.

CHESTNUT SCHIZURA

Schizura badia   93-0099 (8006)   **Common**

TL 17–20 mm. Straw-colored FW is often tinged pinkish. Veins are blackish. Crescent-shaped reniform spot joins a triangle of brown shading that widens toward outer margin. Whitish apical patch is often present. Thorax is strikingly black. **HOSTS:** Northern wild-raisin and other viburnum species. **NOTE:** Two broods.

UNICORN PROMINENT

Schizura unicornis   93-0100 (8007)   **Common**

TL 18–25 mm. Gray FW is often tinted with pale green and violet brown. Scalloped AM and PM lines are double. ST line is marked with a large straw-colored patch. Basal area is pale green overlaid with scalloped black lines. **HOSTS:** Deciduous trees, including oak, maple, willow, and hickory. **NOTE:** Two broods.

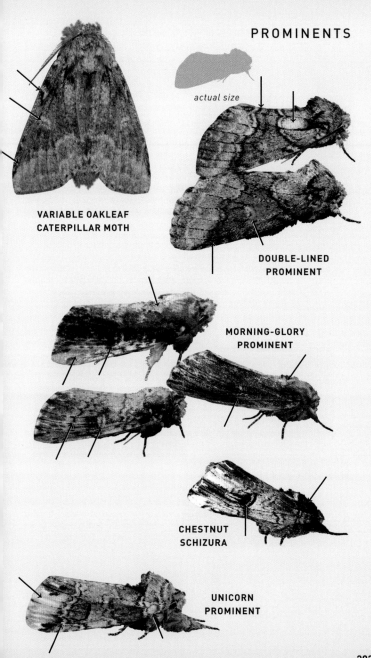

PROMINENTS

actual size

VARIABLE OAKLEAF CATERPILLAR MOTH

DOUBLE-LINED PROMINENT

MORNING-GLORY PROMINENT

CHESTNUT SCHIZURA

UNICORN PROMINENT

RED-HUMPED CATERPILLAR MOTH

Schizura concinna 93-0103 (8010) **Common**
TL 17–21 mm. Paler FW has pinkish brown shading in median area and a reddish streak along inner margin. Thin black basal dash and tiny black reniform dot are the only obvious markings. White apical dash is small. **HOSTS:** Deciduous trees and woody plants, including apple, blueberry, elm, and hickory. **NOTE:** Two broods.

BLACK-BLOTCHED SCHIZURA

Schizura leptinoides 93-0104 (8011) **Common**
TL 22–26 mm. Gray FW has white peppering along black veins. Reddish brown PM line is double. Reniform spot is a black crescent within a dark blotch. A black basal dash is noticeable. **HOSTS:** Mostly hickory and walnut, also apple, birch, oak, and poplar. **NOTE:** Two broods.

RED-WASHED PROMINENT

Oligocentria semirufescens 93-0105 (8012) **Common**
TL 24–25 mm. FW is grayish or straw colored, variably shaded with reddish violet and brown. Reniform spot is a black crescent or dot. Typically shows a short black basal dash and a contrasting white patch at apex. Darker individuals have dusky brown FW with white patches at apex and anal angle. **HOSTS:** Primarily poplar and willow, also alder, birch, maple, and rose. **NOTE:** Two broods.

WHITE-STREAKED PROMINENT

Oligocentria lignicolor 93-0110 (8017) **Common**
TL 25–26 mm. Pale gray FW has white streaks extending between dusky veins. Reniform spot is a tiny blackish dot. Thorax has dusky dorsal stripe. **HOSTS:** Beech, birch, chestnut, and oak.

PINK PROMINENT

Hyparpax aurora 93-0115 (8022) **Uncommon**
TL 17–22 mm. Powdery pink FW has broad pale yellow median band that stops short of costa. Pink crescent curves inward from costal streak, touching the point of angled pink basal patch. **HOSTS:** Scrub oak and viburnum. **NOTE:** Two broods.

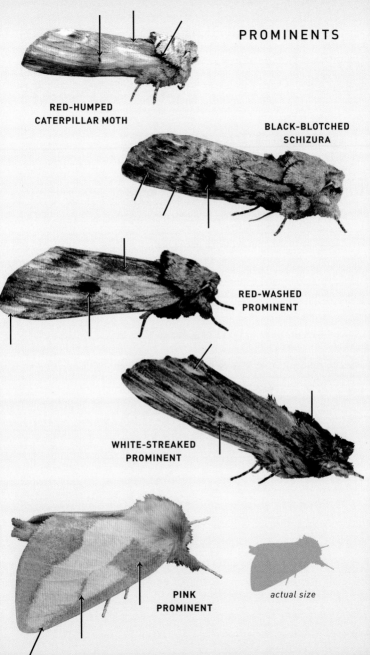

PROMINENTS

RED-HUMPED
CATERPILLAR MOTH

BLACK-BLOTCHED
SCHIZURA

RED-WASHED
PROMINENT

WHITE-STREAKED
PROMINENT

PINK
PROMINENT

actual size

WHITE-HEADED PROMINENT

Symmerista albifrons   93-0127 (7951)   **Common**
TL 18–22 mm. FW is ash gray with brown patch surrounding reniform spot. PM line is indistinct or absent. White costal bar extending from apex to AM line has a rounded or blunt spur jutting into median area. **HOSTS:** Oak. **NOTE:** *Symmerista* species are often impossible to tell apart in the field.

RED-HUMPED OAKWORM

Symmerista canicosta   93-0128 (7952)   **Common**
TL 18–22 mm. Ash gray FW is clouded with brown in outer median area. PM line is double, sometimes indistinct. White costal bar extending from apex to AM line has a sharp spur jutting into median area. **HOSTS:** Beech, chestnut, and oak. **NOTE:** Two broods.

ORANGE-HUMPED OAKWORM

Symmerista leucitys   93-0129 (7953)   **Common**
TL 20–25 mm. Ash gray FW has a trace of brown shading in outer median area. PM line is double, sometimes indistinct. White costal bar extending from apex to AM line has a blunt triangular spur jutting into median area. **HOSTS:** Maple.

GRAY-PATCHED PROMINENT

Dasylophia thyatiroides   93-0134 (7958)   **Common**
TL 24 mm. Streaky gray FW has pale orange basal patch. Curved AM and PM lines are boldly edged black near inner margin, especially in female. Blunt-fronted thorax and pale brushlike labial palps give the appearance of a snapped-off twig. **HOSTS:** Beech. **NOTE:** Two broods.

WHITE-HEADED PROMINENT

RED-HUMPED OAKWORM

ORANGE-HUMPED OAKWORM

actual size

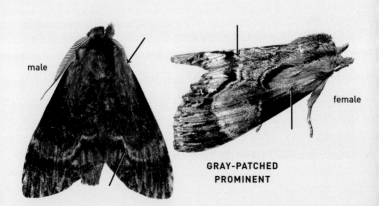

male

female

GRAY-PATCHED PROMINENT

Tussock Moths
Family Erebidae, Subfamily Lymantriinae

Chunky, extremely hairy moths that inhabit woodlands and larger gardens. Most fly between midsummer and early fall. They often have variable and confusing FW patterns that make specific identification a challenge. They rest with their long hairy forelegs sprawled out in front. Males have broad, feathery antennae. Females tend to be larger than males. Most are nocturnal and will come to light, but some can also be found flying during the day.

GYPSY MOTH *Lymantria dispar* 93-0141 (8318) **Common**
TL 26 mm. Sexually dimorphic. Yellowish brown FW of male has dusky scalloped lines and black crescent-shaped reniform spot. Larger female has ivory white FW with faint jagged lines and black reniform crescent. Antennae are broadly bipectinate in male. **HOSTS:** Oak, also other deciduous trees and shrubs. **NOTE:** Male is a conspicuous day-flier (though also attracted to lights at night), whereas the nearly flightless female is usually encountered on a tree trunk with her egg mass. Deliberately introduced from Europe in 1868–1869 and now widespread throughout ne. N. America.

VARIABLE TUSSOCK MOTH
Dasychira vagans 93-0146 (8294) **Common**
TL 26 mm. Variable. FW is peppery with indistinct lines. Reniform area is often sprinkled whitish, especially near costa. Sometimes has a black basal dash. **HOSTS:** Deciduous trees, including apple, birch, poplar, and willow.

YELLOW-BASED TUSSOCK MOTH
Dasychira basiflava 93-0148 (8296) **Common**
TL 20–24 mm. Variable. FW often has extensive warm brown shading in basal area and along ST line. Sometimes has whitish outer median area widening toward costa. Some individuals show dark streaks in basal and inner median areas. White crescent often marks inner ST line. **HOSTS:** Oak.

STREAKED TUSSOCK MOTH
Dasychira obliquata 93-0154 (8302) **Common**
TL 20–25 mm. Ash gray FW has distinct rusty brown bands edging crisp black AM and PM lines. Often has whitish shading around reniform spot. Nearly always has well-defined black streaks extending through basal and inner median areas. **HOSTS:** Oak, also beech, birch, elm, and hickory.

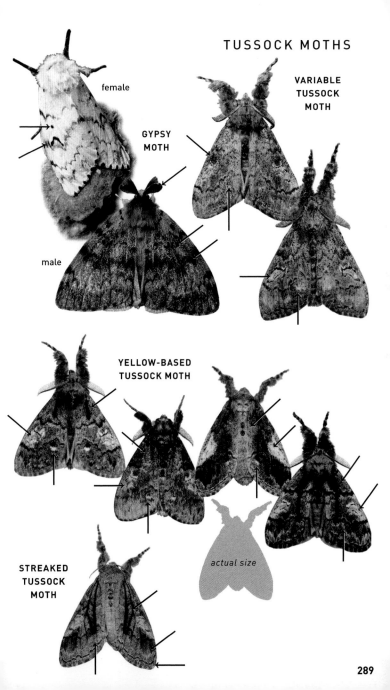

TUSSOCK MOTHS

female

GYPSY MOTH

male

VARIABLE TUSSOCK MOTH

YELLOW-BASED TUSSOCK MOTH

STREAKED TUSSOCK MOTH

actual size

NORTHERN PINE TUSSOCK MOTH

Dasychira plagiata   93-0156 (8304)   **Common**
TL 20–25 mm. Grayish brown FW is marked with bold black AM and PM lines and brown basal area. Usually shows some whitish shading around olive brown reniform spot. Inner ST line is marked with bold white spot. **HOSTS:** Coniferous trees. **RANGE:** S. Canada and n. U.S.

PINE TUSSOCK MOTH

Dasychira pinicola   93-0157 (8305)   **Common**
TL 20–25 mm. Resembles Northern Pine Tussock Moth, but basal area of FW is usually marked with a well-defined black streak. **HOSTS:** Coniferous trees. **RANGE:** S. ON and QU and possibly ne. U.S.

RUSTY TUSSOCK MOTH

Orgyia antiqua   93-0160 (8308)   **Common**
TL 12–16 mm. Rusty brown FW of male has obscure darker lines. Inner ST line is marked with bold white spot. Female (not shown) is wingless. **HOSTS:** Deciduous trees and shrubs, including alder, cherry, maple, pine, and willow. **NOTE:** A conspicuous day-flier.

DEFINITE TUSSOCK MOTH

Orgyia definita   93-0166 (8314)   **Common**
TL 15–17 mm. Grayish brown FW of male has sharply defined AM and PM lines, often edged with wide brown bands. Outer ST line is marked with a row of black dashes. Inner ST line has a bold white crescent. Female (not shown) is wingless. **HOSTS:** Deciduous trees, including basswood, birch, oak, and maple. **NOTE:** Two broods.

WHITE-MARKED TUSSOCK MOTH

Orgyia leucostigma   93-0168 (8316)   **Common**
TL 15–22 mm. FW pattern and color are variable. Resembles Definite Tussock Moth but often is more uniformly gray or brown, usually with less obvious blackish streaks in outer ST area. Female (not shown) is wingless. **HOSTS:** Various deciduous trees. **NOTE:** Two broods.

SATIN MOTH   *Leucoma salicis*   93-0170 (8319)   **Uncommon**
TL 22–27 mm. Satin white FW has tinge of yellow along costa. White abdomen has blackish bands at each segment. Superficially similar to white tiger moths, but legs are banded black and white. **HOSTS:** Poplar and willow. **RANGE:** Locally in Canada and n. U.S. **NOTE:** Introduced from Europe in 1920.

TUSSOCK MOTHS

NORTHERN PINE TUSSOCK MOTH

PINE TUSSOCK MOTH

RUSTY TUSSOCK MOTH

actual size

DEFINITE TUSSOCK MOTH

WHITE-MARKED TUSSOCK MOTH

SATIN MOTH

LICHEN MOTHS
Family Erebidae, Subfamily Arctiinae, Tribe Lithosiini

Small, often strikingly colorful moths whose larvae feed mostly on lichen in wooded areas. Most species are nocturnal and will visit lights in small numbers. A small number, like the Black-and-yellow Lichen Moth, are primarily diurnal and can be found taking nectar from flowers.

KENTUCKY LICHEN MOTH
Cisthene kentuckiensis 93-0178 (8061) **Common**
TL 8–10 mm. Blackish FW has wide golden yellow median band that narrows at midpoint before extending along basal section of inner margin. **HOSTS:** Lichen.

PACKARD'S LICHEN MOTH
Cisthene packardii 93-0189 (8072) **Common**
TL 8–10 mm. Resembles Kentucky Lichen Moth, but FW has broken reddish median band. A yellow streak extends parallel to inner margin in basal area. **HOSTS:** Lichen.

BLACK-AND-YELLOW LICHEN MOTH
Lycomorpha pholus 93-0201 (8087) **Common**
TL 13–17 mm. Golden yellow FW has a bluish black outer half. **HOSTS:** Lichen. **NOTE:** Resembles net-winged beetles in the genus *Calopteron*.

SCARLET-WINGED LICHEN MOTH
Hypoprepia miniata 93-0204 (8089) **Common**
TL 15–21 mm. Lead gray FW has wide scarlet border and shading along central veins. Thorax and head are red. **HOSTS:** Tree lichen.

PAINTED LICHEN MOTH
Hypoprepia fucosa 93-0205 (8090) **Common**
TL 16 mm. Resembles Scarlet-winged Lichen Moth, but FW has wide yellow border and shading along central veins tinged red in ST area. Thorax has reddish stripes and collar. **HOSTS:** Lichen and moss.

LITTLE WHITE LICHEN MOTH
Clemensia albata 93-0215 (8098) **Common**
TL 9–13 mm. Peppery white FW has light brown streaks extending between veins. Fragmented lines are boldest at costa. Reniform spot is a black crescent. **HOSTS:** Lichen. **NOTE:** Two or more broods.

LICHEN MOTHS

**KENTUCKY
LICHEN MOTH**

**PACKARD'S
LICHEN MOTH**

**BLACK-AND-YELLOW
LICHEN MOTH**

**SCARLET-
WINGED
LICHEN MOTH**

**PAINTED
LICHEN
MOTH**

actual size

**LITTLE WHITE
LICHEN MOTH**

BICOLORED MOTH *Eilema bicolor* 93-0217 (8043) **Common**
TL 14–16 mm. Lead gray FW has contrasting yellow costal stripe. Thorax has mustard yellow collar. **HOSTS:** Coniferous trees and the lichen that grows on them.

PALE LICHEN MOTH
Crambidia pallida 93-0219 (8045.1) **Common**
TL 11 mm. Grayish brown FW is marked with a netlike pattern of pale veins. **HOSTS:** Lichen. **NOTE:** Two broods.

PEARLY-WINGED LICHEN MOTH
Crambidia casta 93-0225 (8051) **Common**
TL 16–20 mm. Satin white FW is gray on underside. Abdomen and thorax are white. **HOSTS:** Lichen.

Tiger Moths
Family Erebidae, Subfamily Arctiinae, Tribe Arctiini

A varied group of strikingly attractive moths found in woodlands, fields, and gardens. The *Haploa* and *Cycnia* moths are broad-winged and flimsy-looking. The smaller *Virbia* moths (formerly placed in genus *Holomelina*) are both nocturnal and diurnal and rest with their wings tightly closed. Virginia Ctenucha and Yellow-collared Scape Moth are primarily day-fliers but will also come to light at night. The other species are more robust and hairy, often with striped, banded, or spotted patterns. Some species are more familiar as larvae, such as the confiding Woolly Bear Caterpillar of the Isabella Tiger Moth. Most species will visit lights in varying numbers.

ARGE MOTH *Grammia arge* 93-0240 (8199) **Common**
TL 20–26 mm. Straw-colored FW is marked with a fractured pattern of narrow black stripes and wedges between veins. Outer basal dash is a single streak. Straw-colored HW has a pink flush at base and black spots along ST line. **HOSTS:** Various low plants and vines, including sunflower, cotton, and grape. **NOTE:** Two broods.

PHYLLIRA TIGER MOTH
Grammia phyllira 93-0242 (8194) **Common**
TL 17–21 mm. Black FW has whitish border and stripe extending through central area. PM and ST lines fuse to form a B-shape. AM line is perpendicular to inner margin but is often fragmented. Salmon pink HW has a fragmented black terminal line. **HOSTS:** Low plants, including corn, lupine, and tobacco. **NOTE:** One or two broods.

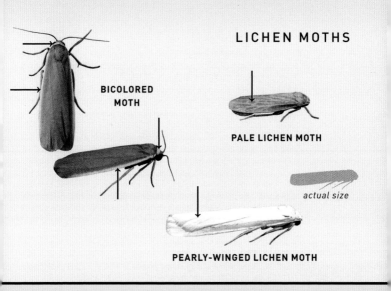

BICOLORED MOTH

PALE LICHEN MOTH

actual size

PEARLY-WINGED LICHEN MOTH

TIGER MOTHS

ARGE MOTH

PHYLLIRA TIGER MOTH

actual size

VIRGIN TIGER MOTH

Grammia virgo 93-0244 (8197) **Common**

TL 24–37 mm. Black FW has fine cream-colored border and stripes along veins. W-shaped ST line touches slightly kinked PM line. AM line meets costa at a right angle. Red HW is boldly marked with black spots in median and terminal areas. **HOSTS:** Low plants, including clover, lettuce, and plantain.

ANNA TIGER MOTH

Grammia anna 93-0245 (8176) **Common**

TL 23–28 mm. Resembles Little Virgin Tiger Moth, but some individuals have fragmented AM and PM lines on FW. Golden yellow HW typically has a wide black terminal line and a single black spot near costa, but can be all black in some females. **HOSTS:** Low plants, including dandelion and plantain.

PARTHENICE TIGER MOTH

Grammia parthenice 93-0246 (8196) **Common**

TL 18–28 mm. Resembles Virgin Tiger Moth, but pale veins are often thinner and salmon pink HW lacks black patches in median area. AM is perpendicular to costa. **HOSTS:** Low plants, including dandelion, ironweed, and thistle. **NOTE:** Two broods.

LITTLE VIRGIN TIGER MOTH

Grammia virguncula 93-0247 (8175) **Common**

TL 19–25 mm. Resembles Virgin Tiger Moth but lacks straight PM line above W-shaped ST line. Yellow HW is extensively spotted black. **HOSTS:** Low plants, including dandelion, knotweed, and plantain.

FIGURED TIGER MOTH

Grammia figurata 93-0253 (8188) **Common**

TL 16–22 mm. Black FW has single stripe extending through central area. Well-defined AM line is perpendicular to inner margin. Bright red (sometimes yellow) HW has a broad black terminal line and one or more black spots in median area. **HOSTS:** Low plants, including alfalfa and plantain. **NOTE:** One or two broods.

WILLIAMS' TIGER MOTH

Grammia williamsii 93-0264 (8186) **Common**

TL 16–18 mm. Black FW has single whitish stripe extending through central area. Fragmented AM line is perpendicular to inner margin but is sometimes absent. Salmon pink or yellow HW has a broad black terminal line and spots in median area. **HOSTS:** Low plants, including ragwort.

TIGER MOTHS

VIRGIN TIGER MOTH

PARTHENICE TIGER MOTH

ANNA TIGER MOTH

LITTLE VIRGIN TIGER MOTH

WILLIAMS' TIGER MOTH

actual size

FIGURED TIGER MOTH

HARNESSED TIGER MOTH

Apantesis phalerata   93-0278 (8169)   **Common**
TL 16–22 mm. Similar to *Grammia* tiger moths, but veins are black and pale PM line present only in black section beside costa. Typically has black spots on collar. Females (not shown) can have reduced bands, appearing more blackish. HW is usually reddish (especially northward) with a fragmented black terminal line. Variable and very similar to Nais Tiger Moth; collar usually useful, but some intermediates may not be identifiable. **HOSTS:** Low plants, including clover, corn, dandelion, and plantain. **NOTE:** Two broods.

NAIS TIGER MOTH   *Apantesis nais*   93-0280 (8171)   **Common**
TL 16–22 mm. Resembles Harnessed Tiger Moth (and often indistinguishable), but typically has no black spots on collar and HW is usually pale yellow, sometimes with a reddish wash at base with a wide black terminal band, often fragmented into a row of black spots. **HOSTS:** Low plants, including clover, various grasses, plantain, and violet. **NOTE:** Two broods.

ST. LAWRENCE TIGER MOTH

Platarctia parthenos   93-0288 (8162)   **Common**
TL 27–33 mm. Chocolate brown FW is marked with rows of cream-colored spots and bars along AM, PM, and ST lines. Black HW has two broad golden yellow bands. **HOSTS:** Deciduous trees and plants, including alder, birch, lettuce, and willow.

GREAT TIGER MOTH   *Arctia caja*   93-0290 (8166)   **Common**
TL 28–37 mm. Chocolate brown FW is boldly marked with wavy cream-colored bands. The pattern varies among individuals. Orange HW has large blue spots outlined in black. **HOSTS:** Deciduous trees, including alder, cherry, poplar, and willow.

JOYFUL VIRBIA   *Virbia laeta*   93-0294 (8114)   **Common**
TL 11–13 mm. Lead gray FW sometimes has a thin pink costal streak. Rosy HW has a broad black border. Gray thorax has a pink collar. **HOSTS:** Dandelion and plantain.

TAWNY VIRBIA   *Virbia opella*   93-0297 (8118)   **Common**
TL 12–16 mm. FW is variably yellowish to chocolate brown, often with slightly darker veins. An inconspicuous discal crescent is sometimes visible. Orange HW has a blackish border and discal spot. Undersides of all wings are pale orange in female. **HOSTS:** Low plants, including dandelion.

TIGER MOTHS

HARNESSED TIGER MOTH

NAIS TIGER MOTH

ST. LAWRENCE TIGER MOTH

actual size

GREAT TIGER MOTH

JOYFUL VIRBIA

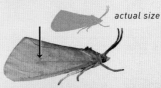

actual size

TAWNY VIRBIA

299

ORANGE VIRBIA
Virbia aurantiaca   93-0299 (8121)   **Common**
TL 10–14 mm. FW is variably pale orange to brown, usually without obvious markings. Sometimes has a small dusky discal spot and shading along ST line. Orange HW has an almost complete black border and a small black discal spot. **HOSTS:** Low plants and crops, including corn, dandelion, pigweed, and plantain.

BOG VIRBIA   *Virbia lamae*   93-0302 (8120)   **Uncommon**
TL 11–14 mm. Chocolate brown FW typically has conspicuous pale spot in inner median area. Darker ST band is bordered with faint pale smudges. Orange HW has a broad black border and black discal spot. **HOSTS:** Plantain.

RUSTY VIRBIA   *Virbia ferruginosa*   93-0306 (8123)   **Common**
TL 13–16 mm. FW is variably pale orange to pinkish brown, usually without obvious markings. Sometimes has a small dusky discal spot and shading along ST line. A whitish spot or bar may be present in inner median area. HW is yellow or pale orange with a fragmented black border and black discal spot. **HOSTS:** Low plants, including dandelion.

AGREEABLE TIGER MOTH
Spilosoma congrua   93-0309 (8134)   **Common**
TL 15–24 mm. FW is typically white, sometimes variably marked with brown spotting in PM and ST areas. White abdomen lacks any color or spots. Coxa and femur of forelegs are yellow-orange. **HOSTS:** Low plants, including plantain and pigweed. Larvae have also been reported to bore into stems of mushrooms.

DUBIOUS TIGER MOTH
Spilosoma dubia   93-0310 (8136)   **Common**
TL 17–21 mm. White FW usually has obvious brown spotting along AM, PM, and ST lines. HW is white with a fragmented blackish ST line and discal spot. Abdomen is marked with yellow and black spotting. Coxa and femur of forelegs are partly orange-yellow. **HOSTS:** Wild cherry and plantain.

PINK-LEGGED TIGER MOTH
Spilosoma latipennis   93-0311 (8133)   **Common**
TL 17–25 mm. Snowy white FW is without markings. White thorax is loosely hairy. White abdomen lacks any spots or color. HW is white. Coxa and femur of forelegs are pink. **HOSTS:** Deciduous trees and low plants, including ash, dandelion, and plantain.

TIGER MOTHS

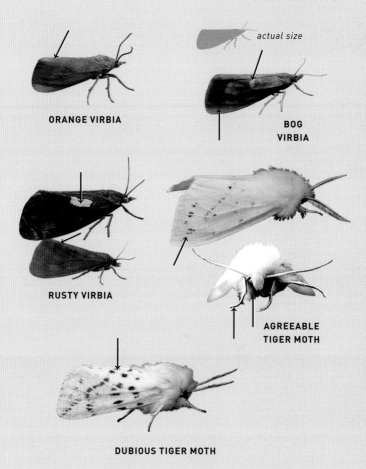

actual size

ORANGE VIRBIA

BOG VIRBIA

RUSTY VIRBIA

AGREEABLE TIGER MOTH

DUBIOUS TIGER MOTH

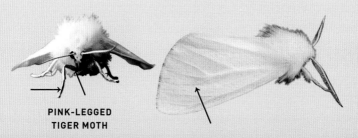

PINK-LEGGED TIGER MOTH

VIRGINIAN TIGER MOTH
Spilosoma virginica 93-0316 (8137)   **Common**
TL 17–26 mm. FW is pure white, sometimes with a few tiny black dots. White HW sometimes has black spots in ST area. Abdomen is marked with yellow patches and rows of black spots. Coxa and femur of forelegs are yellow-orange and black. Legs are striped. **HOSTS:** Deciduous trees and low plants, including birch, cabbage, maple, tobacco, walnut, and willow. **NOTE:** Two broods.

SALT MARSH MOTH
Estigmene acrea 93-0317 (8131)   **Common**
TL 29 mm. White FW is marked with fragmented lines of black dots and dashes, often boldest along costa. Underside is orange in male. HW is orange in male and white in female, with small black blotches. Orange abdomen has a white tip and rows of black dots on each segment. Legs are striped. **HOSTS:** Deciduous trees and low plants, including apple, cabbage, corn, potato, and tobacco. **NOTE:** Two broods.

FALL WEBWORM
Hyphantria cunea 93-0319 (8140)   **Common**
TL 14–19 mm. FW pattern is variable but typically is uniformly white in the northern part of range and marked with brown spots to the south. Sometimes has brown FW with white veins. HW is white, sometimes with a fragmented brown ST line. White abdomen typically has brown bands near tip. Coxa and femur of forelegs are yellow. **HOSTS:** Wide variety of deciduous trees, including ash, hickory, maple, oak, and walnut.

GIANT LEOPARD MOTH
Hypercompe scribonia 93-0323 (8146)   **Common**
TL 33–35 mm. White FW is boldly marked with glossy blue-black spots that are mostly hollow toward inner margin. Thorax has blue-black spots. Abdomen is blue-black dorsally with orange lateral stripes and segment edges. **HOSTS:** Deciduous trees and low plants, including cabbage, cherry, maple, sunflower, and willow.

RUBY TIGER MOTH
Phragmatobia fuliginosa 93-0332 (8156)   **Common**
TL 15–18 mm. Semi-translucent FW is rusty brown with a small blackish reniform spot. Brown HW has pinkish shading along inner margin and a black discal spot. Reddish abdomen is marked with rows of black spots. **HOSTS:** Low plants, including dock, goldenrod, ironweed, plantain, and sunflower. **NOTE:** Two broods.

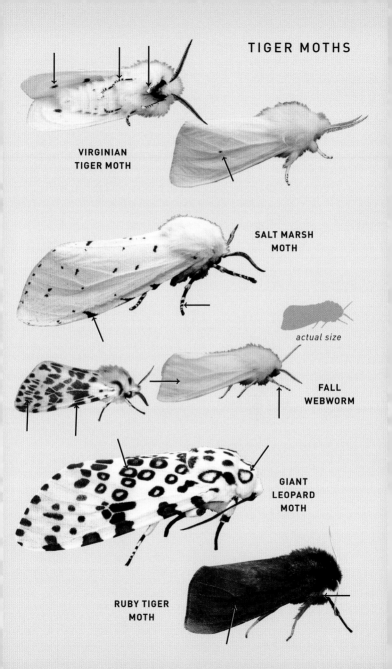

TIGER MOTHS

VIRGINIAN TIGER MOTH

SALT MARSH MOTH

actual size

FALL WEBWORM

GIANT LEOPARD MOTH

RUBY TIGER MOTH

LINED RUBY TIGER MOTH

Phragmatobia lineata   93-0333 (8157)   **Common**
TL 16–21 mm. Resembles Ruby Tiger Moth, but FW has well-defined PM line and fragmented AM and ST lines. HW is mostly pinkish with brown terminal line and costal shading. **HOSTS:** Primarily boneset. **NOTE:** Two broods.

LARGE RUBY TIGER MOTH

Phragmatobia assimilans   93-0334 (8158)   **Common**
TL 20 mm. Resembles Ruby Tiger Moth. Lines, if present, are typically rather broad and fragmented. Pinkish red HW has a distinct blackish terminal line. **HOSTS:** Balsam poplar, birch, blackberry, dandelion, plantain, and raspberry.

ISABELLA TIGER MOTH

Pyrrharctia isabella   93-0335 (8129)   **Common**
TL 24–33 mm. Pale orange FW is marked with faint brown lines and spots of varying intensity. Pale orange (male) or rose (female) HW has a few blackish spots. Abdomen is mostly orange with a row of black dorsal spots. **HOSTS:** Deciduous trees and low plants, including aster, birch, elm, maple, and sunflower. **NOTE:** Two broods.

CLYMENE MOTH   *Haploa clymene*   93-0341 (8107)   **Common**

TL 22–28 mm. Creamy white (rarely pale orange) FW has black costal streak and outer margin. Black streak along inner margin has a barlike extension, forming an upside-down cross on folded wings. **HOSTS:** *Eupatorium* species, also oak, peach, and willow.

REVERSED HAPLOA

Haploa reversa   93-0343 (8109)   **Common**
TL 22–28 mm. White FW has a narrow brown border broken at apex. An oblique brown band extends from midpoint of costa to anal angle. Beyond this, pattern is broken into four or five white spots. **HOSTS:** Deciduous trees, including apple, ash, and elm.

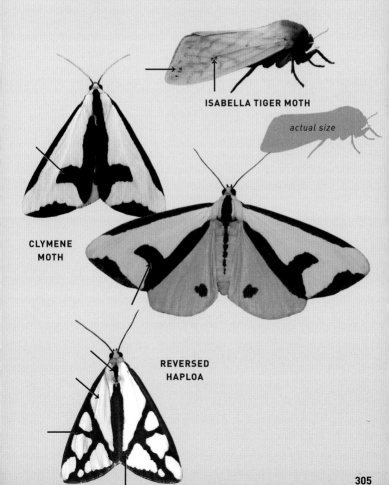

TIGER MOTHS

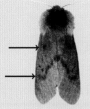

**LINED RUBY
TIGER MOTH**

**LARGE RUBY
TIGER MOTH**

ISABELLA TIGER MOTH

actual size

**CLYMENE
MOTH**

**REVERSED
HAPLOA**

THE NEIGHBOR
Haploa contigua 93-0344 (8110)   **Common**

TL 19–26 mm. White FW has a black border broken at apex and anal angle. A perpendicular black band extends from beyond midpoint of costa to anal angle. Beyond this, pattern is broken into two large white patches. **HOSTS:** Trembling aspen, probably other plants.

LECONTE'S HAPLOA
Haploa lecontei 93-0345 (8111)   **Common**

TL 19–26 mm. FW pattern is variable but typically is white with black border broken at apex and anal angle. A black line slants from inner ST area to apex. Some individuals are mostly white; others are boldly marked, imparting a spotted appearance. **HOSTS:** Trees and shrubs, including apple, blackberry, and peach.

CONFUSED HAPLOA
Haploa confusa 93-0346 (8112)   **Common**

TL 20–22 mm. Resembles Reversed Haploa, but blackish brown FW is boldly marked with white spots that are sometimes fused. **HOSTS:** Hound's-tongue.

ORNATE MOTH   *Utetheisa ornatrix*
93-0348 (8105)   **Common**

TL 16–24 mm. Rose pink FW typically has several rows of black-studded white bands. Pale individuals are mostly pinkish with just a few black spots. **HOSTS:** Mostly legumes, such as lespedeza and lupine, also various trees and low plants. **NOTE:** A rare immigrant to north part of range. Also known as Bella Moth and Rattlebox Moth.

BANDED TUSSOCK MOTH
Halysidota tessellaris 93-0360 (8203)   **Common**

TL 22–25 mm. Pale tan FW has irregular pattern of slightly darker, black-edged bands. Thorax has turquoise and yellow dorsal stripes. **HOSTS:** Deciduous trees and shrubs, including alder, ash, birch, elm, oak, and willow. **NOTE:** Two broods.

HICKORY TUSSOCK MOTH
Lophocampa caryae 93-0370 (8211)   **Common**

TL 20–28 mm. Peppery cream-colored FW is boldly marked with irregular bands of semi-translucent spots between brown veins. Thorax has thick brown lateral stripes. **HOSTS:** Deciduous trees, including ash, elm, hickory, maple, and oak.

TIGER MOTHS

THE NEIGHBOR

CONFUSED HAPLOA

LECONTE'S HAPLOA

ORNATE MOTH

actual size

BANDED TUSSOCK MOTH

HICKORY TUSSOCK MOTH

SPOTTED TUSSOCK MOTH

Lophocampa maculata 93-0373 (8214) **Common**

TL 20–28 mm. Pale yellow FW is marked with brown veins and irregular bands. Thorax is pale tan with thick brown lateral stripes. **HOSTS:** Deciduous trees, including birch, maple, oak, poplar, and willow.

DELICATE CYCNIA

Cycnia tenera 93-0404 (8230) **Common**

TL 16–22 mm. Satin white FW is marked with whiter veins and a yellow costal streak that fades before apex. Head and collar are yellow. **HOSTS:** Indian hemp and milkweed.

OREGON CYCNIA

Cycnia oregonensis 93-0405 (8231) **Common**

TL 16–22 mm. Pearly gray FW has contrasting white veins. Head and collar sides are mustard yellow. **HOSTS:** Indian hemp. **NOTE:** Two broods.

MILKWEED TUSSOCK MOTH

Euchaetes egle 93-0412 (8238) **Common**

TL 17–22 mm. Mousy gray FW is lightly flecked whitish. HW is gray. Head has some yellow around eyes. **HOSTS:** Milkweed. **NOTE:** Two broods.

VIRGINIA CTENUCHA

Ctenucha virginica 93-0435 (8262) **Common**

TL 25–27 mm. Broad, dark grayish brown FW has metallic blue sheen at base. Fringe is partly white. Abdomen and thorax are metallic blue contrasting with orange head and sides of collar. **HOSTS:** Grasses, iris, and sedge. **NOTE:** Two broods.

YELLOW-COLLARED SCAPE MOTH

Cisseps fulvicollis 93-0440 (8267) **Common**

TL 16–20 mm. Narrow, sooty brown FW has yellow streak that extends along basal half of costa. Dull metallic blue thorax has contrasting golden collar. **HOSTS:** Grasses, lichen, and spike-rush. **NOTE:** Two broods.

TIGER MOTHS

SPOTTED
TUSSOCK
MOTH

DELICATE
CYCNIA

actual size

OREGON
CYCNIA

MILKWEED
TUSSOCK
MOTH

VIRGINIA
CTENUCHA

YELLOW-
COLLARED
SCAPE MOTH

309

Litter Moths
Family Erebidae, Subfamily Hermeniinae

Delta-shaped, flat-winged noctuid moths found in woodlands, fields, and gardens. Some species, notably in the genera *Zanclognatha* and *Renia,* have long, often upturned, labial palps. Although this group is initially confusing, subtle differences in pattern and form offer important clues to identification. Most species are nocturnal and will come to lights in small numbers. *Idia* species readily visit sugar bait painted on tree trunks.

AMERICAN IDIA *Idia americalis* 93-0469 (8322) **Common**
TL 13–14 mm. Pale gray FW has jagged black lines boldest at costa. Orbicular and reniform spots are rusty brown. A band of warm brown shading is often present beyond ST line. Darker individuals have blackish gray median area. **HOSTS:** Lichen. **NOTE:** Two or more broods.

COMMON IDIA *Idia aemula* 93-0471 (8323) **Common**
TL 11–16 mm. FW is variably pale grayish brown to dark gray, peppered with dusky scales. Jagged lines are often heaviest at costa. Orbicular and reniform spots are typically pale yellow. Darker individuals often have pale yellow ST line. **HOSTS:** Dead leaves and living foliage of coniferous trees. **NOTE:** Two or more broods.

ROTUND IDIA *Idia rotundalis* 93-0474 (8326) **Common**
TL 11–13 mm. Shiny sooty brown FW has obscure dusky lines. Pale gray orbicular and reniform spots are small and inconspicuous. **HOSTS:** Coral fungus and dead leaves.

FORBES' IDIA *Idia forbesii* 93-0475 (8327) **Common**
TL 9–11 mm. Dark gray FW has scalloped black lines accented with white at costa. Blackish median band is conspicuous. Wavy ST line is highlighted with white dots. **HOSTS:** Unknown. **RANGE:** Se. Canada and e. U.S.

ORANGE-SPOTTED IDIA
Idia diminuendis 93-0477 (8329) **Common**
TL 9–11 mm. Grayish brown FW has inconspicuous jagged lines. Small pale orange orbicular and reniform spots are well defined. **HOSTS:** Unknown.

SMOKY IDIA *Idia scobialis* 93-0478 (8330) **Common**
TL 10–14 mm. Blackish FW has jagged cream-colored lines that are boldest at costa. Orbicular and reniform spots are whitish. **HOSTS:** Unknown.

LITTER MOTHS

AMERICAN IDIA

actual size

COMMON IDIA

ROTUND IDIA

FORBES' IDIA

ORANGE-SPOTTED IDIA

SMOKY IDIA

GLOSSY BLACK IDIA

Idia lubricalis   93-0482 (8334)   **Common**
TL 18–21 mm. Shiny sooty brown FW has paler band beyond jagged ST line. Toothed AM and PM lines are edged pale yellow. **HOSTS:** Fungi, grasses, lichen, and rotten wood.

DARK-BANDED OWLET

Phalaenophana pyramusalis   93-0487 (8338)   **Common**
TL 12–14 mm. Gray FW has straight AM and slightly wavy PM lines bordered with darker brown bands. Reniform spot contains two black dots. **HOSTS:** Wilted and decaying leaves. **NOTE:** One or two broods.

LETTERED FAN-FOOT

Zanclognatha lituralis   93-0489 (8340)   **Common**
TL 12–15 mm. Pale gray FW has dotted lines that end as bold black spots along costa. Reniform spot is a thin black crescent. **HOSTS:** Dead leaves of deciduous trees. **NOTE:** Two broods.

VARIABLE FAN-FOOT

Zanclognatha laevigata   93-0492 (8345)   **Common**
TL 18–21 mm. FW is variable in color and pattern. Straight AM and bulging PM lines are often bordered with brown or blackish bands. Median area can be pale tan, orange, or dark gray. Wavy ST line curves toward apex. **HOSTS:** Unknown, but probably dead leaves.

GRAYISH FAN-FOOT

Zanclognatha pedipilalis   93-0495 (8348)   **Common**
TL 14–17 mm. FW is pale grayish tan (darker in second brood). AM line is sharply bent near costa. PM line has a rounded point to bulge. Straight ST line fades before reaching apex. **HOSTS:** Dead leaves of deciduous trees. **NOTE:** Two broods.

COMPLEX FAN-FOOT

Zanclognatha protumnusalis   93-0496 (8349)   **Common**
TL 12–13 mm. FW is yellowish tan to gray. Jagged AM and PM lines are thicker at costa. Reniform spot is sometimes black. Straight ST line typically lacks yellowish edge. Variation suggests more than one species may be involved. **HOSTS:** Coniferous trees.

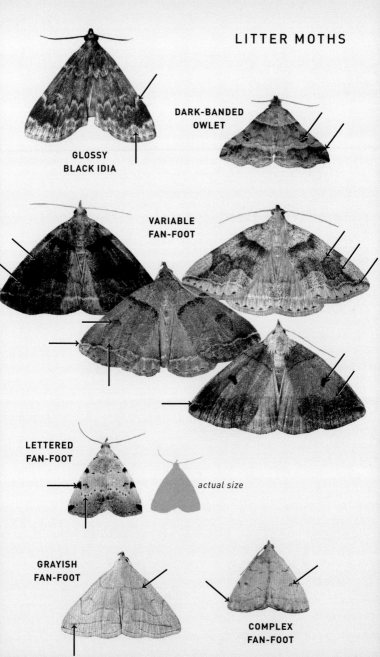

LITTER MOTHS

GLOSSY BLACK IDIA

DARK-BANDED OWLET

VARIABLE FAN-FOOT

LETTERED FAN-FOOT

actual size

GRAYISH FAN-FOOT

COMPLEX FAN-FOOT

EARLY FAN-FOOT
Zanclognatha cruralis   93-0498 (8351)   **Common**
TL 15–17 mm. FW is pale yellowish tan (darker in second brood). AM line is sharply kinked near costa. PM line has indentation in bulge. **HOSTS:** Balsam fir and dead leaves of deciduous trees. **NOTE:** Two broods.

WAVY-LINED FAN-FOOT
Zanclognatha jacchusalis   93-0500 (8353)   **Common**
TL 17–18 mm. FW is yellowish to brown, lightly peppered with brown scales. AM line is wavy, curving toward costa. PM line is toothed. **HOSTS:** Probably dead leaves.

MORBID OWLET
Chytolita morbidalis   93-0502 (8355)   **Common**
TL 16–19 mm. Pale FW has wavy AM line and bulging PM line. Scalloped ST line is accented with a row of outward-pointing dusky wedges. Labial palps are long. **HOSTS:** Dead leaves of deciduous trees.

STONE-WINGED OWLET
Chytolita petrealis   93-0503 (8356)   **Common**
TL 16–19 mm. Resembles Morbid Owlet but has bolder rusty AM and PM lines and more conspicuous reniform spot. **HOSTS:** Dead leaves and tamarack.

TWO-STRIPED OWLET
Macrochilo bivittata   93-0506 (8359)   **Uncommon**
TL 14–15 mm. Straw-colored FW is lightly peppered with brown scales between pale veins. Thick brown streak extends parallel to inner margin. Shorter streak passes close to short apical dash. **HOSTS:** Unknown. **RANGE:** Locally in se. Canada and e. U.S.

SLANT-LINED OWLET
Macrochilo absorptalis   93-0508 (8357)   **Common**
TL 12–14 mm. Sandy gray FW has slanting PM line that curves inward before reaching costa. Straight ST line reaches apex. Reniform spot has two tiny black dots. **HOSTS:** Sedges.

TWO-LINED OWLET
Macrochilo litophora   93-0510 (8358)   **Common**
TL 12–14 mm. Straw-colored FW is lightly peppered with brown scales. Parallel brown AM and PM lines are strongly angled before reaching costa. **HOSTS:** Bluegrass and clover. **RANGE:** Se. Canada and e. U.S.

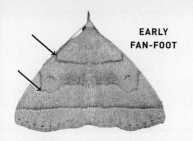

EARLY FAN-FOOT

LITTER MOTHS

WAVY-LINED FAN-FOOT

MORBID OWLET

STONE-WINGED OWLET

TWO-STRIPED OWLET

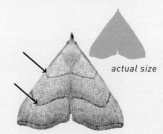

actual size

SLANT-LINED OWLET

TWO-LINED OWLET

BRONZY MACROCHILO
Macrochilo orciferalis   93-0511 (8360)   **Common**
TL 14 mm. Narrow bronze brown FW has paler subapical dash. Some individuals are paler, with streaks of brown shading along veins and a black bar that cuts through orbicular and reniform spots. **HOSTS:** Unknown. **RANGE:** Se. Canada and e. U.S.

PALE PHALAENOSTOLA
Phalaenostola metonalis   93-0512 (8362)   **Common**
TL 13–14 mm. Sandy brown FW has brown median band. Slightly wavy ST line merges with short apical dash. Reniform spot is a narrow crescent. Remarkably long, divergent labial palps are noticeable. Male has broadly bipectinate antennae. **HOSTS:** Primarily dead leaves, also dandelion and lettuce.

DARK PHALAENOSTOLA
Phalaenostola eumelusalis   93-0513 (8363)   **Common**
TL 14 mm. Brown FW has conspicuous wide dusky median band. Wavy ST line is accented with two blackish bulges before merging with short apical dash. Upturned labial palps are moderately long. Male has narrowly bipectinate antennae. **HOSTS:** Unknown.

BLACK-BANDED OWLET
Phalaenostola larentioides   93-0514 (8364)   **Common**
TL 10–13 mm. Violet gray FW has wavy AM and PM lines. Wide bands of black shading pass through median area and along pale ST line. **HOSTS:** Dead grass and leaves, also clover.

SMOKY TETANOLITA
Tetanolita mynesalis   93-0516 (8366)   **Common**
TL 11–13 mm. Gray FW has inconspicuous AM and PM lines. Pale yellow orbicular and reniform spots are well defined. Whitish ST line is fragmented into a row of dots. **HOSTS:** Probably dead leaves.

BENT-WINGED OWLET
Bleptina caradrinalis   93-0520 (8370)   **Common**
TL 12–17 mm. FW is pale sandy brown to violet gray with indistinct, jagged AM and PM lines. Slightly wavy, pale-edged ST line is conspicuous on darker individuals. Reniform spot can be either orange or black. Male has concave costal edge. **HOSTS:** Dead leaves.

BRONZY MACROCHILO

PALE PHALAENOSTOLA

DARK PHALAENOSTOLA

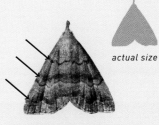

BLACK-BANDED OWLET

actual size

SMOKY TETANOLITA

BENT-WINGED OWLET

SOCIABLE RENIA

Renia factiosalis   93-0530 (8379)   **Common**
TL 14 mm. Brown FW has jagged yellow-edged AM and PM
lines. Narrow reniform spot is orange with two tiny black dots.
Irregular ST line is bordered dark brown. Male has a tuft of
scales beyond midpoint of antennae. **HOSTS:** Dead leaves, also
barberry, clover, and hickory.

DISCOLORED RENIA

Renia discoloralis   93-0532 (8381)   **Common**
TL 19–24 mm. Variable. FW is typically sandy brown with fragmented pale-edged AM and PM lines. Incomplete dusky median band is often present. Pale reniform spot has a black bar
in center. Darker individuals are chocolate brown with a whitish
orbicular spot. Male has a tuft beyond midpoint of antennae.
HOSTS: Dead leaves.

YELLOW-SPOTTED RENIA

Renia flavipunctalis   93-0536 (8384.1)   **Common**
TL 16–17 mm. Violet gray FW has PM line that curves smoothly
inward before reaching costa. Reniform spot is yellow or black.
Indistinct ST line is bordered with a band of brown shading.
Male has a tuft beyond midpoint of antennae. **HOSTS:** Dead
leaves.

SOBER RENIA

Renia sobrialis   93-0539 (8387)   **Common**
TL 13–15 mm. Purplish gray FW has jagged AM and PM lines.
Incomplete blackish median band is often present. Orbicular
and reniform spots are orange. Irregular ST line often is reduced to a row of whitish dots. Male has a tuft of scales near
midpoint of antennae. **HOSTS:** Dead leaves.

AMBIGUOUS MOTH

Lascoria ambigualis   93-0547 (8393)   **Common**
TL 12–14 mm. Violet gray FW has straight AM line that is
broadly edged black. Median and PM lines are scalloped. Male
has black spot in mouth of notch midway along outer margin.
Reniform spot is an oblique white crescent, often fragmented in
female. **HOSTS:** Chrysanthemum, ragweed, and horseradish.
NOTE: Two broods.

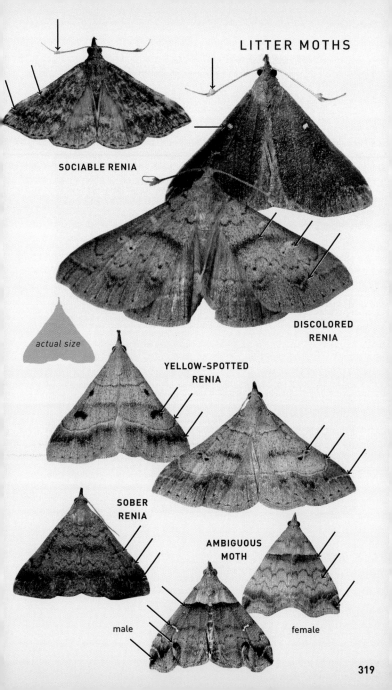

LITTER MOTHS

SOCIABLE RENIA

DISCOLORED RENIA

actual size

YELLOW-SPOTTED RENIA

SOBER RENIA

AMBIGUOUS MOTH

male

female

DARK-SPOTTED PALTHIS

Palthis angulalis   93-0551 (8397)   **Common**
TL 18 mm. Tan FW has oblique brown median band that stops short of costa. Reniform spot is a slanting brown crescent. Apical patch is rusty brown. Outer third of FW is tightly creased. Male has long upturned labial palps. **HOSTS:** Coniferous and deciduous trees, including ash, alder, maple, spruce, and willow. **NOTE:** Two broods

FAINT-SPOTTED PALTHIS

Palthis asopialis   93-0552 (8398)   **Common**
TL 16 mm. Resembles Dark-spotted Palthis, but grayish brown FW has a conspicuous black patch near apex. Has a grotesquely humpbacked profile. **HOSTS:** Bean, coralberry, corn, oak, and Spanish needles. **NOTE:** One or two broods.

WHITE-SPOTTED REDECTIS

Redectis vitrea   93-0555 (8401)   **Common**
TL 15 mm. Grayish tan FW has indistinct, scalloped lines. Outer median area is spangled with brassy scales. Reniform spot has a single white spot edged with orange fragments. Head and thorax are whitish. Male has long, upturned labial palps. **HOSTS:** Crabgrass.

Pangraptine Owlets
Family Erebidae, Subfamily Pangraptinae

Lost Owlet is similar in shape to both the litter moths and the snouts, whereas Decorated Owlet resembles a geometer. Both will visit lights.

DECORATED OWLET

Pangrapta decoralis   93-0559 (8490)   **Uncommon**
TL 11–15 mm. Pale violet gray FW has AM and PM lines that are bordered with rusty brown bands. Black discal spots mark all wings. HW has scalloped outer margin. **HOSTS:** Blueberry, mostly on sandy soils. **NOTE:** A geometrid-like moth that holds its wings in a distinctive shallow dihedral.

LOST OWLET   *Ledaea perditalis*   93-0560 (8491)   **Common**
TL 13–16 mm. Gray FW has curved, double PM line that forms a solid black bar at inner margin. Orbicular and reniform spots are small black dots. Slightly scalloped white ST line is edged with black wedges. **HOSTS:** Buttonbush and woolgrass.

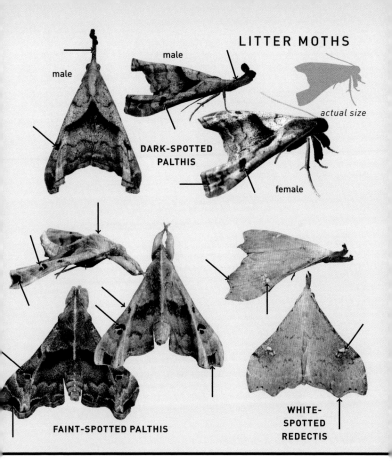

LITTER MOTHS

male

male

actual size

DARK-SPOTTED PALTHIS

female

FAINT-SPOTTED PALTHIS

WHITE-SPOTTED REDECTIS

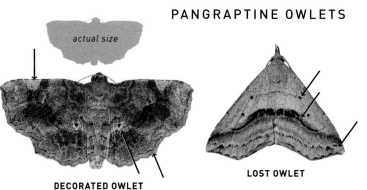

PANGRAPTINE OWLETS

actual size

DECORATED OWLET

LOST OWLET

Deltoid noctuids characterized by their ample, strikingly patterned FW. Long labial palps give them a snoutlike appearance. These woodland moths are mostly nocturnal and are attracted to lights in small numbers. Green Cloverworm is commonly flushed from grassy areas during daylight, and also regularly encountered at sugar bait in the fall.

FLOWING-LINE SNOUT
Hypena manalis   93-0561 (8441)   **Common**
TL 13–16 mm. Grayish brown FW has a round-edged dark brown patch covering most of median area. Black apical dash angles toward inconspicuous dotted ST line. **HOSTS:** Possibly dandelion and dock. **NOTE:** One or two broods.

BALTIMORE SNOUT
Hypena baltimoralis   93-0562 (8442)   **Common**
TL 16–18 mm. Pale tan FW has dark brown median patch that has a straight edge parallel to inner margin. Black apical dash angles toward round-tipped tooth in median patch. Females are usually paler. **HOSTS:** Maple. **NOTE:** Two broods.

DIMORPHIC SNOUT
Hypena bijugalis   93-0564 (8443)   **Common**
TL 14–17 mm. Sexually dimorphic. Sooty black FW of male has a square white patch where PM line meets inner margin. Female is pale gray with a large dark brown median patch. A toothed bulge projects from distal edge of median patch. **HOSTS:** Dogwood. **NOTE:** One or two broods.

MOTTLED SNOUT
Hypena palparia   93-0565 (8444)   **Common**
TL 15–19 mm. Grayish brown FW is speckled with brown scales. Jagged AM and PM lines edge darker brown median area that reaches inner margin. Males are usually darker than females. **HOSTS:** Eastern hornbeam, ironwood, and hazel. **NOTE:** Two broods.

WHITE-LINED SNOUT
Hypena abalienalis   93-0566 (8445)   **Common**
TL 14–18 mm. Sexually dimorphic. Chocolate brown FW of male has lacy grayish ST area. Female is similar but has jagged white AM line. **HOSTS:** Slippery elm.

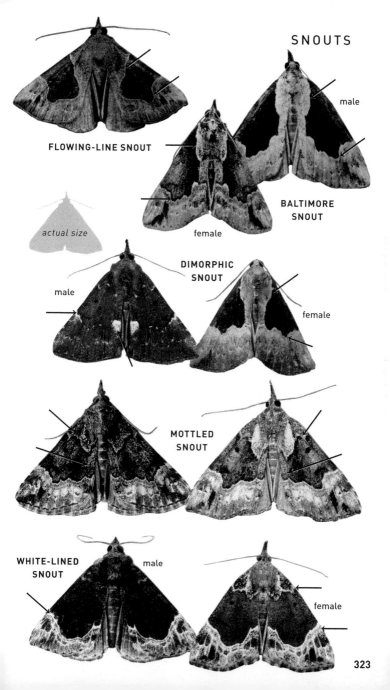

SNOUTS

FLOWING-LINE SNOUT

BALTIMORE SNOUT

male

female

actual size

DIMORPHIC SNOUT

male

female

MOTTLED SNOUT

WHITE-LINED SNOUT

male

female

323

DECEPTIVE SNOUT

Hypena deceptalis   93-0567 (8446)   **Common**

TL 16–20 mm. Sexually dimorphic. Dark brown FW of male is densely peppered with blackish scales. Kinked AM and almost straight PM line edge darker median area. Female is paler overall, especially beyond PM line. **HOSTS:** Basswood. **NOTE:** Two broods.

GRAY-EDGED SNOUT

Hypena madefactalis   93-0568 (8447)   **Common**

TL 19 mm. Sexually dimorphic. FW of male is sooty brown. Female is paler with rusty brown median band and jagged AM line. Both sexes have a lilac gray band beyond wavy PM line. **HOSTS:** Black walnut and butternut. **NOTE:** One or two broods.

SORDID SNOUT

Hypena sordidula   93-0570 (8448)   **Uncommon**

TL 14–17 mm. Sexually dimorphic. Sooty black FW of male has indistinct wavy lines. PM line is highlighted with white at costa. Female is brown with paler outer margin. **HOSTS:** Alder and butternut.

SPECKLED SNOUT

Hypena atomaria   93-0573 (8450)   **Uncommon**

TL 14–18 mm. Pale tan FW is strongly peppered with brown scales. Brown AM line is W-shaped. PM line is slightly curved. Dotted ST line is accented with white along veins. **HOSTS:** Unknown. **NOTE:** One or two broods. **RANGE:** S. Canada and ne. U.S.

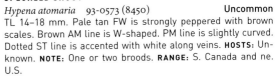

LARGE SNOUT   *Hypena edictalis*   93-0575 (8452)   **Common**

TL 18–20 mm. Pale tan FW has darker violet brown median area. Kinked AM and PM lines are edged pale yellow. Orbicular and reniform spots are black. Darker individuals are sooty brown with contrasting pale lines. **HOSTS:** Unknown.

HOP VINE MOTH   *Hypena humuli*   93-0584 (8461)   **Common**

TL 14–20 mm. Mottled FW has darker brown patch along costa that covers small black orbicular spot. PM line fades before reaching inner margin. Apical dash is short. **HOSTS:** Common hop and stinging nettle. **NOTE:** Up to three broods.

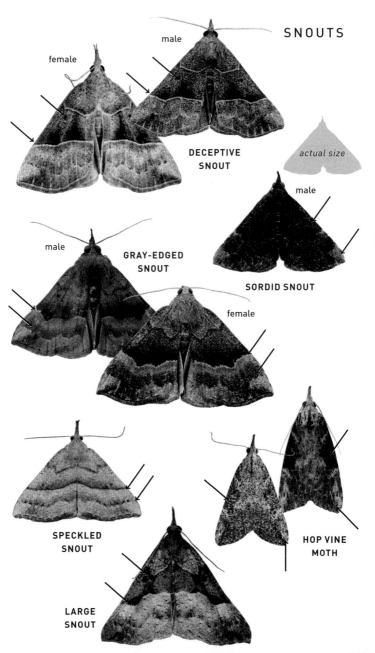

SNOUTS

female

male

DECEPTIVE
SNOUT

actual size

male

SORDID SNOUT

male

GRAY-EDGED
SNOUT

female

SPECKLED
SNOUT

HOP VINE
MOTH

LARGE
SNOUT

GREEN CLOVERWORM
Hypena scabra   93-0588 (8465)   **Common**
TL 15–21 mm. FW is variable but is typically grayish brown with darker outer median area. Black PM line is straight at inner margin. Often there is a short black streak in inner median area. Apical dash is long, reaching inner margin. **HOSTS:** Low plants and crops, including alfalfa, bean, clover, ragweed, raspberry, and strawberry. **NOTE:** Several broods.

RED-FOOTED SNOUT
Hypena eductalis   93-0589 (8455)   **Uncommon**
TL 16 mm. Earth brown FW has pale bluish gray band beyond straight PM line. Yellow-edged AM line is W-shaped. Orbicular spot is a black dot. **HOSTS:** Alder and basswood.

ASSORTED OWLETS
Family Erebidae, Subfamilies Rivulinae, Hyperiinae, Scoliopteryginae, Calpinae, Hypocalinae, Scolecocampinae, Phytometrinae, Hypenodinae, and Boletobiinae

A diverse assemblage of very small to medium-sized noctuid moths that inhabit woodlands, fields, and gardens. Most rest on flat wings, though a few, such as Canadian Owlet and Moonseed Moth, rest with tightly compressed wings. Some, such as Spotted Grass Moth, may be flushed from long grass or leaf litter. Most come to light in small numbers. The Herald and *Dyspyralis* species will also visit sugar bait.

YELLOW-LINED OWLET
Colobochyla interpuncta   93-0590 (8411)   **Uncommon**
TL 11–13 mm. Violet gray FW has parallel yellow-edged rusty AM, median, and PM lines that fade before reaching costa. Orbicular and reniform spots are tiny black dots. **HOSTS:** Willow. **NOTE:** Two broods.

GOLD-LINED MELANOMMA
Melanomma auricinctaria   93-0591 (8412)   **Uncommon**
WS 18 mm. Broad gray FW has darker shading along basal section of costa. Angled blackish median band is conspicuous. Large black reniform spot has metallic silvery dots in middle and edge. Outer ST line is studded with metallic silvery dots. Male has broadly bipectinate antennae. **HOSTS:** Huckleberry. **NOTE:** Two broods.

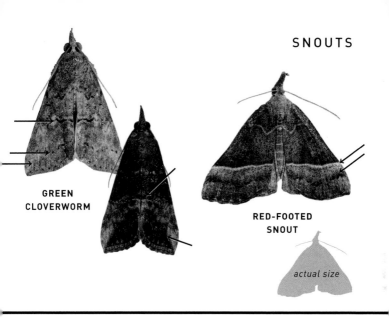

GREEN CLOVERWORM

RED-FOOTED SNOUT

actual size

ASSORTED OWLETS

YELLOW-LINED OWLET

actual size

GOLD-LINED MELANOMMA

SPOTTED GRASS MOTH

Rivula propinqualis 93-0592 (8404) **Common**
TL 10–11 mm. Straw-colored FW has warm brown border. AM line is W-shaped. PM line curves sharply before reaching costa. Brown shading covers two black dots in purple reniform spot. **HOSTS:** Grasses.

THE HERALD

Scoliopteryx libatrix 93-0601 (8555) **Common**
TL 23 mm. Purplish gray FW has wide streak of mottled orange scales through basal and median areas that resemble glowing embers. Whitish PM line is double, curving sharply inward near costa. Basal and orbicular spots are white. **HOSTS:** Poplar and willow. **NOTE:** Adults hibernate through winter months.

YELLOW SCALLOP MOTH

Anomis erosa 93-0602 (8545) **Uncommon**
TL 15–19 mm. Peppery yellow FW has rusty AM and median lines that join at inner margin. PM and ST lines are edged with incomplete violet bands. Brown orbicular spot has tiny white dot in center. **HOSTS:** Mallow. **NOTE:** A tropical species that is an irregular immigrant to ne. N. America, mostly in the fall.

CANADIAN OWLET

Calyptra canadensis 93-0612 (8536) **Uncommon**
TL 19–22 mm. Pinkish brown FW is finely vermiculated with white lines, appearing like a crumpled dead leaf. Slightly wavy brown PM line sweeps across FW from apex to midpoint of inner margin. **HOSTS:** Meadow rue.

MOONSEED MOTH

Plusiodonta compressipalpis 93-0622 (8534) **Uncommon**
TL 14–18 mm. Fawn-colored FW has brown median band that tapers to a tuft of hairlike scales protruding from inner margin. Swirling AM and PM lines are edged with lilac and gray lines. AM and ST lines are spangled with gold. **HOSTS:** Moonseed. **NOTE:** Two broods.

SMALL NECKLACE MOTH

Hypsoropha hormos 93-0629 (8528) **Common**
TL 14–18 mm. Pale gray FW has brown and purplish shading in basal and median areas. Indistinct PM line widens toward inner margin, forming a string of three or four white dots that increase in size. **HOSTS:** Persimmon and sassafras.

SPOTTED GRASS MOTH

THE HERALD

actual size

**YELLOW SCALLOP
MOTH**

CANADIAN OWLET

**MOONSEED
MOTH**

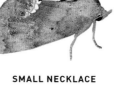

**SMALL NECKLACE
MOTH**

COMMON ARUGISA

Arugisa lutea   93-0634 (8509)   **Common**
TL 9–12 mm. Shiny tan pale FW has blotch of dusky shading at midsection of AM line. Curved median line is fragmented. Orbicular and reniform spots are small black dots. **HOSTS:** Live and dead grasses.

DEAD-WOOD BORER MOTH

Scolecocampa liburna   93-0637 (8514)   **Uncommon**
TL 19–24 mm. Straw-colored FW has fragmented AM and PM lines reduced to rows of brown dots. Tiny black basal and orbicular spots are black. Hollow reniform spot is outlined brown. Dotted ST line has dusky blotch beyond midpoint. **HOSTS:** Possibly fungus in decaying logs and stumps.

THIN-WINGED OWLET

Nigetia formosalis   93-0655 (8440)   **Uncommon**
TL 12 mm. Sharply pointed white FW has a slanting black median bar that connects with black costal streak. Bands of brown and gray shading pass on either side of white ST line. **HOSTS:** Unknown.

LARGE HYPENODES

Hypenodes caducus   93-0661 (8420)   **Uncommon**
TL 7–9 mm. Gray FW has blackish bar at base of pale costa. Inner median band is blackish. Reniform spot is a black wedge. White lines are conspicuous at inner margin. **HOSTS:** Unknown. **NOTE:** Two broods.

BROKEN-LINE HYPENODES

Hypenodes fractilinea   93-0662 (8421)   **Common**
TL 6–8 mm. Gray FW has dotted median line that bulges around small black reniform spot. Inner median area is shaded brown. Terminal line is a row of tiny black wedges. **HOSTS:** Unknown. **NOTE:** Two broods.

VISITATION MOTH

Dyspyralis illocata   93-0669 (8426)   **Common**
TL 7–9 mm. Straw-colored FW has broad dusky gray median band. Wavy lines are often inconspicuous. Reniform spot is a small black crescent. **HOSTS:** Unknown.

ASSORTED OWLETS

COMMON ARUGISA

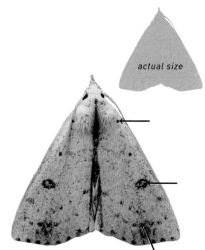

actual size

**DEAD-WOOD
BORER MOTH**

THIN-WINGED OWLET

LARGE HYPENODES

**BROKEN-LINE
HYPENODES**

VISITATION MOTH

SPOT-EDGED DYSPYRALIS
Dyspyralis puncticosta   93-0670 (8427)   **Common**
TL 8–9 mm. Pale gray FW is peppered with black scales. Wavy lines end as bold black patches along costa. Reniform spot is a thin black crescent. **HOSTS:** Unknown.

NIGELLA DYSPYRALIS
Dyspyralis nigellus   93-0671 (8428)   **Uncommon**
TL 9–10 mm. Slate gray FW has jagged black lines. Black median band cuts through white reniform spot. PM and ST lines are accented with white. **HOSTS:** Unknown.

WAVED BLACK
Parascotia fuliginaria   93-0673 (8418)   **Uncommon**
WS 18–28 mm. Gray or blackish wings are marked with jagged cream-colored lines and checkered fringe. Male has broadly bipectinate antennae. **HOSTS:** Lichen and damp fungi on rotting wood. **RANGE:** Locally in s. ON and ne. U.S. **NOTE:** This introduced European species is distinctive, but shape and resting pose suggest a geometrid moth.

COMMON FUNGUS MOTH
Metalectra discalis   93-0679 (8499)   **Common**
WS 20–27 mm. Pale yellow wings are heavily mottled black and brown. All lines are edged with wide dark brown bands. Orbicular and reniform spots are black. **HOSTS:** Dry fungi.

FOUR-SPOTTED FUNGUS MOTH
Metalectra quadrisignata   93-0680 (8500)   **Common**
WS 18–35 mm. Pale reddish brown wings are peppered with dusky scales. All lines are indistinct apart from fragmented blackish median band. Reniform spot and subapical patch are black. **HOSTS:** Fungi.

BLACK FUNGUS MOTH
Metalectra tantillus   93-0682 (8502)   **Common**
WS 20–25 mm. Sooty brown wings are marked with pale fragmented lines. Orbicular and reniform spots are black. Terminal line is a row of black and pale yellow dots. **HOSTS:** Dry fungi.

SIX-SPOTTED GRAY
Spargaloma sexpunctata   93-0715 (8479)   **Common**
TL 15–18 mm. Pale gray FW has brown median band. Scalloped AM and PM lines are inconspicuous. Brown triangular subapical patch is accented with three short black dashes. **HOSTS:** Dogbane.

ASSORTED OWLETS

**SPOT-EDGED
DYSPYRALIS**

NIGELLA DYSPYRALIS

WAVED BLACK

actual size

**COMMON
FUNGUS MOTH**

**FOUR-SPOTTED
FUNGUS MOTH**

**BLACK FUNGUS
MOTH**

**SIX-SPOTTED
GRAY**

PINK-BORDERED YELLOW

Phytometra rhodarialis   93-0717 (8481)   **Common**
TL 10–11 mm. Yellow FW has bright pink shading beyond straight PM line. Basal half of costa and small claviform spot are also pink. Tiny black discal spot touches PM line. **HOSTS:** Unknown.

DOTTED GRAYLET

Hyperstrotia pervertens   93-0729 (9037)   **Common**
TL 8–10 mm. Ash gray FW has faint gray-edged AM and PM lines and a darker median band. Pale gray reniform spot contains one or two tiny black dots. **HOSTS:** Bur oak and American elm.

WHITE-LINED GRAYLET

Hyperstrotia villificans   93-0730 (9038)   **Uncommon**
TL 8–9 mm. Resembles Dotted Graylet but has angled AM and PM lines edged white near inner margin. Median area is mottled brown. Indistinct reniform spot has a tiny black dot in inner half. **HOSTS:** American elm.

YELLOW-SPOTTED GRAYLET

Hyperstrotia flaviguttata   93-0731 (9039)   **Uncommon**
TL 8–9 mm. Resembles White-lined Graylet, but silvery gray FW has faintly dotted AM and PM lines. Fragmented rusty brown median band is accented with yellow spots at midpoint and inner margin. **HOSTS:** Scrub oak on well-drained sandy soils. **RANGE:** E. U.S.

BLACK-PATCHED GRAYLET

Hyperstrotia secta   93-0732 (9040)   **Uncommon**
TL 8–9 mm. Silvery gray FW has diffuse white-edged AM and PM lines and yellowish bands in median and ST areas. Inner median area is marked with a black patch. **HOSTS:** Red oak and white oak.

THIN-LINED OWLET

Isogona tenuis   93-0734 (8493)   **Common**
TL 13–16 mm. Pale grayish brown FW has pale yellow veins extending across wing. Yellow-edged AM line curves inward near costa. Strongly angled PM line is connected to yellow apical dash. Large hollow reniform spot is outlined pale yellow. **HOSTS:** Hackberry.

ASSORTED OWLETS

PINK-BORDERED YELLOW

actual size

DOTTED GRAYLET

WHITE-LINED GRAYLET

YELLOW-SPOTTED GRAYLET

BLACK-PATCHED GRAYLET

THIN-LINED OWLET

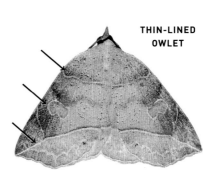

Underwings, Zales, and Related Owlets Family Erebidae, Subfamily Erebinae

A large group of medium to large woodland moths that typically rest with wings held flat. The underwings derive their name from their colorful HW patterns, usually concealed at rest. Underwings and zales frequently visit sugar bait, often the best method of attracting these moths. A few species, such as Clover Looper, Forage Looper, and Toothed Somberwing, may be flushed from vegetation during the day. All will come to light in small numbers.

BLACK WITCH
Ascalapha odorata   93-0759 (8649)   **Uncommon**
WS 110–150 mm. Sexually dimorphic. Dark brown FW of male has wavy black lines. Metallic blue comma-shaped reniform spot is edged orange and black. Yellow-dotted ST line is edged with bands of brown and iridescent blue. Female is similar but has zigzag whitish median bands on all wings. **HOSTS:** Leguminous trees, including cassia and catclaw. **NOTE:** An irregular immigrant (sometimes hurricane driven) from southern states and Mexico.

MOON-LINED MOTH
Spiloloma lunilinea   93-0760 (8769)   **Common**
TL 22–27 mm. Milky brown FW has warm brown shading in inner median and ST areas. Fragmented AM and PM lines are obvious only at costa. Median line is double at inner margin. **HOSTS:** Honey locust.

THE BETROTHED
Catocala innubens   93-0761 (8770)   **Common**
TL 30–38 mm. Mottled brown FW of typical form has jagged AM and PM lines edged whitish. Small subreniform spot is pale. Darker streaks occur in median area and along slanting apical dash. Dark form is dark chocolate brown as far as whitish ST line. HW is orange with uneven black bands and pale fringe. **HOSTS:** Honey locust.

THE PENITENT
Catocala piatrix   93-0762 (8771)   **Common**
TL 36–44 mm. Grayish brown FW typically has brown shading in basal area and beyond jagged PM line. AM line has inward-pointing tooth near inner margin. Oblique whitish bar extends from costa to teardrop-shaped subreniform spot. HW is orange with uneven black bands and pale orange fringe. **HOSTS:** Deciduous trees, including ash, butternut, hickory, and walnut.

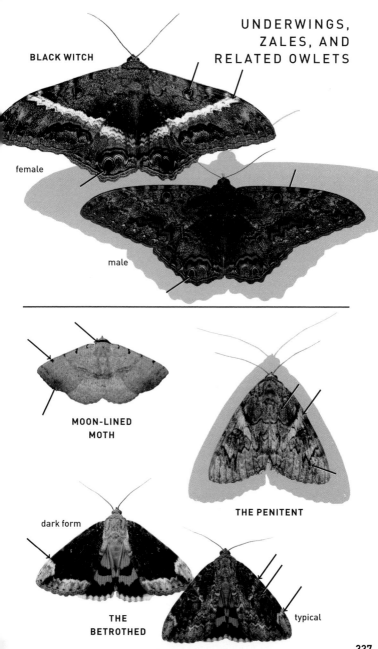

UNDERWINGS,
ZALES, AND
RELATED OWLETS

BLACK WITCH

female

male

MOON-LINED
MOTH

THE PENITENT

dark form

THE
BETROTHED

typical

EPIONE UNDERWING

Catocala epione   93-0764 (8773)   **Common**

TL 29–34 mm. Ash gray FW has broad bands of warm brown shading along black AM and PM lines. PM line has a single outward-pointing tooth. Reniform spot is warm brown. Small white subreniform spot is outlined black. Jagged ST line is broadly edged white. HW is black with a wide white fringe. **HOSTS:** Hickory.

SWEETFERN UNDERWING

Catocala antinympha   93-0766 (8775)   **Uncommon**

TL 24–28 mm. Slate gray FW has inconspicuous lines. Jagged PM line is edged with a band of brown shading. Subreniform and reniform spots are dusted with pale gray scales. HW is golden yellow with irregular black bands and fringe. **HOSTS:** Sweet fern.

THE OLD MAID

Catocala badia coelebs   93-0767 (8777)   **Uncommon**

TL 27–31 mm. Gray FW has thick black bands along AM and PM lines. An oblique whitish bar extends from costa to brown subreniform spot. HW is golden yellow with irregular black bands and mostly gray fringe. **HOSTS:** Sweet gale. **NOTE:** The noncoastal subspecies of Bay Underwing, *C. badia*.

HABILIS UNDERWING

Catocala habilis   93-0768 (8778)   **Common**

TL 29–35 mm. Ash gray FW has finely etched blackish AM and PM lines. Whitish ST line is edged with a band of pale brown shading. Inner section of PM line forms a black dash parallel to inner margin. HW is orange with irregular black bands and pale orange fringe. **HOSTS:** Hickory and walnut.

ROBINSON'S UNDERWING

Catocala robinsonii   93-0769 (8780)   **Common**

TL 37–42 mm. Pale gray FW has jagged AM and PM lines finely etched black. Reniform spot is often clouded warm brown. Zigzag ST line is whitish, sometimes edged with a pale brown band. Female (not shown) has a black basal dash. HW is black with narrow white fringe. **HOSTS:** Hickory, oak, and walnut.

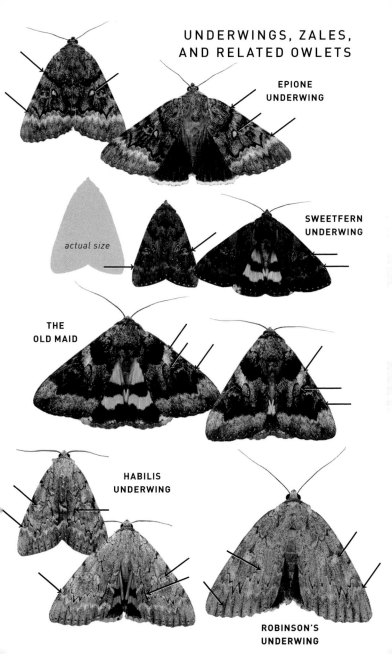

UNDERWINGS, ZALES, AND RELATED OWLETS

EPIONE
UNDERWING

SWEETFERN
UNDERWING

actual size

THE
OLD MAID

HABILIS
UNDERWING

ROBINSON'S
UNDERWING

ANGUS' UNDERWING
Catocala angusi   93-0770 (8783)   **Common**
TL 32–39 mm. Dimorphic. In typical form (not shown) FW is pale
gray with jagged AM and PM lines edged warm brown. Reniform spot is brown. Inner section of PM line forms a black dash
parallel to inner margin. Female has black basal dash. Form
"lucetta" (shown) resembles typical but has broad black streak
extending from base to apex broken in median area. HW is
black with a gray fringe, white at apex. **HOSTS:** Hickory and pecan.

JUDITH'S UNDERWING
Catocala judith   93-0771 (8781)   **Common**
TL 24–29 mm. Ash gray FW has jagged black AM and PM lines.
Zigzag ST line is whitish. Terminal line is a row of black and
white dots. HW is black with pale gray fringe. **HOSTS:** Hickory
and walnut.

OBSCURE UNDERWING
Catocala obscura   93-0773 (8784)   **Common**
TL 32–38 mm. Medium gray FW has jagged AM and PM lines
finely etched in black. Zigzag ST line is pale gray. Terminal line
is a row of black and white dots. HW is black with white fringe.
HOSTS: Hickory, pecan, and walnut.

RESIDUA UNDERWING
Catocala residua   93-0774 (8785)   **Common**
TL 32–38 mm. Resembles Obscure Underwing but often has
whiter ST line and some brown shading along inner PM line.
HW is black with gray fringe. **HOSTS:** Hickory and pecan.

YELLOW-GRAY UNDERWING
Catocala retecta   93-0777 (8788)   **Common**
TL 32–39 mm. Gray FW has jagged black AM and PM lines
edged with warm brown bands. Warm brown reniform spot is
edged pale gray. Three black dashes extend from base to apex,
with another parallel to inner margin. HW is black with broad
white fringe. **HOSTS:** Hickory and walnut.

WIDOW UNDERWING
Catocala vidua   93-0782 (8792)   **Common**
TL 37–44 mm. Ash gray FW is boldly marked with black lines.
Thick black basal dash cuts through AM line. Curved black api-
cal dash pierces whitish ST line, touching white-edged reniform
spot. Inner PM line meanders to form thick black dash parallel
to inner margin. HW is black with broad white fringe. **HOSTS:**
Hickory and walnut.

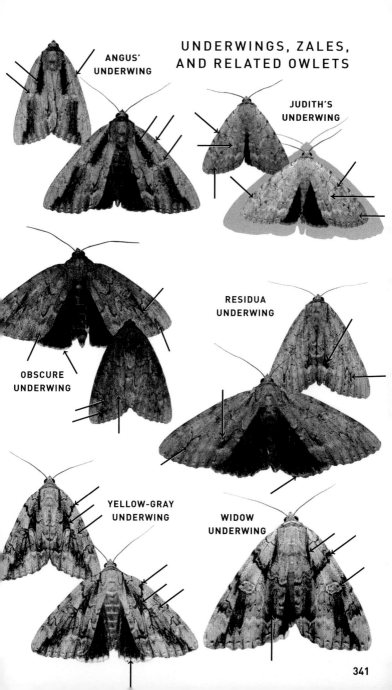

UNDERWINGS, ZALES, AND RELATED OWLETS

ANGUS'
UNDERWING

JUDITH'S
UNDERWING

OBSCURE
UNDERWING

RESIDUA
UNDERWING

YELLOW-GRAY
UNDERWING

WIDOW
UNDERWING

TEARFUL UNDERWING
Catocala lacrymosa   93-0783 (8794)   **Common**
TL 32–43 mm. Dimorphic. FW is variable, but typical form (not shown) is gray with thick black AM and PM lines edged whitish at inner margin. Reniform spot and band inside jagged ST line are warm brown. Form "evelina" (shown) resembles typical but has basal area and inner margin clouded with dusky green shading. HW is black with broad white fringe. **HOSTS:** Hickory.

OLDWIFE UNDERWING
Catocala palaeogama   93-0784 (8795)   **Common**
TL 32–37 mm. FW is variable but typically is grayish brown with black AM line widening at costa. Reniform spot is warm brown. Subreniform spot is pale. Inner PM line meanders to form a black dash parallel to inner margin. HW is orange with irregular black bands and yellow fringe. **HOSTS:** Hickory and walnut.

CLOUDED UNDERWING
Catocala nebulosa   93-0787 (8796)   **Uncommon**
TL 39–45 mm. Yellowish brown FW has violet shading along inner margin and at apex. Black AM line borders dark brown basal area. Inner PM line often meanders to form a black bar parallel to inner margin. HW is orange with a brown base, irregular black bands, and pale orange fringe. **HOSTS:** Hickory and walnut.

YOUTHFUL UNDERWING
Catocala subnata   93-0788 (8797)   **Common**
TL 39–47 mm. Pale gray FW has fragmented black AM and PM lines. Basal area, reniform spot, and band inside zigzag whitish ST line are warm brown. Short black dashes occur at apex and anal angle. Inner PM line meanders to form a dash parallel to inner margin. Basal dash is present in female (not shown). HW is golden yellow with irregular black bands and pale yellowish fringe. **HOSTS:** Butternut and hickory.

SAD UNDERWING
Catocala maestosa   93-0789 (8793)   **Common**
TL 40–50 mm. Gray FW has finely etched AM and PM lines bordered with pale brown bands. Curved black apical dash passes brown reniform spot before ending at midpoint of costa. HW is black with broad white fringe. **HOSTS:** Hickory and walnut.

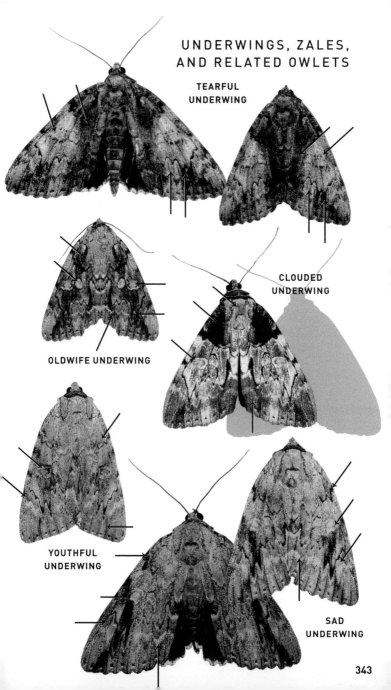

UNDERWINGS, ZALES, AND RELATED OWLETS

TEARFUL UNDERWING

CLOUDED UNDERWING

OLDWIFE UNDERWING

YOUTHFUL UNDERWING

SAD UNDERWING

THE BRIDE *Catocala neogama* 93-0790 (8798) **Common**
TL 37–44 mm. Medium gray FW has jagged AM and PM lines often edged with brown bands. Reniform spot is warm brown. Inner PM line meanders to form a dash parallel to inner margin. Black basal dash and apical dash pronounced in some individuals. HW is golden yellow with irregular black bands and pale yellowish fringe. **HOSTS:** Hickory, butternut, and black walnut.

ILIA UNDERWING *Catocala ilia* 93-0792 (8801) **Common**
TL 34–45 mm. Peppery FW is variable but typically is gray with jagged AM and PM lines bordered with darker brown bands. Median area is often paler. Reniform spot is boldly outlined white or all white. Black basal dash is usually present. HW is reddish with irregular black bands and pale orange fringe. **HOSTS:** Oak.

YELLOW-BANDED UNDERWING
Catocala cerogama 93-0794 (8802) **Common**
TL 34–42 mm. Gray FW has black AM and PM lines that fade before reaching inner margin but are connected by black bar in median area. Reniform spot is warm brown, edged white. Oblique whitish band extends from costa to white subreniform spot. Dark form has mostly blackish median area. HW is black, brown at base, with an even yellow band and checkered fringe. **HOSTS:** Basswood.

WHITE UNDERWING
Catocala relicta 93-0795 (8803) **Common**
TL 37–47 mm. White FW is variably peppered with yellowish and gray scales. Parallel lines are often bordered with bands of darker shading, especially median band. Reniform spot is often blackish. Dark individuals (not shown) have mostly blackish FW with white subreniform spot and edging to lines. HW is black with an even white band and fringe. **HOSTS:** Poplar and willow.

MARBLED UNDERWING
Catocala marmorata 93-0796 (8804) **Common**
TL 47–49 mm. Grayish brown FW has inconspicuous, jagged AM and PM lines edged whitish. A broad black streak extends from midpoint of costa, through reniform spot to outer margin near apex. Whitish ST line is bordered with a brown band. HW is pinkish red with irregular black bands and pale fringe. **HOSTS:** Poplar and willow.

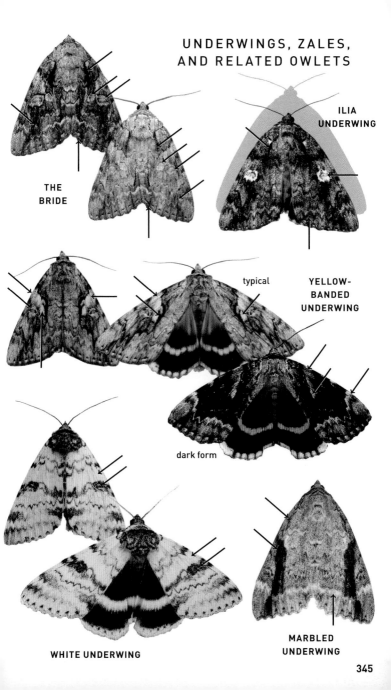

UNDERWINGS, ZALES, AND RELATED OWLETS

ILIA UNDERWING

THE BRIDE

typical

YELLOW-BANDED UNDERWING

dark form

WHITE UNDERWING

MARBLED UNDERWING

ONCE-MARRIED UNDERWING
Catocala unijuga   93-0797 (8805)   **Common**
TL 37–47 mm. Peppery gray FW has jagged AM and PM lines edged whitish. Reniform spot is clouded with darker shading, typically with whitish patch in front of it. Zigzag ST line is broadly edged whitish. HW is pinkish red with black bands and white fringe. **HOSTS:** Poplar and willow.

MOTHER UNDERWING
Catocala parta   93-0798 (8806)   **Common**
TL 38–43 mm. Gray FW has jagged AM and PM lines edged whitish. Reniform spot is clouded with brown and outlined black. An oblique white bar passes inside grayish subreniform spot. Thick black dashes are present in basal and subapical areas and parallel to inner margin. HW is yellow-orange with irregular black bands and pale fringe. **HOSTS:** Poplar and willow.

BRISEIS UNDERWING
Catocala briseis   93-0804 (8817)   **Common**
TL 32–37 mm. Sooty brown FW has inconspicuous lines. Subreniform spot is often sprinkled with whitish scales. A band of warm brown shading passes inside whitish zigzag ST line. HW is orange-red with even black bands and pale fringe. **HOSTS:** Poplar and willow.

SEMIRELICT UNDERWING
Catocala semirelicta   93-0806 (8821)   **Uncommon**
TL 33–39 mm. FW is variable but typically is pale gray with jagged AM and PM lines edged with white. Wide blackish median band cuts through dusky reniform spot. Subreniform spot is paler, sometimes tinged with brown. Some individuals have a blackish bar parallel to inner margin from base to PM line. HW is pinkish red with black bands and white fringe. **HOSTS:** Poplar and willow.

DARLING UNDERWING
Catocala cara   93-0812 (8832)   **Common**
TL 37–44 mm. Violet brown FW is sprinkled with green scales along jagged lines. Outline to subreniform is openly joined to PM line. HW is bright carmine with black bands and checkered fringe. **HOSTS:** Poplar and willow.

PINK UNDERWING
Catocala concumbens   93-0814 (8833)   **Common**
TL 32–39 mm. Uniformly gray FW is tinted with lilac shading along fine jagged lines. Reniform spot is edged whitish. HW is pink with black bands and wide white fringe. **HOSTS:** Poplar and willow.

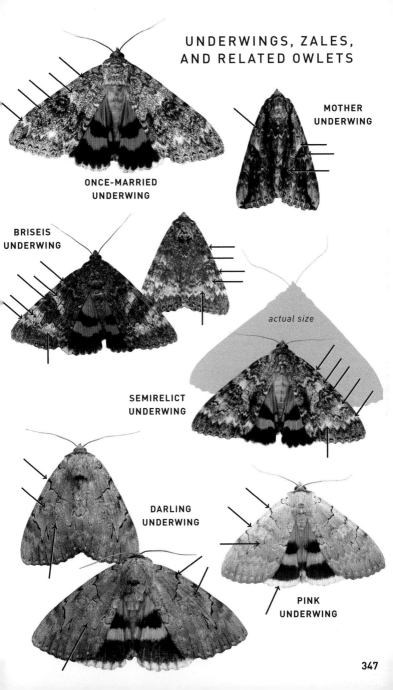

UNDERWINGS, ZALES, AND RELATED OWLETS

ONCE-MARRIED
UNDERWING

MOTHER
UNDERWING

BRISEIS
UNDERWING

actual size

SEMIRELICT
UNDERWING

DARLING
UNDERWING

PINK
UNDERWING

THE SWEETHEART
Catocala amatrix   93-0815 (8834)   **Common**
TL 39–48 mm. FW is variable but is typically pale gray with lilac and brown shading. Jagged AM and PM lines widen at costa. Wide black streak extends from base to apex, interrupted by pale subreniform spot. Paler individuals of form "selecta" lack this blackish streak. HW is reddish pink with black bands and checkered fringe. **HOSTS:** Poplar and willow.

MAGDALEN UNDERWING
Catocala illecta   93-0826 (8840)   **Common**
TL 39–48 mm. Uniformly gray FW has fine AM and PM lines. Outline of hollow subreniform spot is openly joined to PM line. Brownish reniform spot has a few whitish scales in center. HW is golden yellow with black bands and checkered fringe. **HOSTS:** Honey locust and leadplant.

SORDID UNDERWING
Catocala sordida   93-0832 (8846)   **Uncommon**
TL 20–24 mm. Purplish gray FW has fragmented lines that widen at costa. Dusky shading extends along basal half of inner margin. Dark reniform spot has a black streak connecting it to costa. HW is golden yellow with black bands and checkered fringe. **HOSTS:** Blueberry.

SCARLET UNDERWING
Catocala coccinata   93-0837 (8851)   **Uncommon**
TL 30–37 mm. Gray FW has toothed AM line pierced by a long black basal dash. Inner section of jagged PM line forms a black dash parallel to inner margin. Reniform spot and accents along ST line are tinted pale green. HW is scarlet with black bands and checkered fringe. **HOSTS:** Oak.

ULTRONIA UNDERWING
Catocala ultronia   93-0841 (8857)   **Common**
TL 25–33 mm. Bluish gray FW has wide streak of blackish shading along inner margin. Brown subapical dash is connected to outer PM line. HW is red with black bands and a checkered fringe. Paler individuals have thinner black dashes and less dark shading along inner margin. **HOSTS:** Primarily cherry and plum, also apple and hawthorn.

UNDERWINGS, ZALES,
AND RELATED OWLETS

form "selecta"

THE
SWEETHEART

typical

MAGDALEN
UNDERWING

SORDID
UNDERWING

SCARLET
UNDERWING

ULTRONIA
UNDERWING

WONDERFUL UNDERWING

Catocala mira 93-0844 (8863) **Common**

TL 22–27 mm. Pale gray FW has whitish subreniform spot connected to costa by oblique whitish bar. Gray reniform spot is edged whitish. Inner section of PM line forms a dash parallel to inner margin. HW is golden yellow with wavy black bands and checkered fringe. **HOSTS:** Hawthorn.

WOODY UNDERWING

Catocala grynea 93-0845 (8864) **Common**

TL 22–27 mm. Smooth violet gray FW has chestnut streak along inner margin. Fragmented AM and PM lines widen at costa. Inner section of PM line forms a black dash parallel to inner margin. HW is golden yellow with black bands and checkered fringe. **HOSTS:** Apple, cherry, hawthorn, and plum.

HAWTHORN UNDERWING

Catocala crataegi 93-0846 (8858) **Common**

TL 22–27 mm. Pale gray FW has a greenish tinge when fresh. Thick black AM line merges with extensive black shading along inner margin. Oblique white bar extends from costa to brown subreniform spot. HW is golden yellow with wavy black bands and checkered pale orange fringe. **HOSTS:** Apple and hawthorn.

PRAECLARA UNDERWING

Catocala praeclara 93-0847 (8865) **Common**

TL 22–27 mm. Pale greenish gray FW is finely peppered with black along veins. Thin black AM line is edged chestnut. Chestnut-edged inner section of PM line forms a black dash parallel to inner margin. HW is golden yellow with thick black bands and pale fringe. **HOSTS:** Chokeberry, hawthorn, and Juneberry.

CHARMING UNDERWING

Catocala blandula 93-0851 (8867) **Common**

TL 22–27 mm. Gray FW has oblique AM line bordered with brown shading on basal side. Inner section of PM line forms a black dash parallel to inner margin. AM and PM lines touch (or almost do) at inner margin. HW is golden yellow with black bands and checkered fringe. **HOSTS:** Apple and hawthorn.

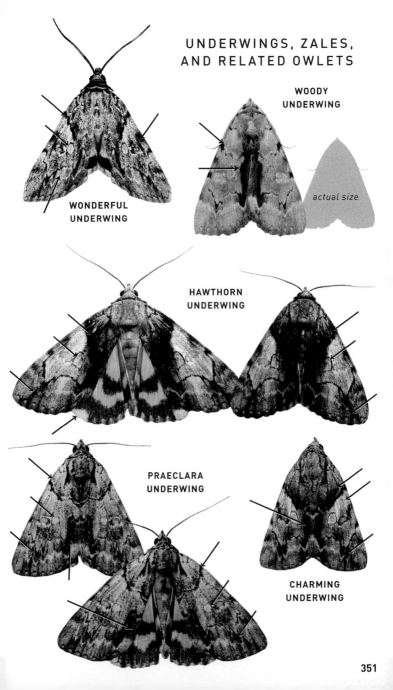

UNDERWINGS, ZALES, AND RELATED OWLETS

WONDERFUL
UNDERWING

WOODY
UNDERWING

actual size

HAWTHORN
UNDERWING

PRAECLARA
UNDERWING

CHARMING
UNDERWING

351

CLINTON'S UNDERWING

Catocala clintonii   93-0853 (8872)   **Common**

TL 25–29 mm. Smooth pale gray FW has band of pale brown shading beyond finely jagged PM line. Black basal dash touches incomplete AM line. Inner section of PM line forms a black dash parallel to inner margin. HW is golden yellow with black bands and pale fringe. **HOSTS:** Apple, cherry, elm, hawthorn, and plum.

SIMILAR UNDERWING

Catocala similis   93-0855 (8873)   **Common**

TL 20–25 mm. Pale gray FW has darker grayish brown median area. AM and PM lines are partly edged brown. White-edged reniform spot is open on costal side and touches smaller subreniform spot. HW is golden yellow with thick black bands and a paler fringe. **HOSTS:** Oak and pecan.

LITTLE UNDERWING

Catocala minuta   93-0856 (8874)   **Common**

TL 19–24 mm. Mottled FW is variable but typically is grayish brown with indistinct blackish lines. Dark form has blackish shading in basal area or along inner margin. Jagged whitish ST line widens at costa. HW is golden yellow with black bands and pale orange fringe. **HOSTS:** Honey locust.

THE LITTLE NYMPH

Catocala micronympha   93-0857 (8876)   **Common**

TL 17–26 mm. FW is variable but typically is pale gray tinted pale green. Fragmented AM and PM lines are often edged brown. Sometimes has a blackish bar curving from midpoint of costa through reniform spot to apex. Zigzag ST line is whitish, widening at costa. Dark individuals have FW with blackish brown shading as far as ST line. HW is golden yellow with thick black marginal band broken toward inner margin. **HOSTS:** Oak.

CONNUBIAL UNDERWING

Catocala connubialis   93-0858 (8877)   **Common**

TL 20–25 mm. FW is variable but is usually whitish with crisp jagged lines. Some individuals have whitish median area with grayish brown shading in basal area and beyond PM line. Subreniform spot can be outlined black. Reniform spot is blackish. HW is golden yellow with black bands and pale fringe. **HOSTS:** Oak.

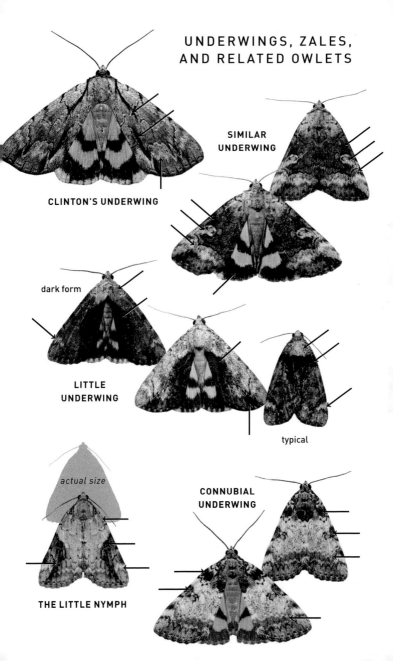

UNDERWINGS, ZALES, AND RELATED OWLETS

SIMILAR UNDERWING

CLINTON'S UNDERWING

dark form

LITTLE UNDERWING

typical

actual size

THE LITTLE NYMPH

CONNUBIAL UNDERWING

GIRLFRIEND UNDERWING

Catocala amica   93-0859 (8878)   **Common**
TL 17–24 mm. Pale gray FW has hairlike quality. Fragmented
AM and PM lines are often edged brown. Median line widens at
costa, forming a blackish triangle. Sometimes a black bar
curves from costa through reniform spot to apex. HW is golden
yellow with a single, thick black marginal band broken toward
inner margin. **HOSTS:** Oak.

LITTLE LINED UNDERWING

Catocala lineella   93-0860 (8878.1)   **Common**
TL 22–24 mm. Resembles Girlfriend Underwing but has whitish
FW boldly marked with jagged black lines. Hollow subreniform
spot is outlined black. HW is golden yellow with a single thick
black marginal band broken toward inner margin. **HOSTS:** Oak.

COMMON OAK MOTH

Phoberia atomaris   93-0862 (8591)   **Common**
TL 18–23 mm. FW is variably pale grayish tan to brown, often
with paler veins. Reniform spot is variably filled with black
scales. Jagged ST line is edged with a brown band. **HOSTS:** Oak.

BLACK-DOTTED BROWN

Cissusa spadix   93-0864 (8592)   **Common**
TL 17–22 mm. Peppery FW is variably pale tan to reddish brown.
Wavy yellow-edged AM and median lines are almost parallel.
PM line fades before reaching inner margin. Faintly scalloped
ST line is accented with two black spots near apex. **HOSTS:** Un-
known.

INDOMITABLE MELIPOTIS

Melipotis indomita   93-0871 (8600)   **Common**
TL 21–26 mm. Gray FW has a complex pattern of black and
brown shading. Oblique white median band sometimes contains a few reddish scales. Large pale reniform spot is crossed
with dark veins. ST area is pale gray. HW is pale yellow with
blackish border and broken white fringe. **HOSTS:** Mesquite.

FIGURE-SEVEN MOTH

Drasteria grandirena   93-0915 (8641)   **Uncommon**
TL 18–20 mm. Lilac gray FW has complex pattern of brown and
black shading along AM and PM lines. Oblique pale yellow median band contains two brown lines. Large reniform spot is
partly filled with white. Brown ST line is edged white. Black HW
has whitish basal stripes and ST line. **HOSTS:** Witch hazel.

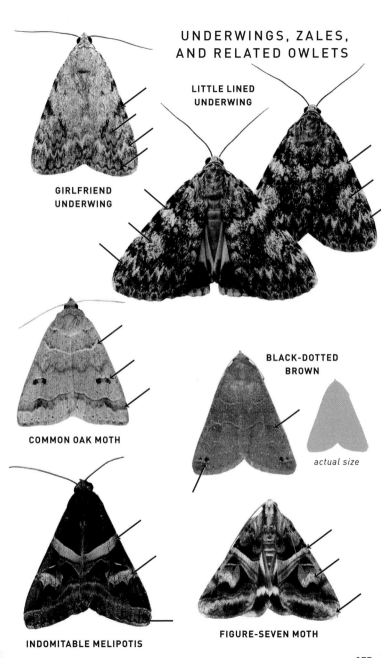

UNDERWINGS, ZALES, AND RELATED OWLETS

LITTLE LINED UNDERWING

GIRLFRIEND UNDERWING

COMMON OAK MOTH

BLACK-DOTTED BROWN

actual size

INDOMITABLE MELIPOTIS

FIGURE-SEVEN MOTH

CLOVER LOOPER
Caenurgina crassiuscula   93-0923 (8738)   **Common**
TL 17–22 mm. FW is variably pale tan to grayish brown. Brown AM and PM bands converge at inner margin. **HOSTS:** Mostly legumes, also a variety of grasses and herbaceous plants. **NOTE:** Three or more broods.

FORAGE LOOPER
Caenurgina erechtea   93-0924 (8739)   **Common**
TL 17–23 mm. Pale brown or gray FW has AM and incomplete PM bands that do not meet at inner margin. Pale individuals have uniformly grayish FW with faint lines. **HOSTS:** Alfalfa, grasses, clover, and ragweed. **NOTE:** Several broods.

TOOTHED SOMBERWING
Euclidia cuspidea   93-0929 (8731)   **Common**
TL 23 mm. Violet gray FW has thick black AM line with an inward-pointing bulge almost touching small black spot near inner margin. Inconspicuous PM line has outward-pointing black tooth. Zigzag ST line ends in toothed subapical patch. **HOSTS:** Clover, grasses, lupine, and sweet fern. **NOTE:** Two or more broods.

VETCH LOOPER
Caenurgia chloropha   93-0938 (8733)   **Common**
TL 15–20 mm. FW is pale tan to brown. Typically there is a blackish blotch just beyond bulging midpoint of PM line. ST line is a row of tiny black dots. **HOSTS:** Primarily legumes, also grasses and herbaceous plants. **NOTE:** Three or more broods.

BLACK BIT MOTH
Celiptera frustulum   93-0940 (8747)   **Common**
TL 19–21 mm. Grayish brown FW has bold inward-pointing black wedge situated inside kinked AM line. Large subreniform and reniform spots touch. Double PM line is edged pale orange. **HOSTS:** Locust. **NOTE:** Two broods.

SMALL MOCIS *Mocis latipes*   93-0942 (8743)   **Common**
TL 19–23 mm. Yellowish tan FW has outer median area and band beyond PM line shaded brown. Hollow subreniform spot is almost fused with dark-centered reniform spot. Sometimes has a black spot where AM line meets inner margin. **HOSTS:** Mostly grasses, also bean and turnip. **NOTE:** An irregular fall immigrant in the north.

UNDERWINGS, ZALES, AND RELATED OWLETS

CLOVER LOOPER

TOOTHED SOMBERWING

actual size

pale

FORAGE LOOPER

typical

VETCH LOOPER

BLACK BIT MOTH

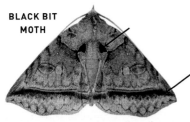

SMALL MOCIS

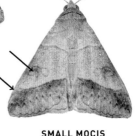

TEXAS MOCIS *Mocis texana* 93-0944 (8745) **Common**

TL 22–26 mm. Very similar to Small Mocis but slightly larger and lacks subreniform spot. Hollow reniform spot is often touched by thin dusky median line. Some individuals have a tiny black dot along inner margin in basal area. **HOSTS:** Mostly grasses, also bean and turnip. **NOTE:** A rare fall immigrant in the north.

FOUR-LINED CHOCOLATE

Argyrostrotis quadrifilaris 93-0954 (8762) **Common**

TL 16–22 mm. Dark chocolate brown FW has cream-colored AM and PM lines that converge slightly toward inner margin. Whitish fringe darkens toward inner margin. **HOSTS:** Cotton. **NOTE:** Two broods. **RANGE:** E. U.S.

SHORT-LINED CHOCOLATE

Argyrostrotis anilis 93-0956 (8764) **Common**

TL 14–22 mm. Chocolate brown FW has oblique white AM line that fades before reaching costa. Incomplete whitish PM line curves toward outer margin. **HOSTS:** Possibly pinks. **NOTE:** Two broods.

MAPLE LOOPER MOTH

Parallelia bistriaris 93-0961 (8727) **Common**

TL 23 mm. Earth brown FW has slightly darker median area bordered with parallel yellowish AM and PM lines. Outer margin is pale gray beyond indistinct, jagged ST line. **HOSTS:** Maple, birch, and walnut.

FALSE UNDERWING

Allotria elonympha 93-0962 (8721) **Common**

TL 19–24 mm. Peppery grayish brown FW has wide black band in basal area. Orbicular spot is a black dot. ST line has two black blotches. Dark individuals have FW blackish as far as PM line. HW is yellow with a wide blackish border. **HOSTS:** Black gum, hickory, and walnut.

DETRACTED OWLET

Lesmone detrahens 93-0970 (8651) **Common**

WS 27–31 mm. FW is variably brown to violet-gray with faint yellow-edged AM and PM lines curving inward near costa. Darker bands pass through median area and inside wavy ST line. Reniform spot is a small white dot. **HOSTS:** Unknown. **NOTE:** A rare fall immigrant to north part of range.

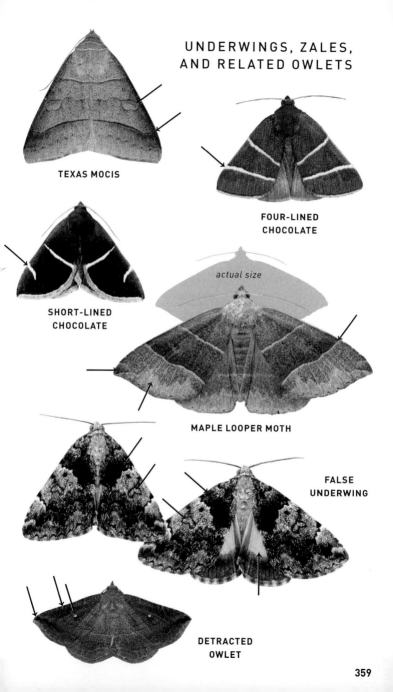

UNDERWINGS, ZALES, AND RELATED OWLETS

TEXAS MOCIS

FOUR-LINED CHOCOLATE

SHORT-LINED CHOCOLATE

actual size

MAPLE LOOPER MOTH

FALSE UNDERWING

DETRACTED OWLET

LUNATE ZALE *Zale lunata* 93-1023 (8689) **Common**
WS 40–55 mm. Variable. Brown FW has a barklike pattern of thin wavy black lines. Costa and median area are often clouded violet brown. Double ST line is boldest from midpoint of outer margin to inner margin. Sometimes has whitish bands along AM and ST lines. **HOSTS:** Trees and woody plants, including apple, cherry, oak, plum, and willow. **NOTE:** Two broods.

MAPLE ZALE *Zale galbanata* 93-1026 (8692) **Common**
WS 39–41 mm. Grayish brown FW has a barklike pattern of thin wavy black lines. Basal and median areas are often shaded brown. Wavy double PM line widens near costa. Sometimes has whitish bands along AM and ST lines. **HOSTS:** Maple. **NOTE:** Two broods.

BLACK ZALE *Zale undularis* 93-1030 (8695) **Common**
WS 38–46 mm. Slate gray FW has AM and ST lines narrowly edged with bands of warm brown. ST line is marked with a small whitish blotch. Some individuals have a contrasting whitish band beyond PM line. **HOSTS:** Locust and dogwood.

COLORFUL ZALE *Zale minerea* 93-1032 (8697) **Common**
WS 37–50 mm. Pattern is highly variable, with larger females being darker than males. Typically FW is pale yellow with darker basal area and wavy lines creating a barklike pattern. Median area is often reddish brown or orange. Sometimes has blackish triangular subapical patch. Some individuals have whitish patches along ST line on all wings. **HOSTS:** Deciduous trees, including beech, birch, maple, and poplar.

HAZEL ZALE *Zale phaeocapna* 93-1033 (8698) **Common**
WS 40 mm. FW is pale grayish brown with barklike pattern of thin wavy black lines. Basal area is often brown. Wavy double PM line widens near costa. Often there is a brownish triangular subapical patch. **HOSTS:** Hazel. **RANGE:** Locally in se. Canada and e. U.S.

FALSE PINE LOOPER ZALE
Zale duplicata 93-1038 (8703) **Common**
WS 38 mm. Purplish gray FW has thick chestnut and black bands along AM and median lines. Thin PM line has two bluntly pointed bulges near costa. A warm brown patch is often present beyond thin black reniform spot. **HOSTS:** Pine.

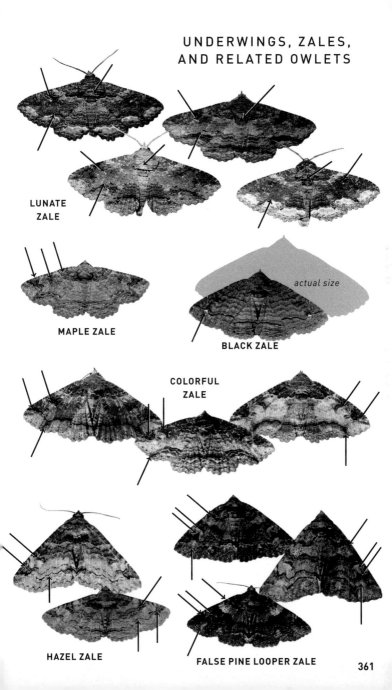

UNDERWINGS, ZALES, AND RELATED OWLETS

LUNATE ZALE

MAPLE ZALE

actual size

BLACK ZALE

COLORFUL ZALE

HAZEL ZALE

FALSE PINE LOOPER ZALE

361

BROWN-SPOTTED ZALE *Zale helata* 93-1039 (8704) **Common**
WS 35–41 mm. Brownish gray FW has brown bands along AM, median, and PM lines. AM line has sharp tooth. Thin PM line has two sharply pointed bulges near costa. A warm brown patch is present beyond thin black reniform spot. Inner ST line is often edged whitish. **HOSTS:** Pine and tamarack.

WASHED-OUT ZALE *Zale metatoides* 93-1042 (8707) **Common**
WS 32–40 mm. Very similar to Brown-spotted Zale, but paler FW has warm brown basal area. Faint lines are edged with orange-brown bands. PM line has two rounded bulges near costa. HW has a pale-edged brown ST line. **HOSTS:** Pine.

INTENT ZALE *Zale intenta* 93-1049 (8713.1) **Common**
WS 37–45 mm. Ash gray FW is finely vermiculated with black lines. Angled black AM line borders dark gray basal area. Warm brown reniform spot is partly edged white. **HOSTS:** Black cherry and white pine. **NOTE:** One or two broods. Was previously considered conspecific with Bold-based Zale, Z. lunifera, now recognized to only occur coastally south from NJ.

ONE-LINED ZALE *Zale unilineata* 93-1052 (8716) **Common**
WS 40–50 mm. Pale brown FW has slightly wavy yellowish PM line that becomes chestnut near apex. Reniform spot is a yellow-edged black crescent. HW has a bold black median line. **HOSTS:** Locust.

HORRID ZALE *Zale horrida* 93-1053 (8717) **Common**
WS 35–40 mm. Dark gray FW has wavy black AM and PM lines that are edged pale yellow at costa. Outer margin beyond ST line is straw colored, finely vermiculated with brown lines. Thorax has three tufts of cinnamon scales. **HOSTS:** Viburnum.

LOCUST UNDERWING
Euparthenos nubilis 93-1055 (8719) **Common**
TL 30–37 mm. Variable. FW of male is gray with whitish median band and shading around reniform spot. Straight AM line borders darker basal area. Mottled brown FW of female has white outer section of PM line. Orange HW has four wavy black bands and paler fringe. **HOSTS:** Primarily black locust. **NOTE:** Two broods.

FEEBLE GRASS MOTH *Amolita fessa* 93-1060 (9818) **Common**
TL 13–17 mm. Peppery straw-colored FW has a bold purplish brown streak that gently curves from base to apex. A less distinct line curves from outer margin to inner median area. Orbicular and reniform spots are small black dots. **HOSTS:** Grasses.

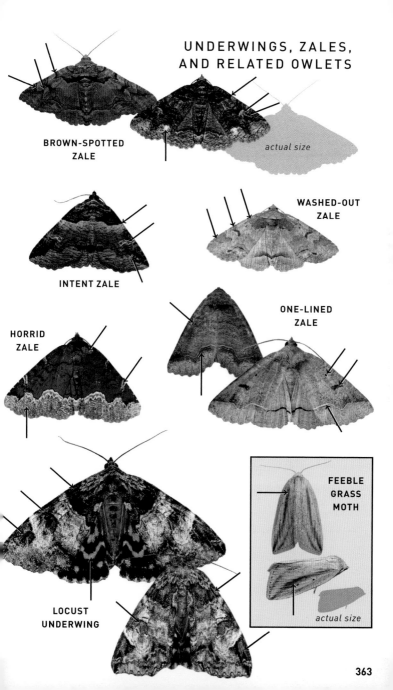

UNDERWINGS, ZALES, AND RELATED OWLETS

BROWN-SPOTTED ZALE

actual size

INTENT ZALE

WASHED-OUT ZALE

HORRID ZALE

ONE-LINED ZALE

LOCUST UNDERWING

FEEBLE GRASS MOTH

actual size

Eulepidotine Owlets
Family Erebidae, Subfamily Eulepidotinae

Velvetbean Caterpillar Moth rests with wings spread and resembles a geometer. An immigrant from southern areas, it is not encountered every year. The panopodas are deltoid noctuids that inhabit woodlands. Curve-lined Owlet is a distinctive species whose long-snouted, large-eyed appearance brings to mind a shrew with wings. All will come to light in small numbers.

VELVETBEAN CATERPILLAR MOTH
Anticarsia gemmatalis 93-1077 (8574)　　　　　　**Uncommon**
WS 33–40 mm. Brownish tan wings are variably shaded or mottled dark brown. Orange-edged brown PM line angles across FW from apex to inner margin. Hollow reniform spot is hourglass-shaped. **HOSTS:** Low plants and crops, including alfalfa, peanut, soybean, and velvetbean. **NOTE:** An irregular, though sometimes common, immigrant in northern part of range. Attracted to sugar bait.

RED-LINED PANOPODA
Panopoda rufimargo 93-1089 (8587)　　　　　　**Common**
TL 22–25 mm. Straw-colored FW has slightly darker median area between almost parallel, reddish-edged AM and PM lines. Reniform spot is typically yellowish but can be black. Dotted ST line sometimes has a dark blotch at midpoint. **HOSTS:** Beech and oak.

BROWN PANOPODA
Panopoda carneicosta 93-1090 (8588)　　　　　　**Common**
TL 21–25 mm. Grayish brown FW has slightly wavy yellow-edged AM and PM lines. Orbicular spot is a black dot. Reniform spot is a black L-shaped figure, sometimes reduced or absent. **HOSTS:** Basswood, hickory, oak, and willow.

CURVE-LINED OWLET
Phyprosopus callitrichoides 93-1101 (8525)　　　　　　**Uncommon**
TL 16–18 mm. Purplish brown FW has a kinked AM line. Gently curving PM line is edged white and sweeps across FW from apex to inner margin. Reniform spot contains two small black dots. Pointed downturned snout imparts a shrewlike appearance. **HOSTS:** Greenbrier.

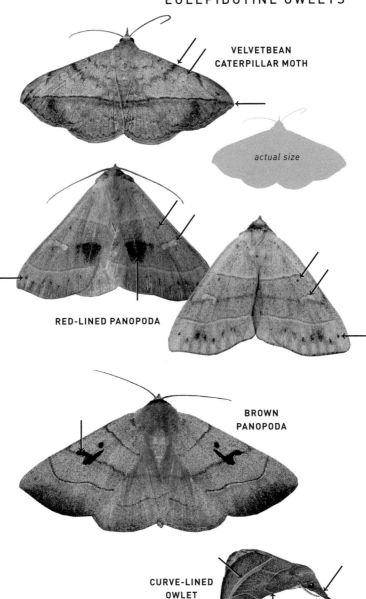

EULEPIDOTINE OWLETS

VELVETBEAN CATERPILLAR MOTH

actual size

RED-LINED PANOPODA

BROWN PANOPODA

CURVE-LINED OWLET

MARATHYSSAS AND PAECTES Family Euteliidae

Small to medium-sized moths, most of which have spectacularly acrobatic resting positions. They occur in a variety of habitats, even in highly urban areas. All are nocturnal and will come to lights in low numbers.

DARK MARATHYSSA

Marathyssa inficita 93-1103 (8955) **Common**
TL 14–17 mm. Violet gray FW is marked with obscure blackish lines and bands of pale crimson in basal area and ST areas. Male has filiform antennae with small teeth. **HOSTS:** Staghorn sumac and poison ivy. **NOTE:** Two broods.

LIGHT MARATHYSSA

Marathyssa basalis 93-1104 (8956) **Common**
TL 15–18 mm. Resembles Dark Marathyssa, but paler ash gray FW has a broad straw-colored streak extending from base to apex. A network of white veins and lines covers wing. Male has bipectinate antennae. **HOSTS:** Poison ivy.

EYED PAECTES *Paectes oculatrix* 93-1106 (8957) **Common**
TL 14–16 mm. Grayish brown FW has straw-colored basal patch. Pale crimson streaks extend through median area parallel to costa. Curved black PM line outlines an eyelike pattern in ST area. **HOSTS:** Poison ivy. **NOTE:** Two or more broods.

PYGMY PAECTES *Paectes pygmaea* 93-1107 (8959) Uncommon
TL 11–12 mm. Grayish brown FW has oval straw-colored basal patch edged by curved double AM line. Smoothly curved double PM line is sharply kinked before reaching costa. Pale gray apex is marked with thin black dashes. **HOSTS:** Sweet gum. **NOTE:** Two broods.

BARRENS PAECTES

Paectes abrostolella 93-1108 (8959.1) **Uncommon**
TL 12–14 mm. Resembles Pygmy Paectes, but FW is paler milky brown with straw-colored basal patch. Whitish apex is marked with thin black dashes. **HOSTS:** Unknown; usually found in prairie habitats. **RANGE:** W. U.S, locally east to se. ON.

LARGE PAECTES

Paectes abrostoloides 93-1111 (8962) **Common**
TL 15–17 mm. Brownish FW has bluish gray ST band. Curved AM line is double, bordered by a straw-colored crescent. Scalloped PM line is double and strongly kinked before reaching costa, showing a smaller kink at midpoint. Black apical dashes almost touch point of PM line. **HOSTS:** Sweet gum.

MARATHYSSAS AND PAECTES

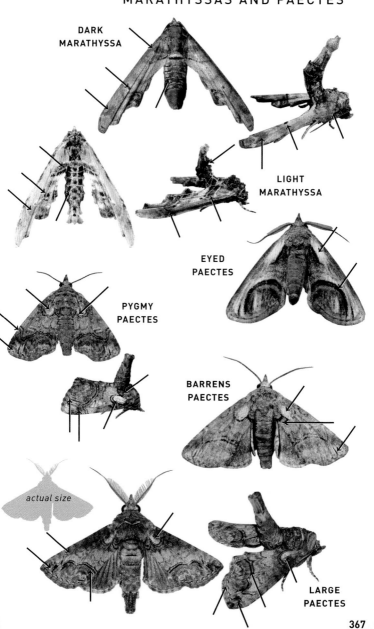

DARK MARATHYSSA

LIGHT MARATHYSSA

EYED PAECTES

PYGMY PAECTES

BARRENS PAECTES

actual size

LARGE PAECTES

367

BEAUTIFUL EUTELIA

Eutelia pulcherrimus   93-1118 (8968)   **Uncommon**
TL 14–20 mm. Multicolored FW has abstract pattern of pale orange, lilac, and maroon, overlaid with a network of white lines and veins. Apex is white. Tip of abdomen has pincerlike appendages. **HOSTS:** Poison sumac.

NOLAS   Family Nolidae, Subfamily Nolinae

Small deltoid noctuid moths that rest with their rounded wings in a flat position. They are predominantly gray or white with patterns of dotted or broken lines. Many species have raised tufts of hairlike scales on the FW. Mostly found in woodlands and old fields, they are nocturnal and are attracted to lights in small numbers.

CONFUSED MEGANOLA

Meganola minuscula   93-1121 (8983)   **Common**
TL 8–12 mm. Gray FW has indistinct lines ending as blackish spots along costa. Dotted PM line bulges around faint reniform spot. Three tufts of raised scales extend parallel to costa, making FW appear lumpy. **HOSTS:** Oak and willow. **NOTE:** One or two broods.

ASHY MEGANOLA

Meganola spodia   93-1123 (8983.2)   **Uncommon**
TL 8–13 mm. Resembles Confused Meganola, but whitish FW has double PM line. Orbicular spot is filled with raised pale yellowish scales. ST line is a row of black wedges. **HOSTS:** Bur oak. **RANGE:** Se. Canada and e. U.S. **NOTE:** One or two broods.

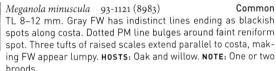

BLURRY-PATCHED NOLA

Nola cilicoides   93-1130 (8990)   **Common**
TL 9–10 mm. White FW has two raised tufts of white scales in basal and median areas. Wide fawn-colored median band passes through raised blackish reniform spot. **HOSTS:** Fringed loosestrife.

SORGHUM WEBWORM

Nola cereella   93-1131 (8991)   **Common**
TL 7–10 mm. Creamy white FW has up to five tufts of fawn scales extending parallel to costa. Midpoint of ST line is accented with blackish wedges. **HOSTS:** Grasses and sorghum seed heads.

BEAUTIFUL EUTELIA

MARATHYSSAS AND PAECTES

actual size

NOLAS

actual size

CONFUSED MEGANOLA

ASHY MEGANOLA

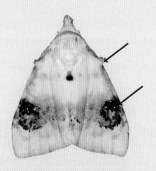

BLURRY-PATCHED NOLA

SORGHUM WEBWORM

THREE-SPOTTED NOLA

Nola triquetrana   93-1132 (8992)   **Common**
TL 9–10 mm. Gray FW has basal section of costa edged black.
AM line is strongly kinked near costa, forming a V-shape. Midpoint of costa is marked with a blackish triangle. Toothed PM
and ST lines are faint. **HOSTS:** Witch hazel.

WOOLLY NOLA   *Nola ovilla*   93-1135 (8995)   **Uncommon**

TL 9–10 mm. Resembles Three-spotted Nola, but peppery FW
has kinked AM line and costal triangle is more diffuse. PM line
is dotted and inconspicuous. Terminal line is dotted when fresh.
HOSTS: Oak. **RANGE:** Se. Canada and ne. U.S.

Baileyas and Nycteolas
Family Noctuidae, Subfamilies Risobinae and Chloephorinae

Predominantly gray, deltoid noctuid moths that typically rest with their
rounded wings in a shallow tentlike position. The baileyas sometimes curl
the abdomen tip upward above the level of the wings. The *Nycteola* species
are small with pointed labial palps, lending them a snoutlike appearance;
they could be mistaken for tortricids because of their small size and shape.
They inhabit woodlands and will visit lights in small numbers.

SMALL CHARACOMA

Garella nilotica   93-1141 (8974)   **Uncommon**
TL 8–9 mm. Variable. Typically, FW is pale gray with brown or
chestnut shading in basal and median areas. Some individuals
have blackish streaks extending through median area. Others
are uniformly grayish brown with bold black AM line. **HOSTS:**
Black almond and willow. **NOTE:** One or two broods.

FRIGID OWLET

Nycteola frigidana   93-1142 (8975)   **Uncommon**
TL 12–14 mm. Gray FW has double AM and PM lines. Outer median area shaded darker, and a checkered pattern is often
present in basal area. ST area usually pale. **HOSTS:** Poplar and
willow.

GRAY MIDGET

Nycteola cinereana   93-1144 (8977)   **Uncommon**
TL 13–16 mm. Resembles Frigid Owlet, and is likewise variable,
but FW is more uniformly gray with double AM and PM lines.
Thin black and white shoulder stripes are often conspicuous.
HOSTS: Poplar. **RANGE:** S. Canada and n. U.S. **NOTE:** Possibly
overwinters as an adult.

NOLAS

actual size

THREE-SPOTTED NOLA

WOOLLY NOLA

BAILEYAS AND NYCTEOLAS

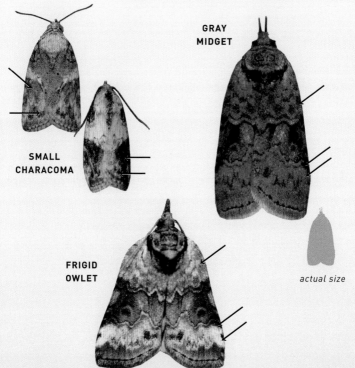

GRAY MIDGET

SMALL CHARACOMA

FRIGID OWLET

actual size

FORGOTTEN FRIGID OWLET
Nycteola metaspilella 93-1145 (8978) **Uncommon**
TL 12–14 mm. Resembles Frigid Owlet but PM line is indistinct or absent. AM line has dark wedge near inner margin. **HOSTS:** Willow.

DOUBLEDAY'S BAILEYA
Baileya doubledayi 93-1148 (8969) **Uncommon**
TL 14–17 mm. Gray FW has wide black and white shoulder stripes. White PM and ST lines pass either side of black wedges near inner margin and costa. Tear-shaped black reniform spot is outlined white. **HOSTS:** Alder. **NOTE:** Two broods.

EYED BAILEYA
Baileya ophthalmica 93-1149 (8970) **Common**
TL 13–18 mm. Peppery grayish brown FW has narrow black, white, and buff shoulder stripes. Large white reniform spot has black dot in center. Wavy PM line fades before reaching costa. Toothed black ST line is edged white. **HOSTS:** Beech, butternut, eastern hornbeam, and ironwood.

SLEEPING BAILEYA
Baileya dormitans 93-1150 (8971) **Uncommon**
TL 14–18 mm. Ash gray FW has broad whitish median band. Toothed ST line is obvious as a thick curved bulge near costa. Reniform spot is a tiny black speck. Two or more black dashes form bold subapical patch. **HOSTS:** Ironwood, also ash, beech, butternut, and walnut.

PALE BAILEYA *Baileya levitans* 93-1152 (8972) **Uncommon**
TL 14–18 mm. Resembles Eyed Baileya, but brownish FW is speckled white in outer median area. White reniform spot has a black dot in center. Midpoint of double AM line is kinked. Curved PM line is most obvious near costa. **HOSTS:** Unknown.

SMALL BAILEYA *Baileya australis* 93-1154 (8973) **Common**
TL 12–16 mm. Resembles Sleeping Baileya, but brownish FW has outer section of wavy PM line almost straight. Brown reniform spot is incompletely outlined black. Two or more black dashes form subapical patch. **HOSTS:** Unknown. **NOTE:** Three broods.

BAILEYAS AND NYCTEOLAS

FORGOTTEN FRIGID OWLET

DOUBLEDAY'S BAILEYA

EYED BAILEYA

actual size

SLEEPING BAILEYA

PALE BAILEYA

SMALL BAILEYA

LOOPERS Family Noctuidae, Subfamily Plusiinae

A distinctive group of sleek noctuid moths that mostly occur in open habitats, such as old fields and barrens. Many have diagnostic silvery stigmas on the FW. Several have tall thoracic crests and tufts of scales at the anal angle of the FW. Some are migratory, appearing well north of their normal ranges late in the fall, often during drought years or periods of favorable winds. The larvae of some widespread species can be serious pests on commercial crops. A few species, most notably Celery Looper, are active during daylight, though most are nocturnal and come to lights in small numbers.

OVAL NETTLE MOTH
Abrostola ovalis   93-1161 (8880)   **Uncommon**
TL 17 mm. Gray FW has oval straw-colored basal patch. Large pale gray claviform and orbicular spots are fused into an hourglass shape. Thorax has "goggle-like" collar behind head. **HOSTS:** Stinging nettle.

SPECTACLED NETTLE MOTH
Abrostola urentis   93-1162 (8881)   **Common**
TL 17 mm. Pale gray FW has bands of darker shading in median area and beyond ST line. Large pale gray claviform and orbicular spots are fused into an hourglass shape. Thorax has "goggle-like" collar behind head. **HOSTS:** Stinging nettle.

GOLDEN LOOPER
Argyrogramma verruca   93-1166 (8885)   **Uncommon**
TL 16–19 mm. Golden brown FW is peppered with rusty brown scales. Toothed AM and PM lines are accented with bands of lilac shading. Two-part golden stigma has a hollow inner part and a smaller, solid outer spot. **HOSTS:** Low plants, including arrowhead, curled dock, and tobacco. **NOTE:** Two or more broods. Occurs mostly as a rare immigrant in north part of range.

PINK-WASHED LOOPER
Enigmogramma basigera   93-1167 (8886)   **Uncommon**
TL 16–19 mm. Pinkish gray FW has contrasting patch of warm brown shading in inner median area, forming a saddle. Two-part silvery stigma has an inverted U-shaped inner part and a solid outer spot. **HOSTS:** Umbellate water pennywort. **RANGE:** Sw. ON and e. U.S; rare in northern part of range.

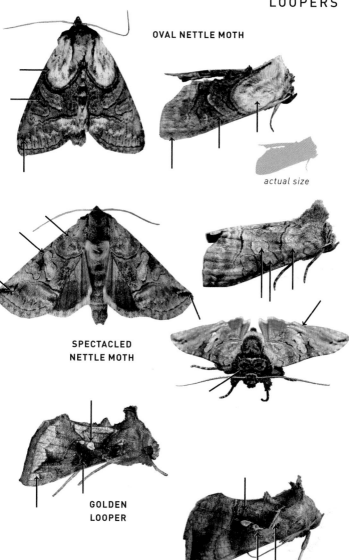

OVAL NETTLE MOTH

actual size

SPECTACLED
NETTLE MOTH

GOLDEN
LOOPER

PINK-WASHED LOOPER

NI MOTH *Trichoplusia ni* 93-1168 (8887) **Common**

TL 17–19 mm. Mottled grayish brown FW is peppered with whitish scales along jagged lines. Two-part silvery stigma has an inverted U-shaped inner part and a solid outer spot. **HOSTS:** Low plants and crops, including asparagus, cabbage, corn, tobacco, and watermelon. **NOTE:** Also known as Cabbage Looper.

SHARP-STIGMA LOOPER

Ctenoplusia oxygramma 93-1169 (8889) **Uncommon**

TL 19–22 mm. Gray FW is peppered with golden scales along inconspicuous jagged lines. Blackish median patch is pierced by an oblique silver-edged stigma. **HOSTS:** Aster, goldenrod, horseweed, and tobacco. **NOTE:** A rare fall immigrant in northern part of range.

SOYBEAN LOOPER

Chrysodeixis includens 93-1170 (8890) **Common**

TL 16–20 mm. Grayish FW has a distinctly bronzy sheen. Typically has a blackish patch between stigma and PM line. Two-part silvery stigma has an inverted U-shaped inner part and a solid outer spot. **HOSTS:** Low plants and crops, including goldenrod, lettuce, soybean, and tobacco. **NOTE:** Two or more broods. A regular fall immigrant in northern part of range.

GRAY LOOPER *Rachiplusia ou* 93-1176 (8895) **Common**

TL 17–22 mm. Ash gray FW has brown shading along indistinct lines. Jagged ST line is distinct only at apex. Two-part silvery stigma has an inverted V-shaped inner part and a solid outer spot. **HOSTS:** Low plants, including clover, mint, corn, and cosmos. **NOTE:** Two or more broods. A rare fall immigrant in northern part of range.

UNSPOTTED LOOPER

Allagrapha aerea 93-1177 (8898) **Common**

TL 16–22 mm. Pinkish FW has bands of orange-brown shading along wavy AM and PM lines. Inconspicuous reniform spot is filled with brown scales. **HOSTS:** Low plants, including aster, dandelion, and stinging nettle. **NOTE:** Two broods.

DARK-SPOTTED LOOPER

Diachrysia aereoides 93-1178 (8896) **Common**

TL 19–21 mm. Pinkish FW has bands of orange-brown shading along almost straight AM and PM lines. Claviform and reniform spots are outlined in brown. **HOSTS:** Aster, meadowsweet, and mint. **NOTE:** Two broods.

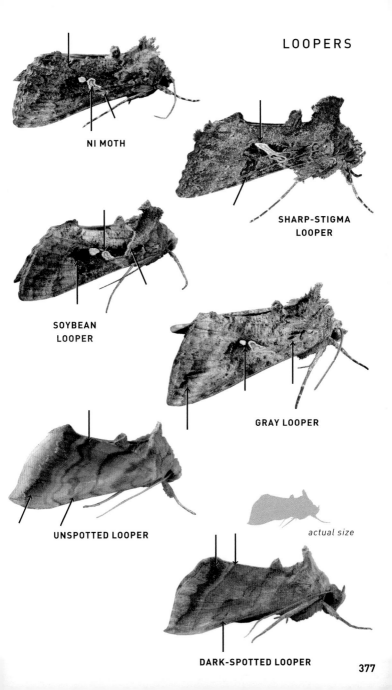

LOOPERS

NI MOTH

SHARP-STIGMA LOOPER

SOYBEAN LOOPER

GRAY LOOPER

UNSPOTTED LOOPER

actual size

DARK-SPOTTED LOOPER

HOLOGRAM MOTH

Diachrysia balluca   93-1179 (8897)   **Common**

TL 24–28 mm. Hook-tipped FW is glossy pinkish mauve with shiny green shading in inner median area and beyond PM line. Front of thorax and head are orange. **HOSTS:** Hops, trembling aspen, wood nettle, and raspberry. **NOTE:** Also known as Green-patched Looper.

STRAIGHT-LINED LOOPER

Pseudeva purpurigera   93-1184 (8899)   **Common**

TL 19 mm. Bronzy brown FW has bands of pink shading along lines. Brown-edged pink PM line is straight but angles inward near costa. Rests with wings tightly compressed. **HOSTS:** Meadow rue.

FORMOSA LOOPER

Chrysanympha formosa   93-1186 (8904)   **Uncommon**

TL 16–19 mm. Silvery gray FW has warm brown shading in inner median area. Blackish AM line is wildly sinuous, extending into median area. Evenly curved black ST line follows contour of outer margin. **HOSTS:** Blueberry and dwarf huckleberry, often on sandy soils.

PINK-PATCHED LOOPER

Eosphoropteryx thyatyroides   93-1187 (8905)   **Uncommon**

TL 17–20 mm. Silvery gray FW has brown streak through central median area. Basal area is pink. Two-part silvery stigma has squiggly inner part and a solid outer spot. Reniform spot contains one or two black dots. **HOSTS:** Meadow rue. **NOTE:** One or two broods.

COMMON LOOPER

Autographa precationis   93-1191 (8908)   **Common**

TL 18–20 mm. Grayish brown FW has bronze and lilac sheen. Stigma is variable, typically fused but sometimes appearing as two distinct spots: outer spot is always solid; inner part is a slanting inverted V-shape. Thin collar is reddish. **HOSTS:** Low plants, including bean, cabbage, dandelion, and plantain. **NOTE:** Three or more broods.

WAVY CHESTNUT Y

Autographa mappa   93-1194 (8912)   **Uncommon**

TL 20–22 mm. Light pinkish brown FW is uniquely patterned with wavy chestnut bands. Two-part silver or gold stigma has inner part shaped like an inverted V and a solid outer spot. **HOSTS:** Blueberry and nettle, often in bogs and fens. **RANGE:** S. Canada and n. U.S.

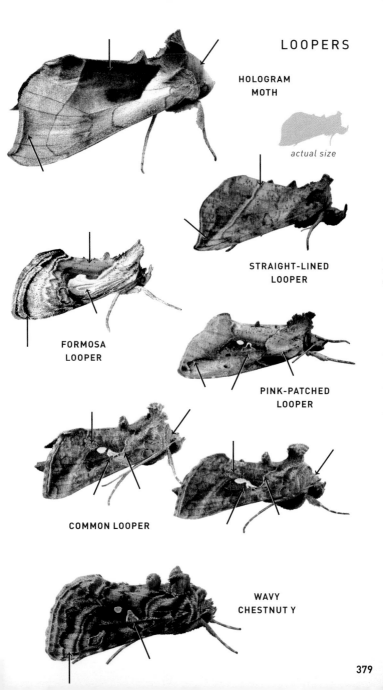

LOOPERS

HOLOGRAM MOTH

actual size

STRAIGHT-LINED LOOPER

FORMOSA LOOPER

PINK-PATCHED LOOPER

COMMON LOOPER

WAVY CHESTNUT Y

379

TWO-SPOTTED LOOPER

Autographa bimaculata　93-1200 (8911)　**Uncommon**
TL 20–22 mm. Pinkish brown FW has purple and brassy green sheen. Median area is shaded chocolate brown. Two-part silvery stigma has a partly hollow inner part and a solid outer spot. **HOSTS:** Dandelion.

LARGE LOOPER

Autographa ampla　93-1204 (8923)　**Common**
TL 21–23 mm. Silvery FW has dark grayish brown saddle covering inner median area. Inner AM and PM lines are edged pink. White hook-shaped stigma touches AM line. **HOSTS:** Various trees, including alder, birch, poplar, and willow.

BILOBED LOOPER

Megalographa biloba　93-1209 (8907)　**Common**
TL 19–20 mm. Brown FW has bronze shading in median area. Large satin white bilobed stigma covers most of central median area. **HOSTS:** Low plants, including alfalfa, cabbage, and tobacco. **NOTE:** Several broods. An erratic visitor in north part of range.

EIGHT-LETTERED LOOPER

Syngrapha octoscripta　93-1212 (8926)　**Uncommon**
TL 17–20 mm. Bluish gray FW has jagged lines accented with white. Inner PM line is typically edged chestnut. Silvery stigma is variable but is sometimes M-shaped, as shown. **HOSTS:** Blueberry.

GREEN-SPOTTED LOOPER

Syngrapha viridisigma　93-1213 (8929)　**Uncommon**
TL 20–22 mm. Gray FW has jagged lines edged whitish near inner margin. Metallic pale green stigma is variable, appearing M-shaped on some individuals. **HOSTS:** Coniferous trees, including spruce, fir, and pine.

EPIGAEA LOOPER

Syngrapha epigaea　93-1215 (8927)　**Uncommon**
TL 23 mm. Silvery FW is brindled with fine blackish lines. Median area has a black bar inside kinked silvery stigma. Rust-edged AM and PM lines are obvious only near inner margin. **HOSTS:** Blueberry.

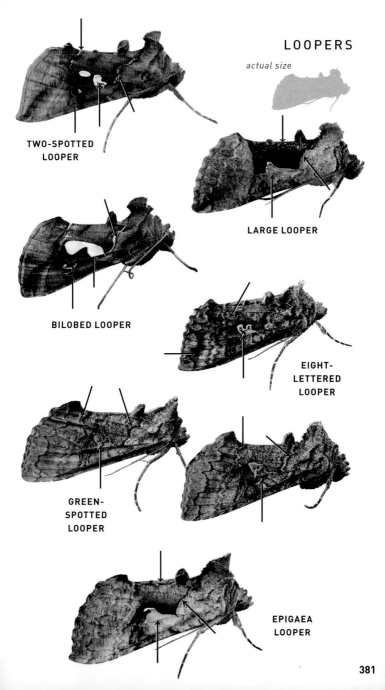

LOOPERS

actual size

TWO-SPOTTED LOOPER

LARGE LOOPER

BILOBED LOOPER

EIGHT-LETTERED LOOPER

GREEN-SPOTTED LOOPER

EPIGAEA LOOPER

ABSTRUSE LOOPER

Syngrapha abstrusa 93-1224 (8940) **Common**
TL 16–17 mm. Very similar to Hooked Silver Y, but silvery white stigma is typically in two parts, with an M-shaped inner part and a solid outer spot. **HOSTS:** Coniferous trees, including white spruce and jack pine.

HOOKED SILVER Y *Syngrapha alias* 93-1225 (8939) **Common**

TL 16–17 mm. Dark gray FW has jagged black lines. Inner median area is blackish. Silvery stigma is slanted H-shape. **HOSTS:** Coniferous trees, including white spruce and balsam fir.

SALT-AND-PEPPER LOOPER

Syngrapha rectangula 93-1227 (8942) **Common**
TL 17–19 mm. Pied FW has jagged black lines that are broadly edged white. White stigma is variable, often joined to costa by an oblique white bar. **HOSTS:** Coniferous trees, including fir, hemlock, pine, and spruce.

CELERY LOOPER *Anagrapha falcifera* 93-1234 (8924) **Common**

TL 18–22 mm. Grayish brown FW has contrasting brown inner median area. Slanting silvery white stigma touches white-edged inner section of AM line. **HOSTS:** Low plants, including beet, celery, clover, corn, and dandelion. **NOTE:** Several broods.

WHITE-STREAKED LOOPER

Plusia venusta 93-1235 (8953) **Uncommon**
TL 17–19 mm. Shiny brown FW has streaks of pink and pale yellow along costa and inner margin. Narrow white lengthwise streak extends through central median area. Reniform spot is a tiny black dot. **HOSTS:** Wetland sedges and grasses.

PUTNAM'S LOOPER

Plusia putnami 93-1236 (8950) **Uncommon**
TL 18–20 mm. Orange FW is sprinkled with rusty scales. Parallel brown lines are accented with gold near inner margin. Silvery white stigma consists of two spots, innermost larger. Silvery white apical dashes are short. **HOSTS:** Bur reed, grasses, and sedges in damp woodlands. **NOTE:** Two broods.

CONNECTED LOOPER

Plusia contexta 93-1239 (8952) **Uncommon**
TL 18–19 mm. Golden yellow FW has streak of purplish shading along costa. Silvery stigma spots are fused. Uppermost white apical dash is noticeably longer. **HOSTS:** Grasses. **NOTE:** Two broods.

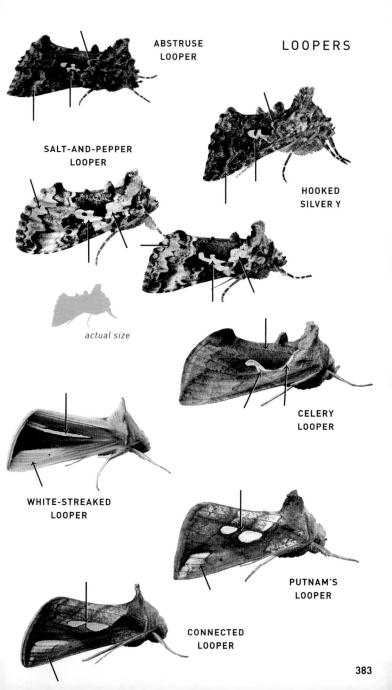

LOOPERS

ABSTRUSE
LOOPER

SALT-AND-PEPPER
LOOPER

HOOKED
SILVER Y

actual size

CELERY
LOOPER

WHITE-STREAKED
LOOPER

PUTNAM'S
LOOPER

CONNECTED
LOOPER

Glyphs
Family Noctuidae, Subfamilies Bagisarinae and Eustrotiinae

Colorful small to medium-sized noctuid moths, many with cryptic lichenlike markings. All are nocturnal and will come to lights. A few, such as Bog Deltote and Pale Glyph, can be flushed from vegetation during daylight.

EIGHT-SPOT *Amyna axis* 93-1253 (9070) **Uncommon**
TL 12–14 mm. Brown FW has hourglass-shaped reniform spot with a white or pale orange spot in inner half. ST line is often edged with a chocolate brown band. **HOSTS:** Goosefoot. **NOTE:** A tropical species that immigrates northward some years, occasionally reaching ne. N. America in the fall.

BLACK-BORDERED LEMON
Marimatha nigrofimbria 93-1284 (9044) **Common**
TL 10–12 mm. Lemon yellow FW has tiny blackish claviform and reniform dots. Terminal line is black. Fringe is dark purplish gray. **HOSTS:** Crabgrass and morning glory.

BOG DELTOTE *Deltote bellicula* 93-1289 (9046) **Uncommon**
TL 10–12 mm. Violet gray FW has chocolate brown median and ST bands. Inner half of curved PM line is edged white. Orbicular and reniform spots are connected with a pale orange bar. **HOSTS:** Unknown; usually restricted to acidic bogs and fens. **NOTE:** Two broods.

LARGE MOSSY GLYPH
Protodeltote muscosula 93-1290 (9047) **Common**
TL 10–12 mm. Peppery gray FW has white-edged lines and spots. Fresh individuals have mossy green shading in basal, median, and ST areas. Inner PM line is broadly edged white. **HOSTS:** Saw grass and other swamp grasses.

PALE GLYPH
Protodeltote albidula 93-1291 (9048) **Common**
TL 12–14 mm. Pale FW is lightly peppered with brown scales and fawn-colored lines. Indistinct orbicular and reniform spots are outlined white. **HOSTS:** Grasses. **RANGE:** S. Canada and n. U.S.

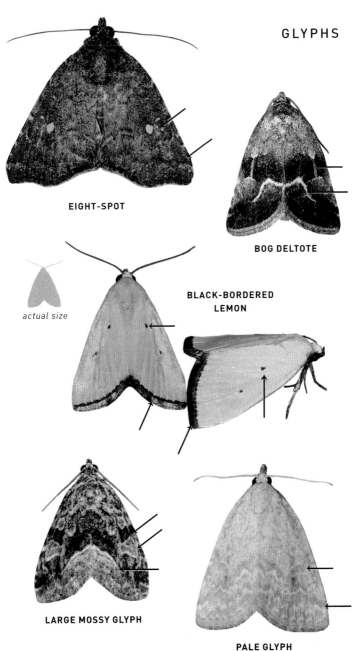

GLYPHS

EIGHT-SPOT

BOG DELTOTE

BLACK-BORDERED
LEMON

actual size

LARGE MOSSY GLYPH

PALE GLYPH

SMALL MOSSY GLYPH

Lithacodia musta   93-1292 (9051)   **Common**

TL 8–10 mm. Mossy green FW has double AM and PM lines filled with pale orange. Inner PM line is edged white. Black claviform spot is partly outlined white. Black orbicular spot is outlined orange. Large reniform spot is partly filled with orange scales. **HOSTS:** Unknown.

BLACK-DOTTED GLYPH

Maliattha synochitis   93-1295 (9049)   **Common**

TL 9–10 mm. White FW is mottled green in basal, median, and ST areas. Triangular green patch in inner median area forms a distinct saddle. Elliptical black orbicular spot and subapical dashes are sharpest markings.   **HOSTS:** Smartweed.

RED-SPOTTED GLYPH

Maliattha concinnimacula   93-1296 (9050)   **Uncommon**

TL 10–12 mm. Light green FW is marked with jagged white lines. Red claviform and reniform spots are outlined white. Black orbicular spot is almost connected to costa by black bar. ST line ends at black subapical patch. **HOSTS:** Unknown.

CURVED HALTER MOTH

Capis curvata   93-1297 (9059)   **Rare**

TL 14–15 mm. Shiny chocolate brown FW has slightly oblique white ST line. Orbicular and reniform spots are sometimes faintly marked with small white dots. **HOSTS:** Unknown, but often found in damp woodlands.

BIRD-DROPPING MOTHS
Family Noctuidae, Subfamily Acontiinae

Small moths, most of which are accomplished bird-dropping mimics. Commonly encountered at woodland edges and old fields, sometimes during daytime, in midsummer. Most are nocturnal and will come to lights, though some, like Olive-shaded Bird-dropping Moth, may be flushed from vegetation during the day.

OLIVE-SHADED BIRD-DROPPING MOTH

Ponometia candefacta   93-1314 (9090)   **Common**

TL 12 mm. White FW has median and outer ST areas clouded yellowish green and gray. Inner median area is darker green. Gray reniform spot is outlined white. **HOSTS:** Ragweed. **NOTE:** Up to three broods.

GLYPHS

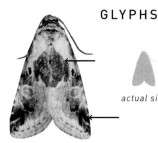

actual size

BLACK-DOTTED GLYPH

SMALL MOSSY GLYPH

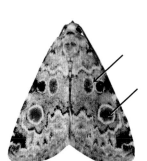

RED-SPOTTED GLYPH

CURVED HALTER MOTH

BIRD-DROPPING MOTHS

actual size

**OLIVE-SHADED
BIRD-DROPPING MOTH**

SMALL BIRD-DROPPING MOTH
Ponometia erastrioides 93-1319 (9095) **Common**
TL 9–10 mm. White FW has mottled dusky green and gray median band that stops short of costa. Orbicular spot is a tiny black dot. Inconspicuous reniform spot is clouded with dusky shading. **HOSTS:** Ragweed. **NOTE:** Up to three broods.

EXPOSED BIRD-DROPPING MOTH
Tarache aprica 93-1343 (9136) **Uncommon**
TL 9–15 mm. Sexually dimorphic. FW of male is white with mottled gray and brown shading in ST area. AM and PM lines end as dusky patches along costa. FW of female is mostly blue-gray with darker lines and contrasting white patches along costa. **HOSTS:** Hollyhock.

COMMON SPRAGUEIA
Spragueia leo 93-1387 (9127) **Common**
TL 7–10 mm. Orange FW has black costal streak broken by black spots. Orange bands interrupt broad black streaks extending through median area and inner margin. **HOSTS:** Bindweed.

PANTHEAS AND YELLOWHORNS
Family Noctuidae, Subfamily Pantheinae

Chunky moths with a slightly hairy appearance. The yellowhorns take their name from their yellowish pectinate antennae. They are common in mixed woodlands and larger gardens from spring to mid-summer. All will come to lights, some in moderate numbers.

EASTERN PANTHEA
Panthea furcilla 93-1396 (9182) **Common**
TL 20–25 mm. Peppery FW is variably whitish to dark gray with crisp black lines. AM and median lines are almost straight; PM line bends sharply toward median line before reaching inner margin. **HOSTS:** Coniferous trees, including pine, spruce, and tamarack. **NOTE:** Two broods.

BLACK ZIGZAG
Panthea acronyctoides 93-1398 (9177) **Uncommon**
TL 21–22 mm. White FW is boldly marked with black zigzag lines. Tiny black orbicular dot sits within a white patch. Fringe is boldly checkered black and white. **HOSTS:** Coniferous trees, including hemlock, pine, and spruce.

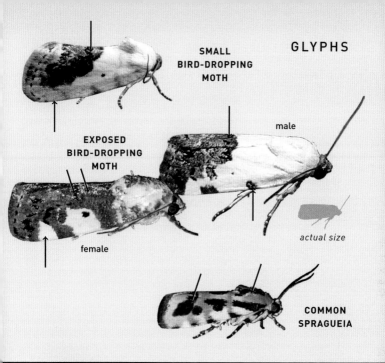

GLYPHS

SMALL BIRD-DROPPING MOTH

EXPOSED BIRD-DROPPING MOTH

male

actual size

female

COMMON SPRAGUEIA

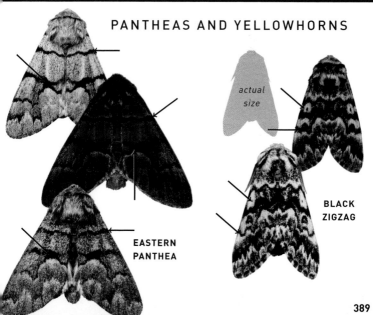

PANTHEAS AND YELLOWHORNS

actual size

BLACK ZIGZAG

EASTERN PANTHEA

389

SADDLED YELLOWHORN
Colocasia flavicornis   93-1400 (9184)   **Uncommon**
TL 18–22 mm. Gray FW has blackish patch covering inner median area. Kinked AM and PM lines are connected by black bar in central median area. White orbicular spot is outlined black. Antennae are yellow. **HOSTS:** Deciduous trees, including beech, elm, ironwood, oak, and maple. **NOTE:** Two broods. Also called simply Yellowhorn.

CLOSE-BANDED YELLOWHORN
Colocasia propinquilinea   93-1401 (9185)   **Common**
TL 20–24 mm. Resembles Saddled Yellowhorn, but FW lacks black inner median patch. AM and PM lines almost touch in inner median area. Orbicular and reniform spots are incompletely outlined black. Antennae are yellow. **HOSTS:** Deciduous trees, including beech, elm, oak, and poplar. **NOTE:** One or two broods.

THE LAUGHER
Charadra deridens   93-1406 (9189)   **Common**
TL 20–24 mm. Peppery FW is variably whitish to dark gray. AM and PM lines are constricted, sometimes connected, in central median area. Conspicuous orbicular spot is outlined white. **HOSTS:** Deciduous trees, including beech, birch, elm, maple, and oak. **NOTE:** One or two broods.

Hieroglyphic Moth
Family Noctuidae, Subfamily Diphtherinae

A distinctive species whose crisp black pattern on orange background calls to mind ancient Egyptian artwork. A very rare immigrant to most of ne. N. America, and not frequently encountered. Will come to light.

HIEROGLYPHIC MOTH
Diphthera festiva   93-1410 (8560)   **Uncommon**
TL 20–24 mm. Pale yellow to orange FW has unique pattern of metallic ink blue lines and dots. Black HW has white fringe. **HOSTS:** Trees, shrubs, and low plants, including pecan and sweet potato. **NOTE:** A largely tropical moth, resident in se. U.S., that occasionally strays northward as far as MI.

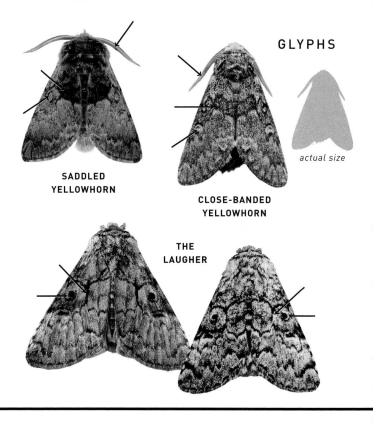

GLYPHS

SADDLED YELLOWHORN

CLOSE-BANDED YELLOWHORN

actual size

THE LAUGHER

HIEROGLYPHIC MOTH

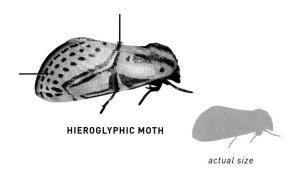

HIEROGLYPHIC MOTH

actual size

BROTHERS   Family Noctuidae, Subfamily Dilobinae

Chunky, slightly hairy moths that resemble the yellowhorns in size and shape. Will visit lights in small numbers.

ABRUPT BROTHER
Raphia abrupta   93-1411 (9192)   **Uncommon**
TL 17–19 mm. Gray FW has curved AM and PM lines that are double near inner margin. Paler orbicular and reniform spots are narrowly outlined black. HW is gray with darker terminal line and pale fringe. **HOSTS:** Unknown, presumably various deciduous trees. **NOTE:** Two broods.

THE BROTHER *Raphia frater*   93-1412 (9193)   **Common**
TL 18–19 mm. Resembles slightly smaller Abrupt Brother but has strikingly white HW. Some individuals have a darker gray patch in inner median area. **HOSTS:** Deciduous trees, including alder, birch, cottonwood, poplar, and willow.

BALSAS   Family Noctuidae, Subfamily Balsinae

Small, rounded-winged moths. Predominantly gray, they are patterned with black lines and streaks. They are commonly encountered in woodlands and gardens in the summer months. All will come to lights, sometimes in moderate numbers.

MANY-DOTTED APPLEWORM
Balsa malana   93-1417 (9662)   **Common**
TL 13–16 mm. Peppery ash gray FW has streaky pattern of toothed lines and blackish veins in ST area. Incomplete oblique black median line forks at costa, forming a vague Y-shape. **HOSTS:** Apple, cherry, elm, pear, and plum. **NOTE:** Two broods.

THREE-LINED BALSA
Balsa tristrigella   93-1418 (9663)   **Common**
TL 11–12 mm. Ash gray FW has finely striated pattern of deeply toothed lines and black veins. Lines are thicker toward costa. ST area is marked with a row of brown streaks. **HOSTS:** Hawthorn.

WHITE-BLOTCHED BALSA
Balsa labecula   93-1419 (9664)   **Common**
TL 13–16 mm. Lilac gray FW is finely peppered with black scales along white veins. Round orbicular spot is white. Longest black dash in ST area almost touches whitish reniform spot. **HOSTS:** Apple, chokeberry, hawthorn, and serviceberry.

BROTHERS

actual size

ABRUPT BROTHER

THE BROTHER

BALSAS

**MANY-DOTTED
APPLEWORM**

**THREE-LINED
BALSA**

actual size

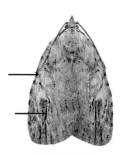

**WHITE-BLOTCHED
BALSA**

DAGGERS Family Noctuidae, Subfamily Acronictinae

A large group of predominantly gray noctuid moths that often have black daggerlike dashes on the FW. Some species are difficult to identify, so care must be taken. Found in woodlands and larger gardens. They are nocturnal and will visit lights and sugar bait in small numbers.

RUDDY DAGGER

Acronicta rubricoma   93-1420 (9199)   Uncommon

TL 20–24 mm. Peppery gray FW has double AM and PM lines. Orbicular spot is outlined black. Large reniform spot is blackish. Basal and anal dashes are thin and indistinct. **HOSTS:** Elm, hackberry, and sumac. **NOTE:** Two broods.

AMERICAN DAGGER

Acronicta americana   93-1421 (9200)   Common

TL 27–38 mm. Large size. Pale gray FW has double PM line edged white. Inconspicuous orbicular and reniform spots are narrowly outlined black. Thin anal dash cuts through PM line. **HOSTS:** Deciduous trees and woody plants, including alder, ash, basswood, elm, chestnut, and hickory. **NOTE:** Two broods.

FINGERED DAGGER

Acronicta dactylina   93-1424 (9203)   Common

TL 24–29 mm. Pale gray FW has toothed PM line accented with black wedges. Orbicular spot is outlined black. Reniform spot is filled with gray and black scales. Thin anal dash cuts through PM line. **HOSTS:** Alder, birch, poplar, and willow.

COTTONWOOD DAGGER

Acronicta lepusculina   93-1425 (9205)   Uncommon

TL 24–27 mm. Whitish FW is sprinkled with gray scales. All lines are obvious only as bold blackish spots along costa. Black anal dash forms a spot where it cuts through PM line. **HOSTS:** Poplar and willow. **NOTE:** Two broods.

UNMARKED DAGGER

Acronicta innotata   93-1428 (9207)   Common

TL 19–22 mm. Creamy white FW often has faint brownish shading along lines. Shallowly scalloped PM line has rounded bulge near inner margin. Reniform spot is a thin black crescent. **HOSTS:** Alder, birch, hickory, poplar, and willow.

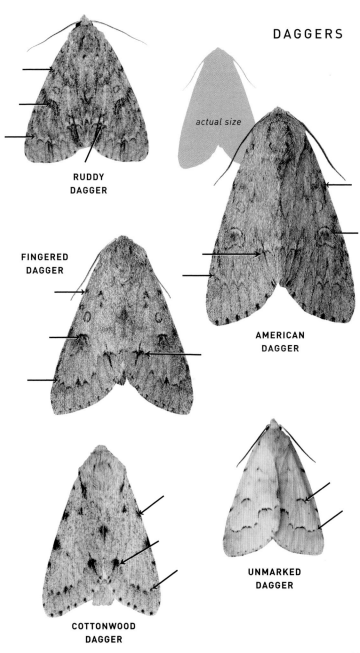

DAGGERS

actual size

RUDDY
DAGGER

FINGERED
DAGGER

AMERICAN
DAGGER

COTTONWOOD
DAGGER

UNMARKED
DAGGER

BIRCH DAGGER

Acronicta betulae   93-1429 (9208)   **Uncommon**
TL 18–22 mm. Pale, yellowish gray FW often has bands of warm brown shading along lines. Jagged PM line has pointed bulge near inner margin. AM and median lines are faintly outlined in brown. **HOSTS:** Birch. **NOTE:** Two broods.

RADCLIFFE'S DAGGER

Acronicta radcliffei   93-1430 (9209)   **Uncommon**
TL 18–20 mm. Grayish brown FW has crisp black AM and PM lines that are narrowly edged white. Long basal and anal dashes slice through lines but do not meet in median area. Orbicular and reniform spots are incompletely edged black. **HOSTS:** Apple, cherry, chokeberry, and hawthorn. **NOTE:** Two broods.

TRITON DAGGER

Acronicta tritona   93-1432 (9211)   **Uncommon**
TL 18–20 mm. Purplish gray FW has rusty median and ST bands. Faint AM line is touched by thin black basal dash. Jagged PM line is edged whitish and pierced by black anal dash. **HOSTS:** Cranberry, blueberry, and rhododendron. **NOTE:** Two broods.

GRAY DAGGER   *Acronicta grisea*   93-1433 (9212)   **Common**

TL 18–20 mm. Peppery gray FW has AM and PM lines edged pale gray. Round orbicular spot is whitish with gray center. Long black basal and anal dashes do not meet in median area. **HOSTS:** Deciduous trees, including alder, apple, birch, and cherry.

CONNECTED DAGGER

Acronicta connecta   93-1436 (9219)   **Uncommon**
TL 19–20 mm. Gray FW has conspicuous streak of dusky shading connecting thin black basal and anal dashes. Pale orbicular spot is separated from brownish reniform spot by patch of dusky shading. **HOSTS:** Willow. **NOTE:** Two broods.

FUNERARY DAGGER

Acronicta funeralis   93-1438 (9221)   **Uncommon**
TL 17–21 mm. Whitish FW has fragmented AM and median lines that are obvious only as blackish spots along costa. Wide black basal and anal dashes almost touch in inner median area. **HOSTS:** Deciduous trees, including apple, birch, elm, maple, and willow. **NOTE:** Two broods.

BIRCH DAGGER

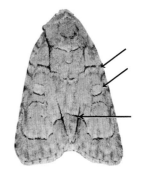

RADCLIFFE'S DAGGER

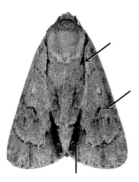

TRITON DAGGER

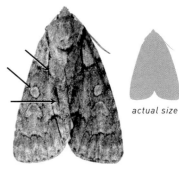

actual size

GRAY DAGGER

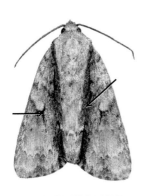

CONNECTED DAGGER

FUNERARY DAGGER

397

DELIGHTFUL DAGGER

Acronicta vinnula 93-1442 (9225) **Common**
TL 15–17 mm. Whitish or gray FW has conspicuous black-edged white orbicular spot. Basal dash widens where it touches indistinct AM line. Bulging PM line is edged white. **HOSTS:** Elm. **NOTE:** Two broods.

SPLENDID DAGGER

Acronicta superans 93-1443 (9226) **Common**
TL 22–25 mm. Whitish FW is heavily mottled with bronze green shading along lines and dashes. Thick blackish basal and anal dashes connect with broad dusky median band. **HOSTS:** Apple, cherry, hawthorn, and mountain ash.

PLEASANT DAGGER

Acronicta laetifica 93-1444 (9227) **Uncommon**
TL 20–22 mm. Pale gray FW has thick black basal dash that has a short spur where it touches faint AM line. White-edged PM line is pierced by long black anal and subapical dashes. Orbicular and reniform spots are connected by short black bar. **HOSTS:** Ironwood. **NOTE:** Two broods.

SPEARED DAGGER

Acronicta hasta 93-1445 (9229) **Common**
TL 22–23 mm. Similar to Pleasant Dagger, but darker gray with a more peppery appearance. Black basal dash ends with three prongs. **HOSTS:** Cherry. **NOTE:** Two broods.

NONDESCRIPT DAGGER

Acronicta spinigera 93-1452 (9235) **Common**
TL 21–25 mm. Pale gray FW is marked with inconspicuous lines and thin black basal, subapical, and anal dashes. Round orbicular spot is partly outlined black. **HOSTS:** Basswood, also apple, birch, cherry, and elm. **NOTE:** Two broods.

OCHRE DAGGER

Acronicta morula 93-1453 (9236) **Common**
TL 22–30 mm. Gray FW has yellowish brown shading along lines and dashes. Inconspicuous AM line is touched by thin black basal dash. White-edged PM line is pierced by anal and subapical dashes. Thorax has a wide ochre dorsal stripe. **HOSTS:** Elm, also apple, basswood, and hawthorn. **NOTE:** Two broods.

DAGGERS

SPLENDID DAGGER

actual size

DELIGHTFUL DAGGER

PLEASANT DAGGER

SPEARED DAGGER

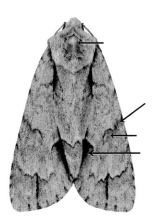

NONDESCRIPT DAGGER

OCHRE DAGGER

INTERRUPTED DAGGER

Acronicta interrupta   93-1454 (9237)   **Common**
TL 21 mm. Smooth ash gray FW has black basal dash that
merges into indistinct AM line. White-edged PM line is pierced
by thin black anal dash. **HOSTS:** Deciduous trees, including apple, birch, cherry, elm, and oak. **NOTE:** Two broods.

GREAT OAK DAGGER

Acronicta lobeliae   93-1455 (9238)   **Common**
TL 21–32 mm. Whitish FW has pattern of indistinct white-edged
lines and crisp black dashes. Black bar connects inconspicuous orbicular and reniform spots. **HOSTS:** Oak. **NOTE:** Two
broods. Also known as Lobelia Dagger.

FRAGILE DAGGER   *Acronicta fragilis*   93-1458 (9241)   **Common**
TL 15–17 mm. Whitish FW has jagged black AM and PM lines
edged white. Conspicuous white orbicular spot is outlined
black. A line of thick black dashes extends through basal, inner
median, and anal angle areas. **HOSTS:** Apple, birch, plum, willow, and white spruce. **NOTE:** Two broods.

OVATE DAGGER   *Acronicta ovata*   93-1463 (9243)   **Common**
TL 15–19 mm. Gray FW has dark basal dash that connects to
partly shaded double AM line. Orbicular and reniform spot are
often shaded brown. Pale ST line visible and thin anal dash
present. **HOSTS:** Beech, chestnut, and oak. **NOTE:** Two broods.

MEDIUM DAGGER

Acronicta modica   93-1465 (9244)   **Common**
TL 18–22 mm. Thin black anal dash is usually only distinct
marking on pale gray FW. Whitish ST line usually visible. **HOSTS:**
Oak. **NOTE:** Two broods.

HESITANT DAGGER

Acronicta haesitata   93-1466 (9245)   **Common**
TL 24 mm. Gray FW has dark basal dash that connects to partly
shaded double AM line. Orbicular and bottom half of reniform
spot outlined in white. Pale ST line visible, but anal dash usually
absent. **HOSTS:** Oak. **NOTE:** Two broods.

DAGGERS

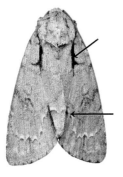

INTERRUPTED DAGGER

GREAT OAK DAGGER

actual size

FRAGILE DAGGER

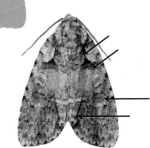

OVATE DAGGER

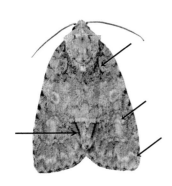

MEDIUM DAGGER

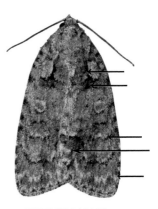

HESITANT DAGGER

SMALL OAK DAGGER

Acronicta increta   93-1467 (9249)   **Common**
TL 15–20 mm. Variably light to dark gray FW has dark basal
dash that connects to shaded double AM line. Orbicular and reniform spots often shaded brown. ST line usually indistinct, and
anal dash is absent. **HOSTS:** Primarily chestnut and oak. **NOTE:**
Two broods. Also known as Raspberry Bud Dagger, a misnomer
as this species does not feed on raspberries.

RETARDED DAGGER

Acronicta retardata   93-1470 (9251)   **Common**
TL 14–16 mm. FW is typically pale gray with whitish median
area. Double AM line has small black triangle at midpoint.
White orbicular and reniform spots are dark centered. Darker
individuals are uniformly dark gray with contrasting whitish
spots. **HOSTS:** Maple. **NOTE:** Two or more broods.

AFFLICTED DAGGER

Acronicta afflicta   93-1471 (9254)   **Uncommon**
TL 20 mm. Sooty gray FW has obscure dark lines and dashes.
Dark-centered white orbicular spot is conspicuous. **HOSTS:**
Oak. **NOTE:** Two broods.

YELLOW-HAIRED DAGGER

Acronicta impleta   93-1474 (9257)   **Uncommon**
TL 21–27 mm. Peppery gray FW has fragmented, double AM
and PM lines. Dark-centered orbicular and reniform spots are
thinly outlined black. Jagged ST line is boldly edged white, especially at inner margin. **HOSTS:** Hickory and walnut, also alder,
ash, elm, and maple. **NOTE:** Two broods.

NIGHT-WANDERING DAGGER

Acronicta noctivaga   93-1476 (9259)   **Uncommon**
TL 20 mm. Whitish FW is heavily peppered with black scales.
Jagged AM and PM lines are double and filled with white. Bold
black dashes pass through basal, inner median, and anal angle
areas. Black median band passes through mostly black reniform spot. **HOSTS:** Poplar. **NOTE:** Two broods.

IMPRESSED DAGGER

Acronicta impressa   93-1477 (9261)   **Uncommon**
TL 18–24 mm. Peppery gray FW has jagged AM and PM lines.
Pale gray orbicular spot is outlined black. Inconspicuous basal
and anal dashes are clouded with gray shading. Inner median
area is often darker gray. **HOSTS:** Deciduous trees and woody
plants. **RANGE:** S. Canada and n. U.S. **NOTE:** Two broods.

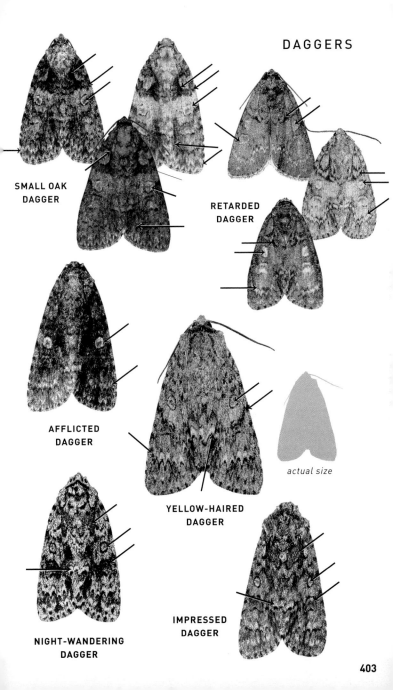

DAGGERS

SMALL OAK
DAGGER

RETARDED
DAGGER

AFFLICTED
DAGGER

YELLOW-HAIRED
DAGGER

actual size

NIGHT-WANDERING
DAGGER

IMPRESSED
DAGGER

LONG-WINGED DAGGER

Acronicta longa   93-1478 (9264)   **Uncommon**
TL 18–24 mm. Whitish FW has zigzag AM, median, and PM lines broadly edged light brown. Round orbicular spot is outlined black. Black anal dash is usually noticeable. **HOSTS:** Deciduous trees, including birch, cherry, and oak. **NOTE:** Two broods.

STREAKED DAGGER

Acronicta lithospila   93-1480 (9266)   **Uncommon**
TL 18–23 mm. Gray FW has white streaks along darker veins. Thin black basal and anal dashes are lost among the streakiness. **HOSTS:** Oak and chestnut, also hickory and walnut. **NOTE:** Two broods.

SMEARED DAGGER

Acronicta oblinita   93-1485 (9272)   **Uncommon**
TL 20–28 mm. Peppery gray FW has blurry dark streaks extending throughout wing. Jagged PM line is indistinct, accented with dusky triangles. **HOSTS:** Trees, shrubs, and forbs, including apple, corn, elm, pine, and willow. **NOTE:** Two broods.

LANCEOLATE DAGGER

Acronicta lanceolaria   93-1488 (9274)   **Uncommon**
TL 22 mm. Pointed gray FW has no obvious markings apart from faint whitish streaks. Short black anal dash touches outer margin. **HOSTS:** Trees and woody plants, including willow, poplar, and tamarack. **RANGE:** S. Canada and n. U.S.

HENRY'S MARSH MOTH

Simyra insularis   93-1493 (9280)   **Uncommon**
TL 20–22 mm. Pale creamy brown FW has contrasting whitish veins. Three streaks of dark brown shading extend across wing. **HOSTS:** Cattail, grasses, sedges, smartweed, poplar, and willow. **NOTE:** Two broods.

GREEN MARVEL   *Agriopodes fallax* 93-1494 (9281)   **Uncommon**
TL 17–20 mm. Pale green FW has chunky black fragments forming AM and PM lines. A black square separates inconspicuous orbicular and reniform spots. Fringe is checkered black and white. **HOSTS:** Viburnum. **NOTE:** Two broods.

THE HEBREW

Polygrammate hebraeicum   93-1497 (9285)   **Uncommon**
TL 13–15 mm. White FW has complex pattern of fragmented black lines. Orbicular spot is a black dot. Terminal line and fringe are checkered black and white. **HOSTS:** Black gum.

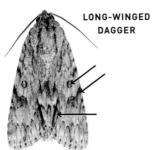

LONG-WINGED DAGGER

DAGGERS

STREAKED DAGGER

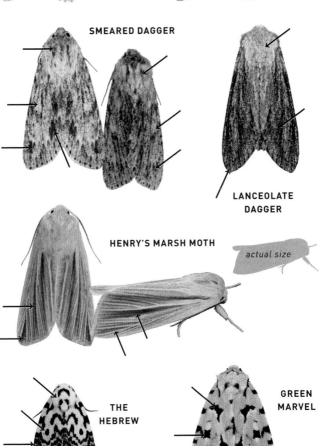

SMEARED DAGGER

LANCEOLATE DAGGER

HENRY'S MARSH MOTH

actual size

THE HEBREW

GREEN MARVEL

405

HARRIS'S THREE-SPOT
Harrisimemna trisignata   93-1498 (9286)   Uncommon
TL 17–20 mm. White FW has pattern of jagged black lines with
large warm brown spots at base, near apex, and at anal angle.
HOSTS: Trees and woody plants, including apple, blueberry,
cherry, honeysuckle, and willow.

OWL-EYED BIRD-DROPPING MOTH
Cerma cora   93-1500 (9061)   Uncommon
TL 15–17 mm. Olive green and white FW is marked with complex pattern of sinuous black lines. White orbicular spot is
boldly outlined black. **HOSTS:** Pin cherry.

TUFTED BIRD-DROPPING MOTH
Cerma cerintha   93-1501 (9062)   Common
TL 15–17 mm. White FW has mosaic-like pattern of brown,
blue, and moss green in basal and ST areas. Pale greenish blue
scallops form a fragmented median band. **HOSTS:** Fruit-bearing
trees, including apple, plum, peach, and cherry.

HOODED OWLETS
Family Noctuidae, Subfamily Cuculliinae

A distinctive group of species that rest with their wings folded and their
forelegs outstretched. A thick thoracic crest typically curls forward over the
head to create a "hooded" appearance. These moths are called "sharks" in
Europe. Found in woodlands and larger gardens, they are nocturnal and will
visit lights in small numbers.

GOLDENROD HOODED OWLET
Cucullia asteroides   93-1504 (10200)   Common
TL 26–29 mm. Ash gray FW has obvious reddish brown blotches
along costal margin. Orbicular and reniform spots are partly
outlined blackish. White HW has a narrow (broader in females)
dusky ST line. **HOSTS:** Aster and goldenrod. **NOTE:** Two broods.
Also known as The Asteroid.

GRAY HOODED OWLET
Cucullia florea   93-1508 (10197)   Common
TL 22–24 mm. Resembles Goldenrod Hooded Owlet, but FW
has narrow blackish streak along inner margin. Costal margin
is mottled with faint brown blotches. HW is grayish with dusky
brown veins. **HOSTS:** Aster and goldenrod.

DAGGERS

**HARRIS'S
THREE-SPOT**

**OWL-EYED
BIRD-DROPPING MOTH**

**TUFTED
BIRD-DROPPING
MOTH**

actual size

HOODED OWLETS

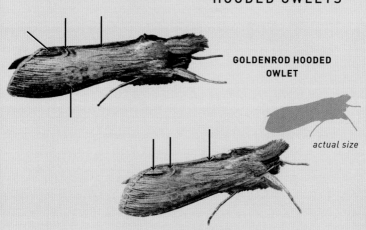

**GOLDENROD HOODED
OWLET**

actual size

GRAY HOODED OWLET

BROWN HOODED OWLET

Cucullia convexipennis   93-1513 (10202)   **Common**
TL 22–27 mm. Creamy gray FW has brown streaks along costa and inner margin. Blackish dashes form a subapical patch. Dusky HW has a whitish fringe. Abdomen has tufts of brown scales protruding above folded wings. **HOSTS:** Aster and goldenrod. **NOTE:** Also known as Brown-bordered Cucullia.

DUSKY HOODED OWLET

Cucullia intermedia   93-1514 (10194)   **Common**
TL 23–27 mm. Ash gray FW is marked with faint jagged lines. Thin black basal dash extends to deepest tooth in AM line. ST area is marked with whitish streaks between thin black veins. HW is dusky brown with whitish fringe. **HOSTS:** Wild lettuce. **NOTE:** Two broods. Also known as Intermediate Cucullia.

AMPHIPYRINE SALLOWS
Family Noctuidae, Subfamily Amphipyrinae

The *Amphipyra* are medium-sized moths that rest with their wings flat. They often run around on bark in a mouselike fashion and regularly visit sugar bait. The others in this group are chunkier moths that usually rest with their wings tented over their back. Most are inhabitants of woodland and field edges. They are nocturnal and will visit lights in small numbers, though Goldenrod Stowaway may be encountered resting on flowers during the day.

COPPER UNDERWING

Amphipyra pyramidoides   93-1544 (9638)   **Common**
TL 23–28 mm. Shiny grayish brown FW is peppered with pale brown hairlike scales. Outer margin is paler beyond slightly jagged PM line. Elliptical orbicular spot is narrowly outlined whitish. Legs are banded black and white. **HOSTS:** Trees and vines, including birch, elm, oak, Virginia creeper, and willow.

MOUSE MOTH

Amphipyra tragopoginis   93-1545 (9639)   **Common**
TL 18–22 mm. Grayish brown FW is sprinkled with pale brown hairlike scales. Black orbicular dot and two black dots at either end of reniform spot are the only obvious markings. ST line is a row of short black streaks along veins. **HOSTS:** Hawthorn and a variety of low plants, including columbine, geranium, plantain, and stinging nettle. **RANGE:** S. Canada and ne. U.S.

HOODED OWLETS

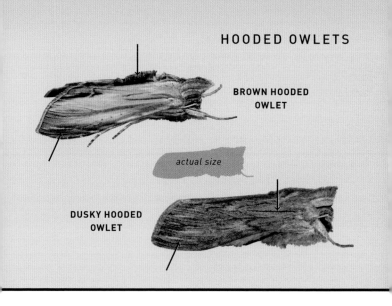

BROWN HOODED OWLET

actual size

DUSKY HOODED OWLET

AMPHIPYRINE SALLOWS

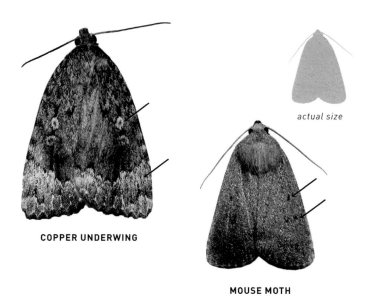

actual size

COPPER UNDERWING

MOUSE MOTH

SMOOTH AMPHIPYRA
Amphipyra glabella   93-1546 (9640)   **Common**
TL 18–22 mm. Grayish brown FW is sprinkled with pale brown hairlike scales. Outer margin is contrastingly paler beyond toothed ST line. **HOSTS:** Balsam poplar.

FIGURE-EIGHT SALLOW
Psaphida resumens   93-1548 (10019)   **Common**
TL 20–21 mm. Medium gray FW has mossy green accents along indistinct lines. Large white-edged claviform and orbicular spots are fused into figure-eight shape. Short black basal dash passes inside claviform spot. Black anal dash cuts through thick white ST band. **HOSTS:** Maple and oak.

THAXTER'S SALLOW
Psaphida thaxterianus   93-1549 (10020)   **Uncommon**
TL 17–20 mm. Resembles Figure-eight Sallow but has darker FW with a wide white band beyond ST line. No anal dash. Round orbicular spot is outlined black. White tegulae on thorax are well defined. **HOSTS:** Oak. **RANGE:** Sw. ON and ne. U.S.

ROLAND'S SALLOW
Psaphida rolandi   93-1550 (10014)   **Uncommon**
TL 17–21 mm. FW is variably gray to sooty black with indistinct lines. Conspicuous orbicular spot is whitish with gray center. **HOSTS:** Oak.

CHOSEN SALLOW
Psaphida electilis   93-1552 (10012)   **Uncommon**
TL 21–22 mm. Slate gray FW has black basal dash typically edged warm brown. Claviform spot is often solid black. Large orbicular and reniform spots are brown. Jagged white-edged ST line is edged brown. In southern part of range, FW is mostly gray with broad black streak extending from base to ST line. **HOSTS:** Hickory and walnut.

FAWN SALLOW
Psaphida styracis   93-1553 (10016)   **Uncommon**
TL 17–21 mm. Peppery fawn-colored FW has pale gray outer margin beyond curved PM line. Pale orbicular and reniform spots are incompletely outlined rusty brown. Hairy thorax is warm brown. **HOSTS:** Oak.

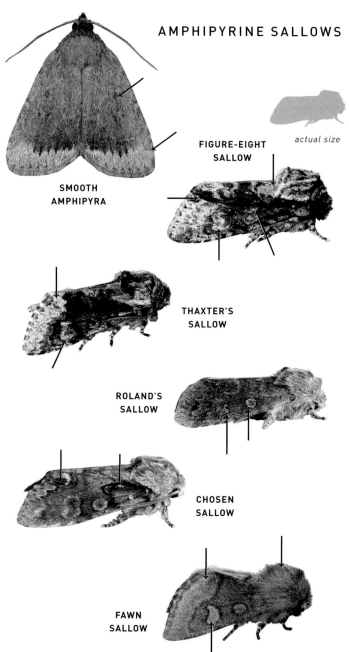

AMPHIPYRINE SALLOWS

actual size

SMOOTH AMPHIPYRA

FIGURE-EIGHT SALLOW

THAXTER'S SALLOW

ROLAND'S SALLOW

CHOSEN SALLOW

FAWN SALLOW

411

GROTE'S SALLOW
Copivaleria grotei 93-1557 (10021) **Common**
TL 21 mm. Gray FW is sprinkled with white scales. Indistinct black lines and outlines to spots are accented with mossy green scales. Large white reniform spot stands out from otherwise marbled pattern. **HOSTS:** Ash.

THE JOKER *Feralia jocosa* 93-1561 (10005) **Common**
TL 18–22 mm. Pale green FW (rarely tawny brown) has jagged lines that are double and filled with white. Green orbicular and reniform spots are outlined white. Terminal line and fringe are checkered black and white. **HOSTS:** Coniferous trees, including balsam fir, hemlock, spruce, and tamarack.

MAJOR SALLOW *Feralia major* 93-1563 (10007) **Common**
TL 20–22 mm. Variable. Pale to mint green FW is typically peppered with black scales in median area. Jagged lines are often indistinct. Inconspicuous orbicular and reniform spots are partly outlined white. **HOSTS:** Pine and spruce.

COMSTOCK'S SALLOW
Feralia comstocki 93-1564 (10008) **Common**
TL 18–21 mm. Green FW has white-edged reniform spot surrounded by three blocks of blackish shading. **HOSTS:** Hemlock, black spruce, and white pine.

BLACK-BARRED BROWN
Plagiomimicus pityochromus 93-1661 (9754) **Uncommon**
TL 14–18 mm. Peppery grayish brown FW has warmer brown shading in median area. Blackish claviform and orbicular spots are fused into hourglass-shaped bar. Pale gray PM line curves around dusky subapical patch. **HOSTS:** Giant ragweed.

GOLD MOTH *Basilodes pepita* 93-1676 (9781) **Common**
TL 18–24 mm. Metallic gold FW has strongly angled AM and PM lines finely etched in brown. Round orbicular and reniform spots are narrowly outlined brown. Reniform spot contains a tiny black dot near center. **HOSTS:** Crown-beard.

GOLDENROD STOWAWAY
Cirrhophanus triangulifer 93-1681 (9766) **Common**
TL 20–21 mm. Shiny pale yellow FW has orange streaks along veins. Sinuous PM line is double. **HOSTS:** Spanish needles. **NOTE:** Often found on yellow flowers (especially goldenrod) while at rest during daylight.

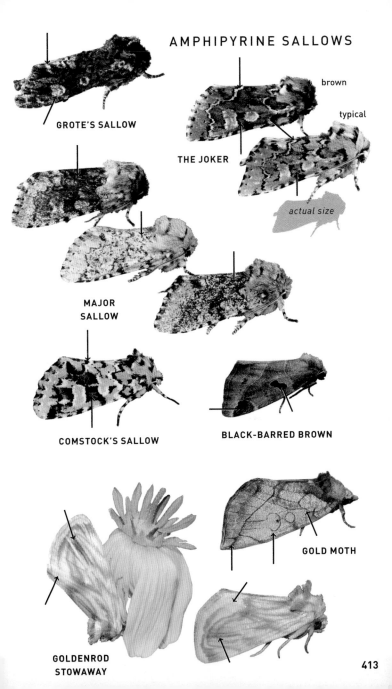

AMPHIPYRINE SALLOWS

GROTE'S SALLOW

brown

THE JOKER

typical

actual size

MAJOR SALLOW

COMSTOCK'S SALLOW

BLACK-BARRED BROWN

GOLD MOTH

GOLDENROD STOWAWAY

OBTUSE YELLOW

Azenia obtusa 93-1724 (9725) **Uncommon**

TL 12–14 mm. Yellow FW has variable pattern of dotted purplish brown lines. Wide, angled median band is typically broken into three patches. ST line is a row of dots ending in larger subapical patch. **HOSTS:** Unknown.

ONCOCNEMIDINE SALLOWS
Family Noctuidae, Subfamily Oncocnemidinae

These medium-sized, predominantly gray moths will often sit with their wings slightly folded at rest but may sometimes be found with them held flat. Toadflax Brocade is the only one to habitually fold its wings tight to the body. Fine-lined Sallow may superficially resemble the hooded owlets. The *Sympistis* is a large group, of which we include a select few; most are gray with distinct black markings. All of the oncocnemidine sallows are nocturnal and will visit lights in small numbers.

FINE-LINED SALLOW

Catabena lineolata 93-1765 (10033) **Common**

TL 14 mm. Ash gray FW has crisp black and white dashes and jagged lines, creating a finely striated effect. Thorax has a blunt, forward-pointing crest. **HOSTS:** Goldenrod and hoary vervain. **NOTE:** Two broods.

TOADFLAX BROCADE

Calophasia lunula 93-1771 (10177) **Uncommon**

TL 14–17 mm. Mottled grayish brown FW has darker patch in inner median area. Elliptical orbicular spot and bar-shaped reniform spots are white. ST area is marked with a row of black and white dashes. Hairy thorax is double-crested. **HOSTS:** Butter-and-eggs (toadflax). **NOTE:** Two broods. An introduced European species.

BROWN-LINED SALLOW

Sympistis badistriga 93-1821 (10059) **Uncommon**

TL 17–18 mm. Peppery gray FW has streaks of brown shading between veins. Narrow white-edged AM and PM lines are strongly curved. Thick black basal dash reaches inner PM line. Another dash extends from ST area to bulge in AM line. Thorax has thick black semi-collar. **HOSTS:** Honeysuckle.

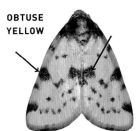

OBTUSE YELLOW

AMPHIPYRINE SALLOWS

actual size

ONCOCNEMIDINE SALLOWS

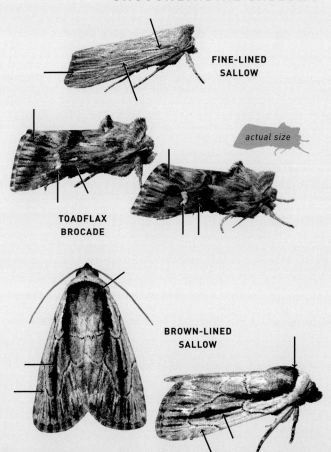

FINE-LINED SALLOW

actual size

TOADFLAX BROCADE

BROWN-LINED SALLOW

BROAD-LINED SALLOW

Sympistis dinalda   93-1823 (10066.1)   **Uncommon**
TL 17–19 mm. Ash gray FW has crisp black AM and PM lines that are gently sinuous. Bold black basal dash extends through median area, joining PM line. Another dash cuts through bulge of PM line, not reaching AM line. Thorax has broad white collar. **HOSTS:** Black walnut.

FRINGE-TREE SALLOW

Sympistis chionanthi   93-1906 (10067)   **Common**
TL 18–22 mm. Ash gray FW has angular lines crisply etched in black. Gray orbicular and reniform spots are outlined white. Dark subapical patch contains short black dashes. Thick black anal dash cuts through jagged white ST line. **HOSTS:** Black ash and fringe tree.

BLACK-BANDED BEAUTY

Sympistis piffardi   93-1909 (10123)   **Uncommon**
TL 16–19 mm. Ash gray FW has contrasting blackish median band. Blackish subapical patch blends into ST line. ST area is marked with a row of fine black dashes. HW is black with a large white basal patch. **HOSTS:** Meadowsweet. **RANGE:** S. Canada and ne. U.S.

WOOD-NYMPHS AND FORESTERS
Family Noctuidae, Subfamily Agaristinae

The nocturnal, woodland-dwelling wood-nymphs have long forelegs covered in downy tufts that are splayed outward at rest. They freely come to lights. Grapevine Epimenis is an early season day-flier often found at woodland edges where grapevines are abundant. The foresters are also day-flying moths, best sought in flowery meadows and open woodlands in midsummer.

PEARLY WOOD-NYMPH

Eudryas unio   93-1964 (9299)   **Common**
TL 21 mm. White FW has white-speckled crimson shading along costa and outer margin. Scalloped ST line is edged olive green. Reniform spot is clouded olive green. Thorax has a ridge of curly, glossy black scales. **HOSTS:** Evening primrose, grape, hibiscus, and Virginia creeper.

BEAUTIFUL WOOD-NYMPH

Eudryas grata   93-1966 (9301)   **Common**
TL 24 mm. Resembles Pearly Wood-Nymph, but ST area is darker red with brighter yellow-green edging, and ST line is evenly curved. **HOSTS:** *Ampelopsis,* grape, and Virginia creeper.

ONCOCNEMIDINE SALLOWS

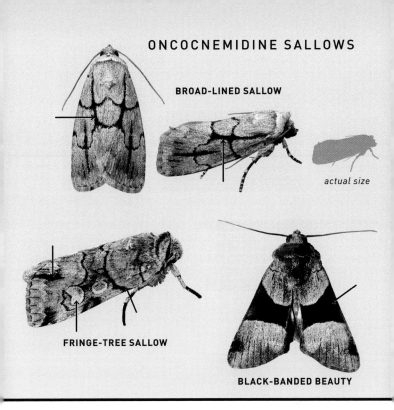

BROAD-LINED SALLOW

actual size

FRINGE-TREE SALLOW

BLACK-BANDED BEAUTY

WOOD-NYMPHS AND FORESTERS

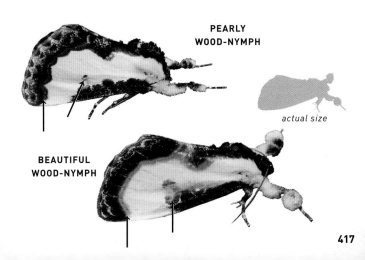

PEARLY WOOD-NYMPH

actual size

BEAUTIFUL WOOD-NYMPH

GRAPEVINE EPIMENIS
Psychomorpha epimenis   93-1975 (9309)   **Uncommon**
TL 12–14 mm. Velvety blackish FW has bold white crescent in outer median area. Evenly curved ST line is accented with metallic blue scales. Black HW has a broad vermillion band. **HOSTS:** Grape.

EIGHT-SPOTTED FORESTER
Alypia octomaculata   93-1979 (9314)   **Common**
TL 16–20 mm. Velvety black FW is accented with metallic blue scales. Two large cream-colored spots mark central median area. Black HW has two large white patches, the outer of which may be reduced in size. Black thorax has pale yellow tegulae. Legs are adorned with showy orange tufts. Antennae are black. **HOSTS:** *Ampelopsis,* grape, and Virginia creeper.

GROUNDLINGS
Family Noctuidae, Subfamily Condicinae

A group of mostly small to medium-sized deltoid noctuid moths that rest with their wings flat or slightly tented. Found in woodlands and larger gardens, they are nocturnal and will come to light in low numbers.

WHITE-DOTTED GROUNDLING
Condica videns   93-1989 (9690)   **Common**
TL 13–18 mm. Shiny tawny brown FW is peppered with white scales along darker veins. Costa is tinged reddish. A blackish streak cuts through inner half of fragmented white reniform spot. **HOSTS:** Aster and goldenrod.

MOBILE GROUNDLING
Condica mobilis   93-1992 (9693)   **Common**
TL 15–22 mm. FW is variably orange to reddish brown, lightly peppered with white scales along darker veins. Claviform and orbicular spots are indistinct. Reniform spot typically has a white dot in inner half. **HOSTS:** Beggar ticks.

DUSKY GROUNDLING
Condica vecors   93-1995 (9696)   **Common**
TL 16–18 mm. Mottled brown FW is peppered with white scales along veins. Club-shaped claviform spot is black. Reniform spot has conspicuous white dot in inner half. **HOSTS:** Reported on lettuce.

WOOD-NYMPHS AND FORESTERS

actual size

**GRAPEVINE
EPIMENIS**

**EIGHT-SPOTTED
FORESTER**

GROUNDLINGS

**WHITE-DOTTED
GROUNDLING**

**MOBILE
GROUNDLING**

**DUSKY
GROUNDLING**

actual size

419

THE COBBLER *Condica sutor* 93-1998 (9699)   **Uncommon**
TL 16–18 mm. Grayish tan FW is peppered with whitish scales along darker veins. All lines are blurry and indistinct. Orbicular and reniform spots are incompletely outlined white. ST area is marked with black and white dashes. **HOSTS:** Celery, marigold, and creeping-oxeye.

THE CONFEDERATE
Condica confederata 93-2015 (9714)   **Uncommon**
TL 18–22 mm. Mottled pale FW is marked with wide, irregular brown bands in basal and ST areas. Club-shaped claviform spot is black. Pale tan orbicular and reniform spots are outlined white. Female typically has brown FW with less extensive pale markings. **HOSTS:** Spanish needles.

COMMON PINKBAND
Ogdoconta cinereola 93-2018 (9720)   **Common**
TL 12–13 mm. Hoary brown FW has inner basal area and ST band shaded pink. All lines and outlines to spots are whitish and indistinct. **HOSTS:** Wild and cultivated plants, including artichoke, bean, and sunflower. **NOTE:** Three or more broods.

WATER-LILY MOTH
Homophoberia cristata 93-2024 (9056)   **Uncommon**
TL 14–17 mm. Brown or grayish brown FW is straw-colored beyond wavy PM line. Scalloped AM line is accented with straw-colored crescents. Small orbicular and reniform spots are partly outlined pale yellow. Male has bipectinate antennae. **HOSTS:** Yellow water lily. **NOTE:** Found mostly in wetlands.

BLACK WEDGE-SPOT
Homophoberia apicosa 93-2025 (9057)   **Uncommon**
TL 11–13 mm. Similar to larger Water-lily Moth, but dark gray FW has a pinkish band beyond wavy PM line. Claviform spot is a black backward-pointing wedge. Oblique reniform spot is broadly outlined pale yellow. Thorax has a white spot behind a slight crest. Often rests with tip of abdomen raised above wings. **HOSTS:** Lady's thumb. **NOTE:** Two broods. Found mostly around wetlands.

GREEN LEUCONYCTA
Leuconycta diphteroides 93-2026 (9065)   **Common**
TL 15–16 mm. Pale green FW is marked with scalloped white-edged lines. An incomplete black median band extends from costa to area between indistinct orbicular and reniform spots. Terminal line and fringe are checkered. **HOSTS:** Goldenrod and aster.

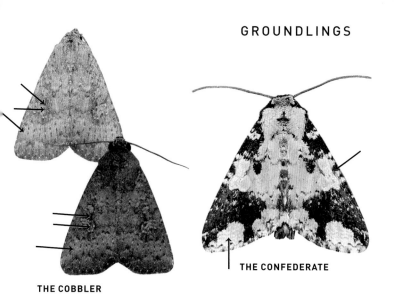

THE CONFEDERATE

THE COBBLER

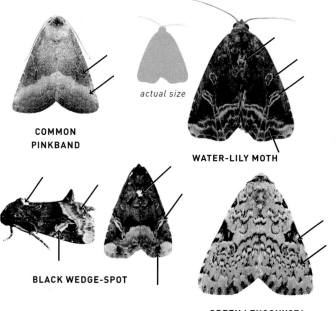

COMMON
PINKBAND

actual size

WATER-LILY MOTH

BLACK WEDGE-SPOT

GREEN LEUCONYCTA

MARBLED-GREEN LEUCONYCTA

Leuconycta lepidula   93-2027 (9066)   **Common**
TL 16 mm. Resembles Green Leuconycta, but broad gray median band is almost complete. Large pale green orbicular and reniform spots are incompletely outlined white. ST line is a row of black dashes along whitish veins. **HOSTS:** Reported on dandelion. **NOTE:** Two broods.

VERBENA MOTH

Crambodes talidiformis   93-2030 (9661)   **Common**
TL 16 mm. Narrow, straw-colored FW has streaky pattern of brown lines between veins. Costa and inner median area are blackish. Barlike reniform spot is white. Fringe is checkered black and white. **HOSTS:** Vervain. **NOTE:** Two broods.

Flower Moths
Family Noctuidae, Subfamily Heliothinae

Small to medium-sized, often beautifully patterned noctuids of woodlands, fields, and prairies. The HW color and pattern are important for identifying some species. Many species are regularly encountered during the daytime taking nectar from flowers. A few, such as Corn Earworm, are prone to irruptive northerly movements in late summer and fall. Although most are diurnal, many species are also nocturnal and are attracted to lights in small numbers.

BORDERED SALLOW

Pyrrhia cilisca   93-2040 (11063)   **Common**
TL 17–19 mm. Orange FW is peppered with rusty scales. Curved dark purple PM line has band of lilac shading between it and jagged ST line. HW is pale yellow with wide purplish terminal line. **HOSTS:** Deciduous trees and low plants, including alder, cabbage, rose, sumac, and walnut. **RANGE:** E. Canada and e. U.S. **NOTE:** Two broods.

PURPLE-LINED SALLOW

Pyrrhia exprimens   93-2041 (11064)   **Common**
TL 17–19 mm. Pinkish orange FW has darker veins. Sharply bent, dark purple median and PM lines are edged with bands of purplish brown shading. Reniform spot is partly filled with black. HW is pale yellow with purplish terminal line. **HOSTS:** Deciduous trees and low plants, including cherry, knotweed, rose, sweet fern, and willow.

GROUNDLINGS

**MARBLED-GREEN
LEUCONYCTA**

actual size

VERBENA MOTH

FLOWER MOTHS

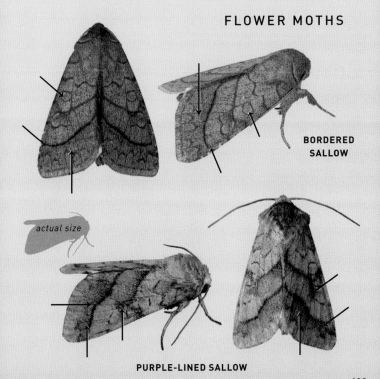

actual size

**BORDERED
SALLOW**

PURPLE-LINED SALLOW

CORN EARWORM

Helicoverpa zea   93-2045 (11068)   **Common**
TL 18–22 mm. FW is yellowish tan to dull orange with a darker band beyond toothed PM line. Reniform spot typically has dusky dot in inner half. HW is whitish with blackish veins and wide terminal line. **HOSTS:** Low plants and crops, including corn, cotton, tomato, and tobacco. **NOTE:** Several broods. A regular immigrant to the north in fall.

DARKER-SPOTTED STRAW MOTH

Heliocheilus phloxiphaga   93-2046 (11072)   **Common**
TL 17–19 mm. Yellowish brown FW has wide band of darker brown shading along strongly angled median line. ST line is obvious as a blackish wedge at costa. Reniform spot is black. HW is whitish with a black discal spot and broad black border. **HOSTS:** Low plants, including aster, delphinium, gladiolus, phlox, and strawberry.

TOBACCO BUDWORM

Heliothis virescens   93-2054 (11071)   **Common**
TL 15–19 mm. Yellowish green FW has darker, parallel lines that fade before reaching costa. AM and PM lines are broadly edged white. HW is white with a dark gray ST line. **HOSTS:** Tobacco, also ageratum, geranium, rose, and members of the nightshade family. **NOTE:** One or two broods.

PRIMROSE MOTH

Schinia florida   93-2082 (11164)   **Common**
TL 15–19 mm. Bright pink FW has contrasting pale yellow border beyond ST line. Some individuals show paler pink or yellow scales along lines and in basal area. **HOSTS:** Seed capsules of evening primrose. **NOTE:** Often found on evening primrose flowers during daytime.

RAGWEED FLOWER MOTH

Schinia rivulosa   93-2091 (11135)   **Common**
TL 14–16 mm. Peppery earth brown FW has paler grayish brown median area and terminal line. White AM line is strongly curved. PM line is gently wavy. **HOSTS:** Ragweed.

THREE-LINED FLOWER MOTH

Schinia trifascia   93-2096 (11149)   **Common**
TL 12–17 mm. Pale olive green FW has contrasting white lines. AM line curves strongly inward before reaching costa. HW is mostly white in male and white with an olive green ST band in female. **HOSTS:** False boneset and joe-pye weed.

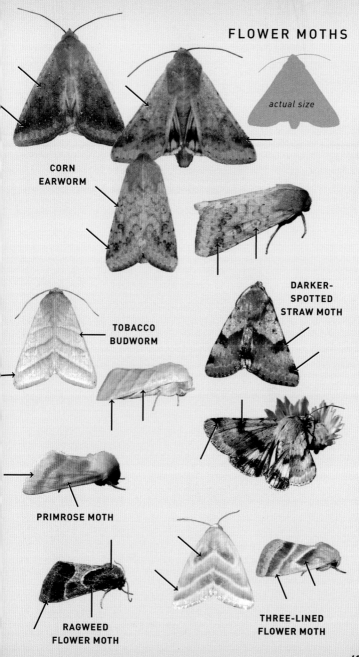

FLOWER MOTHS

actual size

CORN
EARWORM

DARKER-
SPOTTED
STRAW MOTH

TOBACCO
BUDWORM

PRIMROSE MOTH

RAGWEED
FLOWER MOTH

THREE-LINED
FLOWER MOTH

425

LYNX FLOWER MOTH

Schinia lynx 93-2120 (11117) **Common**
TL 10–12 mm. Pale brown FW has curved cream-colored AM and PM lines. Basal and ST areas are marked with wide bands of dark brown or reddish shading. HW is yellow with black discal spot and wide border. **HOSTS:** Fleabane.

ARCIGERA FLOWER MOTH

Schinia arcigera 93-2134 (11128) **Common**
TL 12–13 mm. Maroon brown FW has paler pinkish gray median area and terminal line. White AM line is evenly curved. HW is yellow with a black border and white fringe in male and black with a white fringe in female. **HOSTS:** Aster.

BLEEDING FLOWER MOTH

Schinia sanguinea 93-2145 (11173) **Uncommon**
TL 15–18 mm. Purplish pink FW often has a greenish-tinged median area. Fragmented AM and PM lines are reduced to white dashes along veins. Terminal line and fringe are checkered with whitish streaks along veins. HW is brown or whitish with a broad brown ST band. **HOSTS:** Blazing star. **NOTE:** Includes what was formerly known as Glorious Flower Moth, *S. gloriosa*.

GOLDENROD FLOWER MOTH

Schinia nundina 93-2156 (11177) **Common**
TL 13–15 mm. White FW has irregular bands of pale olive green shading. Orbicular spot is a tiny black dot. Hourglass-shaped reniform spot is thickly outlined in black. HW is white with a brown ST line. **HOSTS:** Aster and goldenrod.

FERN MOTHS Family Noctuidae, Subfamily Eriopinae

Small, complexly patterned noctuids that rest with their wings tightly folded. They have tufts of hairlike scales on the thorax and inner margin of the wing that stick up when at rest. These woodland moths are nocturnal and will regularly come to light.

FLORIDA FERN MOTH

Callopistria floridensis 93-2190 (9630) **Uncommon**
TL 15–16 mm. Brown FW has swirling pattern of ash gray bands and white-edged lines. Costa is marked with dark subapical and median patches. Slanting orbicular and reniform spots are partly outlined white. **HOSTS:** Ferns. **RANGE:** Se. U.S. **NOTE:** Occasionally reported as a greenhouse transplant north of its usual range.

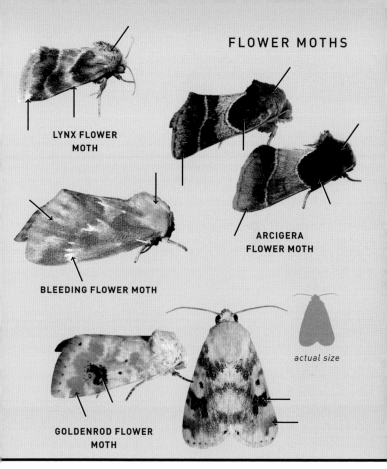

FLOWER MOTHS

LYNX FLOWER MOTH

ARCIGERA FLOWER MOTH

BLEEDING FLOWER MOTH

GOLDENROD FLOWER MOTH

actual size

FERN MOTHS

FLORIDA FERN MOTH

actual size

PINK-SHADED FERN MOTH
Callopistria mollissima   93-2192 (9631)   **Common**
TL 15 mm. Warm brown FW has bright pink bands along slightly jagged black AM and PM lines. Orbicular and reniform spots are partly outlined white. Legs have tufts of hairlike scales. **HOSTS:** New York fern.

SILVER-SPOTTED FERN MOTH
Callopistria cordata   93-2194 (9633)   **Common**
TL 15–16 mm. Pale yellowish tan FW is densely peppered with rusty scales. Large spots and crescents along AM and PM lines are silvery white. **HOSTS:** Ferns.

PHOSPHILAS AND ARMYWORMS
Family Noctuidae, Subfamily Noctuinae, Tribes Pseudeustrotiini, Phosphilini, and Prodeniini

A varied assortment of small- to medium-sized noctuid moths commonly found in woodlands, gardens and fields. The first four are delta-shaped and rest with their wings flat; the remaining three have long, narrow wings that they hold tight to the body. All are nocturnal and will come to light, though Pink-barred Pseudeustrotia may also be flushed from vegetation during the day. Small Mottled Willow and both armyworms are annual immigrants to the northern part of their range and are readily attracted to sugar bait.

PINK-BARRED PSEUDEUSTROTIA
Pseudeustrotia carneola   93-2205 (9053)   **Common**
TL 11–13 mm. Mottled brown FW has an oblique pale pink bar slanting from costa to inner edge of brown reniform spot. Irregular white ST line is broadly edged light brown. **HOSTS:** Dock, goldenrod, and smartweed. **NOTE:** Two broods.

GRAY MARVEL
Anterastria teratophora   93-2207 (9284)   **Uncommon**
TL 11–13 mm. Uniformly grayish brown FW is liberally peppered with whitish scales. Scalloped blackish lines are indistinct. Reniform spot is edged and partly filled with white. **HOSTS:** Mint and bee balm.

FERN MOTHS

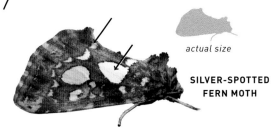

PINK-SHADED FERN MOTH

SILVER-SPOTTED FERN MOTH

actual size

PHOSPHILAS AND ARMYWORMS

PINK-BARRED PSEUDEUSTROTIA

actual size

GRAY MARVEL

TURBULENT PHOSPHILA
Phosphila turbulenta   93-2208 (9618)   **Uncommon**
TL 15–19 mm. Mottled brown FW has darker median area with a black bar in inner half. A thick black anal dash is conspicuous. Double AM and PM lines are filled with pale orange. Reniform spot is partly filled with pale yellow scales. **HOSTS:** Greenbrier. **NOTE:** Two broods.

SPOTTED PHOSPHILA
Phosphila miselioides   93-2209 (9619)   **Uncommon**
TL 18 mm. Grayish brown FW is densely sprinkled with mossy green scales when fresh. Jagged AM and PM lines converge toward inner margin. Large reniform spot is typically snowy white but can also be orange. **HOSTS:** Greenbrier. **NOTE:** Two broods.

SMALL MOTTLED WILLOW
Spodoptera exigua   93-2215 (9665)   **Uncommon**
TL 15–16 mm. FW is variably pale tan to grayish brown with indistinct jagged lines. Round orbicular spot is pale orange and outlined whitish. **HOSTS:** Crops, including apple, bean, beet, corn, and potato. **NOTE:** Also known as Beet Armyworm Moth; an irregular immigrant to ne. N. America.

FALL ARMYWORM
Spodoptera frugiperda   93-2216 (9666)   **Common**
TL 16–19 mm. Sexually dimorphic. FW of male is tan with gray and brown shading covering outer half of wing. An oblique, pale bar passes behind orange orbicular spot, ending abruptly level with inner edge of reniform spot. Apex is whitish. FW of female is uniformly grayish brown with indistinct lines and slanting orbicular spot. **HOSTS:** Grasses, crops, and other low plants. **NOTE:** Several broods in s. U.S.; appears in ne. N. America in variable numbers most years.

YELLOW-STRIPED ARMYWORM
Spodoptera ornithogalli   93-2219 (9669)   **Common**
TL 18–24 mm. Pale grayish brown FW has complex pattern of whitish veins extending across median area. Slanting straw-colored orbicular spot converges toward reniform spot. ST area is accented with black dashes. **HOSTS:** Various crops and low plants; sometimes a pest. **NOTE:** Several broods in s. U.S., but mostly an irregular fall immigrant in the northern part of range.

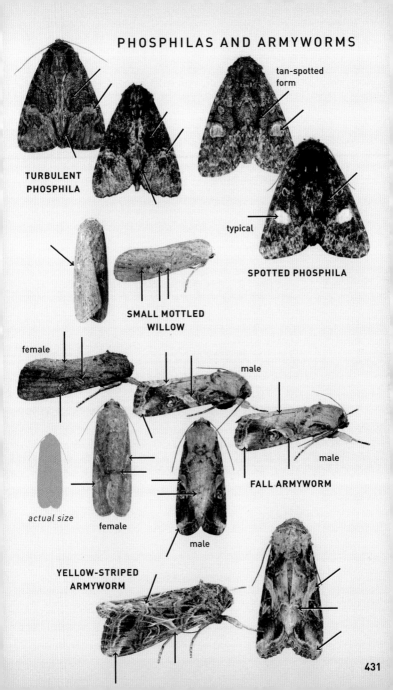

PHOSPHILAS AND ARMYWORMS

TURBULENT PHOSPHILA

tan-spotted form

typical

SPOTTED PHOSPHILA

SMALL MOTTLED WILLOW

female

actual size

female

male

male

male

FALL ARMYWORM

YELLOW-STRIPED ARMYWORM

MIDGETS
Family Noctuidae, Subfamily Noctuinae, Tribe Elaphriini

Small, highly patterned brown moths with short rounded wings. They are locally common in woodlands and larger gardens. All are nocturnal and will come to light in small to moderate numbers.

VARIEGATED MIDGET
Elaphria versicolor   93-2228 (9678)   **Common**
TL 14 mm. Brownish FW has kinked white PM line that widens toward costa. Indistinct orbicular and reniform spots are separated by a black patch. Gray ST area is marked with a pale orange apical patch. **HOSTS:** Fir, pine, and spruce.

CHALCEDONY MIDGET
Elaphria chalcedonia   93-2230 (9679)   **Common**
TL 14 mm. Resembles Variegated Midget, but FW has inner margin shaded dark grayish brown. PM line is edged with a band of diffused white shading. A black dash passes either side of reniform spot. **HOSTS:** Plants in the snapdragon family, including beardtongue, figwort, and monkey flower.

GEORGE'S MIDGET
Elaphria georgei   93-2232 (9680)   **Uncommon**
TL 12 mm. Pale gray FW has wide blackish median band. Basal and ST areas are clouded with pink shading. AM and PM lines are edged white at inner margin. Brownish reniform spot is edged black along rear edge. **HOSTS:** Unknown. **RANGE:** Se. Canada and e. U.S.

PALE-WINGED MIDGET
Elaphria alapalida   93-2234 (9681.1)   **Common**
TL 14 mm. Light brown FW has contrasting warm brown patches at inner margin and in ST area. Small hollow claviform spot is outlined black. Curved white reniform spot has black patches on either side. Apical patch is pale orange. **HOSTS:** Manitoba maple.

GRATEFUL MIDGET
Elaphria grata   93-2238 (9684)   **Common**
TL 13 mm. Reddish brown FW is peppered with white scales along black veins. Slightly curved AM and PM lines are white. Orbicular spot is a small black dot. Hourglass-shaped reniform spot contains two black dots. **HOSTS:** Violet, also clover, oak, and dead leaves. **NOTE:** Two or more broods.

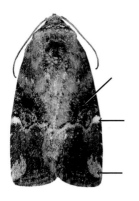

VARIEGATED MIDGET

CHALCEDONY MIDGET

actual size

GEORGE'S MIDGET

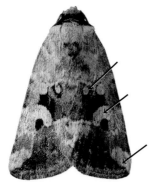

PALE-WINGED MIDGET

GRATEFUL MIDGET

THE WEDGLING *Galgula partita* 93-2249 (9688)   **Common**
TL 11–13 mm. Sexually dimorphic. FW of male is shiny yellowish tan, narrowly bordered with rusty scales. Oblique, gently curved PM line is edged yellow. Midpoint of costa is marked with a blackish blotch. FW of female is shiny dark maroon or gray with some white in inner PM line. **HOSTS:** Wood sorrel. **NOTE:** Several broods.

ASSORTED NOCTUIDS
Family Noctuidae, Subfamily Noctuinae, Tribes Caradrinini, Dypterygiini, and Actinotiini

A varied group of small to medium-sized noctuid moths, some well patterned. Found mostly in woodlands, fields, and gardens, they will come to light in small numbers. Variable Narrow-Wing is an uncommon immigrant to ne. N. America.

CIVIL RUSTIC *Caradrina montana* 93-2260 (9656) **Uncommon**
TL 16–19 mm. Sandy-colored FW has fragmented AM and PM lines. Orbicular spot is a small brown dot. Warm brown reniform spot is partly outlined white with a black dot in inner half. Chestnut-edged ST line is bordered with dusky band. **HOSTS:** Unknown. **RANGE:** W. Canada and w. U.S., also locally in sw. ON and ne. U.S. **NOTE:** Two broods.

SPECKLED RUSTIC
Caradrina multifera 93-2261 (9657)   **Common**
TL 18 mm. Peppery ash gray FW is marked with incomplete, jagged AM and PM lines. Orbicular spot is a small reddish brown dot. Brown reniform spot has a black dot in inner half and is partly outlined with white dots. Whitish ST line is accented with brown wedges. **HOSTS:** Unknown.

MIRANDA MOTH *Proxenus miranda* 93-2266 (9647) **Common**
TL 13–15 mm. Shiny grayish brown FW is marked with indistinct curved AM and PM lines. A small white dot in reniform spot is the only obvious marking. HW is whitish. **HOSTS:** Alfalfa and dandelion. **NOTE:** Two broods.

THE SLOWPOKE *Athetis tarda* 93-2269 (9650)   **Common**
TL 14–15 mm. Grayish brown FW often has a violet gray band beyond PM line. Blackish AM and PM lines are slightly scalloped. Broader, more diffuse median band is sometimes present. Orbicular spot is a tiny black dot. Reniform spot is partly outlined pale yellow. Black ST line is edged yellow. **HOSTS:** Oak. **NOTE:** Two broods.

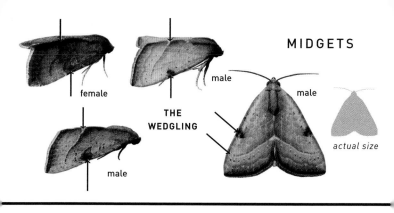

MIDGETS

female

male

male

THE WEDGLING

male

actual size

ASSORTED NOCTUIDS

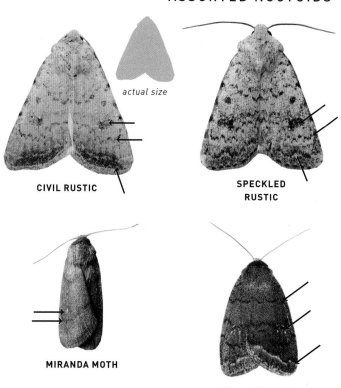

actual size

CIVIL RUSTIC

SPECKLED RUSTIC

MIRANDA MOTH

THE SLOWPOKE

AMERICAN BIRD'S-WING

Dypterygia rozmani   93-2272 (9560)   **Common**
TL 20 mm. Smooth slate gray FW is marked with crisp, wildly
curvaceous black lines. A streaky patch of brown and white
shading at anal angle resembles a bird's wing. Pale streak
along inner margin merges with raised dorsal crest on thorax.
HOSTS: Dock and smartweed.

DELICATE MOTH

Trachea delicata   93-2280 (9626)   **Uncommon**
TL 18–20 mm. Uniformly gray FW is marked with bold black
claviform spot. Lines and outlines to spots are accented with
bright mossy green scales when fresh. **HOSTS:** Unknown, but
often found in sandy soil habitats. **RANGE:** S. Canada and n. U.S.

VARIABLE NARROW-WING

Magusa divaricata   93-2282 (9637.1)   **Uncommon**
TL 18–22 mm. FW is typically chocolate brown with paler gray
shading along inner margin. Some individuals have a thin white
basal dash. Orbicular and reniform spots are typically narrowly
outlined whitish. A whitish or orange orblike apical patch is
usually present. **HOSTS:** Black ironweed and coyotillo. **NOTE:** A
scarce, though regular, immigrant from Cen. America.

GRAY HALF-SPOT

Nedra ramosula   93-2283 (9582)   **Common**
TL 15–25 mm. Light gray FW has streaky pattern of black and
brown lines. A large patch of blackish shading surrounds inner
half of open-sided brown and white reniform spot. Slanting
black apical dash is edged white. **HOSTS:** Saint John's wort.
NOTE: Two broods.

WHITE-EYED BORER

Iodopepla u-album 93-2287 (9522)   **Uncommon**
TL 18 mm. Lilac gray FW has contrasting black and chestnut
median patch. White-edged reniform spot is an inverted U-
shape. Whitish ST line is edged chestnut. **HOSTS:** Unknown, but
usually restricted to dune habitats close to wetlands.

ASSORTED NOCTUIDS

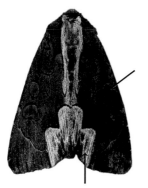

AMERICAN BIRD'S-WING

DELICATE MOTH

actual size

VARIABLE NARROW-WING

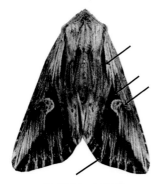

GRAY HALF-SPOT

WHITE-EYED BORER

437

ANGLE SHADES
Family Noctuidae, Subfamily Noctuinae, Tribe Phlogophorini

Medium-sized noctuid moths that are commonly found in woodlands and larger gardens. They roll the outer half of the FW while at rest. All are boldly patterned with dark chevrons in the median area. They regularly come to light in small numbers.

AMERICAN ANGLE SHADES
Euplexia benesimilis   93-2290 (9545)   **Common**
TL 17 mm. Mottled dusky brown FW has pinkish band beyond PM line. Blackish AM and PM lines converge toward inner margin. Large reniform spot is partly filled with and outlined whitish. **HOSTS:** Deciduous trees, ferns, and low plants, including aster, huckleberry, and willow. **NOTE:** Two broods.

OLIVE ANGLE SHADES
Phlogophora iris   93-2291 (9546)   **Common**
TL 25 mm. Straw-colored FW has mossy green shading in inner basal and median areas. Pale lines are edged with lilac and rust. Angled AM and PM lines touch at inner margin. Lilac orbicular and reniform spots fuse together to form an inverted V-shape. **HOSTS:** Low plants, including dandelion, dock, and thistle. **NOTE:** Two broods.

BROWN ANGLE SHADES
Phlogophora periculosa   93-2292 (9547)   **Common**
TL 27 mm. Dimorphic. Resembles Olive Angle Shades, but pinkish FW has sharply demarcated dark or medium brown median area. AM line is straight. Reniform spot is partly filled with dark brown. Outer margin of FW is scalloped. **HOSTS:** Trees and low plants, including alder, balsam fir, cranberry, and plum.

SHARP ANGLE SHADES
Conservula anodonta   93-2293 (9548)   **Uncommon**
TL 17 mm. Resembles Brown Angle Shades, but chocolate brown median patch is wider at costa. Outer margin of FW is not scalloped. Pointed thoracic crest is tipped brown. **HOSTS:** Unknown, but often found in coniferous and mixed woodlands.

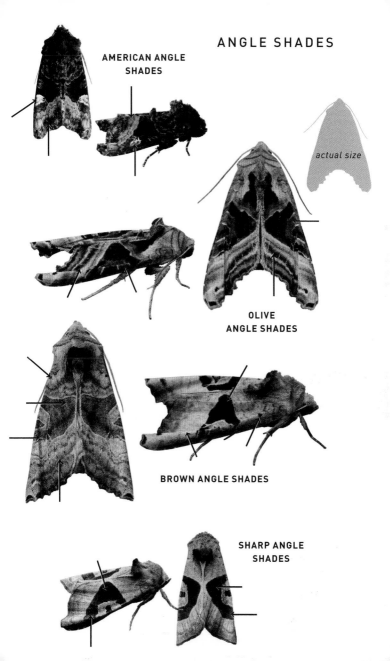

ANGLE SHADES

AMERICAN ANGLE SHADES

actual size

OLIVE ANGLE SHADES

BROWN ANGLE SHADES

SHARP ANGLE SHADES

439

APAMEAS, BROCADES, AND BORERS
Family Noctuidae, Subfamily Noctuinae,
Tribes Apameini and Arzamini

A large and varied group of noctuid moths mostly found in woodlands and old fields. Many are highly host specific. The apameas are medium-sized and rest with wings flat. Some are plainly attired with woodgrain patterns. The brocades are typically smaller, often with a darker median area and well-defined reniform and orbicular spots. The late season borers are bright, medium-sized moths; most are yellow-orange or bronzy with fractured white spots and can be difficult to separate. All of these species will come to light in small or moderate numbers.

MULLEIN APAMEA
Apamea verbascoides 93-2294 (9326) **Common**
TL 22 mm. Light brown FW has pale streak along costa. Bold black dashes pass through basal and inner median areas, ending at white inner PM line. **HOSTS:** Unknown; probably grasses.

BLACK-DASHED APAMEA
Apamea nigrior 93-2296 (9328) **Common**
TL 22 mm. Grayish brown FW has straw-colored veins and shading along costa. Two thin black dashes pass through basal area. Thick black bar in inner median area ends at white inner PM line. Slanting orbicular and reniform spots are outlined in white. **HOSTS:** Unknown; probably grasses.

RICE WORM MOTH
Apamea apamiformis 93-2302 (9343) **Uncommon**
TL 22 mm. Peppery grayish tan FW has indistinct lines and a thin black basal dash. Grayish reniform spot is partly outlined white. Short black dash near anal angle is interrupted by pale ST line. **HOSTS:** Wild rice. **RANGE:** Se. Canada and ne. U.S. **NOTE:** Occurs near wetlands.

AIRY APAMEA *Apamea vultuosa* 93-2303 (9341) **Common**
TL 22 mm. Yellowish FW has rusty brown shading along costa. Reniform spot has a black dot in inner half. ST area has blackish wedge at midpoint and blackish dash at anal angle. **HOSTS:** Grasses.

DUSKY APAMEA
Apamea plutonia 93-2304 (9344) **Uncommon**
TL 20 mm. Peppery sooty gray FW is tinted warm brown in basal and median areas. Jagged lines are interrupted by black veins. Slanting orbicular and reniform spots are partly outlined whitish. **HOSTS:** Grasses. **RANGE:** W. U.S. and Great Lakes region.

APAMEAS, BROCADES, AND BORERS

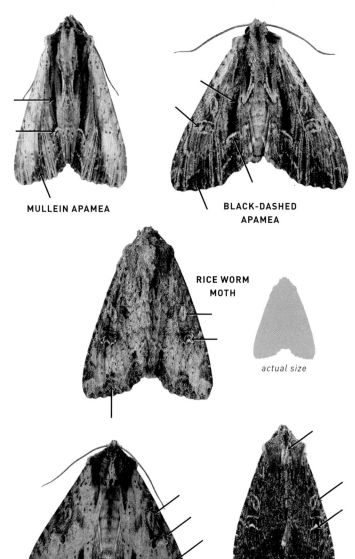

MULLEIN APAMEA

BLACK-DASHED APAMEA

RICE WORM MOTH

actual size

AIRY APAMEA

DUSKY APAMEA

FOX APAMEA *Apamea alia* 93-2307 (9351) **Common**
TL 18–20 mm. Pale grayish tan FW is mottled with rusty brown shading along costa. Reniform spot has a black dot in inner half. Inconspicuous ST line is accented with black dots at mid-point and inner section. **HOSTS:** Grasses. **RANGE:** W. U.S. and Great Lakes region.

SMALL CLOUDED BRINDLE
Apamea unanimis 93-2308 (9362.2) **Uncommon**
TL 19–21 mm. Mottled yellowish brown FW has indistinct pale-edged lines. Outward-curving reniform spot is partly outlined white. **HOSTS:** Grasses. **RANGE:** Se. Canada and ne. U.S. **NOTE:** This European species was first noted near Ottawa in 1991 and is now locally common in parts of ne. N. America.

IGNORANT APAMEA
Apamea indocilis 93-2310 (9362) **Common**
TL 18 mm. Pale gray and brown FW is marked with conspicuous thick black basal and median bars. Large white orbicular and reniform spots are partly outlined black. Two black wedges edge white ST line. **HOSTS:** Grasses and sedges.

IMPULSIVE APAMEA
Apamea impulsa 93-2311 (9360) **Common**
TL 19 mm. Bluish slate FW is marked with crisply etched black lines. Large orbicular and reniform spots are sprinkled with a few pale scales. ST line is a row of short black dashes. **HOSTS:** Grasses. **RANGE:** S. Canada and n. U.S.

RUSTIC SHOULDER-KNOT
Apamea sordens 93-2314 (9364) **Common**
TL 20–22 mm. Pale gray FW has chestnut median area and ac-cents along whitish ST line. Black basal dash is conspicuous. Large gray orbicular spot is outlined black. Reniform spot has black dot in inner half. **HOSTS:** Grasses.

WOOD-COLORED APAMEA

Apamea lignicolora 93-2319 (9333) **Common**
TL 24–26 mm. Yellowish brown FW has slanting pale orange or-bicular spot. Reniform spot has black dot in inner half. Basal area has two black dashes. Outer margin is marked with two blackish triangular patches. **HOSTS:** Quack grass and other grasses.

APAMEAS, BROCADES, AND BORERS

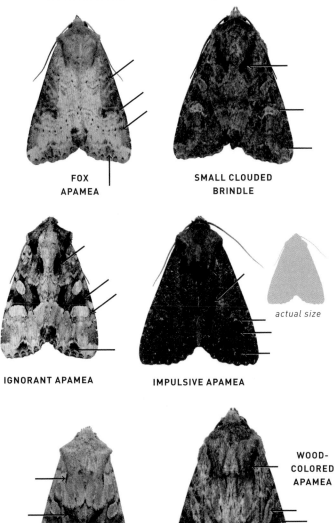

FOX
APAMEA

SMALL CLOUDED
BRINDLE

IGNORANT APAMEA

IMPULSIVE APAMEA

actual size

RUSTIC
SHOULDER-KNOT

WOOD-
COLORED
APAMEA

443

YELLOW THREE-SPOT

Apamea helva   93-2322 (9373)   **Common**
TL 19–24 mm. Orange FW has fragmented scalloped lines
edged with brown bands. Reniform spot has a black dot in inner
half. Brown subapical patch is separated from brown ST line.
HOSTS: Grasses.

YELLOW-HEADED CUTWORM

Apamea amputatrix   93-2333 (9348)   **Common**
TL 26–27 mm. Gray FW has fragmented rusty brown band in
median area and along pale ST line. Ovate orbicular and reniform spots are incompletely outlined white. Darker individuals
are slate gray and rust with orange accents. **HOSTS:** Fruit-bearing trees, grasses, and crops, including cabbage, corn, and lettuce.

RED-WINGED APAMEA

Apamea scoparia   93-2343 (9365)   **Uncommon**
TL 22–24 mm. Reddish brown FW is speckled with white scales
along faint black veins. Inconspicuous orbicular and especially
reniform spots are incompletely outlined whitish. Reniform
spot has a blackish dot in inner half. **HOSTS:** Presumably
grasses.

DOUBTFUL APAMEA

Apamea dubitans   93-2344 (9367)   **Common**
TL 22–23 mm. Dark sooty brown FW is liberally peppered with
whitish scales along veins. Indistinct lines are edged brown.
Curved reniform spot is partly outlined and filled with creamy
white. **HOSTS:** Grasses.

GLASSY CUTWORM

Apamea devastator   93-2350 (9382)   **Common**
TL 22–26 mm. Peppery gray FW has doubled lines filled with
pale gray. Orbicular and reniform spots are incompletely outlined white. A row of black wedges inside ST line can be obvious
when fresh. **HOSTS:** Grasses and crops; sometimes a serious
pest.

SNOWY-VEINED APAMEA

Apamea niveivenosa   93-2355 (9374)   **Uncommon**
TL 19 mm. Pale grayish tan FW has bold white veins and black
dashes in basal and inner median areas. ST line is a row of
black dashes. Narrow, slanting orbicular spot has a black
wedge in front of it. **HOSTS:** Bluegrass. **RANGE:** S. Canada and
ne. U.S.

APAMEAS, BROCADES, AND BORERS

YELLOW THREE-SPOT

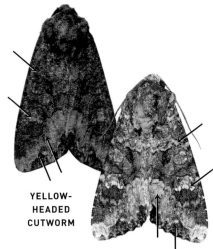

YELLOW-HEADED CUTWORM

DOUBTFUL APAMEA

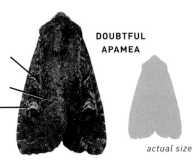

RED-WINGED APAMEA

actual size

GLASSY CUTWORM

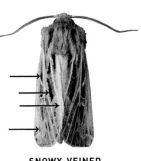

SNOWY-VEINED APAMEA

445

VEILED EAR MOTH
Loscopia velata   93-2358 (9454)   **Common**
TL 18–19 mm. Grayish brown FW has darker brown shading in median area and white peppering along veins. Orbicular and reniform spots are crisply outlined white. Hourglass-shaped reniform spot has a black dot in inner half. **HOSTS:** Grasses. **NOTE:** Two broods.

DOUBLE LOBED
Lateroligia ophiogramma   93-2363 (9385.1)   **Uncommon**
TL 18 mm. FW is variably straw-colored to dark gray with broad chestnut and black patch in outer median area. Black reniform spot has a pale orange dot in center. ST line is a row of orange dots. **HOSTS:** Grasses. **NOTE:** An introduced European species.

DOCK RUSTIC
Resapamea passer   93-2368 (9391)   **Uncommon**
TL 21 mm. FW is variably mousy gray to brown with a club-shaped black claviform spot. PM line is a fragmented row of black crescents. Round orbicular spot is partly outlined black. Reniform spot has yellowish outer edge. **HOSTS:** Dock.

BROKEN-LINED BROCADE
Mesapamea fractilinea   93-2370 (9406)   **Common**
TL 12–16 mm. FW is variably pale tan to dark brown, peppered with black and white scales along veins. Median area is usually darker brown. Reniform spot is filled with and partly edged whitish. **HOSTS:** Corn and grasses.

DARK-WINGED QUAKER
Eremobina claudens   93-2372 (9396)   **Uncommon**
TL 16–18 mm. Pale gray FW has white-edged AM and PM lines. Thin black basal dash and thicker black bar in inner median area are conspicuous. White orbicular and reniform spots are separated by black patch. **HOSTS:** Unknown. **RANGE:** S. Canada and w. and n. U.S.

YELLOW-SPOTTED BROCADE
Oligia chlorostigma   93-2377 (9402)   **Uncommon**
TL 15 mm. Grayish brown FW is peppered with yellow and brown scales. AM line forms a whitish spot at inner margin. Indistinct orbicular and reniform spots are tinted yellowish green. **HOSTS:** Possibly sedges. **RANGE:** Se. Canada and ne. U.S.

APAMEAS, BROCADES, AND BORERS

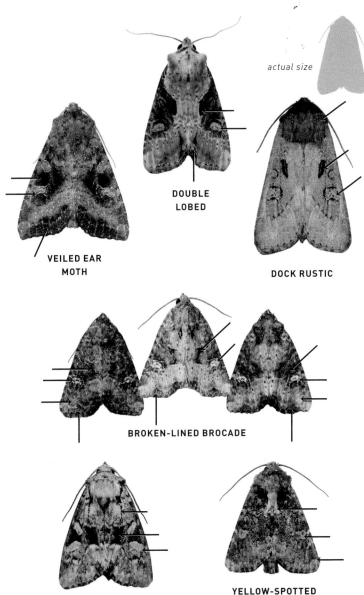

actual size

DOUBLE LOBED

VEILED EAR MOTH

DOCK RUSTIC

BROKEN-LINED BROCADE

DARK-WINGED QUAKER

YELLOW-SPOTTED BROCADE

BLACK-BANDED BROCADE
Oligia modica   93-2378 (9404)   **Common**
TL 17 mm. FW is variably pale tan to bluish gray, with dusky brown median band. Large orbicular and reniform spots are whitish. Lumpy thorax has protruding shoulders reminiscent of some pinions. **HOSTS:** Unknown.

BRIDGHAM'S BROCADE
Oligia bridghamii   93-2382 (9415)   **Uncommon**
TL 17 mm. Rusty brown FW has contrasting pale gray ST band. Indistinct AM and PM lines are edged whitish. Gray orbicular and reniform spots are outlined white. **HOSTS:** Unknown.

SMALL BROCADE
Oligia minuscula   93-2384 (9416)   **Uncommon**
TL 14–16 mm. Violet brown FW is warmer brown in basal and median areas. AM and PM lines are usually connected by black bar in inner median area. Pale-outlined orbicular and reniform spots are sometimes separated by blackish patch. **HOSTS:** Unknown.

OBTUSE BROCADE   *Oligia obtusa* 93-2385 (9418)   **Uncommon**
TL 17 mm. Gray FW has contrasting triangular brown median patch. White-edged AM and PM lines converge toward inner margin. Inner margin has black-edged white streak near base. **HOSTS:** Unknown. **RANGE:** Se. Canada and ne. U.S.

EXHAUSTED BROCADE
Neoligia exhausta   93-2390 (9408)   **Common**
TL 17 mm. Peppery gray FW has darker brown median area. Black bar from AM to terminal lines interrupted by white PM line. Pale reniform spot is partly filled with yellowish brown scales. **HOSTS:** Unknown.

CONNECTED BROCADE
Neoligia subjuncta   93-2392 (9412)   **Uncommon**
TL 13 mm. Dark brown FW has contrasting cream-colored reniform spot and ST band. Inner half of PM line is edged white. Reddish brown shading in outer half of median area projects backward to a point inside reniform spot. **HOSTS:** Unknown.

MULTICOLORED SEDGEMINER
Meropleon diversicolor   93-2413 (9427)   **Uncommon**
TL 16–18 mm. Whitish FW has fragmented darker brown median band and brown, rounded basal area. Slanting orbicular spot is white. **HOSTS:** Sedges.

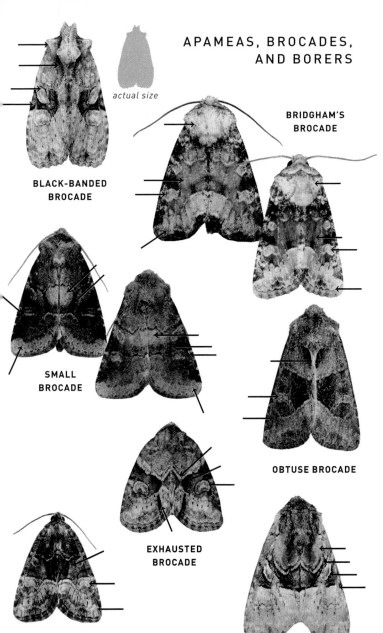

APAMEAS, BROCADES, AND BORERS

actual size

BLACK-BANDED BROCADE

BRIDGHAM'S BROCADE

SMALL BROCADE

OBTUSE BROCADE

EXHAUSTED BROCADE

CONNECTED BROCADE

MULTICOLORED SEDGEMINER

449

NEWMAN'S BROCADE

Meropleon ambifusca   93-2414 (9428)   **Uncommon**
TL 13 mm. Resembles Multicolored Sedgeminer, but FW is grayer with brown shading in basal and ST areas. Thick black dashes mark basal and median areas. Orbicular and reniform spots are separated by black patch. **HOSTS:** Unknown, perhaps sedges.

FINGERED LEMMERIA

Lemmeria digitalis   93-2415 (9429)   **Uncommon**
TL 14 mm. Grayish fawn FW has contrasting rusty brown median band. White AM and PM lines converge toward inner margin. Orange-outlined reniform spot has a dusky dot in inner half. Thorax has a pointed crest. **HOSTS:** Unknown. **RANGE:** Se. Canada and ne. U.S.

REED CANARY GRASS BORER

Xylomoia chagnoni   93-2416 (9433)   **Uncommon**
TL 16 mm. Shiny grayish tan FW is flushed pink when fresh. A crisp black median bar connects indistinct AM and PM lines. Two dusky wedges accent ST line. **HOSTS:** Reed canary grass, usually in damp areas. **RANGE:** Se. Canada and ne. U.S.

INCLUDED CORDGRASS BORER

Photedes includens   93-2421 (9434)   **Uncommon**
TL 12–13 mm. Orange-brown FW has darker brown median area and broad pinkish ST band. Curved reniform spot is white with black outline. **HOSTS:** Coarse grasses and sedges, often near wetlands.

NARROW-WINGED BORER

Photedes defecta   93-2425 (9443)   **Uncommon**
TL 13 mm. Yellowish FW has streaks of warm brown shading between paler veins. Double AM and PM lines are fragmented into rows of dashes. Brown-edged white streak through central median area ends at tiny white reniform spot. **HOSTS:** Unknown, but probably wetland plants. **RANGE:** S. Canada and w. and n. U.S.

SORDID WAINSCOT

Hypocoena inquinata   93-2426 (9437)   **Uncommon**
TL 12–15 mm. Straw-colored FW is peppered with pinkish scales between whitish veins. Black streaks are typically present between veins in basal and median areas. Black terminal line a series of dashes. **HOSTS:** Sedges, often in wetlands. **RANGE:** S. Canada and n. U.S.

APAMEAS, BROCADES, AND BORERS

NEWMAN'S BROCADE

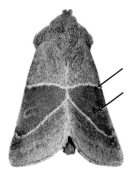

FINGERED LEMMERIA

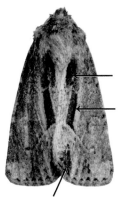

REED CANARY GRASS BORER

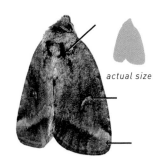

actual size

INCLUDED CORDGRASS BORER

NARROW-WINGED BORER

SORDID WAINSCOT

LARGE WAINSCOT

Rhizedra lutosa 93-2437 (9447.2) **Uncommon**
TL 20–25 mm. Straw-colored FW has faint grayish brown streaks extending along whitish veins. PM line is a row of widely spaced black dots. **HOSTS:** Common reed. **RANGE:** Se. Canada and ne. U.S. **NOTE:** Introduced from Europe.

OBLONG SEDGE BORER

Capsula oblonga 93-2438 (9449) **Uncommon**
TL 25 mm. Peppery pale tan FW is marked with lengthwise streaks of pinkish brown shading. Toothed PM line and terminal line appear as rows of tiny black dots. **HOSTS:** Cattails and bulrushes

SUBFLAVA SEDGE BORER

Capsula subflava 93-2439 (9450) **Uncommon**
TL 19 mm. Pale orange FW has darker veins that are peppered with white scales. Reddish streaks pass through median and ST areas. PM line appears as a row of black dots along veins. **HOSTS:** Bulrushes, cattails, grasses, and rushes.

IRIS BORER

Macronoctua onusta 93-2442 (9452) **Common**
TL 25–27 mm. Pale tan FW has toothed AM and PM lines finely etched in black. Broad slate gray streak along costal edge extends to orbicular and reniform spots. **HOSTS:** Larvae bore into roots of iris.

RENIFORM HELOTROPHA

Helotropha reniformis 93-2443 (9453) **Common**
TL 20–24 mm. Grayish brown FW is peppered with white scales along veins. Curved AM and PM lines are double and filled with pale brown. Curved reniform spot is partially filled with and outlined white, sometimes fused to whitish veins surrounding it. **HOSTS:** Sedges. **RANGE:** S. Canada and w. and n. U.S.

ELDER SHOOT BORER

Achatodes zeae 93-2444 (9520) **Common**
TL 13 mm. Crimson FW is marked with slate gray bands and inconspicuous dotted black lines. ST line is a row of orange dashes, most obvious at apex. Thorax has fiery orange dorsal stripe. **HOSTS:** Elderberry, corn, dahlia, and grasses.

APAMEAS, BROCADES, AND BORERS

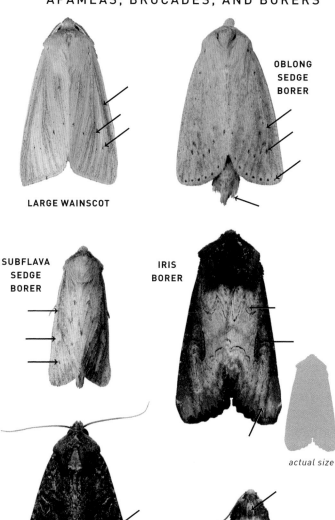

LARGE WAINSCOT

OBLONG SEDGE BORER

SUBFLAVA SEDGE BORER

IRIS BORER

actual size

RENIFORM HELOTROPHA

ELDER SHOOT BORER

AMERICAN EAR MOTH
Amphipoea americana 93-2447 (9457) **Common**
TL 14–20 mm. Rusty orange FW has prominent orange or white reniform spot. Fine AM and PM lines are broadly double and crossed by dark veins, creating a netlike pattern. **HOSTS:** Grasses and sedges, sometimes corn.

ROSY RUSTIC
Hydraecia micacea 93-2458 (9514) **Common**
TL 24 mm. Pinkish brown FW has a rosy flush when fresh. Median area is shaded brown inside straight PM line. Large orbicular and reniform spots are outlined brown. **HOSTS:** Low plants, including burdock, corn, dock, potato, and tomato. **NOTE:** An introduced European species.

MEADOW RUE BORER
Papaipema unimoda 93-2465 (9509) **Uncommon**
TL 18–22 mm. Dark bronzy FW has lilac gray AM and ST areas. Basal area is cream colored with a small white dot. White claviform and orbicular spots are often hollow or C-shaped. Cream-colored reniform spot is thickly outlined with white mosaic-like fragments. **HOSTS:** Meadow rue, coneflower, carrion flower, and Jacob's ladder.

GOLDEN BORER
Papaipema cerina 93-2466 (9464) **Uncommon**
TL 18–25 mm. Pale yellow FW has scalloped chocolate brown lines and a band of brown shading beyond toothed PM line. Apical spot is pale yellow. Gray claviform, orbicular, and reniform spots are outlined brown. **HOSTS:** Lilies and May apple. **RANGE:** Great Lakes region.

ASH-TIP BORER
Papaipema furcata 93-2468 (9495) **Uncommon**
TL 21–26 mm. Pale orange FW has small white spot in basal area. Large white claviform and orbicular spots are separated by smaller dot. Yellow reniform spot is thickly outlined with white mosaic-like fragments. **HOSTS:** Ash and box elder.

IRONWEED BORER
Papaipema cerussata 93-2470 (9505) **Uncommon**
TL 20–22 mm. Bronzy FW has violet gray AM and ST areas. Inner median area is reddish brown. White-edged reniform spot is relatively small and narrow. **HOSTS:** Ironweed.

APAMEAS, BROCADES, AND BORERS

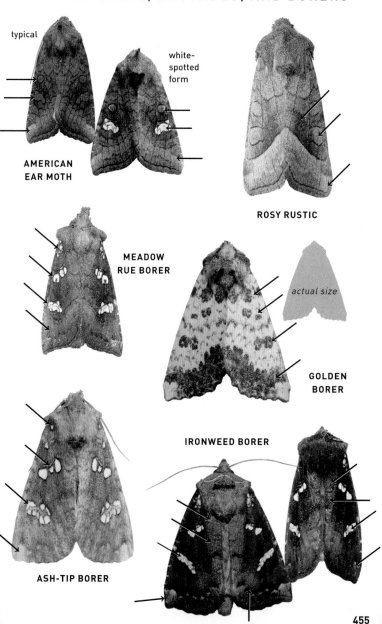

typical

white-spotted form

AMERICAN EAR MOTH

ROSY RUSTIC

MEADOW RUE BORER

actual size

GOLDEN BORER

IRONWEED BORER

ASH-TIP BORER

TURTLEHEAD BORER

Papaipema nepheleptena 93-2473 (9490) **Uncommon**

TL 18 mm. Resembles Ironweed Borer but is less dark and elongated cream-colored reniform spot is thickly outlined with white mosaic-like fragments. **HOSTS:** Turtlehead. **RANGE:** Se. Canada and ne. U.S.

OSMUNDA BORER

Papaipema speciosissima 93-2475 (9482) **Uncommon**

TL 23–27 mm. Lightly peppered orange FW has darker ST area beyond strongly angled, double PM line. Narrow white spots are bar-shaped. **HOSTS:** Flowering ferns.

SENSITIVE FERN BORER

Papaipema inquaesita 93-2476 (9483) **Common**

TL 19 mm. Peppery orange FW is marked with network of dark veins. Median and PM lines are strongly angled. Spots are typically orange but are sometimes partly white. **HOSTS:** Sensitive fern.

UMBELLIFER BORER

Papaipema birdi 93-2478 (9486) **Common**

TL 18 mm. Orange FW is peppered with rusty scales. Basal area is usually cream colored, sometimes orange. Orbicular and claviform spots are large, and thick white fragments surrounding reniform spot often touch PM line. **HOSTS:** Umbellifers, including spotted water hemlock and purplestem angelica.

COLUMBINE BORER

Papaipema leucostigma 93-2488 (9478) **Common**

TL 20 mm. Peppery orange FW has a spiky violet gray band in ST area. Basal area is uniformly orange. Spots typically have little white, especially the reniform spot. Median and PM lines are dark. **HOSTS:** Columbine. **RANGE:** Se. Canada and ne. U.S.

BRACKEN BORER

Papaipema pterisii 93-2489 (9480) **Uncommon**

TL 19 mm. Resembles Columbine Borer, but white claviform and orbicular spots are oblong, typically fused to form an oblique bar. Pale orange reniform spot is partly outlined with white mosaic-like fragments. **HOSTS:** Bracken.

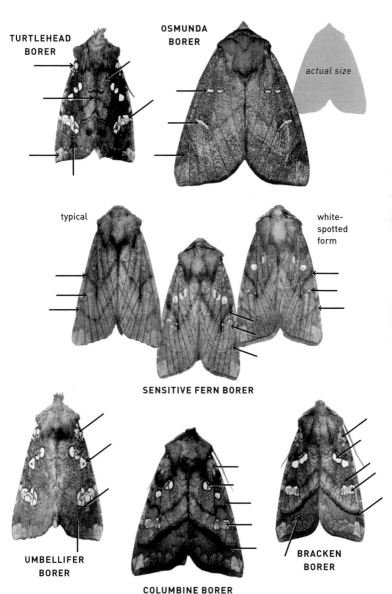

TURTLEHEAD
BORER

OSMUNDA
BORER

actual size

typical

white-
spotted
form

SENSITIVE FERN BORER

UMBELLIFER
BORER

COLUMBINE BORER

BRACKEN
BORER

NORTHERN BURDOCK BORER
Papaipema arctivorens   93-2492 (9471)   **Common**
TL 17–18 mm. Resembles Columbine Borer but is darker, with small white spots in basal area. Median line is often indistinct, and lilac ST band typically blends into dark ST area. **HOSTS:** Thistle, common burdock, teasel, and other plants.

INDIGO STEM BORER
Papaipema baptisiae   93-2494 (9485)   **Uncommon**
TL 20 mm. Resembles Columbine Borer but is lighter and has small white dot in basal area. Median and PM lines are orange. Lilac ST band is more uniform in width. **HOSTS:** Wild indigo, dogbane, and Indian plantain.

BURDOCK BORER
Papaipema cataphracta   93-2497 (9466)   **Uncommon**
TL 18 mm. Golden FW has violet brown bands in AM and ST areas. Basal area and all spots are golden with dark outlines. **HOSTS:** Low plants, including aster, burdock, corn, cottonwood, iris, sunflower, and tomato.

BRONZED BORER
Papaipema aerata   93-2499 (9468)   **Uncommon**
TL 20 mm. Violet gray FW has contrasting bronzy brown median and basal areas that are speckled with pale scales. Lines are indistinct, the most noticeable being the almost straight PM line. Inconspicuous spots are sometimes darker brown. **HOSTS:** Unknown. **RANGE:** Se. Canada and ne. U.S.

ASTER BORER
Papaipema impecuniosa   93-2500 (9473)   **Uncommon**
TL 15 mm. Resembles Burdock Borer, but golden brown FW is more peppery. Median line is dark and sharply pointed. AM line is usually relatively indistinct. **HOSTS:** Aster and sneezeweed.

STALK BORER
Papaipema nebris   93-2501 (9496)   **Common**
TL 16–20 mm. Hoary gray brown FW has broad ash gray band beyond almost straight white PM line. Spots are usually dark but may sometimes be white (not shown). **HOSTS:** Stalks of thick-stemmed plants; sometimes a pest of corn.

APAMEAS, BROCADES, AND BORERS

NORTHERN BURDOCK BORER

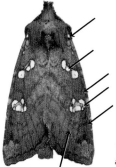

INDIGO STEM BORER

actual size

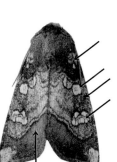

BURDOCK BORER

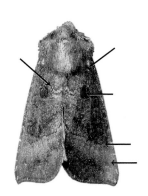

BRONZED BORER

ASTER BORER

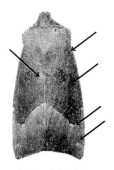

STALK BORER

459

JOE-PYE-WEED BORER

Papaipema eupatorii   93-2502 (9501)   **Uncommon**
TL 18–20 mm. Similar to Stalk Borer, but straight PM line is edged pale violet gray. ST line often visible as a linear sprinkling of white scales. **HOSTS:** Joe-pye weed. **NOTE:** Also called Eupatorium Borer.

CONEFLOWER BORER

Papaipema nelita   93-2506 (9502)   **Uncommon**
TL 20 mm. Resembles Stalk Borer, but FW is usually darker. Brown PM line is slightly scalloped. Orbicular and claviform spots are dark and relatively distinct; may rarely be white. Thorax is dark, liberally sprinkled with white scales. **HOSTS:** Cutleaf coneflower.

BLACK-TAILED DIVER

Bellura vulnifica   93-2514 (9523.1)   **Uncommon**
TL 19–27 mm. Peppery tan FW has diffuse blackish median band inside strongly angled AM line. PM line is scalloped. Indistinct spots are peppered with blackish scales. **HOSTS:** White water lily and other Nymphaea spp. **NOTE:** One or two broods. Was previously considered conspecific with White-tailed Diver.

CATTAIL BORER

Bellura obliqua   93-2517 (9525)   **Uncommon**
TL 22–28 mm. Grayish brown FW has pale costal streak that blends into slanting pale basal area and tegulae of thorax. Blackish PM line is shallowly toothed. Streaky orbicular spot is whitish. Oblique reniform spot is partly outlined white or pale orange. **HOSTS:** Cattail, pickerelweed, arrowhead, and skunk cabbage. **NOTES:** Two broods. Genetic studies suggest that what is currently recognized in e. N.A. as Cattail Borer may actually be a complex of two or more species. Many individuals with shorter, rounder wings and more uniform orbicular spots may prove to be a separate species once the genus has been examined and revised.

PICKERELWEED BORER

Bellura densa   93-2518 (9526)   **Uncommon**
TL 19–26 mm. Resembles larger Cattail Borer, but FW is browner with fawn-colored costal streak. Orbicular and reniform spots are orange, outlined brown. **HOSTS:** Cattail, pickerelweed, and water hyacinth. **NOTE:** Two broods.

APAMEAS, BROCADES, AND BORERS

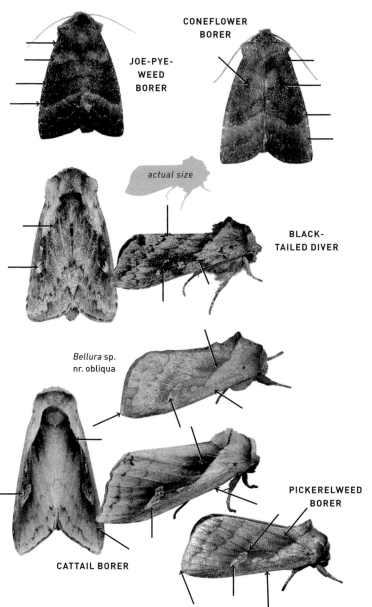

JOE-PYE-WEED BORER

CONEFLOWER BORER

actual size

BLACK-TAILED DIVER

Bellura sp. nr. obliqua

PICKERELWEED BORER

CATTAIL BORER

461

Swordgrasses, Pinions, and Xylenine Sallows Family Noctuidae, Subfamily Noctuinae, Tribe Xylenini

A moderately large group of thick-bodied noctuids that inhabit woodlands and old fields. Most species rest with wings flat, but swordgrasses hold their wings tightly curled around the abdomen, forming a tapered point. Some pinions bear a thick ruff of hairlike scales across the thorax that look like epaulets, and show a bend in the costa at the PM line. Most sallows have squared-off wings. Many are typically late season fliers; some overwinter as adults and fly for a brief period early in the spring. They are nocturnal and come to light and sugar bait, some in large numbers.

AMERICAN SWORDGRASS
Xylena nupera   93-2519 (9873)   Uncommon
TL 31 mm. Pale tan FW has darker shading along costa and inner margin. A series of black dashes extends across wing from base to jagged ST line. Thorax is black dorsally. **HOSTS:** Deciduous trees and grasses, including cherry, poplar, and willow.

DOT-AND-DASH SWORDGRASS
Xylena curvimacula   93-2520 (9874)   Uncommon
TL 25–28 mm. Grayish brown FW has contrasting cream-colored streak extending from base to apex. Looped AM line is edged with black basal dash. Crescent-shaped reniform spot is edged whitish. Thorax is chestnut brown. **HOSTS:** Deciduous trees and plants, including alder, birch, dandelion, and poplar.

GRAY SWORDGRASS
Xylena cineritia   93-2522 (9876)   Uncommon
TL 21–25 mm. Bluish gray FW has pale pinkish streak extending through wing parallel to blackish costa. Dark orbicular spot almost touches tawny reniform spot. Thorax is black dorsally. **HOSTS:** Deciduous trees and shrubs, including alder, birch, maple, meadowsweet, and poplar.

ASHEN BRINDLE
Lithomoia germana   93-2524 (9878)   Uncommon
TL 27 mm. Ash gray FW has darker median band and zigzag blackish lines. Large pale reniform spot is outlined white. Wings are held tightly rolled at rest. Raises abdomen at rest. **HOSTS:** Deciduous trees and woody shrubs, including alder, birch, blueberry, poplar, and willow. **RANGE:** Locally in se. Canada and ne. U.S.

SWORDGRASSES, PINIONS, AND XYLENINE SALLOWS

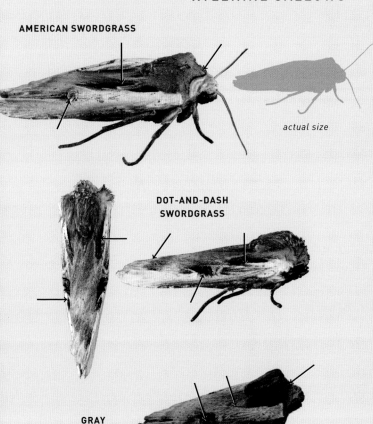

AMERICAN SWORDGRASS

actual size

DOT-AND-DASH SWORDGRASS

GRAY SWORDGRASS

ASHEN BRINDLE

GOAT SALLOW *Homoglaea hircina* 93-2527 (9881)   **Common**
TL 17–18 mm. Grayish brown FW is variably shaded warm brown in median area. Curved AM and PM lines are widely edged pale gray. ST line is accented with a row of blackish dots. **HOSTS:** Alder, basswood, birch, poplar, and willow.

FALSE PINION
Litholomia napaea 93-2530 (9884)   **Uncommon**
TL 16–17 mm. Ash gray FW has crisp black lines. Slightly wavy black median line is often edged warm brown. Large round orbicular spot is filled with white scales. Reniform spot has black spot in inner half. **HOSTS:** Trembling aspen. **RANGE:** S. Canada and n. U.S.

SINGED PINION
Lithophane semiusta 93-2531 (9885)   **Common**
TL 18–19 mm. Yellowish brown FW has rust-colored shading along lines and in median area. Slanting orbicular spot and reniform spots are outlined pale yellow. ST area is darker within dotted terminal line. **HOSTS:** Basswood, chokecherry, and trembling aspen. **RANGE:** Se. Canada and ne. U.S.

DIMORPHIC PINION
Lithophane petefacta 93-2532 (9886)   **Common**
TL 18–20 mm. Dimorphic. FW typically is pale grayish cream with olive brown bands in median and ST areas. Rectangular black patch in inner median area is sharply defined. Dark form (uncommon; not shown) resembles dark Hemina Pinion with prominent black patch. **HOSTS:** Mostly chokecherry, oak, and maple, also larvae of lepidoptera.

BETHUNE'S PINION
Lithophane bethunei 93-2533 (9887)   **Common**
TL 18–20 mm. Resembles typical form of Dimorphic Pinion, but paler, straw-colored FW has warm brown bands in median and ST areas. Jagged lines are accented with pairs of tiny black dots along veins. Dusky patch in inner median area is faint. **HOSTS:** Deciduous trees, including ash, birch, chokecherry, elm, maple, and willow.

NAMELESS PINION
Lithophane innominata 93-2534 (9888)   **Common**
TL 19–20 mm. Resembles typical form of Dimorphic Pinion, but rectangular blackish patch in inner median area is diffuse. Brown terminal shading often has darker patches at midpoint and anal angle. **HOSTS:** Deciduous trees and shrubs, including alder, apple, hemlock, oak, spruce, and willow.

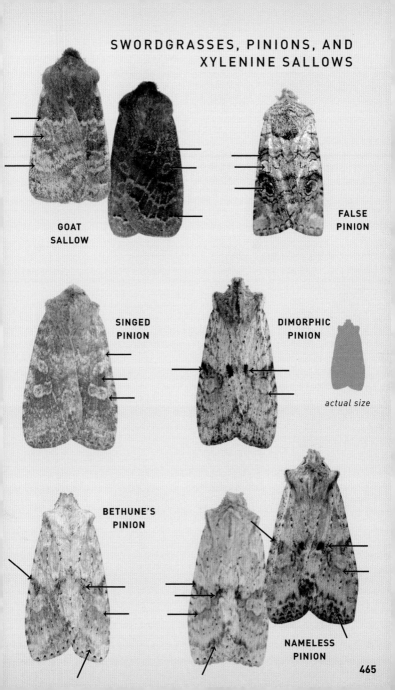

SWORDGRASSES, PINIONS, AND XYLENINE SALLOWS

GOAT SALLOW

FALSE PINION

SINGED PINION

DIMORPHIC PINION

actual size

BETHUNE'S PINION

NAMELESS PINION

WANTON PINION

Lithophane petulca   93-2536 (9889)   **Common**
TL 18–20 mm. Dimorphic. FW of light form is light grayish brown with darker brown bands in median and ST areas. Faint dusky patch is often present in inner median area. Dark form has dusky brown shading covering inner half of FW, contrasting with pale costal streak and reniform spot. **HOSTS:** Birch, also alder, basswood, elm, trembling aspen, and willow.

DASHED GRAY PINION

Lithophane disposita   93-2537 (9892)   **Common**
TL 20 mm. Light greenish gray FW has thin black basal dash and large orbicular and reniform spots narrowly outlined black. ST area shaded gray at midpoint and anal angle. **HOSTS:** Chokecherry, elm, and willow.

HEMINA PINION

Lithophane hemina   93-2538 (9893)   **Common**
TL 20–22 mm. Dimorphic. FW of light form typically is warm brown with darker brown bands in median and ST areas. Blackish rectangular patch in inner median area is usually well defined. Dark form has sooty shading covering inner half of FW with sharply contrasting pale costal streak and orbicular and reniform spots. **HOSTS:** Deciduous trees, including birch, chokecherry, and oak.

AMANDA'S PINION

Lithophane amanda   93-2544 (9891)   **Uncommon**
TL 20–23 mm. Grayish tan FW has tawny streak passing through outer half of pale reniform spot. A large dusky smudge is typically present in inner median area. **HOSTS:** Deciduous trees, including birch and willow. **RANGE:** S. Canada and n. U.S.

PLUSH-NAPED PINION

Lithophane pexata   93-2545 (9922)   **Common**
TL 20–21 mm. Grayish FW is variably suffused warm brown along inner margin and ST line. Thick white shoulder stripe is edged black along rounded inner edge. Pale reniform spot has a chestnut dot in inner half. **HOSTS:** Alder.

THAXTER'S PINION

Lithophane thaxteri   93-2547 (9928)   **Uncommon**
TL 18–20 mm. Ash gray FW has unique marbled pattern. Basal, inner median, and reniform areas are tinged warm brown. **HOSTS:** Trees and shrubs, including birch, blueberry, sweet gale, tamarack, and willow. **RANGE:** Canada and n. U.S.

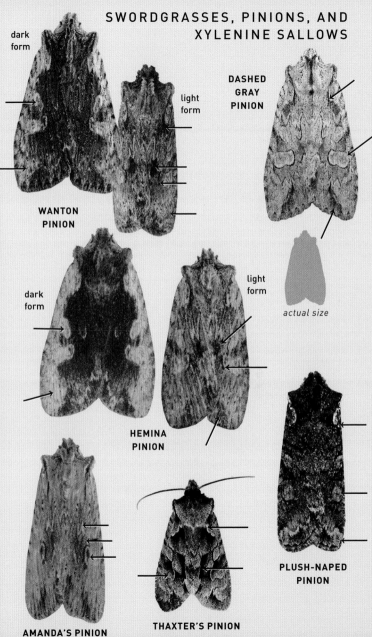

SWORDGRASSES, PINIONS, AND XYLENINE SALLOWS

dark form

light form

DASHED GRAY PINION

WANTON PINION

dark form

light form

actual size

HEMINA PINION

PLUSH-NAPED PINION

AMANDA'S PINION

THAXTER'S PINION

467

HOARY PINION *Lithophane fagina* 93-2548 (9917) **Uncommon**
TL 21–24 mm. Pale ash gray FW has whitish streak along costal margin. Finely etched black lines are wildly jagged, creating streaky appearance. **HOSTS:** Birch and cherry.

BAILEY'S PINION *Lithophane baileyi* 93-2549 (9902) **Common**
TL 20–21 mm. FW is variably whitish to bluish gray with indistinct lines. Whitish shoulder spot is bordered on inner edge by thick black basal dash. Whitish U-shaped orbicular spot is open-sided to costa. Pale reniform spot has a chestnut dot in inner half. **HOSTS:** Deciduous trees, including apple, birch, cherry, and willow.

ASHEN PINION
Lithophane antennata 93-2577 (9910) **Common**
TL 23–25 mm. Medium gray FW has indistinct blackish lines and outlines to spots. Pale gray shoulder spot is bordered on inner edge by thin black basal dash. Hollow claviform spot is wedge-shaped. Orbicular spot is hourglass-shaped, filled with two gray dots. Gray reniform spot is partly filled with brown scales. **HOSTS:** Deciduous trees, including apple, ash, elm, maple, oak, and willow.

TRIPLE-SPOTTED PINION
Lithophane laticinerea 93-2580 (9914) **Common**
TL 22–25 mm. Resembles Ashen Pinion, but smooth gray FW has whitish figure eight–shaped orbicular spot filled with three distinct gray spots. Pale reniform spot is sometimes weakly tinged with brown, often with a black dot in inner half. **HOSTS:** Deciduous trees, including ash, basswood, elm, maple, and poplar. **RANGE:** S. Canada and n. U.S.

GROTE'S PINION *Lithophane grotei* 93-2581 (9915) **Common**
TL 22–26 mm. Rough gray FW has jagged black lines. Inconspicuous pale gray shoulder patch is weakly edged with dark gray basal dash. Whitish hourglass-shaped orbicular spot is filled with two gray spots. Indistinct gray reniform spot has a blackish dot in inner half. **HOSTS:** Apple, birch, chokecherry, maple, and oak.

DOWDY PINION
Lithophane unimoda 93-2582 (9916) **Common**
TL 21–22 mm. Dull gray FW has inconspicuous darker lines. Whitish outer half of hourglass-shaped orbicular spot is often the only obvious marking. **HOSTS:** Deciduous trees, including cherry, maple, and oak.

SWORDGRASSES, PINIONS, AND XYLENINE SALLOWS

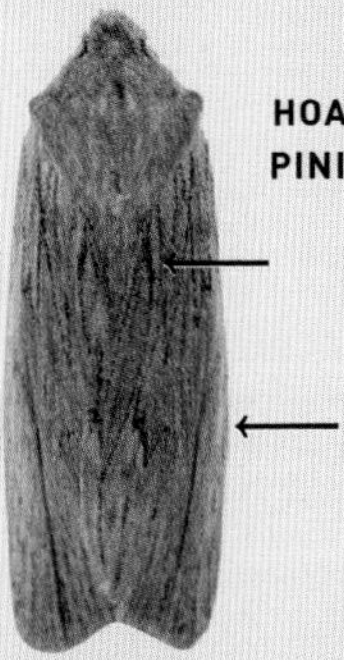

HOARY PINION

BAILEY'S PINION

actual size

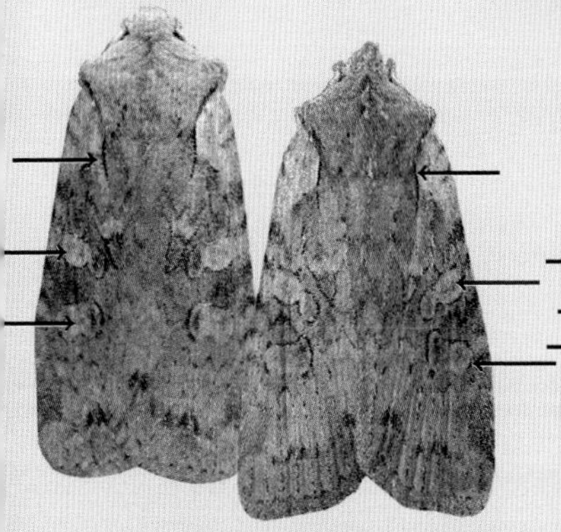

ASHEN PINION

TRIPLE-SPOTTED PINION

GROTE'S PINION

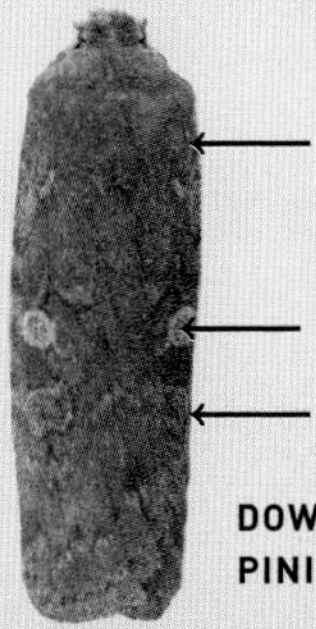

DOWDY PINION

469

MUSTARD SALLOW

Pyreferra hesperidago   93-2583 (9929)   **Common**
TL 18–20 mm. Yellowish FW is finely peppered with orange scales. Rusty brown AM and median lines are slightly wavy. PM line is straight but kinks abruptly inward near costa. Reniform spot has a blackish dot in inner half. **HOSTS:** Witch hazel and ironwood.

CITRINE SALLOW

Pyreferra citromba   93-2584 (9930)   **Uncommon**
TL 17 mm. Resembles Mustard Sallow, but pale yellow FW has straight AM and median lines. Inconspicuous reniform spot is filled with slightly darker scales. **HOSTS:** Witch hazel. **RANGE:** Se. Canada and ne. U.S.

STRAIGHT-TOOTHED SALLOW

Eupsilia vinulenta   93-2587 (9933)   **Common**
TL 20 mm. FW is variably pale orange to rusty brown or maroon with purplish lines. AM line is straight, median line strongly angled, and PM line jagged. Reniform spot is either white or orange with tiny satellite dots on either side. **HOSTS:** Deciduous trees, including cherry, maple, and oak.

THREE-SPOTTED SALLOW

Eupsilia tristigmata   93-2590 (9935)   **Common**
TL 18 mm. Resembles typical light form of Straight-toothed Sallow, but white or orange reniform spot usually has obvious black dot in inner half. AM line is slightly wavy. **HOSTS:** Deciduous trees, including birch, butternut, cherry, oak, and willow.

MORRISON'S SALLOW

Eupsilia morrisoni   93-2591 (9936)   **Common**
TL 18–21 mm. Peppery pale brown FW has inconspicuous AM and PM lines edged paler. Faint brown median line is angled at midpoint. Indistinct reniform spot has black dot in inner half. **HOSTS:** Apple, birch, cherry, and elm.

SWORDGRASSES, PINIONS, AND XYLENINE SALLOWS

MUSTARD SALLOW

CITRINE SALLOW

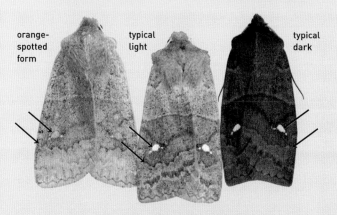

orange-spotted form

typical light

typical dark

STRAIGHT-TOOTHED SALLOW

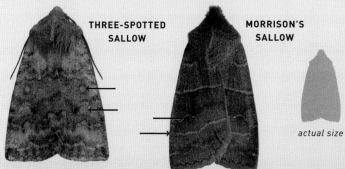

THREE-SPOTTED SALLOW

MORRISON'S SALLOW

actual size

LOST SALLOW
Eupsilia devia 93-2594 (9939) **Uncommon**
TL 17–19 mm. Lilac gray FW is strongly dusted with white scales. Median area and band beyond ST line are darker brown. Whitish AM and ST lines curve gently outward. Faint reniform spot is partly edged white. **HOSTS:** Primarily aster and goldenrod, also chokecherry and oak.

UNSATED SALLOW
Metaxaglaea inulta 93-2597 (9943) **Common**
TL 23–26 mm. Brown FW often has violet sheen when fresh. Purplish AM and PM lines curve gently inward near costa. Hollow orbicular and reniform spots converge and sometimes touch. ST line is edged warm brown. **HOSTS:** Arrow-wood, nannyberry, and wayfaring tree.

ROADSIDE SALLOW
Metaxaglaea viatica 93-2598 (9944) **Common**
TL 22–28 mm. Dull chestnut brown FW has bands of purplish brown shading beyond scalloped PM and ST lines. Large hollow orbicular and reniform spots converge but do not touch. Reniform spot has faint dusky spot in inner half. **HOSTS:** Apple, crab apple, mountain ash, and cherry.

SLOPING SALLOW
Epiglaea decliva 93-2602 (9946) **Common**
TL 22–26 mm. Earth brown FW has slightly toothed, purplish AM and PM lines. Tips of teeth in PM line form a row of dots. Large orbicular and reniform spots are darker than ground color and partly outlined pale yellow. Reniform spot has blackish dot in inner half. ST line is warm brown edged pale yellow. **HOSTS:** Cherry and oak.

WAXED SALLOW
Chaetaglaea cerata 93-2604 (9948) **Uncommon**
TL 24 mm. Pale grayish tan FW has whitish veins. Gently curved AM and PM lines are edged pale yellow. Slightly darker orbicular and reniform spots have pale outlines. Reniform spot has tiny black dot in inner half. Thin yellow streak extends along inner margin. **HOSTS:** Unknown. **RANGE:** Se. ON and possibly ne. U.S.

SILKY SALLOW *Chaetaglaea sericea* 93-2607 (9950) **Common**
TL 20–23 mm. Resembles Waxed Sallow, but darker FW is marked with distinct whitish veins. A wide yellow streak extends along inner margin. **HOSTS:** Blueberry, cherry, and oak.

SWORDGRASSES, PINIONS, AND XYLENINE SALLOWS

LOST SALLOW

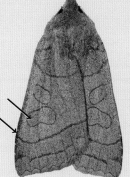

actual size

UNSATED SALLOW

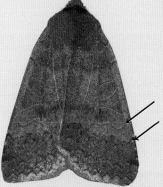

ROADSIDE SALLOW

SLOPING SALLOW

WAXED SALLOW

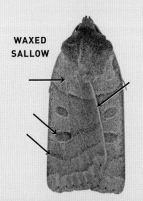

SILKY SALLOW

SCALLOPED SALLOW

Eucirroedia pampina   93-2609 (9952)   **Common**
TL 21–25 mm. Orange FW has bold rusty AM and PM lines that converge toward inner margin. Large orbicular and reniform spots are purplish. Outer margin is boldly scalloped. Typically rests with its angled wings and abdomen raised. **HOSTS:** Deciduous trees and plants, including cherry, oak, and poplar. **NOTE:** May be flushed from leaf litter during the day.

BICOLORED SALLOW

Sunira bicolorago   93-2616 (9957)   **Common**
TL 18–20 mm. Peppery pale orange FW typically has wavy lines bordered with purplish bands. Scalloped PM line is accented with faint black dots along veins. Reniform spot has a blackish dot in inner half. Some individuals (bicolored) show dark shading across apical half of wing. **HOSTS:** Deciduous trees and low plants, including cabbage, cherry, elm, maple, and tobacco.

DOTTED SALLOW   *Anathix ralla*   93-2619 (9961)   **Common**

TL 17–21 mm. Orange FW has slightly scalloped, double AM and PM lines. Angled brown median band is often conspicuous. ST and terminal lines are rows of black dots. Orbicular and reniform spots have diffuse blackish dots in inner halves. **HOSTS:** Aspen.

PUTA SALLOW   *Anathix puta*   93-2620 (9962)   **Uncommon**

TL 14–15 mm. FW is variably grayish brown to pale orange, typically with contrasting pale gray veins. Double AM and PM lines are filled with pale gray. Angled median line touches blackish spot in inner half of reniform spot. Midpoint of inconspicuous ST line is accented with black dots. **HOSTS:** Trembling aspen.

APPROACHABLE SALLOW

Anathix aggressa   93-2621 (9963)   **Uncommon**
TL 15–17 mm. Similar to smaller Puta Sallow, but FW is usually paler grayish tan with contrasting whitish veins. Scalloped AM and PM lines are often inconspicuous. Angled median line touches grayish spot in inner half of reniform spot. **HOSTS:** Poplar. **RANGE:** W. Canada and U.S., also sw. ON.

PINK-BARRED SALLOW

Xanthia tatago   93-2622 (9965)   **Uncommon**
TL 16–17 mm. Bright yellow FW is boldly marked with purplish brown shading and spots. ST line is a row of blackish dots. Terminal line is checkered. Fringe is pinkish. Slightly crested golden yellow thorax has wide purplish collar. **HOSTS:** Willow.

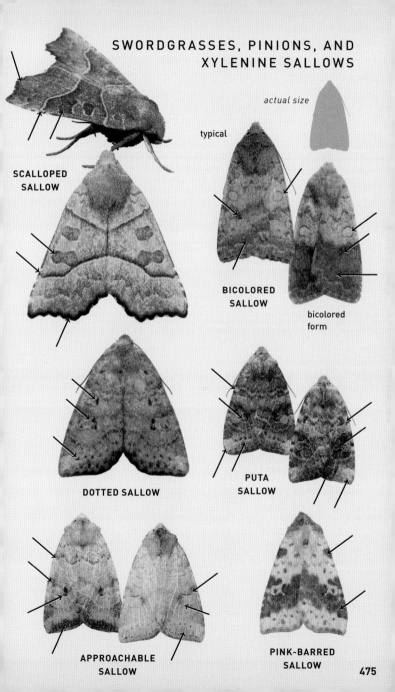

SWORDGRASSES, PINIONS, AND XYLENINE SALLOWS

actual size

SCALLOPED SALLOW

typical

BICOLORED SALLOW

bicolored form

DOTTED SALLOW

PUTA SALLOW

APPROACHABLE SALLOW

PINK-BARRED SALLOW

BLACK-DISC SALLOW

Brachylomia discinigra   93-2656 (9999)   **Uncommon**
TL 19–22 mm. Peppery gray FW has darker median area and mottled white basal patch. Double AM and PM lines are filled with pale gray. Kinked blackish median band is conspicuous. Faint gray spots are outlined whitish. **HOSTS:** Unknown. **RANGE:** Canada and possibly n. U.S.

COMMON HYPPA

Hyppa xylinoides   93-2664 (9578)   **Common**
TL 21–24 mm. Ash gray FW has darker gray median area. A thick black bar in inner median area is edged maroon. Jagged AM line and curved PM line are whitish. Two black basal dashes merge with blackish tegulae on thorax. **HOSTS:** Trees and low plants, including alder, cranberry, rose, and Saint John's wort. **NOTE:** Two broods.

AMERICAN DUN-BAR

Cosmia calami   93-2672 (9815)   **Common**
TL 15–17 mm. Straw-colored FW has whitish AM and PM lines converging toward inner margin. Blurry brown median line angles between indistinct orbicular and reniform spots. Usually rests with wings tented over back. **HOSTS:** Oak.

PALE ENARGIA   *Enargia decolor*   93-2674 (9549)   **Common**
TL 17–23 mm. Peppery FW is variably straw colored to orange with parallel, strongly angled lines. Large orbicular and reniform spots are narrowly outlined brown. **HOSTS:** Trembling aspen, large-toothed aspen, alder, white birch, and balsam poplar.

SMOKED SALLOW

Enargia infumata   93-2675 (9550)   **Common**
TL 19 mm. Resembles Pale Enargia, but flies earlier in the season, and reniform spot usually has a small blackish dot in inner half. **HOSTS:** Trembling aspen, white birch, willow, and balsam poplar. **NOTE:** Includes Lesser Eyed Sallow, previously recognized as a separate species, *E. mephisto.*

EVEN-LINED SALLOW

Ipimorpha pleonectusa   93-2679 (9555)   **Common**
TL 18–20 mm. Brownish FW is often tinged olive green when fresh. Straight cream-colored AM and PM lines are roughly parallel. Slightly darker claviform, orbicular, and reniform spots are large and narrowly outlined pale yellow. Thorax has sharp dorsal ridge. **HOSTS:** Aspen, balsam poplar, and willow.

SWORDGRASSES, PINIONS, AND XYLENINE SALLOWS

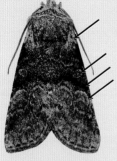

BLACK-DISC SALLOW

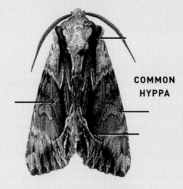

COMMON HYPPA

AMERICAN DUN-BAR

SMOKED SALLOW

actual size

PALE ENARGIA

EVEN-LINED SALLOW

WANDERING BROCADE

Fishia illocata   93-2695 (9420)   **Common**
TL 23 mm. Lilac gray FW has rosy pink shading in median area. A black median bar connects AM and PM lines. Large orbicular and reniform spots are mostly white. **HOSTS:** Alder, birch, and willow.

ADORABLE BROCADE

Platypolia mactata   93-2699 (9419)   **Common**
TL 20 mm. Resembles Wandering Brocade but lacks rosy shading and median bar is typically thicker. Scalloped AM and PM lines are edged white. Large pale gray orbicular and reniform spots are narrowly outlined black. **HOSTS:** Unknown.

ACADIAN SALLOW

Xylotype acadia   93-2701 (9980)   **Uncommon**
TL 19–22 mm. Ash gray FW is boldly marked with scalloped white AM and PM lines that converge toward inner margin. Large pale orbicular and reniform spots are outlined white. Black dashes in inner median area and anal angle are conspicuous. **HOSTS:** Alder, bog laurel, chokecherry, pine, and tamarack.

PRIVATE SALLOW

Sutyna privata   93-2707 (9989)   **Uncommon**
TL 19–22 mm. Peppery ash gray FW has darker gray basal and median areas. All lines and spots are indistinct and edged white. Thick black bar in inner median area is conspicuous. ST line has black wedges at midpoint and anal angle. **HOSTS:** Blackberry.

GROTE'S SATYR

Ufeus satyricus   93-2709 (11051)   **Uncommon**
TL 23–25 mm. Grayish brown FW is peppered with paler scales. Curved black PM line strongly marked. Reniform spot is a black dot or streak. ST area is accented with thin black dashes. **HOSTS:** Trembling aspen.

FOLDED SATYR

Ufeus plicatus   93-2710 (11052)   **Uncommon**
TL 22 mm. Closely resembles Grote's Satyr (some intermediates may not be identifiable), but PM line typically has slightly pointed bulge at midpoint. Conspicuous blackish streak extends through pale reniform spot. **HOSTS:** Trembling aspen. **RANGE:** Incompletely known.

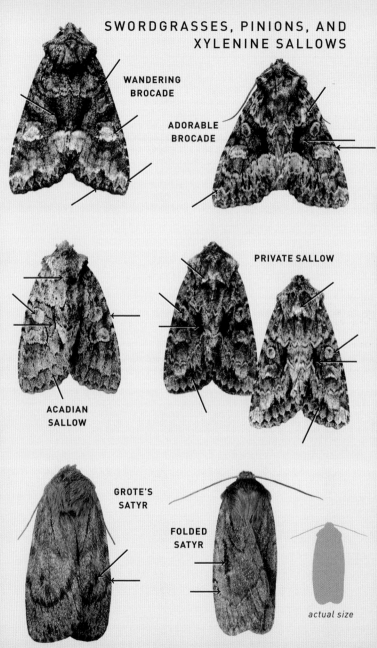

SWORDGRASSES, PINIONS, AND XYLENINE SALLOWS

WANDERING BROCADE

ADORABLE BROCADE

PRIVATE SALLOW

ACADIAN SALLOW

GROTE'S SATYR

FOLDED SATYR

actual size

CLOAKED MARVEL

Chytonix palliatricula   93-2713 (9556)   **Common**
TL 17 mm. Gray FW typically has straw-colored shading in median area. Crisp black lines converge toward inner margin. Thick black bar in inner median area ends as an elongated white dot. Southern individuals average darker than northern ones. Some individuals have extensive white in the inner median area. **HOSTS:** Grasses and aster blossoms.

MARSH FERN MOTH

Fagitana littera   93-2749 (9629)   **Uncommon**
TL 16 mm. Fawn-colored FW is clouded rusty brown along costa and in median area. White-edged rusty AM and PM lines converge toward inner margin. White reniform spot is 7-shaped. White terminal line contrasts with pale orange fringe. **HOSTS:** Ferns, including eastern marsh fern, Virginia chain fern, and royal fern.

Spring Quakers, Woodlings, and Woodgrains   Family Noctuidae,
Subfamily Noctuinae, Tribe Orthosiini

Medium-sized, plain noctuid moths, many of which are on the wing early in the season. A few species are highly variable. They are commonly found in woodlands and larger gardens. All are nocturnal and will come to light. *Orthosia* species can often be attracted to sugar bait.

RUBY QUAKER

Orthosia rubescens   93-2770 (10487)   **Common**
TL 20 mm. FW is extremely variable, but typically is mottled reddish brown with paler basal area. Blackish subapical spot is often noticeable. Reniform spot has a blackish dot in inner half. ST line is indistinct. Antennae of male are bipectinate. **HOSTS:** Deciduous trees, including aspen, cherry, maple, and oak.

GARMAN'S QUAKER

Orthosia garmani   93-2771 (10488)   **Common**
TL 18–22 mm. FW is variably grayish brown to reddish brown with a pale band along outer margin. Inner section of irregular ST line is accented with blackish wedges. **HOSTS:** Chokecherry and sugar maple.

SWORDGRASSES, PINIONS, AND XYLENINE SALLOWS

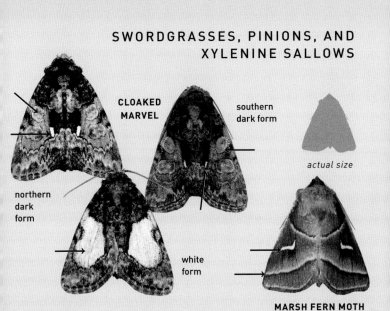

CLOAKED MARVEL

southern dark form

northern dark form

white form

actual size

MARSH FERN MOTH

SPRING QUAKERS, WOODLINGS, AND WOODGRAINS

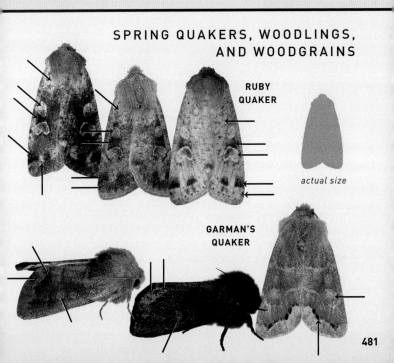

RUBY QUAKER

actual size

GARMAN'S QUAKER

SUBDUED QUAKER
Orthosia revicta   93-2773 (10490)   **Common**
TL 19–22 mm. Pale gray FW is suffused with reddish brown shading in basal and median areas. Peppery pale veins cut through chestnut-edged yellow ST line. Large orbicular and reniform spots are outlined reddish and pale yellow. **HOSTS:** Deciduous trees, including ash, birch, beech, elm, maple, oak, poplar, and willow.

GRAY QUAKER   *Orthosia alurina*   93-2774 (10491)   **Common**
TL 19–21 mm. Uniformly pale gray FW has inconspicuous lines edged chestnut. Brownish median band is often noticeable. Large reniform spot has a small black dot in inner half. **HOSTS:** A variety of trees, including basswood, black cherry, chokecherry, and serviceberry.

SPECKLED GREEN FRUITWORM MOTH
Orthosia hibisci   93-2778 (10495)   **Common**
TL 20–23 mm. Grayish brown FW is variably mottled brown. White-outlined reniform spot has large black dot in inner half. Whitish ST line (sometimes not well defined) is edged brown, forming a dark subapical patch. **HOSTS:** Deciduous trees and woody plants, including apple, chokecherry, elm, hickory, poplar, spruce, and willow.

NORMAN'S QUAKER
Crocigrapha normani   93-2784 (10501)   **Common**
TL 18–19 mm. FW is variably pale tan to reddish brown with a straight, pale-edged AM line. Reniform spot has black dot in inner half. ST line is absent. Apical patch is whitish. **HOSTS:** Deciduous trees, including ash, birch, ironwood, maple, oak, and pin cherry.

INTRACTABLE QUAKER
Himella fidelis   93-2785 (10502)   **Common**
TL 13–18 mm. FW is variably grayish tan to reddish brown. Inconspicuous AM and PM lines end as black dots near inner margin. Midpoint of yellowish ST line is typically marked with two black wedges. Large orbicular and reniform spots are outlined pale yellow. **HOSTS:** Elm, flowering crab apple, and oak.

GRIEVING WOODLING   *Egira dolosa*   93-2795 (10513)   **Common**
TL 19–20 mm. Peppery gray FW has white-edged orbicular spot fused to whitish inner median area. Reniform spot is partly outlined white. Darker individuals are completely sooty black with narrow white collar on thorax. **HOSTS:** Birch, poplar, and willow. **RANGE:** S. Canada and ne. U.S.

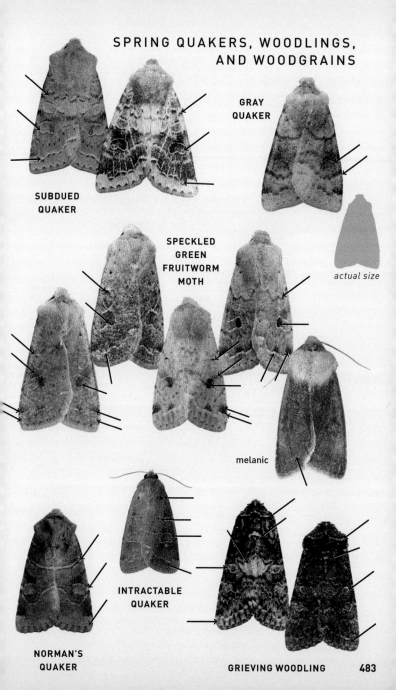

SPRING QUAKERS, WOODLINGS, AND WOODGRAINS

GRAY QUAKER

SUBDUED QUAKER

actual size

SPECKLED GREEN FRUITWORM MOTH

melanic

INTRACTABLE QUAKER

NORMAN'S QUAKER

GRIEVING WOODLING

483

ALTERNATE WOODLING
Egira alternans 93-2799 (10517) **Common**
TL 18–21 mm. Pale gray FW is shaded reddish brown in basal and median areas. Often has a thick black bar in inner median area. Large whitish orbicular spot is fused to a pale band that extends to inner margin. Reddish brown reniform spot is outlined whitish. **HOSTS:** Black cherry, honeysuckle, and willow. **RANGE:** E. U.S.

DISTINCT QUAKER

Achatia distincta 93-2800 (10518) **Common**
TL 20 mm. Pale gray FW is marked with thin black AM and PM lines that are connected in inner median area with a kinked bar. Orbicular and reniform spots are partly filled with warm brown. Black dashes pass through ST area. **HOSTS:** Deciduous trees and woody plants, including ash, birch, butternut, grape, maple, and oak.

GRAY WOODGRAIN
Morrisonia mucens 93-2801 (10519) **Common**
TL 17–20 mm. Pale gray FW has barklike pattern of warm brown streaks. Darkest markings are two thin black basal dashes and a thick dusky bar in inner median area. Jagged PM line is whitish at inner margin. Two dusky wedges point inward from outer margin. **HOSTS:** Unknown. **RANGE:** E. U.S.

BICOLORED WOODGRAIN

Morrisonia evicta 93-2802 (10520) **Common**
TL 19–21 mm. Grayish brown FW has contrasting pale costal streak. Black basal dash and veins create a woodgrain effect. Slanting orbicular spot is fused to brown-filled reniform spot. Some individuals have dark brown shading along inner margin of FW. **HOSTS:** Cherry.

CONFUSED WOODGRAIN

Morrisonia confusa 93-2803 (10521) **Common**
TL 18–22 mm. Tan-colored FW has barklike pattern of brown streaks between white-speckled veins. Basal area is marked with two black dashes. Jagged PM line is edged white at inner margin. **HOSTS:** Deciduous trees and woody plants, including beech, birch, elm, cherry, maple, and oak.

FLUID ARCHES *Morrisonia latex* 93-2805 (10291) **Common**

TL 22–26 mm. Gray FW has indistinct AM and PM lines. Slanting black line connects outline of large chestnut-filled reniform spot to costa. Midpoint of rounded outer margin is accented with a row of black dashes. **HOSTS:** Deciduous trees, including birch, elm, maple, and oak.

SPRING QUAKERS, WOODLINGS, AND WOODGRAINS

ALTERNATE WOODLING

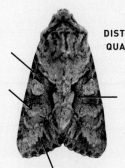

DISTINCT QUAKER

actual size

GRAY WOODGRAIN

typical

light form

BICOLORED WOODGRAIN

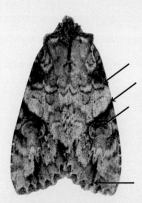

CONFUSED WOODGRAIN

FLUID ARCHES

485

LARGE ARCHES   Family Noctuidae, Subfamily Noctuinae, Tribes Tholerini and Hadenini

Medium-sized midsummer noctuids that often display intricate FW patterns. They mostly occur in woodlands and old fields, but also in larger gardens. Wheat Head Armyworm and The Pink-Streak resemble wainscots. All typically rest with their wings in a shallow tent. They are attracted to light in small to moderate numbers.

BRONZED CUTWORM

Nephelodes minians   93-2810 (10524)   **Common**
TL 21–28 mm. FW is variably pinkish to grayish brown with a violet sheen when fresh. Reddish brown median area is edged with curved orange AM and PM lines. Orbicular and reniform spots are pale orange. ST area is often crossed with blackish veins. **HOSTS:** Corn and grasses.

THE NUTMEG   *Anarta trifolii*   93-2826 (10223)   **Common**
TL 17–19 mm. Grayish brown FW is marked with crisp, often fragmented, black lines. Reniform spot has dark gray dot in inner half. Central section of ST line is W-shaped. HW is whitish with dusky terminal line. **HOSTS:** Various woody and herbaceous plants; a minor crop pest. **NOTE:** Two broods.

STORMY ARCHES   *Polia nimbosa*   93-2867 (10275)   **Common**
TL 29 mm. Whitish FW is dusted with gray scales along costa. AM and PM lines are double. White orbicular and reniform spots are separated by blackish patch. Irregular ST line is accented with black wedges. **HOSTS:** Deciduous trees and low plants, including alder, gooseberry, huckleberry, and maple.

CLOUDY ARCHES   *Polia imbrifera*   93-2868 (10276)   **Common**
TL 25–26 mm. Resembles Stormy Arches, but FW is gray with indistinct AM and PM lines. Orbicular and reniform spots are edged pale gray. Black basal dash is often present. Irregular whitish ST line is accented with black wedges. **HOSTS:** Alder, birch, chokecherry, and willow.

PURPLE ARCHES

Polia purpurissata   93-2872 (10280)   **Common**
TL 27 mm. Purplish gray FW has indistinct AM and PM lines. Orbicular and reniform spots are outlined black. Central and inner sections of ST line have thick black accents. **HOSTS:** Trees and low plants, including alder, birch, blueberry, sweet fern, and willow.

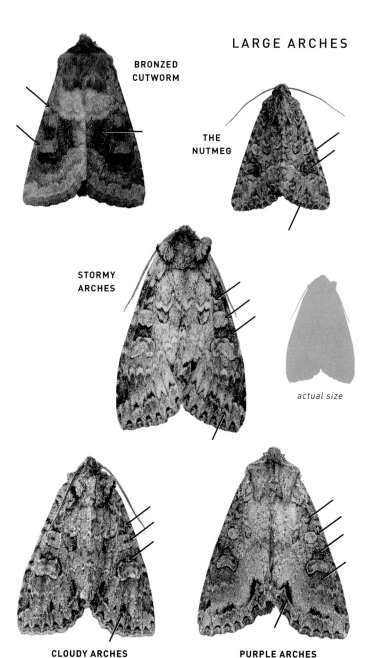

LARGE ARCHES

BRONZED CUTWORM

THE NUTMEG

STORMY ARCHES

actual size

CLOUDY ARCHES

PURPLE ARCHES

487

HITCHED ARCHES
Melanchra adjuncta 93-2874 (10292) **Common**
TL 19–21 mm. Dark gray FW is marked with striking pattern of fragmented white lines. Orbicular spot is narrowly outlined white. Large reniform spot is white with dark central crescent. **HOSTS:** Deciduous trees and low plants, including alder, clover, elm, and plantain. **NOTE:** Two broods.

ZEBRA CATERPILLAR MOTH
Melanchra picta 93-2875 (10293) **Common**
TL 18–22 mm. Maroon FW has yellowish shading along inner margin and white frosting along veins. Gray teardrop-shaped orbicular spot and hourglass-shaped reniform spots are edged white. HW is white. **HOSTS:** Various trees, crops, and low plants. **NOTE:** Two or more broods.

BLACK ARCHES
Melanchra assimilis 93-2877 (10295) **Common**
TL 18–22 mm. Sooty gray FW is marked with crisp black lines and outlines to spots. Inner margin is rusty brown. Inner ST line forms a distinct cream-colored patch. **HOSTS:** Deciduous trees, shrubs, and low plants, including alder, ash, birch, Labrador tea, and willow.

ATLANTIC ARCHES
Lacanobia atlantica 93-2879 (10297) **Uncommon**
TL 20–22 mm. Grayish brown FW has straw-colored shoulder patch extending along costa. Thin black basal dash and black-edged claviform spot are boldest markings. Slanting pale orbicular spot almost touches gray-filled reniform spot. Midpoint of whitish ST line is W-shaped. **HOSTS:** Deciduous trees and low plants, including alfalfa, clover, dandelion, honeysuckle, poplar, and willow. **RANGE:** S. Canada and n. U.S.

SUBDUED ARCHES
Lacanobia subjuncta 93-2881 (10299) **Common**
TL 18–22 mm. Grayish brown FW has warm brown basal patch and shading in outer median area. Basal and inner median areas are marked with black dashes. Midpoint of pale ST line is W-shaped. Inner PM line is a white crescent. **HOSTS:** Deciduous trees and woody and herbaceous plants; sometimes a pest. **NOTE:** Two broods.

LARGE ARCHES

HITCHED ARCHES

ZEBRA CATERPILLAR MOTH

BLACK ARCHES

actual size

ATLANTIC ARCHES

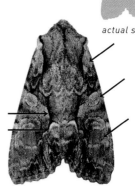

SUBDUED ARCHES

GRAND ARCHES *Lacanobia grandis* 93-2882 (10300) **Common**
TL 22–23 mm. Violet gray FW has reddish brown shading in median area. Scalloped lines fade before reaching costa. Basal and inner median areas are marked with thick black bars. Midpoint of white ST line is W-shaped. **HOSTS:** Deciduous trees, including alder, aspen, cherry, flowering dogwood, and willow.

OTTER ARCHES *Spiramater lutra* 93-2883 (10301) **Common**
TL 20–22 mm. Resembles Scripted Arches but is smaller. Gray FW has rust-colored patches in basal area. Scalloped blackish lines are fine and indistinct. Orbicular and reniform spots are thickly outlined white. Claviform spot larger than orbicular spot. **HOSTS:** Deciduous trees, including aspen, birch, maple, and willow.

WRINKLED TRICHORDESTRA
Trichordestra rugosa 93-2884 (10302) **Uncommon**
TL 17–19 mm. Lilac gray FW has reddish brown shading in median area and beyond slightly kinked yellow ST line. White veins extend through median area. Black basal dash, claviform spot, and patches on either side of orbicular spot create "gothic" pattern. **HOSTS:** Black chokeberry.

TACOMA ARCHES
Trichordestra tacoma 93-2885 (10303) **Uncommon**
TL 19 mm. Pale lilac gray FW has rusty brown shading in basal area. Median area is marked with blackish claviform spot and patches on either side of gray orbicular spot and rust-colored reniform spot. **HOSTS:** Various trees and low plants, including black chokeberry, elderberry, and willow. **RANGE:** S. Canada and n. U.S.

STRIPED GARDEN CATERPILLAR MOTH
Trichordestra legitima 93-2886 (10304) **Common**
TL 20 mm. Resembles Tacoma Arches, but lacks black patches around reniform spot. Pale lilac gray FW has reddish brown shading along costa and in outer median area. Claviform spot is black. Reniform spot has gray dot in inner half. **HOSTS:** Wide variety of crops and low plants; sometimes a pest.

SCRIPTED ARCHES
Mamestra curialis 93-2899 (10272) **Common**
TL 26 mm. Peppery gray FW has indistinct blackish lines. Reniform spots are boldly edged white. Claviform spot same size as orbicular spot. Inner ST area is contrastingly pale gray. **HOSTS:** Low plants and grasses, including clover and dandelion. **RANGE:** Se. Canada and ne. U.S.

LARGE ARCHES

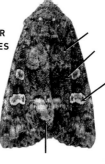

OTTER ARCHES

GRAND ARCHES

actual size

WRINKLED TRICHORDESTRA

TACOMA ARCHES

STRIPED GARDEN CATERPILLAR MOTH

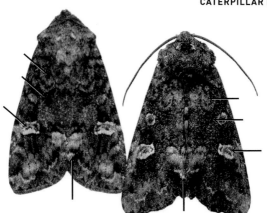

SCRIPTED ARCHES

ROSEWING *Sideridis rosea* 93-2906 (10265) **Common**
TL 23–28 mm. Peppery pale orange FW has chestnut band beyond jagged cream-colored ST line. Rusty brown lines and outlines to spots are often indistinct. Reniform spot has black dot in inner half. **HOSTS:** Russian olive, gooseberry, soapberry, and willow.

THE GERMAN COUSIN
Sideridis congermana 93-2907 (10266) **Uncommon**
TL 21 mm. Rusty brown FW has indistinct pale orange lines and apical patch. Inconspicuous orbicular spot is edged pale gray. White-edged reniform spot is partly filled with white scales. Thorax has pale orange dorsal stripe. **HOSTS:** Unknown.

CAPSULE MOTH
Hadena capsularis 93-2911 (10317) **Common**
TL 15–17 mm. Gray FW has black AM and PM lines connected by wedge-shaped claviform spot. Large round orbicular spot is thickly outlined white. Three black dashes cut through ST area near anal angle. **HOSTS:** Seed capsules of pinks.

WHEAT HEAD ARMYWORM
Dargida diffusa 93-2928 (10431) **Common**
TL 15–19 mm. Straw-colored FW has gray outer margin beyond ST line. Bold white streak extends through wing, contrasting with black basal dash. Slanting black apical dash curves toward black reniform dot. Thorax has whitish stripes. **HOSTS:** Mostly grasses, also corn and wheat. **NOTE:** Two or more broods.

THE PINK-STREAK
Dargida rubripennis 93-2931 (10434) **Uncommon**
TL 18–21 mm. Straw-colored FW has broad white-edged pink streak extending from base to anal angle. A wedge of pink shading slants inward from apex. Thorax is cinnamon with whitish dorsal stripe and collar. Heavy tufts of hairlike scales on foretibia. **HOSTS:** Crabgrass.

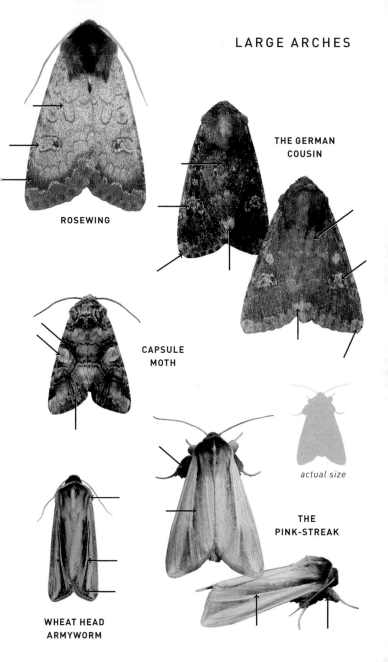

LARGE ARCHES

ROSEWING

THE GERMAN COUSIN

CAPSULE MOTH

WHEAT HEAD ARMYWORM

actual size

THE PINK-STREAK

WAINSCOTS
Family Noctuidae, Subfamily Noctuinae, Tribe Leucaniini

Medium-sized, mostly tan-colored noctuid moths that exhibit faint streaky FW patterns. Distinguishing features are often subtle, making species difficult to tell apart. Ursula and False wainscots have distinctive, thick "leggings." Flying mostly in midsummer and fall, they are often found in old fields and wetlands. All are nocturnal and will come to light in small numbers. The White-Speck will also come to sugar bait and can often be very numerous.

LESSER WAINSCOT
Mythimna oxygala   93-2933 (10436)   **Common**
TL 18 mm. Pale yellow FW is evenly striated with thin brown lines between veins. Whitish streak extending through central median area diverges at black reniform dot. ST line is accented with two black dots. **HOSTS:** Grasses. **RANGE:** Widespread **NOTE:** Three broods. .

THE WHITE-SPECK
Mythimna unipuncta   93-2935 (10438)   **Common**
TL 20–25 mm. FW is variably straw colored to orange-brown, finely peppered with dusky scales. Indistinct orbicular and reniform spots are often orange. A tiny white speck touches inner part of reniform spot. A thin dark line slants inward from apex. **HOSTS:** Mostly grasses and cereals; sometimes a major pest on crops. **NOTE:** Several broods.

LINEN WAINSCOT   *Leucania linita* 93-2938 (10440)   **Common**
TL 18 mm. Pale straw-colored FW is evenly striated with faint brown lines between veins. Darker brown central streak ends at black-edged white reniform dot. PM line is a complete row of tiny dots. **HOSTS:** Orchard grass.

PHRAGMITES WAINSCOT
Leucania phragmitidicola   93-2943 (10444)   **Common**
TL 18–19 mm. Pale tan FW is weakly tinted warm brown through median area. A brown-edged whitish streak extends from base to tiny black reniform dot. PM line is an even row of tiny blackish dots. **HOSTS:** Grasses. **NOTE:** Two broods.

LINDA'S WAINSCOT
Leucania linda   93-2944 (10445)   **Common**
TL 20–21 mm. Resembles Phragmites Wainscot, but FW is strongly tinted reddish brown. PM line is an even row of well-defined blackish dots. **HOSTS:** Unknown. **NOTE:** Two broods.

LESSER
WAINSCOT

THE
WHITE-SPECK

LINEN
WAINSCOT

light

dark

actual size

PHRAGMITES WAINSCOT

LINDA'S WAINSCOT

MANY-LINED WAINSCOT

Leucania multilinea   93-2945 (10446)   **Common**
TL 19–20 mm. Pale tan FW has thin black-edged white streak extending from base to tiny black reniform dot. Faint brown streak extends along inner margin. PM line is accented with two black dots. Thorax has collar of three parallel grayish lines. **HOSTS:** Grasses. **NOTE:** Two broods.

COMMA WAINSCOT

Leucania commoides   93-2947 (10447)   **Common**
TL 20–21 mm. Resembles Many-lined Wainscot, but darker FW is marked with bolder black and white streaks. Median area is often shaded brown. Thorax has narrow dark brown lateral stripes and grayish collar. **HOSTS:** Grasses.

HETERODOX WAINSCOT

Leucania insueta   93-2948 (10449)   **Common**
TL 18–19 mm. Pale tan FW is peppered with dusky scales along pale costal streak. Streaks of brown shading pass through median area and along outer margin. Peppery whitish streaks extend through inner and central median areas. PM line is an even row of black dashes. **HOSTS:** Grasses. **RANGE:** S. Canada and ne. U.S. **NOTE:** Two broods.

SCIRPUS WAINSCOT

Leucania scirpicola   93-2957 (10455)   **Common**
TL 18–21 mm. Resembles Linen Wainscot, but FW is tinted with tawny shading through median area. Dusky median streak passes through bold white discal spot. Thorax has brown lateral stripes. **HOSTS:** Grasses.

ADJUTANT WAINSCOT

Leucania adjuta   93-2960 (10456)   **Common**
TL 18–20 mm. Resembles Many-lined Wainscot, but straw-colored FW is marked with faint brown streaks. Pale central line extends beyond black discal dot and is accented with a black dot at midpoint. Thorax has speckled gray bands behind head. **HOSTS:** Orchard grass. **RANGE:** Sw. ON and e. U.S.

UNARMED WAINSCOT

Leucania inermis   93-2963 (10459)   **Common**
TL 17 mm. Pale grayish tan FW is sprinkled with dusky scales. Zigzag PM line appears as one or two rows of blackish dots. Pale reniform spot has dusky dot in inner half. Foretibia is slightly hairy in both sexes. **HOSTS:** Orchard grass. **RANGE:** Se. Canada and e. U.S. **NOTE:** Two broods.

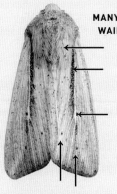

MANY-LINED WAINSCOT

COMMA WAINSCOT

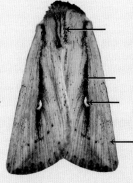

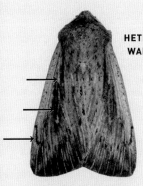

HETERODOX WAINSCOT

SCIRPUS WAINSCOT

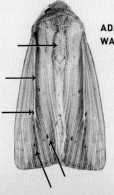

ADJUTANT WAINSCOT

UNARMED WAINSCOT

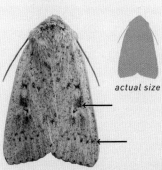

actual size

URSULA WAINSCOT

Leucania ursula   93-2965 (10461)   **Common**
TL 19 mm. Resembles Unarmed Wainscot, but foretibia of male
(shown) has large tufts of hairlike scales. Females of the two
species are virtually identical. **HOSTS:** Crabgrass and honeysuckle. **NOTE:** Two broods.

FALSE WAINSCOT

Leucania pseudargyria   93-2966 (10462)   **Common**
TL 26 mm. Resembles Unarmed and Ursula wainscots but usu-
ally is larger. FW typically has strong reddish tint. A reddish
brown streak cuts through pale orbicular and reniform spots.
Foretibia of male (shown) has massive tufts of hairlike scales.
HOSTS: Grasses.

SMALL ARCHES AND SUMMER QUAKERS
Family Noctuidae, Subfamily Noctuinae, Tribe Eriopygini

A group of small noctuid moths that are on the wing during summer and
early fall. Typically they are found in woodlands and old fields, but sometimes in gardens. The arches are mostly intricately patterned, brightly colored with defined spots. The small summer quakers are mostly brown or
chestnut and typically show a more rounded wing shape. All are nocturnal
and regularly come to light in small or moderate numbers.

THE THINKER

Lacinipolia meditata   93-3016 (10368)   **Common**
TL 15–17 mm. Peppery FW is variably brownish to purplish
gray, often with warm brown shading in basal and median areas. Scalloped lines and spots are edged with gray. Reniform
spot is black at inner end. **HOSTS:** Low plants, including clover,
dandelion, and tobacco. **NOTE:** Two broods.

SNAKY ARCHES

Lacinipolia anguina   93-3019 (10372)   **Uncommon**
TL 15–16 mm. Peppery medium gray FW has darker median
area. White-edged AM and PM lines are indistinct. Gray orbicular and reniform spots are outlined whitish. Whitish inner ST
line is marked with broken black dash. **HOSTS:** Unknown.

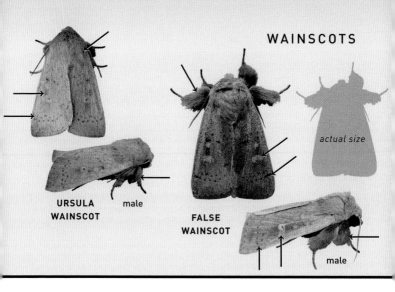

WAINSCOTS

actual size

URSULA WAINSCOT   male

FALSE WAINSCOT   male

SMALL ARCHES AND SUMMER QUAKERS

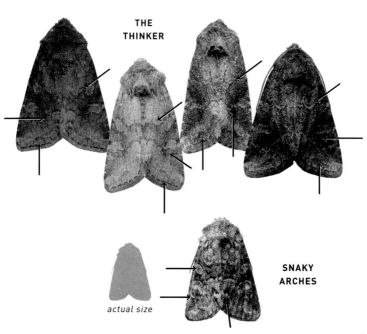

THE THINKER

SNAKY ARCHES

actual size

499

NEIGHBORLY ARCHES

Lacinipolia vicina   93-3040 (10394)   **Uncommon**
TL 15–16 mm. Ash gray FW is peppered with whitish scales.
Black-edged claviform spot is shaded rusty brown. Short black
basal dash cuts through whitish basal line. Slanting orbicular
spot is open-sided toward costa. **HOSTS:** Reported on alfalfa
and dandelion. **RANGE:** W. Canada and U.S. and Great Lakes region.

BRISTLY CUTWORM

Lacinipolia renigera   93-3044 (10397)   **Common**
TL 14–15 mm. Purplish gray FW is mottled pinkish brown along
veins. Lime green basal dash, center of white-edged reniform
spot, and patch near anal angle are obvious when fresh. Claviform spot is solid black. **HOSTS:** Wide variety of crops and low
plants. **NOTE:** Two or more broods.

BRIDLED ARCHES

Lacinipolia lorea   93-3052 (10405)   **Common**
TL 18–20 mm. Yellowish brown FW is paler beyond curved PM
line. Inner median bar is darker brown. Reniform spot has gray
dot in inner half. **HOSTS:** Low plants, including alfalfa, blueberry, clover, dandelion, and sweet fern.

OLIVE ARCHES

Lacinipolia olivacea   93-3053 (10406)   **Common**
TL 14–15 mm. Resembles Snaky Arches but is darker and has
more pointed FW. Peppery whitish FW has darker shading in
basal and median areas. Lines are accented with moss green
scales when fresh. Whitish reniform spot almost touches pale
ST band. **HOSTS:** Low plants, including dandelion, phlox, and
plantain.

LAUDABLE ARCHES

Lacinipolia laudabilis   93-3065 (10411)   **Common**
TL 16 mm. Pale green FW is marked with white-filled double
lines. Grayish brown shading in central median area clashes
with orange patch between orbicular and reniform spots.
HOSTS: Dandelion. **NOTE:** Two broods.

EXPLICIT ARCHES

Lacinipolia explicata   93-3067 (10413)   **Common**
TL 15–17 mm. Whitish FW has basal and median areas shaded
with brown or greenish scales. AM and PM lines are edged
white. White ST line is pierced by a black dash near anal angle.
HOSTS: Unknown. **NOTE:** Two broods.

SMALL ARCHES AND SUMMER QUAKERS

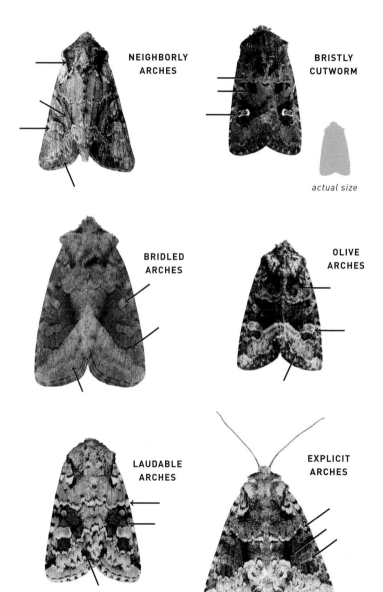

NEIGHBORLY ARCHES

BRISTLY CUTWORM

actual size

BRIDLED ARCHES

OLIVE ARCHES

LAUDABLE ARCHES

EXPLICIT ARCHES

IMPLICIT ARCHES

Lacinipolia implicata   93-3068 (10414)   **Uncommon**

TL 15–17 mm. White FW is tinted pale green when fresh. Grayish brown median area is narrow at inner margin in male. Black AM and PM lines are often incomplete. Basal and inner median areas are marked with black bars. Orbicular and reniform spots typically are separated by warm brown patch. **HOSTS:** Reported on dead leaves, dandelion, and various herbs.

UNITED CUTWORM

Anhimella contrahens   93-3086 (10530)   **Common**

TL 16 mm. Brownish tan FW has peppery veins and a pinkish sheen when fresh. AM and PM lines are edged pale yellow. Orbicular and reniform spots are dusky with incomplete pale outlines. **HOSTS:** Dandelion. **RANGE:** W. Canada and U.S. and Great Lakes region.

NORTHERN SCURFY QUAKER

Homorthodes furfurata   93-3088 (10532)   **Common**

TL 14 mm. FW is variably pale tan to reddish brown, peppered with white along veins. Scalloped lines are inconspicuous. Pale orbicular spot is often the most noticeable marking. Reniform spot has black dot in inner half. Some individuals show an angled dusky median band. **HOSTS:** Maple.

BANDED QUAKER

Protorthodes incincta   93-3105 (10552)   **Common**

TL 16–17 mm. Grayish brown FW is often tinted warm brown in median area. AM and PM lines are inconspicuous. Pale-outlined reniform spot has black dot in inner half. Midpoint of yellowish ST line is accented with blackish wedges. **HOSTS:** Unknown, but often found in sand dunes and prairies. **RANGE:** W. Canada and U.S. and Great Lakes region.

RUDDY QUAKER

Protorthodes oviduca   93-3113 (10563)   **Common**

TL 15 mm. Brown FW is densely peppered with pale gray scales along darker veins and lines. Median area is often chestnut brown. Blackish orbicular and reniform spots are outlined whitish. Slightly wavy ST line is pale orange. **HOSTS:** Dandelion, grasses, and plantain. **NOTE:** Two broods.

SHEATHED QUAKER

Ulolonche culea   93-3118 (10567)   **Uncommon**

TL 18 mm. Yellowish brown FW has crisp yellowish AM and PM lines that converge near inner margin. Pale-outlined reniform spot has black dot in inner half. Shallowly toothed ST line is accented with tiny black dots. **HOSTS:** Red oak.

SMALL ARCHES AND SUMMER QUAKERS

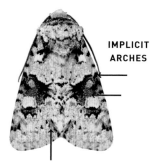

IMPLICIT ARCHES

UNITED CUTWORM

actual size

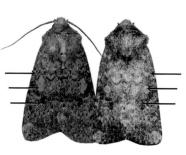

NORTHERN SCURFY QUAKER

BANDED QUAKER

RUDDY QUAKER

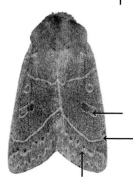

SHEATHED QUAKER

MODEST QUAKER

Ulolonche modesta   93-3120 (10569)   **Common**
TL 15 mm. Ash gray FW has bold, slightly scalloped black lines. White orbicular spot is outlined black. Reniform spot has a fragmented white outline. ST line is a row of black crescents. **HOSTS:** Unknown. **RANGE:** Se. Canada and ne. U.S.

SMALL BROWN QUAKER

Pseudorthodes vecors   93-3128 (10578)   **Common**
TL 15 mm. FW is variably tan to reddish brown with inconspicuous scalloped lines. Reniform spot is filled with either white or orange scales. ST line is a diffuse row of short blackish dashes. **HOSTS:** Dandelion, plantain, and grasses. **NOTE:** Two broods.

RUSTIC QUAKER

Orthodes majuscula   93-3136 (10585)   **Common**
TL 19 mm. Peppery reddish brown FW has crisp pale yellow lines. PM line kinks inward near costa. Large orbicular and reniform spots almost touch. Thoracic collar has a black triangle just behind head. **HOSTS:** Low plants, including dandelion, plantain, and grasses.

CYNICAL QUAKER

Orthodes cynica   93-3138 (10587)   **Common**
TL 15–17 mm. Reddish brown FW is marked with orange-edged black lines. Inconspicuous orbicular and reniform spots do not touch. Wavy ST line is edged pale orange. Scales seem to wear off rapidly. **HOSTS:** Dandelion and goldenrod. **NOTE:** Two broods.

GOODELL'S ARCHES

Orthodes goodelli   93-3141 (10289)   **Common**
TL 17–18 mm. Chestnut brown FW is peppered with black and white scales along veins. AM and PM lines are edged pale fawn. Claviform spot is weakly outlined black. Reniform spot is partly outlined and filled with white scales. **HOSTS:** Unknown. **RANGE:** E. Canada and e. U.S.

DISPARAGED ARCHES

Orthodes detracta   93-3146 (10288)   **Common**
TL 17–18 mm. Gray FW has brown shading in basal and median areas. All lines are indistinct. Claviform spot is black, often with an orange patch beyond it. Orbicular and reniform spots are edged white. **HOSTS:** Deciduous trees and low plants, including blueberry, clover, hickory, and oak.

SMALL ARCHES AND SUMMER QUAKERS

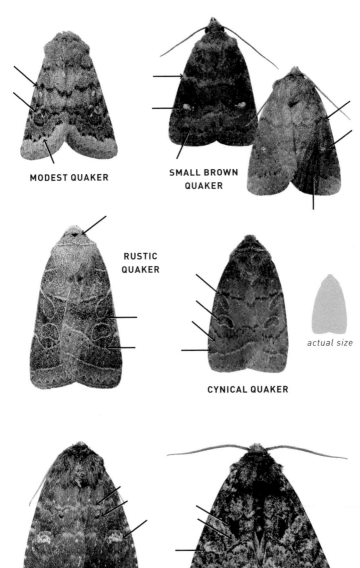

MODEST QUAKER

SMALL BROWN
QUAKER

RUSTIC
QUAKER

CYNICAL QUAKER

actual size

GOODELL'S ARCHES

DISPARAGED ARCHES

SIGNATE QUAKER

Tricholita signata   93-3193 (10627)   **Common**
TL 15–18 mm. FW is variably brown to reddish brown with
white-peppered veins. Angled median band touches reniform
spot. Orbicular spot can be orange or brown. Reniform spot is
either brown or orange with a fractured white border. **HOSTS:**
Low plants, including dandelion and plantain.

SPANISH MOTH
Family Noctuidae, Subfamily Noctuinae, Tribe Glottulini

A distinct species that cannot be confused. The pink, orange, and black FW
may bring to mind traditional Spanish patterning. A southeastern species
that just enters ne. N. America. Comes to light.

SPANISH MOTH   *Xanthopastis timais* 93-3210 (10640)   **Common**
TL 21–24 mm. Pink FW has black shading along costa and outer
median area. Basal dash and edging to orbicular and reniform
spots are bright golden yellow. **HOSTS:** Figs, spider lily, and nar-
cissus.

DARTS
Family Noctuidae, Subfamily Noctuinae, Tribe Noctuini

Medium-sized moths with long, moderately narrow FW. Many are late season fliers found in old fields and gardens. They are mostly nocturnal and
will come to light, but a few can be found taking nectar from flowers during
daylight hours. Some, such as Ipsilon Dart and Pearly Underwing, can frequently be found at sugar bait.

PEARLY UNDERWING

Peridroma saucia   93-3211 (10915)   **Common**
TL 25 mm. Mottled FW is variably pale tan to chestnut brown.
Jagged AM and PM lines are double, though often indistinct.
Large oval orbicular spot is outlined black. Costa is checkered
with black spots. Thorax has raised frosty dorsal stripe. **HOSTS:**
Wide variety of trees, crops, and low plants. **NOTE:** Two or more
broods. Also known as Variegated Cutworm.

GREEN CUTWORM   *Anicla infecta*   93-3212 (10911)   **Common**
TL 17–20 mm. Pale lilac gray FW is variably peppered with
dusky scales. Outer margin is violet brown beyond wavy white
ST line. Reniform spot is filled with a mosaic of black fragments. Thorax has thick black collar behind head. **HOSTS:** Low
plants, including beet, clover, grasses, tobacco.

SMALL ARCHES AND SUMMER QUAKERS

SIGNATE QUAKER

actual size

SPANISH MOTH

actual size

SPANISH MOTH

DARTS

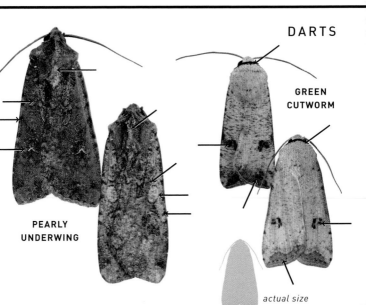

GREEN CUTWORM

PEARLY UNDERWING

actual size

SLIPPERY DART
Anicla lubricans   93-3214 (10901)   **Common**
TL 17–20 mm. Ash gray FW has bands of reddish brown shading in median area and beyond faint PM line. Lines are obvious as black spots along costa. Reniform spot has fragmented black center. HW is pearly gray with terminal line and white fringe. Thorax has narrow black collar. **HOSTS:** Unknown. **NOTE:** Two broods.

SNOWY DART
Anicla illapsa   93-3216 (10903)   **Common**
TL 17–19 mm. Resembles Slippery Dart but has more northerly distribution. HW is strikingly white. **HOSTS:** Unknown. **NOTE:** Two broods.

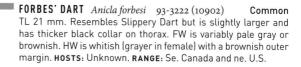

FORBES' DART   *Anicla forbesi*   93-3222 (10902)   **Common**
TL 21 mm. Resembles Slippery Dart but is slightly larger and has thicker black collar on thorax. FW is variably pale gray or brownish. HW is whitish (grayer in female) with a brownish outer margin. **HOSTS:** Unknown. **RANGE:** Se. Canada and ne. U.S.

WESTERN BEAN CUTWORM
Striacosta albicosta   93-3228 (10878)   **Uncommon**
TL 19–20 mm. Purplish gray FW has straw-colored costal streak that fades before apex. Incomplete AM line separates thick black basal dash from hollow claviform spot. Brown orbicular and reniform spots are outlined white. HW is strikingly white. **HOSTS:** Low plants and crops, including bean, corn, and tomato. **NOTE:** An invasive species from w. N. America.

FINNISH DART
Actebia fennica   93-3229 (10924)   **Uncommon**
TL 20–22 mm. Violet gray FW has indistinct blackish lines and outlines to spots. Male (shown) has distinctive pale orange streak along inner margin. Narrow claviform spot is outlined black. Two black dashes point inward from inconspicuous ST line. **HOSTS:** Deciduous trees and low plants, including blueberry, elm, and clover.

INCLINED DART
Dichagyris acclivis   93-3232 (10870)   **Common**
TL 18 mm. Grayish FW has paler brown shading along basal half of costa. Short claviform spot is outlined black. Orbicular spot is streaklike. Pale reniform spot is flanked by short black streaks. ST line is a row of pale dashes. **HOSTS:** Unknown. **RANGE:** E. U.S. and sw. ONT.

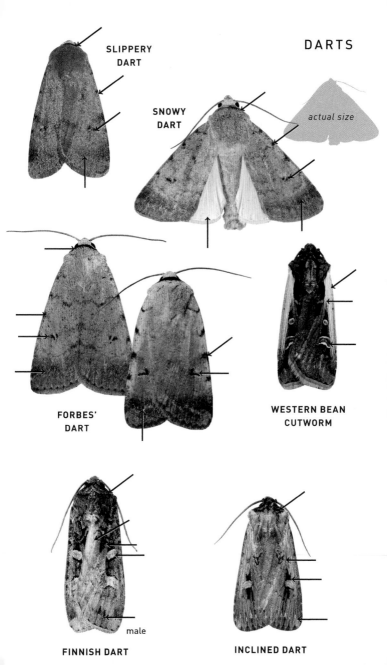

DARTS

SLIPPERY DART

SNOWY DART

actual size

FORBES' DART

WESTERN BEAN CUTWORM

FINNISH DART

male

INCLINED DART

509

REAPER DART *Euxoa messoria* 93-3319 (10705) **Common**
TL 20 mm. Mottled brown FW has double, slightly scalloped AM
and PM lines. Large ovate orbicular spot is narrowly outlined
black. Reniform spot is thickly edged black on basal side.
HOSTS: Many forbs and woody plants; sometimes a pest.

DIVERGENT DART
Euxoa divergens 93-3320 (10702) **Uncommon**
TL 17–21 mm. Grayish brown FW has whitish veins on either
side of black median streak. Orbicular and reniform spots are
edged whitish. Scalloped PM and ST lines are edged pale tan.
HOSTS: Unknown.

WHITE CUTWORM *Euxoa scandens* 93-3329 (10715) **Common**
TL 20–22 mm. Sandy gray FW is tinted warm brown when fresh.
Dotted AM and PM lines are indistinct. Whitish orbicular spot is
finely edged black. White-edged reniform spot has a black dot in
inner half. ST line is a row of white dots. **HOSTS:** Crops and other
low plants, often on sandy soils. **RANGE:** S. Canada and ne. U.S.

TESSELLATE DART *Euxoa tessellata* 93-3395 (10805) **Common**
TL 19 mm. FW is variably grayish to dusky brown, often tinted
lilac. AM and PM lines are double. Pale gray orbicular spot has
black shading on either side of it. Gray reniform spot has pale
dot in middle. **HOSTS:** Low plants and crops, including corn,
squash, and tobacco.

WHITE-STRIPED DART
Euxoa albipennis 93-3397 (10807) **Common**
TL 18–19 mm. FW is variably dark gray to bronzy brown, often
darker along costa and beyond ST line. Large gray orbicular
spot is open-sided toward costa. Reniform spot has a black dot
in inner half. **HOSTS:** Unknown. **RANGE:** Se. Canada and ne. U.S.

FLEECE-WINGED DART
Euxoa velleripennis 93-3411 (10803) **Common**
TL 19 mm. Dark gray FW has indistinct blackish lines. Dark
gray orbicular and reniform spots have fragmented black outlines. HW is white with a dusky terminal line in male, grayer in
female. **HOSTS:** Unknown.

OBELISK DART *Euxoa obeliscoides* 93-3428 (10817) **Common**
TL 19 mm. Dark grayish brown FW has contrasting whitish costal streak ending at PM line. Scalloped AM and PM lines fade
before reaching costa. Large pale orbicular and reniform spots
are partly filled with brown. **HOSTS:** Unknown.

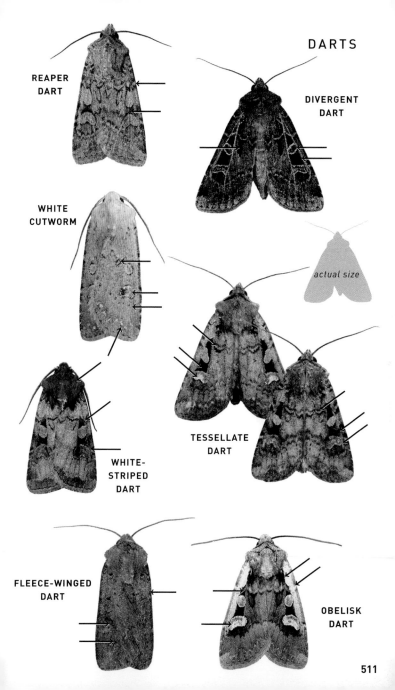

DARTS

REAPER
DART

DIVERGENT
DART

WHITE
CUTWORM

actual size

WHITE-
STRIPED
DART

TESSELLATE
DART

FLEECE-WINGED
DART

OBELISK
DART

FILLET DART *Euxoa redimicula* 93-3440 (10851) **Common**
TL 15–17 mm. Violet gray FW has contrasting thick black basal dash and median streak. Large orbicular and reniform spots are pale gray. Sinuous ST line has a band of darker shading beyond it. **HOSTS:** Unknown.

 RUBBED DART *Euxoa detersa* 93-3461 (10838) **Common**
TL 17–18 mm. Ash gray FW is marbled with white and brown scales. Scalloped lines are indistinct. Brownish orbicular and reniform spots are outlined black. Darker individuals have dusky FW with white orbicular spot. **HOSTS:** Low plants and crops, including corn, cranberry, and tobacco.

SOFT DART *Feltia mollis* 93-3488 (10644) **Uncommon**
TL 17–19 mm. Pale grayish tan FW is tinged warm brown in median and ST areas. Large pale gray orbicular spot interrupts a sharply defined black bar in central median area. Claviform spot is incompletely edged black. **HOSTS:** Blueberry. **RANGE:** S. Canada and n. U.S.

 KNEE-JOINT DART
Feltia geniculata 93-3495 (10680) **Common**
TL 18–19 mm. Peppery gray FW has purplish brown bands in median area and beyond PM line. Whitish orbicular and reniform are open-ended toward costa. Central median area is black. Hollow claviform spot ends as a black dash. **HOSTS:** Unknown; probably crops and low plants.

 DINGY CUTWORM *Feltia jaculifera* 93-3498 (10670) **Common**
TL 21 mm. Grayish FW has complex pattern of dark markings between whitish veins. Reniform spot is often pale orange. Long black claviform spot is separated from black basal patch by incomplete white AM line. **HOSTS:** Various trees, crops, and grasses.

 SUBGOTHIC DART
Feltia subgothica 93-3501 (10674) **Common**
TL 19–20 mm. Warm brown FW has pattern similar to that of Dingy Cutworm, but lacks whitish veins. Reniform spot is partly filled with brown. **HOSTS:** Many low plants and crops.

 MASTER'S DART *Feltia herilis* 93-3503 (10676) **Common**
TL 22–24 mm. Violet gray FW pattern similar to that of Subgothic Dart but is darker. Pale yellow streak extends through central median area. Crescent-shaped reniform spot is pale yellow. **HOSTS:** Various low plants and crops.

RUBBED DART

FILLET DART

SOFT DART

KNEE-JOINT DART

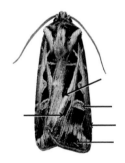

DINGY CUTWORM

SUBGOTHIC DART

MASTER'S DART

actual size

SUBTERRANEAN DART

Feltia subterranea   93-3504 (10664)   **Common**
TL 21–24 mm. FW is yellowish brown, with extensive gray shading covering inner half on female (not shown). Bulging double AM line touches orbicular spot. Black bar connects orbicular and reniform spots. **HOSTS:** Unknown.

OLD MAN DART   *Agrotis vetusta*   93-3506 (10641)   **Common**
TL 18–24 mm. Lilac gray FW has fragmented AM and PM lines accented with white. Reniform spot has a black dot in inner half. **HOSTS:** Plants and crops, including bean, corn, lettuce, tobacco, and tomato.

SWORDSMAN DART

Agrotis gladiaria   93-3515 (10648)   **Common**
TL 18–20 mm. Grayish brown FW is marked with pale veins. Claviform, orbicular, and reniform spots are crisply outlined with black. Dotted ST line is accented with white dots. **HOSTS:** Low plants and crops, including bean, corn, tobacco, and tomato.

VENERABLE DART

Agrotis venerabilis   93-3516 (10651)   **Common**
TL 18–22 mm. Straw-colored or brown FW has dark costal shading. Long claviform spot and reniform spot are blackish. Streaky orbicular spot is white. **HOSTS:** Low plants and crops, including alfalfa, chickweed, corn, tobacco, and tomato.

VOLUBLE DART   *Agrotis volubilis*   93-3521 (10659)   **Common**
TL 20–22 mm. Straw-colored or brown FW has slate gray costal shading. Orbicular and reniform spots are gray. Basal dash joins black-edged claviform spot. **HOSTS:** Many low plants and crops.

OBLIQUE DART   *Agrotis obliqua*   93-3522 (10660)   **Common**
TL 20–22 mm. Resembles Voluble Dart, but pinkish brown FW has faint gray costal shading. Orbicular and reniform spots are often joined by a black streak. Basal dash joins black-edged claviform spot. Plain ST area is faintly marked with thin black veins. **HOSTS:** Unknown. **RANGE:** Widespread.

RASCAL DART   *Agrotis malefida*   93-3526 (10661)   **Common**
TL 22–25 mm. Yellowish brown FW has dusky costal streak. Wavy AM line is double and filled with pale gray. Claviform and reniform spots are black. **HOSTS:** Low plants and crops, including clover, corn, and tomato.

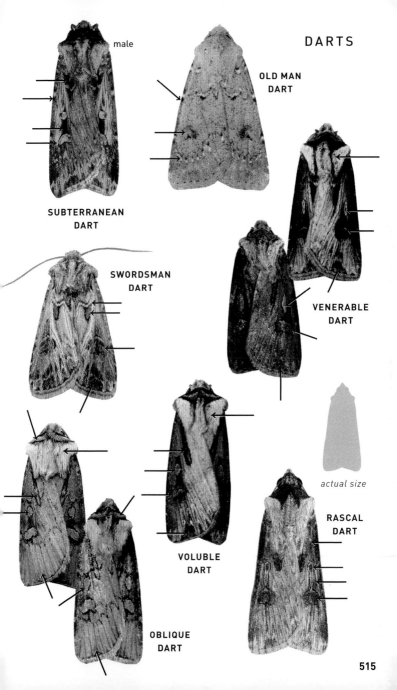

DARTS

male

OLD MAN
DART

SUBTERRANEAN
DART

SWORDSMAN
DART

VENERABLE
DART

actual size

VOLUBLE
DART

RASCAL
DART

OBLIQUE
DART

IPSILON DART *Agrotis ipsilon* 93-3528 (10663) **Common**
TL 22 mm. Brownish FW has variable gray shading along costa and median area. Hollow claviform spot and teardrop-shaped orbicular spot are finely outlined black. **HOSTS:** Low plants and crops, including bean, corn, potato, and tobacco. **NOTE:** Several broods.

FLAME-SHOULDERED DART

Ochropleura implecta 93-3529 (10891) **Common**
TL 15 mm. Chocolate brown FW has contrasting straw-colored costal streak. PM line is a row of black dots. Black basal dash is long. Orbicular spot is edged white. ST line is a faint row of orange dashes. **HOSTS:** Clover and other low plants. **NOTE:** Two broods.

SMALLER PINKISH DART

Diarsia jucunda 93-3533 (10919) **Common**
TL 19–20 mm. Grayish tan FW is variably shaded with pinkish brown shading. Lines are indistinct. Large white-edged orbicular and reniform spots usually have patches of black or chestnut shading between them. Has a long-snouted appearance. **HOSTS:** Grasses.

REDDISH SPECKLED DART

Cerastis tenebrifera 93-3536 (10994) **Common**
TL 18–19 mm. Chestnut brown FW has indistinct peppery AM and PM lines. Orbicular and reniform spots are pale yellow. Reniform spot has black dot in inner half. Wavy ST line is pale yellow. **HOSTS:** Dandelion, grape, and lettuce.

FISH'S DART *Cerastis fishii* 93-3537 (10997) **Uncommon**

TL 18–20 mm. Uniformly chestnut brown FW has inconspicuous lines. Hourglass-shaped reniform spot is partly edged yellow with black dot in inner half. Black subapical patch is part of dotted ST line. **HOSTS:** Blueberry.

WILLOW DART
Cerastis salicarum 93-3542 (10996) **Common**
TL 19–20 mm. Pale gray brown FW is darker beyond strongly angled median band. Clublike claviform spot is dark brown. Inconspicuous reniform spot is brown with a black dot in inner half. Whitish ST line is almost straight. **HOSTS:** Unknown, possibly willow. **RANGE:** S. Canada and n. U.S.

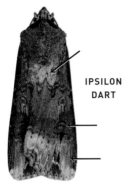

IPSILON DART

FLAME-SHOULDERED DART

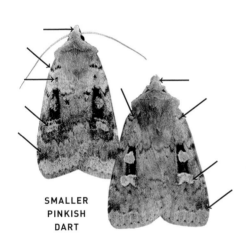

SMALLER PINKISH DART

REDDISH SPECKLED DART

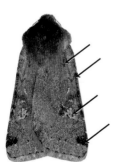

actual size

FISH'S DART

WILLOW DART

BENT-LINE DART

Cheophora fungorum   93-3543 (10998)   **Uncommon**
TL 21–27 mm. FW is variably pale tan to orange-brown. Bent AM and PM lines are dark brown. Blackish shading between inconspicuous orbicular and reniform spots bleeds into costal margin. HW is pale yellow with a dark median line. **HOSTS:** Low plants, including clover, dandelion, and tobacco.

LEAFY DART   *Lycophotia phyllophora*   93-3547 (11010)   **Common**

TL 18–20 mm. Pinkish gray FW has darker bands of reddish shading in median area and inside irregular ST line. Slightly scalloped AM and PM lines are double. Round orbicular spot has reddish center. Inconspicuous reniform spot has black dot in inner half. **HOSTS:** Alder, arrow-wood, birch, blueberry, cherry, and willow.

LARGE YELLOW UNDERWING

Noctua pronuba   93-3551 (11003.1)   **Common**
TL 30–35 mm. FW varies from pale tan to sooty brown. Reniform spot is filled with gray and black scales. Black subapical patch is always present. HW is golden yellow with black terminal band. **HOSTS:** Various grasses and low plants. **RANGE:** Widespread. **NOTE:** An introduced European species.

LESSER YELLOW UNDERWING

Noctua comes   93-3552 (11003.2)   **Uncommon**
TL 19–22 mm. FW is variably pale tan to chestnut brown with darker orbicular and reniform spots. Dark brown subapical patch is part of darker band along ST line. HW is golden yellow with black terminal line and narrow crescent near base. **HOSTS:** Various grasses and low plants. **RANGE:** Currently s. ON, but likely expanding. **NOTE:** An introduced European species.

CATOCALINE DART

Cryptocala acadiensis   93-3553 (11012)   **Common**
TL 15–17 mm. FW is variably grayish green to reddish brown with darker, angled median band. Teardrop-shaped orbicular spot is often fused to reniform spot. Blackish subapical patch is often noticeable. **HOSTS:** Arrowhead, cherry, dock, dogbane, elderberry, meadowsweet, yarrow, and others.

CLANDESTINE DART

Spaelotis clandestina   93-3554 (10926)   **Common**
TL 22 mm. Mousy gray FW has inconspicuous jagged AM and PM lines. Almond-shaped orbicular spot is joined to indistinct reniform spot by a black bar. **HOSTS:** Trees and low plants, including apple, blueberry, maple, and pine. **NOTE:** Two broods.

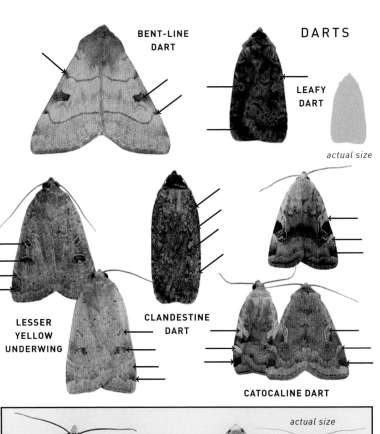

BENT-LINE DART

DARTS

LEAFY DART

actual size

LESSER YELLOW UNDERWING

CLANDESTINE DART

CATOCALINE DART

actual size

LARGE YELLOW UNDERWING

519

GREAT BROCADE

Eurois occulta   93-3560 (10929)   **Uncommon**
TL 29–35 mm. Large. Peppery gray FW has indistinct scalloped AM and PM lines. Whitish orbicular spot is often joined to indistinct reniform spot by a black bar. **HOSTS:** Tamarack, trembling aspen, alder, and willow. **NOTE:** Two broods, but most common in Aug.

DOUBLE DART

Graphiphora augur   93-3563 (10928)   **Common**
TL 27–29 mm. Mousy gray-brown FW is tinted purple when fresh. Jagged AM and PM lines are often fragmented. Orbicular and reniform spots typically have incomplete black outlines. Blackish wedge behind reniform spot is boldest marking. **HOSTS:** Birch and willow. **RANGE:** S. Canada and n. U.S.

GREEN ARCHES

Anaplectoides prasina   93-3564 (11000)   **Common**
TL 27–28 mm. Grayish brown FW has extensive mossy green accents along veins that fade rapidly with wear. Inconspicuous, scalloped AM and PM lines are double and partly filled with white. Typically has large whitish patch between reniform spot and ST line. **HOSTS:** Trees and low plants, including apple, cranberry, currant, honeysuckle, and knotweed.

DAPPLED DART

Anaplectoides pressus   93-3565 (11001)   **Common**
TL 18–20 mm. Pale grayish tan FW is peppered with brown scales. Yellow-green accents along veins fade rapidly with wear. Large claviform, orbicular, and reniform spots are partly outlined black. **HOSTS:** Corn salad.

SIGMOID DART

Eueretagrotis sigmoides   93-3568 (11007)   **Common**
TL 24 mm. Grayish brown FW has contrasting straw-colored costal streak that ends at blackish subapical patch. Thick black basal dash is almost connected to black median bar. Outer margin of wing is pale beyond wavy ST line. **HOSTS:** Unknown.

TWO-SPOT DART

Eueretagrotis perattentus   93-3569 (11008)   **Common**
TL 21 mm. Reddish brown FW has slightly paler costal streak. Thick black basal dash is widely separated from black median bar. Area between PM and ST lines is dark. **HOSTS:** Blueberry and fire cherry.

DARTS

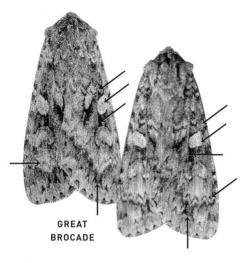

GREAT BROCADE

DOUBLE DART

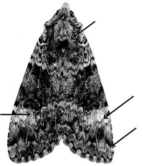

GREEN ARCHES

DAPPLED DART

actual size

SIGMOID DART

TWO-SPOT DART

521

ATTENTIVE DART
Eueretagrotis attentus   93-3570 (11009)   **Common**
TL 16–19 mm. Reddish brown FW has slightly paler costal streak. Black basal dash is the only obvious marking. Orbicular and reniform spots are narrowly outlined black. **HOSTS:** Birch, blueberry, elderberry, strawberry, and willow.

SMITH'S DART   *Xestia smithii*   93-3572 (10944)   **Common**
TL 20–23 mm. FW is variably pale tan to violet gray with chocolate brown lines and shading. Large round orbicular spot is outlined brown. Reniform spot has a black dot in inner half. Subapical patch is blackish brown. **HOSTS:** Trees and low plants, including alder, birch, and violet.

NORMAN'S DART
Xestia normaniana   93-3573 (10943)   **Common**
TL 20–22 mm. Pale grayish tan FW has brownish lines and peppery shading in median area. Black median bar passes on either side of slanting orbicular spot and curls around outer edge of reniform spot. Basal dot and subapical patch are black. **HOSTS:** Low plants, including blueberry, raspberry, and plantain.

NORTHERN VARIABLE DART
Xestia badicollis   93-3584 (10968)   **Common**
TL 18–21 mm. FW is ash gray variably shaded pinkish brown. Black basal and median dashes are boldest markings. Toothed black PM line is edged white. Area between slanting orbicular spot and pale reniform spot is chestnut. **HOSTS:** White pine, also fir, hemlock, spruce, and tamarack.

DULL REDDISH DART
Xestia dilucida   93-3586 (10969)   **Common**
TL 18–21 mm. Ash gray FW has reddish brown shading along inner margin. Toothed black AM and PM lines are indistinct. Whitish reniform spot is conspicuous. **HOSTS:** Blueberry, leather-leaf, sweet gale, and tamarack. **NOTE:** Form "youngii" was formerly recognized as a full species, *Xestia youngii*.

SETACEOUS HEBREW CHARACTER
Xestia c-nigrum   93-3588 (10942)   **Common**
TL 15–19 mm. Coppery brown (male, shown) or bluish gray (female) FW has triangular, straw-colored orbicular spot that widens toward costa. Black basal dash, median bar, and subapical patches are conspicuous. Straight AM line may be useful in separating from Greater Black-letter Dart. **HOSTS:** Various low plants, crops, and grasses. **NOTE:** Two broods.

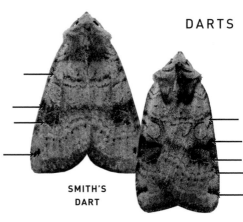

DARTS

**ATTENTIVE
DART**

**SMITH'S
DART**

NORMAN'S DART

**NORTHERN
VARIABLE
DART**

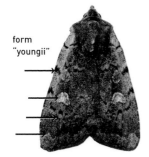

form
"youngii"

DULL REDDISH DART

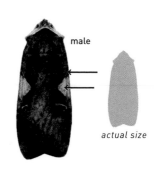

male

actual size

**SETACEOUS HEBREW
CHARACTER**

523

GREATER BLACK-LETTER DART

Xestia dolosa   93-3589 (10942.1)   **Common**
TL 20–21 mm. Very similar to smaller Setaceous Hebrew Character. Scalloped AM line may be useful in separating the two species. **HOSTS:** A wide variety of trees, crops, and low plants, including barley, clover, and tobacco. **NOTE:** Two broods.

PALE-BANDED DART

Agnorisma badinodis   93-3626 (10955)   **Uncommon**
TL 21 mm. Grayish brown FW has darker brown bands in median and ST areas. Kinked AM and shallowly curved PM lines are edged pale yellow. Intersection of orbicular spot and AM line is marked with a small black triangle. **HOSTS:** Apple, aster, chickweed, and dock.

COLLARED DART

Agnorisma bugrai   93-3627 (10954)   **Uncommon**
TL 17–20 mm. Grayish brown FW has band of darker shading inside sinuous ST line. Slightly kinked, double AM and evenly curved PM lines are filled with pale gray. Large gray orbicular spot has blackish patches on each side. Inner margin edged pale. **HOSTS:** Unknown.

PINK-SPOTTED DART

Pseudohermonassa bicarnea   93-3629 (10950)   **Common**
TL 18–24 mm. Blue-gray FW has pinkish patches in basal and subapical areas. Slanting gray orbicular spot cuts through black median bar. ST line is an even row of straw-colored dots. **HOSTS:** Deciduous trees and low plants, including blueberry, birch, and maple.

MORRISON'S SOOTY DART

Pseudohermonassa tenuicula   93-3630 (10951)   **Uncommon**
TL 18–20 mm. Violet gray FW has thick black basal dash and median bar. Pale yellow PM line is bent at costa. Slanting gray orbicular and reniform spots are partly edged yellow. Inner and outer margin edged pale. **HOSTS:** Unknown.

BROWN-COLLARED DART

Protolampra brunneicollis   93-3649 (11006)   **Common**
TL 20–22 mm. FW is variably pale tan to violet brown with inconspicuous lines and outlines to spots. PM line is a row of black dots. Subapical spot is blackish. Velvety, deep brown collar is darkest marking. **HOSTS:** Low plants, including blueberry, clover, dandelion, and tobacco. **NOTE:** Two broods.

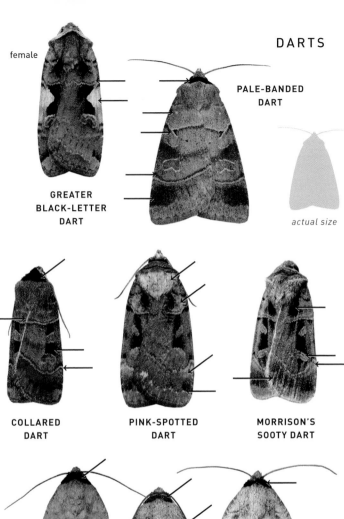

DARTS

female

PALE-BANDED
DART

GREATER
BLACK-LETTER
DART

actual size

COLLARED
DART

PINK-SPOTTED
DART

MORRISON'S
SOOTY DART

BROWN-COLLARED DART

GREATER RED DART
Abagrotis alternata 93-3680 (11029)   **Common**
TL 20–23 mm. Peppery FW is variably pale tan to reddish brown with inconspicuous AM and PM lines. Usually has pale terminal band beyond irregular ST line. Orbicular and reniform spots are dark brown, edged whitish. **HOSTS:** Deciduous trees and low plants, including apple, cabbage, hickory, oak, spruce, and walnut.

CUPID DART *Abagrotis cupida* 93-3685 (11043)   **Common**
TL 17–18 mm. Speckled FW is orange-brown with slightly paler terminal band and black subapical patch. Orbicular and reniform spots are often blackish. **HOSTS:** Apple, grape, peach, and willow. **RANGE:** Se. Canada and ne. U.S. **NOTE:** Two broods.

GREATER RED DART

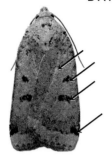

CUPID DART

actual size

Hydrangea Leaftier

Carmine Snout Moth

ACKNOWLEDGMENTS

Common Looper

This book would not have been possible without the goodwill and assistance of many people. I owe a huge debt of gratitude to the following:

Mike King for his amazing eye for detail and cheerful company on countless moth-catching trips. Mike also made many custom-built moth traps for me over the years and meticulously proofed the species accounts in their early stages. Mary de Bruyn also proofed later versions of the species accounts not once, but twice—a most valuable contribution that is much appreciated. Paul Prior likewise read through many accounts, providing many constructive comments that allowed me to understand the meaning of brevity! Steve Laforest and Carolyn King have joined me on many mothing weekends all over southern Ontario. Their boundless energy, logistical support, and delightful company are deeply appreciated. Dr. Donald Lafontaine, Christian Schmidt, and Jeff Crolla helped with tricky identifications throughout the project. Parker Backstrom essentially became "our man in the south" and kindly allowed us to use a huge number of his excellent moth photographs in the guide. The book will be of far greater appeal due to his important contribution. Jason Dombroskie allowed us to plunder his extensive photo library, providing photographs of several elusive species from the north. John Walas compiled a detailed list of the moths of his local area that was of great use when compiling the range maps. Likewise, Rosalind Chaundy provided species lists from her study sites in northern Ontario. Paul Pratt also provided much local information that was of great value. I'd like to thank Mark Peck, Brad Hubley, and Antonia Guidotti at the Royal Ontario Museum, Toronto, for kindly arranging access to the extensive Lepidoptera collection. Phil Milton and Ian Chrysler provided much insight regarding photographic techniques. Phil also provided me with top-notch moth traps during my annual visits to the UK.

I owe much to the folks who got me into moths in the first place. Ian Hunter and the late Dennis Batchelor provided the initial spark while I was working at Sandwich Bay Bird Observatory Trust way back in the early eighties. Francis Solly, Phil Milton, and Jon and Simon Curson rekindled my interest in later years.

Many people have kindly allowed access to their properties for my mothing activities. These include, in no particular order:

In Ontario, my long-suffering neighbors in Toronto—Henny and Howard and Mick and Barb for putting up with copious amounts of moth trap–related light pollution! Doug and Lois Thomas for unrivaled access to their great property at Portage Lake. Barry and Nancy Freeman, Elden and Jane Freeman, and Shawn and Noga Freeman welcomed me onto their properties at Portage Lake. Mary Gartshore and Peter Carson provided endless support and great moths in the South Walsingham area. Dale and Lloyd Leadbeater at Raven Lake were superb hosts during moth night events for the annual Carden Nature Festival. Karen and Brian Henshaw kindly gave me free run of their moth-rich garden at Brooklin. John Fulford and Sally Thomas welcomed moth traps into their garden while on holidays in Southampton. David Brewer provided some nice mothing opportunities at Puslinch. Alan McEachran and Cynthia Russel invited us several times to catch moths around their cottage at Dickey Lake. Steve Pike and Maurice Bottos provided great company and mothing locations in the Leamington area. Kim Baker and family allowed me to employ unorthodox catching techniques on high-flying moths at their home in Bracebridge. Emily Slavik and Kipling Campbell of Ontario Parks enthusiastically facilitated several moth events at Rondeau Provincial Park.

Elsewhere, Dave Shepherd and Julie Cappelman cheerfully put up with my moth traps in their back yard at Portugal Cove South in Newfoundland, even though the locals thought a UFO had landed behind their house on the first night! Merrill Lynch kindly arranged permission for us to catch moths at Nag's Head in North Carolina. My sister Rosemary let me run a moth trap on her balcony in Ramsgate, UK—often for weeks at a time! I am deeply indebted to them all.

Of course, this book would not have been possible without the boundless enthusiasm and energy of my coauthor and friend, Seabrooke. From start to finish, her commitment to the project was absolute, which can be a tall order for something that lasts several years. And, needless to say, I'd like to thank Russell Galen, Lisa White, and all the wonderful staff at Houghton Mifflin for actually believing we could pull this off!

Finally, I thank my gloriously patient wife Katie, my son James, and my families on both sides of the Atlantic for all the love and support I could ever hope for throughout this project. James in particular became my "right-hand man" during many moth events.

—David Beadle

An incredible number of people are involved, directly or indirectly, in the making of a guide like this. From conceptualization to publication it will have been four years, during which time I've had not one, not two, but three serious computer failures. I've tried hard to ensure that I back up my data regularly, but I know files and e-mails have been lost along the way. I am extremely grateful to everyone who has helped in one way or another with the realization of this guide, and if I've forgotten to include someone's name here it's due to hardware malfunction and a faulty memory, for which I apologize.

It's hard to know where to start in expressing my thanks with this project, but perhaps, chronologically, the first people to deserve it were my hosts on Vancouver Island in 2007, who provided me with the blacklight and sheet that got it all started. Writers Julie Zickefoose, Scott Weidensaul, Dick Cannings, and David Sibley offered early advice and encouragement on how to go about finding a home for our guide. Our literary agent, Russell Galen, believed in us from the start, and it's entirely due to his commitment to our book that this guide is now part of the Peterson Field Guide series.

In preparing the manuscript I am indebted to all of my fellow moth-ers who sent me their personal checklists, which were invaluable in helping me build range maps: Carol Statton DiFiori, Bill Garthe, Bill Glaser, Anita Gould, Robert Grosek, John Himmelman,

Jeff Hooper, Cindy Mead, Jenn Forman Orth, Bob Patterson, Nelson Poirier, and Marie Winn. Mark Peck generously sent me a copy of Riotte's annotated list of Ontario Lepidoptera so I could return Dave's. Many others contributed their photographs and provided last-minute images when we realized we still needed something; our photographers are listed at the end of this book.

Christian Schmidt of the Canadian National Collection has been invaluable, providing me with documents detailing the most up-to-date taxonomy at the time of manuscript preparation, as well as lending his expertise in checking our identification and ranges, and patiently answering my many questions along the way. Thanks to Andrew Couturier for discussions on how to go about preparing the range maps, and to Andrew Jano who helped me learn ArcView GIS software for this purpose.

My mother, Sheridan, assisted with the proofing of species' common and scientific names to ensure no typos or taxonomic changes had slipped in when we drafted our initial list of species to include. My sister Gaelan helped out with the preparation of numerous images for the guide, for which services I exchanged an afternoon of housework at her apartment; I still feel I got the easier end of the deal. Tim Mudie lent a hand in resizing about a thousand of the images when it was discovered I'd forgotten that step during the file prep, and also prepared all of the flight period bars displayed beneath the range maps, saving me a great deal of time and tedium.

Our wonderful editor, Lisa White, deserves recognition simply for her patience with us over our multiple requests for deadline extensions, but she's been incredibly helpful at all stages along the way. The manuscript was copyedited by Elizabeth Pierson, whose keen eye and attention to detail has made this guide immeasurably better and saved us from some embarrassment. Beth Burleigh Fuller, Brian Moore, and the entire team of people behind-the-scenes at HMH have done a fabulous job pulling it all together into a cohesive whole that actually looks and functions like a field guide, and Taryn Roeder and Katrina Kruse and their publicity and marketing crews have done an amazing job getting the book out there.

Thanks to my coauthor and friend, Dave, for helping cultivate my interest in moths in those early days of 2007; for not only tolerating my many requests for help with IDs but actually encouraging me to send them; for building my moth trap, which I still run and use today; for agreeing to tackle this mountain of a project with me when I suggested it, still a relative newbie, in early 2008; for lending me many books and references, most of which I still haven't returned; and for all the effort that's gone into preparing this guide, from the manuscript itself to the hundreds of e-mails exchanged over the course of the project, especially following my departure from Toronto before we'd even signed the contract.

Mom, Dad, Gaelan, Rheanna, and Tahlia have all been extremely supportive from the moment that I announced I had this crazy idea; thanks to all of you for all your love and encouragement (and an ear when I needed to vent) along the way. Perhaps most of all I thank my partner, Dan, who may have been regretting his support at times when I disappeared into my study for days on end at the approach of a deadline, leaving him to take care of the chores and walk the dogs largely on his own. Thank you for your patience and understanding through this project, for bringing moths to my attention at the porch light or in the garden, for saving moths for me in the fridge, and for not only putting up with my moth gear scattered about the house every summer but actually encouraging me to set it out and run it. A moth addict couldn't ask for a better facilitator than you.

—Seabrooke Leckie

Boxwood Leaftier

GLOSSARY

Abdomen: The third, and terminal, body section of an insect; in Lepidoptera it comprises 10 segments.

AM area: See *Basal area.*

AM line: The antemedial line that separates the basal and median areas of the forewing. Often an important identification feature on noctuid moths.

Anal angle: The angle formed where the inner and outer margins of a wing converge.

Anal dash: A contrastingly colored streak passing through the ST area and PM area, and sometimes also the median area, near the anal angle, parallel to the inner margin.

Antennae: Segmented sensory appendages located at the inside edge of each eye.

Apex: The pointed tip of the forewing.

Apical dash: A contrastingly colored streak passing through the ST area and PM area near the apex of the wing, parallel to the costa.

Basal area: The area at the base of the forewing, often divided from the median area by an AM line. Also called AM area.

Basal dash: A contrastingly colored streak passing through the basal area of the forewing parallel to the inner margin.

Basal line: A contrastingly colored line cutting across the basal area of the forewing.

Bipectinate antennae: Featherlike antennae with two branches on most segments.

Brindled: Showing a lightly striped pattern.

Brood: A single generation.

Case: A silken, cocoonlike structure formed as a shelter by the larvae of some species often incorporating plant material.

Caterpillar: The larval form of all Lepidoptera.

Claviform spot: A round or wedgelike spot positioned between the orbicular spot and the inner margin on the forewing. It is especially noticeable on some noctuid moths.

Cocoon: A protective covering made by a caterpillar from silk or other materials prior to pupation.

Collar: The dorsal part of the prothorax immediately behind the head of a moth.

Costa or costal margin: The leading edge of the wing—usually refers to the forewing.

Costa streak: A contrastingly colored edge or border along the costa of the forewing.

Coxa: The basal segment of an insect leg—the segment that attaches to the body.

Crepuscular: Active at dawn or dusk.

Cutworm: A popular name referring to the caterpillars of certain noctuid moths that are considered agricultural pests. The name is often used for the adult moths, as well.

Dashes: Short, contrastingly colored lines in the forewing patterns of some moths, especially daggers and underwings.

Deltoid: Roughly triangular in shape.

Dimorphic: Having two distinctly different forms within a species; the difference may be in size, shape, color, or pattern. Often used to refer to the difference between the male and female of a species (see *Sexual dimorphism*).

Discal spot or dot: A small dotlike marking in the center of the wings, especially noticeable on many geometrid moths.

Diurnal: Active during daylight hours.

Dorsal: Referring to the upper surface of a moth.

Exoskeleton: The hard outer body armor of an insect.

Femur: The segment of an insect leg between the coxa and the tibia.

Filiform antennae: Threadlike antennae with no branches on the segments.

Flight period: The period of time when adults of a species can be found.

Forelegs: The front legs of an insect.

Foretibia: The middle section of the front legs of an insect—the second section from the body, after the coxa.

Frass: Pelletlike excrement of caterpillars.

Fringe: Hairlike scales on the outer margin of the wings.

FW: The forewing of a moth.

Habitat: The surroundings, specialized or general, in which a species lives.

Hind legs: The rear legs of an insect.

Holarctic: Occurring in the northern parts of both North America and Eurasia.

Hooked: Referring to the swept-back shape of the apex on the forewing of some moths, such as Arched Hooktip.

Host plants: The plant species on which a caterpillar feeds.

HW: The hindwing of a moth.

Immigrant: A species that is prone to erratic or regular flights in response to drought or other environmental conditions.

Inner margin: The inner edge of the wing, closest to the abdomen.

Labial palps: A pair of sensory appendages extending forward, and often curving upward, from the lower part of the head. They are particularly noticeable on many deltoid noctuid moths such as the *Zanclognatha* species.

Larva: The caterpillar stage in the life cycle of Lepidoptera.

Leaf mine: An excavation in plant tissue that results from the tunneling of moth larvae.

Light trap: See *Moth trap*.

Lepicloptera: The taxonomic order of insects that includes moths and butterflies.

Macromoths: A broad term referring to the more evolutionarily recent moth families organized in the second half of taxonomic lists. The majority of species are relatively large, though some species are smaller than many micromoths.

Median area: The central portion of the forewing.

Median line: A contrastingly colored line that passes through the median area of the forewing, usually between the orbicular and reniform spots.

Melanic: A dark (often all-black) color form resulting from an excess of pigment.

Micromoths: A term that refers to the tiny or small moths that are more evolutionarily primitive and organized in the first half of taxonomic lists. Note that some micromoths, such as the carpenterworms, are larger than any macromoths.

Moth trap: A means of catching and holding moths, usually using lights. Also called light trap when lightbulb is used as lure.

Noctuid: A moth species in the family Noctuidae.

Nocturnal: Active at night.

Orbicular spot: A round spot or outline in the inner median area of the forewing. An important identification clue for many species of noctuid moths.

Outer margin: The edge of the wing farthest from the body when wing is extended for flight.

Palps: see *Labial palps*.

Pectinate antennae: Featherlike antennae with branches on only one side of most segments.

Peppered: Showing a finely speckled pattern. Usually refers to the wings, especially of geometrid moths.

Pheromone: A chemical substance secreted by animals, often as a sex attractant. Commercially available pheromones can sometimes be used to attract rarely seen moths, such as the clearwing borers in the family Sesiidae.

PM area: The area in the outer third of the wing often bordered by the PM line and the ST line.

PM line: The postmedial line that separates the median area from the postmedial (PM) area on the forewing. Often an important identification feature on noctuid moths.

Proboscis: The coiled-up tubular tongue of the adult moth, used for taking nectar and water from flowers.

Prothorax: The first of three thoracic segments on an insect—the one closest to the head.

Pupation: The final stage of metamorphosis whereby larval features are replaced with adult characteristics.

Reniform spot: A kidney-shaped spot or outline in the outer median area of the forewing. An important identification clue for many species of noctuid moths.

Scales: Modified setae (see below) that are flattened or hairlike. Scales normally cover the body and wings of most Lepidoptera.

Setae: Bristles that emerge from the exoskeleton in insects. They are modified to form scales in adult Lepidoptera.

Sexual dimorphism: A difference in pattern or color between males and females of the same species.

Shading: Broad areas of color or tinting on the wings of a moth.

ST area: The area in the outer part of the wing often bordered by the ST line and the fringe.

Stigma: The contrastingly colored spot in the median area of the forewing between the orbicular and reniform spots. Found primarily in the loopers (subfamily Plusinae).

ST line: The subterminal line often present between the PM line and the terminal line. Often an important identification feature on noctuid moths.

Subreniform spot: A small spot or outline between the reniform spot and the inner margin of the forewing. An important identification feature on some noctuid moths.

Tarsus: The small terminal segment on an insect's leg.

Tegulae: Appendages attached to the prothorax and covering the forewing base.

Terminal line: The outermost line on a moth's wings, before the fringe.

Thorax: The middle of the three main body segments on an insect. It comprises three parts: the prothorax, mesothorax, and metathorax.

Tibia: The long, narrow leg segment (sometimes spiny) of an insect, between the femur and the tarsus.

TL: The total length of a moth as measured from the front of the head to the tip of the wings or abdomen.

Vagrant: A rare immigrant species that is not to be expected in a certain area.

Veins: Branches of tubular rods that support the wing membranes.

WS: The wingspan of a moth as measured from one wingtip to the other. An important measurement for most geometrid moths and some spread-winged noctuids.

RESOURCES

Maple Spanworm

If you've been bitten by the mothing bug, here are some additional resources that may help you to expand your identification skills and familiarize yourself with what can be found in your area. Some of the publications may be out of print, but used copies should be readily available online with a little digging.

In addition to the resources below, here are two more suggestions. Many moth enthusiasts have started posting online photographs and lists of the moths they have found. A web search for "moths of <your state/province>" will often turn up local websites. Many of these moth-ers are happy to offer their help, and they may even be willing to get together for a night of mothing.

Also see if there are entomologist or naturalist associations for your state or region. These groups can be amazing fonts of knowledge, with friendly, enthusiastic people who are delighted to welcome new people to their passion. Many will hold public moth nights that you can attend.

Printed Guides and Checklists

Covell, Charles V., Jr. 1999. *The Butterflies and Moths (Lepidoptera) of Kentucky: An Annotated Checklist.* Frankfort: Kentucky State Nature Preserves Commission.

Covell, Charles V., Jr. 2005. *A Field Guide to Moths of Eastern North America.* Martinsville: Virginia Museum of Natural History.

Eaton, Eric R., and Kenn Kaufman. 2007. *Kaufman Field Guide to Insects of North America.* New York: Houghton Mifflin.

Forbes, William T. M. 1923–1960. *The Lepidoptera of New York and Neighboring States.* 4 pts. Ithaca, NY: Cornell University.

Handfield, Louis. 1999. *Le Guide des Papillons du Québec.* Boucherville, QC: Broquet.

Heitzman, J. Richard, and Joan E. Heitzman. 1996. *Butterflies and Moths of Missouri.* 2d ed. Jefferson City: Missouri Dept. Conservation.

Himmelman, John. 2002. *Discovering Moths: Nighttime Jewels in Your Own Backyard.* Camden, ME: Down East Books.

Hodges, R. W., et al. 1983. *Check List of the Lepidoptera of America North of Mexico.* London: E. W. Classey.

Leverton, Roy. 2001. *Enjoying Moths.* London: Academic Press. [Although this book uses British moths as examples, the information it contains is applicable anywhere.]

Powell, Jerry A., and Paul A. Opler. 2009. *Moths of Western North America.* Berkeley: University of California Press.

Rings, Roy W., Eric H. Metzler, Fred J. Arnold, and David H. Harris. 1992. *The Owlet Moths of Ohio: Order Lepidoptera, Family Noctuidae.* Ohio Biological Survey Bulletin. New Series vol. 9, no. 2.

Riotte, J. C. E. 1992. *Annotated List of Ontario Lepidoptera.* Toronto: Royal Ontario Museum.

Sogaard, Jim. 2009. *Moths & Caterpillars of the North Woods.* Duluth, MN: Kollath-Stensaas Publishing.

Wagner, David L. 2005. *Caterpillars of Eastern North America: A Guide to Identification and Natural History.* Princeton, NJ: Princeton University Press.

Internet Resources

BugGuide.Net. Hosted by Iowa State University Entomology. An incredible resource for all insects, not just moths. Includes user-submitted photographs as well as information on identification, range, food plants, etc., where it is available. An "ID Request" feature allows you to upload your own photographs for expert identification. http://bugguide.net.

Butterflies and Moths of North America. A searchable database of Lepidoptera records for North America. Provides maps, written accounts, and photographs for many species. Butterflies are very well covered, and moths receive some treatment as well. http://www.butterfliesandmoths.org.

The Lepidopterists' Society. Some information is contained at the site itself, but it also provides an excellent list of additional resources, both in print and online. Although this is not strictly an identification or information website, the Lepidopterists' Society provides an excellent opportunity to learn more from like-minded people. This is the largest North American lepidopteran organization and is continental in scope. You can also look for more regional societies or associations in your area. http://www.lepsoc.org.

Microleps.org. An outstanding resource for micromoths. In addition to photographs (including spread-wing specimens), this site also provides information on host plants, feeding habits, flight period, etc. http://microleps.org.

Moths of Canada. A series of publications and online pages produced by the Canadian Biodiversity Information Facility of the Government of Canada. Excellent photographs of pinned specimens are accompanied by metric rulers for size reference. http://www.cbif.gc.ca/spp_pages/misc_moths/phps/mothindex_e.php.

North American Moth Photographers Group (MPG). Hosted by the Mississippi Entomological Museum at Mississippi State University. The best moth website out there; contains a compilation of images for the majority of North American species. http://moth photographersgroup.msstate.edu.

Tortricid.net. Originally begun as an identification resource for the large micromoth family Tortricidae—a role now filled more thoroughly by MPG—this website serves as an excellent source of additional information about the group. http://www.tortricidae.com.

Photography Credits

Many photographers made valuable contributions to this guide by donating excellent material for the plates. They are listed here in alphabetical order, with the moth images they provided noted by Hodges numbers.

Jerry Armstrong: 4699, 8704

Parker Backstrom: 2596, 4675, 4698, 4896, 5219, 6076, 6077, 6322, 6588, 6659, 6733, 6818, 6823, 6843, 7033, 7059, 7164, 7417, 7653, 7674, 7683, 7685, 7706, 7708, 7712, 7716, 7771, 7775, 7778, 7783, 7789, 7793, 7816, 7853, 7855, 7890, 7903, 7942, 8061, 8105, 8296, 8302, 8481, 8490, 8493, 8503, 8509, 8525, 8528, 8588, 8592, 8651, 8733, 8762, 8769, 8771, 8773, 8780, 8783, 8784, 8785, 8788, 8793, 8794, 8796, 8797, 8804, 8840, 8851, 8876, 8877, 8885, 8889, 8962, 9037, 9038, 9039, 9044, 9051, 9127, 9136, 9208, 9209, 9227, 9241, 9525, 9556, 9650, 9766, 9781, 9944, 10411, 10413, 10517, 10567, 10664, 10694, 10901, 10998, 11071, 11135

Giff Beaton: 2552

John M. Bills, Jr.: 7704

Maurice Bottos: 8796, 8863

John Davis: 7210, 9221, 10702

Jason J. Dombroskie: 0018, 0022, 0229, 6431, 6436, 6665, 6743, 7047, 7235, 7285, 7425, 8051, 8162, 8904, 9884, 10123

Mark Dreiling: 7094, 7709, 7985, 8411, 9070, 9182, 9192, 9264, 9266, 10488, 10502, 10519, 10661, 10903, 11177

Bill Evans: 6666

Ronnie Gaubert: 7730

Jeff Hollenbeck: 10455

Mary Hopson: 7166

Eddie Huber: 7046

Ali Iyoob: 7719

Michael King: 2536, 9630, 10817

Tim Lethbridge: 11173

Larry Line: 6449, 6987

J. Merrill Lynch: 6834, 7974, 8107, 9505

Cynthia Mead: 7873

Phil Milton: 8308

Tom Murray: 8188, 8560, 9056, 9199, 9618, 10456

Randy Newman: 7861

Jenn Forman Orth: 8169

Karl Overman: 11072

Tracy Palmer/Bird Nerd Nature Photography: 2549

Nelson Poirier Photo: 6884, 7294, 7437, 7767, 7811, 7933, 8912, 9501, 9928, 9980, 10266, 10462

Peter W. Post: 7730, 7873

Delise and Matthew Priebe: 9526

Glenn Richardson: 7764

Lynette Schimming: 8109

Harvey Schmidt: 8308

Nolie Schneider: 0021, 6729, 7165, 7294, 7430, 7884, 8006, 8175, 8939, 8990, 9434, 10954

Robert Siegel, MD, PhD, Stanford University: 10640

Marvin Smith: 6711, 7855, 8194, 8600, 8959

Rick Snider: 8649

Francis Solly: 7892

Jeremy B. Tatum: 8975

Renn Tumlison: 7767, 8872

Wade Wander: 4639, 4700, 8176, 10488, 11149

Laney P. Williams, Jr.: 9694, 9714

Carol Wolf: 7046, 7441, 8140, 9482

Karen Yukich: 8318

Robert Lord Zimlich: 9950

Squash Vine Borer

CHECKLIST

One of the great joys of mothing is keeping a "life list" of species you have seen. An offshoot of this is recording what species have occurred at your favorite mothing locations and even what species you are able to see each year. It is hard to deny that there is some excitement in finding a species that's new to you, even if your be-all-and-end-all focus of the activity isn't in building your list. You'll be surprised at how quickly your list grows, too—each year, and each new location, has the potential to add new species even if you've been mothing for a long time.

The list presented here contains only the species shown in this field guide, and it follows the same order. There are probably hundreds more moths that occur in your region that we haven't shown. Most of these will be uncommon or rare and may occur only locally or patchily. We have left space for you to write in your additions at the end.

As we noted in the chapter How to Use This Book, only the Noctuoidea superfamily has received an official MPG prefix (93); however, in this checklist we provide unofficial numbers in parentheses for all of the other groups. These two-digit numbers may be used as a prefix, in combination with the four-digit Hodges number as a suffix, to create a similar six-digit number, in order to help sort species by current taxonomy. Although the prefix for the Noctuoidea is assigned at the superfamily level, our unofficial numbers are given at the family level, which is necessary to ensure proper taxonomic organization.

For all groups up to the superfamily Noctuoidea, the checklist provides only the Hodges number. Beginning with the Noctuoidea, it provides both the MPG and Hodges numbers.

MPG #	Hodges #	Scientific Name	Common Name

☐	0647	*Micrurapteryx salicifoliella*	Willow Leaf Blotch Miner
☐	0657	*Parectopa robiniella*	Locust Digitate Leafminer
☐	0663	*Neurobathra strigifinitella*	Finite-channeled Leafminer
☐	0686.97	*Parornix spp.*	Parornix species complex
☐	0698	*Leucospilapteryx venustella*	Snakeroot Leafminer
☐	0723	*Cremastobombycia solidaginis*	Goldenrod Leafminer
☐	0765	*Phyllonorycter lucidicostella*	Lesser Maple Leaf Blotch Miner
☐	0784	*Phyllonorycter propinquinella*	Cherry Blotch Miner
☐	0790	*Phyllonorycter robiniella*	Black Locust Leafminer
☐	0832	*Cameraria ostryarella*	Hornbeam Leafminer

Ermine and Needleminer Moths – Families Lyonetiidae and Yponomeutidae (08)

☐	462	*Philonome clemensella*	Clemens' Philonome
☐	2401	*Atteva aurea*	Ailanthus Webworm
☐	2413	*Swammerdamia caesiella*	Gray-blue Swammerdamia
☐	2420	*Yponomeuta multipunctella*	American Ermine
☐	2421	*Yponomeuta padella*	Orchard Ermine
☐	2423.1	*Yponomeuta cagnagella*	Spindle Ermine
☐	2427	*Zelleria haimbachi*	Pine Needle Sheathminer
☐	2435	*Argyresthia alternatella*	Honey-comb Micro
☐	2457	*Argyresthia goedartella*	Bronze Alder Moth
☐	2467	*Argyresthia oreasella*	Cherry Shoot Borer

Falcate-winged Moths – Family Ypsolophidae (09)

☐	2371	*Ypsolopha canariella*	Canary Ypsolopha
☐	2375	*Ypsolopha dentella*	European Honeysuckle Moth
☐	2380	*Ypsolopha falciferella*	Scythed Ypsolopha

Sedge, Diamondback, and False Diamondback Moths – Families Glyphipterigidae, Plutellidae, and Acrolepiidae (10)

☐	2346	*Diploschizia impigritella*	Yellow Nutsedge Moth
☐	2363	*Plutella porrectella*	Dame's Rocket Moth
☐	2366	*Plutella xylostella*	Diamondback Moth
☐	2490	*Acrolepiopsis incertella*	Carrionflower Moth

Grass Miner Moths – Family Elachistidae (11)

☐	0857	*Agonopterix lythrella*	Red Agonopterix
☐	0859	*Agonopterix curvilineella*	Curve-line Agonopterix
☐	0862	*Agonopterix clemensella*	Clemens' Agonopterix
☐	0864	*Agonopterix atrodorsella*	Brown-collared Agonopterix
☐	0867	*Agonopterix pulvipennella*	Featherduster Agonopterix
☐	0874.1	*Agonopterix alstromeriana*	Poison Hemlock Agonopterix
☐	0878	*Agonopterix canadensis*	Canadian Agonopterix
☐	0882	*Agonopterix robiniella*	Four-dotted Agonopterix
☐	0911	*Bibarrambla alenella*	Bog Bibarrambla
☐	0912	*Semioscopis packardella*	Packard's Semioscopis
☐	0914	*Semioscopis inornata*	Plain Semioscopis
☐	0916	*Semioscopis aurorella*	Aurora Semioscopis

☐	0922	*Depressaria pastinacella*	Parsnip Webworm
☐	0926	*Depressaria alienella*	Yarrow Webworm
☐	0951	*Machimia tentoriferella*	Gold-striped Leaftier
☐	0957	*Psilocorsis reflexella*	Dotted Leaftier
☐	0986	*Ethmia bipunctella*	Viper's Bugloss Moth
☐	0992	*Ethmia zelleriella*	Zeller's Ethmia
☐	0999	*Ethmia longimaculella*	Streaked Ethmia
☐	1011	*Antaeotricha schlaegeri*	Schlaeger's Fruitworm Moth
☐	1463	*Chrysoclista linneella*	Linden Bark-Borer

Concealer and Scavenger Moths – Families Xyloryctidae, Oecophoridae, and Autostichidae (12)

☐	1042	*Decantha boreasella*	Reticulated Decantha
☐	1046	*Epicallima argenticinctella*	Orange-headed Epicallima
☐	1048	*Dafa formosella*	Beautiful Dafa
☐	1058	*Polix coloradella*	The Skunk
☐	1068	*Eido trimaculella*	Three-spotted Concealer Moth
☐	1134	*Oegoconia novimundi*	Four-spotted Yellowneck
☐	1144	*Gerdana caritella*	Gerdana Moth
☐	1162	*Blastobasis glandulella*	Acorn Moth

Casebearer Moths – Family Coleophoridae (13)

☐	1257	*Coleophora atromarginata*	American Pistol Casebearer
☐	1271	*Coleophora pruniella*	Cherry Casebearer
☐	1387	*Coleophora mayrella*	Metallic Casebearer
☐	1388	*Coleophora trifolii*	Large Clover Casebearer
☐	1443	*Mompha eloisella*	Red-streaked Mompha
☐	1673	*Scythris limbella*	Chenopodium Scythris

Cosmet Moths – Family Cosmopterigidae (14)

☐	1467	*Euclemensia bassettella*	Kermes Scale Moth
☐	1472	*Cosmopterix pulchrimella*	Chambers' Cosmopterix
☐	1476	*Cosmopterix montisella*	Mountain Cosmopterix
☐	1515	*Limnaecia phragmitella*	Shy Cosmet
☐	1609	*Stilbosis tesquella*	Hog-peanut Leaf-Sewer
☐	1615	*Walshia miscecolorella*	Sweetclover Root Borer
☐	1631/ 1632	*Perimede ricina/ falcata*	Perimede species complex

Twirler Moths – Family Gelechiidae (15)

☐	1685	*Metzneria lappella*	Burdock Seedhead Moth
☐	1718	*Chrysoesthia lingulacella*	Silver-banded Moth
☐	1721	*Enchrysa dissectella*	Orange-crescent Moth
☐	1761	*Aristotelia roseosuffusella*	Pink-washed Aristotelia
☐	1783	*Recurvaria nanella*	Lesser Bud Moth
☐	1793	*Coleotechnites australis*	Southern Needleminer
☐	1851	*Arogalea cristifasciella*	White Stripe-backed Moth
☐	1852	*Athrips mouffetella*	Ten-spotted Honeysuckle Moth

☐	1857	*Telphusa latifasciella*	White-banded Telphusa
☐	1858	*Telphusa longifasciella*	Y-backed Telphusa
☐	1864	*Pseudochelaria walsinghami*	Walsingham's Moth
☐	1874.2	*Carpatolechia fugitivella*	Elm Leaf-Sewer
☐	1881	*Neotelphusa sequax*	Crepuscular Rock-rose Moth
☐	1986	*Gnorimoschema gallaesolidaginis*	Goldenrod Gall Moth
☐	2077	*Chionodes formosella*	Spring Oak Leafroller
☐	2093	*Chionodes mediofuscella*	Black-smudged Chionodes
☐	2209	*Stegasta bosqueella*	Red-necked Peanutworm Moth
☐	2225	*Battaristis concinnusella*	Music-loving Moth
☐	2229	*Battaristis vittella*	Orange Stripe-backed Moth
☐	2237	*Anacampsis innocuella*	Dark-headed Aspen Leafroller
☐	2244	*Anacampsis nonstrigella*	Unstriped Anacampsis
☐	2257	*Anarsia lineatella*	Peach Twig Borer
☐	2267	*Helcystogramma fernaldella*	Fernald's Helcystogramma
☐	2268	*Helcystogramma hystricella*	Lanceolate Moth
☐	2281	*Dichomeris ligulella*	Palmerworm Moth
☐	2282	*Dichomeris marginella*	Juniper Webworm
☐	2283	*Dichomeris punctidiscella*	Spotted Dichomeris
☐	2289	*Dichomeris ochripalpella*	Shining Dichomeris
☐	2291	*Dichomeris bilobella*	Bilobed Dichomeris
☐	2291.2	*Dichomeris copa*	Copa Dichomeris
☐	2295	*Dichomeris flavocostella*	Cream-edged Dichomeris
☐	2297	*Dichomeris inserrata*	Indented Dichomeris
☐	2297.2	*Dichomeris bolize*	Glaser's Dichomeris
☐	2299	*Dichomeris leuconotella*	Two-spotted Dichomeris
☐	2307	*Dichomeris nonstrigella*	Little Devil
☐	2309	*Dichomeris picrocarpa*	Black-edged Dichomeris
☐	2310.1	*Dichomeris inversella*	Inversed Dichomeris

Leaf Skeletonizers – Family Zygaenidae (16)

☐	4624	*Harrisina americana*	Grapeleaf Skeletonizer
☐	4639	*Pyromorpha dimidiata*	Orange-patched Smoky Moth

Slug Moths – Family Limacodidae (17)

☐	4652	*Tortricidia testacea*	Early Button Slug Moth
☐	4654	*Tortricidia flexuosa*	Abbreviated Button Slug Moth
☐	4659	*Packardia geminata*	Jeweled Tailed Slug Moth
☐	4661	*Packardia elegans*	Elegant Tailed Slug Moth
☐	4665	*Lithacodes fasciola*	Yellow-shouldered Slug Moth
☐	4667	*Apoda y-inversum*	Yellow-collared Slug Moth
☐	4669	*Apoda biguttata*	Shagreened Slug Moth
☐	4671	*Prolimacodes badia*	Skiff Moth
☐	4675	*Isochaetes beutenmuelleri*	Spun Glass Slug Moth
☐	4677	*Phobetron pithecium*	Hag Moth
☐	4681	*Isa textula*	Crowned Slug Moth

☐	4685	*Adoneta spinuloides*	Purple-crested Slug Moth
☐	4697	*Euclea delphinii*	Spiny Oak-slug Moth
☐	4698	*Parasa chloris*	Smaller Parasa
☐	4699	*Parasa indetermina*	Stinging Rose Caterpillar Moth
☐	4700	*Acharia stimulea*	Saddleback Caterpillar Moth

Clearwing Borers – Family Sesiidae (18)

☐	2513	*Pennisetia marginatum*	Raspberry Crown Borer
☐	2532	*Albuna fraxini*	Virginia Creeper Clearwing
☐	2536	*Melittia cucurbitae*	Squash Vine Borer
☐	2542	*Sesia apiformis*	European Hornet Moth
☐	2543	*Sesia tibiale*	American Hornet Moth
☐	2546	*Synanthedon acerrubri*	Red Maple Borer
☐	2549	*Synanthedon scitula*	Dogwood Borer
☐	2550	*Synanthedon pictipes*	Lesser Peachtree Borer
☐	2552	*Synanthedon rileyana*	Riley's Clearwing
☐	2553	*Synanthedon tipuliformis*	Currant Clearwing
☐	2554	*Synanthedon acerni*	Maple Callus Borer
☐	2583	*Synanthedon exitiosa*	Peachtree Borer
☐	2589	*Podosesia syringae*	Lilac Borer
☐	2596	*Carmenta bassiformis*	Eupatorium Borer

Metalmark Moths – Family Choreutidae (19)

☐	2650	*Choreutis pariana*	Apple Leaf Skeletonizer

Carpenterworm and Leopard Moths – Family Cossidae (20)

☐	2675	*Acossus centerensis*	Poplar Carpenterworm
☐	2693	*Prionoxystus robiniae*	Robin's Carpenterworm
☐	2694	*Prionoxystus macmurtei*	Little Carpenterworm
☐	2700	*Zeuzera pyrina*	Leopard Moth

Tortrix Leafrollers – Family Tortricidae, Subfamily Tortricinae, Tribes Tortricini, Euliini, and Cnephasiini (21)

☐	3501	*Acleris forskaleana*	Hairnet Acleris
☐	3503	*Acleris semipurpurana*	Oak Leafshredder
☐	3506	*Acleris macdunnoughi*	MacDunnough's Acleris
☐	3510	*Acleris nivisellana*	Snowy-shouldered Acleris
☐	3517	*Acleris subnivana*	Common Acleris
☐	3520	*Acleris fuscana*	Small Aspen Leaftier
☐	3521	*Acleris semiannula*	Half-ringed Acleris
☐	3526	*Acleris negundana*	Speckled Acleris
☐	3531	*Acleris hastiana*	Hasty Acleris
☐	3532	*Acleris fragariana*	Strawberry Acleris
☐	3533	*Acleris celiana*	Celiana's Acleris
☐	3539	*Acleris chalybeana*	Lesser Maple Leafroller
☐	3540	*Acleris logiana*	Black-headed Birch Leafroller
☐	3542	*Acleris flavivittana*	Multiform Leafroller
☐	3548	*Acleris variana*	Eastern Black-headed Budworm

☐	3550	*Acleris youngana*	Young's Acleris
☐	3551	*Acleris inana*	Dark-spotted Acleris
☐	3556	*Acleris nigrolinea*	Black-lined Acleris
☐	3557	*Acleris maximana*	Great Acleris
☐	3565	*Eulia ministrana*	Ferruginous Eulia
☐	3573	*Decodes basiplagana*	Gray-marked Tortricid

Cochylid Moths – Family Tortricidae, Subfamily Tortricinae, Tribe Cochylini (22)

☐	3754.2	*Aethes argentilimitana*	Silver-bordered Aethes
☐	3754.3	*Aethes atomosana*	Two-spotted Aethes
☐	3755.1	*Aethes biscana*	Reddish Aethes
☐	3758.2	*Aethes mymara*	Dark-spotted Aethes
☐	3759	*Aethes patricia*	Patricia's Aethes
☐	3760.2	*Aethes sexdentata*	Six-toothed Aethes
☐	3767	*Cochylis aurorana*	Pink-mottled Cochylid
☐	3769	*Cochylis bucera*	Horned Cochylid
☐	3777	*Cochylis hospes*	Banded Sunflower Moth
☐	3778	*Cochylis nana*	Broad-patch Cochylid
☐	3780	*Cochylis ringsi*	Rings' Cochylid
☐	3807	*Phalonidia lepidana*	Brown-patched Phalonidia
☐	3813	*Phtheochroa birdana*	Bird's Cochylid
☐	3822	*Phtheochroa riscana*	Marbled Cochylid
☐	3825	*Phtheochroa vitellinana*	Silver-lined Cochylid
☐	3837	*Rolandylis maiana*	Kearfott's Rolandylis
☐	3843	*Thyraylia bana*	Dark-banded Cochylid
☐	3847	*Thyraylia hollandana*	Holland's Cochylid
☐	3848	*Atroposia oenotherana*	Primrose Cochylid

Archips Leafrollers – Family Tortricidae, Subfamily Tortricinae, Tribe Archipini (23)

☐	3594	*Pandemis limitata*	Three-lined Leafroller
☐	3597	*Argyrotaenia velutinana*	Red-banded Leafroller
☐	3621	*Argyrotaenia quadrifasciana*	Four-lined Leafroller
☐	3623	*Argyrotaenia quercifoliana*	Lined Oak Leafroller
☐	3624	*Argyrotaenia alisellana*	White-spotted Leafroller
☐	3625	*Argyrotaenia mariana*	Gray-banded Leafroller
☐	3632	*Choristoneura fractivittana*	Broken-banded Leafroller
☐	3635	*Choristoneura rosaceana*	Oblique-banded Leafroller
☐	3637	*Choristoneura conflictana*	Large Aspen Tortrix
☐	3638	*Choristoneura fumiferana*	Spruce Budworm
☐	3643	*Choristoneura pinus*	Jack Pine Budworm
☐	3648	*Archips argyrospila*	Fruit Tree Leafroller
☐	3653	*Archips semiferana*	White-spotted Oak Leafroller
☐	3655	*Archips fervidana*	Oak Webworm
☐	3658	*Archips purpurana*	Omnivorous Leafroller
☐	3661	*Archips cerasivorana*	Ugly-nest Caterpillar Moth
☐	3664	*Archips strianus*	Striated Tortrix
☐	3666	*Archips dissitana*	Boldy-marked Archips

☐	3667	*Archips pachardiana*	Spring Spruce Needle
☐	3672	*Syndemis afflictana*	Black-and-gray Banded Leafroller
☐	3682	*Clepsis persicana*	White-triangle Clepsis
☐	3684	*Clepsis clemensiana*	Clemens' Clepsis
☐	3686	*Clepsis melaleucanus*	Black-patched Clepsis
☐	3688	*Clepsis peritana*	Garden Tortrix
☐	3691	*Adoxophyes negundana*	Shimmering Adoxophyes

Sparganothid Leafrollers – Family Tortricidae, Subfamily Tortricinae, Tribe Sparganothidini (24)

☐	3695	*Sparganothis sulfureana*	Sparganothis Fruitworm
☐	3699	*Sparganothis tristriata*	Three-streaked Sparganothis
☐	3711	*Sparganothis unifasciana*	One-lined Sparganothis
☐	3716	*Cenopis diluticostana*	Oak Cenopis
☐	3720	*Cenopis reticulatana*	Reticulated Fruitworm
☐	3725	*Cenopis pettitana*	Maple-basswood Leafroller
☐	3727	*Cenopis niveana*	Aproned Cenopis
☐	3740	*Platynota idaeusalis*	Tufted Apple Bud Moth
☐	3741	*Platynota semiustana*	Singed Platynota
☐	3743	*Platynota exasperatana*	Exasperating Platynota
☐	3748	*Amorbia humerosana*	White-line Leafroller

Olethreutine Moths – Family Tortricidae, Subfamily Olethreutinae (25)

☐	2707	*Bactra verutana*	Javelin Moth
☐	2712	*Paralobesia viteana*	Grape Berry Moth
☐	2738	*Endothenia hebesana*	Dull-barred Endothenia
☐	2747	*Hulda impudens*	Impudent Hulda
☐	2749	*Eumarozia malachitana*	Sculptured Moth
☐	2765	*Apotomis deceptana*	Deceptive Apotomis
☐	2769	*Pseudosciaphila duplex*	Poplar Leafroller
☐	2770	*Orthotaenia undulana*	Dusky Leafroller
☐	2775	*Olethreutes nitidana*	Shining Olethreutes
☐	2786	*Olethreutes punctanum*	Punctuated Olethreutes
☐	2788	*Olethreutes inornatana*	Inornate Olethreutes
☐	2791	*Olethreutes exoletum*	Wretched Olethreutes
☐	2794	*Olethreutes quadrifidum*	Quartered Olethreutes
☐	2800	*Olethreutes nigranum*	Dark Olethreutes
☐	2820	*Olethreutes malana*	Malana Leafroller
☐	2823	*Olethreutes fasciatana*	Banded Olethreutes
☐	2827	*Olethreutes ferriferana*	Hydrangea Leaftier
☐	2838.1	*Olethreutes ferrolineana*	Iron-lined Olethreutes
☐	2847	*Olethreutes glaciana*	Frosty Olethreutes
☐	2848	*Olethreutes bipartitana*	Divided Olethreutes
☐	2860	*Metendothenia separatana*	Pink-washed Leafroller
☐	2862	*Hedya nubiferana*	Green Budworm
☐	2867	*Rhyacionia buoliana*	European Pine Shoot Moth
☐	2892	*Retinia albicapitana*	Northern Pitch Twig Moth

☐	2898	*Retinia gemistrigulana*	Gray Retinia
☐	2913	*Phaneta umbrastriana*	Shaded Phaneta
☐	2927	*Phaneta ochrocephala*	Pale-headed Phaneta
☐	2928	*Phaneta raracana*	Reddish Phaneta
☐	2929	*Phaneta ochroterminana*	Buff-tipped Phaneta
☐	2936	*Phaneta tomonana*	Aster-head Phaneta
☐	3009	*Eucosma robinsonana*	Robinson's Eucosma
☐	3074	*Eucosma tocullionana*	White Pine Cone Borer
☐	3116	*Eucosma dorsisignatana*	Triangle-backed Eucosma
☐	3116.1	*Eucosma similiana*	Similar Eucosma
☐	3120	*Eucosma derelicta*	Derelict Eucosma
☐	3184	*Epiblema tripartitana*	Three-parted Epiblema
☐	3186	*Epiblema scudderiana*	Scudder's Epiblema
☐	3202	*Epiblema otiosana*	Bidens Borer
☐	3203	*Epiblema brightonana*	Brighton's Epiblema
☐	3210	*Notocelia illotana*	Dirty Notocelia
☐	3217	*Suleima cinerodorsana*	Ashy Suleima
☐	3219	*Sonia canadana*	Canadian Sonia
☐	3226	*Gypsonoma haimbachiana*	Cottonwood Twig Borer
☐	3230	*Proteoteras aesculana*	Maple Twig Borer
☐	3233	*Proteoteras crescentana*	Black-crescent Proteoteras
☐	3235	*Proteoteras moffatiana*	Maple Shoot Borer
☐	3246	*Pseudexentera cressoniana*	Shagbark Hickory Leafroller
☐	3247	*Pseudexentera mali*	Pale Apple Leafroller
☐	3254	*Pseudexentera maracana*	Banded Pseudexentera
☐	3258	*Pseudexentera virginiana*	Virginia Pseudexentera
☐	3264	*Gretchena amatana*	Likeable Gretchena
☐	3306	*Epinotia nisella*	Yellow-headed Aspen Leaftier
☐	3310	*Epinotia transmissana*	Walker's Epinotia
☐	3334	*Catastega aceriella*	Maple Trumpet Skeletonizer
☐	3351	*Epinotia lindana*	Diamondback Epinotia
☐	3354	*Ancylis nubeculana*	Little Cloud Ancylis
☐	3361	*Ancylis semiovana*	Half-oval Ancylis
☐	3370	*Ancylis platanana*	Sycamore Leaffolder
☐	3379	*Ancylis diminutana*	Shattered Ancylis
☐	3404/ 3406	*Dichrorampha simulana/ bittana*	Variable Dichrorampha species complex
☐	3419	*Pammene felicitana*	Happy Pammene
☐	3426	*Grapholita molesta*	Oriental Fruit Moth
☐	3428	*Grapholita packardi*	Cherry Fruitworm
☐	3439	*Grapholita interstinctana*	Clover Head Caterpillar Moth
☐	3461	*Cydia albimaculana*	White-marked Cydia
☐	3486	*Cydia toreuta*	Eastern Pine Seedworm
☐	3492	*Cydia pomonella*	Codling Moth
☐	3494	*Cydia latiferreana*	Filbertworm Moth

☐	3495	*Gymnandrosoma punctidiscanum*	Dotted Gymnandrosoma
☐	3497	*Ecdytolopha insiticiana*	Locust Twig Borer

False Burnet and Many-plumed Moths – Families Urodidae and Alucitidae (26)

☐	2313	*Alucita montana*	Six-plume Moth
☐	2415.1	*Wockia asperipunctella*	Shaggy-spotted Wockia

Plume Moths – Family Pterophoridae (27)

☐	6091	*Geina periscelidactylus*	Grape Plume Moth
☐	6093	*Geina bucksi*	Buck's Plume Moth
☐	6102	*Dejongia lobidactylus*	Lobed Plume Moth
☐	6105	*Cnaemidophorus rhododactyla*	Rose Plume Moth
☐	6107	*Gillmeria pallidactyla*	Yarrow Plume Moth
☐	6109	*Platyptilia carduidactylus*	Artichoke Plume Moth
☐	6118	*Amblyptilia pica*	Geranium Plume Moth
☐	6157	*Adaina montanus*	Mountain Plume Moth
☐	6168	*Oidaematophorus eupatorii*	Eupatorium Plume Moth
☐	6186	*Hellinsia inquinatus*	Black-marked Plume Moth
☐	6203	*Hellinsia homodactylus*	Plain Plume Moth
☐	6234	*Emmelina monodactyla*	Morning-glory Plume Moth

Fruitworm Moths – Family Carposinidae (28)

☐	2315	*Carposina fernaldana*	Currant Fruitworm Moth
☐	2319	*Bondia crescentella*	Crescent-marked Bondia

Assorted Pyralids – Family Pyralidae, Subfamilies Pyralinae, Epipaschiinae, and Galleriinae (29)

☐	5510	*Pyralis farinalis*	Meal Moth
☐	5511	*Aglossa costiferalis*	Calico Pyralid
☐	5512	*Aglossa disciferalis*	Pink-masked Pyralid
☐	5516	*Aglossa pinguinalis*	Large Tabby
☐	5517	*Aglossa caprealis*	Stored Grain Moth
☐	5518	*Aglossa cuprina*	Grease Moth
☐	5524	*Hypsopygia costalis*	Clover Hayworm
☐	5526	*Pseudasopia intermedialis*	Red-shawled Moth
☐	5533	*Dolichomia olinalis*	Yellow-fringed Dolichomia
☐	5552	*Galasa nigrinodis*	Boxwood Leaftier
☐	5556	*Tosale oviplagalis*	Dimorphic Tosale
☐	5571	*Condylolomia participalis*	Drab Condylolomia
☐	5577	*Epipaschia superatalis*	Dimorphic Epipaschia
☐	5579	*Macalla zelleri*	Zeller's Macalla
☐	5588	*Oneida lunulalis*	Orange-tufted Oneida
☐	5604	*Pococera militella*	Sycamore Webworm
☐	5606	*Pococera asperatella*	Maple Webworm
☐	5608	*Pococera expandens*	Striped Oak Webworm
☐	5622	*Galleria mellonella*	Greater Wax Moth
☐	5629	*Aphomia sociella*	Bee Moth

Phycitine Moths – Family Pyralidae, Subfamily Phycitinae (30)

☐	5651	*Acrobasis indigenella*	Leaf Crumpler Moth
☐	5653	*Acrobasis vaccinii*	Cranberry Fruitworm
☐	5655	*Acrobasis tricolorella*	Tricolored Acrobasis
☐	5659	*Acrobasis palliolella*	Mantled Acrobasis
☐	5661	*Acrobasis juglandis*	Pecanleaf Casebearer
☐	5664	*Acrobasis caryae*	Hickory Shoot Borer
☐	5670	*Acrobasis aurorella*	Pigeon Acrobasis
☐	5673	*Acrobasis angusella*	Hickory Leafstem Borer
☐	5674	*Acrobasis demotella*	Walnut Shoot Moth
☐	5721	*Apomyelois bistriatella*	Two-striped Apomyelois
☐	5744	*Etiella zinckenella*	Gold-banded Etiella
☐	5766	*Immyrla nigrovittella*	Black-banded Immyrla
☐	5773	*Salebriaria engeli*	Engel's Salebriaria
☐	5783	*Ortholepis pasadamia*	Striped Birch Pyralid
☐	5794	*Sciota vetustella*	Belted Leafroller
☐	5796	*Sciota subcaesiella*	Locust Leafroller
☐	5797	*Sciota virgatella*	Black-spotted Leafroller
☐	5799	*Sciota basilaris*	Yellow-shouldered Leafroller
☐	5808	*Tlascala reductella*	Tlascala Moth
☐	5812	*Telethusia ovalis*	Oval Telethusia
☐	5829	*Pyla fusca*	Speckled Black Pyla
☐	5841	*Dioryctria abietivorella*	Evergreen Coneworm
☐	5843	*Dioryctria reniculelloides*	Spruce Coneworm
☐	5847	*Dioryctria disclusa*	Webbing Coneworm
☐	5852	*Dioryctria zimmermani*	Zimmerman Pine Moth
☐	5896	*Elasmopalpus lignosellus*	Lesser Cornstalk Borer
☐	5995	*Euzophera semifuneralis*	American Plum Borer
☐	5997	*Euzophera ostricolorella*	Root Collar Borer
☐	5999	*Eulogia ochrifrontella*	Broad-banded Eulogia
☐	6005	*Moodna ostrinella*	Darker Moodna
☐	6007	*Vitula edmandsii*	Dried-fruit Moth
☐	6011	*Vitula broweri*	Brower's Vitula
☐	6053	*Peoria approximella*	Carmine Snout Moth

Moss-eating Crambids – Family Crambidae, Subfamily Scopariinae (31)

☐	4716	*Scoparia biplagialis*	Double-striped Scoparia
☐	4719	*Scoparia basalis*	Many-spotted Scoparia
☐	4738	*Eudonia strigalis*	Striped Eudonia

Grass-Veneers – Family Crambidae, Subfamily Crambinae (32)

☐	5342	*Crambus bidens*	Biden's Grass-Veneer
☐	5343	*Crambus perlella*	Immaculate Grass-Veneer
☐	5344	*Crambus unistriatellus*	Wide-stripe Grass-Veneer
☐	5355	*Crambus praefectellus*	Common Grass-Veneer
☐	5357	*Crambus leachellus*	Leach's Grass-Veneer

☐	5361	*Crambus albellus*	Small White Grass-Veneer
☐	5362	*Crambus agitatellus*	Double-banded Grass-Veneer
☐	5363	*Crambus saltuellus*	Pasture Grass-Veneer
☐	5365	*Crambus girardellus*	Girard's Grass-Veneer
☐	5378	*Crambus laqueatellus*	Eastern Grass-Veneer
☐	5379	*Neodactria luteolellus*	Mottled Grass-Veneer
☐	5391	*Chrysoteuchia topiarius*	Topiary Grass-Veneer
☐	5399	*Agriphila ruricolellus*	Lesser Vagabond Sod Webworm
☐	5403	*Agriphila vulgivagellus*	Vagabond Crambus
☐	5408	*Catoptria latiradiellus*	Three-spotted Crambus
☐	5413	*Pediasia trisecta*	Sod Webworm
☐	5419	*Microcrambus biguttellus*	Gold-stripe Grass-Veneer
☐	5420	*Microcrambus elegans*	Elegant Grass-Veneer
☐	5435	*Fissicrambus mutabilis*	Changeable Grass-Veneer
☐	5439	*Thaumatopsis pexellus*	Woolly Grass-Veneer
☐	5451	*Parapediasia teterrella*	Bluegrass Webworm
☐	5454	*Euchromius ocelleus*	Belted Grass-Veneer
☐	5464	*Urola nivalis*	Snowy Urola
☐	5465	*Vaxi auratella*	Curve-lined Argyria
☐	5466	*Vaxi critica*	Straight-lined Argyria
☐	5488	*Haimbachia albescens*	Silvered Haimbachia

Donacaulas – Family Crambidae, Subfamily Schoenobiinae (33)

☐	5316	*Donacaula melinellus*	Delightful Donacaula
☐	5319	*Donacaula longirostrallus*	Long-beaked Donacaula
☐	5321	*Donacaula roscidellus*	Brown Donacaula

Aquatic Crambids – Family Crambidae, Subfamily Acentropinae (34)

☐	4747	*Nymphula ekthlipsis*	Nymphula Moth
☐	4748	*Elophila icciusalis*	Pondside Crambid
☐	4751	*Elophila gyralis*	Waterlily Borer
☐	4754	*Synclita tinealis*	Black Duckweed Moth
☐	4755	*Synclita obliteralis*	Waterlily Leafcutter
☐	4759	*Parapoynx maculalis*	Polymorphic Pondweed Moth
☐	4760	*Parapoynx obscuralis*	Obscure Pondweed Moth
☐	4761	*Parapoynx badiusalis*	Chestnut-marked Pondweed Moth
☐	4764	*Parapoynx allionealis*	Watermilfoil Leafcutter
☐	4774	*Petrophila bifascialis*	Two-banded Petrophila
☐	4787	*Eoparargyractis plevie*	Plevie's Aquatic Moth

Assorted Crambids – Family Crambidae, Subfamilies Odontiinae, Glaphyriinae, and Evergestinae (35)

☐	4789	*Metrea ostreonalis*	Oystershell Metrea
☐	4794	*Eustixia pupula*	Spotted Peppergrass Moth
☐	4796	*Microtheoris ophionalis*	Yellow-veined Moth
☐	4826	*Mimoschinia rufofascialis*	Rufous-banded Crambid
☐	4846	*Hellula rogatalis*	Cabbage Webworm

☐	4870	*Glaphyria sequistrialis*	White-roped Glaphyria
☐	4873	*Glaphyria fulminalis*	Black-patched Glaphyria
☐	4879	*Xanthophysa psychialis*	Xanthophysa Moth
☐	4888	*Lipocosmodes fuliginosalis*	Sooty Lipocosmodes
☐	4889	*Dicymolomia julianalis*	Julia's Dicymolomia
☐	4895	*Chalcoela iphitalis*	Sooty-winged Chalcoela
☐	4896	*Chalcoela pegasalis*	Pegasus Chalcoela
☐	4897	*Evergestis pallidata*	Purple-backed Cabbageworm
☐	4901	*Evergestis unimacula*	Large-spotted Evergestis

Pyraustine Moths – Family Crambidae, Subfamily Pyraustinae (36)

☐	4936	*Saucrobotys futilalis*	Dogbane Saucrobotys
☐	4937	*Nascia acutella*	Streaked Orange Moth
☐	4945	*Crocidophora tuberculalis*	Pale-winged Crocidophora
☐	4949	*Ostrinia nubilalis*	European Corn Borer
☐	4950	*Fumibotys fumalis*	Mint Root Borer
☐	4951	*Perispasta caeculalis*	Titian Peale's Crambid
☐	4952	*Eurrhypara hortulata*	Small Magpie
☐	4953	*Phlyctaenia coronata*	Crowned Phlyctaenia
☐	4958	*Anania funebris*	White-spotted Sable
☐	4975	*Achyra rantalis*	Garden Webworm
☐	4986.1	*Sitochroa palealis*	Carrot Seed Moth
☐	5004	*Loxostege sticticalis*	Beet Webworm
☐	5017	*Loxostege cerealis*	Alfalfa Webworm
☐	5034	*Pyrausta signatalis*	Raspberry Pyrausta
☐	5040	*Pyrausta bicoloralis*	Bicolored Pyrausta
☐	5058	*Pyrausta orphisalis*	Orange-spotted Pyrausta
☐	5071	*Pyrausta acrionalis*	Mint-loving Pyrausta
☐	5079	*Udea rubigalis*	Celery Leaftier
☐	5117	*Loxostegopsis merrickalis*	Merrick's Crambid
☐	5142	*Diacme elealis*	Paler Diacme
☐	5143	*Diacme adipaloides*	Darker Diacme
☐	5156	*Nomophila nearctica*	Lucerne Moth
☐	5159	*Desmia funeralis*	Grape Leaffolder
☐	5160	*Desmia maculalis*	White-headed Grape Leaffolder
☐	5169	*Hymenia perspectalis*	Spotted Beet Webworm
☐	5170	*Spoladea recurvalis*	Hawaiian Beet Webworm
☐	5175	*Diathrausta harlequinalis*	Harlequin Webworm
☐	5176	*Anageshna primordialis*	Yellow-spotted Webworm
☐	5182	*Blepharomastix ranalis*	Hollow-spotted Blepharomastix
☐	5204	*Diaphania hyalinata*	Melonworm Moth
☐	5219	*Palpita kimballi*	Kimball's Palpita
☐	5226	*Palpita magniferalis*	Splendid Palpita
☐	5228	*Polygrammodes flavidalis*	Ironweed Root Moth
☐	5241	*Pantographa limata*	Basswood Leafroller
☐	5250	*Lygropia rivulalis*	Bog Lygropia

☐	5255	*Diastictis ventralis*	White-spotted Brown Moth
☐	5275	*Herpetogramma pertextalis*	Bold-feathered Grass Moth
☐	5277	*Herpetogramma thestealis*	Zigzag Herpetogramma
☐	5281	*Pilocrocis ramentalis*	Scraped Pilocrocis

Window-winged Moths – Family Thyrididae (37)

☐	6076	*Thyris maculata*	Spotted Thyris
☐	6077	*Thyris sepulchralis*	Mournful Thyris

Habrosynes, Thyatirids, and Hooktips – Family Depranidae (38)

☐	6235	*Habrosyne scripta*	Lettered Habrosyne
☐	6236	*Habrosyne gloriosa*	Glorious Habrosyne
☐	6237	*Pseudothyatira cymatophoroides*	Tufted Thyatirid
☐	6240	*Euthyatira pudens*	Dogwood Thyatirid
☐	6251	*Drepana arcuata*	Arched Hooktip
☐	6252	*Drepana bilineata*	Two-lined Hooktip
☐	6253	*Eudeilinia herminiata*	Northern Eudeilinia
☐	6255	*Oreta rosea*	Rose Hooktip

Scoopwings – Family Uraniidae (39)

☐	7650	*Callizzia amorata*	Gray Scoopwing
☐	7653	*Calledapteryx dryopterata*	Brown Scoopwing

Carpets and Pugs – Family Geometridae, Subfamily Larentiinae (40)

☐	7187	*Dysstroma truncata*	Marbled Carpet
☐	7189	*Dysstroma hersiliata*	Orange-barred Carpet
☐	7196	*Eulithis diversilineata*	Lesser Grapevine Looper
☐	7197	*Eulithis gracilineata*	Greater Grapevine Looper
☐	7201	*Eulithis testata*	The Chevron
☐	7203	*Eulithis molliculata*	Dimorphic Eulithis
☐	7206	*Eulithis explanata*	White Eulithis
☐	7208	*Eulithis serrataria*	Serrated Eulithis
☐	7210	*Eustroma semiatrata*	Black-banded Carpet
☐	7213	*Ecliptopera silaceata*	Small Phoenix
☐	7216	*Plemyria georgii*	George's Carpet
☐	7217	*Thera juniperata*	Juniper Carpet
☐	7218	*Thera contractata*	Contracted Spanworm
☐	7229	*Hydriomena perfracta*	Shattered Hydriomena
☐	7235	*Hydriomena divisaria*	Black-dashed Hydriomena
☐	7236	*Hydriomena renunciata*	Renounced Hydriomena
☐	7237	*Hydriomena transfigurata*	Transfigured Hydriomena
☐	7285	*Triphosa haesitata*	Tissue Moth
☐	7290	*Coryphista meadii*	Barberry Geometer
☐	7292	*Rheumaptera prunivorata*	Cherry Scallop Shell
☐	7293	*Rheumaptera hastata*	Spear-marked Black
☐	7294	*Rheumaptera subhastata*	White-banded Black
☐	7307	*Mesoleuca ruficillata*	White-ribboned Carpet
☐	7312	*Spargania magnoliata*	Double-banded Carpet

☐	7320	*Perizoma alchemillata*	Small Rivulet
☐	7329	*Anticlea vasiliata*	Variable Carpet
☐	7330	*Anticlea multiferata*	Many-lined Carpet
☐	7333	*Stamnodes gibbicostata*	Shiny Gray Carpet
☐	7368	*Xanthorhoe labradorensis*	Labrador Carpet
☐	7388	*Xanthorhoe ferrugata*	Red Twin-Spot
☐	7390	*Xanthorhoe lacustrata*	Toothed Brown Carpet
☐	7394	*Epirrhoe alternata*	White-banded Toothed Carpet
☐	7399	*Euphyia intermediata*	Sharp-angled Carpet
☐	7414	*Orthonama obstipata*	The Gem
☐	7416	*Costaconvexa centrostrigaria*	Bent-line Carpet
☐	7417	*Disclisioprocta stellata*	Somber Carpet
☐	7422	*Hydrelia inornata*	Unadorned Carpet
☐	7423	*Hydrelia albifera*	Fragile White Carpet
☐	7425	*Venusia cambrica*	The Welsh Wave
☐	7428	*Venusia comptaria*	Brown-shaded Carpet
☐	7430	*Trichodezia albovittata*	White-striped Black
☐	7433	*Epirrita autumnata*	Autumnal Moth
☐	7437	*Operophtera bruceata*	Bruce Spanworm
☐	7440	*Eubaphe mendica*	The Beggar
☐	7441	*Eubaphe meridiana*	The Little Beggar
☐	7445	*Horisme intestinata*	Brown Bark Carpet
☐	7459	*Eupithecia columbiata*	Columbia Pug
☐	7474	*Eupithecia miserulata*	Common Pug
☐	7488	*Eupithecia tripunctaria*	White-spotted Pug
☐	7551	*Eupithecia interruptofasciata*	Juniper Pug
☐	7575	*Eupithecia mutata*	Cloaked Pug
☐	7586.1	*Eupithecia absinthiata*	Wormwood Pug
☐	7605	*Eupithecia ravocostaliata*	Tawny Pug
☐	7625	*Pasiphila rectangulata*	Green Pug
☐	7635	*Acasis viridata*	Olive-and-black Carpet
☐	7637	*Cladara limitaria*	Mottled Gray Carpet
☐	7639	*Cladara atroliturata*	The Scribbler
☐	7640	*Lobophora nivigerata*	Powdered Bigwing
☐	7645	*Heterophleps refusaria*	Three-patched Bigwing
☐	7647	*Heterophleps triguttaria*	Three-spotted Fillip
☐	7648	*Dyspteris abortivaria*	The Bad-Wing

Waves – Family Geometridae, Subfamily Sterrhinae (41)

☐	7094	*Lobocleta ossularia*	Drab Brown Wave
☐	7114	*Idaea demissaria*	Red-bordered Wave
☐	7126	*Idaea dimidiata*	Single-dotted Wave
☐	7132	*Pleuroprucha insulsaria*	Common Tan Wave
☐	7136	*Cyclophora packardi*	Packard's Wave
☐	7139	*Cyclophora pendulinaria*	Sweetfern Geometer
☐	7146	*Haematopis grataria*	Chickweed Geometer

☐	7147	*Timandra amaturaria*	Cross-lined Wave
☐	7157	*Scopula cacuminaria*	Frosted Tan Wave
☐	7159	*Scopula limboundata*	Large Lace-Border
☐	7164	*Scopula junctaria*	Simple Wave
☐	7165	*Scopula quadrilineata*	Four-lined Wave
☐	7166	*Scopula frigidaria*	Frigid Wave
☐	7169	*Scopula inductata*	Soft-lined Wave
☐	7180	*Leptostales ferruminaria*	Light-ribboned Wave

Emeralds – Family Geometridae, Subfamily Geometrinae (42)

☐	7033	*Nemoria lixaria*	Red-bordered Emerald
☐	7046	*Nemoria bistriaria*	Red-fringed Emerald
☐	7047	*Nemoria rubrifrontaria*	Red-fronted Emerald
☐	7048	*Nemoria mimosaria*	White-fringed Emerald
☐	7053	*Dichorda iridaria*	Showy Emerald
☐	7058	*Synchlora aerata*	Wavy-lined Emerald
☐	7059	*Synchlora frondaria*	Southern Emerald
☐	7071	*Chlorochlamys chloroleucaria*	Blackberry Looper
☐	7084	*Hethemia pistasciaria*	Pistachio Emerald

Infants – Family Geometridae, Subfamily Archiearinae (43)

☐	6256	*Archiearis infans*	The Infant
☐	6257	*Leucobrephos brephoides*	Scarce Infant

Typical Geometers – Family Geometridae, Subfamily Ennominae (44)

☐	6258	*Alsophila pometaria*	Fall Cankerworm Moth
☐	6261	*Heliomata cycladata*	Common Spring Moth
☐	6271.1	*Mellilla xanthometata*	Orange Wing
☐	6272	*Eumacaria madopata*	Brown-bordered Geometer
☐	6273	*Speranza pustularia*	Lesser Maple Spanworm
☐	6274	*Speranza ribearia*	Currant Spanworm
☐	6283	*Speranza sulphurea*	Sulphur Granite
☐	6286	*Speranza brunneata*	Rannoch Looper
☐	6292	*Speranza exauspicata*	Speckled Granite
☐	6299	*Speranza coortaria*	Four-spotted Granite
☐	6303	*Speranza subcessaria*	Barred Granite
☐	6304	*Speranza bitactata*	Split-lined Granite
☐	6321	*Epelis truncataria*	Black-banded Orange
☐	6326	*Macaria aemulataria*	Common Angle
☐	6330	*Macaria notata*	Birch Angle
☐	6339	*Macaria transitaria*	Blurry Chocolate Angle
☐	6340	*Macaria minorata*	Minor Angle
☐	6341	*Macaria bicolorata*	Bicolored Angle
☐	6342	*Macaria bisignata*	Red-headed Inchworm
☐	6343	*Macaria sexmaculata*	Six-spotted Angle
☐	6344	*Macaria signaria*	Pale-marked Angle
☐	6347	*Macaria pinistrobata*	White Pine Angle

☐	6348	*Macaria fissinotata*	Hemlock Angle
☐	6351	*Macaria oweni*	Owen's Angle
☐	6362	*Digrammia continuata*	Curve-lined Angle
☐	6386	*Digrammia ocellinata*	Faint-spotted Angle
☐	6397	*Digrammia mellistrigata*	Yellow-lined Angle
☐	6405	*Digrammia gnophosaria*	Hollow-spotted Angle
☐	6430	*Orthofidonia flavivenata*	Yellow-veined Geometer
☐	6431	*Hesperumia sulphuraria*	Sulphur Wave
☐	6436	*Ematurga amitaria*	Cranberry Spanworm
☐	6449	*Glena cribrataria*	Dotted Gray
☐	6570	*Aethalura intertexta*	Four-barred Gray
☐	6582	*Iridopsis vellivolata*	Large Purplish Gray
☐	6583	*Iridopsis ephyraria*	Pale-winged Gray
☐	6584	*Iridopsis humaria*	Small Purplish Gray
☐	6588	*Iridopsis larvaria*	Bent-line Gray
☐	6590	*Anavitrinella pampinaria*	Common Gray
☐	6594	*Cleora sublunaria*	Double-lined Gray
☐	6597	*Ectropis crepuscularia*	Small Engrailed
☐	6598	*Protoboarmia porcelaria*	Porcelain Gray
☐	6599	*Epimecis hortaria*	Tulip-tree Beauty
☐	6620	*Melanolophia canadaria*	Canadian Melanolophia
☐	6621	*Melanolophia signataria*	Signate Melanolophia
☐	6638	*Eufidonia notataria*	Powder Moth
☐	6639	*Eufidonia discospilata*	Sharp-lined Powder Moth
☐	6640	*Biston betularia*	Pepper-and-salt Geometer
☐	6651	*Lycia ursaria*	Stout Spanworm
☐	6654	*Hypagyrtis unipunctata*	One-spotted Variant
☐	6656	*Hypagyrtis piniata*	Pine Measuringworm Moth
☐	6658	*Phigalia titea*	The Half-Wing
☐	6659	*Phigalia denticulata*	Toothed Phigalia
☐	6660	*Phigalia strigataria*	Small Phigalia
☐	6662	*Paleacrita vernata*	Spring Cankerworm
☐	6665	*Erannis tiliaria*	Linden Looper
☐	6666	*Lomographa semiclarata*	Bluish Spring Moth
☐	6667	*Lomographa vestaliata*	White Spring Moth
☐	6668	*Lomographa glomeraria*	Gray Spring Moth
☐	6677	*Cabera erythemaria*	Yellow-dusted Cream
☐	6678	*Cabera variolaria*	The Vestal
☐	6711	*Ilecta intractata*	Black-dotted Ruddy
☐	6720	*Lytrosis unitaria*	Common Lytrosis
☐	6724	*Euchlaena serrata*	The Saw-Wing
☐	6725	*Euchlaena muzaria*	Muzaria Euchlaena
☐	6729	*Euchlaena johnsonaria*	Johnson's Euchlaena
☐	6733	*Euchlaena amoenaria*	Deep Yellow Euchlaena
☐	6737	*Euchlaena tigrinaria*	Mottled Euchlaena
☐	6739	*Euchlaena irraria*	Least-marked Euchlaena

☐	6740	*Xanthotype urticaria*	False Crocus Geometer
☐	6743	*Xanthotype sospeta*	Crocus Geometer
☐	6753	*Pero honestaria*	Honest Pero
☐	6755	*Pero morrisonaria*	Morrison's Pero
☐	6763	*Phaeoura quernaria*	Oak Beauty
☐	6796	*Campaea perlata*	Pale Beauty
☐	6797	*Ennomos magnaria*	Maple Spanworm
☐	6798	*Ennomos subsignaria*	Elm Spanworm
☐	6804	*Petrophora subaequaria*	Northern Petrophora
☐	6806	*Tacparia atropunctata*	Northern Pale Alder
☐	6807	*Tacparia detersata*	Pale Alder
☐	6812	*Homochlodes fritillaria*	Pale Homochlodes
☐	6817	*Selenia alciphearia*	Northern Thorn
☐	6818	*Selenia kentaria*	Kent's Geometer
☐	6819	*Metanema inatomaria*	Pale Metanema
☐	6820	*Metanema determinata*	Dark Metanema
☐	6821	*Metarranthis warneri*	Warner's Metarranthis
☐	6822	*Metarranthis duaria*	Ruddy Metarranthis
☐	6823/25	*Metarranthis*	Scalloped Metarranthis complex
☐	6832	*Metarranthis obfirmaria*	Yellow-washed Metarranthis
☐	6834	*Cepphis decoloraria*	Dark Scallop Moth
☐	6835	*Cepphis armataria*	Scallop Moth
☐	6836	*Plagodis pulveraria*	American Barred Umber
☐	6837	*Probole alienaria*	Alien Probole
☐	6838	*Probole amicaria*	Friendly Probole
☐	6840	*Plagodis serinaria*	Lemon Plagodis
☐	6841	*Plagodis kuetzingi*	Purple Plagodis
☐	6842	*Plagodis phlogosaria*	Straight-lined Plagodis
☐	6843	*Plagodis fervidaria*	Fervid Plagodis
☐	6844	*Plagodis alcoolaria*	Hollow-spotted Plagodis
☐	6863	*Caripeta divisata*	Gray Spruce Looper
☐	6864	*Caripeta piniata*	Northern Pine Looper
☐	6867	*Caripeta angustiorata*	Brown Pine Looper
☐	6884	*Besma endropiaria*	Straw Besma
☐	6885	*Besma quercivoraria*	Oak Besma
☐	6888	*Lambdina fiscellaria*	Hemlock Looper
☐	6894	*Lambdina fervidaria*	Curve-lined Looper
☐	6898	*Cingilia catenaria*	Chain-dotted Geometer
☐	6906	*Nepytia canosaria*	False Hemlock Looper
☐	6912	*Sicya macularia*	Sharp-lined Yellow
☐	6941	*Eusarca confusaria*	Confused Eusarca
☐	6963	*Tetracis crocallata*	Yellow Slant-Line
☐	6964	*Tetracis cachexiata*	White Slant-Line
☐	6965	*Eugonobapta nivosaria*	Snowy Geometer
☐	6966	*Eutrapela clemataria*	Curve-toothed Geometer
☐	6974	*Patalene olyzonaria*	Juniper-twig Geometer

☐	6982	*Prochoerodes lineola*	Large Maple Spanworm
☐	6987	*Antepione thisoaria*	Variable Antepione
☐	7010	*Nematocampa resistaria*	Horned Spanworm

Sack-Bearers – Family Mimallonidae (45)

☐	7659	*Lacosoma chiridota*	Scalloped Sack-Bearer
☐	7662	*Cicinnus melsheimeri*	Melsheimer's Sack-Bearer

Apatelodid Moths – Family Apatelodidae (46)

☐	7663	*Apatelodes torrefacta*	Spotted Apatelodes
☐	7665	*Olceclostera angelica*	The Angel

Tent Caterpillar and Lappet Moths – Family Lasiocampidae (47)

☐	7670	*Tolype velleda*	Large Tolype
☐	7673	*Tolype laricis*	Larch Tolype
☐	7674	*Tolype notialis*	Small Tolype
☐	7683	*Artace cribrarius*	Dot-lined White Moth
☐	7685	*Heteropacha rileyana*	Riley's Lappet Moth
☐	7687	*Phyllodesma americana*	Lappet Moth
☐	7698	*Malacosoma disstria*	Forest Tent Caterpillar Moth
☐	7701	*Malacosoma americana*	Eastern Tent Caterpillar Moth

Royal Silkworm Moths – Family Saturniidae, Subfamily Ceratocampinae (48)

☐	7704	*Eacles imperialis*	Imperial Moth
☐	7706	*Citheronia regalis*	Regal Moth
☐	7708	*Citheronia sepulcralis*	Pine Devil
☐	7709	*Syssphinx bicolor*	Honey Locust Moth
☐	7712	*Syssphinx bisecta*	Bisected Honey Locust Moth
☐	7715	*Dryocampa rubicunda*	Rosy Maple Moth
☐	7716	*Anisota stigma*	Spiny Oakworm Moth
☐	7719	*Anisota senatoria*	Orange-tipped Oakworm Moth
☐	7723	*Anisota virginiensis*	Pink-striped Oakworm Moth

Buck Moths – Family Saturniidae, Subfamily Hemileucinae (49)

☐	7730	*Hemileuca maia*	Eastern Buck Moth
☐	7746	*Automeris io*	Io Moth

Giant Silkworm Moths – Family Saturniidae, Subfamily Saturniinae (50)

☐	7757	*Antheraea polyphemus*	Polyphemus Moth
☐	7758	*Actias luna*	Luna Moth
☐	7764	*Callosamia promethea*	Promethea Moth
☐	7765	*Callosamia angulifera*	Tulip-tree Silkmoth
☐	7767	*Hyalophora cecropia*	Cecropia Moth
☐	7768	*Hyalophora columbia*	Columbia Silkmoth

Large Sphinx Moths – Family Sphingidae, Subfamily Sphinginae (51)

☐	7771	*Agrius cingulata*	Pink-spotted Hawkmoth
☐	7775	*Manduca sexta*	Carolina Sphinx

☐	7776	*Manduca quinquemaculatus*	Five-spotted Hawkmoth
☐	7778	*Manduca rustica*	Rustic Sphinx
☐	7783	*Manduca jasminearum*	Ash Sphinx
☐	7784	*Dolba hyloeus*	Pawpaw Sphinx
☐	7786	*Ceratomia amyntor*	Elm Sphinx
☐	7787	*Ceratomia undulosa*	Waved Sphinx
☐	7789	*Ceratomia catalpae*	Catalpa Sphinx
☐	7793	*Paratrea plebeja*	Plebian Sphinx
☐	7796	*Lintneria eremitus*	Hermit Sphinx
☐	7802	*Sphinx chersis*	Great Ash Sphinx
☐	7807	*Sphinx canadensis*	Canadian Sphinx
☐	7809	*Sphinx kalmiae*	Laurel Sphinx
☐	7810.1	*Sphinx poecila*	Northern Apple Sphinx
☐	7811	*Sphinx luscitiosa*	Clemens' Sphinx
☐	7812	*Sphinx drupiferarum*	Wild Cherry Sphinx
☐	7816	*Lapara coniferarum*	Southern Pine Sphinx
☐	7817	*Lapara bombycoides*	Northern Pine Sphinx

Eyed Sphinx Moths – Family Sphingidae, Subfamily Smerinthinae (52)

☐	7821	*Smerinthus jamaicensis*	Twin-spotted Sphinx
☐	7822	*Smerinthus cerisyi*	One-eyed Sphinx
☐	7824	*Paonias excaecata*	Blinded Sphinx
☐	7825	*Paonias myops*	Small-eyed Sphinx
☐	7827	*Amorpha juglandis*	Walnut Sphinx
☐	7828	*Pachysphinx modesta*	Modest Sphinx

Small Sphinx Moths – Family Sphingidae, Subfamily Macroglossinae (53)

☐	7853	*Hemaris thysbe*	Hummingbird Clearwing
☐	7855	*Hemaris diffinis*	Snowberry Clearwing
☐	7859	*Eumorpha pandorus*	Pandorus Sphinx
☐	7861	*Eumorpha achemon*	Achemon Sphinx
☐	7870	*Sphecodina abbottii*	Abbott's Sphinx
☐	7871	*Deidamia inscriptum*	Lettered Sphinx
☐	7873	*Amphion floridensis*	Nessus Sphinx
☐	7884	*Darapsa versicolor*	Hydrangea Sphinx
☐	7885	*Darapsa myron*	Virginia Creeper Sphinx
☐	7886	*Darapsa choerilus*	Azalea Sphinx
☐	7890	*Xylophanes tersa*	Tersa Sphinx
☐	7892	*Hyles euphorbiae*	Spurge Hawkmoth
☐	7893	*Hyles gallii*	Gallium Sphinx
☐	7894	*Hyles lineata*	White-lined Sphinx

SUPERFAMILY NOCTUOIDEA (93)
Prominents – Family Notodontidae

☐	93-0003	7895	*Clostera albosigma*	Sigmoid Prominent
☐	93-0004	7896	*Clostera inclusa*	Angle-lined Prominent
☐	93-0006	7898	*Clostera strigosa*	Striped Chocolate-Tip
☐	93-0009	7901	*Clostera apicalis*	Apical Prominent

☐	93-0010	7917	*Hyperaeschra georgica*	Georgian Prominent
☐	93-0012	7922	*Pheosia rimosa*	Black-rimmed Prominent
☐	93-0013	7924	*Odontosia elegans*	Elegant Prominent
☐	93-0015	7926	*Notodonta scitipennis*	Finned-willow Prominent
☐	93-0017	7928	*Notodonta torva*	Northern Finned Prominent
☐	93-0018	7929	*Nerice bidentata*	Double-toothed Prominent
☐	93-0019	7931	*Gluphisia septentrionis*	Common Gluphisia
☐	93-0021	7933	*Gluphisia avimacula*	Four-spotted Gluphisia
☐	93-0022	7934	*Gluphisia lintneri*	Lintner's Gluphisia
☐	93-0024	7936	*Furcula borealis*	White Furcula
☐	93-0025	7937	*Furcula cinerea*	Gray Furcula
☐	93-0027	7939	*Furcula occidentalis*	Western Furcula
☐	93-0029	7941	*Furcula modesta*	Modest Furcula
☐	93-0030	7942	*Cerura scitiscripta*	Black-etched Prominent
☐	93-0033	7902	*Datana ministra*	Yellow-necked Caterpillar Moth
☐	93-0034	7903	*Datana angusii*	Angus' Datana
☐	93-0035	7904	*Datana drexelii*	Drexel's Datana
☐	93-0037	7906	*Datana contracta*	Contracted Datana
☐	93-0038	7907	*Datana integerrima*	Walnut Caterpillar Moth
☐	93-0039	7908	*Datana perspicua*	Spotted Datana
☐	93-0046	7915	*Nadata gibbosa*	White-dotted Prominent
☐	93-0048	7919	*Peridea basitriens*	Oval-based Prominent
☐	93-0049	7920	*Peridea angulosa*	Angulose Prominent
☐	93-0050	7921	*Peridea ferruginea*	Chocolate Prominent
☐	93-0051	7930	*Ellida caniplaga*	Linden Prominent
☐	93-0066	7974	*Misogada unicolor*	Drab Prominent
☐	93-0067	7975	*Macrurocampa marthesia*	Mottled Prominent
☐	93-0075	7983	*Heterocampa obliqua*	Oblique Heterocampa
☐	93-0077	7985	*Heterocampa subrotata*	Small Heterocampa
☐	93-0082	7990	*Heterocampa umbrata*	White-blotched Heterocampa
☐	93-0086	7994	*Heterocampa guttivitta*	Saddled Prominent
☐	93-0087	7995	*Heterocampa biundata*	Wavy-lined Heterocampa
☐	93-0090	7998	*Lochmaeus manteo*	Variable Oakleaf Caterpillar Moth
☐	93-0091	7999	*Lochmaeus bilineata*	Double-lined Prominent
☐	93-0098	8005	*Schizura ipomoeae*	Morning-glory Prominent
☐	93-0099	8006	*Schizura badia*	Chestnut Schizura
☐	93-0100	8007	*Schizura unicornis*	Unicorn Prominent
☐	93-0103	8010	*Schizura concinna*	Red-humped Caterpillar Moth
☐	93-0104	8011	*Schizura leptinoides*	Black-blotched Schizura
☐	93-0105	8012	*Oligocentria semirufescens*	Red-washed Prominent
☐	93-0110	8017	*Oligocentria lignicolor*	White-streaked Prominent
☐	93-0115	8022	*Hyparpax aurora*	Pink Prominent
☐	93-0127	7951	*Symmerista albifrons*	White-headed Prominent
☐	93-0128	7952	*Symmerista canicosta*	Red-humped Oakworm
☐	93-0129	7953	*Symmerista leucitys*	Orange-humped Oakworm
☐	93-0134	7958	*Dasylophia thyatiroides*	Gray-patched Prominent

Tussock Moths – Family Erebidae, Subfamily Lymantriinae

☐	93-0141	8318	*Lymantria dispar*	Gypsy Moth
☐	93-0146	8294	*Dasychira vagans*	Variable Tussock Moth
☐	93-0148	8296	*Dasychira basiflava*	Yellow-based Tussock Moth
☐	93-0154	8302	*Dasychira obliquata*	Streaked Tussock Moth
☐	93-0156	8304	*Dasychira plagiata*	Northern Pine Tussock Moth
☐	93-0157	8305	*Dasychira pinicola*	Pine Tussock Moth
☐	93-0160	8308	*Orgyia antiqua*	Rusty Tussock Moth
☐	93-0166	8314	*Orgyia definita*	Definite Tussock Moth
☐	93-0168	8316	*Orgyia leucostigma*	White-marked Tussock Moth
☐	93-0170	8319	*Leucoma salicis*	Satin Moth

Lichen Moths – Family Erebidae, Subfamily Arctiinae, Tribe Lithosiini

☐	93-0178	8061	*Cisthene kentuckiensis*	Kentucky Lichen Moth
☐	93-0189	8072	*Cisthene packardii*	Packard's Lichen Moth
☐	93-0201	8087	*Lycomorpha pholus*	Black-and-yellow Lichen Moth
☐	93-0204	8089	*Hypoprepia miniata*	Scarlet-winged Lichen Moth
☐	93-0205	8090	*Hypoprepia fucosa*	Painted Lichen Moth
☐	93-0215	8098	*Clemensia albata*	Little White Lichen Moth
☐	93-0217	8043	*Eilema bicolor*	Bicolored Moth
☐	93-0219	8045.1	*Crambidia pallida*	Pale Lichen Moth
☐	93-0225	8051	*Crambidia casta*	Pearly-winged Lichen Moth

Tiger Moths – Family Erebidae, Subfamily Arctiinae, Tribe Arctiini

☐	93-0240	8199	*Grammia arge*	Arge Moth
☐	93-0242	8194	*Grammia phyllira*	Phyllira Tiger Moth
☐	93-0244	8197	*Grammia virgo*	Virgin Tiger Moth
☐	93-0245	8176	*Grammia anna*	Anna Tiger Moth
☐	93-0246	8196	*Grammia parthenice*	Parthenice Tiger Moth
☐	93-0247	8175	*Grammia virguncula*	Little Virgin Tiger Moth
☐	93-0253	8188	*Grammia figurata*	Figured Tiger Moth
☐	93-0264	8186	*Grammia williamsii*	Williams' Tiger Moth
☐	93-0278	8169	*Apantesis phalerata*	Harnessed Tiger Moth
☐	93-0280	8171	*Apantesis nais*	Nais Tiger Moth
☐	93-0288	8162	*Platarctia parthenos*	St. Lawrence Tiger Moth
☐	93-0290	8166	*Arctia caja*	Great Tiger Moth
☐	93-0294	8114	*Virbia laeta*	Joyful Virbia
☐	93-0297	8118	*Virbia opella*	Tawny Virbia
☐	93-0299	8121	*Virbia aurantiaca*	Orange Virbia
☐	93-0302	8120	*Virbia lamae*	Bog Virbia
☐	93-0306	8123	*Virbia ferruginosa*	Rusty Virbia
☐	93-0309	8134	*Spilosoma congrua*	Agreeable Tiger Moth
☐	93-0310	8136	*Spilosoma dubia*	Dubious Tiger Moth
☐	93-0311	8133	*Spilosoma latipennis*	Pink-legged Tiger Moth
☐	93-0316	8137	*Spilosoma virginica*	Virginian Tiger Moth
☐	93-0317	8131	*Estigmene acrea*	Salt Marsh Moth

☐	93-0319	8140	*Hyphantria cunea*	Fall Webworm
☐	93-0323	8146	*Hypercompe scribonia*	Giant Leopard Moth
☐	93-0332	8156	*Phragmatobia fuliginosa*	Ruby Tiger Moth
☐	93-0333	8157	*Phragmatobia lineata*	Lined Ruby Tiger Moth
☐	93-0334	8158	*Phragmatobia assimilans*	Large Ruby Tiger Moth
☐	93-0335	8129	*Pyrrharctia isabella*	Isabella Tiger Moth
☐	93-0341	8107	*Haploa clymene*	Clymene Moth
☐	93-0343	8109	*Haploa reversa*	Reversed Haploa
☐	93-0344	8110	*Haploa contigua*	The Neighbor
☐	93-0345	8111	*Haploa lecontei*	Leconte's Haploa
☐	93-0346	8112	*Haploa confusa*	Confused Haploa
☐	93-0348	8105	*Utetheisa ornatrix*	Ornate Moth
☐	93-0360	8203	*Halysidota tessellaris*	Banded Tussock Moth
☐	93-0370	8211	*Lophocampa caryae*	Hickory Tussock Moth
☐	93-0373	8214	*Lophocampa maculata*	Spotted Tussock Moth
☐	93-0404	8230	*Cycnia tenera*	Delicate Cycnia
☐	93-0405	8231	*Cycnia oregonensis*	Oregon Cycnia
☐	93-0412	8238	*Euchaetes egle*	Milkweed Tussock Moth
☐	93-0435	8262	*Ctenucha virginica*	Virginia Ctenucha
☐	93-0440	8267	*Cisseps fulvicollis*	Yellow-collared Scape Moth

Litter Moths – Family Erebidae, Subfamily Hermeniinae

☐	93-0469	8322	*Idia americalis*	American Idia
☐	93-0471	8323	*Idia aemula*	Common Idia
☐	93-0474	8326	*Idia rotundalis*	Rotund Idia
☐	93-0475	8327	*Idia forbesii*	Forbes' Idia
☐	93-0477	8329	*Idia diminuendis*	Orange-spotted Idia
☐	93-0478	8330	*Idia scobialis*	Smoky Idia
☐	93-0482	8334	*Idia lubricalis*	Glossy Black Idia
☐	93-0487	8338	*Phalaenophana pyramusalis*	Dark-banded Owlet
☐	93-0489	8340	*Zanclognatha lituralis*	Lettered Fan-Foot
☐	93-0492	8345	*Zanclognatha laevigata*	Variable Fan-Foot
☐	93-0495	8348	*Zanclognatha pedipilalis*	Grayish Fan-Foot
☐	93-0496	8349	*Zanclognatha protumnusalis*	Complex Fan-Foot
☐	93-0498	8351	*Zanclognatha cruralis*	Early Fan-Foot
☐	93-0500	8353	*Zanclognatha jacchusalis*	Wavy-lined Fan-Foot
☐	93-0502	8355	*Chytolita morbidalis*	Morbid Owlet
☐	93-0503	8356	*Chytolita petrealis*	Stone-winged Owlet
☐	93-0506	8359	*Macrochilo bivittata*	Two-striped Owlet
☐	93-0508	8357	*Macrochilo absorptalis*	Slant-lined Owlet
☐	93-0510	8358	*Macrochilo litophora*	Two-lined Owlet
☐	93-0511	8360	*Macrochilo orciferalis*	Bronzy Macrochilo
☐	93-0512	8362	*Phalaenostola metonalis*	Pale Phalaenostola
☐	93-0513	8363	*Phalaenostola eumelusalis*	Dark Phalaenostola
☐	93-0514	8364	*Phalaenostola larentioides*	Black-banded Owlet
☐	93-0516	8366	*Tetanolita mynesalis*	Smoky Tetanolita

☐	93-0520	8370	*Bleptina caradrinalis*	Bent-winged Owlet
☐	93-0530	8379	*Renia factiosalis*	Sociable Renia
☐	93-0532	8381	*Renia discoloralis*	Discolored Renia
☐	93-0536	8384.1	*Renia flavipunctalis*	Yellow-spotted Renia
☐	93-0539	8387	*Renia sobrialis*	Sober Renia
☐	93-0547	8393	*Lascoria ambigualis*	Ambiguous Moth
☐	93-0551	8397	*Palthis angulalis*	Dark-spotted Palthis
☐	93-0552	8398	*Palthis asopialis*	Faint-spotted Palthis
☐	93-0555	8401	*Redectis vitrea*	White-spotted Redectis

Pangraptine Owlets – Family Erebidae, Subfamily Pangraptinae

| ☐ | 93-0559 | 8490 | *Pangrapta decoralis* | Decorated Owlet |
| ☐ | 93-0560 | 8491 | *Ledaea perditalis* | Lost Owlet |

Snouts – Family Erebidae, Subfamily Hypeninae

☐	93-0561	8441	*Hypena manalis*	Flowing-line Snout
☐	93-0562	8442	*Hypena baltimoralis*	Baltimore Snout
☐	93-0564	8443	*Hypena bijugalis*	Dimorphic Snout
☐	93-0565	8444	*Hypena palparia*	Mottled Snout
☐	93-0566	8445	*Hypena abalienalis*	White-lined Snout
☐	93-0567	8446	*Hypena deceptalis*	Deceptive Snout
☐	93-0568	8447	*Hypena madefactalis*	Gray-edged Snout
☐	93-0570	8448	*Hypena sordidula*	Sordid Snout
☐	93-0573	8450	*Hypena atomaria*	Speckled Snout
☐	93-0575	8452	*Hypena edictalis*	Large Snout
☐	93-0584	8461	*Hypena humuli*	Hop Vine Moth
☐	93-0588	8465	*Hypena scabra*	Green Cloverworm
☐	93-0589	8455	*Hypena eductalis*	Red-footed Snout

Assorted Owlets – Family Erebidae, Subfamilies Rivulinae, Hyperiinae, Scoliopteryginae, Calpinae, Hypocalinae, Scolecocampinae, Phytometrinae, Hypenodinae, and Boletobiinae

☐	93-0590	8411	*Colobochyla interpuncta*	Yellow-lined Owlet
☐	93-0591	8412	*Melanomma auricinctaria*	Gold-lined Melanomma
☐	93-0592	8404	*Rivula propinqualis*	Spotted Grass Moth
☐	93-0601	8555	*Scoliopteryx libatrix*	The Herald
☐	93-0602	8545	*Anomis erosa*	Yellow Scallop Moth
☐	93-0612	8536	*Calyptra canadensis*	Canadian Owlet
☐	93-0622	8534	*Plusiodonta compressipalpis*	Moonseed Moth
☐	93-0629	8528	*Hypsoropha hormos*	Small Necklace Moth
☐	93-0634	8509	*Arugisa lutea*	Common Arugisa
☐	93-0637	8514	*Scolecocampa liburna*	Dead-wood Borer Moth
☐	93-0655	8440	*Nigetia formosalis*	Thin-winged Owlet
☐	93-0661	8420	*Hypenodes caducus*	Large Hypenodes
☐	93-0662	8421	*Hypenodes fractilinea*	Broken-line Hypenodes
☐	93-0669	8426	*Dyspyralis illocata*	Visitation Moth
☐	93-0670	8427	*Dyspyralis puncticosta*	Spot-edged Dyspyralis

	93-0671	8428	*Dyspyralis nigellus*	Nigella Dyspyralis
☐	93-0671	8428	*Dyspyralis nigellus*	Nigella Dyspyralis
☐	93-0673	8418	*Parascotia fuliginaria*	Waved Black
☐	93-0679	8499	*Metalectra discalis*	Common Fungus Moth
☐	93-0680	8500	*Metalectra quadrisignata*	Four-spotted Fungus Moth
☐	93-0682	8502	*Metalectra tantillus*	Black Fungus Moth
☐	93-0715	8479	*Spargaloma sexpunctata*	Six-spotted Gray
☐	93-0717	8481	*Phytometra rhodarialis*	Pink-bordered Yellow
☐	93-0729	9037	*Hyperstrotia pervertens*	Dotted Graylet
☐	93-0730	9038	*Hyperstrotia villificans*	White-lined Graylet
☐	93-0731	9039	*Hyperstrotia flaviguttata*	Yellow-spotted Graylet
☐	93-0732	9040	*Hyperstrotia secta*	Black-patched Graylet
☐	93-0734	8493	*Isogona tenuis*	Thin-lined Owlet

Underwings, Zales, and Related Owlets – Family Erebidae, Subfamily Erebinae

☐	93-0759	8649	*Ascalapha odorata*	Black Witch
☐	93-0760	8769	*Spiloloma lunilinea*	Moon-lined Moth
☐	93-0761	8770	*Catocala innubens*	The Betrothed
☐	93-0762	8771	*Catocala piatrix*	The Penitent
☐	93-0764	8773	*Catocala epione*	Epione Underwing
☐	93-0766	8775	*Catocala antinympha*	Sweetfern Underwing
☐	93-0767	8777	*Catocala badia coelebs*	The Old Maid
☐	93-0768	8778	*Catocala habilis*	Habilis Underwing
☐	93-0769	8780	*Catocala robinsonii*	Robinson's Underwing
☐	93-0770	8783	*Catocala angusi*	Angus' Underwing
☐	93-0771	8781	*Catocala judith*	Judith's Underwing
☐	93-0773	8784	*Catocala obscura*	Obscure Underwing
☐	93-0774	8785	*Catocala residua*	Residua Underwing
☐	93-0777	8788	*Catocala retecta*	Yellow-gray Underwing
☐	93-0782	8792	*Catocala vidua*	Widow Underwing
☐	93-0783	8794	*Catocala lacrymosa*	Tearful Underwing
☐	93-0784	8795	*Catocala palaeogama*	Oldwife Underwing
☐	93-0787	8796	*Catocala nebulosa*	Clouded Underwing
☐	93-0788	8797	*Catocala subnata*	Youthful Underwing
☐	93-0789	8793	*Catocala maestosa*	Sad Underwing
☐	93-0790	8798	*Catocala neogama*	The Bride
☐	93-0792	8801	*Catocala ilia*	Ilia Underwing
☐	93-0794	8802	*Catocala cerogama*	Yellow-banded Underwing
☐	93-0795	8803	*Catocala relicta*	White Underwing
☐	93-0796	8804	*Catocala marmorata*	Marbled Underwing
☐	93-0797	8805	*Catocala unijuga*	Once-married Underwing
☐	93-0798	8806	*Catocala parta*	Mother Underwing
☐	93-0804	8817	*Catocala briseis*	Briseis Underwing
☐	93-0806	8821	*Catocala semirelicta*	Semirelict Underwing
☐	93-0812	8832	*Catocala cara*	Darling Underwing
☐	93-0814	8833	*Catocala concumbens*	Pink Underwing
☐	93-0815	8834	*Catocala amatrix*	The Sweetheart

☐	93-0826	8840	*Catocala illecta*	Magdalen Underwing
☐	93-0832	8846	*Catocala sordida*	Sordid Underwing
☐	93-0837	8851	*Catocala coccinata*	Scarlet Underwing
☐	93-0841	8857	*Catocala ultronia*	Ultronia Underwing
☐	93-0844	8863	*Catocala mira*	Wonderful Underwing
☐	93-0845	8864	*Catocala grynea*	Woody Underwing
☐	93-0846	8858	*Catocala crataegi*	Hawthorn Underwing
☐	93-0847	8865	*Catocala praeclara*	Praeclara Underwing
☐	93-0851	8867	*Catocala blandula*	Charming Underwing
☐	93-0853	8872	*Catocala clintonii*	Clinton's Underwing
☐	93-0855	8873	*Catocala similis*	Similar Underwing
☐	93-0856	8874	*Catocala minuta*	Little Underwing
☐	93-0857	8876	*Catocala micronympha*	The Little Nymph
☐	93-0858	8877	*Catocala connubialis*	Connubial Underwing
☐	93-0859	8878	*Catocala amica*	Girlfriend Underwing
☐	93-0860	8878.1	*Catocala lineella*	Little Lined Underwing
☐	93-0862	8591	*Phoberia atomaris*	Common Oak Moth
☐	93-0864	8592	*Cissusa spadix*	Black-dotted Brown
☐	93-0871	8600	*Melipotis indomita*	Indomitable Melipotis
☐	93-0915	8641	*Drasteria grandirena*	Figure-seven Moth
☐	93-0923	8738	*Caenurgina crassiuscula*	Clover Looper
☐	93-0924	8739	*Caenurgina erechtea*	Forage Looper
☐	93-0929	8731	*Euclidia cuspidea*	Toothed Somberwing
☐	93-0938	8733	*Caenurgia chloropha*	Vetch Looper
☐	93-0940	8747	*Celiptera frustulum*	Black Bit Moth
☐	93-0942	8743	*Mocis latipes*	Small Mocis
☐	93-0944	8745	*Mocis texana*	Texas Mocis
☐	93-0954	8762	*Argyrostrotis quadrifilaris*	Four-lined Chocolate
☐	93-0956	8764	*Argyrostrotis anilis*	Short-lined Chocolate
☐	93-0961	8727	*Parallelia bistriaris*	Maple Looper Moth
☐	93-0962	8721	*Allotria elonympha*	False Underwing
☐	93-0970	8651	*Lesmone detrahens*	Detracted Owlet
☐	93-1023	8689	*Zale lunata*	Lunate Zale
☐	93-1026	8692	*Zale galbanata*	Maple Zale
☐	93-1030	8695	*Zale undularis*	Black Zale
☐	93-1032	8697	*Zale minerea*	Colorful Zale
☐	93-1033	8698	*Zale phaeocapna*	Hazel Zale
☐	93-1038	8703	*Zale duplicata*	False Pine Looper Zale
☐	93-1039	8704	*Zale helata*	Brown-spotted Zale
☐	93-1042	8707	*Zale metatoides*	Washed-out Zale
☐	93-1049	8713.1	*Zale intenta*	Intent Zale
☐	93-1052	8716	*Zale unilineata*	One-lined Zale
☐	93-1053	8717	*Zale horrida*	Horrid Zale
☐	93-1055	8719	*Euparthenos nubilis*	Locust Underwing
☐	93-1060	9818	*Amolita fessa*	Feeble Grass Moth

Eulepidotine Owlets – Family Erebidae, Subfamily Eulepidotinae

☐	93-1077	8574	*Anticarsia gemmatalis*	Velvetbean Caterpillar Moth
☐	93-1089	8587	*Panopoda rufimargo*	Red-lined Panopoda
☐	93-1090	8588	*Panopoda carneicosta*	Brown Panapoda
☐	93-1101	8525	*Phyprosopus callitrichoides*	Curve-lined Owlet

Marathyssas and Paectes – Family Euteliidae

☐	93-1103	8955	*Marathyssa inficita*	Dark Marathyssa
☐	93-1104	8956	*Marathyssa basalis*	Light Marathyssa
☐	93-1106	8957	*Paectes oculatrix*	Eyed Paectes
☐	93-1107	8959	*Paectes pygmaea*	Pygmy Paectes
☐	93-1108	8959.1	*Paectes abrostolella*	Barrens Paectes
☐	93-1111	8962	*Paectes abrostoloides*	Large Paectes
☐	93-1118	8968	*Eutelia pulcherrimus*	Beautiful Eutelia

Nolas – Family Nolidae, Subfamily Nolinae

☐	93-1121	8983	*Meganola minuscula*	Confused Meganola
☐	93-1123	8983.2	*Meganola spodia*	Ashy Meganola
☐	93-1130	8990	*Nola cilicoides*	Blurry-patched Nola
☐	93-1131	8991	*Nola cereella*	Sorghum Webworm
☐	93-1132	8992	*Nola triquetrana*	Three-spotted Nola
☐	93-1135	8995	*Nola ovilla*	Woolly Nola

Baileyas and Nycteolas – Family Noctuidae, Subfamilies Risobinae and Chloephorinae

☐	93-1141	8974	*Garella nilotica*	Small Characoma
☐	93-1142	8975	*Nycteola frigidana*	Frigid Owlet
☐	93-1144	8977	*Nycteola cinereana*	Gray Midget
☐	93-1145	8978	*Nycteola metaspilella*	Forgotten Frigid Owlet
☐	93-1148	8969	*Baileya doubledayi*	Doubleday's Baileya
☐	93-1149	8970	*Baileya ophthalmica*	Eyed Baileya
☐	93-1150	8971	*Baileya dormitans*	Sleeping Baileya
☐	93-1152	8972	*Baileya levitans*	Pale Baileya
☐	93-1154	8973	*Baileya australis*	Small Baileya

Loopers – Family Noctuidae, Subfamily Plusiinae

☐	93-1161	8880	*Abrostola ovalis*	Oval Nettle Moth
☐	93-1162	8881	*Abrostola urentis*	Spectacled Nettle Moth
☐	93-1166	8885	*Argyrogramma verruca*	Golden Looper
☐	93-1167	8886	*Enigmogramma basigera*	Pink-washed Looper
☐	93-1168	8887	*Trichoplusia ni*	Ni Moth
☐	93-1169	8889	*Ctenoplusia oxygramma*	Sharp-stigma Looper
☐	93-1170	8890	*Chrysodeixis includens*	Soybean Looper
☐	93-1176	8895	*Rachiplusia ou*	Gray Looper
☐	93-1177	8898	*Allagrapha aerea*	Unspotted Looper
☐	93-1178	8896	*Diachrysia aereoides*	Dark-spotted Looper
☐	93-1179	8897	*Diachrysia balluca*	Hologram Moth
☐	93-1184	8899	*Pseudeva purpurigera*	Straight-lined Looper
☐	93-1186	8904	*Chrysanympha formosa*	Formosa Looper

☐	93-1187	8905	*Eosphoropteryx thyatyroides*	Pink-patched Looper
☐	93-1191	8908	*Autographa precationis*	Common Looper
☐	93-1194	8912	*Autographa mappa*	Wavy Chestnut Y
☐	93-1200	8911	*Autographa bimaculata*	Two-spotted Looper
☐	93-1204	8923	*Autographa ampla*	Large Looper
☐	93-1209	8907	*Megalographa biloba*	Bilobed Looper
☐	93-1212	8926	*Syngrapha octoscripta*	Eight-lettered Looper
☐	93-1213	8929	*Syngrapha viridisigma*	Green-spotted Looper
☐	93-1215	8927	*Syngrapha epigaea*	Epigaea Looper
☐	93-1224	8940	*Syngrapha abstrusa*	Abstruse Looper
☐	93-1225	8939	*Syngrapha alias*	Hooked Silver Y
☐	93-1227	8942	*Syngrapha rectangula*	Salt-and-pepper Looper
☐	93-1234	8924	*Anagrapha falcifera*	Celery Looper
☐	93-1235	8953	*Plusia venusta*	White-streaked Looper
☐	93-1236	8950	*Plusia putnami*	Putnam's Looper
☐	93-1239	8952	*Plusia contexta*	Connected Looper

Glyphs – Family Noctuidae, Subfamilies Bagisarinae and Eustrotiinae

☐	93-1253	9070	*Amyna axis*	Eight-Spot
☐	93-1284	9044	*Marimatha nigrofimbria*	Black-bordered Lemon
☐	93-1289	9046	*Deltote bellicula*	Bog Deltote
☐	93-1290	9047	*Protodeltote muscosula*	Large Mossy Glyph
☐	93-1291	9048	*Protodeltote albidula*	Pale Glyph
☐	93-1292	9051	*Lithacodia musta*	Small Mossy Glyph
☐	93-1295	9049	*Maliattha synochitis*	Black-dotted Glyph
☐	93-1296	9050	*Maliattha concinnimacula*	Red-spotted Glyph
☐	93-1297	9059	*Capis curvata*	Curved Halter Moth

Bird-dropping Moths – Family Noctuidae, Subfamily Acontiinae

☐	93-1314	9090	*Ponometia candefacta*	Olive-shaded Bird-dropping Moth
☐	93-1319	9095	*Ponometia erastrioides*	Small Bird-dropping Moth
☐	93-1343	9136	*Tarache aprica*	Exposed Bird-dropping Moth
☐	93-1387	9127	*Spragueia leo*	Common Spragueia

Pantheas and Yellowhorns – Family Noctuidae, Subfamily Pantheinae

☐	93-1396	9182	*Panthea furcilla*	Eastern Panthea
☐	93-1398	9177	*Panthea acronyctoides*	Black Zigzag
☐	93-1400	9184	*Colocasia flavicornis*	Saddled Yellowhorn
☐	93-1401	9185	*Colocasia propinquilinea*	Close-banded Yellowhorn
☐	93-1406	9189	*Charadra deridens*	The Laugher

Hieroglyphic Moth – Family Noctuidae, Subfamily Diphtherinae

☐	93-1410	8560	*Diphthera festiva*	Hieroglyphic Moth

Brothers – Family Noctuidae, Subfamily Dilobinae

☐	93-1411	9192	*Raphia abrupta*	Abrupt Brother
☐	93-1412	9193	*Raphia frater*	The Brother

Balsas – Family Noctuidae, Subfamily Balsinae

	93-1417	9662	*Balsa malana*	Many-dotted Appleworm
☐	93-1417	9662	*Balsa malana*	Many-dotted Appleworm
☐	93-1418	9663	*Balsa tristrigella*	Three-lined Balsa
☐	93-1419	9664	*Balsa labecula*	White-blotched Balsa

Daggers – Family Noctuidae, Subfamily Acronictinae

	93-1420	9199	*Acronicta rubricoma*	Ruddy Dagger
☐	93-1420	9199	*Acronicta rubricoma*	Ruddy Dagger
☐	93-1421	9200	*Acronicta americana*	American Dagger
☐	93-1424	9203	*Acronicta dactylina*	Fingered Dagger
☐	93-1425	9205	*Acronicta lepusculina*	Cottonwood Dagger
☐	93-1428	9207	*Acronicta innotata*	Unmarked Dagger
☐	93-1429	9208	*Acronicta betulae*	Birch Dagger
☐	93-1430	9209	*Acronicta radcliffei*	Radcliffe's Dagger
☐	93-1432	9211	*Acronicta tritona*	Triton Dagger
☐	93-1433	9212	*Acronicta grisea*	Gray Dagger
☐	93-1436	9219	*Acronicta connecta*	Connected Dagger
☐	93-1438	9221	*Acronicta funeralis*	Funerary Dagger
☐	93-1442	9225	*Acronicta vinnula*	Delightful Dagger
☐	93-1443	9226	*Acronicta superans*	Splendid Dagger
☐	93-1444	9227	*Acronicta laetifica*	Pleasant Dagger
☐	93-1445	9229	*Acronicta hasta*	Speared Dagger
☐	93-1452	9235	*Acronicta spinigera*	Nondescript Dagger
☐	93-1453	9236	*Acronicta morula*	Ochre Dagger
☐	93-1454	9237	*Acronicta interrupta*	Interrupted Dagger
☐	93-1455	9238	*Acronicta lobeliae*	Great Oak Dagger
☐	93-1458	9241	*Acronicta fragilis*	Fragile Dagger
☐	93-1463	9243	*Acronicta ovata*	Ovate Dagger
☐	93-1465	9244	*Acronicta modica*	Medium Dagger
☐	93-1466	9245	*Acronicta haesitata*	Hesitant Dagger
☐	93-1467	9249	*Acronicta increta*	Small Oak Dagger
☐	93-1470	9251	*Acronicta retardata*	Retarded Dagger
☐	93-1471	9254	*Acronicta afflicta*	Afflicted Dagger
☐	93-1474	9257	*Acronicta impleta*	Yellow-haired Dagger
☐	93-1476	9259	*Acronicta noctivaga*	Night-wandering Dagger
☐	93-1477	9261	*Acronicta impressa*	Impressed Dagger
☐	93-1478	9264	*Acronicta longa*	Long-winged Dagger
☐	93-1480	9266	*Acronicta lithospila*	Streaked Dagger
☐	93-1485	9272	*Acronicta oblinita*	Smeared Dagger
☐	93-1488	9274	*Acronicta lanceolaria*	Lanceolate Dagger
☐	93-1493	9280	*Simyra insularis*	Henry's Marsh Moth
☐	93-1494	9281	*Agriopodes fallax*	Green Marvel
☐	93-1497	9285	*Polygrammate hebraeicum*	The Hebrew
☐	93-1498	9286	*Harrisimemna trisignata*	Harris's Three-Spot
☐	93-1500	9061	*Cerma cora*	Owl-eyed Bird-dropping Moth
☐	93-1501	9062	*Cerma cerintha*	Tufted Bird-dropping Moth

Hooded Owlets – Family Noctuidae, Subfamily Cuculliinae

☐	93-1504	10200	*Cucullia asteroides*	Goldenrod Hooded Owlet
☐	93-1508	10197	*Cucullia florea*	Gray Hooded Owlet
☐	93-1513	10202	*Cucullia convexipennis*	Brown Hooded Owlet
☐	93-1514	10194	*Cucullia intermedia*	Dusky Hooded Owlet

Amphipyrine Sallows – Family Noctuidae, Subfamily Amphipyrinae

☐	93-1544	9638	*Amphipyra pyramidoides*	Copper Underwing
☐	93-1545	9639	*Amphipyra tragopoginis*	Mouse Moth
☐	93-1546	9640	*Amphipyra glabella*	Smooth Amphipyra
☐	93-1548	10019	*Psaphida resumens*	Figure-eight Sallow
☐	93-1549	10020	*Psaphida thaxterianus*	Thaxter's Sallow
☐	93-1550	10014	*Psaphida rolandi*	Roland's Sallow
☐	93-1552	10012	*Psaphida electilis*	Chosen Sallow
☐	93-1553	10016	*Psaphida styracis*	Fawn Sallow
☐	93-1557	10021	*Copivaleria grotei*	Grote's Sallow
☐	93-1561	10005	*Feralia jocosa*	The Joker
☐	93-1563	10007	*Feralia major*	Major Sallow
☐	93-1564	10008	*Feralia comstocki*	Comstock's Sallow
☐	93-1661	9754	*Plagiomimicus pityochromus*	Black-barred Brown
☐	93-1676	9781	*Basilodes pepita*	Gold Moth
☐	93-1681	9766	*Cirrhophanus triangulifer*	Goldenrod Stowaway
☐	93-1724	9725	*Azenia obtusa*	Obtuse Yellow

Oncocnemidine Sallows – Family Noctuidae, Subfamily Oncocnemidinae

☐	93-1765	10033	*Catabena lineolata*	Fine-lined Sallow
☐	93-1771	10177	*Calophasia lunula*	Toadflax Brocade
☐	93-1821	10059	*Sympistis badistriga*	Brown-lined Sallow
☐	93-1823	10066.1	*Sympistis dinalda*	Broad-lined Sallow
☐	93-1906	10067	*Sympistis chionanthi*	Fringe-tree Sallow
☐	93-1909	10123	*Sympistis piffardi*	Black-banded Beauty

Wood-Nymphs and Foresters – Family Noctuidae, Subfamily Agaristinae

☐	93-1964	9299	*Eudryas unio*	Pearly Wood-Nymph
☐	93-1966	9301	*Eudryas grata*	Beautiful Wood-Nymph
☐	93-1975	9309	*Psychomorpha epimenis*	Grapevine Epimenis
☐	93-1979	9314	*Alypia octomaculata*	Eight-spotted Forester

Groundlings – Family Noctuidae, Subfamily Condicinae

☐	93-1989	9690	*Condica videns*	White-dotted Groundling
☐	93-1992	9693	*Condica mobilis*	Mobile Groundling
☐	93-1995	9696	*Condica vecors*	Dusky Groundling
☐	93-1998	9699	*Condica sutor*	The Cobbler
☐	93-2015	9714	*Condica confederata*	The Confederate
☐	93-2018	9720	*Ogdoconta cinereola*	Common Pinkband
☐	93-2024	9056	*Homophoberia cristata*	Water-lily Moth
☐	93-2025	9057	*Homophoberia apicosa*	Black Wedge-Spot
☐	93-2026	9065	*Leuconycta diphteroides*	Green Leuconycta

☐	93-2027	9066	*Leuconycta lepidula*	Marbled-green Leuconycta
☐	93-2030	9661	*Crambodes talidiformis*	Verbena Moth

Flower Moths – Family Noctuidae, Subfamily Heliothinae

☐	93-2040	11063	*Pyrrhia cilisca*	Bordered Sallow
☐	93-2041	11064	*Pyrrhia exprimens*	Purple-lined Sallow
☐	93-2045	11068	*Helicoverpa zea*	Corn Earworm
☐	93-2046	11072	*Heliocheilus phloxiphaga*	Darker-spotted Straw Moth
☐	93-2054	11071	*Heliothis virescens*	Tobacco Budworm
☐	93-2082	11164	*Schinia florida*	Primrose Moth
☐	93-2091	11135	*Schinia rivulosa*	Ragweed Flower Moth
☐	93-2096	11149	*Schinia trifascia*	Three-lined Flower Moth
☐	93-2120	11117	*Schinia lynx*	Lynx Flower Moth
☐	93-2134	11128	*Schinia arcigera*	Arcigera Flower Moth
☐	93-2145	11173	*Schinia sanguinea*	Bleeding Flower Moth
☐	93-2156	11177	*Schinia nundina*	Goldenrod Flower Moth

Fern Moths – Family Noctuidae, Subfamily Eriopinae

☐	93-2190	9630	*Callopistria floridensis*	Florida Fern Moth
☐	93-2192	9631	*Callopistria mollissima*	Pink-shaded Fern Moth
☐	93-2194	9633	*Callopistria cordata*	Silver-spotted Fern Moth

Phosphilas and Armyworms – Family Noctuidae, Subfamily Noctuinae,
Tribes Pseudeustrotiini, Phosphilini, and Prodeniini

☐	93-2205	9053	*Pseudeustrotia carneola*	Pink-barred Pseudeustrotia
☐	93-2207	9284	*Anterastria teratophora*	Gray Marvel
☐	93-2208	9618	*Phosphila turbulenta*	Turbulent Phosphila
☐	93-2209	9619	*Phosphila miselioides*	Spotted Phosphila
☐	93-2215	9665	*Spodoptera exigua*	Small Mottled Willow
☐	93-2216	9666	*Spodoptera frugiperda*	Fall Armyworm
☐	93-2219	9669	*Spodoptera ornithogalli*	Yellow-striped Armyworm

Midgets – Family Noctuidae, Subfamily Noctuinae, Tribe Elaphriini

☐	93-2228	9678	*Elaphria versicolor*	Variegated Midget
☐	93-2230	9679	*Elaphria chalcedonia*	Chalcedony Midget
☐	93-2232	9680	*Elaphria georgei*	George's Midget
☐	93-2234	9681.1	*Elaphria alapalida*	Pale-winged Midget
☐	93-2238	9684	*Elaphria grata*	Grateful Midget
☐	93-2249	9688	*Galgula partita*	The Wedgling

Assorted Noctuids – Family Noctuidae, Subfamily Noctuinae, Tribes Caradrinini,
Dypterygiini, and Actinotiini

☐	93-2260	9656	*Caradrina montana*	Civil Rustic
☐	93-2261	9657	*Caradrina multifera*	Speckled Rustic
☐	93-2266	9647	*Proxenus miranda*	Miranda Moth
☐	93-2269	9650	*Athetis tarda*	The Slowpoke
☐	93-2272	9560	*Dypterygia rozmani*	American Bird's-Wing
☐	93-2280	9626	*Trachea delicata*	Delicate Moth

	93-2282	9637.1	*Magusa divaricata*	Variable Narrow-Wing
☐	93-2282	9637.1	*Magusa divaricata*	Variable Narrow-Wing
☐	93-2283	9582	*Nedra ramosula*	Gray Half-Spot
☐	93-2287	9522	*Iodopepla u-album*	White-eyed Borer

Angle Shades – Family Noctuidae, Subfamily Noctuinae, Tribe Phlogophorini

☐	93-2290	9545	*Euplexia benesimilis*	American Angle Shades
☐	93-2291	9546	*Phlogophora iris*	Olive Angle Shades
☐	93-2292	9547	*Phlogophora periculosa*	Brown Angle Shades
☐	93-2293	9548	*Conservula anodonta*	Sharp Angle Shades

Apameas, Brocades, and Borers – Family Noctuidae, Subfamily Noctuinae, Tribes Apameini and Arzamini

☐	93-2294	9326	*Apamea verbascoides*	Mullein Apamea
☐	93-2296	9328	*Apamea nigrior*	Black-dashed Apamea
☐	93-2302	9343	*Apamea apamiformis*	Rice Worm Moth
☐	93-2303	9341	*Apamea vultuosa*	Airy Apamea
☐	93-2304	9344	*Apamea plutonia*	Dusky Apamea
☐	93-2307	9351	*Apamea alia*	Fox Apamea
☐	93-2308	9362.2	*Apamea unanimis*	Small Clouded Brindle
☐	93-2310	9362	*Apamea indocilis*	Ignorant Apamea
☐	93-2311	9360	*Apamea impulsa*	Impulsive Apamea
☐	93-2314	9364	*Apamea sordens*	Rustic Shoulder-Knot
☐	93-2319	9333	*Apamea lignicolora*	Wood-colored Apamea
☐	93-2322	9373	*Apamea helva*	Yellow Three-Spot
☐	93-2333	9348	*Apamea amputatrix*	Yellow-headed Cutworm
☐	93-2343	9365	*Apamea scoparia*	Red-winged Apamea
☐	93-2344	9367	*Apamea dubitans*	Doubtful Apamea
☐	93-2350	9382	*Apamea devastator*	Glassy Cutworm
☐	93-2355	9374	*Apamea niveivenosa*	Snowy-veined Apamea
☐	93-2358	9454	*Loscopia velata*	Veiled Ear Moth
☐	93-2363	9385.1	*Lateroligia ophiogramma*	Double Lobed
☐	93-2368	9391	*Resapamea passer*	Dock Rustic
☐	93-2370	9406	*Mesapamea fractilinea*	Broken-lined Brocade
☐	93-2372	9396	*Eremobina claudens*	Dark-winged Quaker
☐	93-2377	9402	*Oligia chlorostigma*	Yellow-spotted Brocade
☐	93-2378	9404	*Oligia modica*	Black-banded Brocade
☐	93-2382	9415	*Oligia bridghamii*	Bridgham's Brocade
☐	93-2384	9416	*Oligia minuscula*	Small Brocade
☐	93-2385	9418	*Oligia obtusa*	Obtuse Brocade
☐	93-2390	9408	*Neoligia exhausta*	Exhausted Brocade
☐	93-2392	9412	*Neoligia subjuncta*	Connected Brocade
☐	93-2413	9427	*Meropleon diversicolor*	Multicolored Sedgeminer
☐	93-2414	9428	*Meropleon ambifusca*	Newman's Brocade
☐	93-2415	9429	*Lemmeria digitalis*	Fingered Lemmeria
☐	93-2416	9433	*Xylomoia chagnoni*	Reed Canary Grass Borer
☐	93-2421	9434	*Photedes includens*	Included Cordgrass Borer
☐	93-2425	9443	*Photedes defecta*	Narrow-winged Borer

☐	93-2426	9437	*Hypocoena inquinata*	Sordid Wainscot
☐	93-2437	9447.2	*Rhizedra lutosa*	Large Wainscot
☐	93-2438	9449	*Capsula oblonga*	Oblong Sedge Borer
☐	93-2439	9450	*Capsula subflava*	Subflava Sedge Borer
☐	93-2442	9452	*Macronoctua onusta*	Iris Borer
☐	93-2443	9453	*Helotropha reniformis*	Reniform Helotropha
☐	93-2444	9520	*Achatodes zeae*	Elder Shoot Borer
☐	93-2447	9457	*Amphipoea americana*	American Ear Moth
☐	93-2458	9514	*Hydraecia micacea*	Rosy Rustic
☐	93-2465	9509	*Papaipema unimoda*	Meadow Rue Borer
☐	93-2466	9464	*Papaipema cerina*	Golden Borer
☐	93-2468	9495	*Papaipema furcata*	Ash-tip Borer
☐	93-2470	9505	*Papaipema cerussata*	Ironweed Borer
☐	93-2473	9490	*Papaipema nepheleptena*	Turtlehead Borer
☐	93-2475	9482	*Papaipema speciosissima*	Osmunda Borer
☐	93-2476	9483	*Papaipema inquaesita*	Sensitive Fern Borer
☐	93-2478	9486	*Papaipema birdi*	Umbellifer Borer
☐	93-2488	9478	*Papaipema leucostigma*	Columbine Borer
☐	93-2489	9480	*Papaipema pterisii*	Bracken Borer
☐	93-2492	9471	*Papaipema arctivorens*	Northern Burdock Borer
☐	93-2494	9485	*Papaipema baptisiae*	Indigo Stem Borer
☐	93-2497	9466	*Papaipema cataphracta*	Burdock Borer
☐	93-2499	9468	*Papaipema aerata*	Bronzed Borer
☐	93-2500	9473	*Papaipema impecuniosa*	Aster Borer
☐	93-2501	9496	*Papaipema nebris*	Stalk Borer
☐	93-2502	9501	*Papaipema eupatorii*	Joe-pye-weed Borer
☐	93-2506	9502	*Papaipema nelita*	Coneflower Borer
☐	93-2514	9523.1	*Bellura vulnifica*	Black-tailed Diver
☐	93-2517	9525	*Bellura obliqua*	Cattail Borer
☐	93-2518	9526	*Bellura densa*	Pickerelweed Borer

Swordgrasses, Pinions, and Xylenine Sallows – Family Noctuidae,
Subfamily Noctuinae, Tribe Xylenini

☐	93-2519	9873	*Xylena nupera*	American Swordgrass
☐	93-2520	9874	*Xylena curvimacula*	Dot-and-dash Swordgrass
☐	93-2522	9876	*Xylena cineritia*	Gray Swordgrass
☐	93-2524	9878	*Lithomoia germana*	Ashen Brindle
☐	93-2527	9881	*Homoglaea hircina*	Goat Sallow
☐	93-2530	9884	*Litholomia napaea*	False Pinion
☐	93-2531	9885	*Lithophane semiusta*	Singed Pinion
☐	93-2532	9886	*Lithophane patefacta*	Dimorphic Pinion
☐	93-2533	9887	*Lithophane bethunei*	Bethune's Pinion
☐	93-2534	9888	*Lithophane innominata*	Nameless Pinion
☐	93-2536	9889	*Lithophane petulca*	Wanton Pinion
☐	93-2537	9892	*Lithophane disposita*	Dashed Gray Pinion
☐	93-2538	9893	*Lithophane hemina*	Hemina Pinion

☐	93-2544	9891	*Lithophane amanda*	Amanda's Pinion
☐	93-2545	9922	*Lithophane pexata*	Plush-naped Pinion
☐	93-2547	9928	*Lithophane thaxteri*	Thaxter's Pinion
☐	93-2548	9917	*Lithophane fagina*	Hoary Pinion
☐	93-2549	9902	*Lithophane baileyi*	Bailey's Pinion
☐	93-2577	9910	*Lithophane antennata*	Ashen Pinion
☐	93-2580	9914	*Lithophane laticinerea*	Triple-spotted Pinion
☐	93-2581	9915	*Lithophane grotei*	Grote's Pinion
☐	93-2582	9916	*Lithophane unimoda*	Dowdy Pinion
☐	93-2583	9929	*Pyreferra hesperidago*	Mustard Sallow
☐	93-2584	9930	*Pyreferra citrombra*	Citrine Sallow
☐	93-2587	9933	*Eupsilia vinulenta*	Straight-toothed Sallow
☐	93-2590	9935	*Eupsilia tristigmata*	Three-spotted Sallow
☐	93-2591	9936	*Eupsilia morrisoni*	Morrison's Sallow
☐	93-2594	9939	*Eupsilia devia*	Lost Sallow
☐	93-2597	9943	*Metaxaglaea inulta*	Unsated Sallow
☐	93-2598	9944	*Metaxaglaea viatica*	Roadside Sallow
☐	93-2602	9946	*Epiglaea decliva*	Sloping Sallow
☐	93-2604	9948	*Chaetaglaea cerata*	Waxed Sallow
☐	93-2607	9950	*Chaetaglaea sericea*	Silky Sallow
☐	93-2609	9952	*Eucirroedia pampina*	Scalloped Sallow
☐	93-2616	9957	*Sunira bicolorago*	Bicolored Sallow
☐	93-2619	9961	*Anathix ralla*	Dotted Sallow
☐	93-2620	9962	*Anathix puta*	Puta Sallow
☐	93-2621	9963	*Anathix aggressa*	Approachable Sallow
☐	93-2622	9965	*Xanthia tatago*	Pink-barred Sallow
☐	93-2656	9999	*Brachylomia discinigra*	Black-disc Sallow
☐	93-2664	9578	*Hyppa xylinoides*	Common Hyppa
☐	93-2672	9815	*Cosmia calami*	American Dun-Bar
☐	93-2674	9549	*Enargia decolor*	Pale Enargia
☐	93-2675	9550	*Enargia infumata*	Smoked Sallow
☐	93-2679	9555	*Ipimorpha pleonectusa*	Even-lined Sallow
☐	93-2695	9420	*Fishia illocata*	Wandering Brocade
☐	93-2699	9419	*Platypolia mactata*	Adorable Brocade
☐	93-2701	9980	*Xylotype acadia*	Acadian Sallow
☐	93-2707	9989	*Sutyna privata*	Private Sallow
☐	93-2709	11051	*Ufeus satyricus*	Grote's Satyr
☐	93-2710	11052	*Ufeus plicatus*	Folded Satyr
☐	93-2713	9556	*Chytonix palliatricula*	Cloaked Marvel
☐	93-2749	9629	*Fagitana littera*	Marsh Fern Moth

Spring Quakers, Woodlings, and Woodgrains – Family Noctuidae, Subfamily Noctuinae, Tribe Orthosiini

☐	93-2770	10487	*Orthosia rubescens*	Ruby Quaker
☐	93-2771	10488	*Orthosia garmani*	Garman's Quaker
☐	93-2773	10490	*Orthosia revicta*	Subdued Quaker

	93-2774	10491	*Orthosia alurina*	Gray Quaker
☐	93-2774	10491	*Orthosia alurina*	Gray Quaker
☐	93-2778	10495	*Orthosia hibisci*	Speckled Green Fruitworm Moth
☐	93-2784	10501	*Crocigrapha normani*	Norman's Quaker
☐	93-2785	10502	*Himella fidelis*	Intractable Quaker
☐	93-2795	10513	*Egira dolosa*	Grieving Woodling
☐	93-2799	10517	*Egira alternans*	Alternate Woodling
☐	93-2800	10518	*Achatia distincta*	Distinct Quaker
☐	93-2801	10519	*Morrisonia mucens*	Gray Woodgrain
☐	93-2802	10520	*Morrisonia evicta*	Bicolored Woodgrain
☐	93-2803	10521	*Morrisonia confusa*	Confused Woodgrain
☐	93-2805	10291	*Morrisonia latex*	Fluid Arches

Large Arches – Family Noctuidae, Subfamily Noctuinae, Tribes Tholerini and Hadenini

☐	93-2810	10524	*Nephelodes minians*	Bronzed Cutworm
☐	93-2826	10223	*Anarta trifolii*	The Nutmeg
☐	93-2867	10275	*Polia nimbosa*	Stormy Arches
☐	93-2868	10276	*Polia imbrifera*	Cloudy Arches
☐	93-2872	10280	*Polia purpurissata*	Purple Arches
☐	93-2874	10292	*Melanchra adjuncta*	Hitched Arches
☐	93-2875	10293	*Melanchra picta*	Zebra Caterpillar Moth
☐	93-2877	10295	*Melanchra assimilis*	Black Arches
☐	93-2879	10297	*Lacanobia atlantica*	Atlantic Arches
☐	93-2881	10299	*Lacanobia subjuncta*	Subdued Arches
☐	93-2882	10300	*Lacanobia grandis*	Grand Arches
☐	93-2883	10301	*Spiramater lutra*	Otter Arches
☐	93-2884	10302	*Trichordestra rugosa*	Wrinkled Trichordestra
☐	93-2885	10303	*Trichordestra tacoma*	Tacoma Arches
☐	93-2886	10304	*Trichordestra legitima*	Striped Garden Caterpillar Moth
☐	93-2899	10272	*Mamestra curialis*	Scripted Arches
☐	93-2906	10265	*Sideridis rosea*	Rosewing
☐	93-2907	10266	*Sideridis congermana*	The German Cousin
☐	93-2911	10317	*Hadena capsularis*	Capsule Moth
☐	93-2928	10431	*Dargida diffusa*	Wheat Head Armyworm
☐	93-2931	10434	*Dargida rubripennis*	The Pink-Streak

Wainscots – Family Noctuidae, Subfamily Noctuinae, Tribe Leucaniini

☐	93-2933	10436	*Mythimna oxygala*	Lesser Wainscot
☐	93-2935	10438	*Mythimna unipuncta*	The White-Speck
☐	93-2938	10440	*Leucania linita*	Linen Wainscot
☐	93-2943	10444	*Leucania phragmitidicola*	Phragmites Wainscot
☐	93-2944	10445	*Leucania linda*	Linda's Wainscot
☐	93-2945	10446	*Leucania multilinea*	Many-lined Wainscot
☐	93-2947	10447	*Leucania commoides*	Comma Wainscot
☐	93-2948	10449	*Leucania insueta*	Heterodox Wainscot
☐	93-2957	10455	*Leucania scirpicola*	Scirpus Wainscot
☐	93-2960	10456	*Leucania adjuta*	Adjutant Wainscot

☐ 93-2963	10459	*Leucania inermis*	Unarmed Wainscot
☐ 93-2965	10461	*Leucania ursula*	Ursula Wainscot
☐ 93-2966	10462	*Leucania pseudargyria*	False Wainscot

Small Arches and Summer Quakers – Family Noctuidae, Subfamily Noctuinae, Tribe Eriopygini

☐ 93-3016	10368	*Lacinipolia meditata*	The Thinker
☐ 93-3019	10372	*Lacinipolia anguina*	Snaky Arches
☐ 93-3040	10394	*Lacinipolia vicina*	Neighborly Arches
☐ 93-3044	10397	*Lacinipolia renigera*	Bristly Cutworm
☐ 93-3052	10405	*Lacinipolia lorea*	Bridled Arches
☐ 93-3053	10406	*Lacinipolia olivacea*	Olive Arches
☐ 93-3065	10411	*Lacinipolia laudabilis*	Laudable Arches
☐ 93-3067	10413	*Lacinipolia explicata*	Explicit Arches
☐ 93-3068	10414	*Lacinipolia implicata*	Implicit Arches
☐ 93-3086	10530	*Anhimella contrahens*	United Cutworm
☐ 93-3088	10532	*Homorthodes furfurata*	Northern Scurfy Quaker
☐ 93-3105	10552	*Protorthodes incincta*	Banded Quaker
☐ 93-3113	10563	*Protorthodes oviduca*	Ruddy Quaker
☐ 93-3118	10567	*Ulolonche culea*	Sheathed Quaker
☐ 93-3120	10569	*Ulolonche modesta*	Modest Quaker
☐ 93-3128	10578	*Pseudorthodes vecors*	Small Brown Quaker
☐ 93-3136	10585	*Orthodes majuscula*	Rustic Quaker
☐ 93-3138	10587	*Orthodes cynica*	Cynical Quaker
☐ 93-3141	10289	*Orthodes goodelli*	Goodell's Arches
☐ 93-3146	10288	*Orthodes detracta*	Disparaged Arches
☐ 93-3193	10627	*Tricholita signata*	Signate Quaker

Spanish Moth – Family Noctuidae, Subfamily Noctuinae, Tribe Glottulini

☐ 93-3210	10640	*Xanthopastis timais*	Spanish Moth

Darts – Family Noctuidae, Subfamily Noctuinae, Tribe Noctuini

☐ 93-3211	10915	*Peridroma saucia*	Pearly Underwing
☐ 93-3212	10911	*Anicla infecta*	Green Cutworm
☐ 93-3214	10901	*Anicla lubricans*	Slippery Dart
☐ 93-3216	10903	*Anicla illapsa*	Snowy Dart
☐ 93-3222	10902	*Anicla forbesi*	Forbes' Dart
☐ 93-3228	10878	*Striacosta albicosta*	Western Bean Cutworm
☐ 93-3229	10924	*Actebia fennica*	Finnish Dart
☐ 93-3232	10870	*Dichagyris acclivis*	Inclined Dart
☐ 93-3319	10705	*Euxoa messoria*	Reaper Dart
☐ 93-3320	10702	*Euxoa divergens*	Divergent Dart
☐ 93-3329	10715	*Euxoa scandens*	White Cutworm
☐ 93-3395	10805	*Euxoa tessellata*	Tessellate Dart
☐ 93-3397	10807	*Euxoa albipennis*	White-striped Dart
☐ 93-3411	10803	*Euxoa velleripennis*	Fleece-winged Dart
☐ 93-3428	10817	*Euxoa obeliscoides*	Obelisk Dart

☐	93-3440	10851	*Euxoa redimicula*	Fillet Dart
☐	93-3461	10838	*Euxoa detersa*	Rubbed Dart
☐	93-3488	10644	*Feltia mollis*	Soft Dart
☐	93-3495	10680	*Feltia geniculata*	Knee-joint Dart
☐	93-3498	10670	*Feltia jaculifera*	Dingy Cutworm
☐	93-3501	10674	*Feltia subgothica*	Subgothic Dart
☐	93-3503	10676	*Feltia herilis*	Master's Dart
☐	93-3504	10664	*Feltia subterranea*	Subterranean Dart
☐	93-3506	10641	*Agrotis vetusta*	Old Man Dart
☐	93-3515	10648	*Agrotis gladiaria*	Swordsman Dart
☐	93-3516	10651	*Agrotis venerabilis*	Venerable Dart
☐	93-3521	10659	*Agrotis volubilis*	Voluble Dart
☐	93-3522	10660	*Agrotis obliqua*	Oblique Dart
☐	93-3526	10661	*Agrotis malefida*	Rascal Dart
☐	93-3528	10663	*Agrotis ipsilon*	Ipsilon Dart
☐	93-3529	10891	*Ochropleura implecta*	Flame-shouldered Dart
☐	93-3533	10919	*Diarsia jucunda*	Smaller Pinkish Dart
☐	93-3536	10994	*Cerastis tenebrifera*	Reddish Speckled Dart
☐	93-3537	10997	*Cerastis fishii*	Fish's Dart
☐	93-3542	10996	*Cerastis salicarum*	Willow Dart
☐	93-3543	10998	*Cheophora fungorum*	Bent-line Dart
☐	93-3547	11010	*Lycophotia phyllophora*	Leafy Dart
☐	93-3551	11003.1	*Noctua pronuba*	Large Yellow Underwing
☐	93-3552	11003.2	*Noctua comes*	Lesser Yellow Underwing
☐	93-3553	11012	*Cryptocala acadiensis*	Catocaline Dart
☐	93-3554	10926	*Spaelotis clandestina*	Clandestine Dart
☐	93-3560	10929	*Eurois occulta*	Great Brocade
☐	93-3563	10928	*Graphiphora augur*	Double Dart
☐	93-3564	11000	*Anaplectoides prasina*	Green Arches
☐	93-3565	11001	*Anaplectoides pressus*	Dappled Dart
☐	93-3568	11007	*Eueretagrotis sigmoides*	Sigmoid Dart
☐	93-3569	11008	*Eueretagrotis perattentus*	Two-spot Dart
☐	93-3570	11009	*Eueretagrotis attentus*	Attentive Dart
☐	93-3572	10944	*Xestia smithii*	Smith's Dart
☐	93-3573	10943	*Xestia normaniana*	Norman's Dart
☐	93-3584	10968	*Xestia badicollis*	Northern Variable Dart
☐	93-3586	10969	*Xestia dilucida*	Dull Reddish Dart
☐	93-3588	10942	*Xestia c-nigrum*	Setaceous Hebrew Character
☐	93-3589	10942.1	*Xestia dolosa*	Greater Black-letter Dart
☐	93-3626	10955	*Agnorisma badinodis*	Pale-banded Dart
☐	93-3627	10954	*Agnorisma bugrai*	Collared Dart
☐	93-3629	10950	*Pseudohermonassa bicarnea*	Pink-spotted Dart
☐	93-3630	10951	*Pseudohermonassa tenuicula*	Morrison's Sooty Dart
☐	93-3649	11006	*Protolampra brunneicollis*	Brown-collared Dart
☐	93-3680	11029	*Abagrotis alternata*	Greater Red Dart
☐	93-3685	11043	*Abagrotis cupida*	Cupid Dart

Additions:

- [ ] _____
- [ ] _____
- [ ] _____
- [ ] _____
- [ ] _____
- [ ] _____
- [ ] _____
- [ ] _____
- [ ] _____
- [ ] _____
- [ ] _____
- [ ] _____
- [ ] _____
- [ ] _____
- [ ] _____
- [ ] _____
- [ ] _____
- [ ] _____
- [ ] _____
- [ ] _____
- [ ] _____
- [ ] _____
- [ ] _____
- [ ] _____
- [ ] _____
- [ ] _____
- [ ] _____
- [ ] _____
- [ ] _____
- [ ] _____
- [ ] _____
- [ ] _____
- [ ] _____
- [ ] _____
- [ ] _____
- [ ] _____
- [ ] _____

INDEX

Boxwood Leaftier

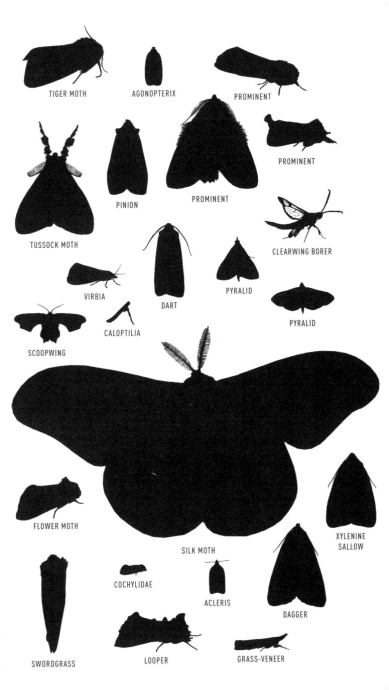

TIGER MOTH

AGONOPTERIX

PROMINENT

TUSSOCK MOTH

PINION

PROMINENT

PROMINENT

VIRBIA

DART

PYRALID

CLEARWING BORER

SCOOPWING

CALOPTILIA

PYRALID

FLOWER MOTH

SILK MOTH

XYLENINE
SALLOW

COCHYLIDAE

ACLERIS

DAGGER

SWORDGRASS

LOOPER

GRASS-VENEER